RUNAWAYS

ESCAPE TO NEW YORK

P9-CSG-940

Writer: Brian K. Vaughan

Pencilers: Adrian Alphona & Takeshi Miyazawa (Issues #7-8)

Inker: Craig Yeung

Colorist: Christina Strain

Letterer: Virtual Calligraphy's Randy Gentile & Dave Sharpe

Cover Artists: Jo Chen, James Jean & Chris Bachalo with Tim Townsend

Assistant Editor: Nathan Cosby

Editors: MacKenzie Cadenhead

Special thanks to C.B. Cebulski

Runaways created by Brian K. Vaughan & Adrian Alphona

Collection Editor: Jennifer Grünwald
Assistant Editor: Michael Short
Senior Editor, Special Projects: Jeff Youngquist
Vice President of Sales: David Gabriel
Production: Jerron Quality Color
Creative Director: Tom Marvelli

Editor in Chief: Joe Quesada
Publisher: Dan Buckley

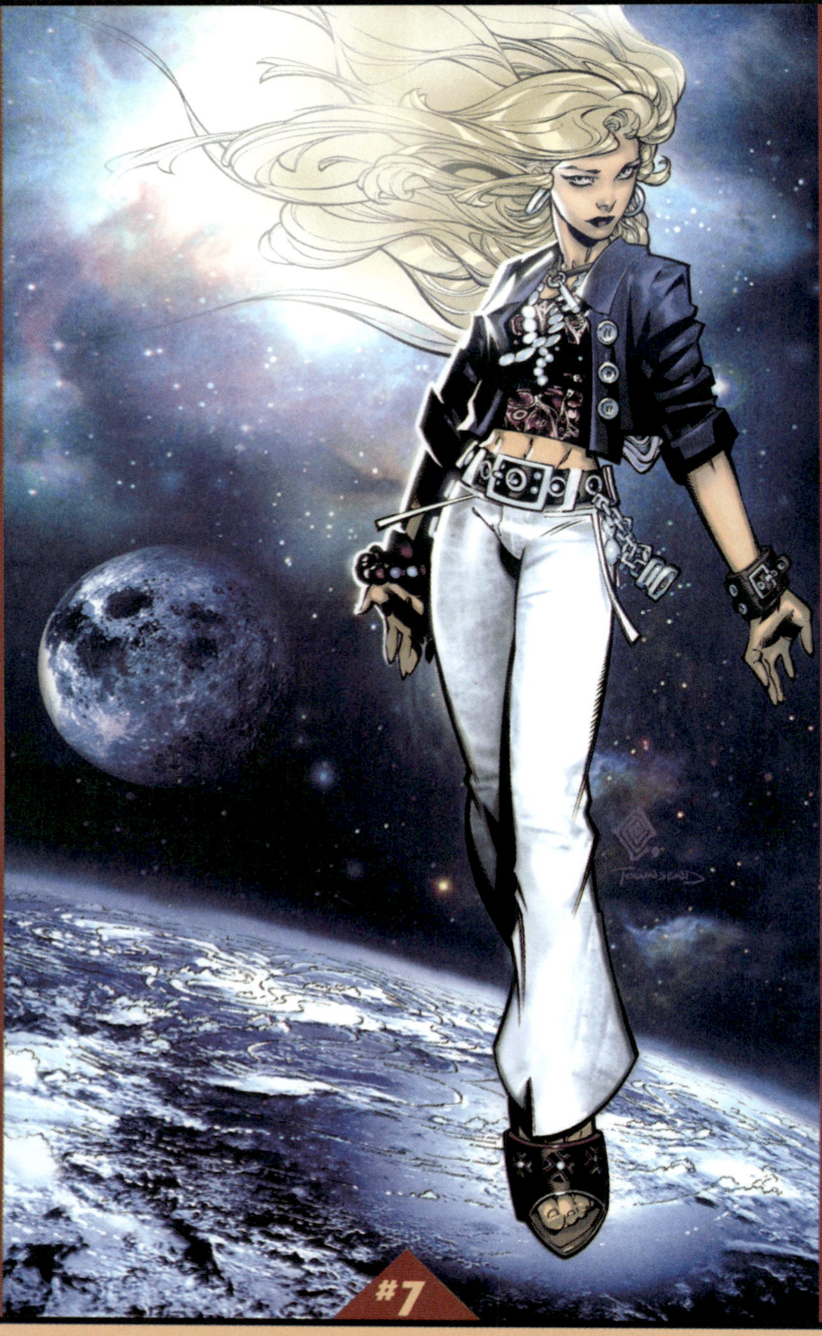

#7

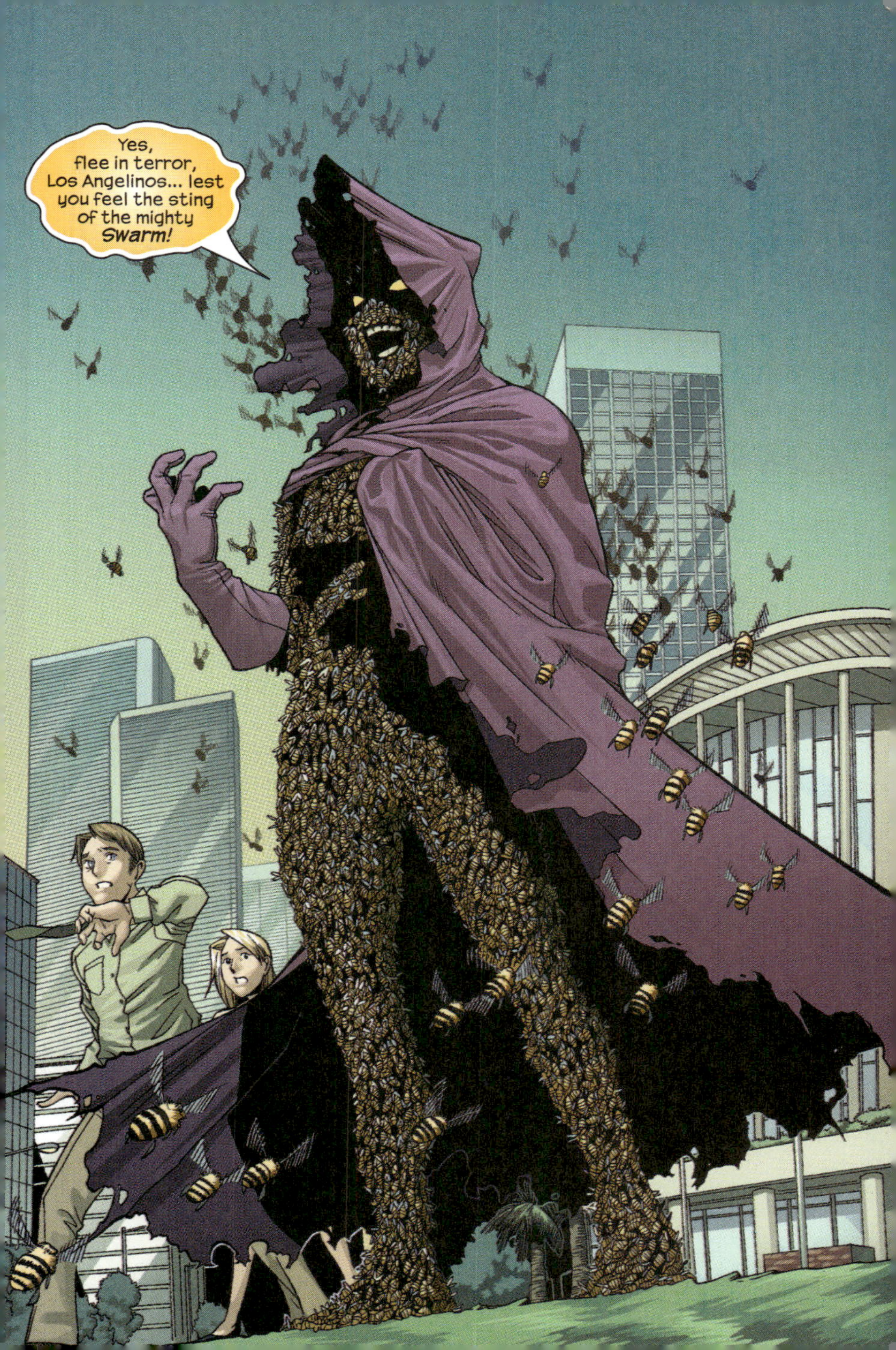
Yes, flee in terror, Los Angelinos... lest you feel the sting of the mighty *Swarm!*

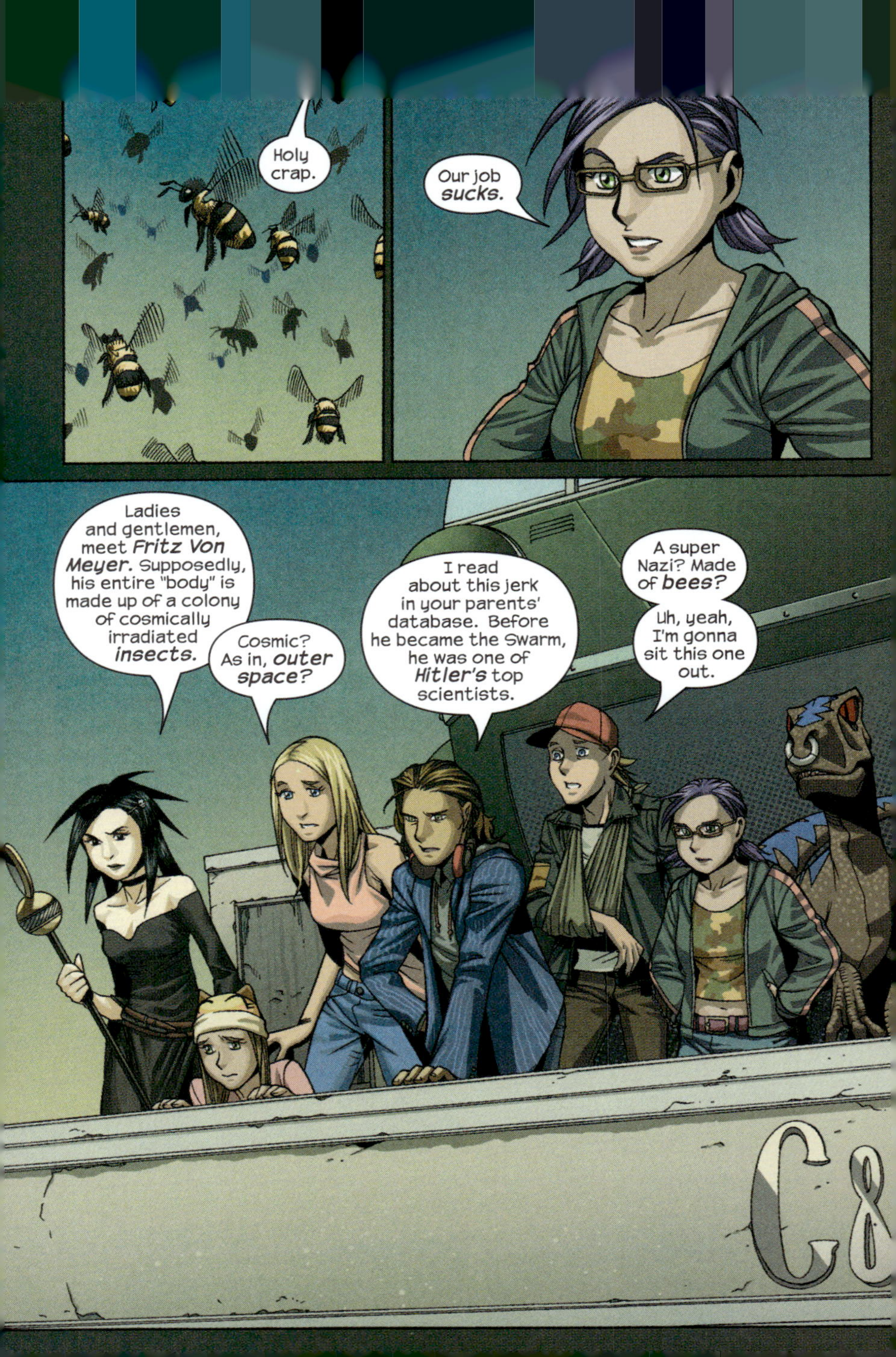
Holy crap.
Our job sucks.
Ladies and gentlemen, meet Fritz Von Meyer. Supposedly, his entire "body" is made up of a colony of cosmically irradiated insects.
Cosmic? As in, outer space?
I read about this jerk in your parents' database. Before he became the Swarm, he was one of Hitler's top scientists.
A super Nazi? Made of bees?
Uh, yeah, I'm gonna sit this one out.
C8

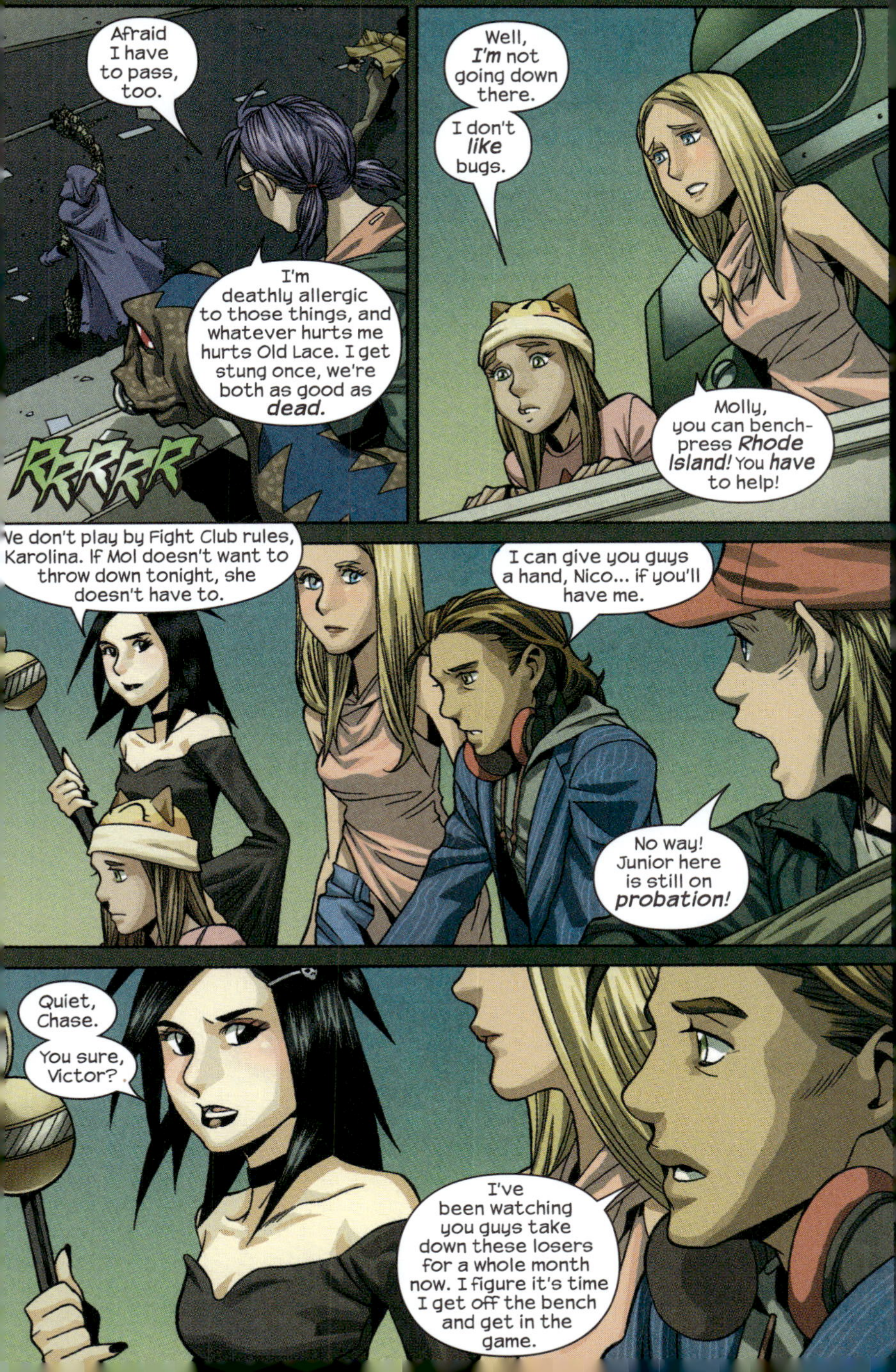

Afraid I have to pass, too.
I'm deathly allergic to those things, and whatever hurts me hurts Old Lace. I get stung once, we're both as good as *dead.*
RRRRR
Well, *I'm* not going down there.
I don't *like* bugs.
Molly, you can bench-press *Rhode Island!* You *have* to help!
We don't play by Fight Club rules, Karolina. If Mol doesn't want to throw down tonight, she doesn't have to.
I can give you guys a hand, Nico... if you'll have me.
No way! Junior here is still on *probation!*
Quiet, Chase.
You sure, Victor?
I've been watching you guys take down these losers for a whole month now. I figure it's time I get off the bench and get in the game.

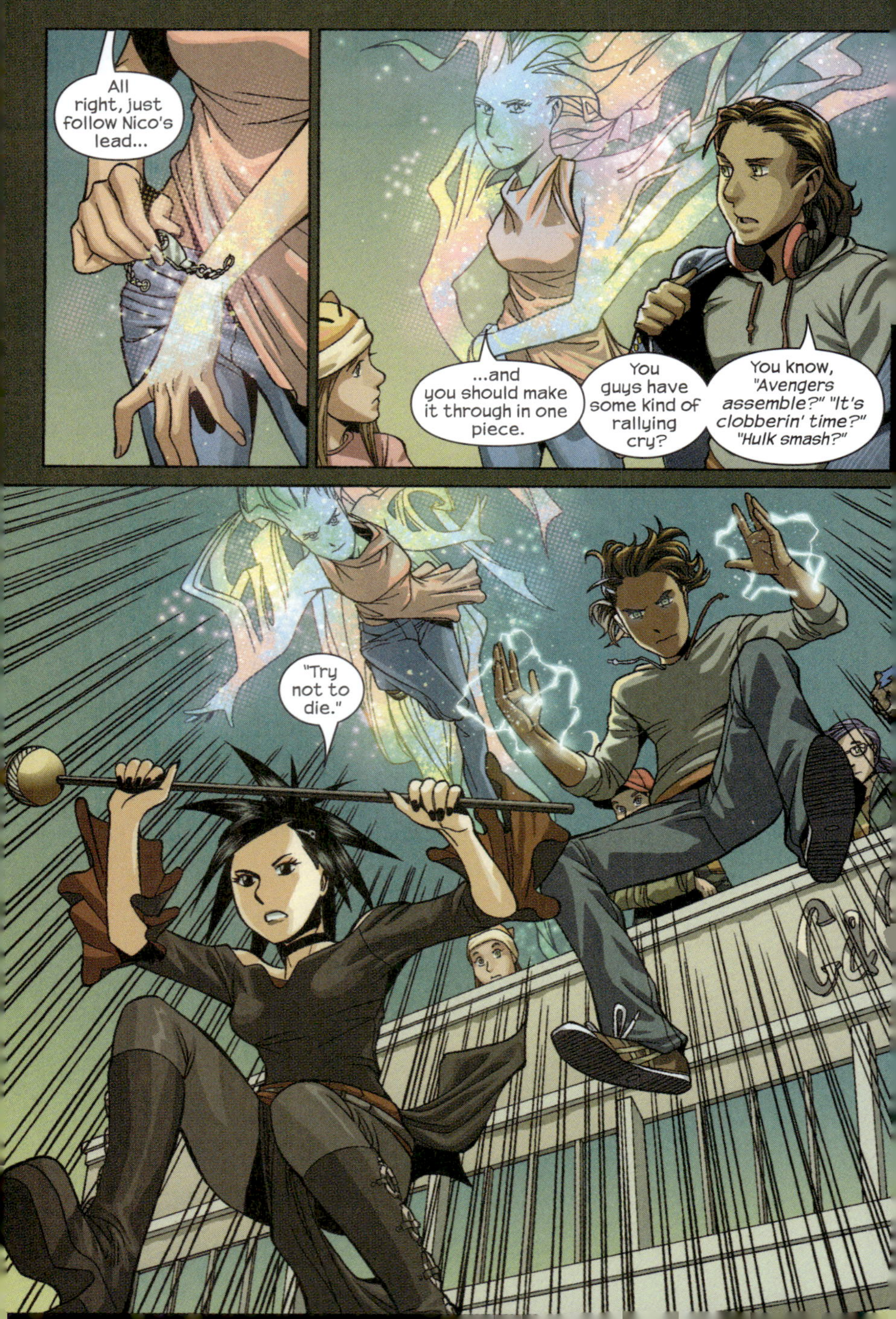
All right, just follow Nico's lead...
...and you should make it through in one piece.
You guys have some kind of rallying cry?
You know, "Avengers assemble?" "It's clobberin' time?" "Hulk smash?"
"Try not to die."

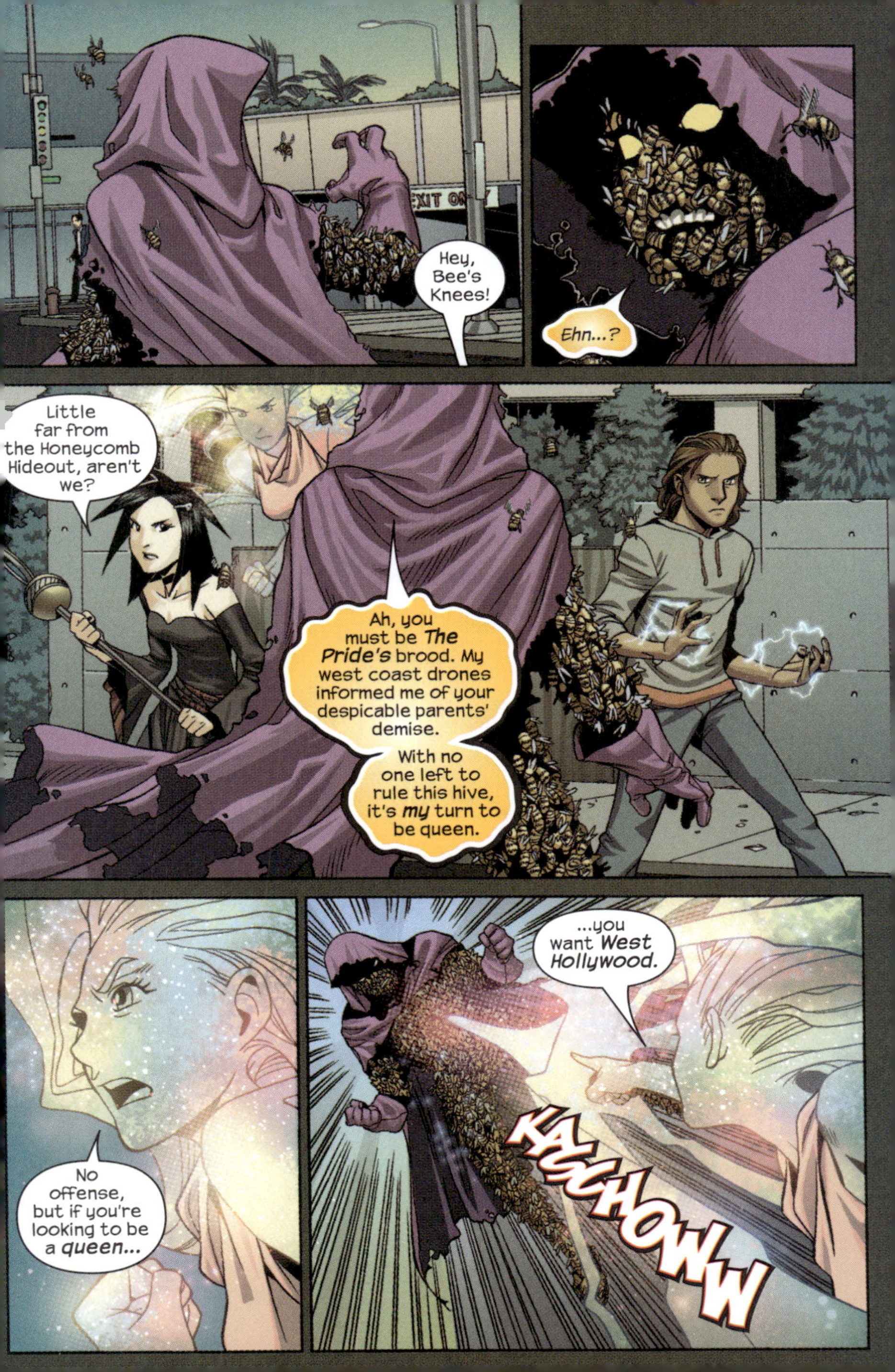
EXIT ON
Hey, Bee's Knees!
Ehn...?
Little far from the Honeycomb Hideout, aren't we?
Ah, you must be *The Pride's* brood. My west coast drones informed me of your despicable parents' demise.
With no one left to rule this hive, it's *my* turn to be queen.
No offense, but if you're looking to be a *queen*...
...you want *West Hollywood.*
KACHOWW

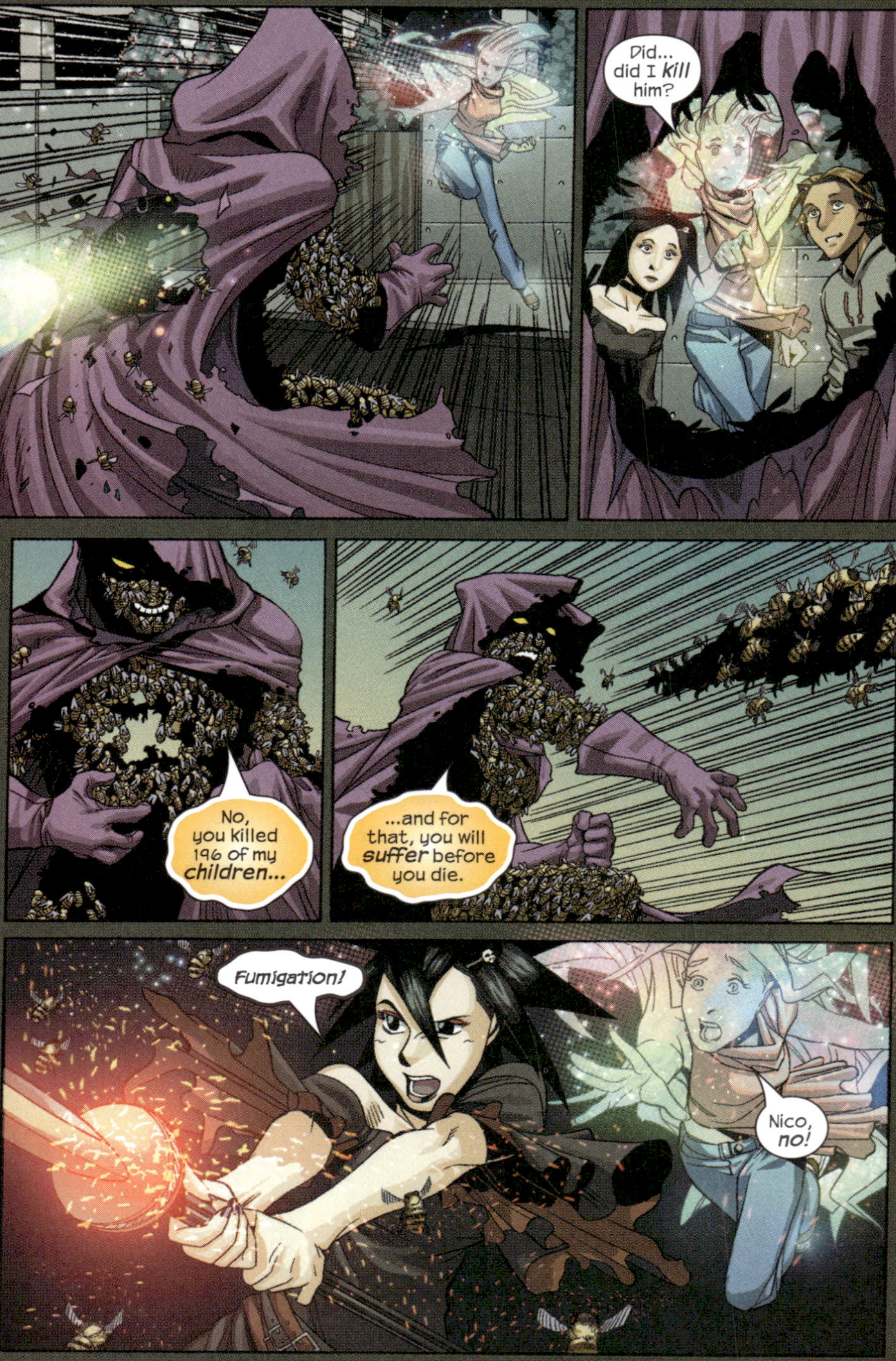
Did... did I kill him?
No, you killed 196 of my children...
...and for that, you will suffer before you die.
Fumigation!
Nico, no!

What the...?

Where *are* we?

Few miles outside of L.A., from the looks of it.

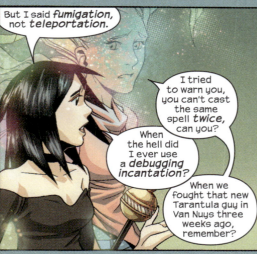

But I said *fumigation*, not *teleportation*.

I tried to warn you, you can't cast the same spell *twice*, can you?

When the hell did I ever use a *debugging incantation*?

When we fought that new Tarantula guy in Van Nuys three weeks ago, remember?

...I'm so stupid.

It's just, there have been *so many* bad guys since our 'rents died, and--

Beat yourself up *later*, girlfriend.

If *we're* out here, that means *Victor's* all alone with Satan's beekeeper.

I know I always say this, Karolina...

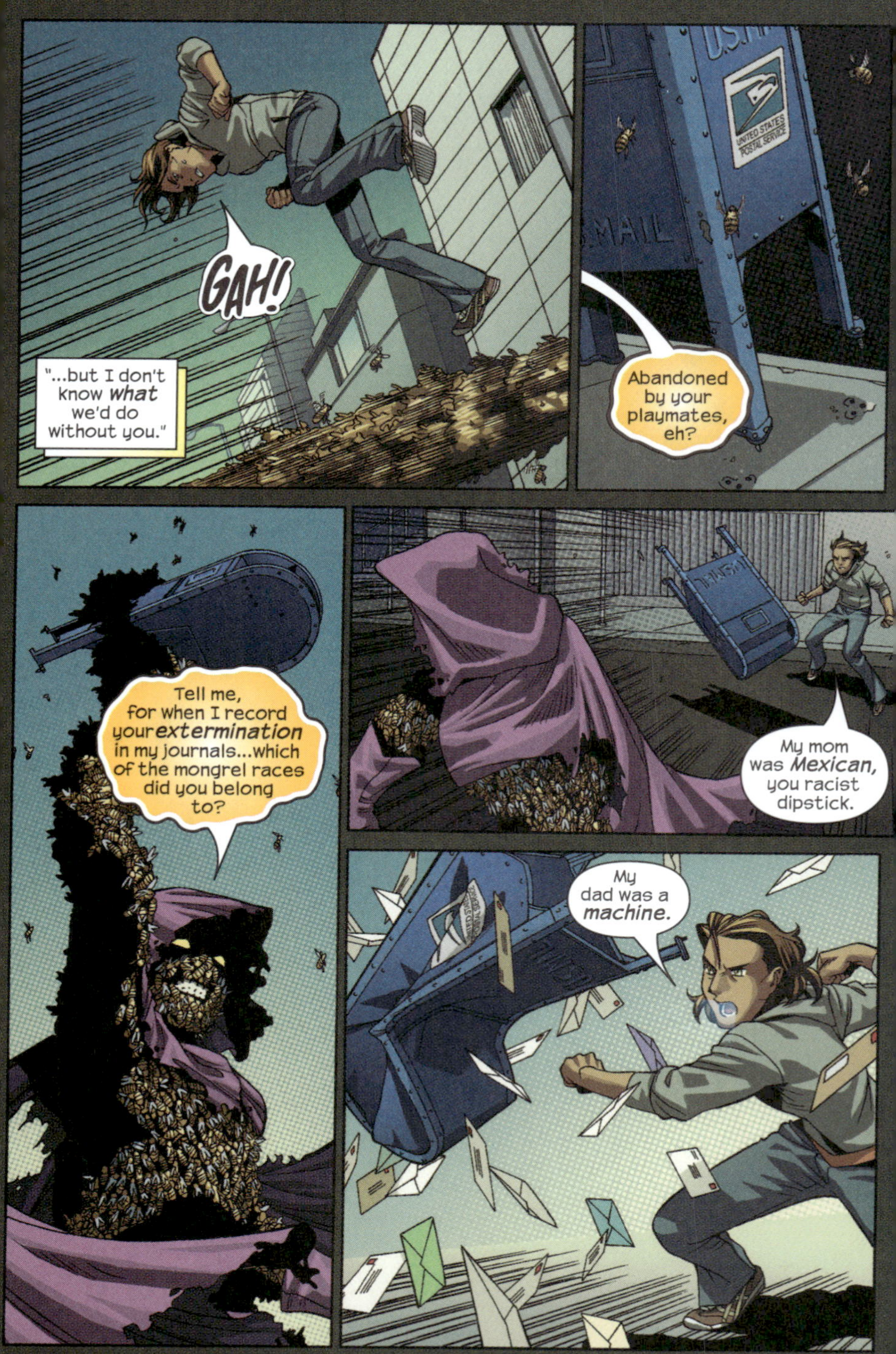
GAH!
"...but I don't know *what* we'd do without you."
Abandoned by your playmates, eh?
Tell me, for when I record your *extermination* in my journals...which of the mongrel races did you belong to?
My mom was *Mexican,* you racist dipstick.
My dad was a *machine.*

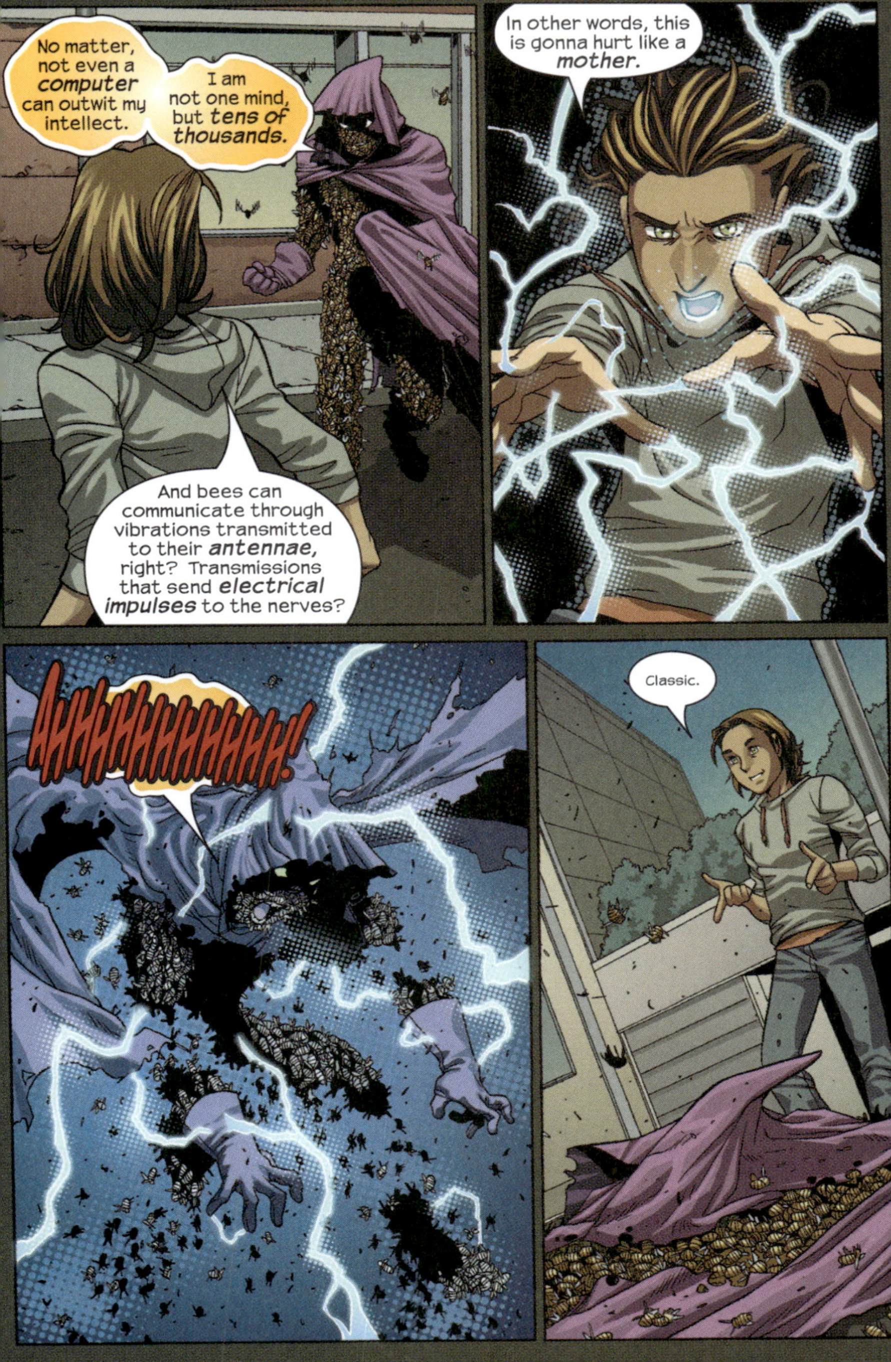
No matter, not even a computer can outwit my intellect.
I am not one mind, but tens of thousands.
And bees can communicate through vibrations transmitted to their antennae, right? Transmissions that send electrical impulses to the nerves?
In other words, this is gonna hurt like a mother.
AHHHHHHHHHHHH!
Classic.

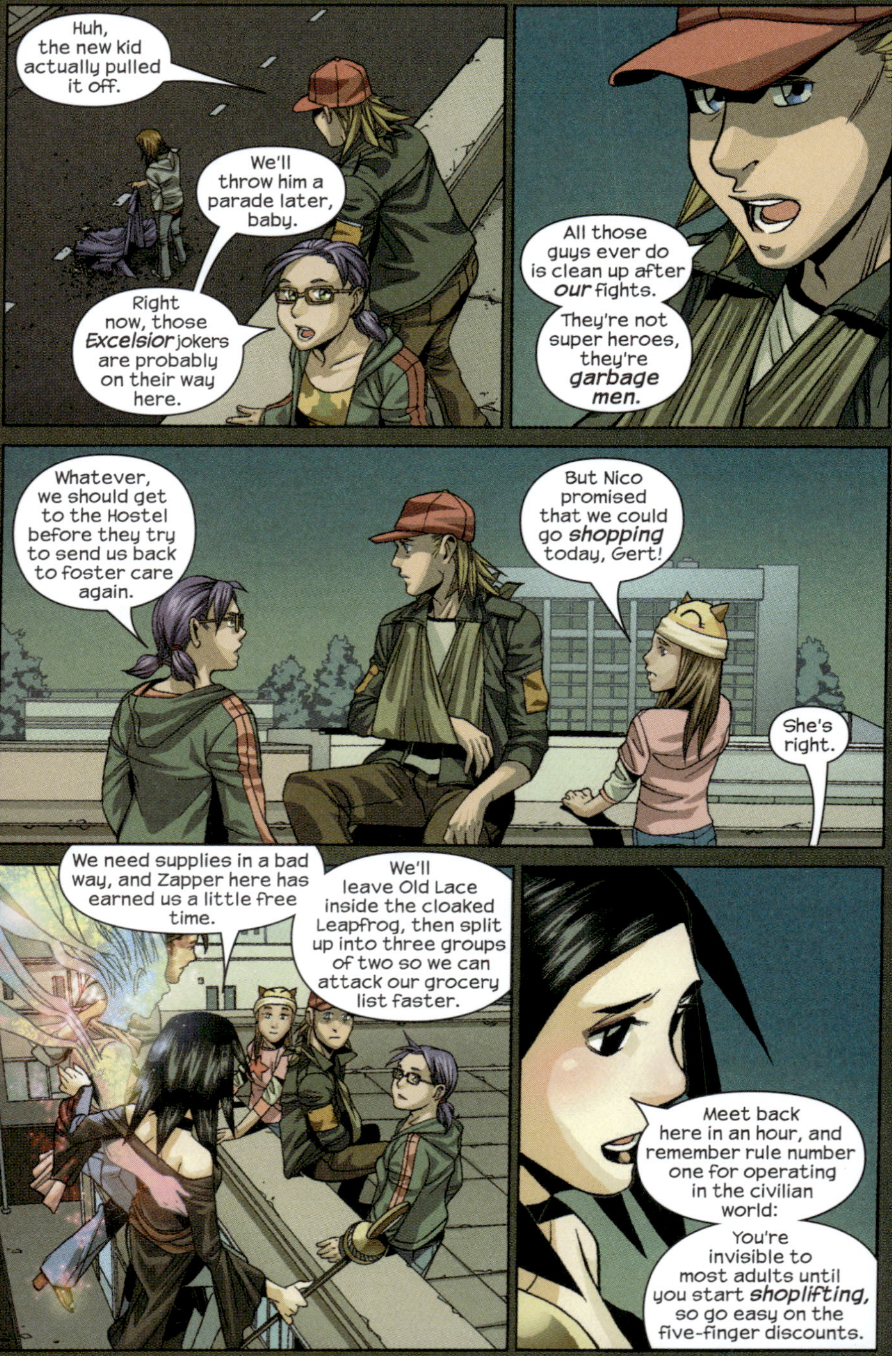
Huh, the new kid actually pulled it off.
We'll throw him a parade later, baby.
Right now, those *Excelsior* jokers are probably on their way here.
All those guys ever do is clean up after *our* fights.
They're not super heroes, they're *garbage men.*
Whatever, we should get to the Hostel before they try to send us back to foster care again.
But Nico promised that we could go *shopping* today, Gert!
She's right.
We need supplies in a bad way, and Zapper here has earned us a little free time.
We'll leave Old Lace inside the cloaked Leapfrog, then split up into three groups of two so we can attack our grocery list faster.
Meet back here in an hour, and remember rule number one for operating in the civilian world:
You're invisible to most adults until you start *shoplifting,* so go easy on the five-finger discounts.

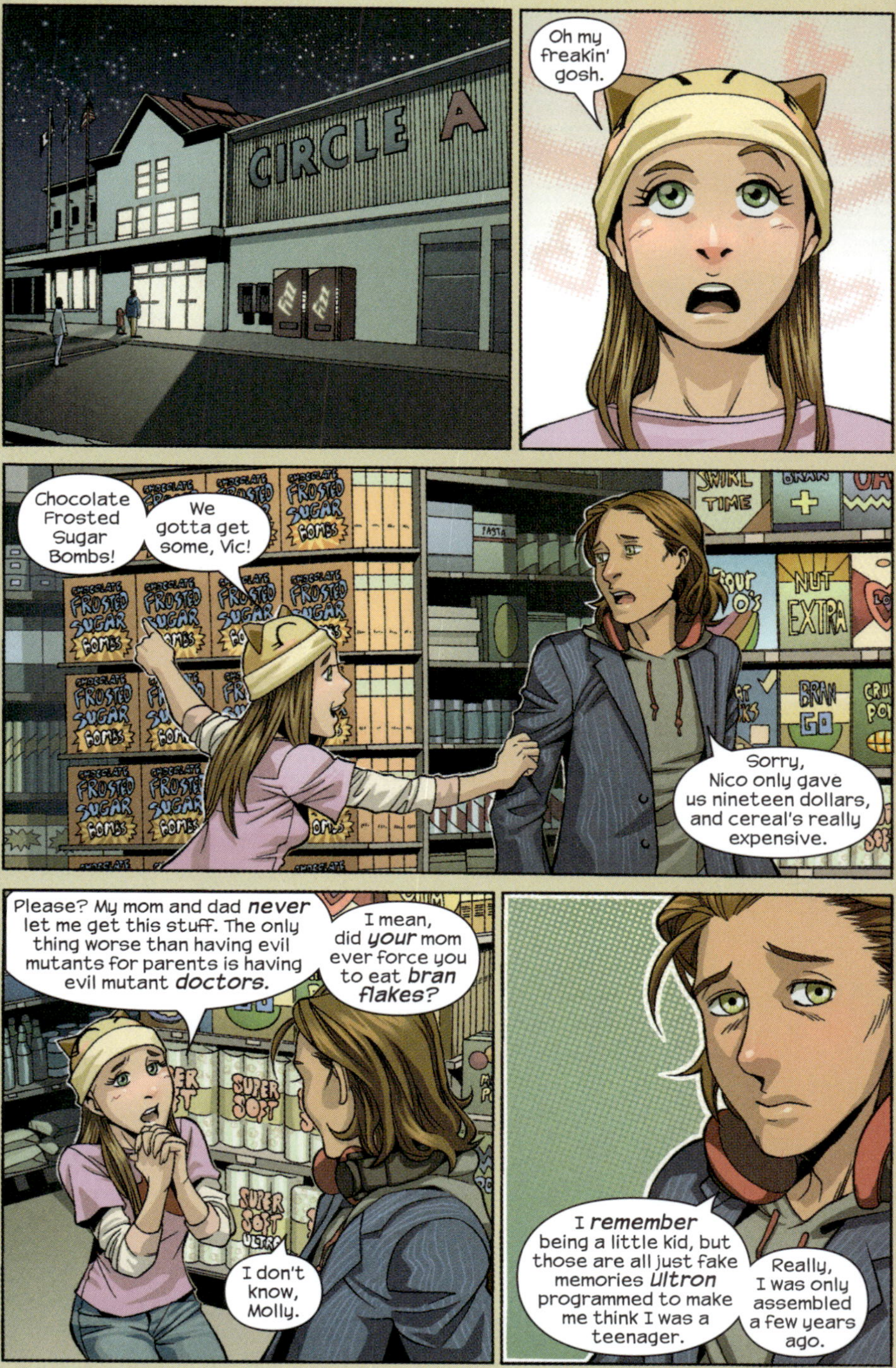
CIRCLE A
Oh my freakin' gosh.
Chocolate Frosted Sugar Bombs!
We gotta get some, Vic!
Sorry, Nico only gave us nineteen dollars, and cereal's really expensive.
Please? My mom and dad **never** let me get this stuff. The only thing worse than having evil mutants for parents is having evil mutant **doctors.**
I mean, did **your** mom ever force you to eat **bran flakes?**
I don't know, Molly.
I **remember** being a little kid, but those are all just fake memories **Ultron** programmed to make me think I was a teenager.
Really, I was only assembled a few years ago.

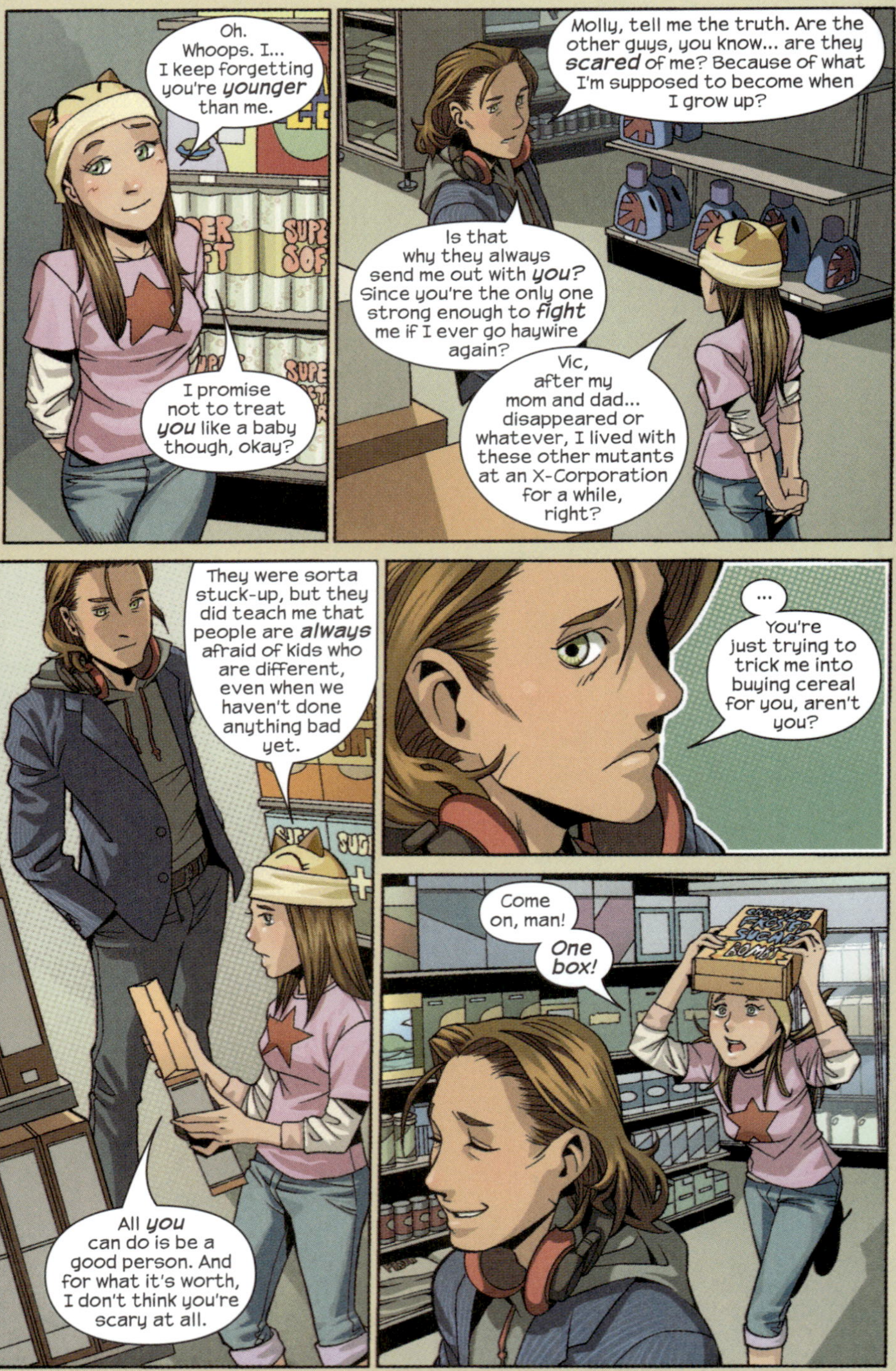
Oh.
Whoops. I... I keep forgetting you're *younger* than me.
I promise not to treat *you* like a baby though, okay?
Molly, tell me the truth. Are the other guys, you know... are they *scared* of me? Because of what I'm supposed to become when I grow up?
Is that why they always send me out with *you?* Since you're the only one strong enough to *fight* me if I ever go haywire again?
Vic, after my mom and dad... disappeared or whatever, I lived with these other mutants at an X-Corporation for a while, right?
They were sorta stuck-up, but they did teach me that people are *always* afraid of kids who are different, even when we haven't done anything bad yet.
All *you* can do is be a good person. And for what it's worth, I don't think you're scary at all.
...
You're just trying to trick me into buying cereal for you, aren't you?
Come on, man!
One box!

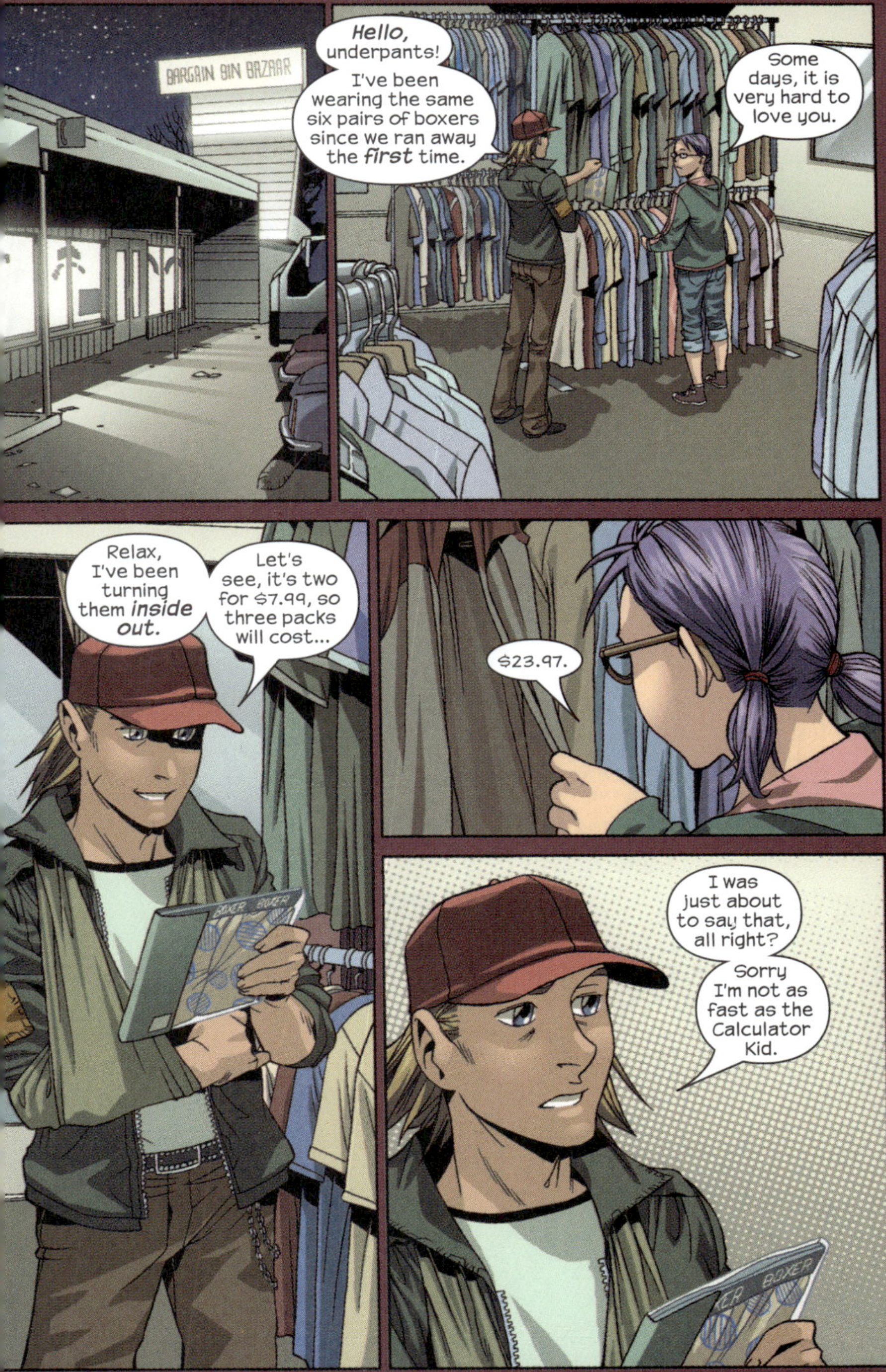
BARGAIN BIN BAZAAR
Hello, underpants!
I've been wearing the same six pairs of boxers since we ran away the *first* time.
Some days, it is very hard to love you.
Relax, I've been turning them *inside out.*
Let's see, it's two for $7.99, so three packs will cost...
$23.97.
I was just about to say that, all right?
Sorry I'm not as fast as the Calculator Kid.
BOXER BOXER

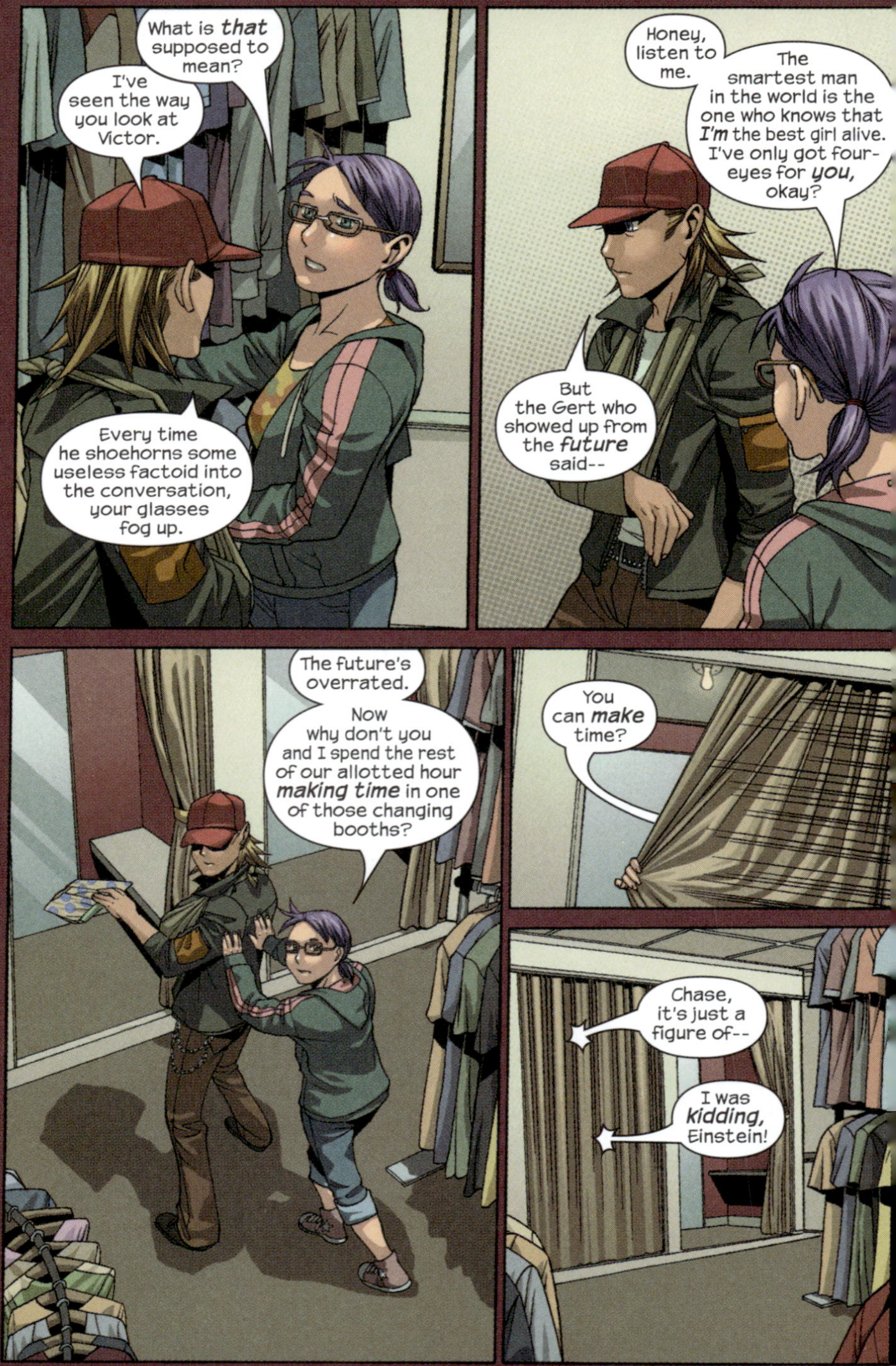
What is *that* supposed to mean?
I've seen the way you look at Victor.
Every time he shoehorns some useless factoid into the conversation, your glasses fog up.
Honey, listen to me.
The smartest man in the world is the one who knows that *I'm* the best girl alive. I've only got four-eyes for *you,* okay?
But the Gert who showed up from the *future* said--
The future's overrated.
Now why don't you and I spend the rest of our allotted hour *making time* in one of those changing booths?
You can *make* time?
Chase, it's just a figure of--
I was *kidding,* Einstein!

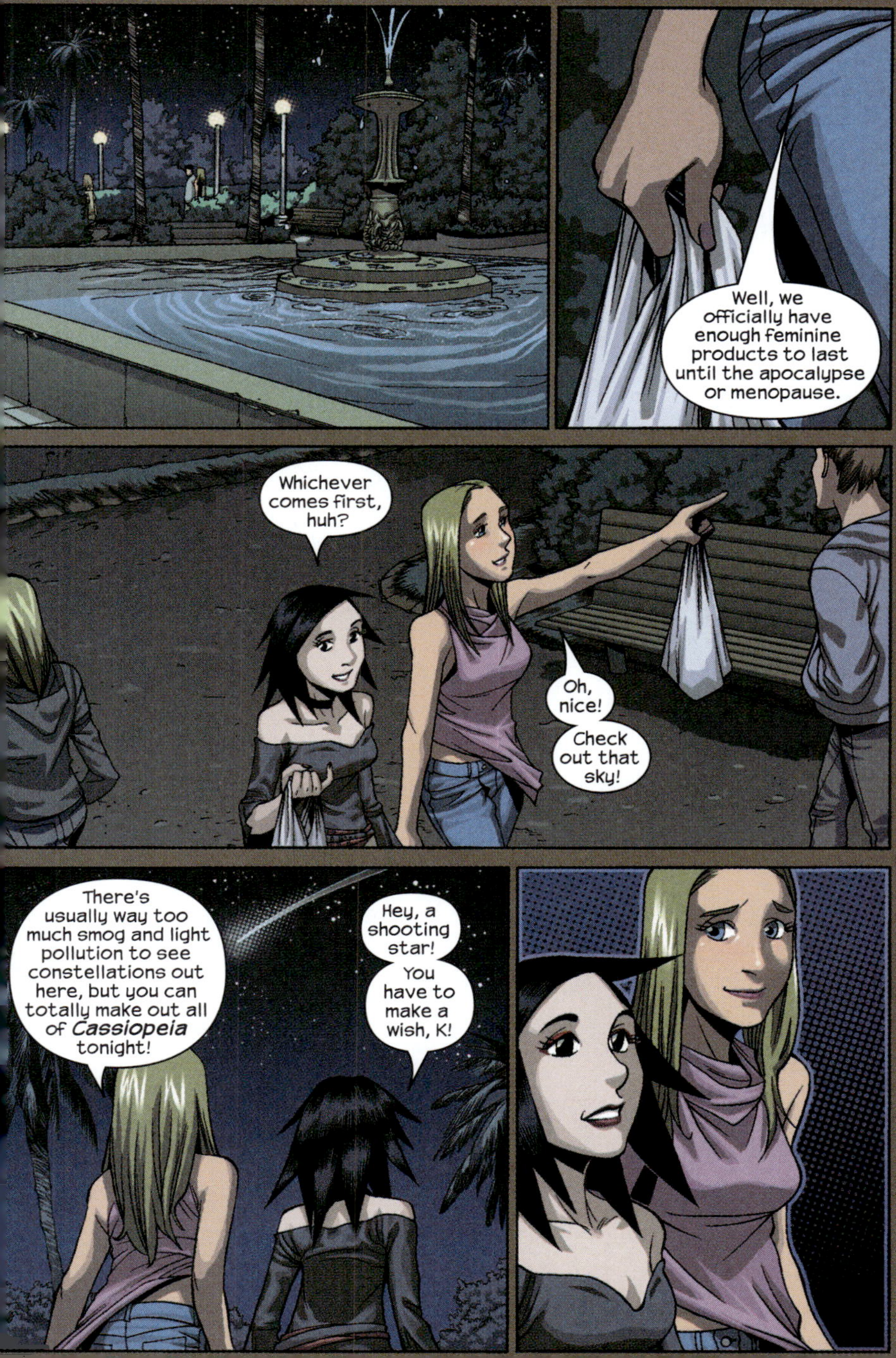
Well, we officially have enough feminine products to last until the apocalypse or menopause.
Whichever comes first, huh?
Oh, nice!
Check out that sky!
There's usually way too much smog and light pollution to see constellations out here, but you can totally make out all of *Cassiopeia* tonight!
Hey, a shooting star!
You have to make a wish, K!

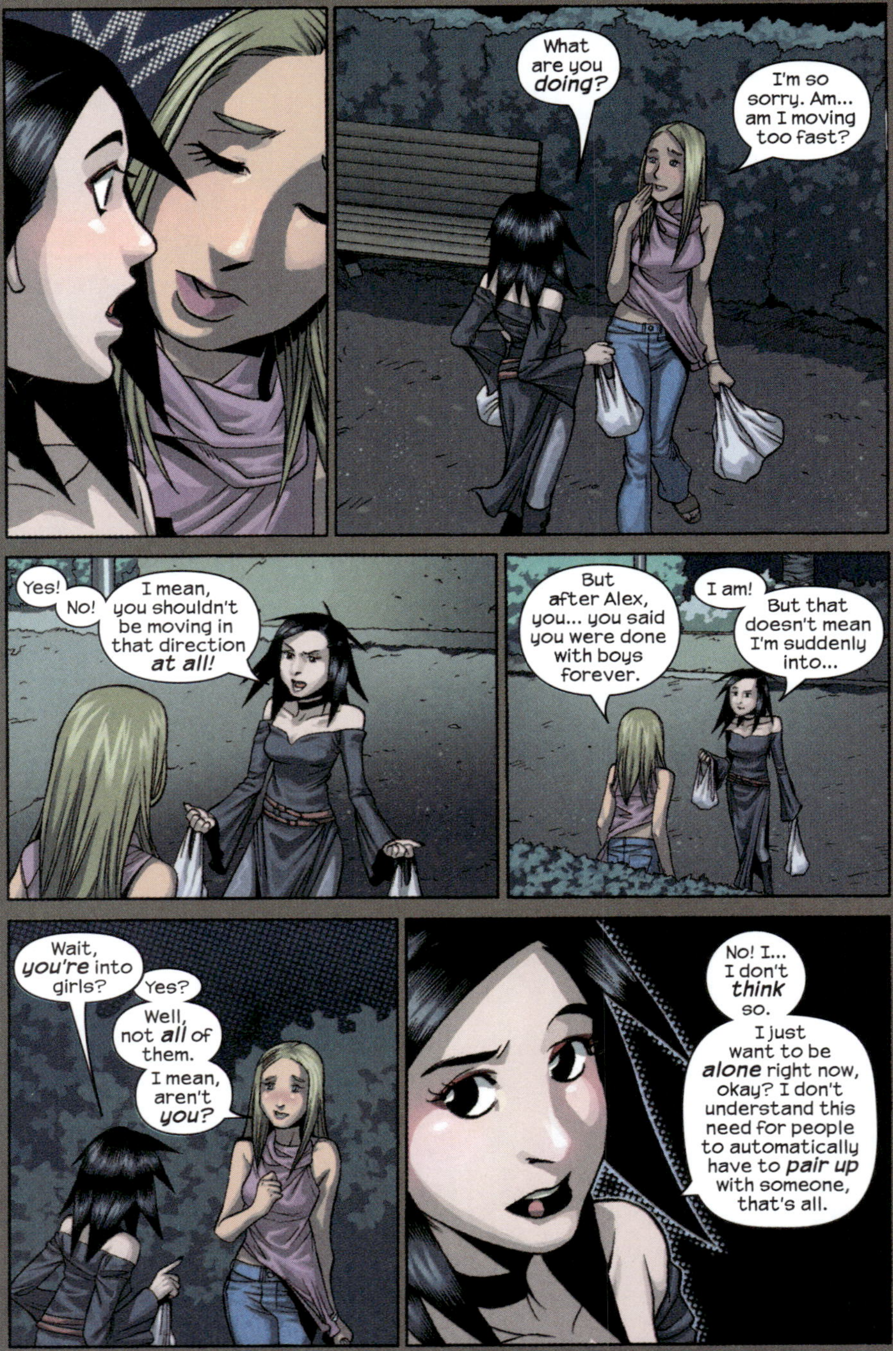
What are you *doing*?
I'm so sorry. Am... am I moving too fast?
Yes!
No!
I mean, you shouldn't be moving in that direction *at all!*
But after Alex, you... you said you were done with boys forever.
I am!
But that doesn't mean I'm suddenly into...
Wait, *you're* into girls?
Yes?
Well, not *all* of them.
I mean, aren't *you?*
No! I... I don't *think* so.
I just want to be *alone* right now, okay? I don't understand this need for people to automatically have to *pair up* with someone, that's all.

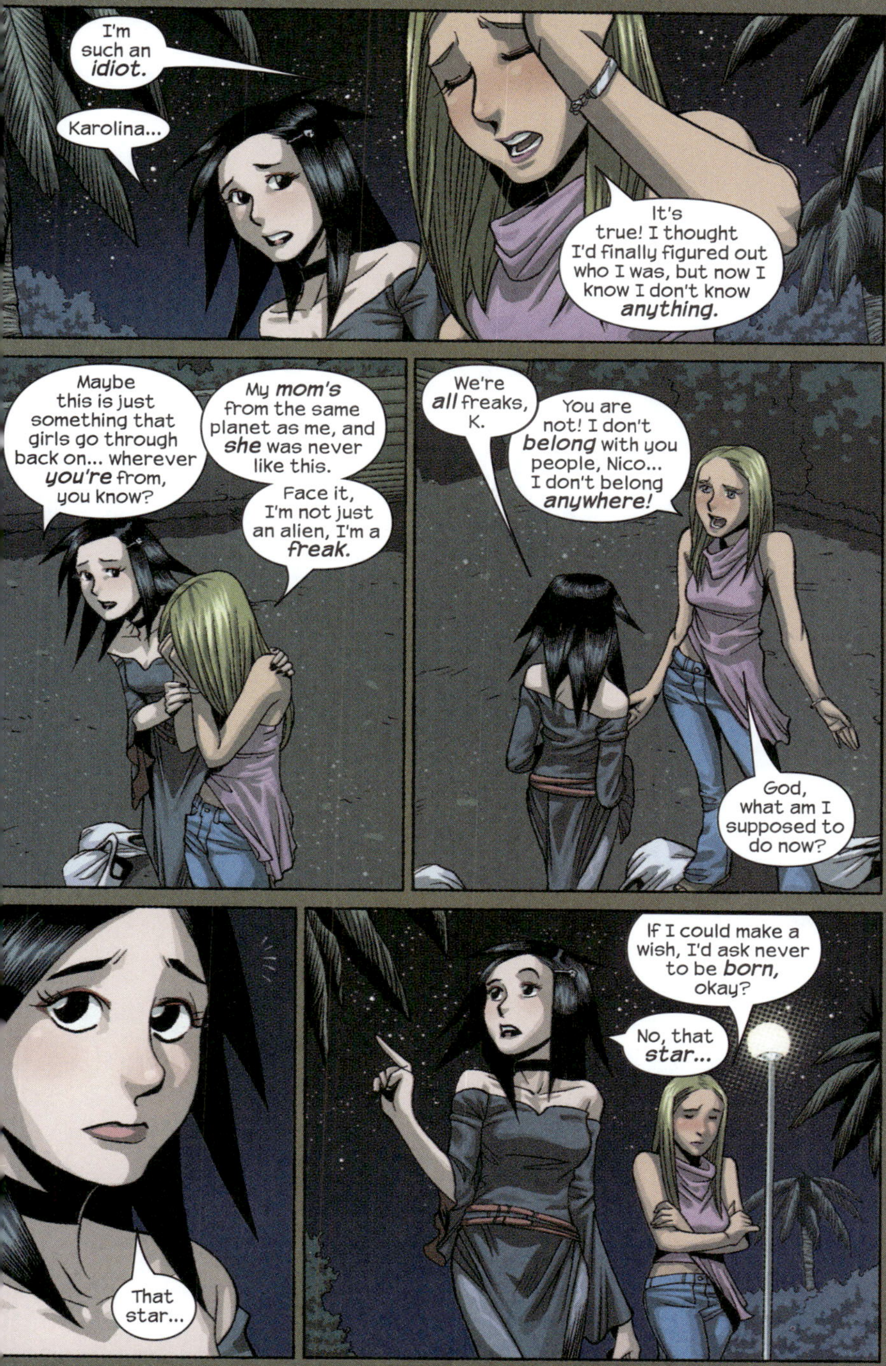
I'm such an idiot.
Karolina...
It's true! I thought I'd finally figured out who I was, but now I know I don't know anything.
Maybe this is just something that girls go through back on... wherever you're from, you know?
My mom's from the same planet as me, and she was never like this.
Face it, I'm not just an alien, I'm a freak.
We're all freaks, K.
You are not! I don't belong with you people, Nico... I don't belong anywhere!
God, what am I supposed to do now?
That star...
If I could make a wish, I'd ask never to be born, okay?
No, that star...

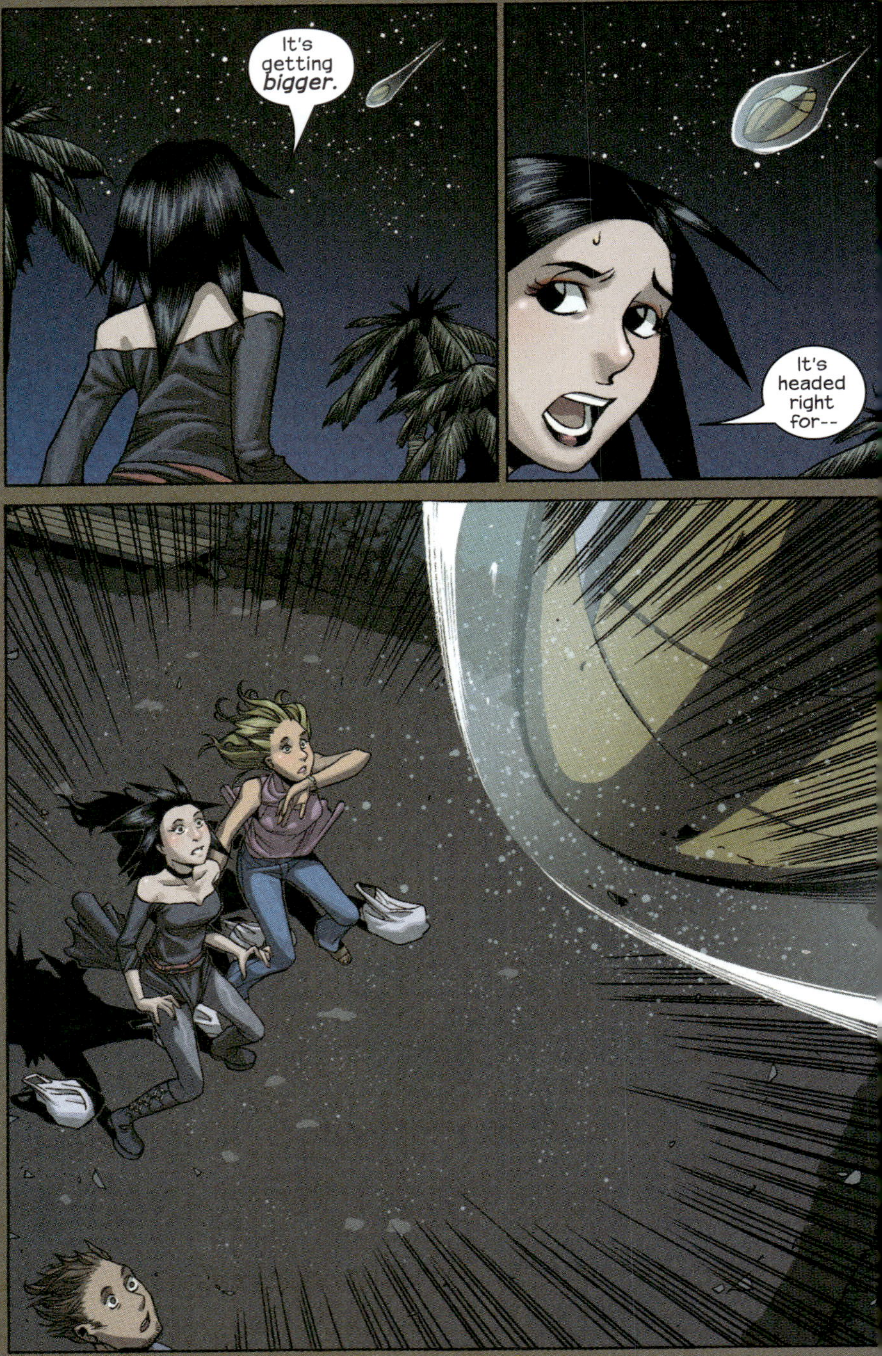
It's getting *bigger.*
It's headed right for--

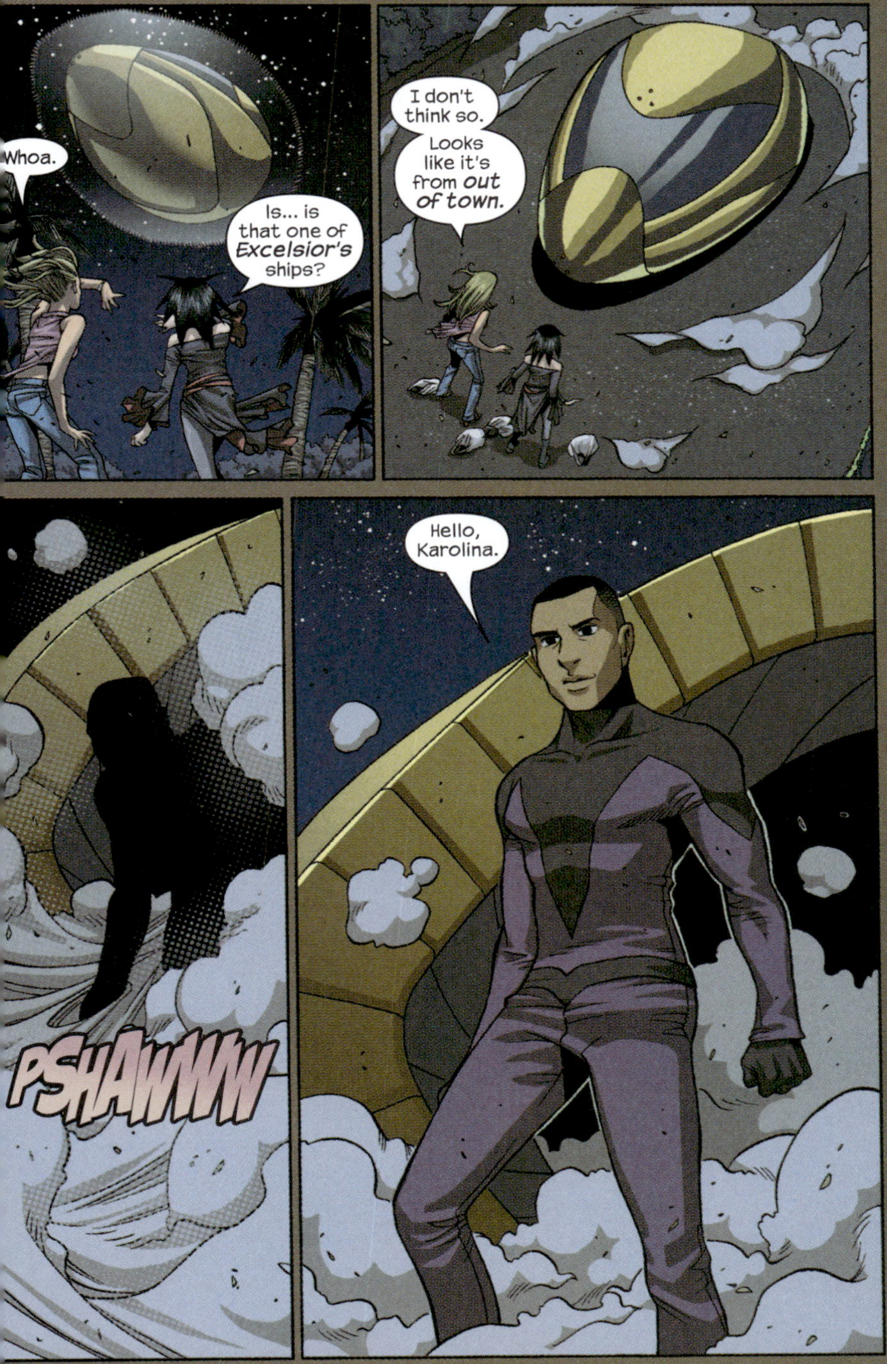
Whoa.
Is... is that one of Excelsior's ships?
I don't think so.
Looks like it's from out of town.
PSHAWWW
Hello, Karolina.

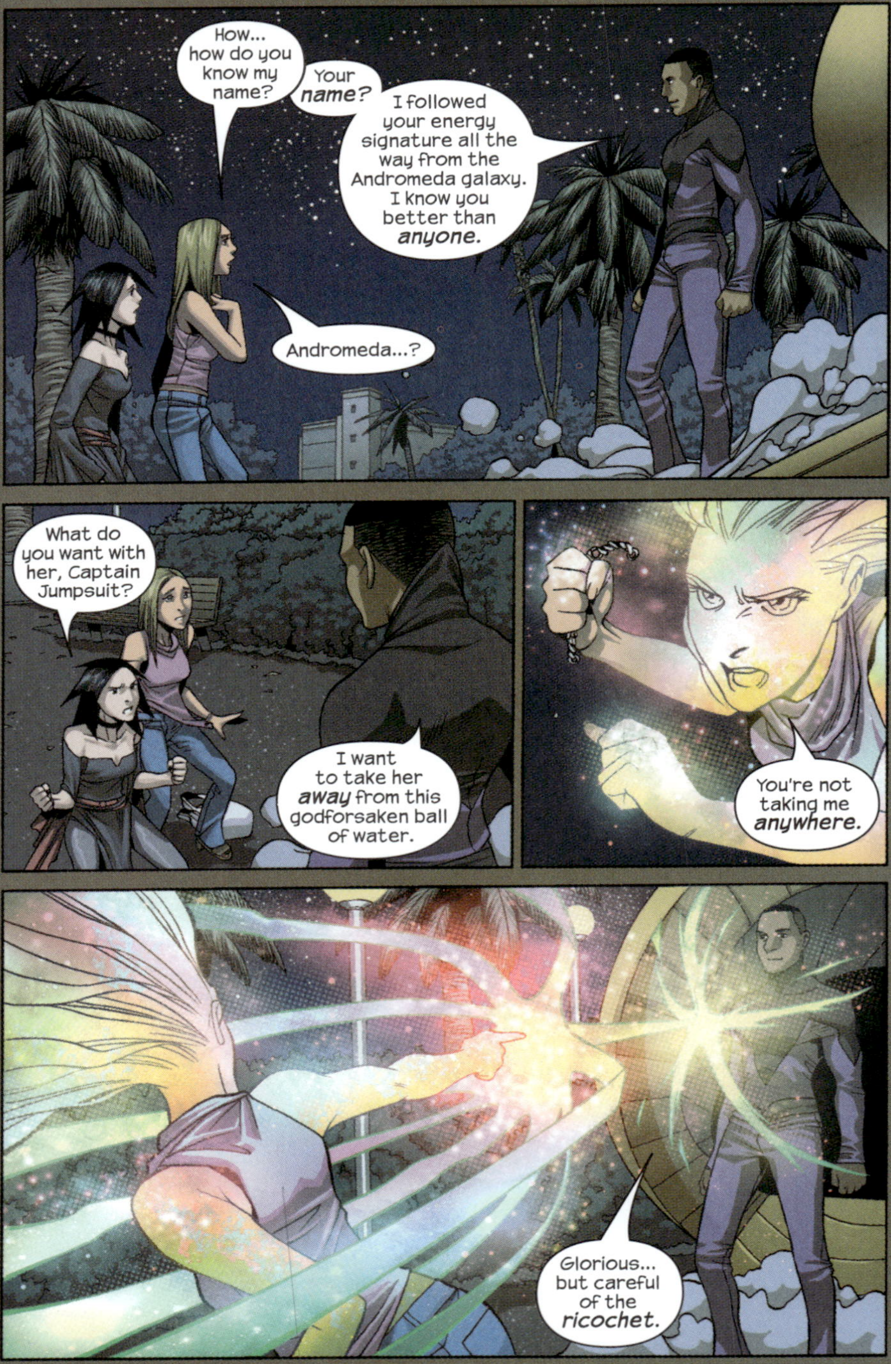
How... how do you know my name?
Your *name?*
I followed your energy signature all the way from the Andromeda galaxy. I know you better than *anyone.*
Andromeda...?
What do you want with her, Captain Jumpsuit?
I want to take her *away* from this godforsaken ball of water.
You're not taking me *anywhere.*
Glorious... but careful of the *ricochet.*

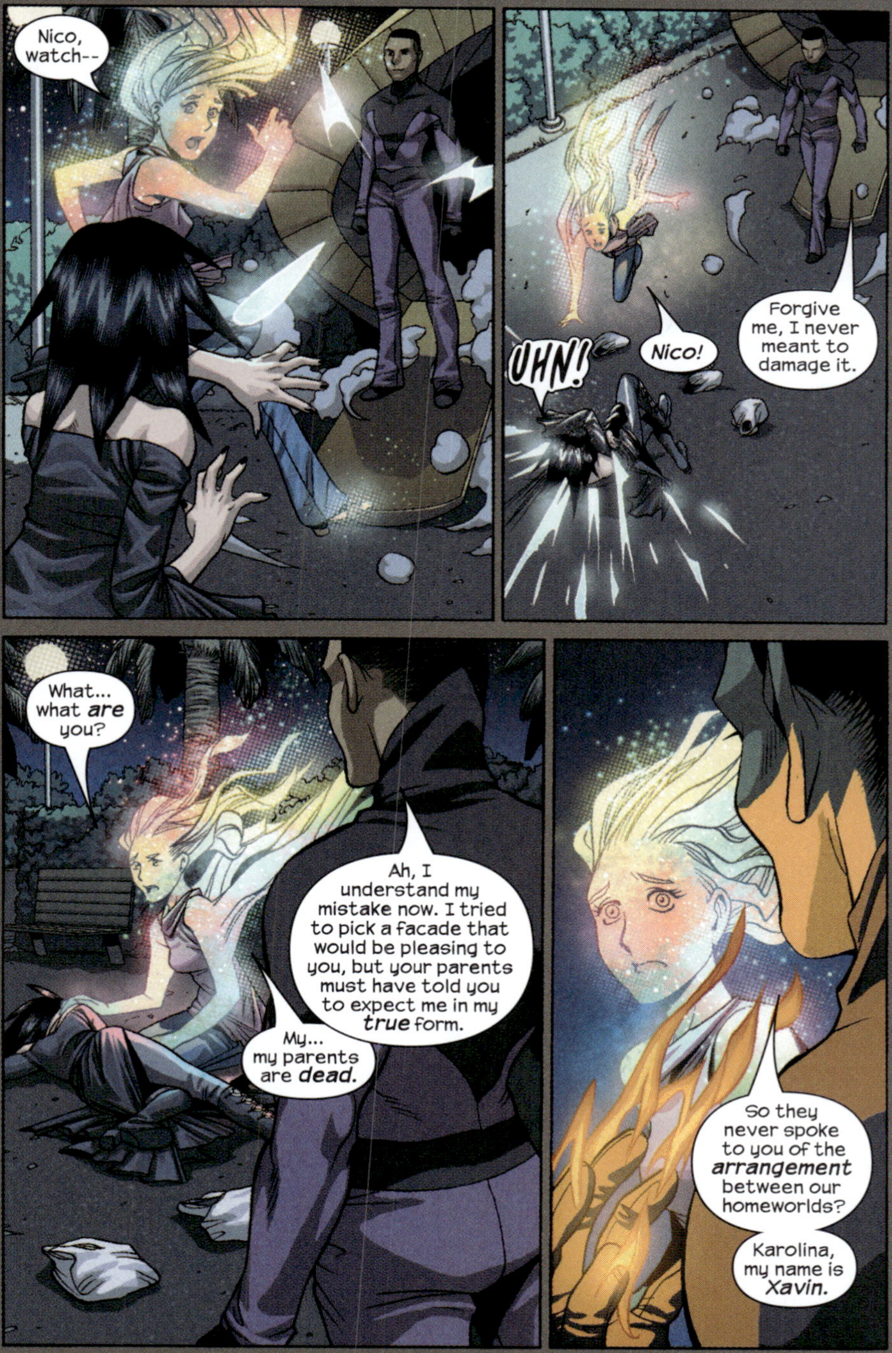
Nico, watch--
Nico!
UHN!
Forgive me, I never meant to damage it.
What... what **are** you?
Ah, I understand my mistake now. I tried to pick a facade that would be pleasing to you, but your parents must have told you to expect me in my **true** form.
My... my parents are **dead.**
So they never spoke to you of the **arrangement** between our homeworlds?
Karolina, my name is **Xavin.**

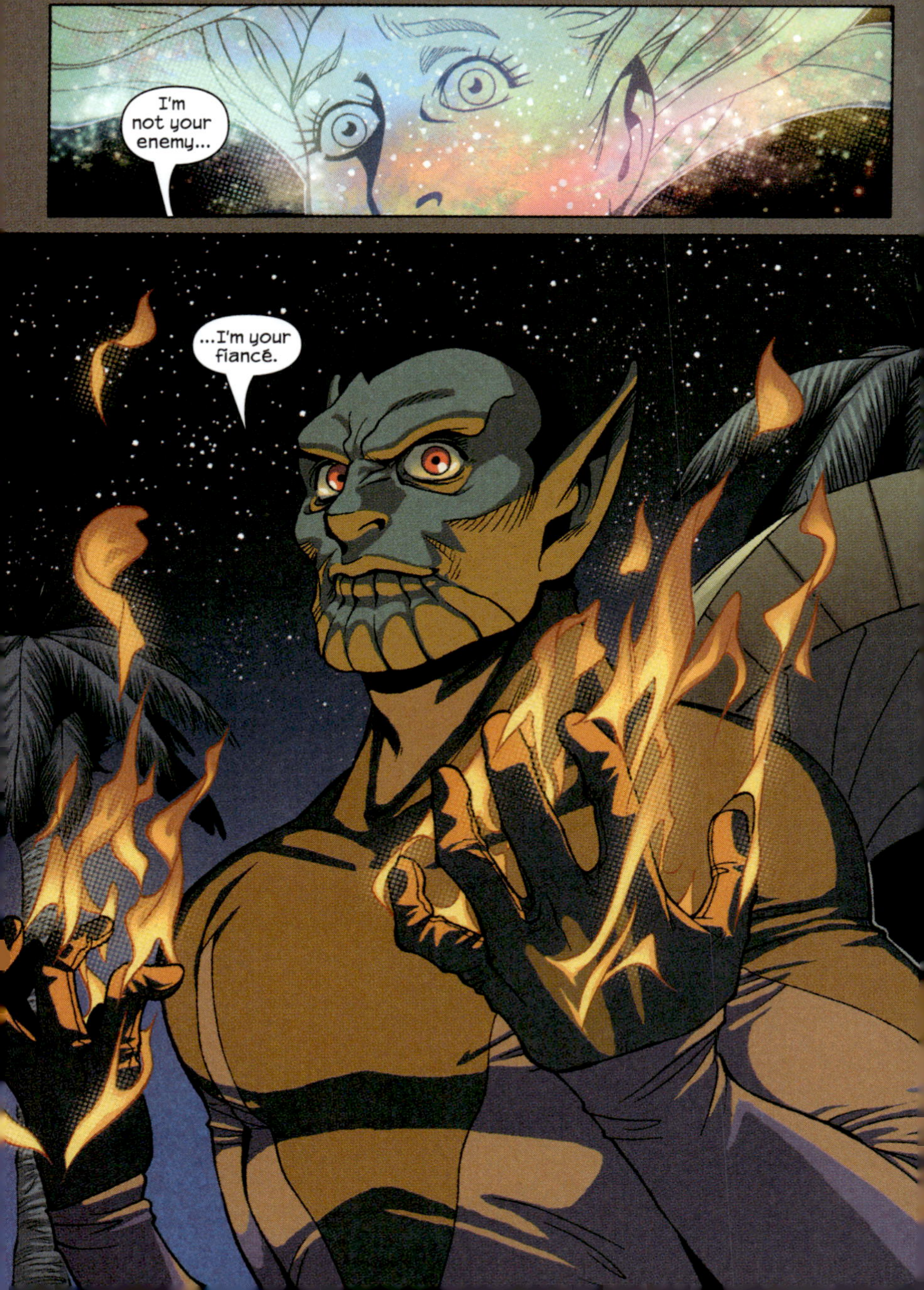
I'm not your enemy...
...I'm your fiancé.

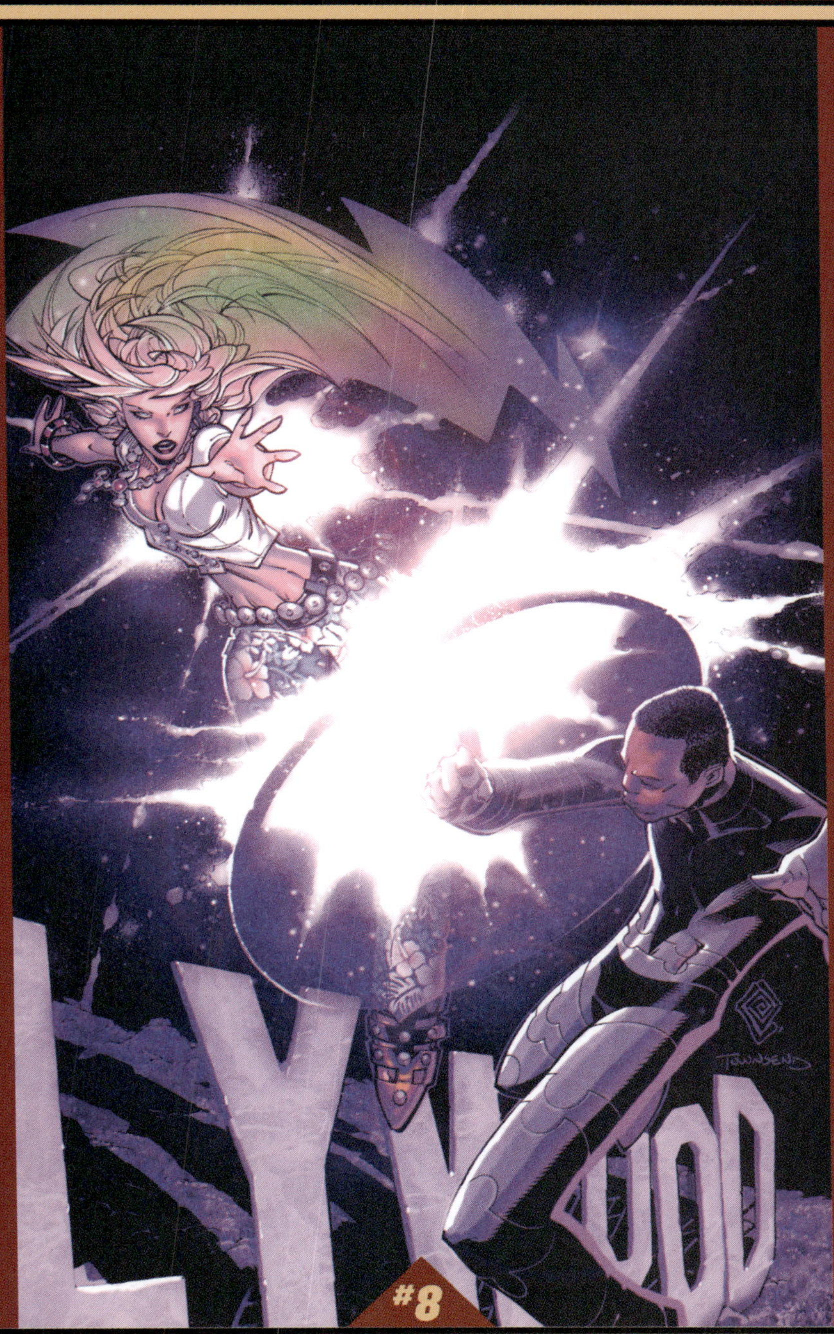
TOWNSEND
#8

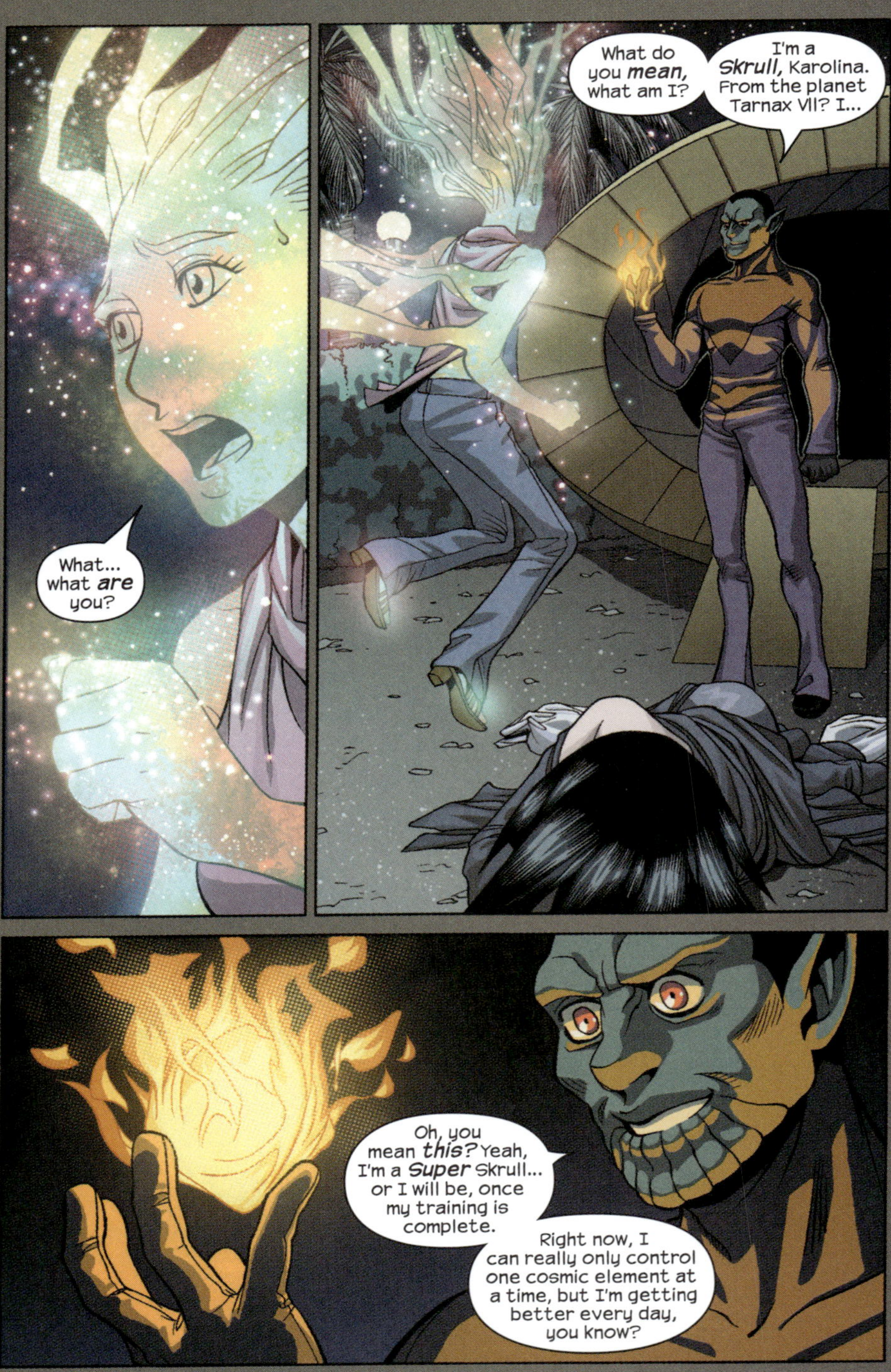
What... what are you?
What do you mean, what am I?
I'm a Skrull, Karolina. From the planet Tarnax VII? I...
Oh, you mean this? Yeah, I'm a Super Skrull... or I will be, once my training is complete.
Right now, I can really only control one cosmic element at a time, but I'm getting better every day, you know?

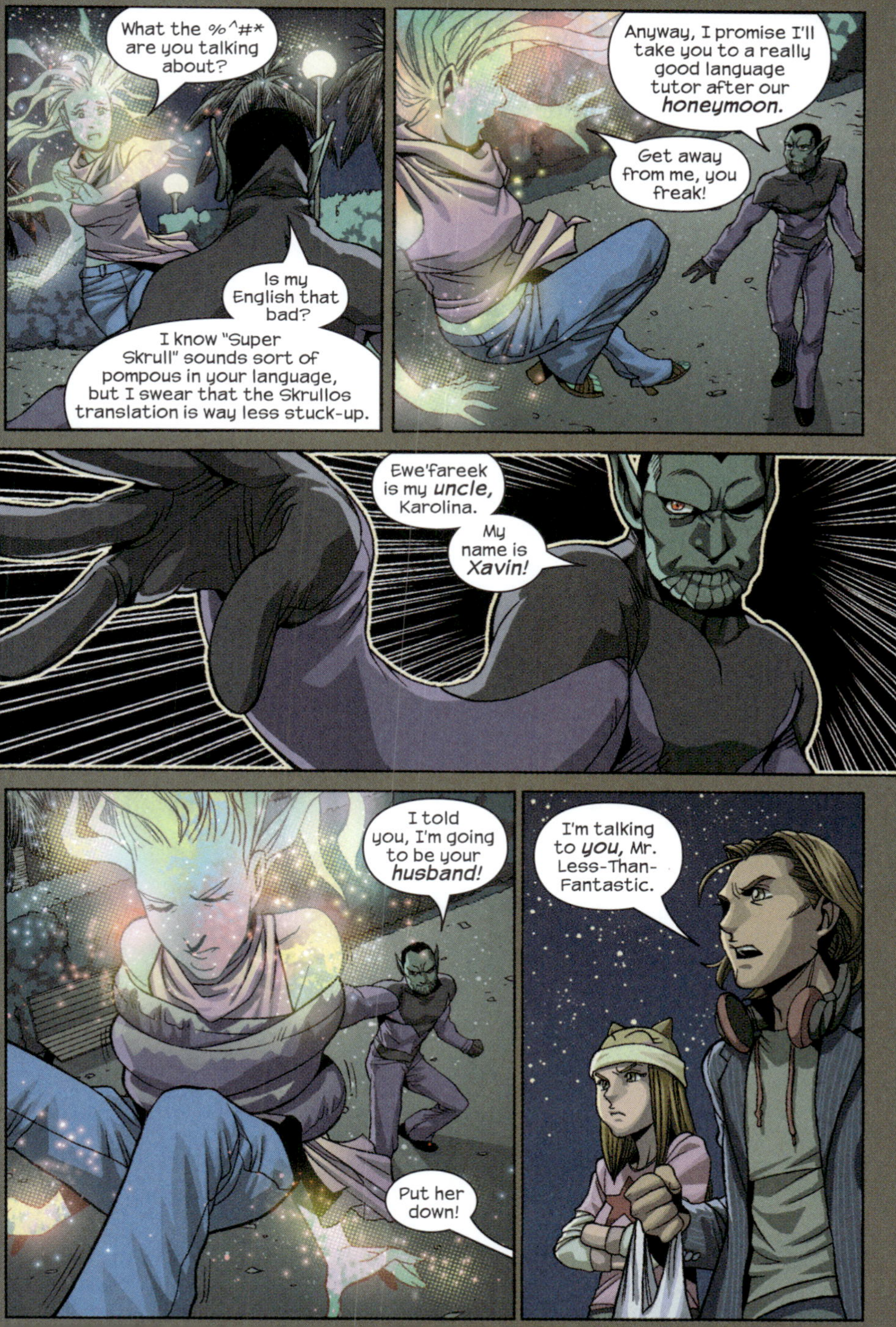
What the %^#* are you talking about?
Is my English that bad?
I know "Super Skrull" sounds sort of pompous in your language, but I swear that the Skrullos translation is way less stuck-up.
Anyway, I promise I'll take you to a really good language tutor after our honeymoon.
Get away from me, you freak!
Ewe'fareek is my uncle, Karolina.
My name is Xavin!
I told you, I'm going to be your husband!
Put her down!
I'm talking to you, Mr. Less-Than-Fantastic.

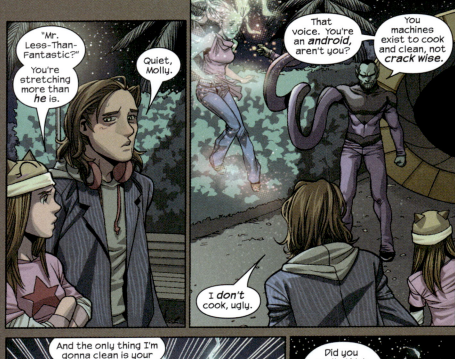

"Mr. Less-Than-Fantastic?" You're stretching more than *he* is.

Quiet, Molly.

That voice. You're an *android*, aren't you?

You machines exist to cook and clean, not *crack wise.*

I *don't* cook, ugly.

And the only thing I'm gonna clean is your *clock.*

Careful with my *cereal,* Victor!

Did you really think something as primitive as *you* could keep me from my betrothed?

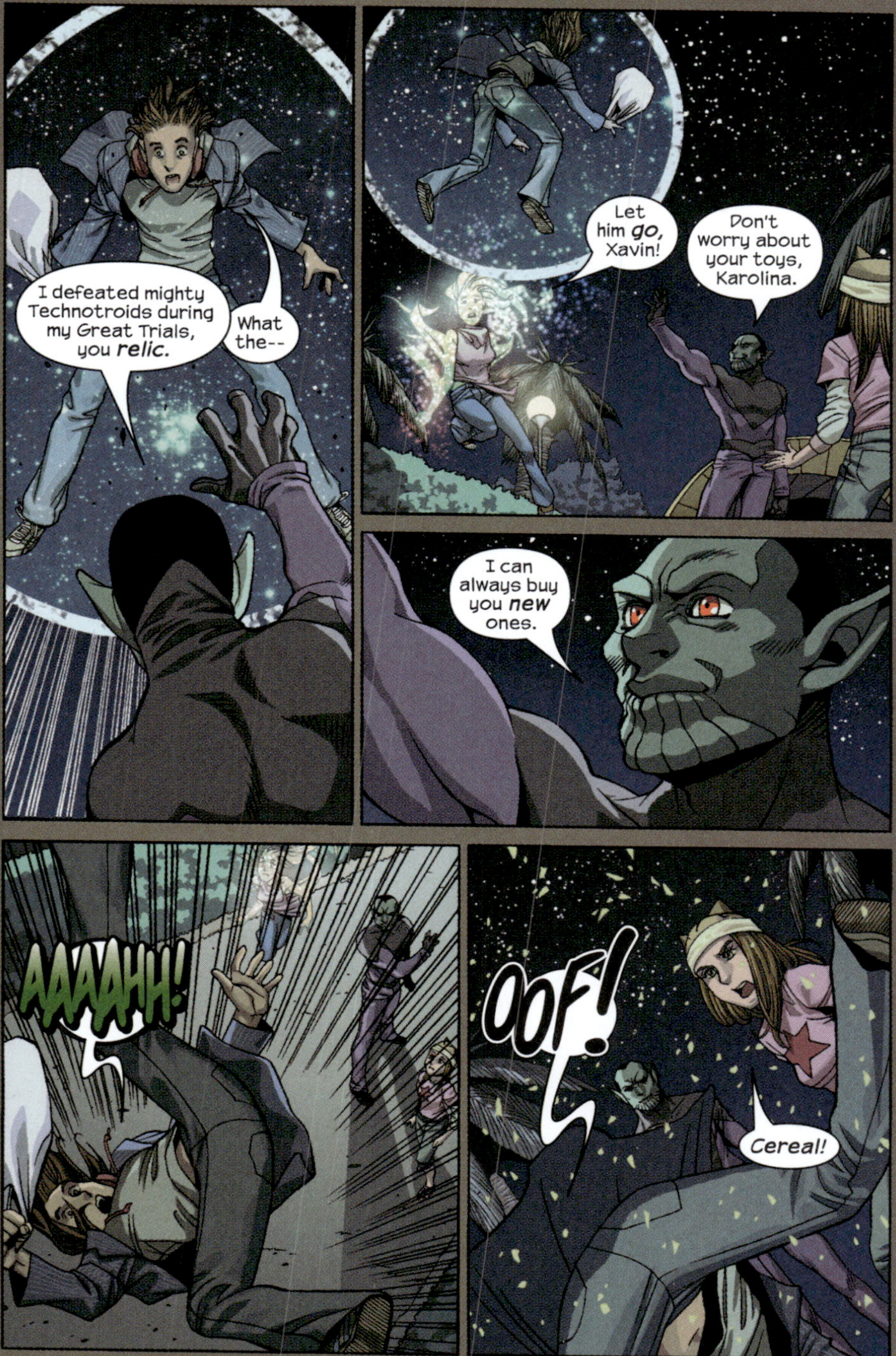

What the--
I defeated mighty Technotroids during my Great Trials, you relic.
Let him go, Xavin!
Don't worry about your toys, Karolina.
I can always buy you new ones.
AAAAHH!
OOF!
Cereal!

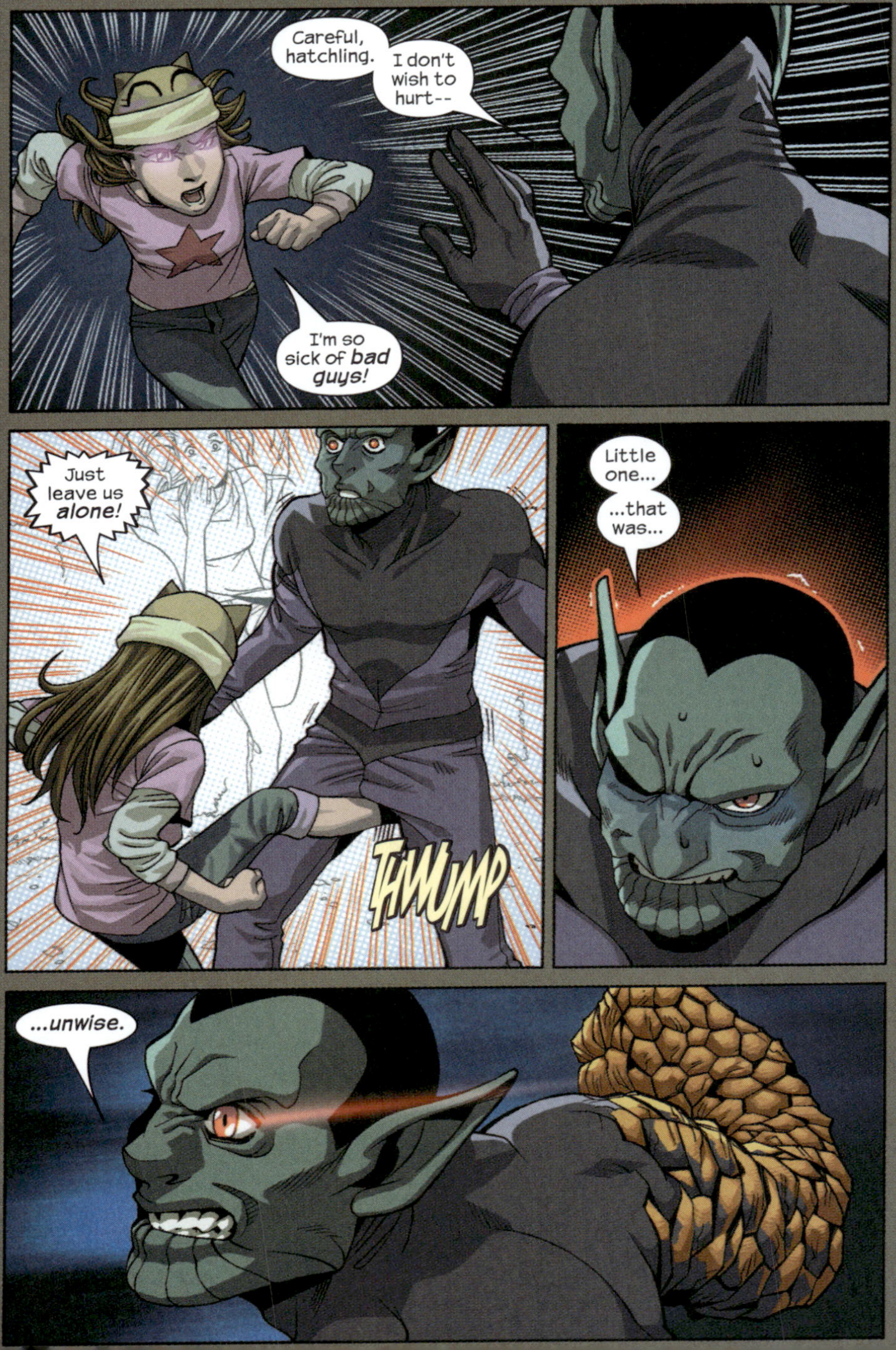
Careful, hatchling.
I don't wish to hurt--
I'm so sick of bad guys!
Just leave us alone!
THWUMP
Little one...
...that was...
...unwise.

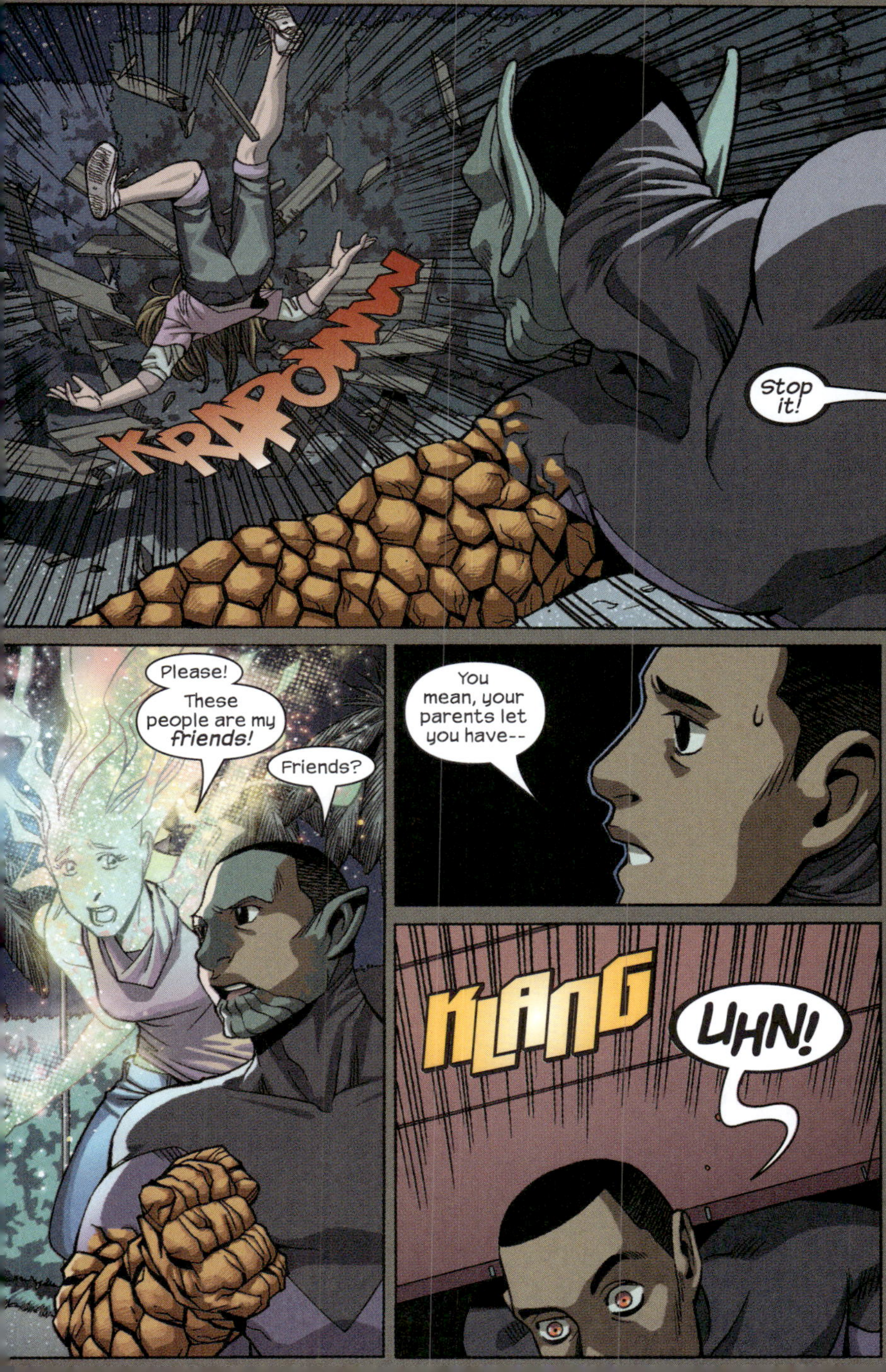
KRAPOWW
Stop it!
Please! These people are my friends!
Friends?
You mean, your parents let you have--
KLANG
UHN!

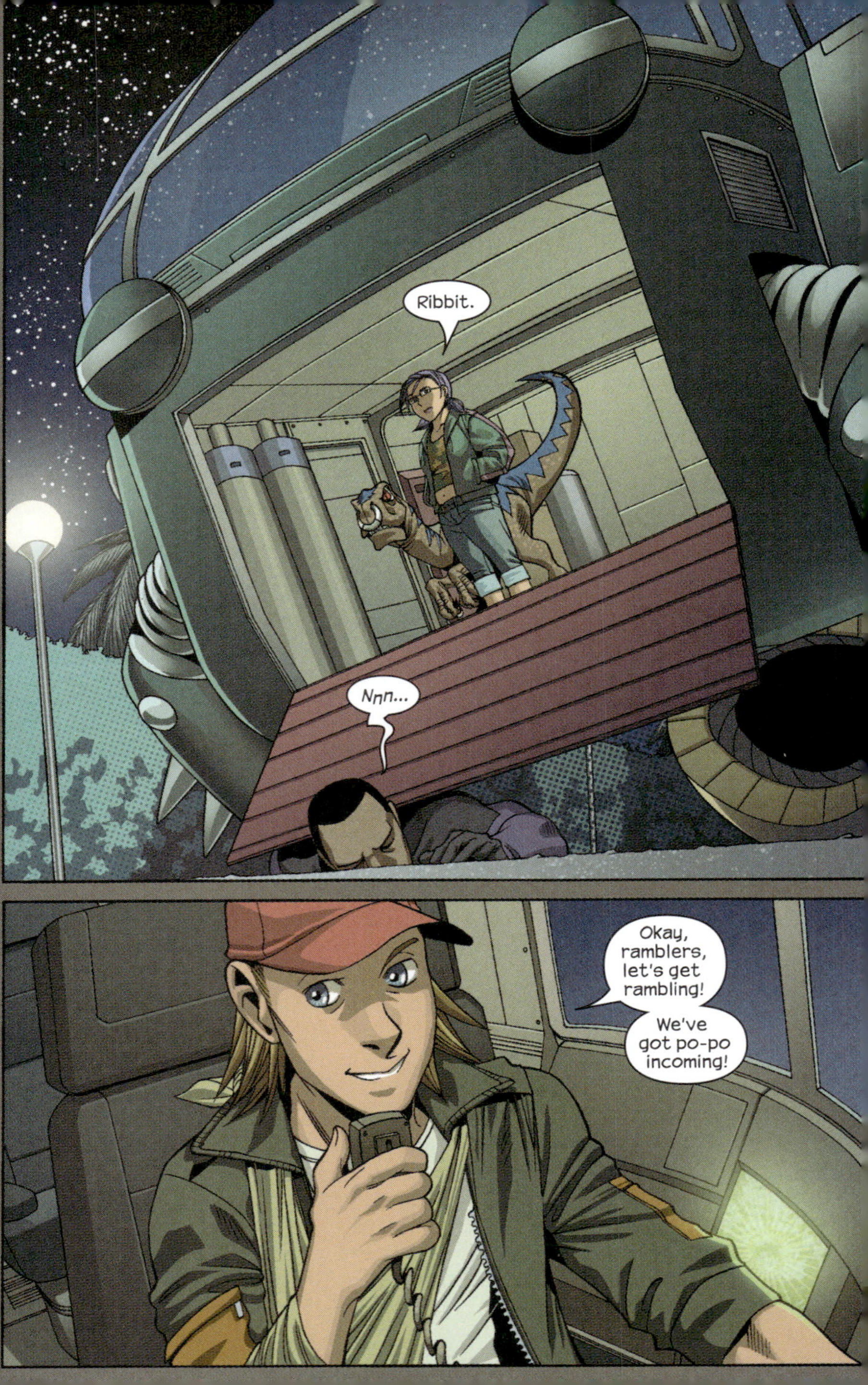
Ribbit.
Nnn...
Okay, ramblers, let's get rambling!
We've got po-po incoming!

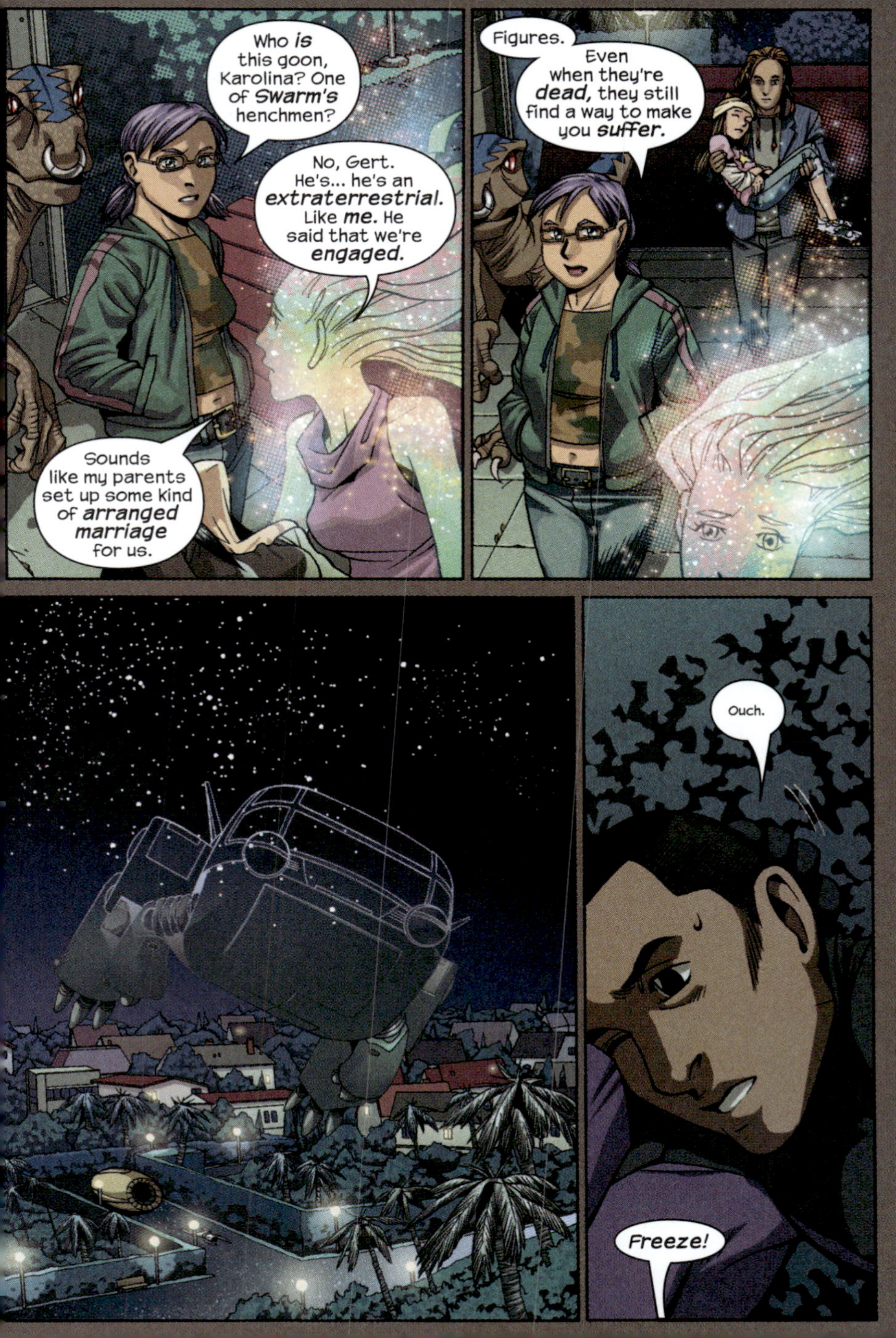

Who is this goon, Karolina? One of Swarm's henchmen?
No, Gert. He's... he's an extraterrestrial. Like me. He said that we're engaged.
Sounds like my parents set up some kind of arranged marriage for us.
Figures.
Even when they're dead, they still find a way to make you suffer.
Ouch.
Freeze!

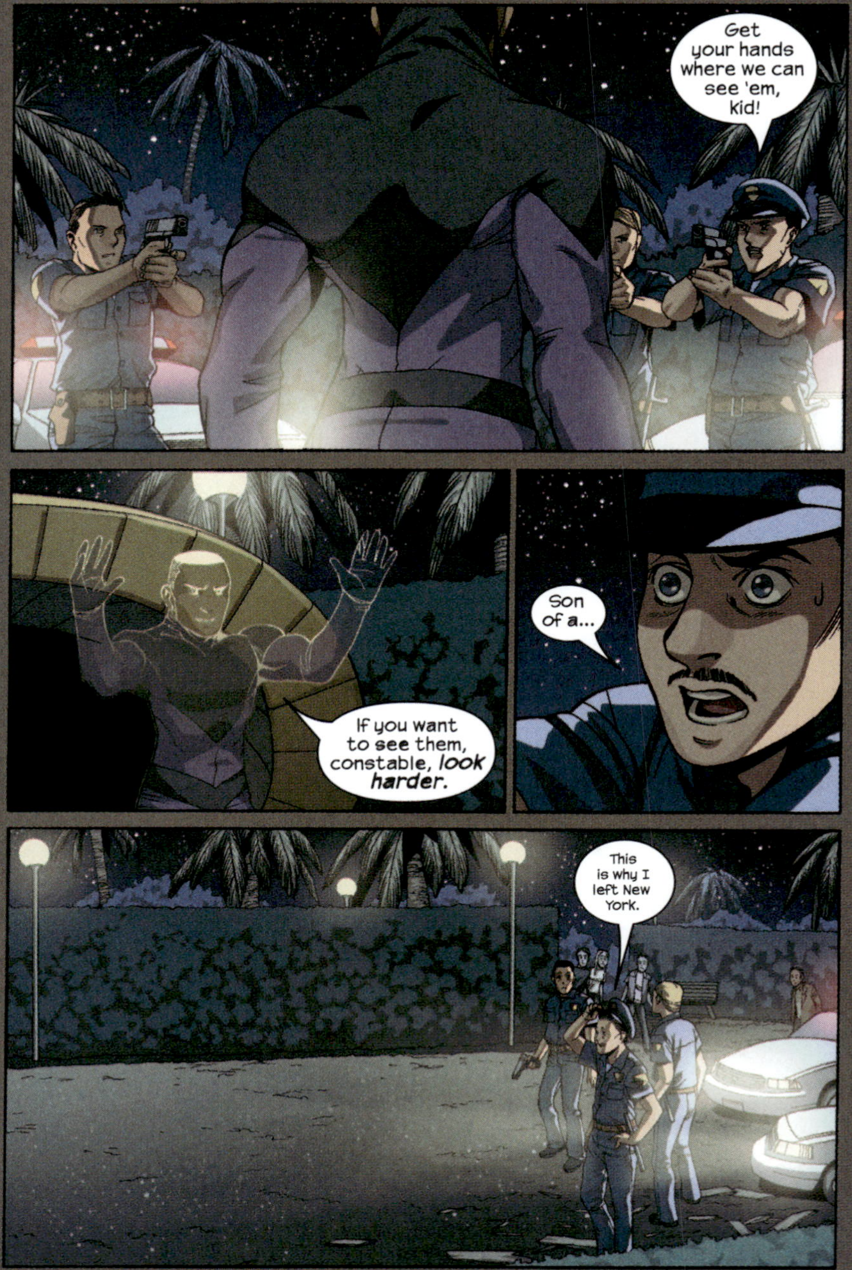

Get your hands where we can see 'em, kid!
If you want to see them, constable, *look harder*.
Son of a...
This is why I left New York.

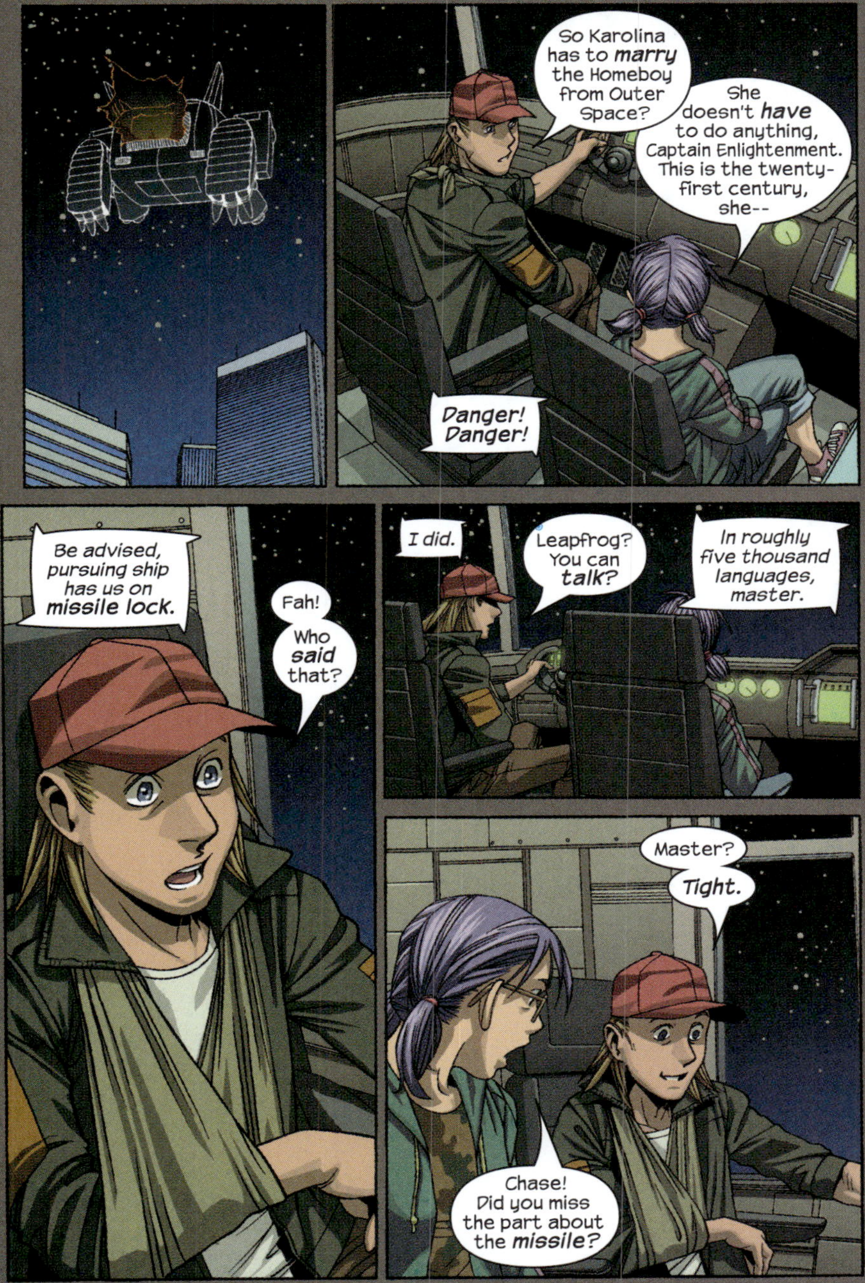
So Karolina has to *marry* the Homeboy from Outer Space?
She doesn't *have* to do anything, Captain Enlightenment. This is the twenty-first century, she--
Danger! Danger!
Be advised, pursuing ship has us on ***missile lock.***
Fah!
Who *said* that?
I did.
Leapfrog? You can *talk?*
In roughly five thousand languages, master.
Master?
Tight.
Chase! Did you miss the part about the *missile?*

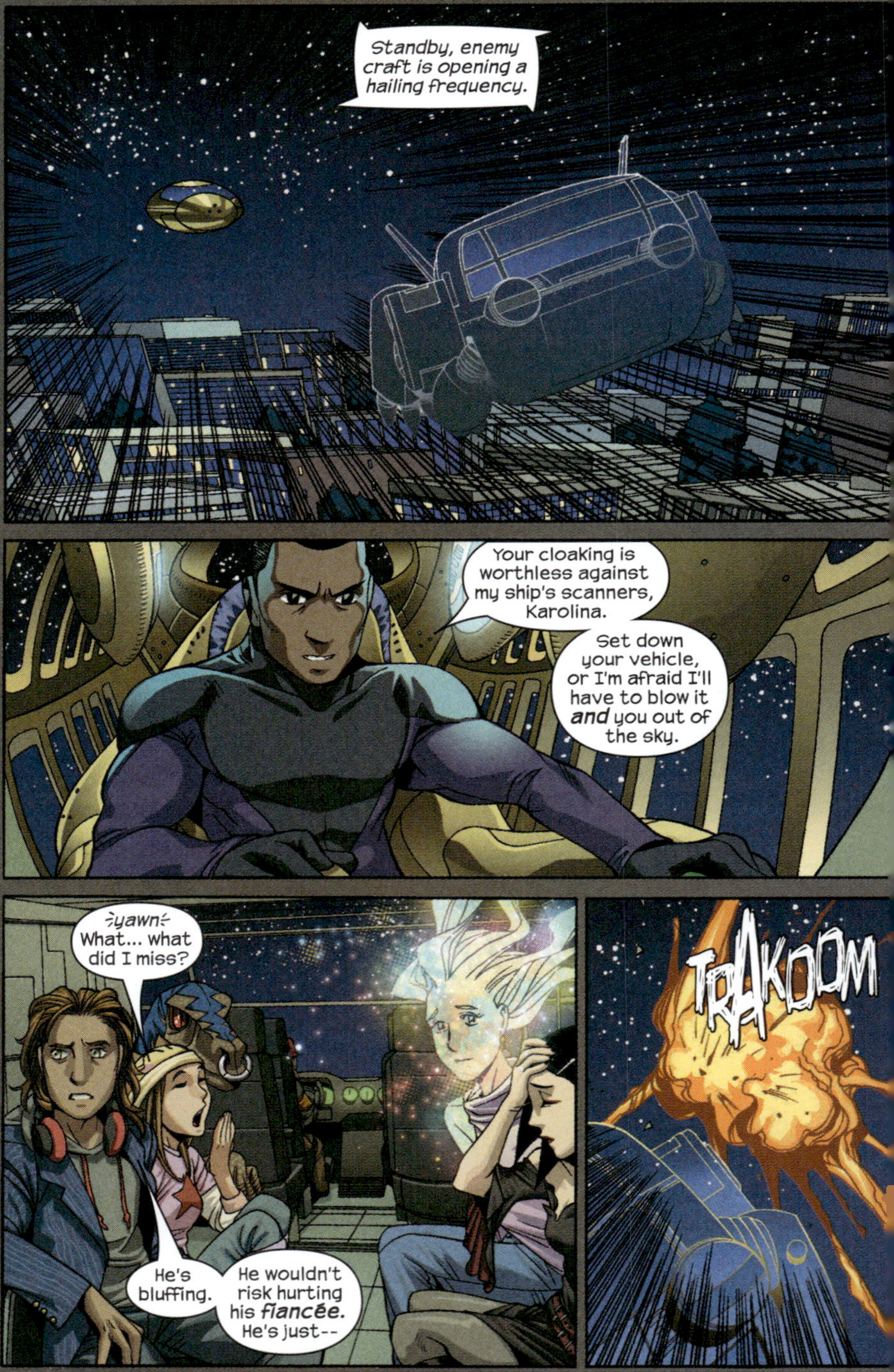
Standby, enemy craft is opening a hailing frequency.
Your cloaking is worthless against my ship's scanners, Karolina.
Set down your vehicle, or I'm afraid I'll have to blow it *and* you out of the sky.
-yawn-
What... what did I miss?
He's bluffing.
He wouldn't risk hurting his *fiancée.* He's just--
TRAKOOM

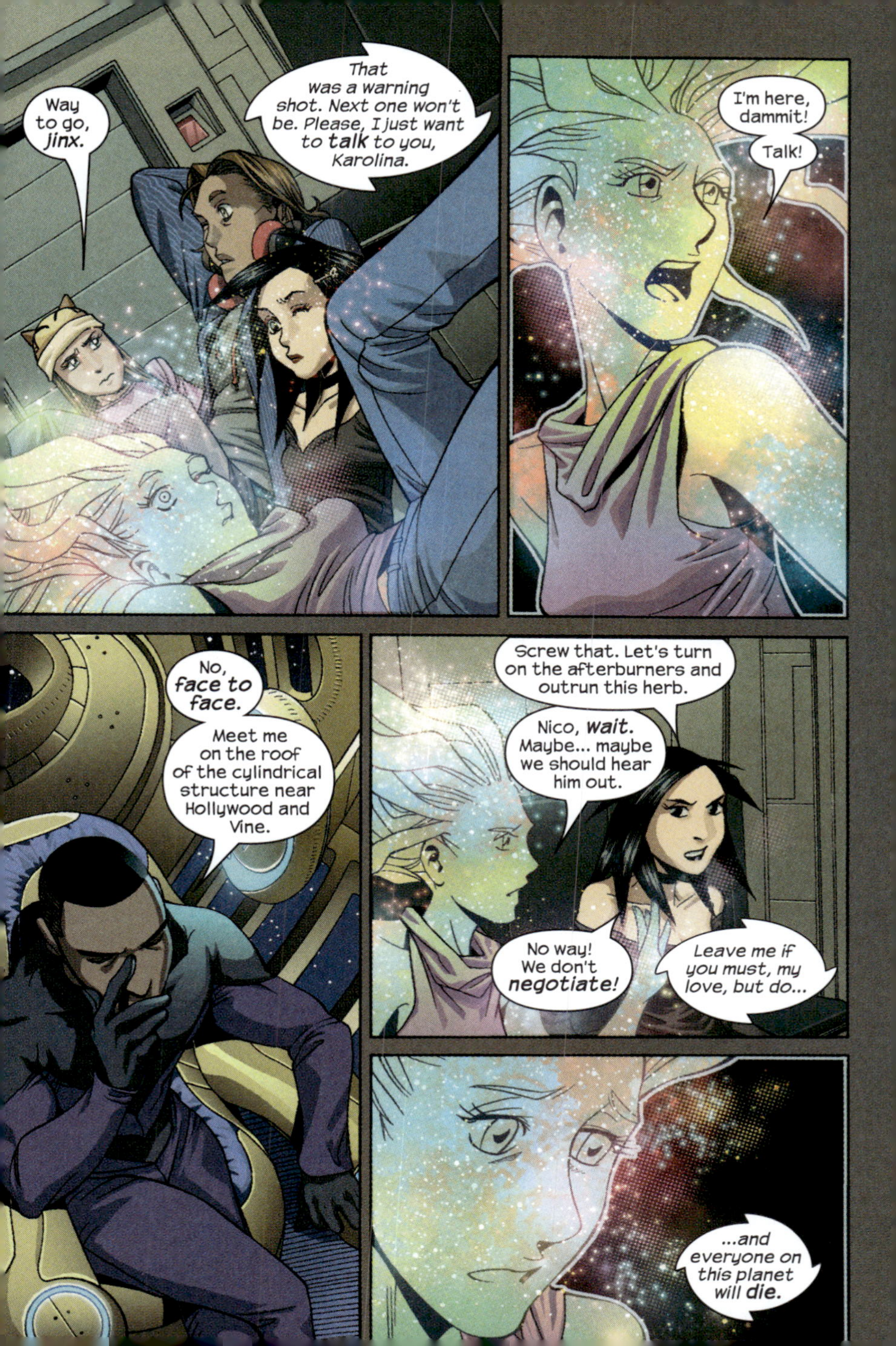
Way to go, jinx.
That was a warning shot. Next one won't be. Please, I just want to talk to you, Karolina.
I'm here, dammit!
Talk!
No, face to face.
Meet me on the roof of the cylindrical structure near Hollywood and Vine.
Screw that. Let's turn on the afterburners and outrun this herb.
Nico, wait. Maybe... maybe we should hear him out.
No way! We don't negotiate!
Leave me if you must, my love, but do...
...and everyone on this planet will die.

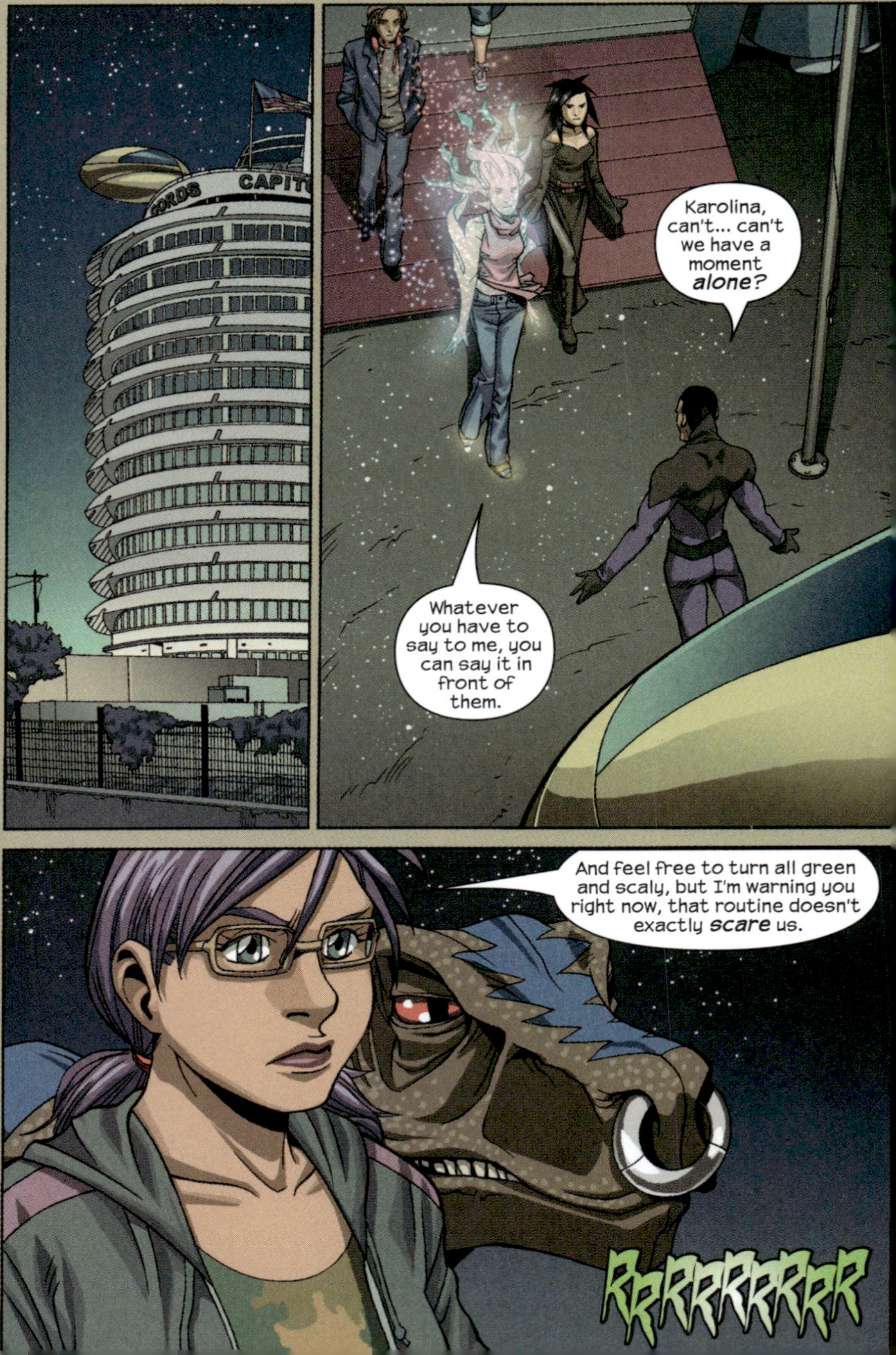
CORDS CAPITO
Karolina, can't... can't we have a moment *alone?*
Whatever you have to say to me, you can say it in front of them.
And feel free to turn all green and scaly, but I'm warning you right now, that routine doesn't exactly *scare* us.
RRRRRRRR

First of all, I apologize for my... **outburst.** Your customs are still unfamiliar to me.

I hail from a distant outpost world of the Skrull Empire. Fifteen years ago, my father, Prince De'zean, led an invasion against Earth. He was stopped by your **parents,** Karolina.

My parents? *HOW?*

In exchange for sparing their adopted home, your mother and father revealed the coordinates of a much more valuable target...

...*Majesdane,* your parents' *birth planet,* which had exiled them for criminal activities decades ago.

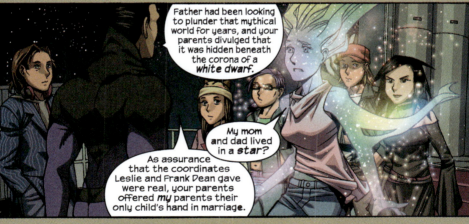

Father had been looking to plunder that mythical world for years, and your parents divulged that it was hidden beneath the corona of a *white dwarf.*

My mom and dad lived in a *star?*

As assurance that the coordinates Leslie and Frank Dean gave were real, your parents offered *my* parents their only child's hand in marriage.

And now you're here to **collect** on your folks' sick agreement?

My "folks" are *dead.*

They were both killed in the bloody war that's been raging between Tarnax VII and Majesdane for the last fifteen years.

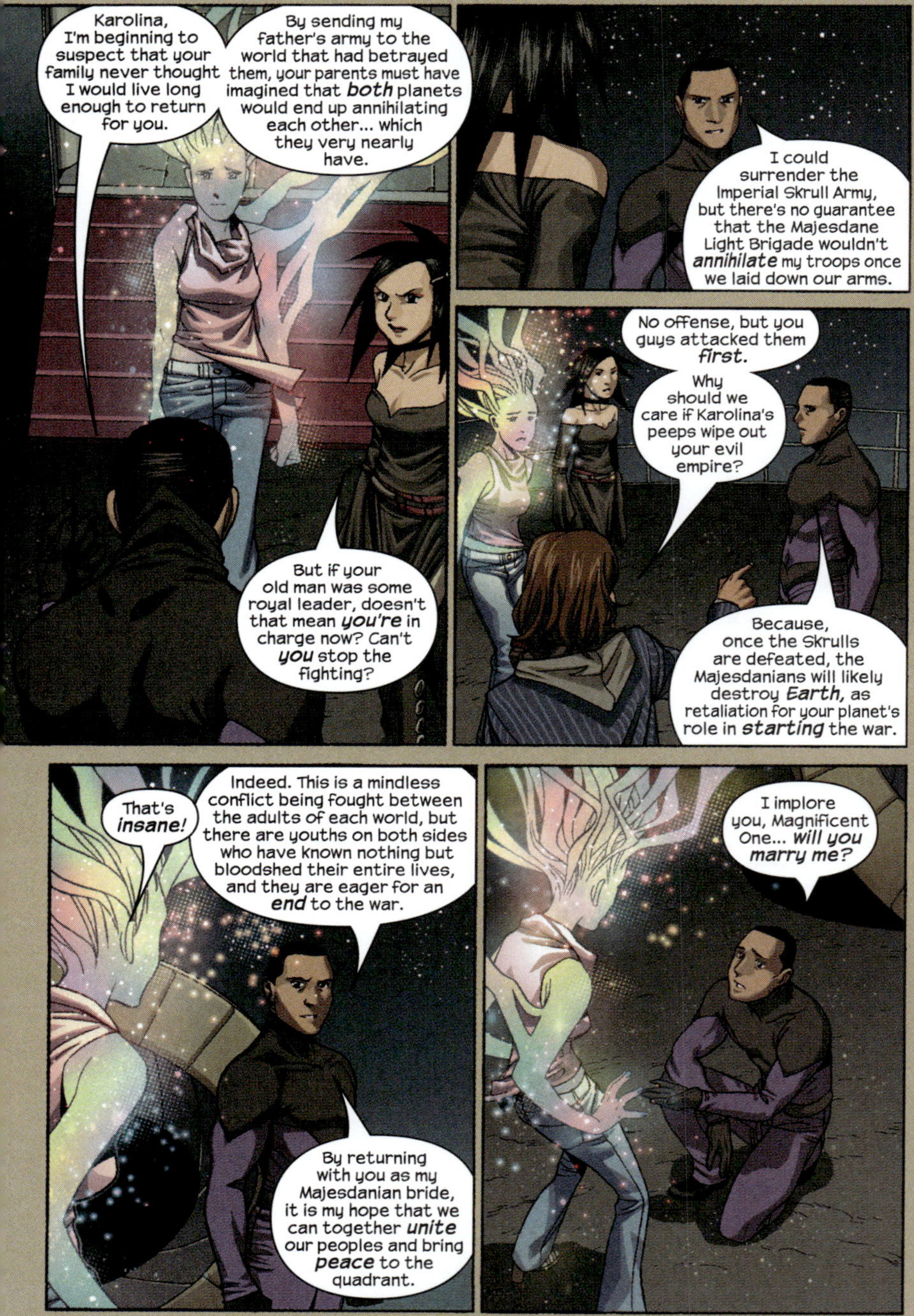

Karolina, I'm beginning to suspect that your family never thought I would live long enough to return for you.
By sending my father's army to the world that had betrayed them, your parents must have imagined that *both* planets would end up annihilating each other... which they very nearly have.
But if your old man was some royal leader, doesn't that mean *you're* in charge now? Can't *you* stop the fighting?
I could surrender the Imperial Skrull Army, but there's no guarantee that the Majesdane Light Brigade wouldn't *annihilate* my troops once we laid down our arms.
No offense, but you guys attacked them *first.*
Why should we care if Karolina's peeps wipe out your evil empire?
Because, once the Skrulls are defeated, the Majesdanians will likely destroy *Earth,* as retaliation for your planet's role in *starting* the war.
That's *insane!*
Indeed. This is a mindless conflict being fought between the adults of each world, but there are youths on both sides who have known nothing but bloodshed their entire lives, and they are eager for an *end* to the war.
By returning with you as my Majesdanian bride, it is my hope that we can together *unite* our peoples and bring *peace* to the quadrant.
I implore you, Magnificent One... *will you marry me?*

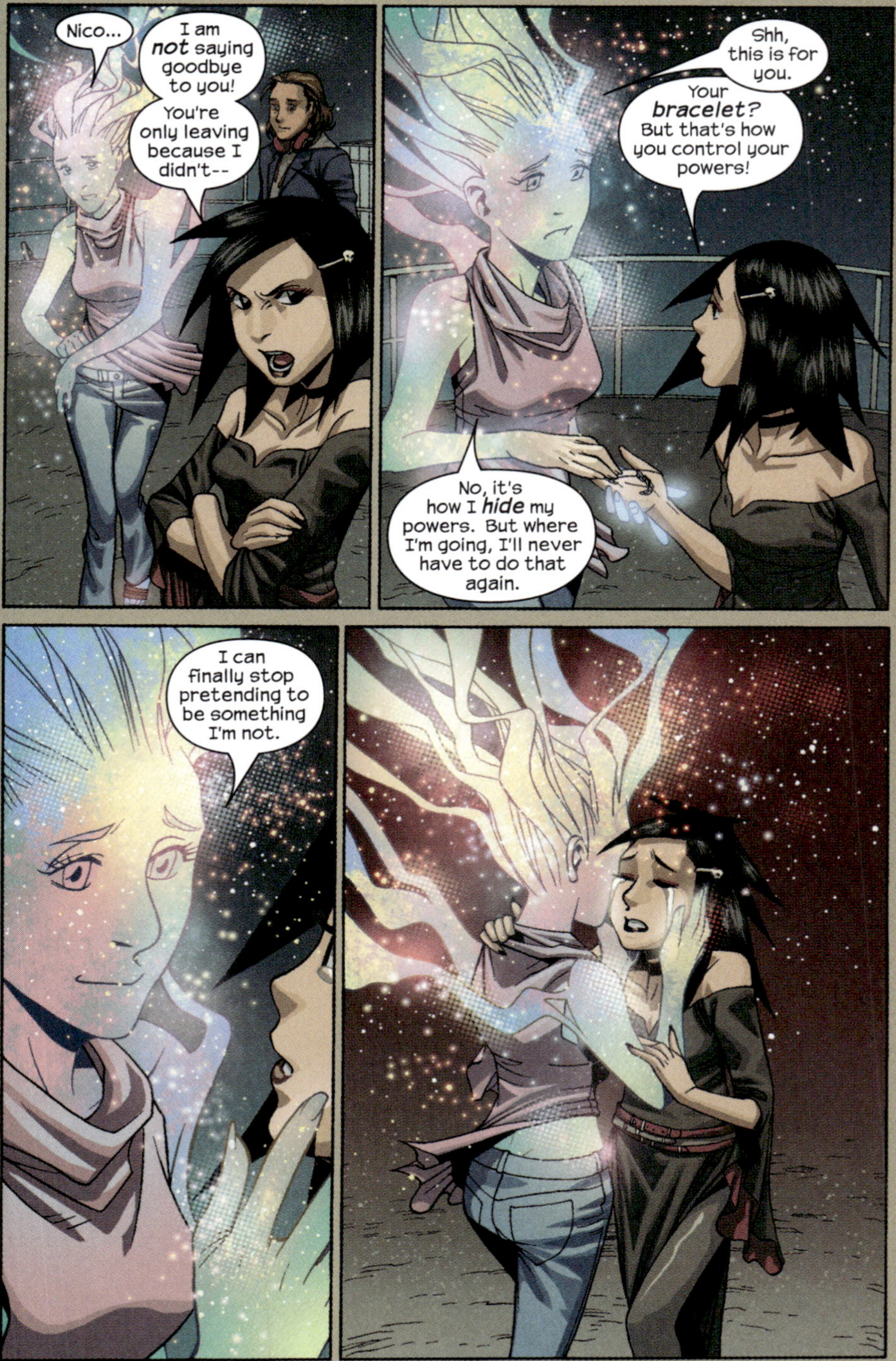

Nico...
I am *not* saying goodbye to you!
You're only leaving because I didn't--
Shh, this is for you.
Your *bracelet?* But that's how you control your powers!
No, it's how I *hide* my powers. But where I'm going, I'll never have to do that again.
I can finally stop pretending to be something I'm not.

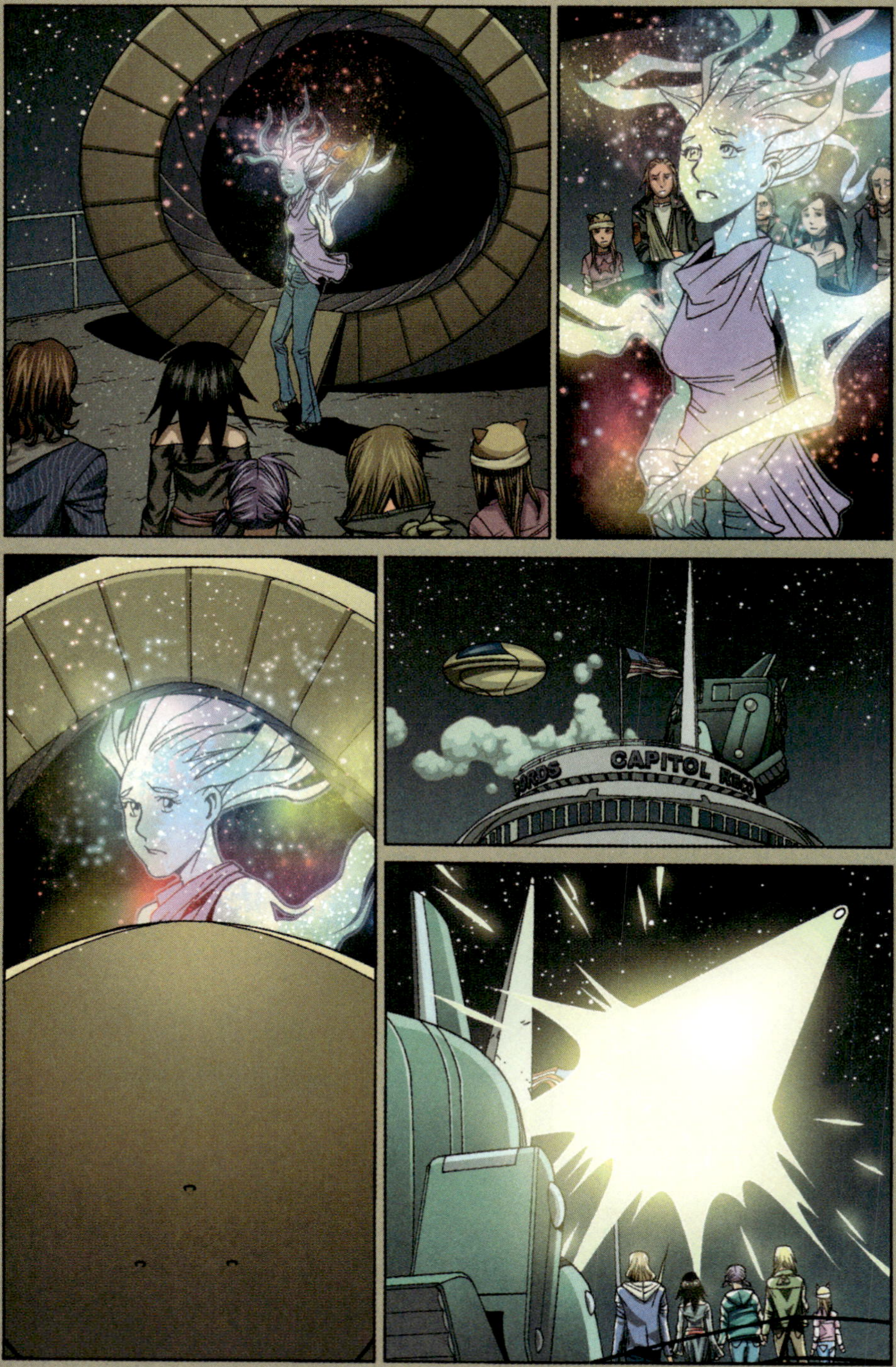
ORDS
CAPITOL REC

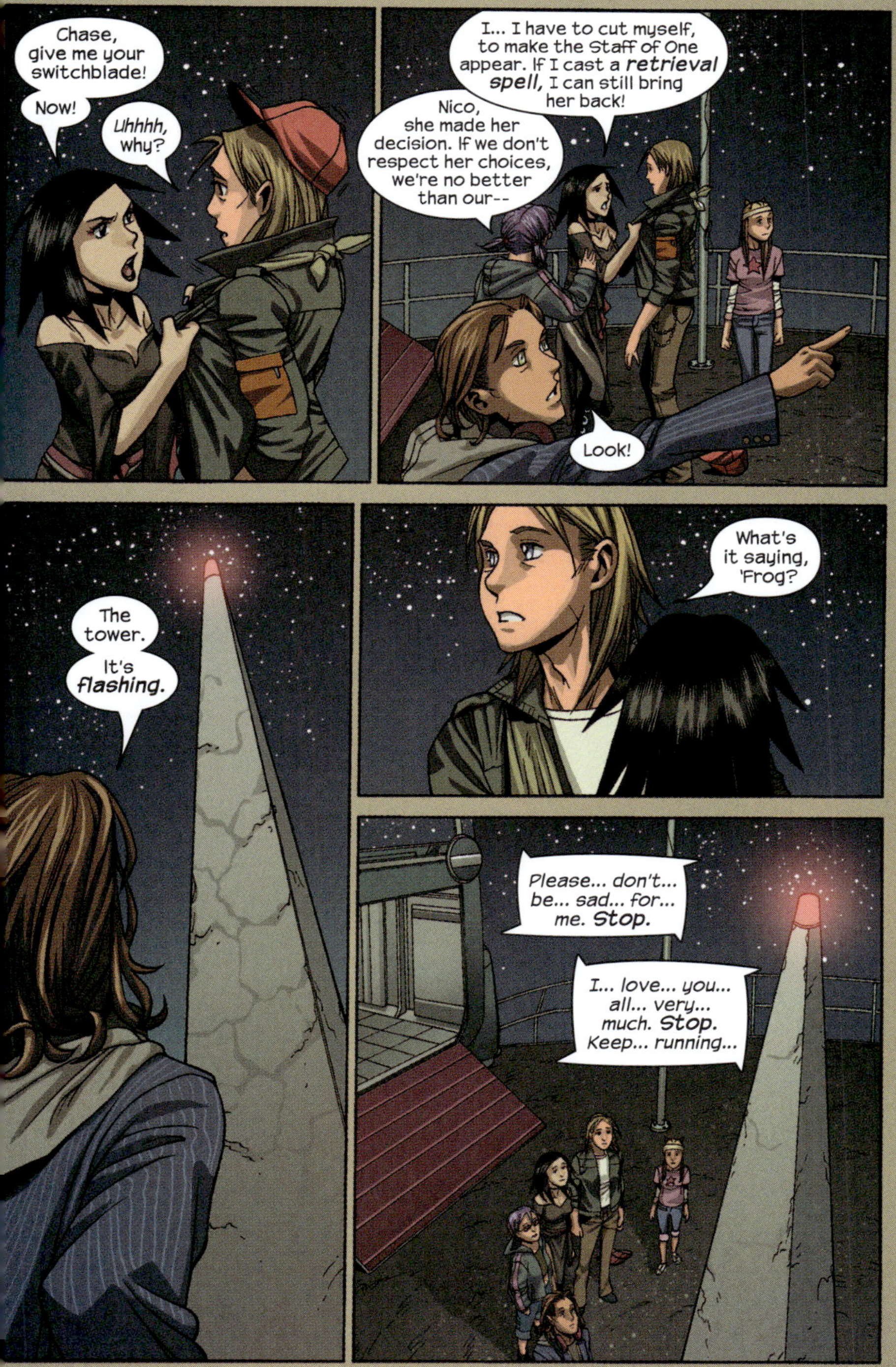

Chase, give me your switchblade!
Now!
Uhhhh, why?
I... I have to cut myself, to make the Staff of One appear. If I cast a **retrieval spell**, I can still bring her back!
Nico, she made her decision. If we don't respect her choices, we're no better than our--
Look!
The tower.
It's *flashing.*
What's it saying, 'Frog?
Please... don't... be... sad... for... me. **Stop.**
I... love... you... all... very... much. **Stop.** Keep... running...

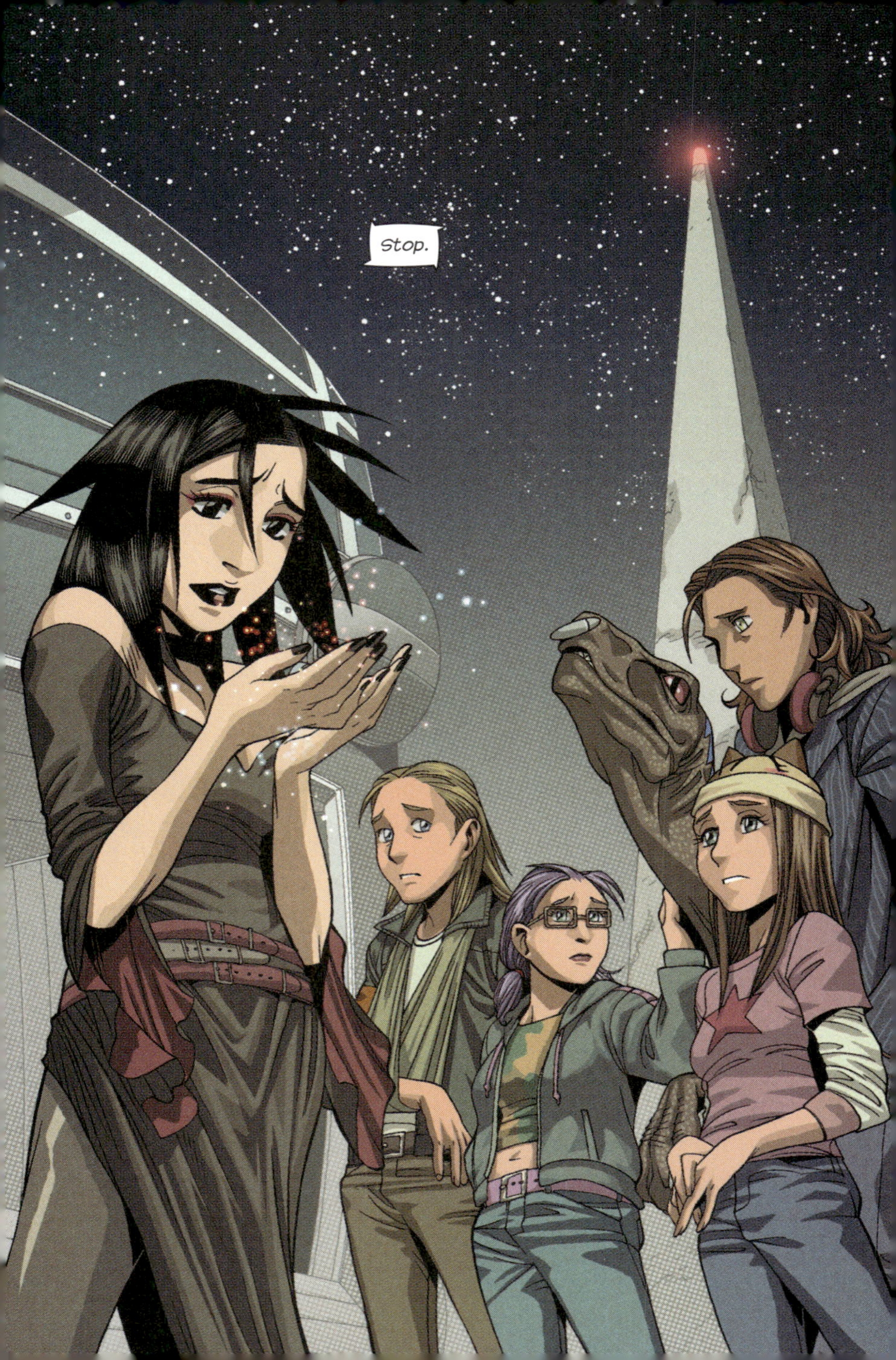
Stop.

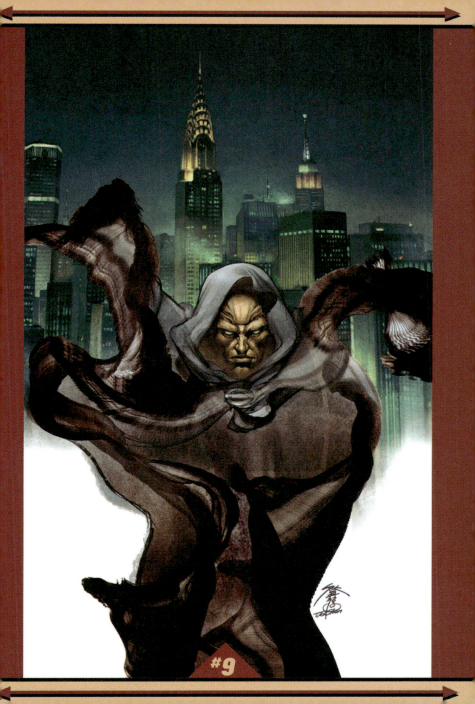

#9

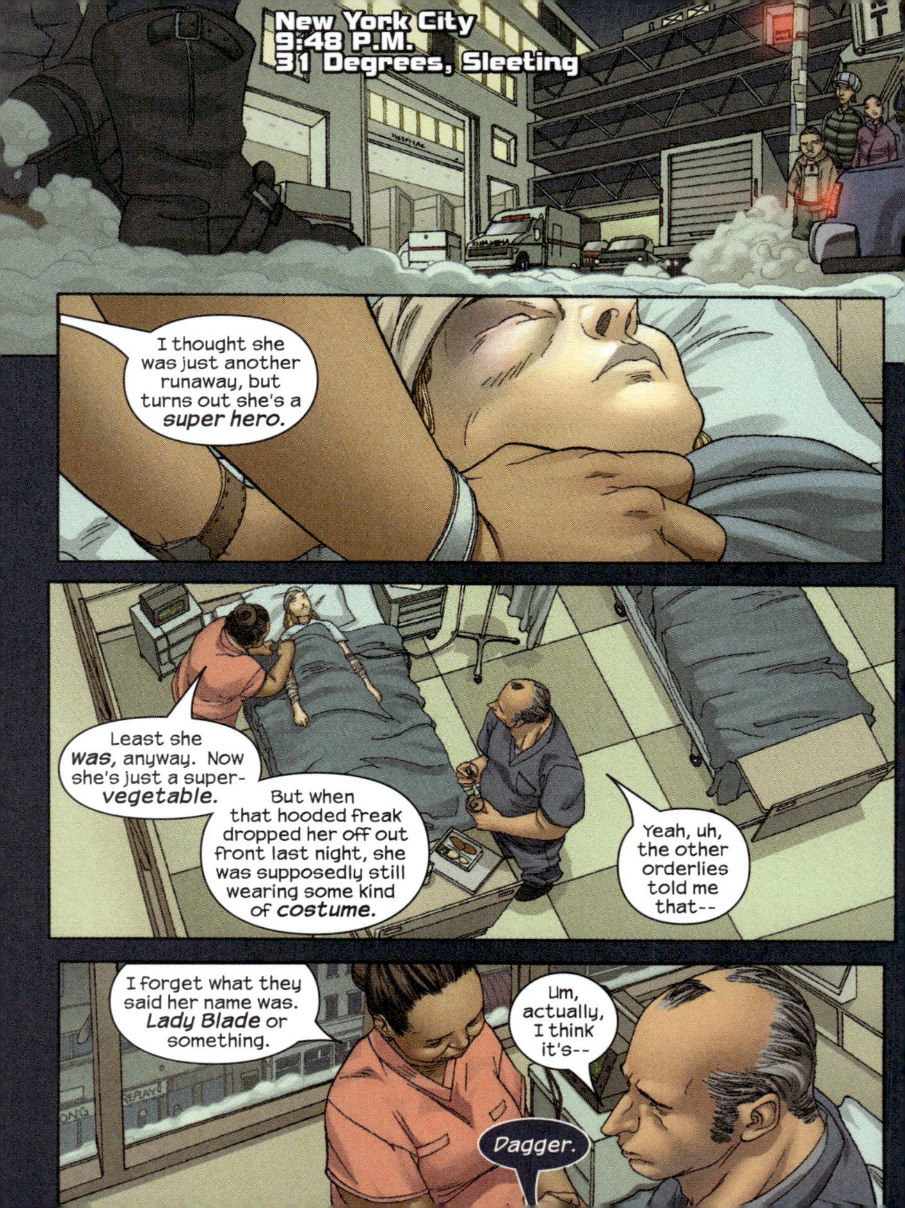
New York City
9:48 P.M.
31 Degrees, Sleeting
I thought she was just another runaway, but turns out she's a *super hero.*
Least she *was,* anyway. Now she's just a super-*vegetable.*
But when that hooded freak dropped her off out front last night, she was supposedly still wearing some kind of *costume.*
Yeah, uh, the other orderlies told me that--
I forget what they said her name was. *Lady Blade* or something.
Um, actually, I think it's--
Dagger.

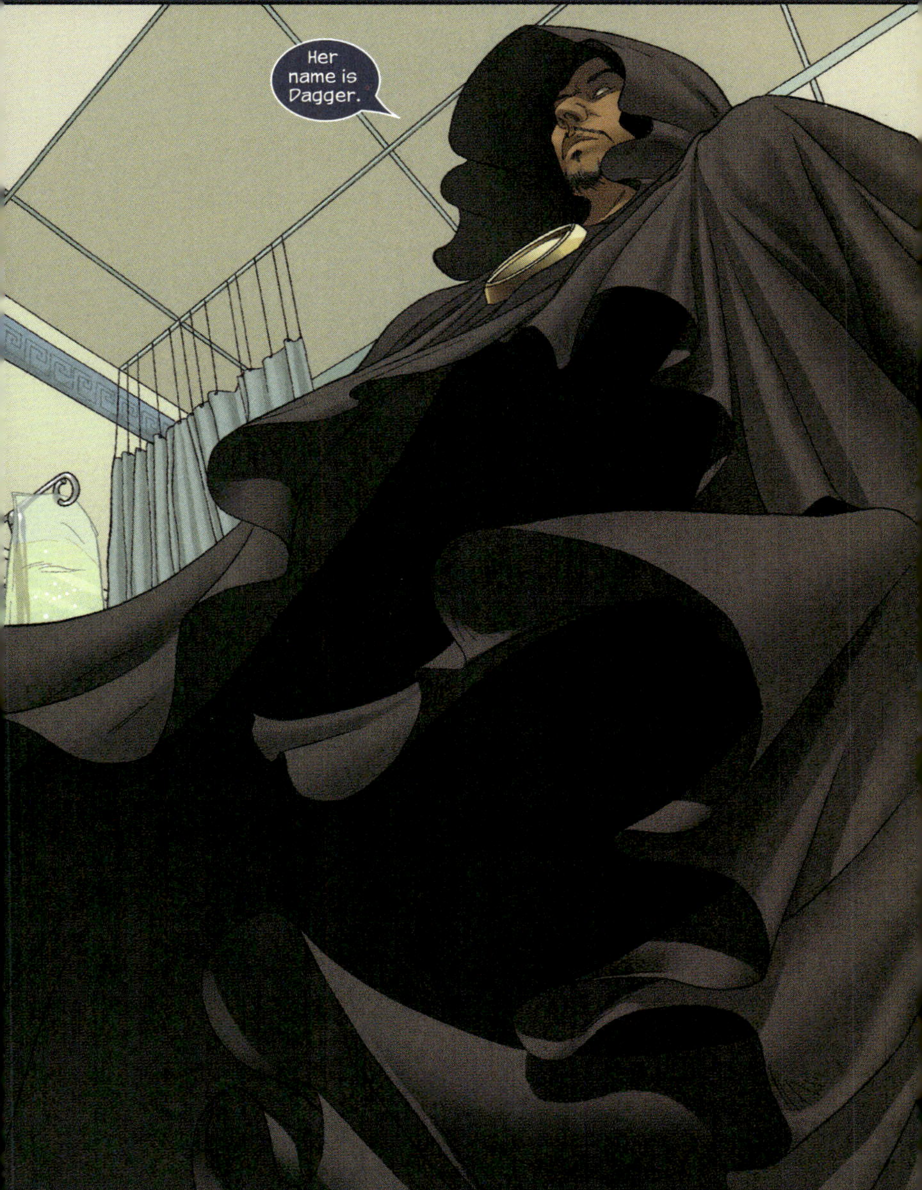
Her name is Dagger.

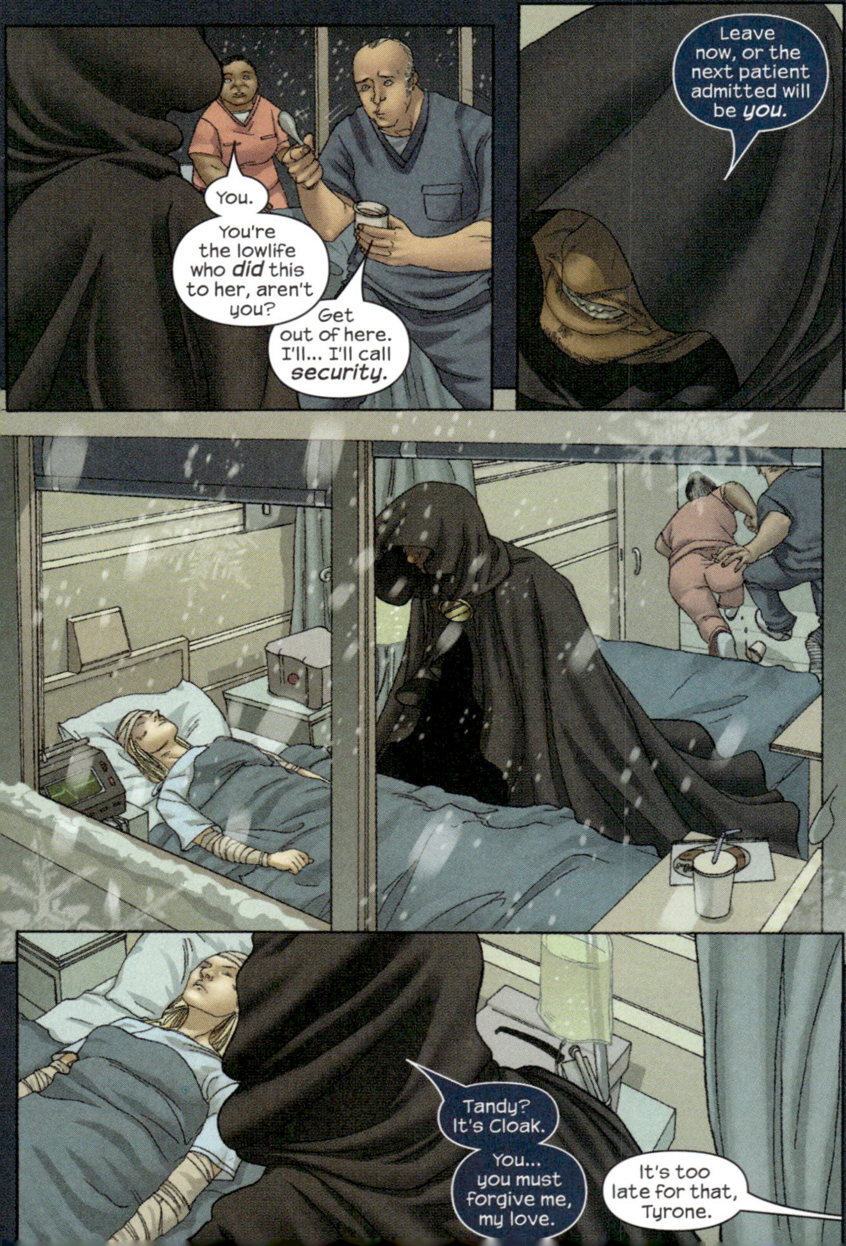
You.
You're the lowlife who *did* this to her, aren't you?
Get out of here. I'll... I'll call *security.*
Leave now, or the next patient admitted will be *you.*
Tandy? It's Cloak.
You... you must forgive me, my love.
It's too late for that, Tyrone.

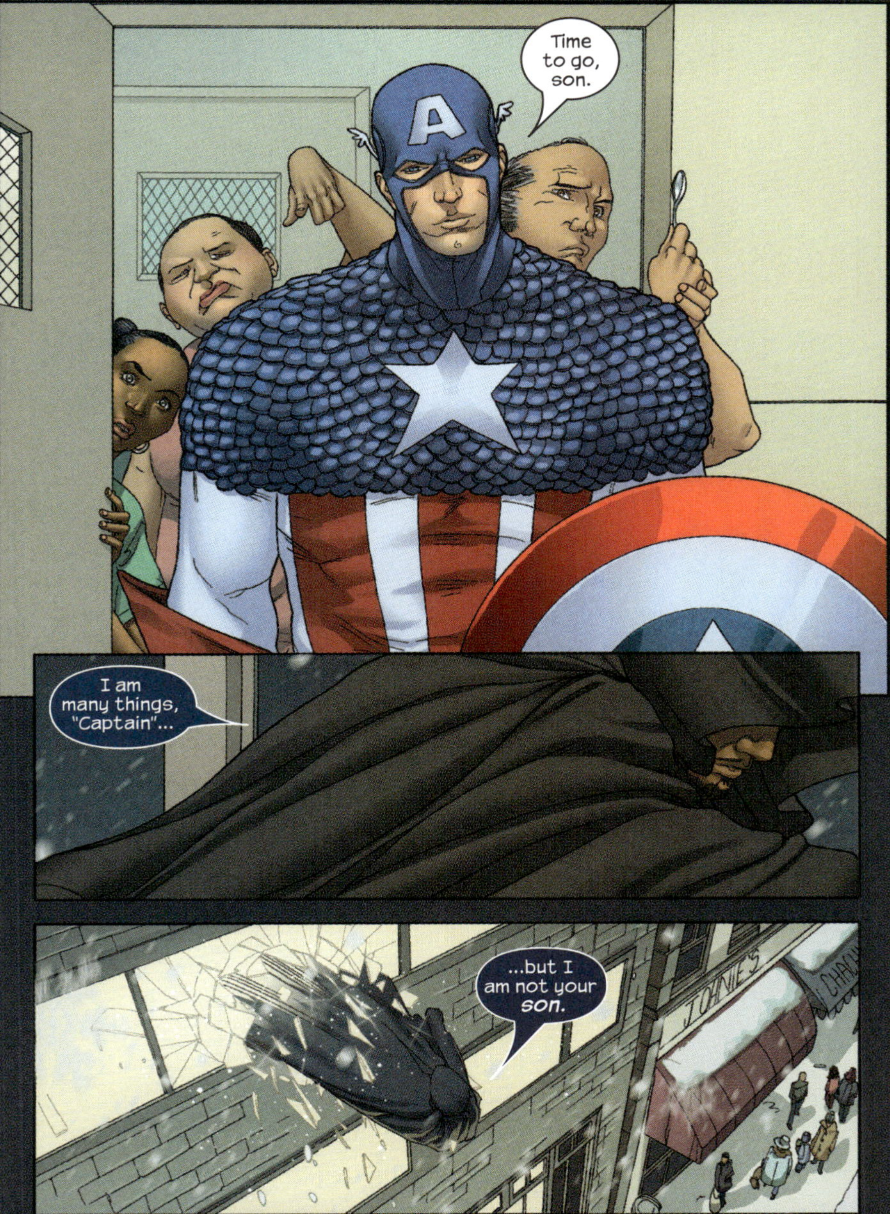
Time to go, son.
I am many things, "Captain"...
...but I am not your *son.*
JOHNIE'S

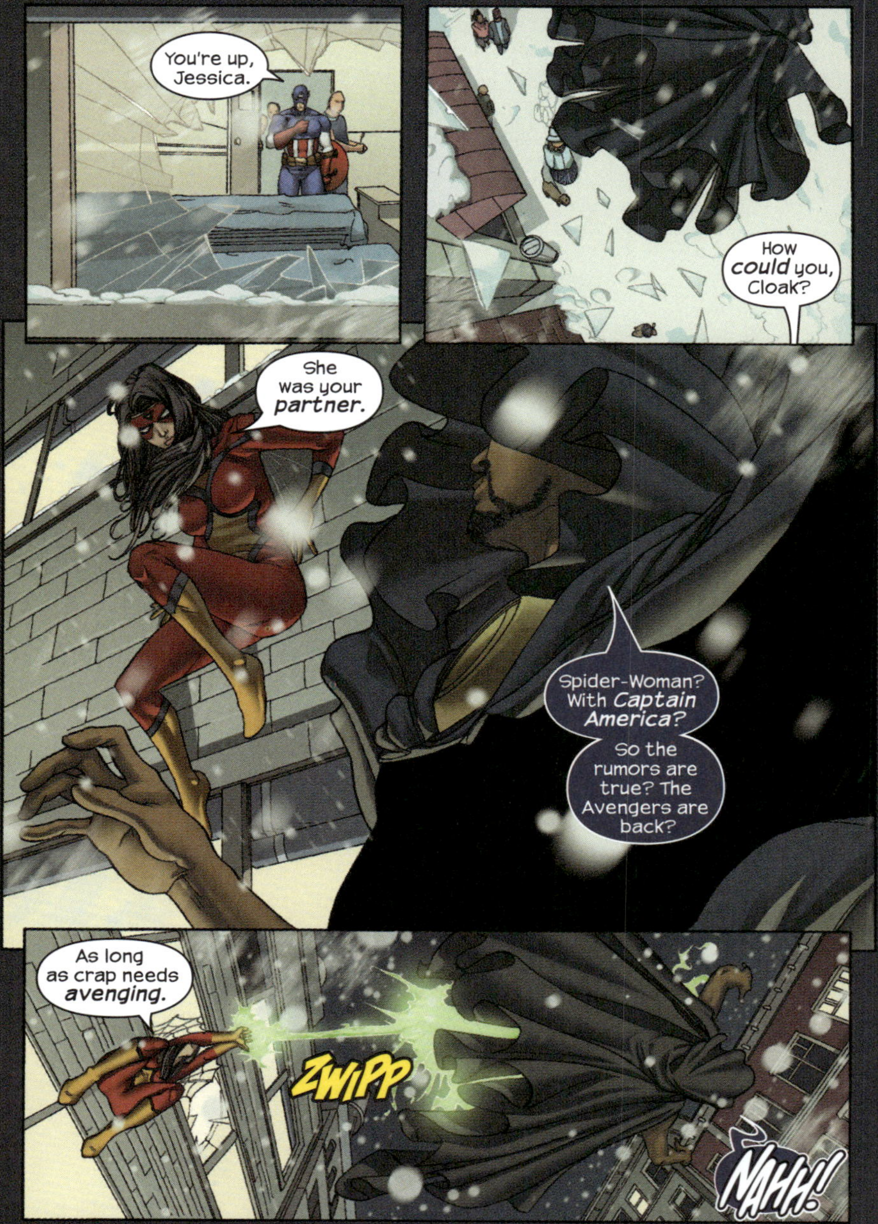
You're up, Jessica.
How *could* you, Cloak?
She was your *partner.*
Spider-Woman? With *Captain America?*
So the rumors are true? The Avengers are back?
As long as crap needs *avenging.*
ZWIPP
NAHH!

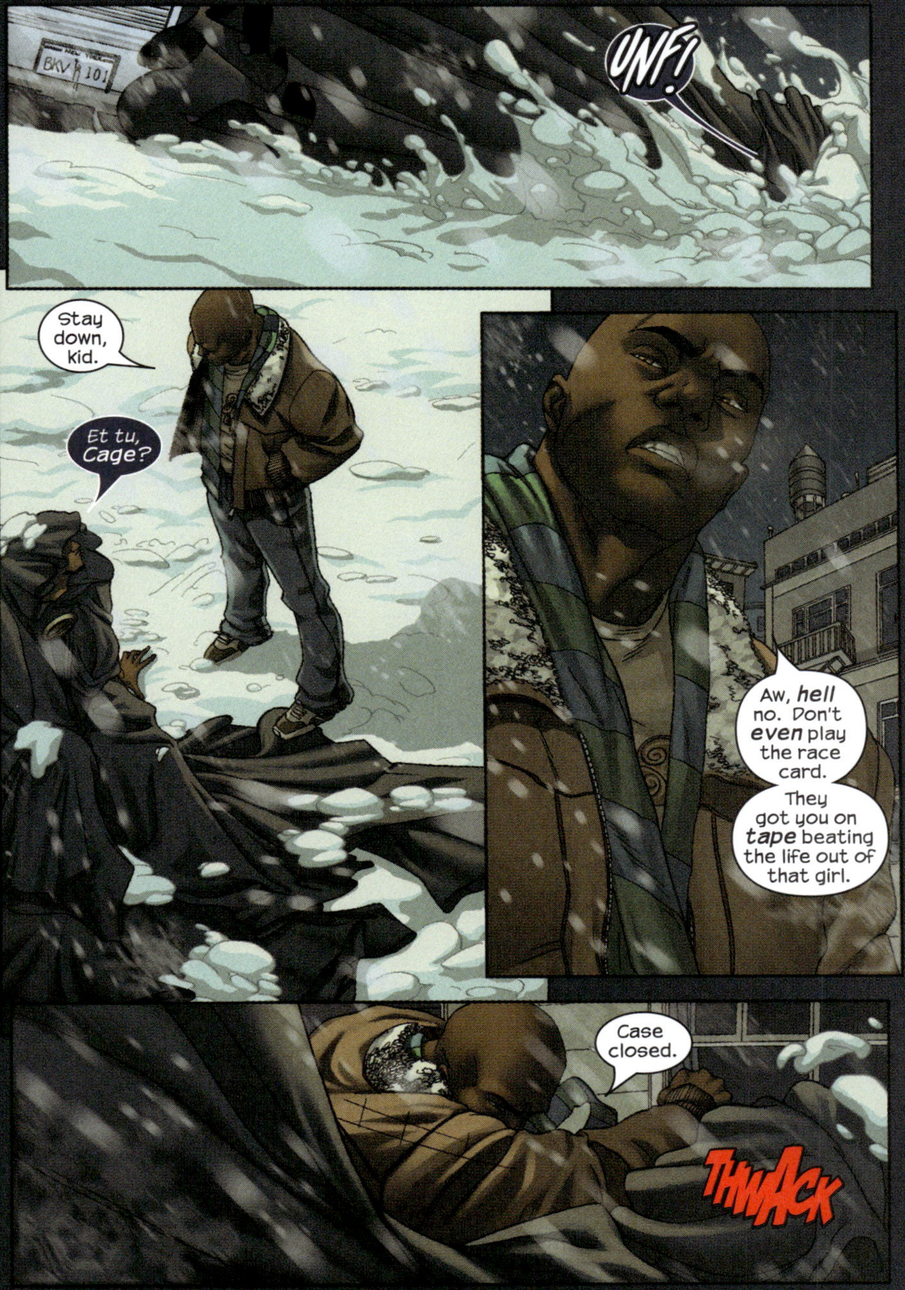

BKV 101
UNF!
Stay down, kid.
Et tu, Cage?
Aw, hell no. Don't even play the race card.
They got you on tape beating the life out of that girl.
Case closed.
THWACK

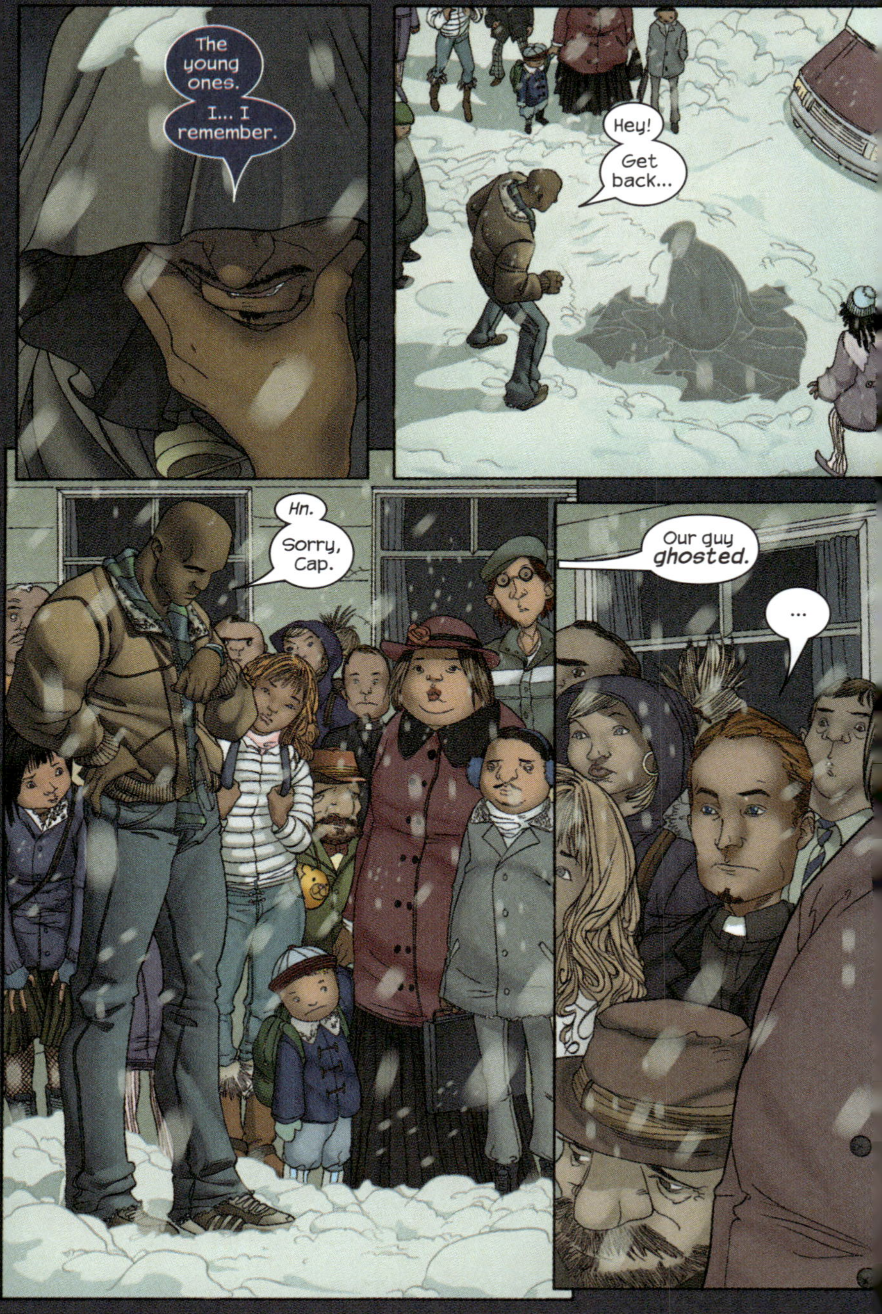
The young ones.
I... I remember.
Hey!
Get back...
Hn.
Sorry, Cap.
Our guy *ghosted.*
...

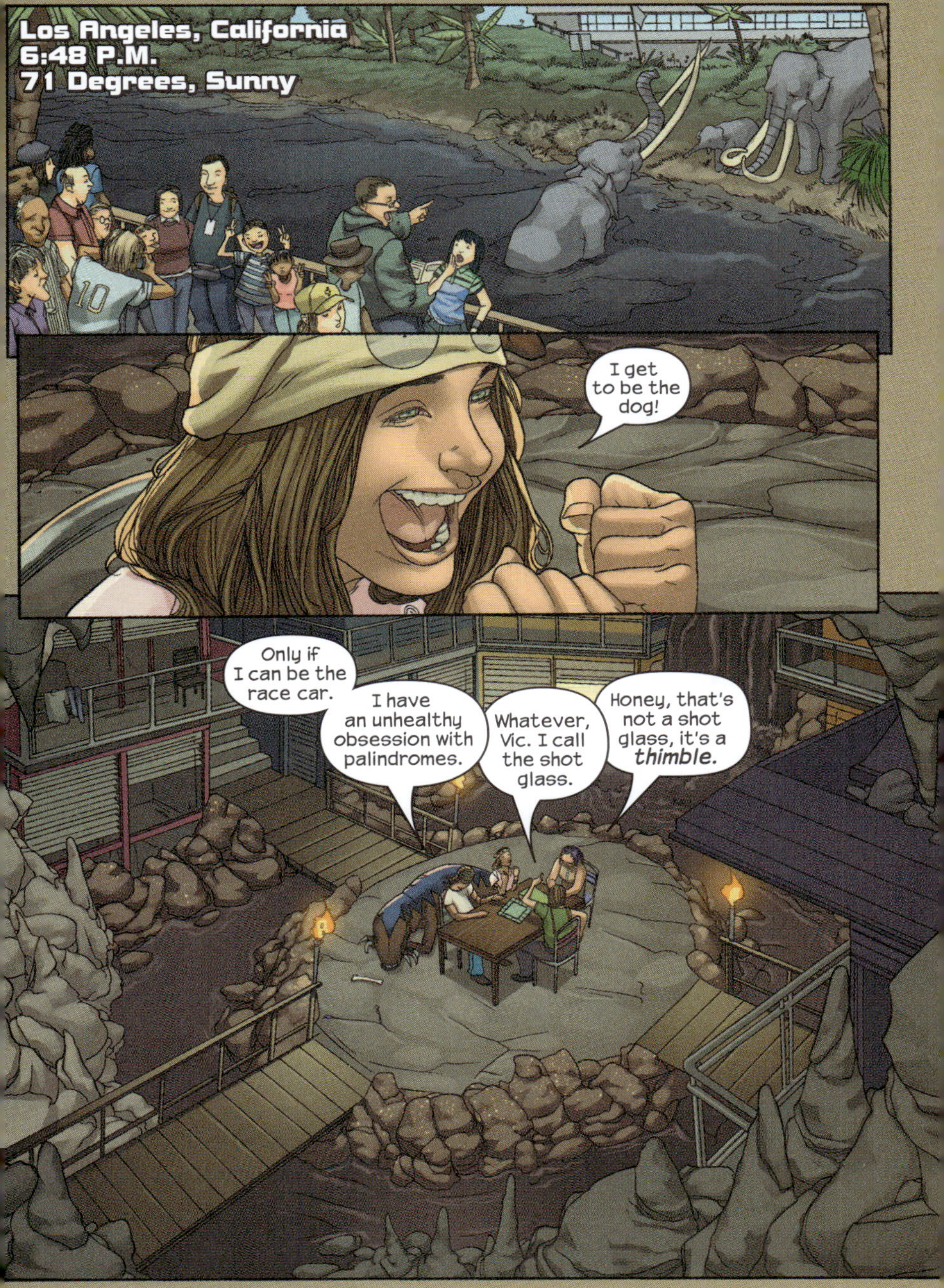
Los Angeles, California
6:48 P.M.
71 Degrees, Sunny
I get to be the dog!
Only if I can be the race car.
I have an unhealthy obsession with palindromes.
Whatever, Vic. I call the shot glass.
Honey, that's not a shot glass, it's a *thimble.*

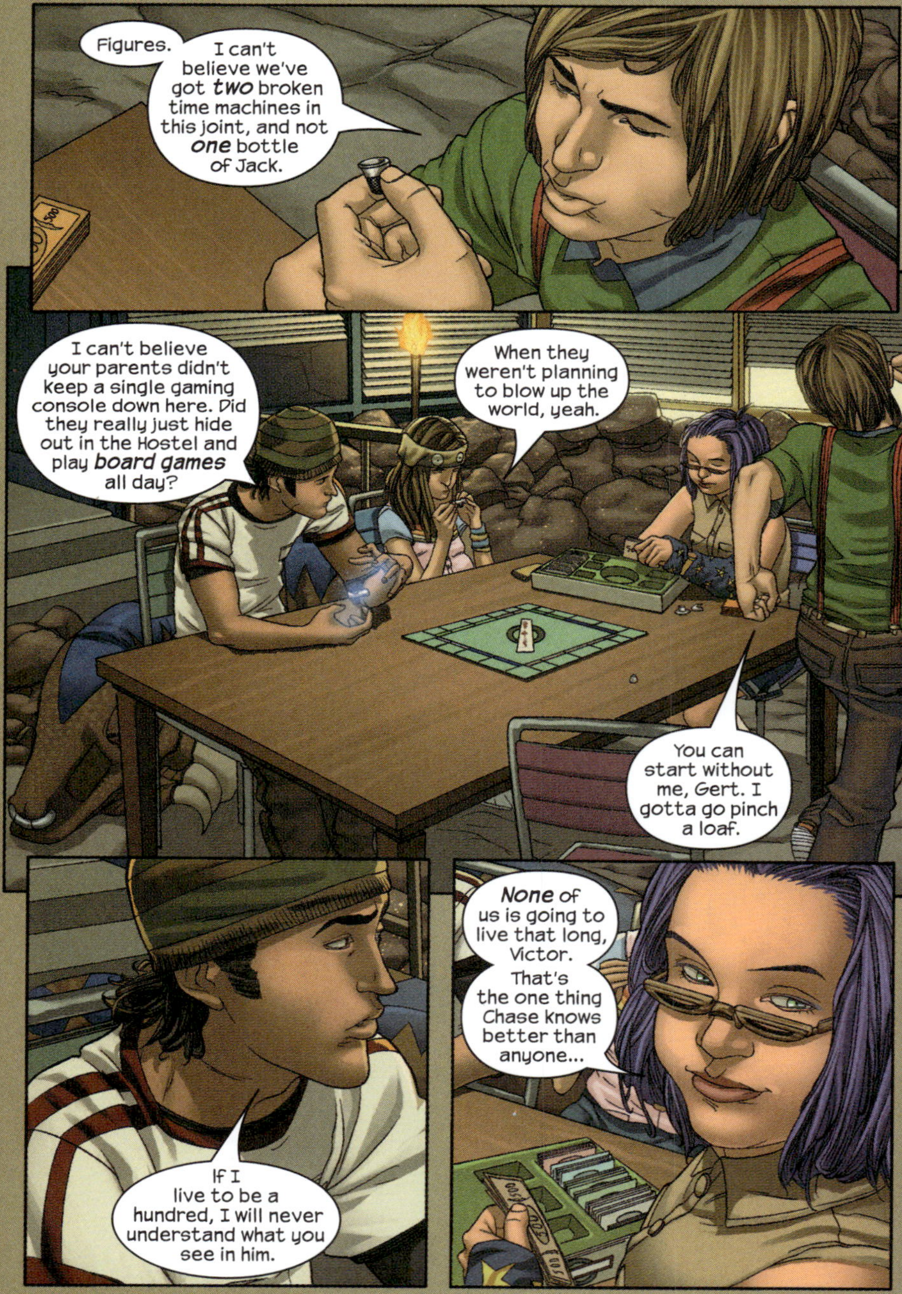
Figures.
I can't believe we've got *two* broken time machines in this joint, and not *one* bottle of Jack.
I can't believe your parents didn't keep a single gaming console down here. Did they really just hide out in the Hostel and play *board games* all day?
When they weren't planning to blow up the world, yeah.
You can start without me, Gert. I gotta go pinch a loaf.
If I live to be a hundred, I will never understand what you see in him.
None of us is going to live that long, Victor.
That's the one thing Chase knows better than anyone...

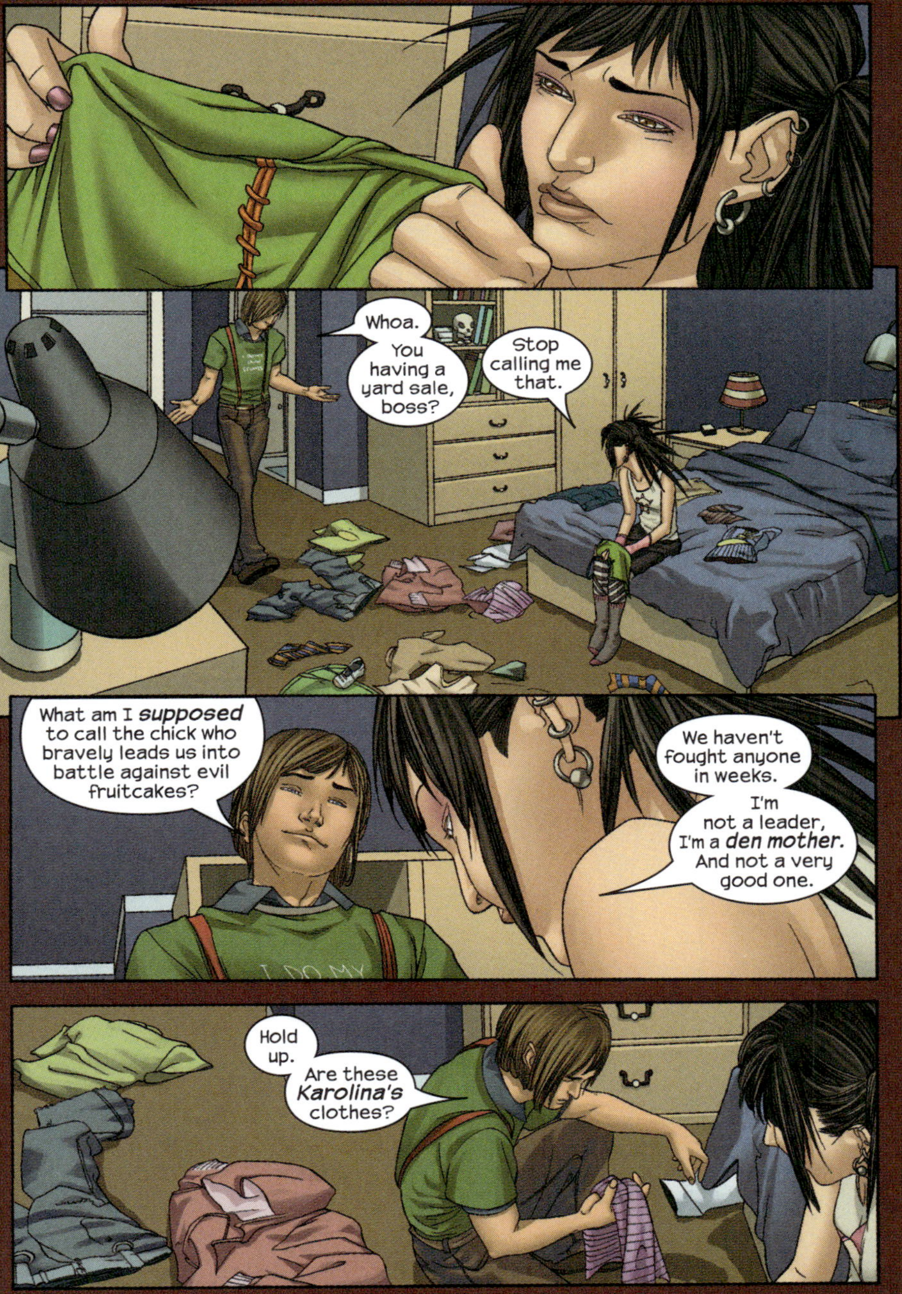
Whoa.
You having a yard sale, boss?
Stop calling me that.
What am I *supposed* to call the chick who bravely leads us into battle against evil fruitcakes?
We haven't fought anyone in weeks.
I'm not a leader, I'm a ***den mother.*** And not a very good one.
Hold up.
Are these ***Karolina's*** clothes?

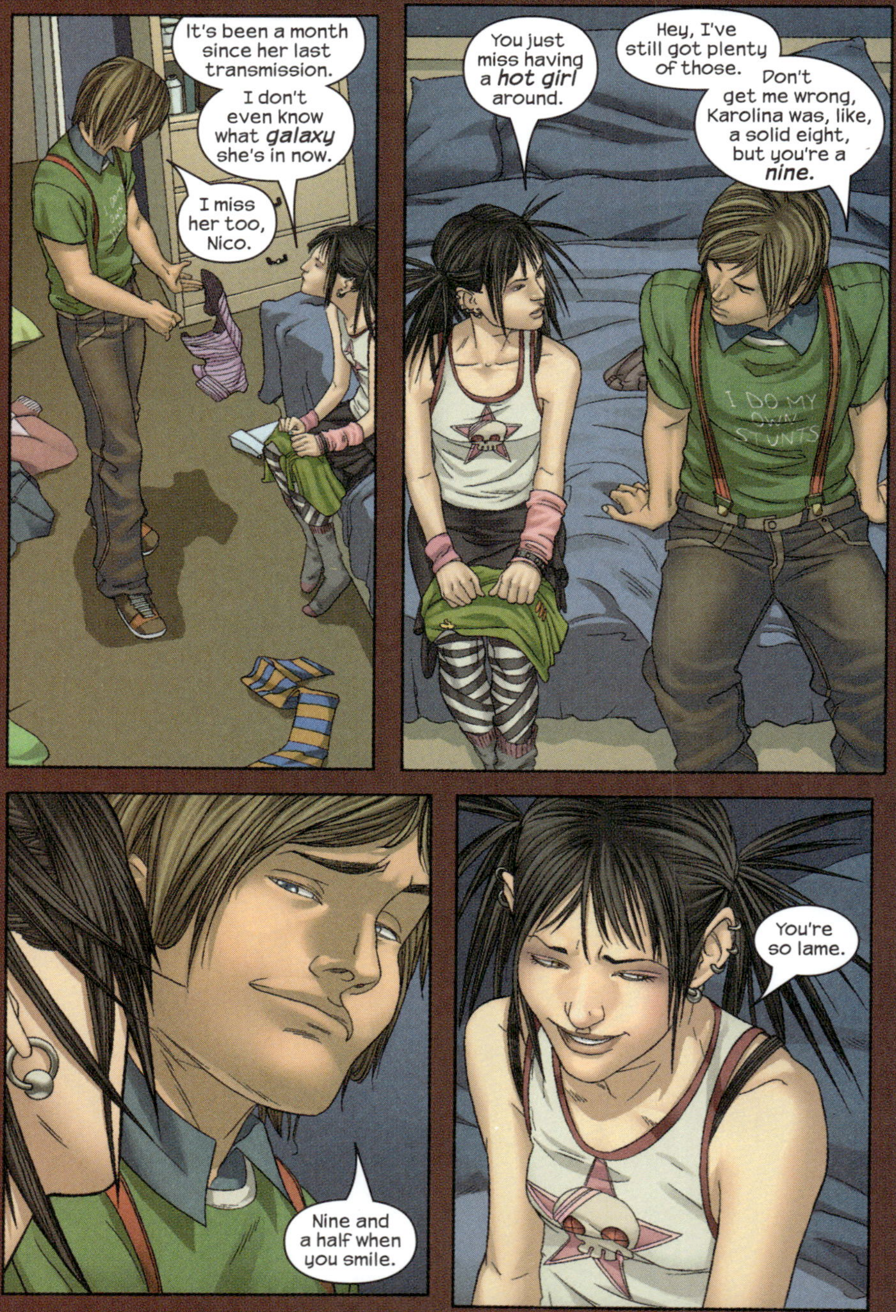
It's been a month since her last transmission.
I don't even know what galaxy she's in now.
I miss her too, Nico.
You just miss having a hot girl around.
Hey, I've still got plenty of those.
Don't get me wrong, Karolina was, like, a solid eight, but you're a nine.
I DO MY OWN STUNTS
Nine and a half when you smile.
You're so lame.

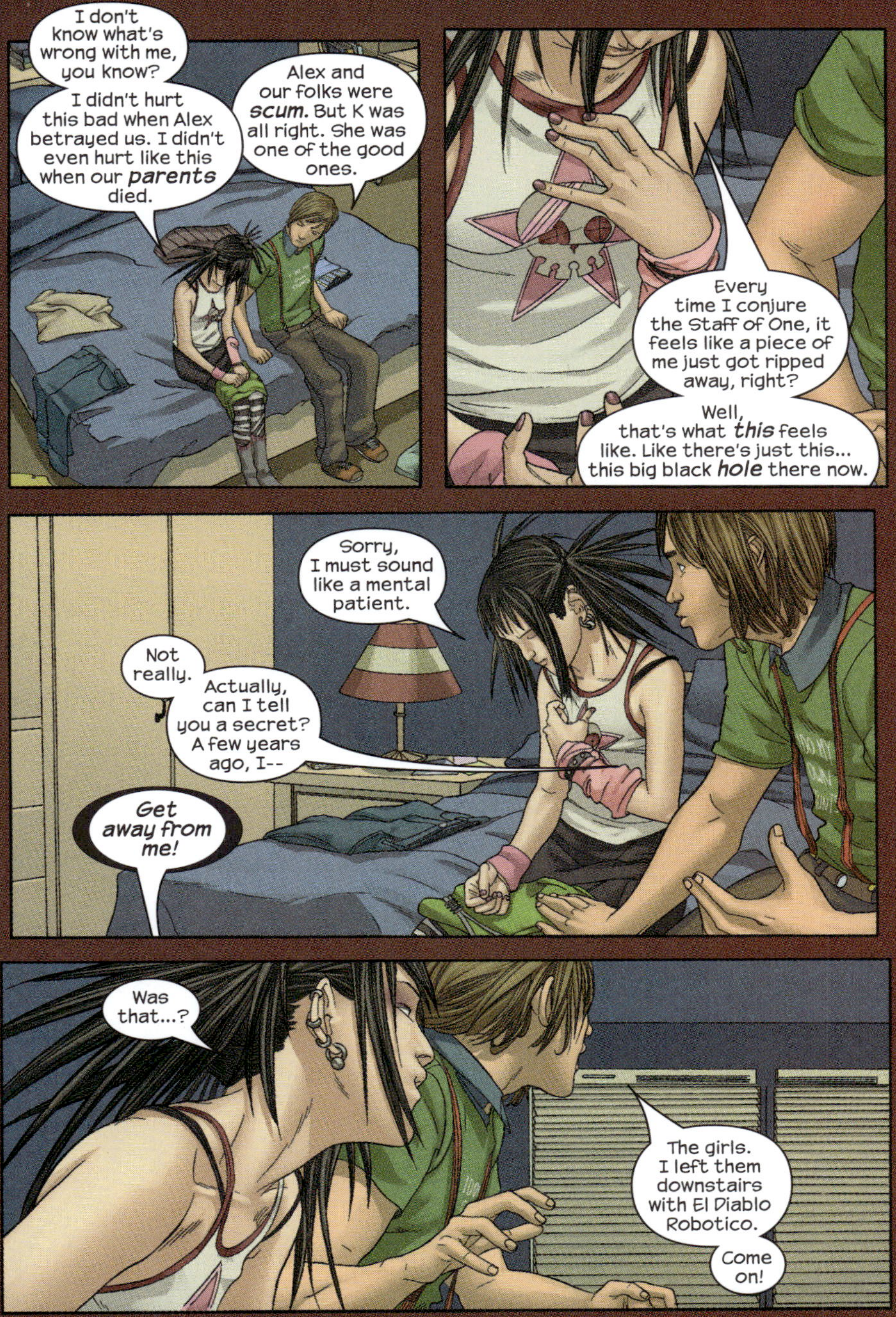

I don't know what's wrong with me, you know?
I didn't hurt this bad when Alex betrayed us. I didn't even hurt like this when our *parents* died.
Alex and our folks were *scum.* But K was all right. She was one of the good ones.
Every time I conjure the Staff of One, it feels like a piece of me just got ripped away, right?
Well, that's what *this* feels like. Like there's just this... this big black *hole* there now.
Sorry, I must sound like a mental patient.
Not really.
Actually, can I tell you a secret? A few years ago, I--
Get away from me!
Was that...?
The girls. I left them downstairs with El Diablo Robotico.
Come on!

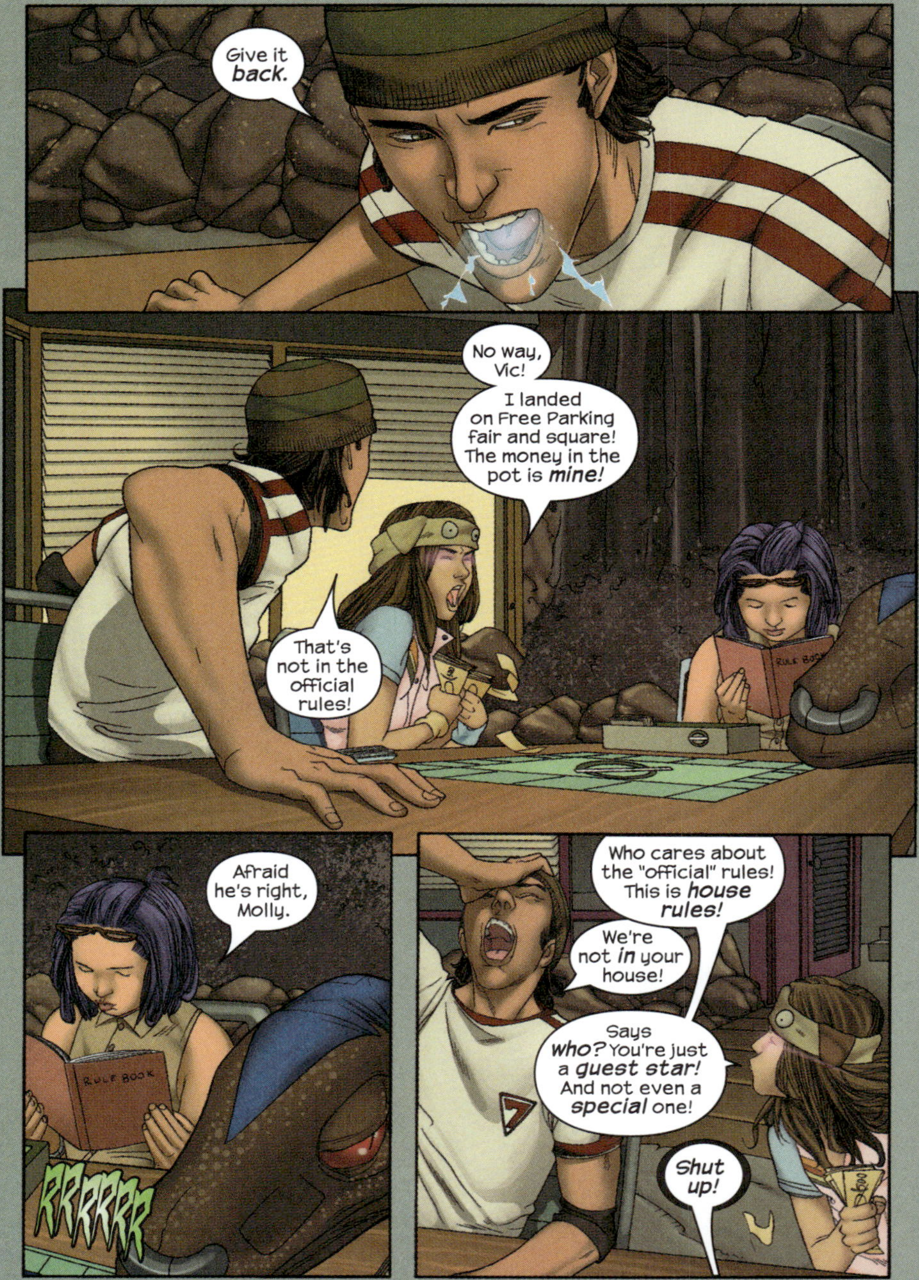
Give it back.
No way, Vic!
I landed on Free Parking fair and square! The money in the pot is mine!
That's not in the official rules!
Afraid he's right, Molly.
RRRRRR
Who cares about the "official" rules! This is house rules!
We're not in your house!
Says who? You're just a guest star! And not even a special one!
Shut up!

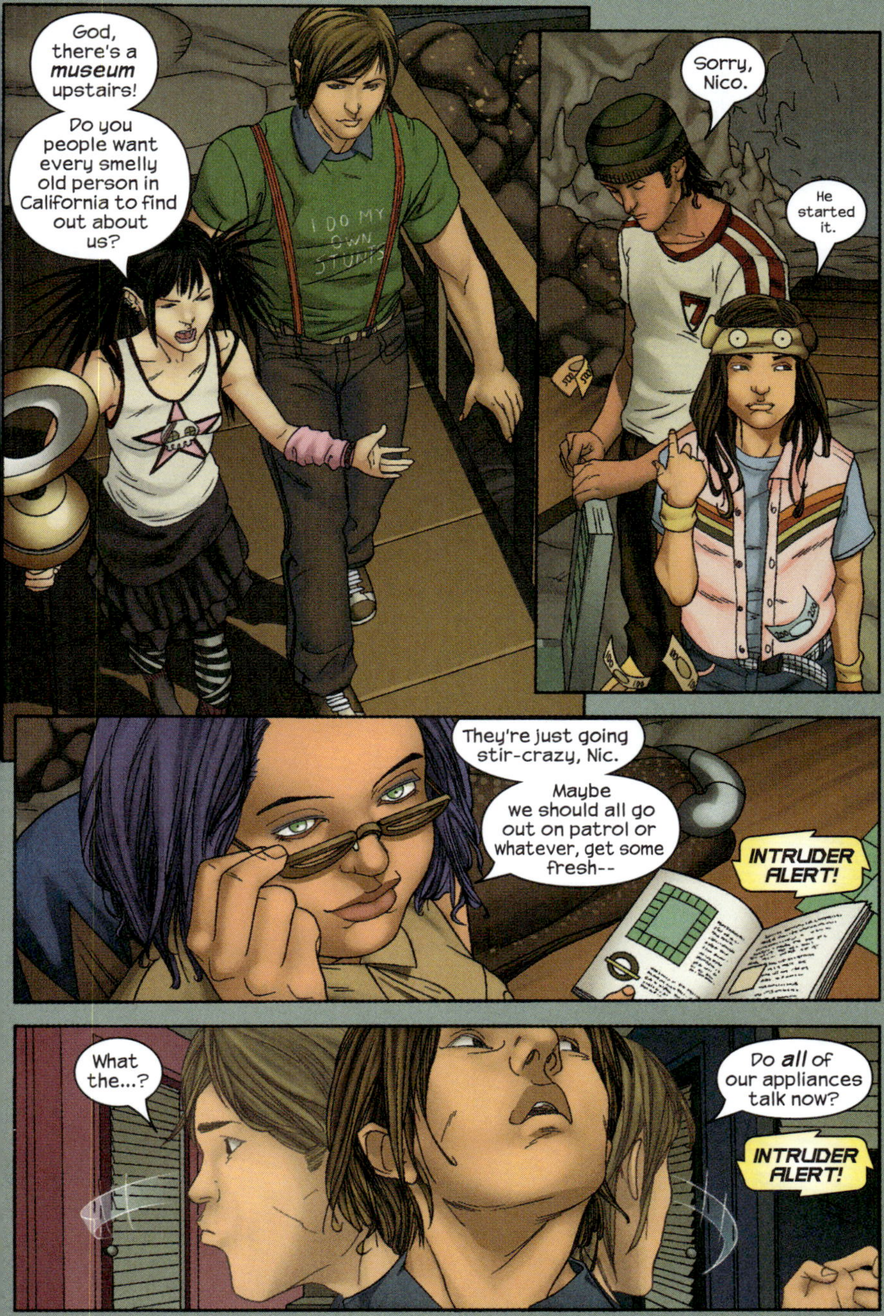
God, there's a ***museum*** upstairs!
Do you people want every smelly old person in California to find out about us?
I DO MY OWN STUNTS
Sorry, Nico.
He started it.
They're just going stir-crazy, Nic.
Maybe we should all go out on patrol or whatever, get some fresh--
INTRUDER ALERT!
What the...?
Do ***all*** of our appliances talk now?
INTRUDER ALERT!

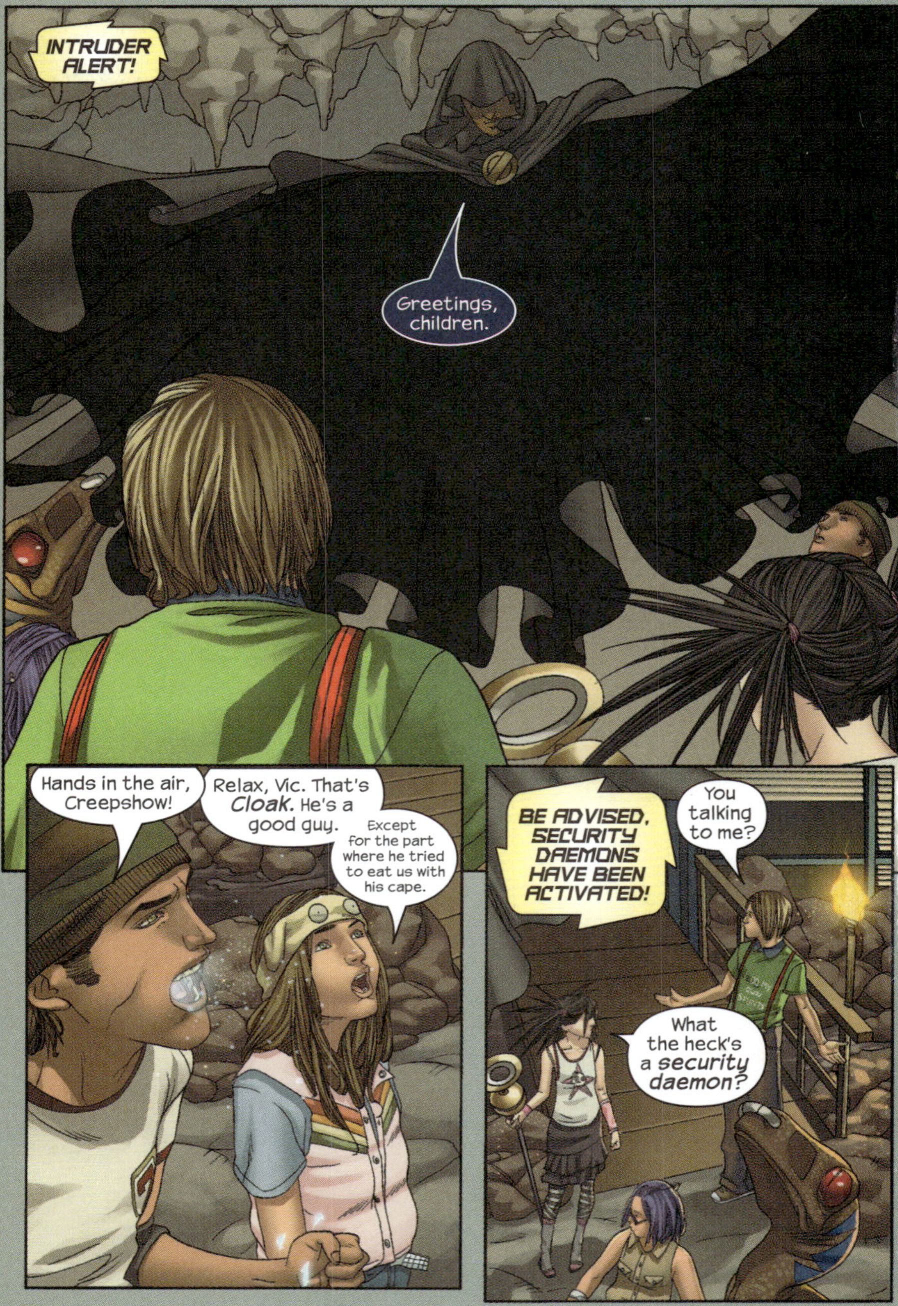
INTRUDER ALERT!
Greetings, children.
Hands in the air, Creepshow!
Relax, Vic. That's *Cloak*. He's a good guy.
Except for the part where he tried to eat us with his cape.
BE ADVISED, SECURITY DAEMONS HAVE BEEN ACTIVATED!
You talking to me?
What the heck's a *security daemon*?

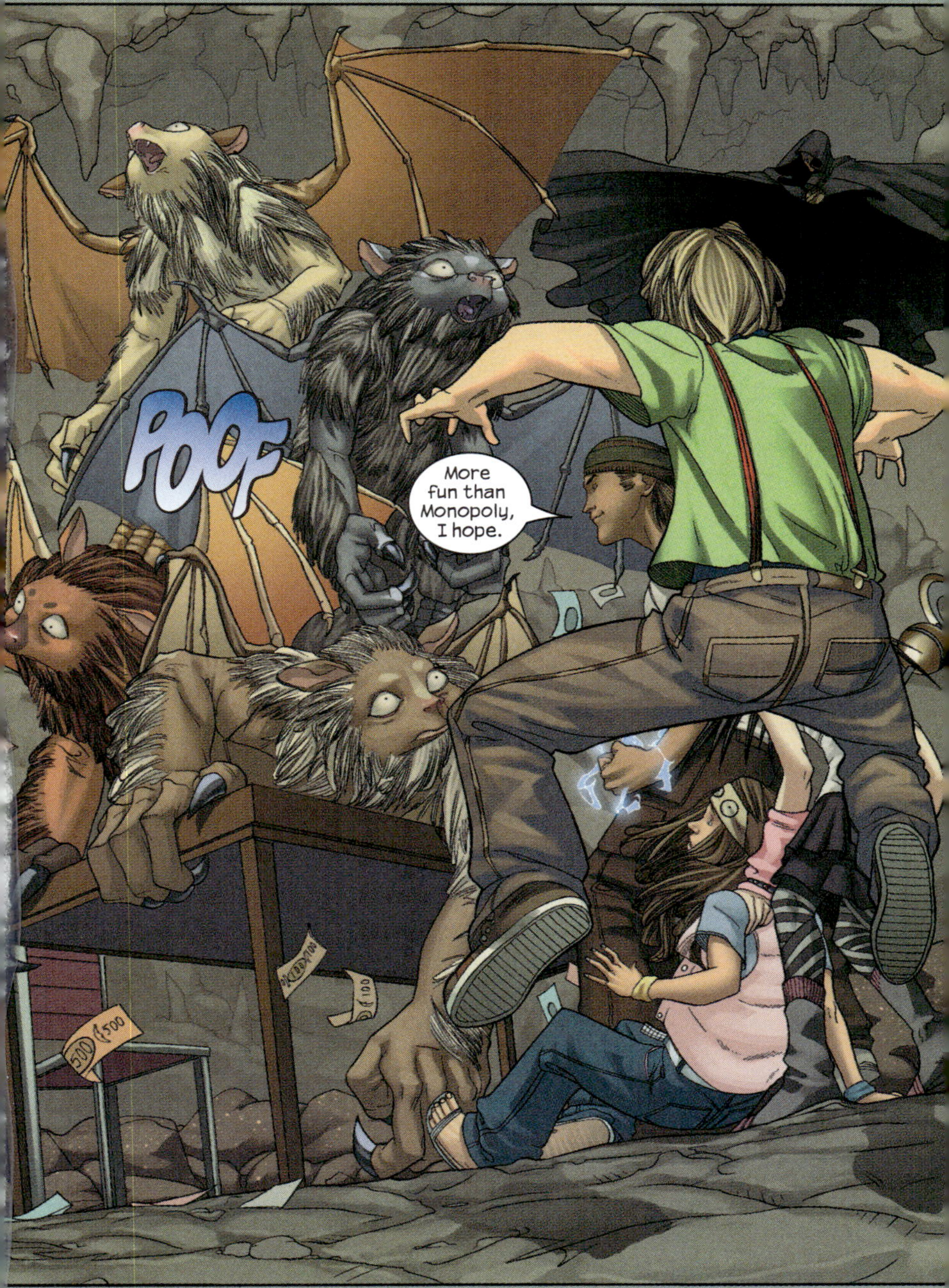
POOF
More fun than Monopoly, I hope.

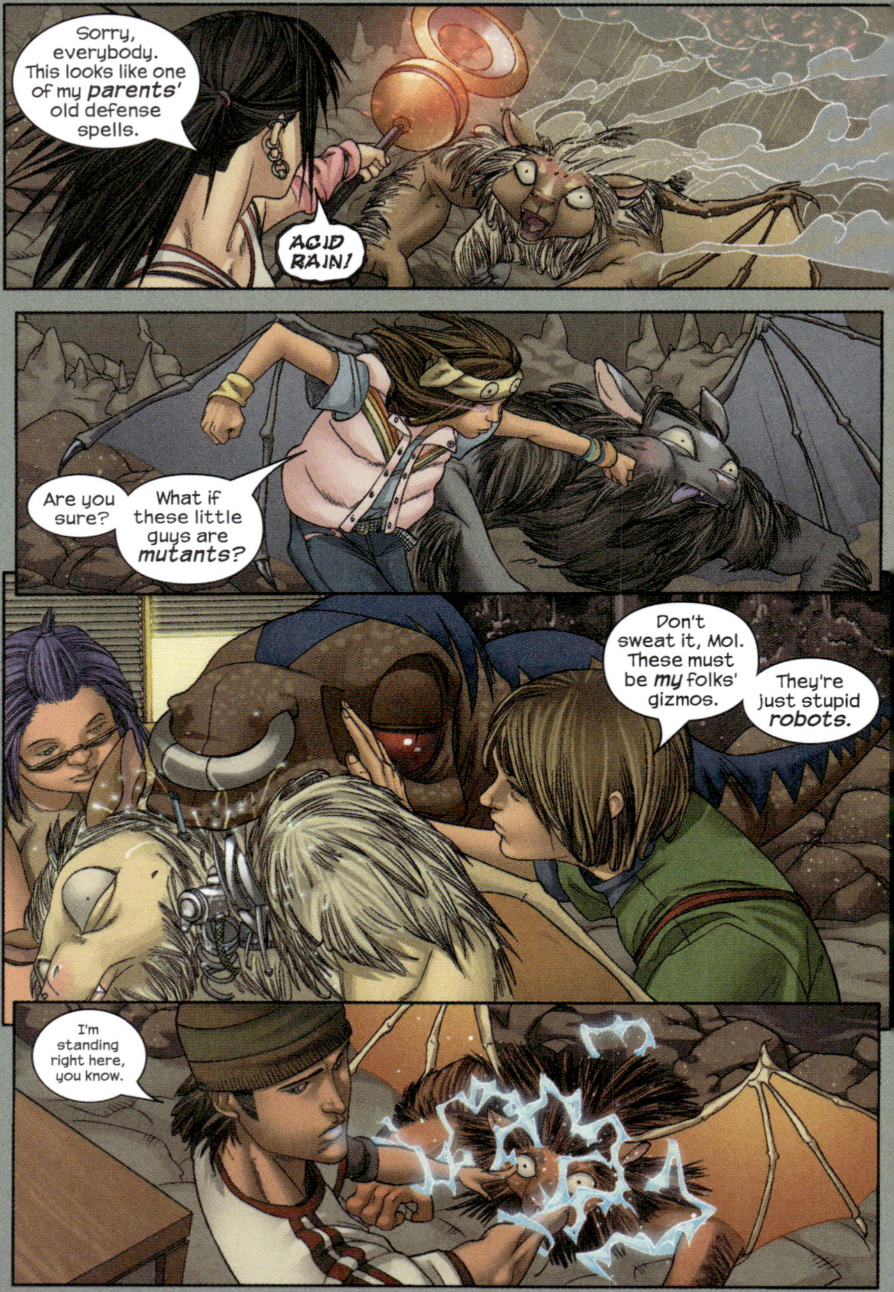
Sorry, everybody. This looks like one of my parents' old defense spells.
ACID RAIN!
Are you sure?
What if these little guys are mutants?
Don't sweat it, Mol. These must be my folks' gizmos.
They're just stupid robots.
I'm standing right here, you know.

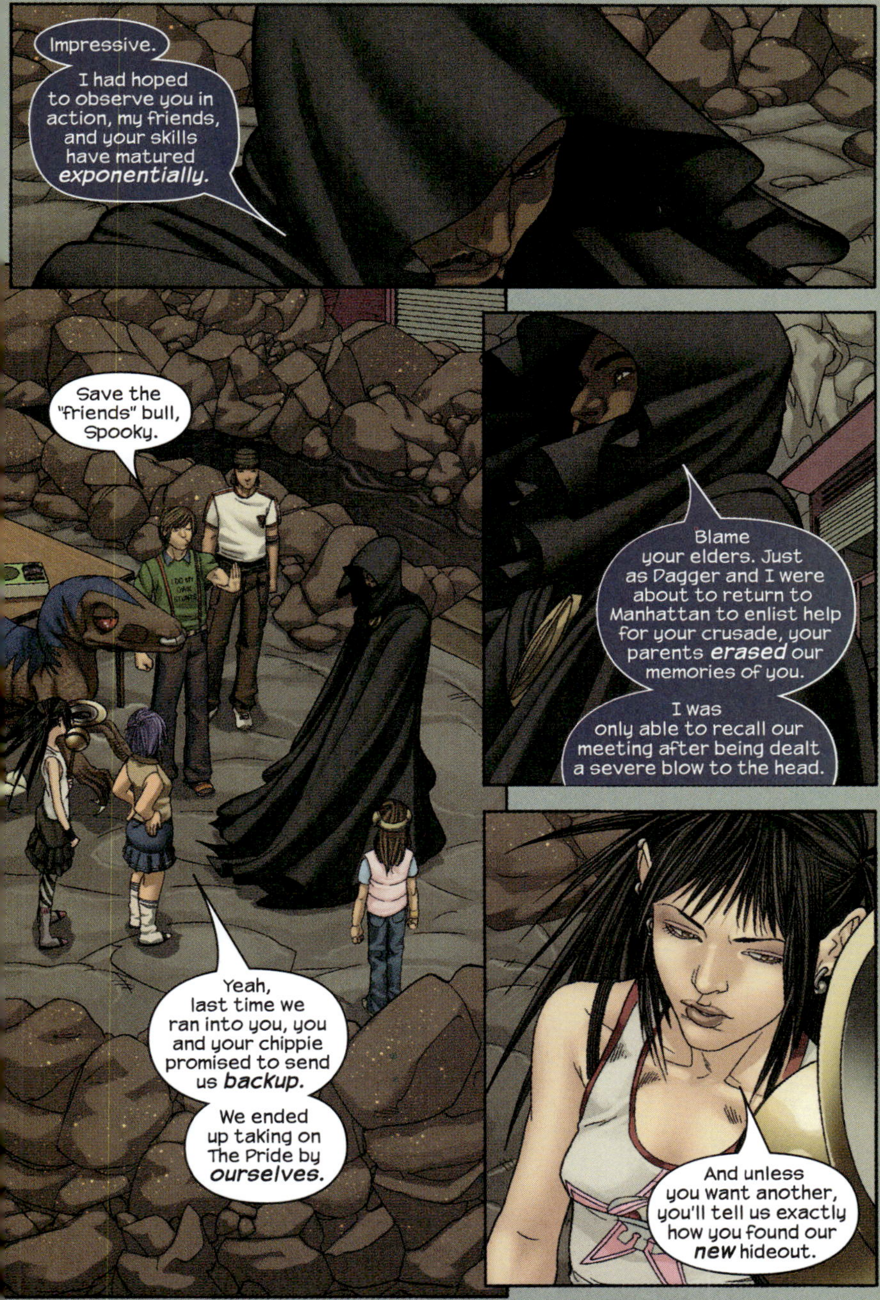
Impressive.
I had hoped to observe you in action, my friends, and your skills have matured *exponentially.*
Save the "friends" bull, Spooky.
Blame your elders. Just as Dagger and I were about to return to Manhattan to enlist help for your crusade, your parents *erased* our memories of you.
I was only able to recall our meeting after being dealt a severe blow to the head.
Yeah, last time we ran into you, you and your chippie promised to send us *backup.*
We ended up taking on The Pride by *ourselves.*
And unless you want another, you'll tell us exactly how you found our *new* hideout.

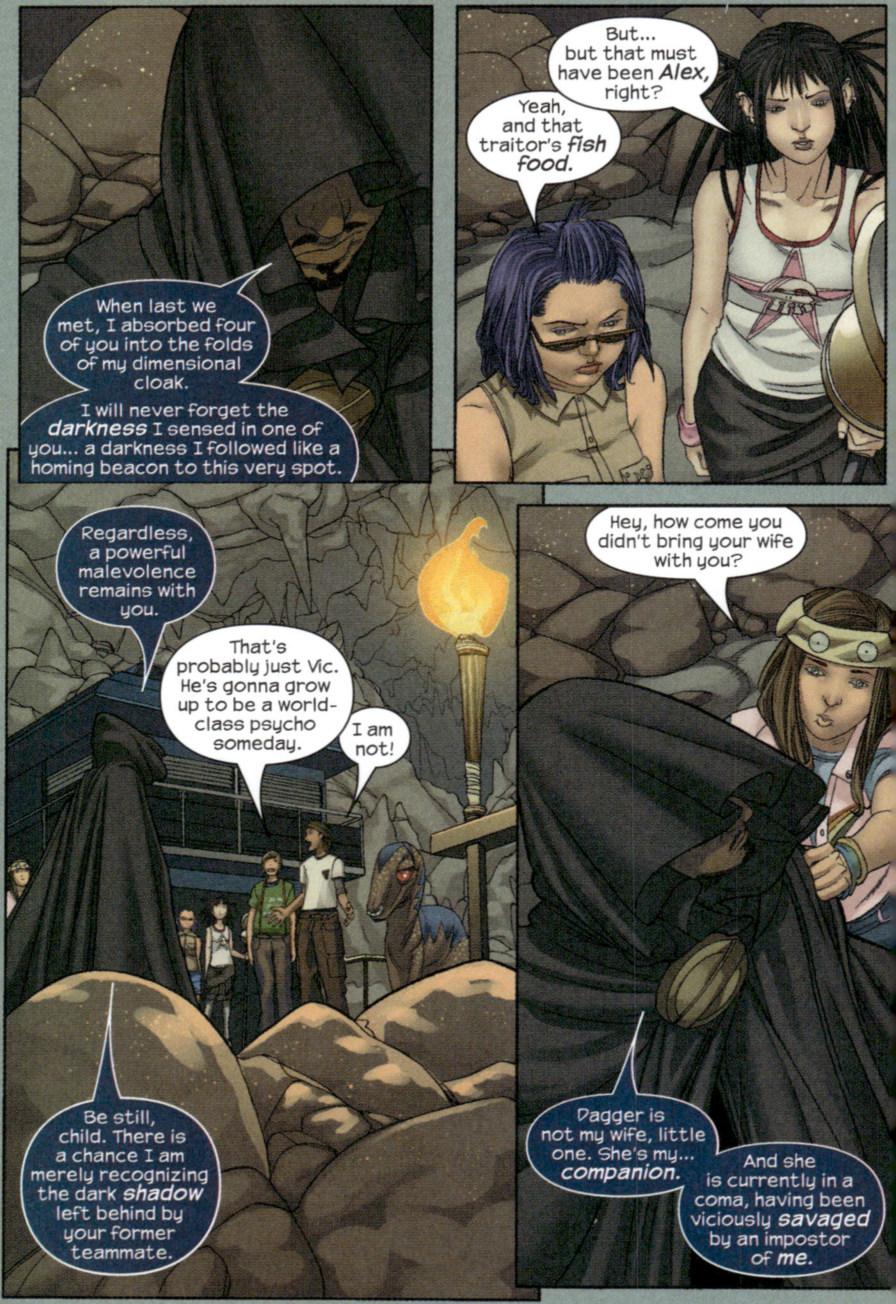

When last we met, I absorbed four of you into the folds of my dimensional cloak.
I will never forget the *darkness* I sensed in one of you... a darkness I followed like a homing beacon to this very spot.
But... but that must have been *Alex,* right?
Yeah, and that traitor's *fish food.*
Regardless, a powerful malevolence remains with you.
That's probably just Vic. He's gonna grow up to be a world-class psycho someday.
I am not!
Be still, child. There is a chance I am merely recognizing the dark *shadow* left behind by your former teammate.
Hey, how come you didn't bring your wife with you?
Dagger is not my wife, little one. She's my... *companion.*
And she is currently in a coma, having been viciously *savaged* by an impostor of *me.*

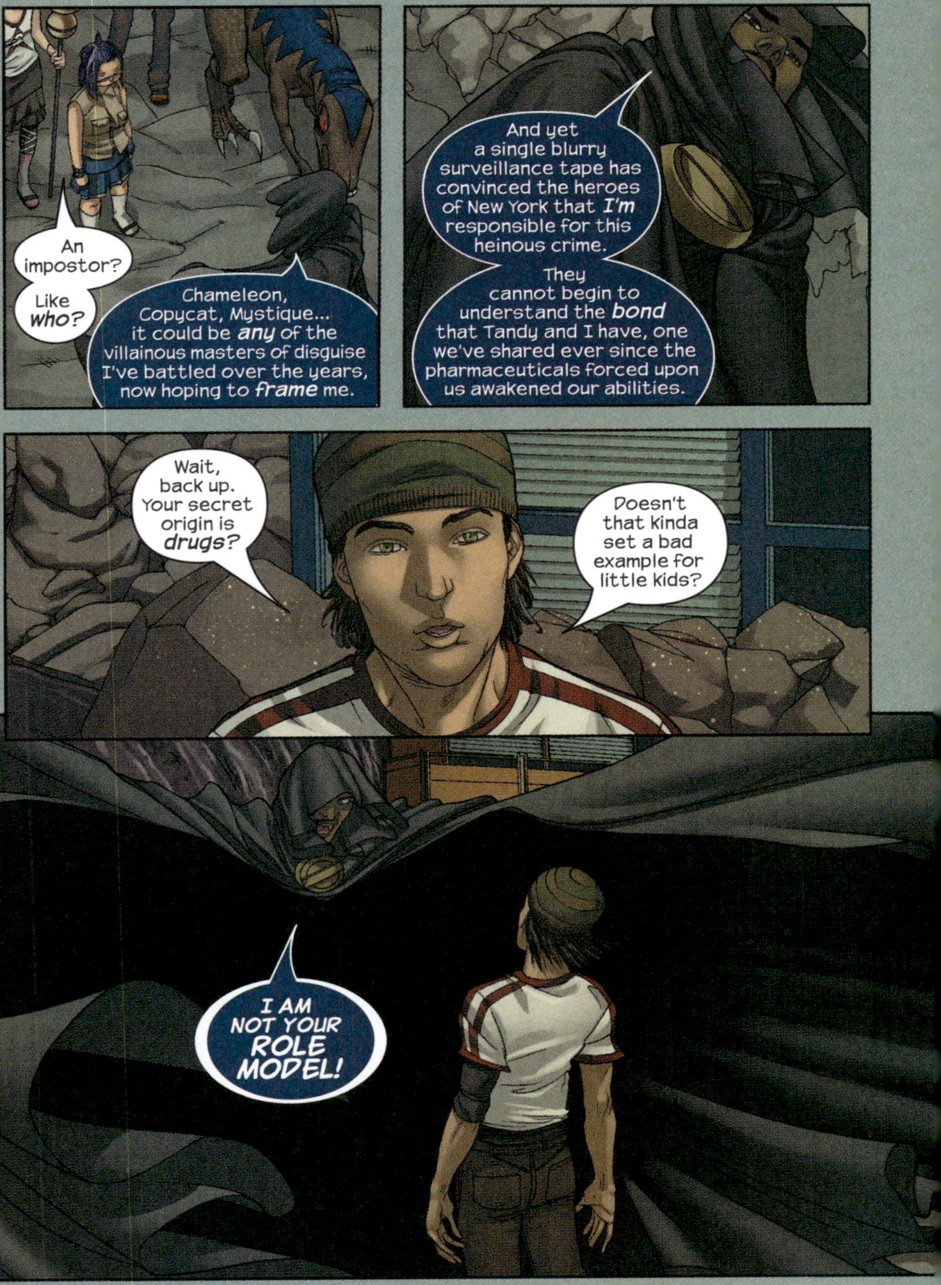

An impostor?
Like who?
Chameleon, Copycat, Mystique... it could be any of the villainous masters of disguise I've battled over the years, now hoping to frame me.
And yet a single blurry surveillance tape has convinced the heroes of New York that I'm responsible for this heinous crime.
They cannot begin to understand the bond that Tandy and I have, one we've shared ever since the pharmaceuticals forced upon us awakened our abilities.
Wait, back up. Your secret origin is drugs?
Doesn't that kinda set a bad example for little kids?
I AM NOT YOUR ROLE MODEL!

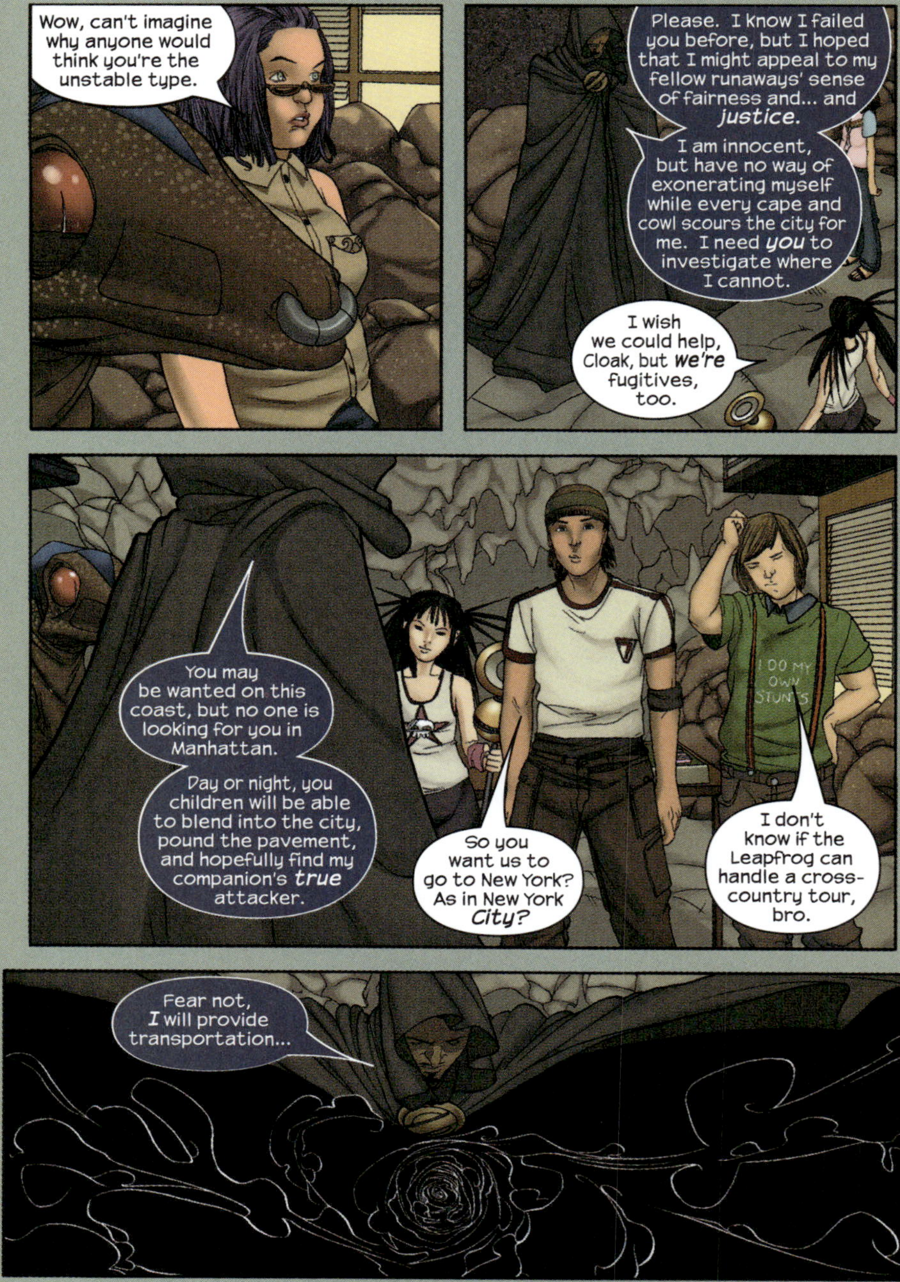
Wow, can't imagine why anyone would think you're the unstable type.
Please. I know I failed you before, but I hoped that I might appeal to my fellow runaways' sense of fairness and... and *justice.*
I am innocent, but have no way of exonerating myself while every cape and cowl scours the city for me. I need *you* to investigate where I cannot.
I wish we could help, Cloak, but *we're* fugitives, too.
You may be wanted on this coast, but no one is looking for you in Manhattan.
Day or night, you children will be able to blend into the city, pound the pavement, and hopefully find my companion's *true* attacker.
So you want us to go to New York? As in New York *City?*
I DO MY OWN STUNTS
I don't know if the Leapfrog can handle a cross-country tour, bro.
Fear not, *I* will provide transportation...

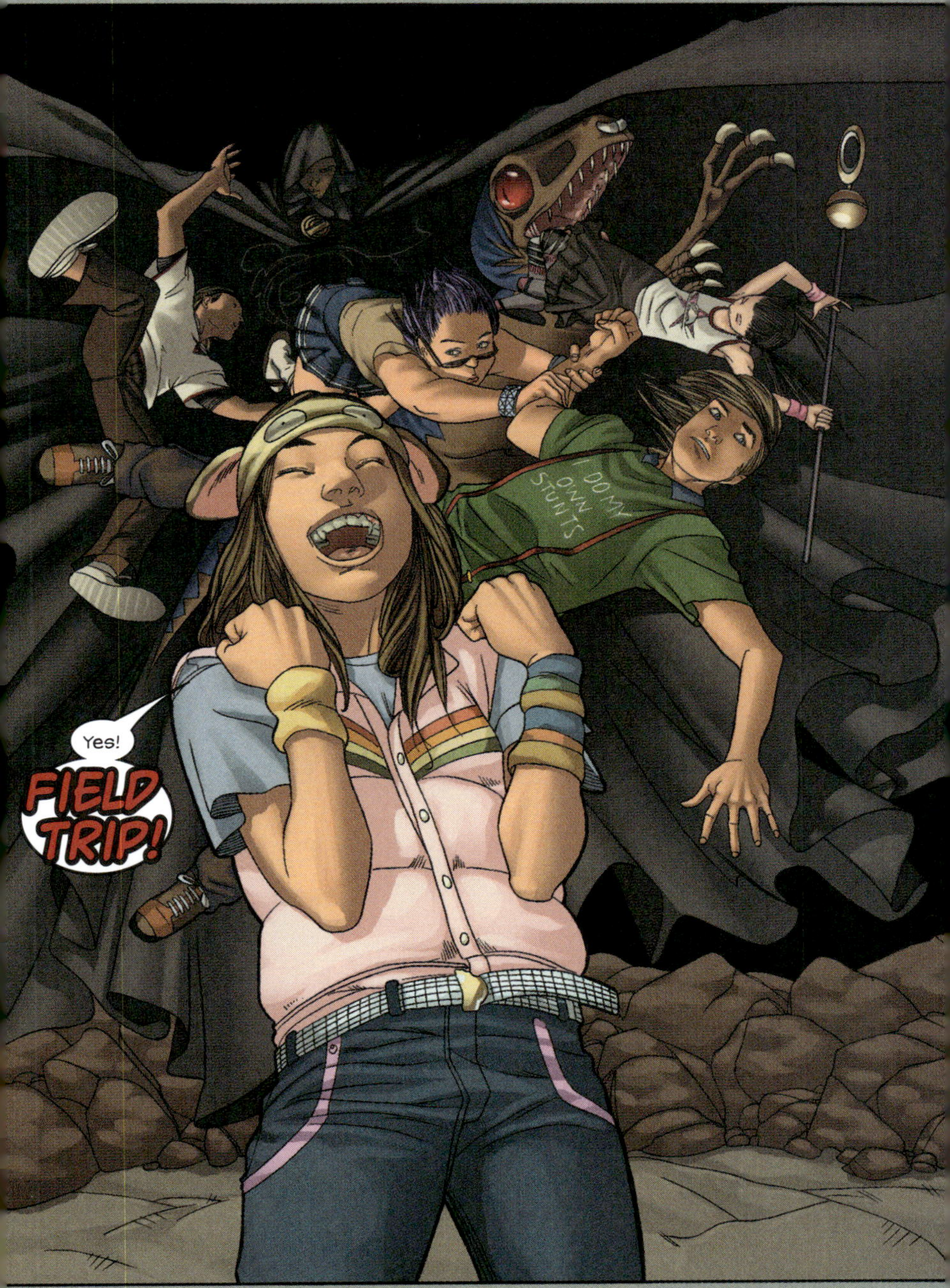
Yes!
FIELD TRIP!

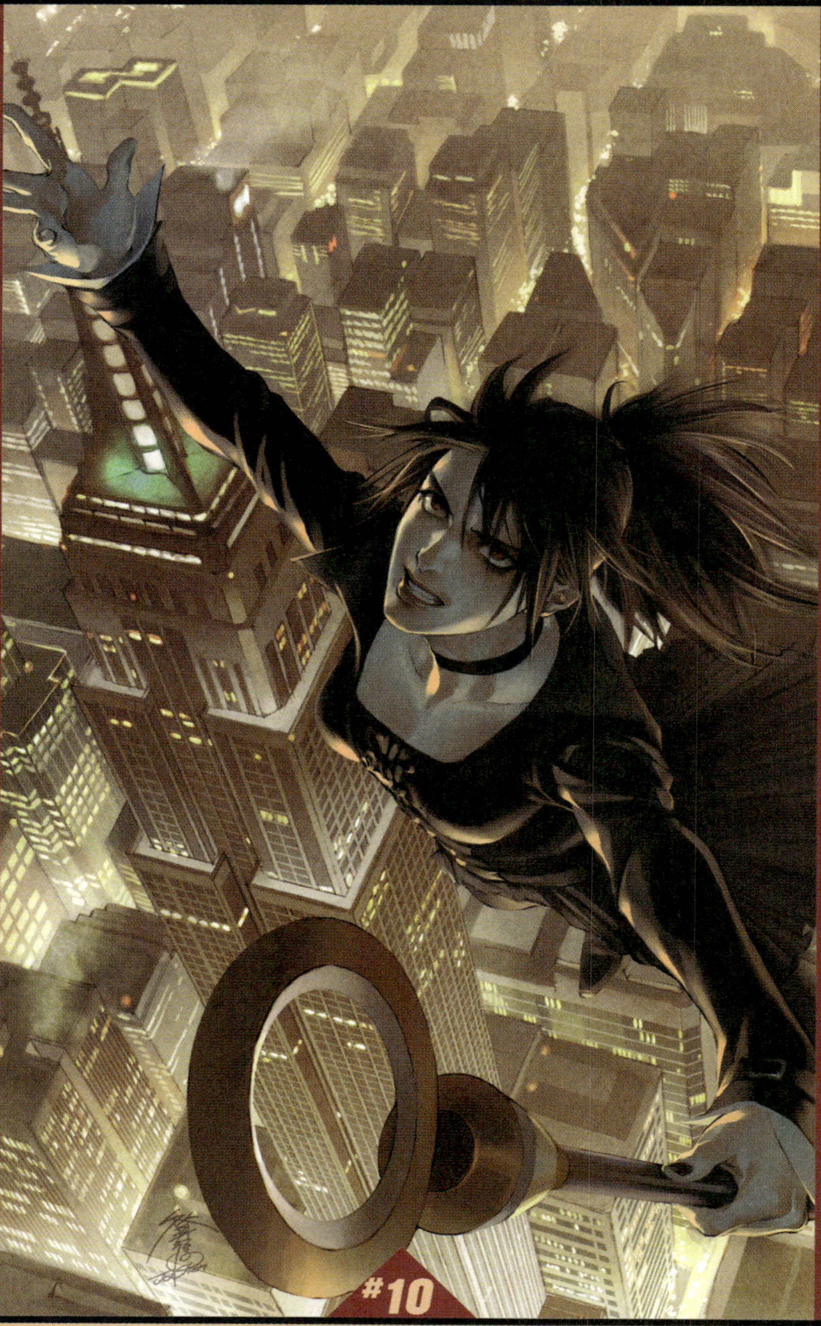
#10

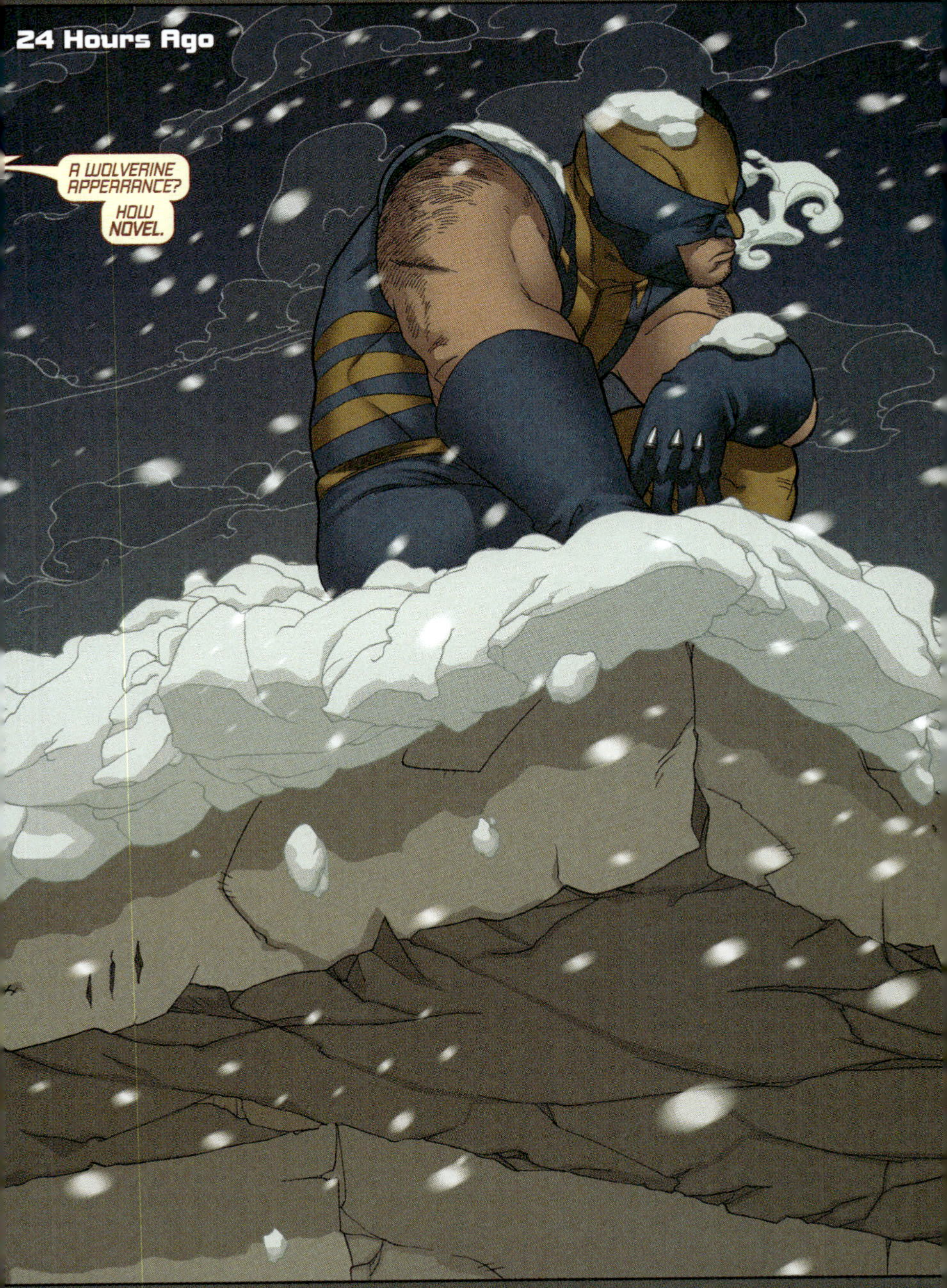
24 Hours Ago
A WOLVERINE APPEARANCE?
HOW NOVEL.

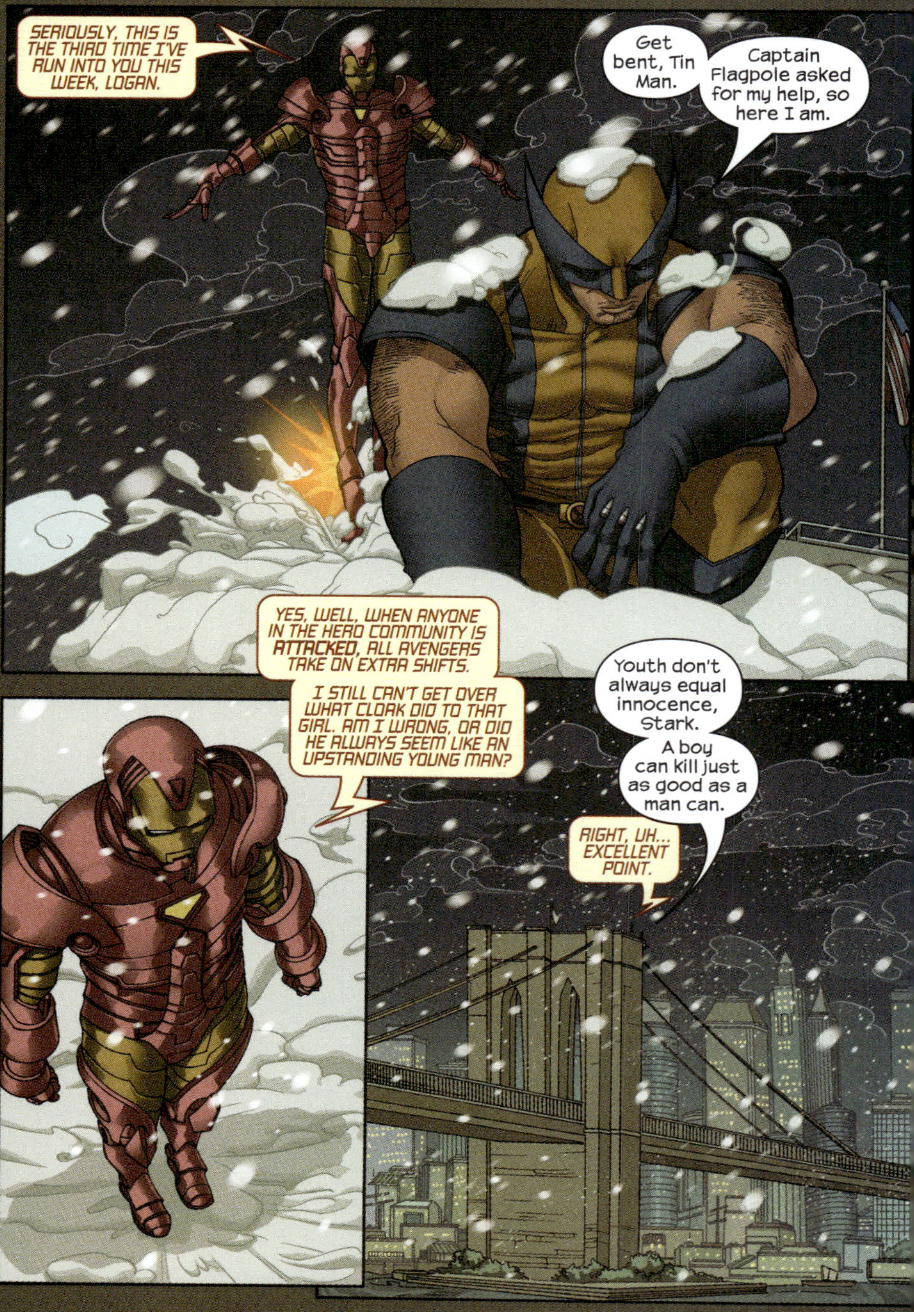
SERIOUSLY, THIS IS THE THIRD TIME I'VE RUN INTO YOU THIS WEEK, LOGAN.
Get bent, Tin Man.
Captain Flagpole asked for my help, so here I am.
YES, WELL, WHEN ANYONE IN THE HERO COMMUNITY IS ATTACKED, ALL AVENGERS TAKE ON EXTRA SHIFTS.
I STILL CAN'T GET OVER WHAT CLOAK DID TO THAT GIRL. AM I WRONG, OR DID HE ALWAYS SEEM LIKE AN UPSTANDING YOUNG MAN?
Youth don't always equal innocence, Stark.
A boy can kill just as good as a man can.
RIGHT, UH... EXCELLENT POINT.

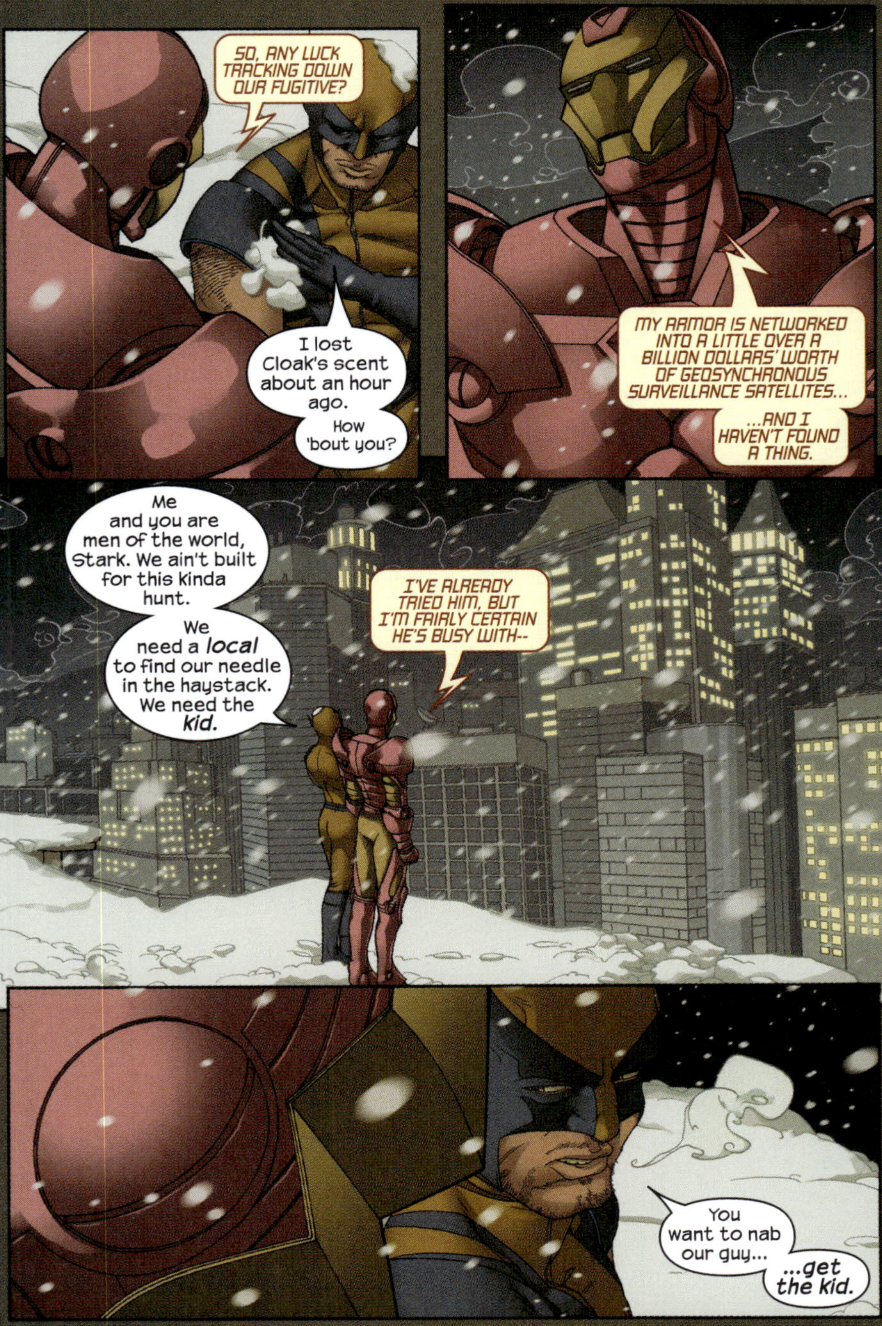
SO, ANY LUCK TRACKING DOWN OUR FUGITIVE?
I lost Cloak's scent about an hour ago.
How 'bout you?
MY ARMOR IS NETWORKED INTO A LITTLE OVER A BILLION DOLLARS' WORTH OF GEOSYNCHRONOUS SURVEILLANCE SATELLITES...
...AND I HAVEN'T FOUND A THING.
Me and you are men of the world, Stark. We ain't built for this kinda hunt.
We need a *local* to find our needle in the haystack. We need the *kid.*
I'VE ALREADY TRIED HIM, BUT I'M FAIRLY CERTAIN HE'S BUSY WITH--
You want to nab our guy...
...get the kid.

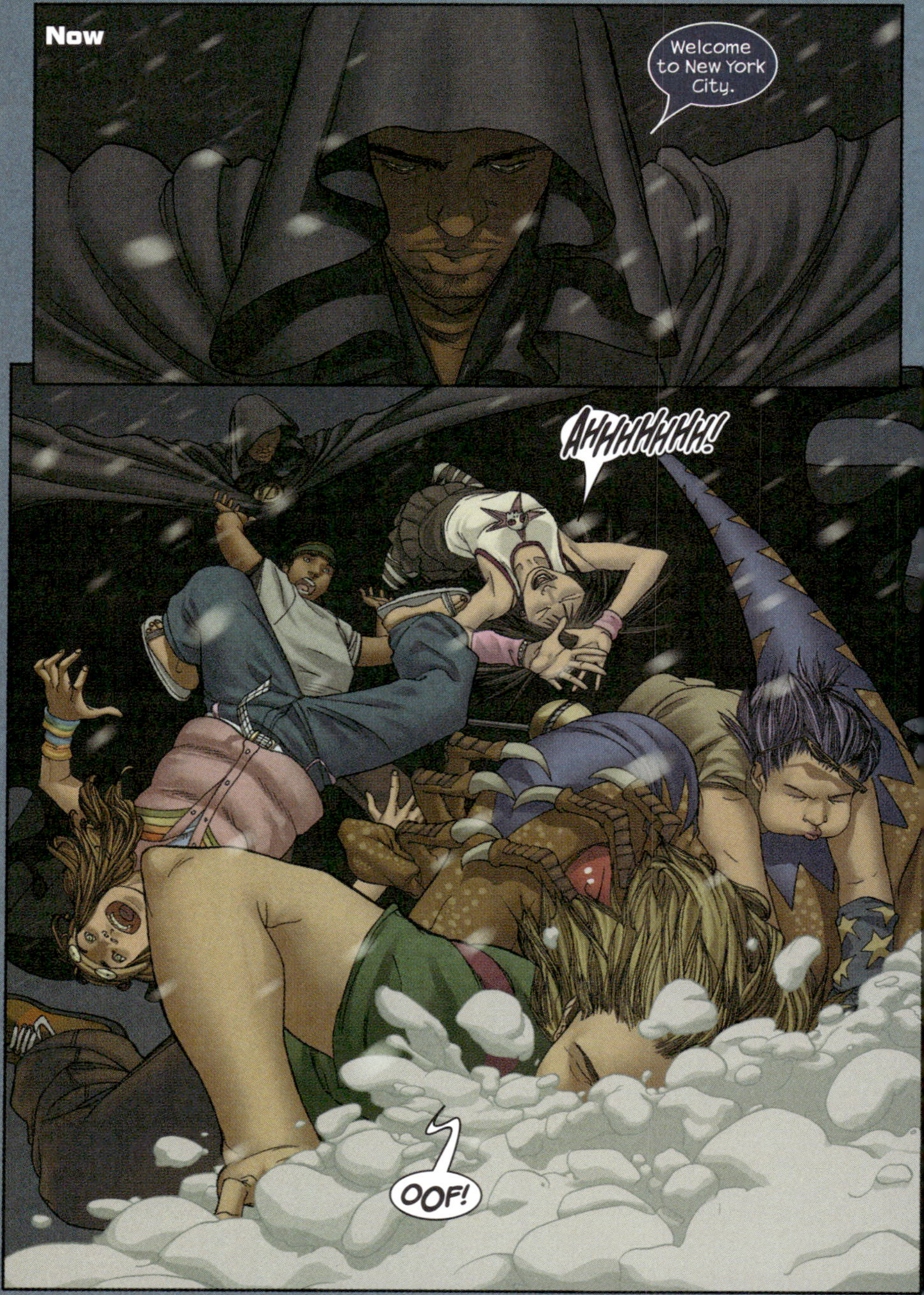
Now
Welcome to New York City.
AHHHHHHH!
OOF!

Well, still beats flying America West.

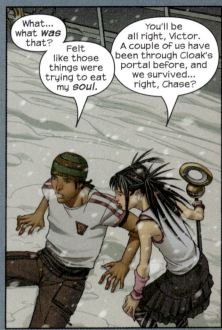

What... what *was* that?

Felt like those things were trying to eat my *soul*.

You'll be all right, Victor. A couple of us have been through Cloak's portal before, and we survived... right, Chase?

Sharks. There... there were *sharks*. In *space*.

Space sharks.

Smells like he went in his *pants*.

Forgive my hastiness.

I realize that the Darkforce Dimension is not the most... *comfortable* way to travel, but time is of the essence.

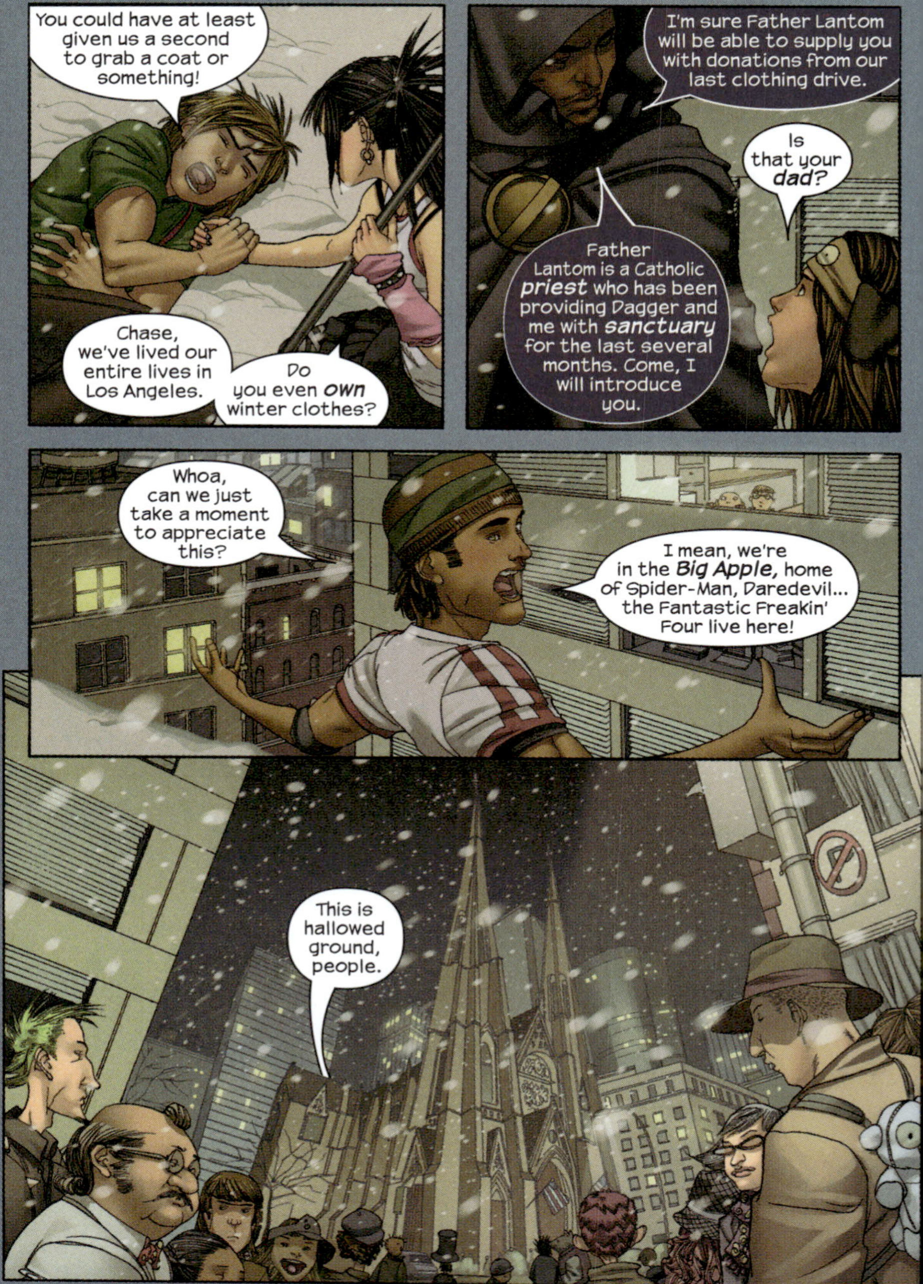
You could have at least given us a second to grab a coat or something!
Chase, we've lived our entire lives in Los Angeles.
Do you even own winter clothes?
I'm sure Father Lantom will be able to supply you with donations from our last clothing drive.
Is that your dad?
Father Lantom is a Catholic priest who has been providing Dagger and me with sanctuary for the last several months. Come, I will introduce you.
Whoa, can we just take a moment to appreciate this?
I mean, we're in the Big Apple, home of Spider-Man, Daredevil... the Fantastic Freakin' Four live here!
This is hallowed ground, people.

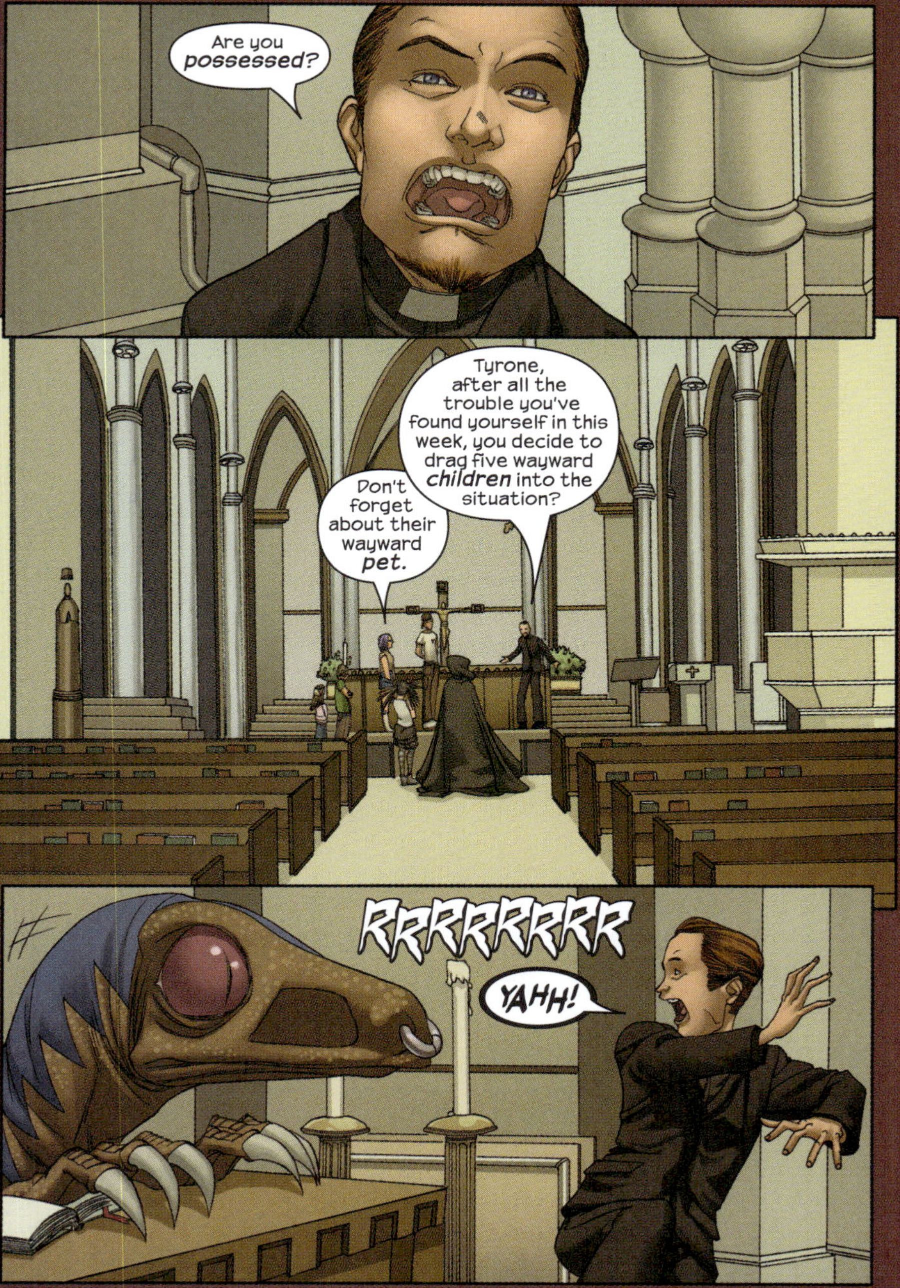
Are you *possessed?*
Tyrone, after all the trouble you've found yourself in this week, you decide to drag five wayward *children* into the situation?
Don't forget about their wayward *pet.*
RRRRRRRR
YAHH!

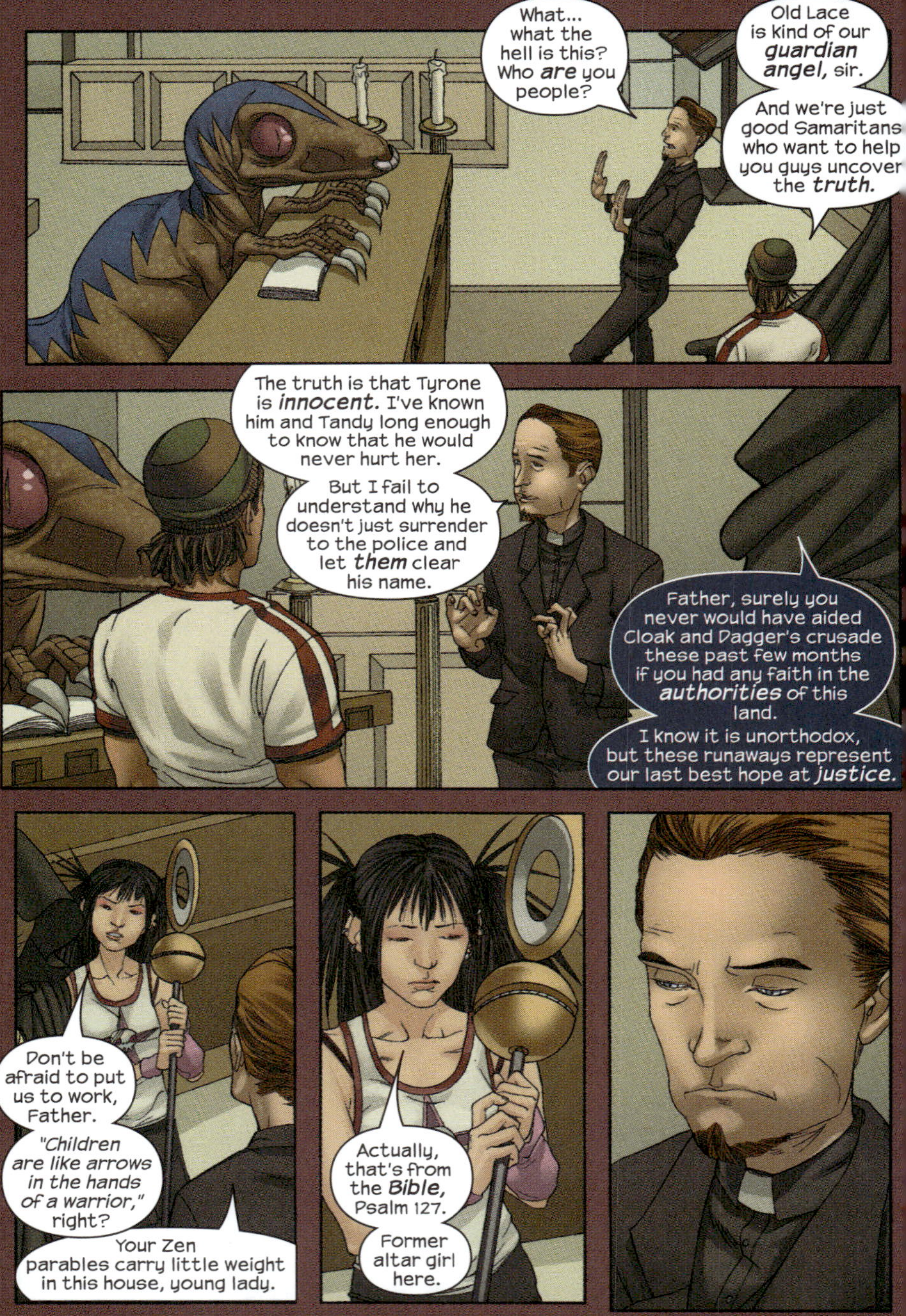
What... what the hell is this? Who are you people?
Old Lace is kind of our guardian angel, sir.
And we're just good Samaritans who want to help you guys uncover the truth.
The truth is that Tyrone is innocent. I've known him and Tandy long enough to know that he would never hurt her.
But I fail to understand why he doesn't just surrender to the police and let them clear his name.
Father, surely you never would have aided Cloak and Dagger's crusade these past few months if you had any faith in the authorities of this land.
I know it is unorthodox, but these runaways represent our last best hope at justice.
Don't be afraid to put us to work, Father.
"Children are like arrows in the hands of a warrior," right?
Your Zen parables carry little weight in this house, young lady.
Actually, that's from the Bible, Psalm 127.
Former altar girl here.

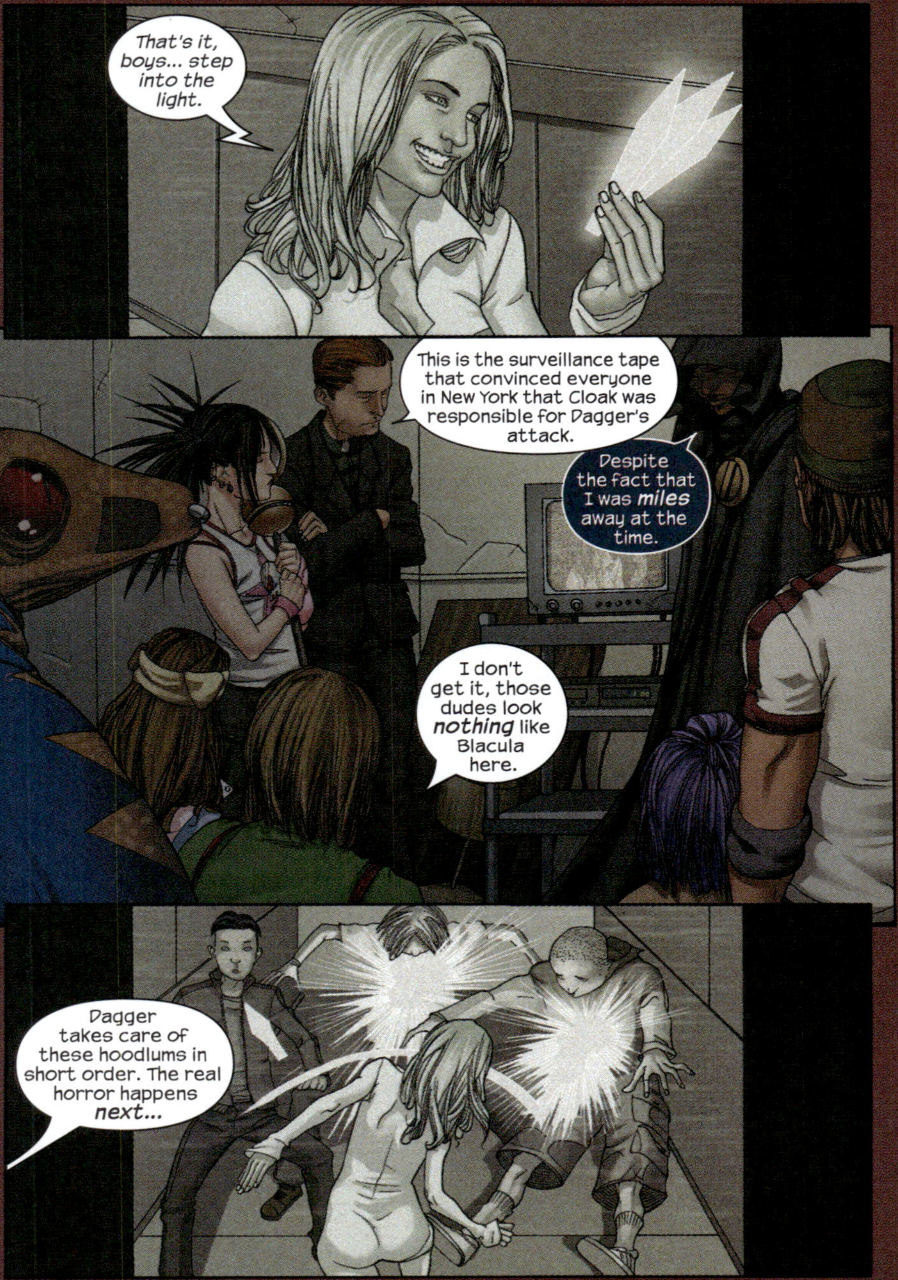
That's it, boys... step into the light.
This is the surveillance tape that convinced everyone in New York that Cloak was responsible for Dagger's attack.
Despite the fact that I was *miles* away at the time.
I don't get it, those dudes look *nothing* like Blacula here.
Dagger takes care of these hoodlums in short order. The real horror happens *next*...

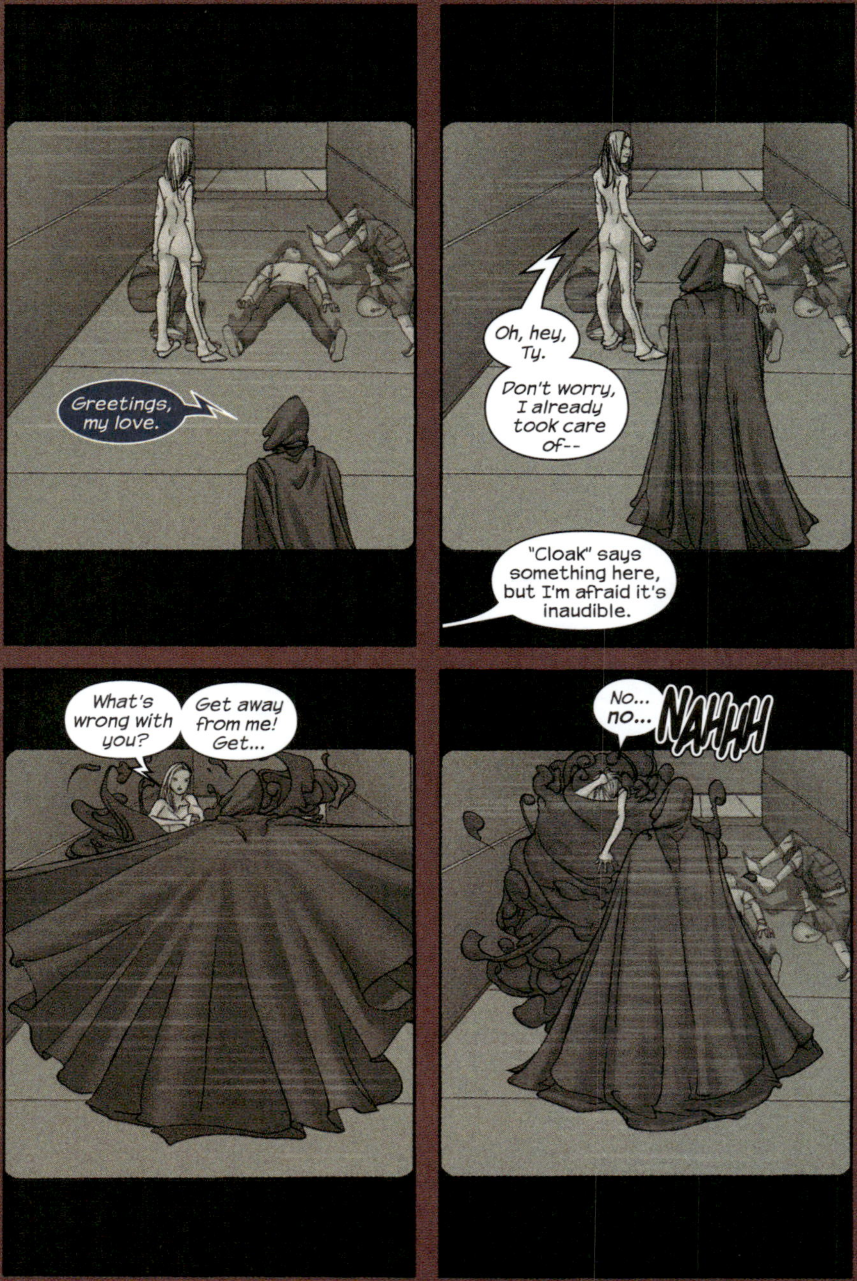
Greetings, my love.
Oh, hey, Ty.
Don't worry, I already took care of--
"Cloak" says something here, but I'm afraid it's inaudible.
What's wrong with you?
Get away from me! Get...
No... no...
NAHHH

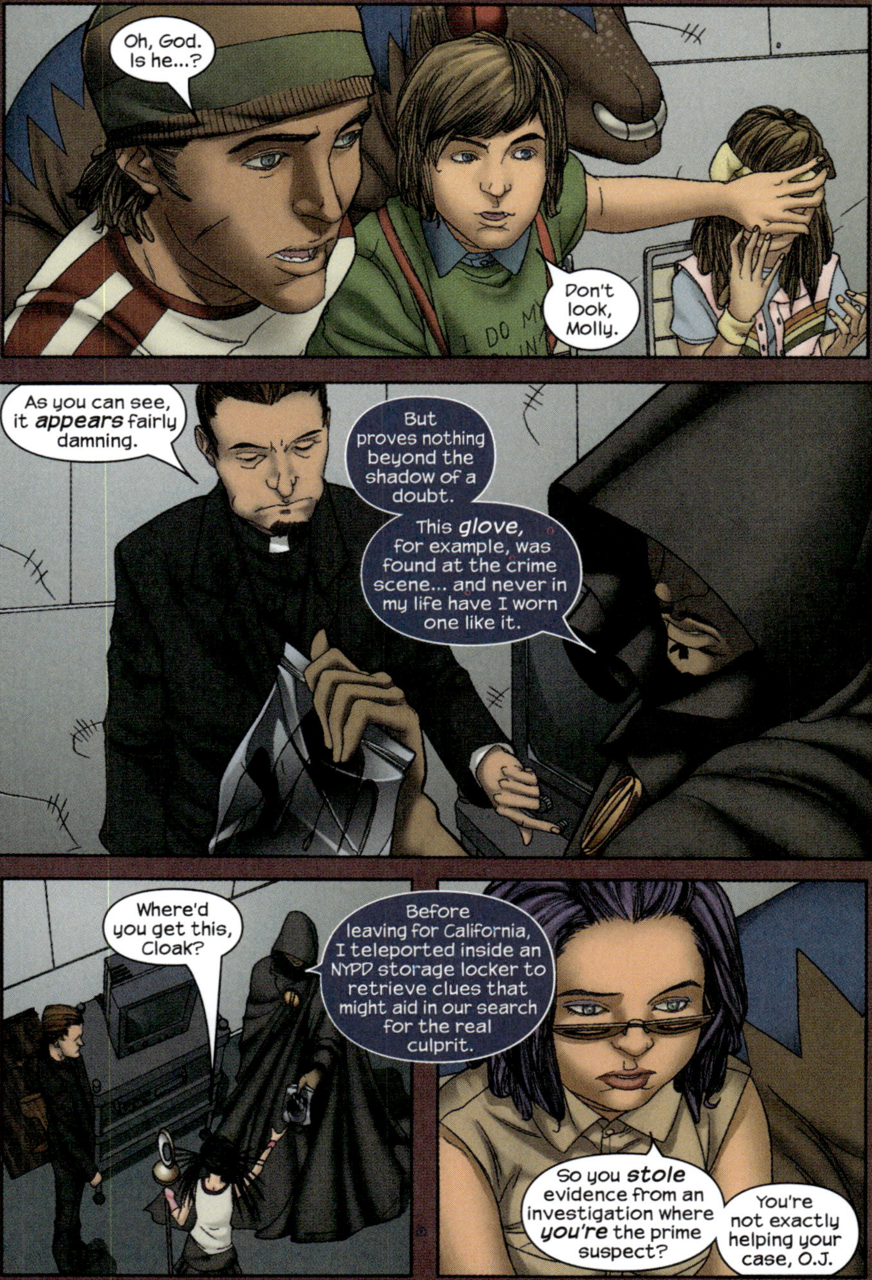
Oh, God. Is he...?
Don't look, Molly.
As you can see, it *appears* fairly damning.
But proves nothing beyond the shadow of a doubt.
This *glove,* for example, was found at the crime scene... and never in my life have I worn one like it.
Where'd you get this, Cloak?
Before leaving for California, I teleported inside an NYPD storage locker to retrieve clues that might aid in our search for the real culprit.
So you *stole* evidence from an investigation where *you're* the prime suspect?
You're not exactly helping your case, O.J.

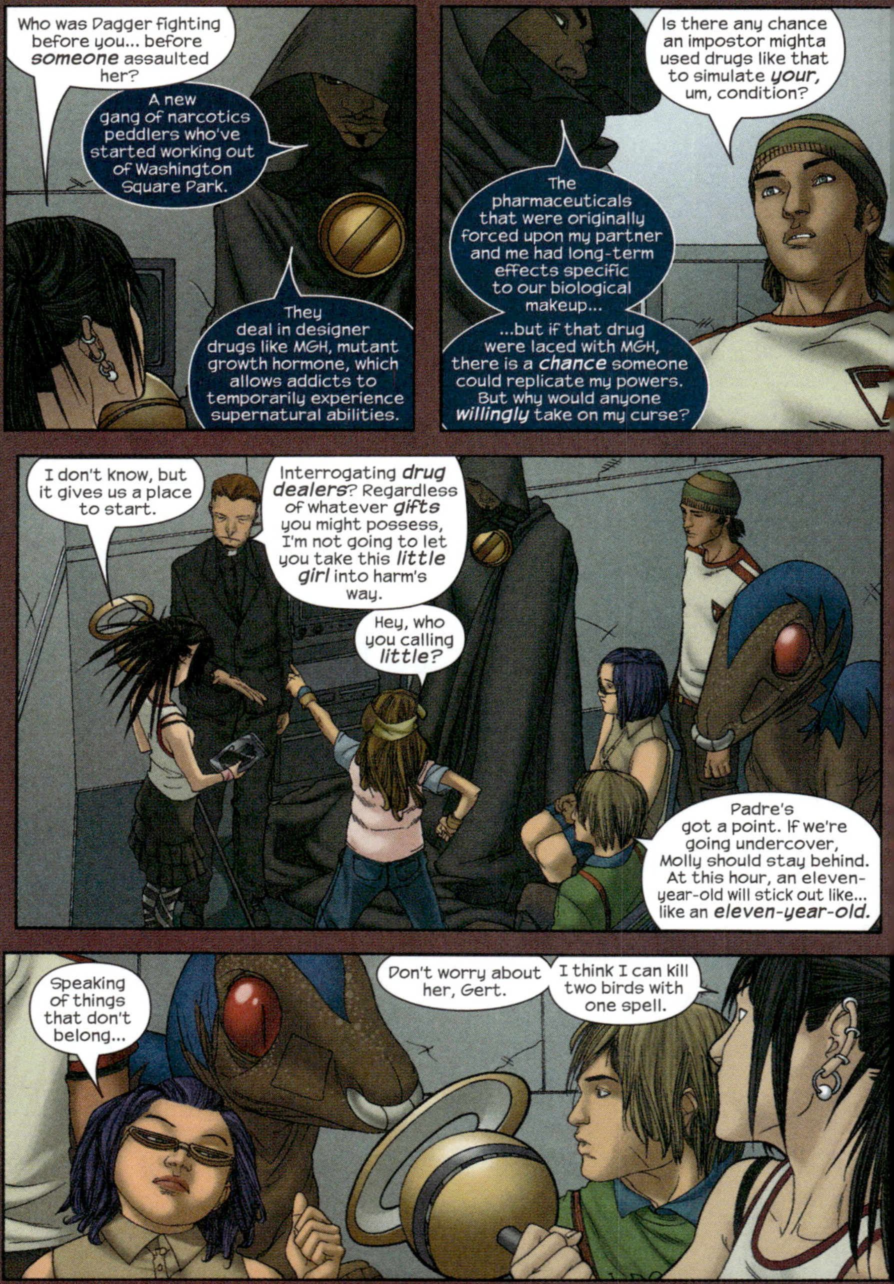

Who was Dagger fighting before you... before *someone* assaulted her?
A new gang of narcotics peddlers who've started working out of Washington Square Park.
They deal in designer drugs like MGH, mutant growth hormone, which allows addicts to temporarily experience supernatural abilities.
Is there any chance an impostor mighta used drugs like that to simulate *your,* um, condition?
The pharmaceuticals that were originally forced upon my partner and me had long-term effects specific to our biological makeup...
...but if that drug were laced with MGH, there is a *chance* someone could replicate my powers. But why would anyone *willingly* take on my curse?
I don't know, but it gives us a place to start.
Interrogating *drug dealers*? Regardless of whatever *gifts* you might possess, I'm not going to let you take this *little girl* into harm's way.
Hey, who you calling *little?*
Padre's got a point. If we're going undercover, Molly should stay behind. At this hour, an eleven-year-old will stick out like... like an *eleven-year-old.*
Speaking of things that don't belong...
Don't worry about her, Gert.
I think I can kill two birds with one spell.

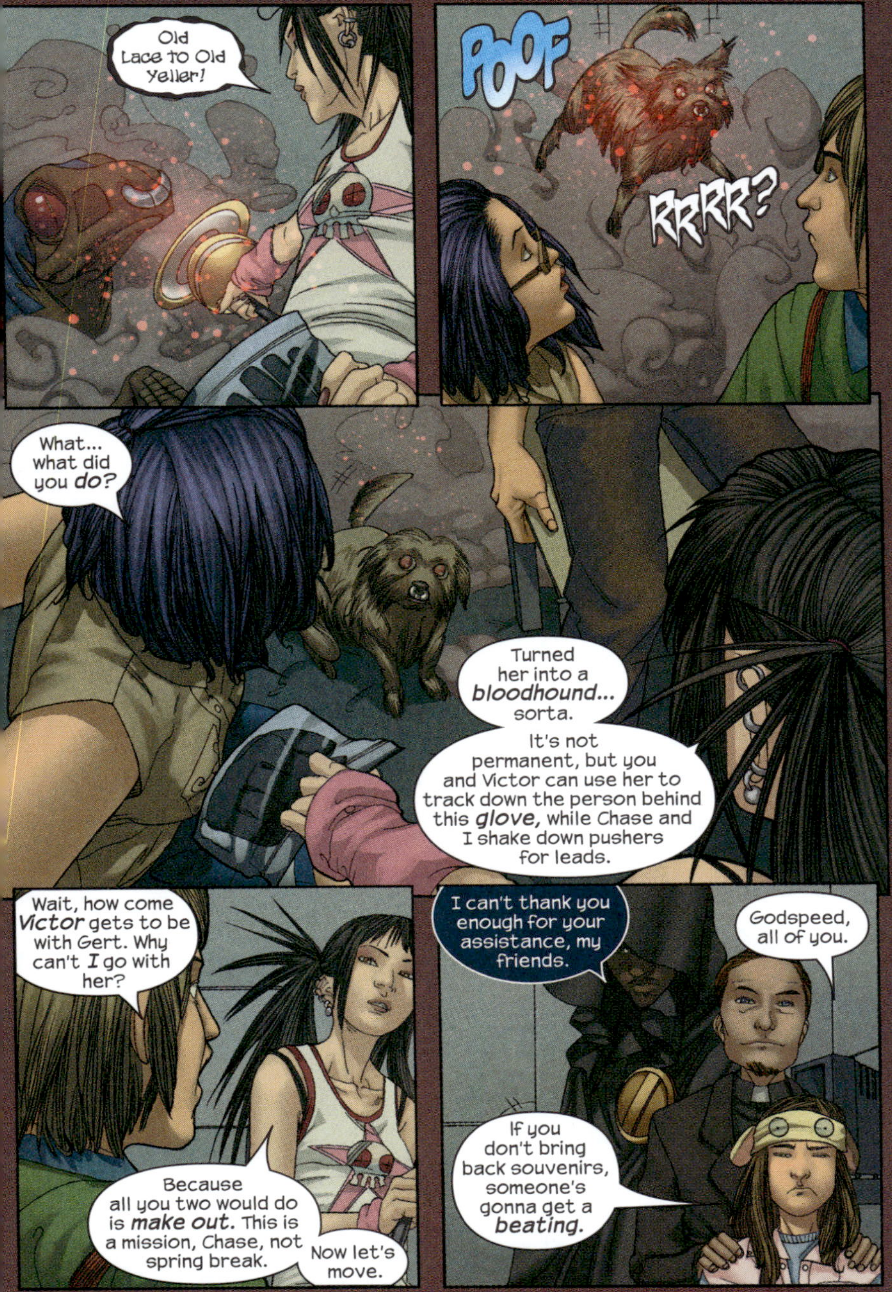
Old Lace to Old Yeller!
POOF
RRRR?
What... what did you *do?*
Turned her into a ***bloodhound...*** sorta.
It's not permanent, but you and Victor can use her to track down the person behind this ***glove,*** while Chase and I shake down pushers for leads.
Wait, how come ***Victor*** gets to be with Gert. Why can't ***I*** go with her?
Because all you two would do is ***make out.*** This is a mission, Chase, not spring break.
Now let's move.
I can't thank you enough for your assistance, my friends.
Godspeed, all of you.
If you don't bring back souvenirs, someone's gonna get a ***beating.***

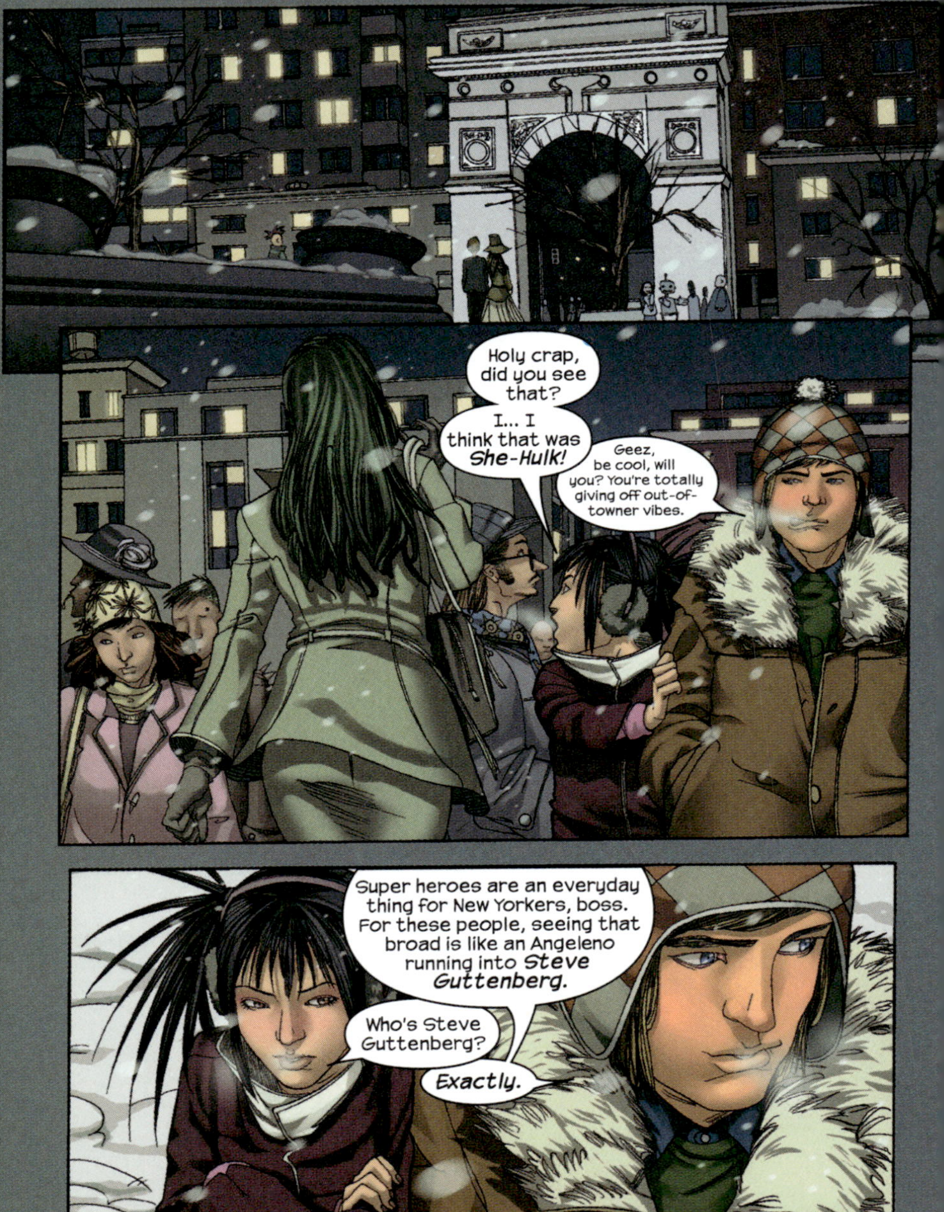
Holy crap, did you see that?
I... I think that was She-Hulk!
Geez, be cool, will you? You're totally giving off out-of-towner vibes.
Super heroes are an everyday thing for New Yorkers, boss. For these people, seeing that broad is like an Angeleno running into Steve Guttenberg.
Who's Steve Guttenberg?
Exactly.

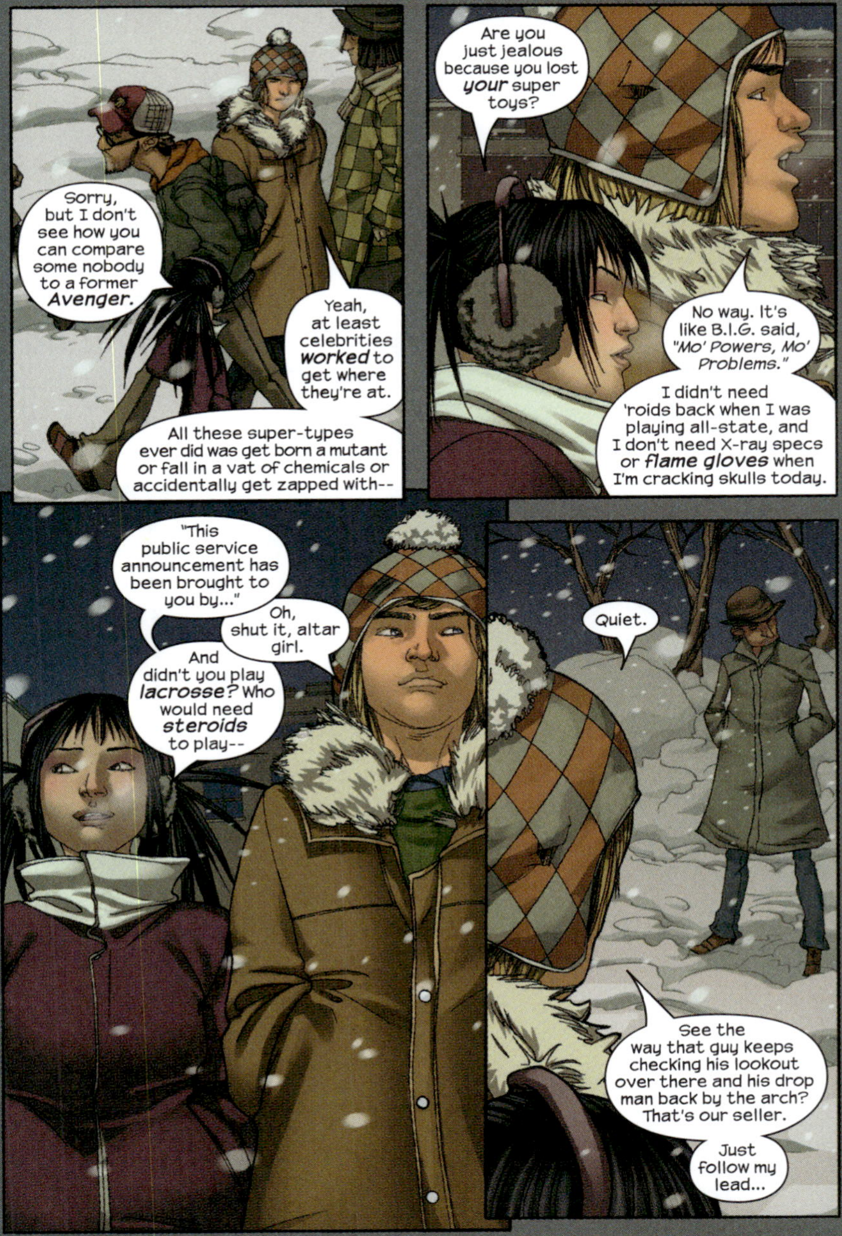
Sorry, but I don't see how you can compare some nobody to a former *Avenger.*
Yeah, at least celebrities **worked** to get where they're at.
All these super-types ever did was get born a mutant or fall in a vat of chemicals or accidentally get zapped with--
Are you just jealous because you lost **your** super toys?
No way. It's like B.I.G. said, *"Mo' Powers, Mo' Problems."*
I didn't need 'roids back when I was playing all-state, and I don't need X-ray specs or **flame gloves** when I'm cracking skulls today.
"This public service announcement has been brought to you by..."
Oh, shut it, altar girl.
And didn't you play ***lacrosse?*** Who would need ***steroids*** to play--
Quiet.
See the way that guy keeps checking his lookout over there and his drop man back by the arch? That's our seller.
Just follow my lead...

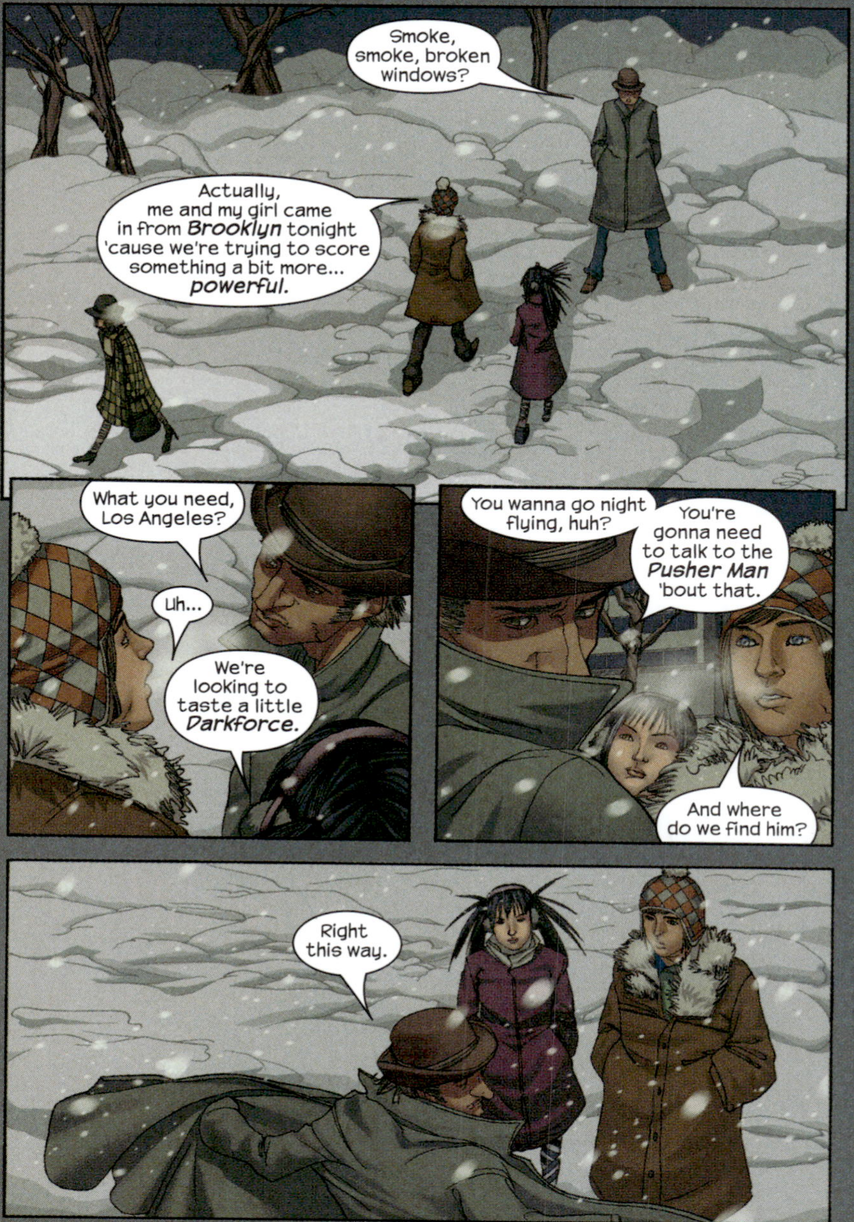
Smoke, smoke, broken windows?
Actually, me and my girl came in from Brooklyn tonight 'cause we're trying to score something a bit more... powerful.
What you need, Los Angeles?
Uh...
We're looking to taste a little Darkforce.
You wanna go night flying, huh?
You're gonna need to talk to the Pusher Man 'bout that.
And where do we find him?
Right this way.

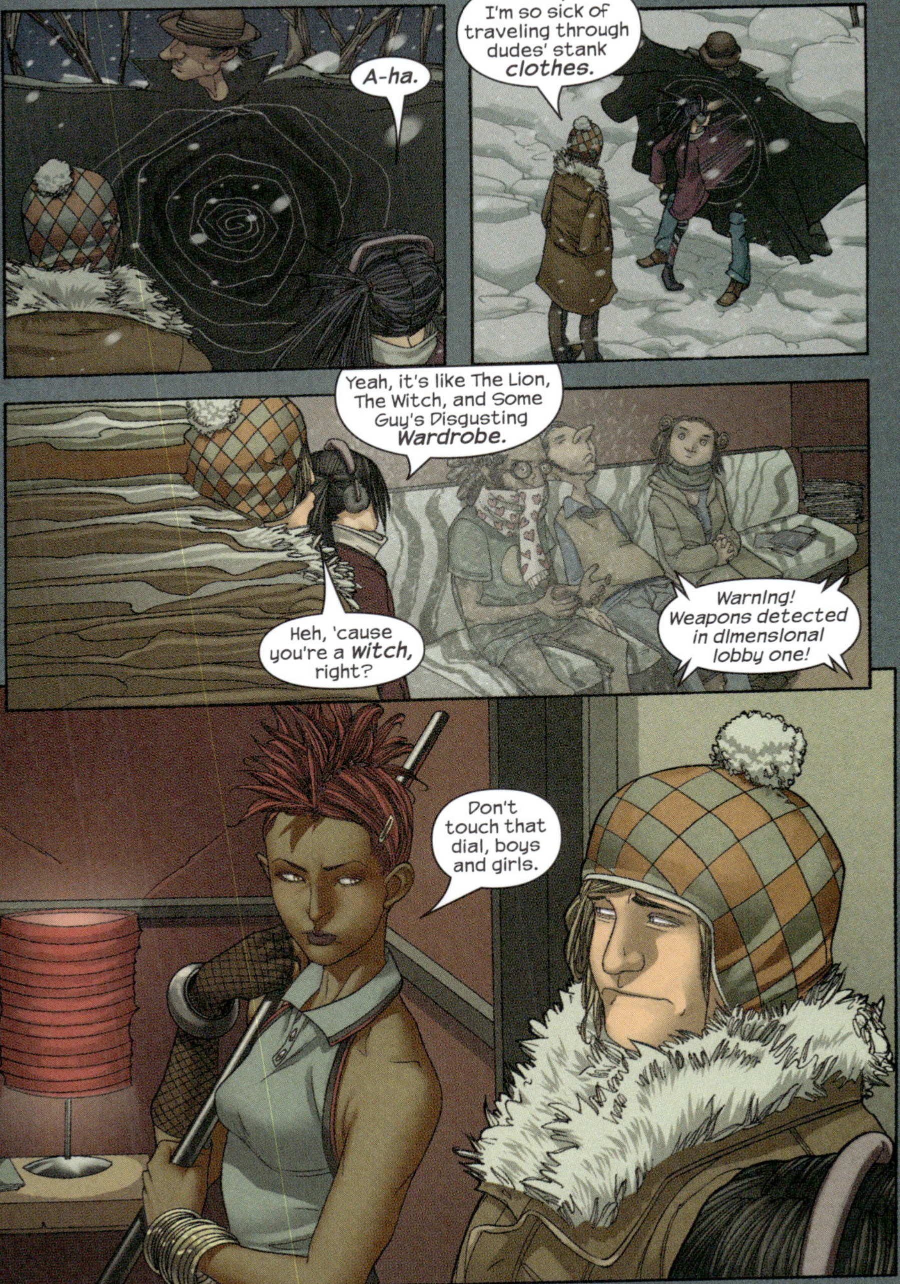
A-ha.
Guh, I'm so sick of traveling through dudes' stank clothes.
Yeah, it's like The Lion, The Witch, and Some Guy's Disgusting Wardrobe.
Heh, 'cause you're a witch, right?
Warning! Weapons detected in dimensional lobby one!
Don't touch that dial, boys and girls.

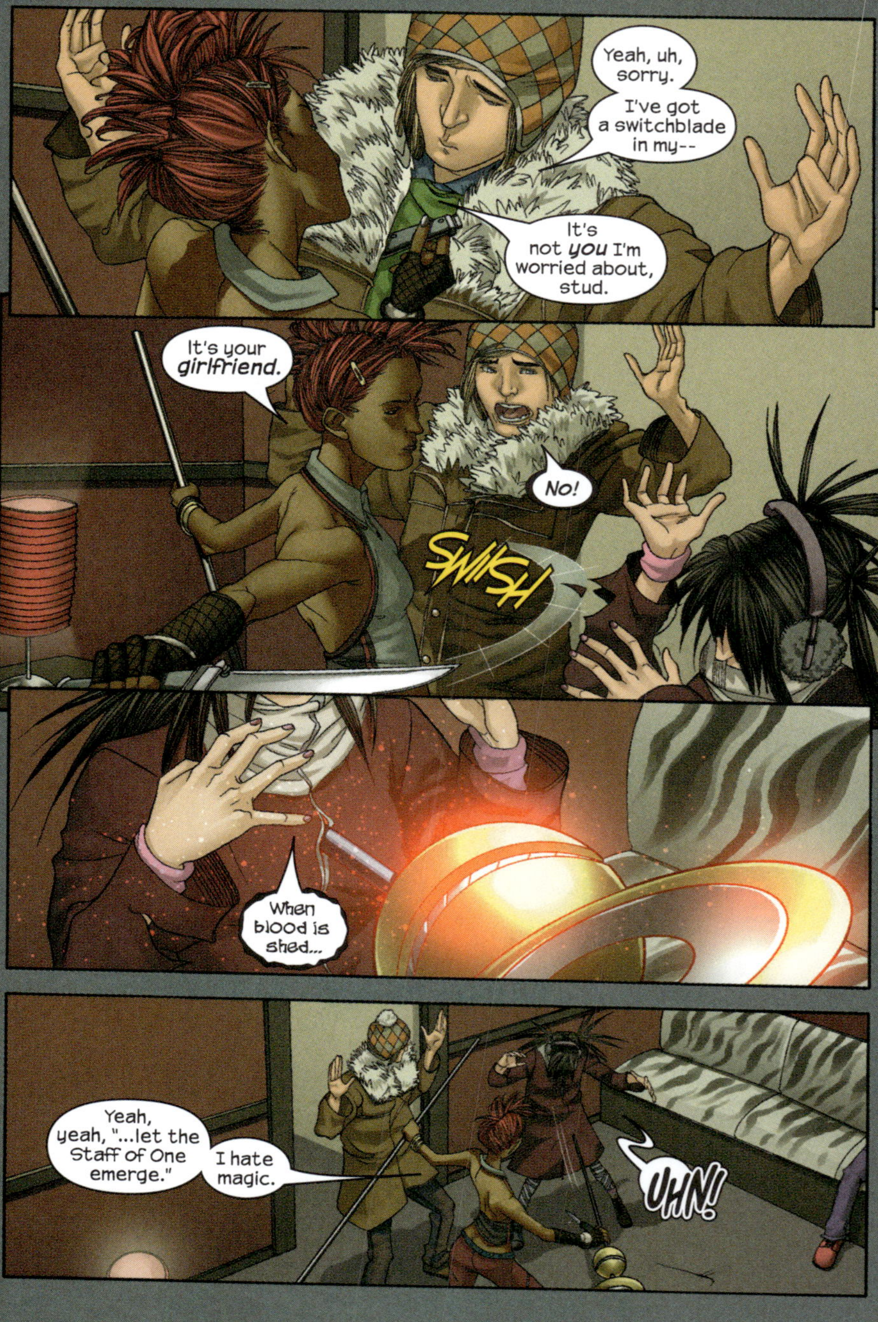
Yeah, uh, sorry.
I've got a switchblade in my--
It's not *you* I'm worried about, stud.
It's your *girlfriend.*
No!
SWISH
When blood is shed...
Yeah, yeah, "...let the Staff of One emerge."
I hate magic.
UHN!

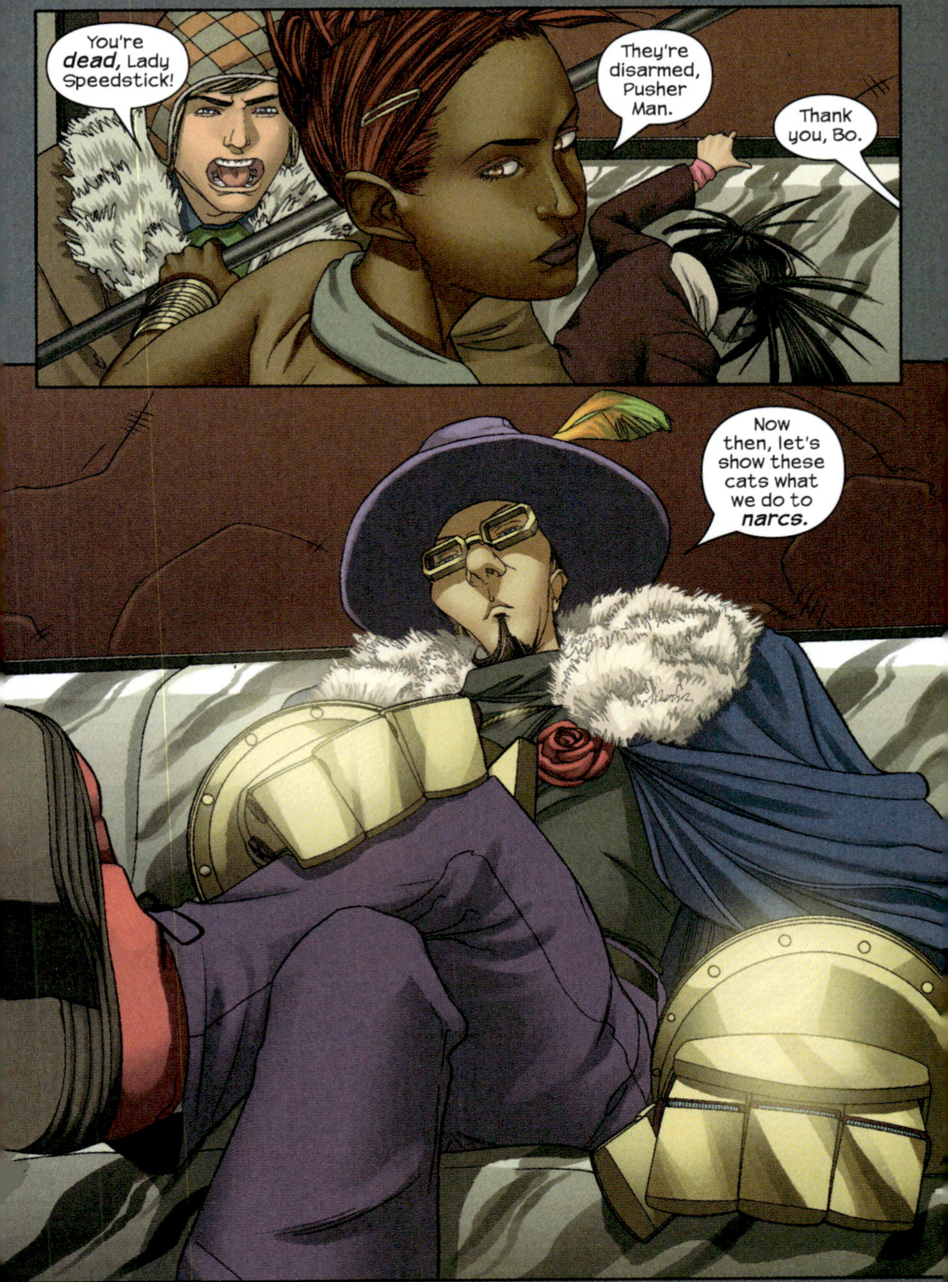
You're *dead,* Lady Speedstick!
They're disarmed, Pusher Man.
Thank you, Bo.
Now then, let's show these cats what we do to *narcs.*

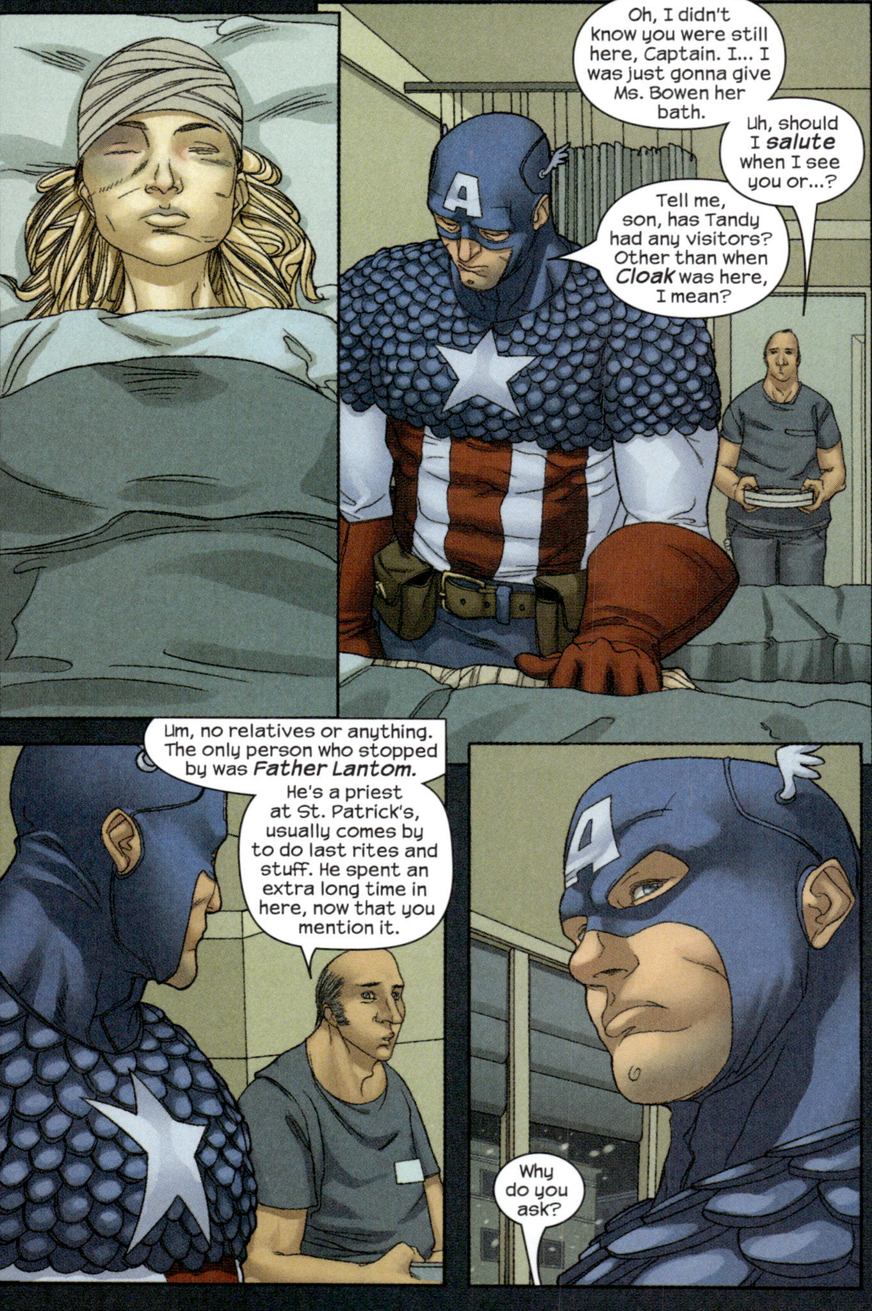

Oh, I didn't know you were still here, Captain. I... I was just gonna give Ms. Bowen her bath.
Uh, should I *salute* when I see you or...?
Tell me, son, has Tandy had any visitors? Other than when *Cloak* was here, I mean?
Um, no relatives or anything. The only person who stopped by was *Father Lantom.*
He's a priest at St. Patrick's, usually comes by to do last rites and stuff. He spent an extra long time in here, now that you mention it.
Why do you ask?

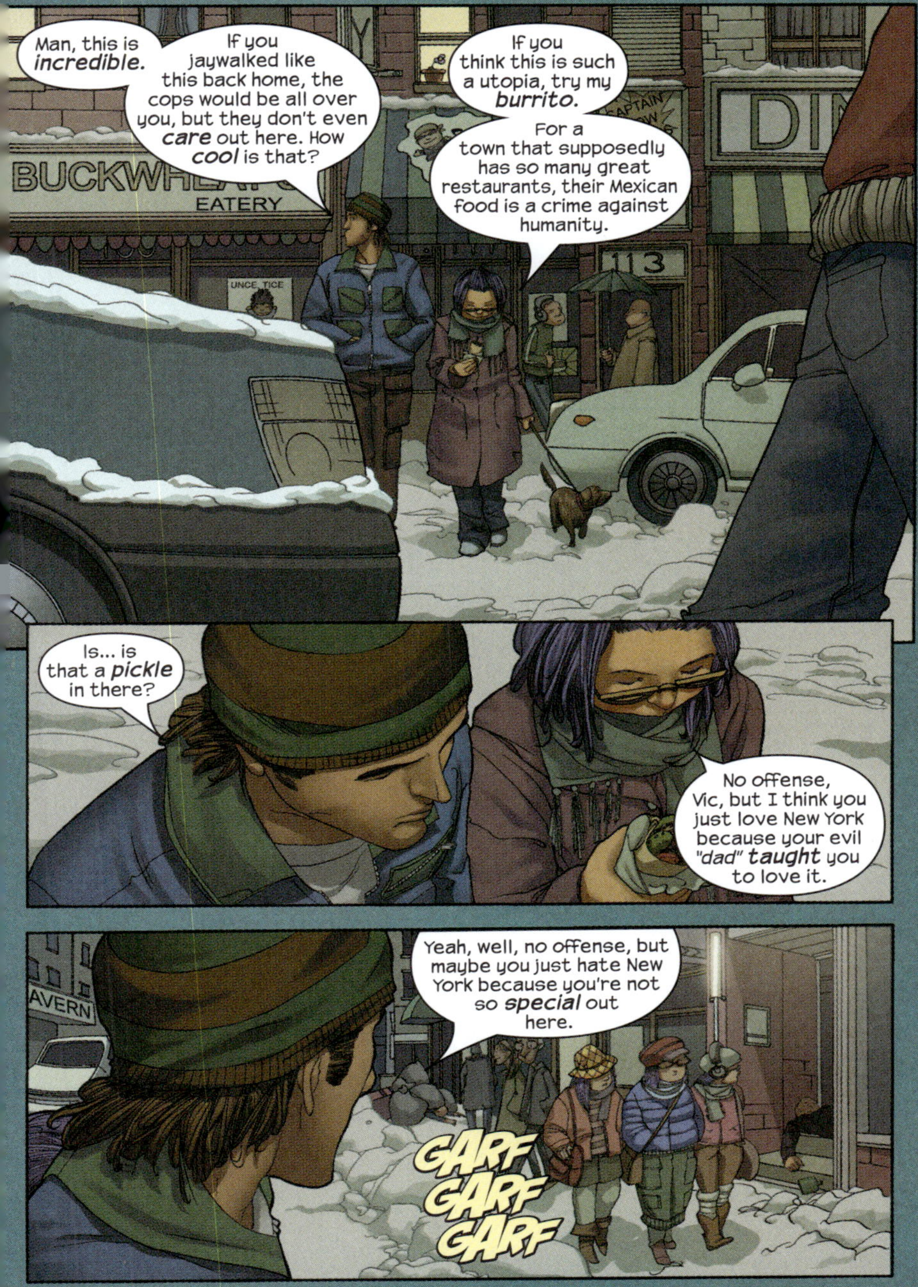
Man, this is *incredible.*
If you jaywalked like this back home, the cops would be all over you, but they don't even *care* out here. How *cool* is that?
If you think this is such a utopia, try my *burrito.*
For a town that supposedly has so many great restaurants, their Mexican food is a crime against humanity.
BUCKWHEAT'S
EATERY
113
Is... is that a *pickle* in there?
No offense, Vic, but I think you just love New York because your evil "dad" *taught* you to love it.
Yeah, well, no offense, but maybe you just hate New York because you're not so *special* out here.
GARF GARF GARF

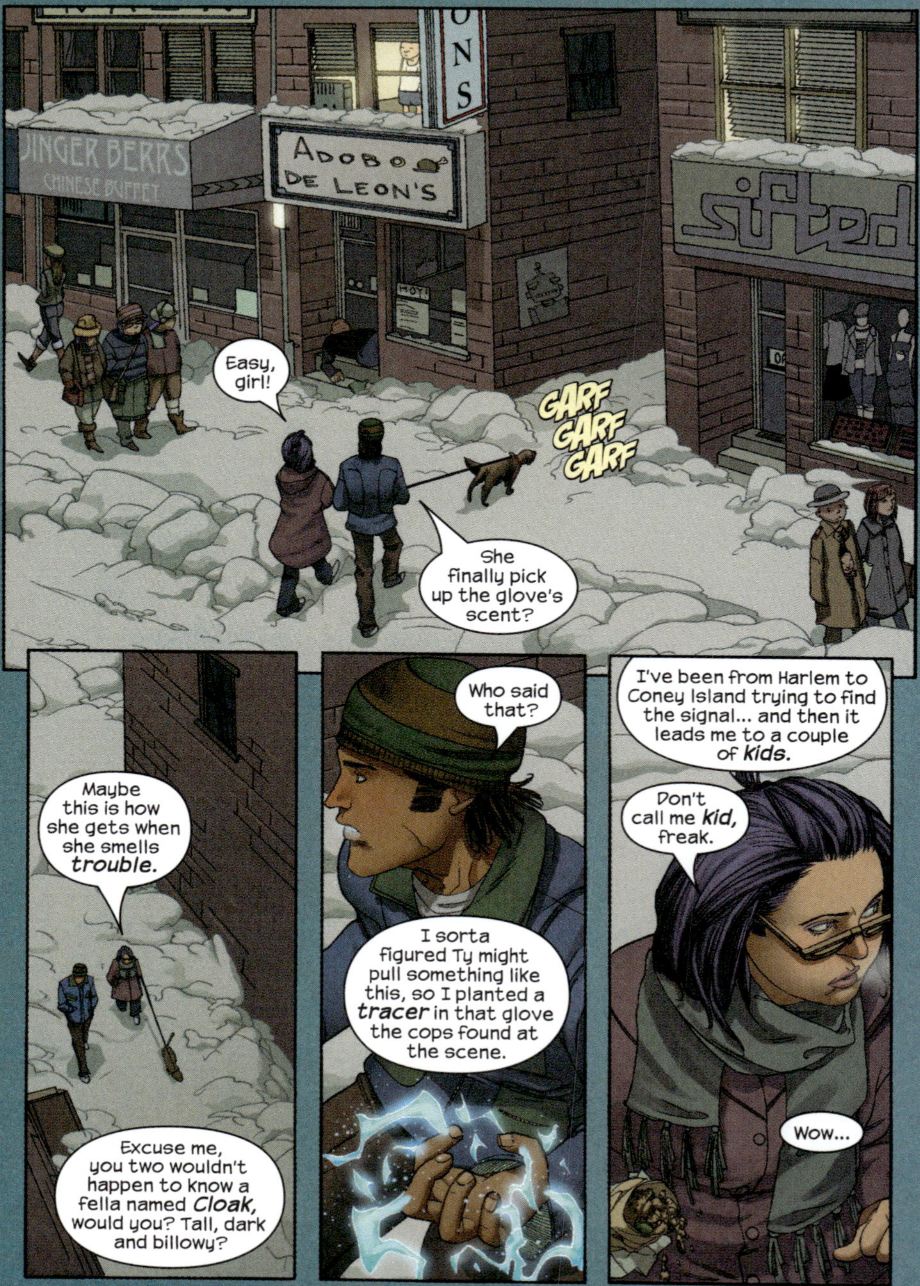
ADOBO
DE LEON'S
sifted
Easy, girl!
GARF GARF GARF
She finally pick up the glove's scent?
Maybe this is how she gets when she smells *trouble.*
Excuse me, you two wouldn't happen to know a fella named *Cloak,* would you? Tall, dark and billowy?
Who said that?
I sorta figured Ty might pull something like this, so I planted a *tracer* in that glove the cops found at the scene.
I've been from Harlem to Coney Island trying to find the signal... and then it leads me to a couple of *kids.*
Don't call me *kid,* freak.
Wow...

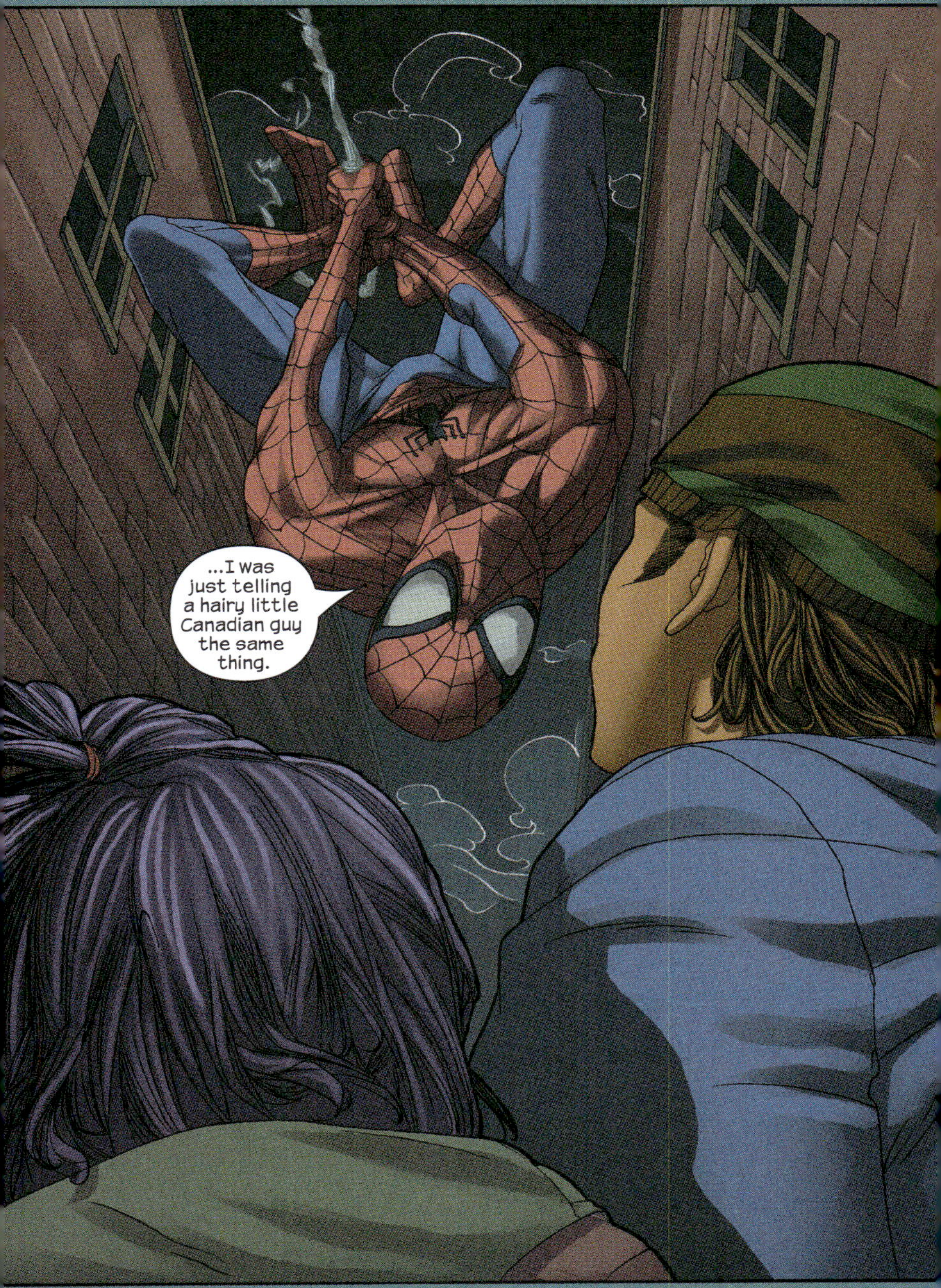
...I was just telling a hairy little Canadian guy the same thing.

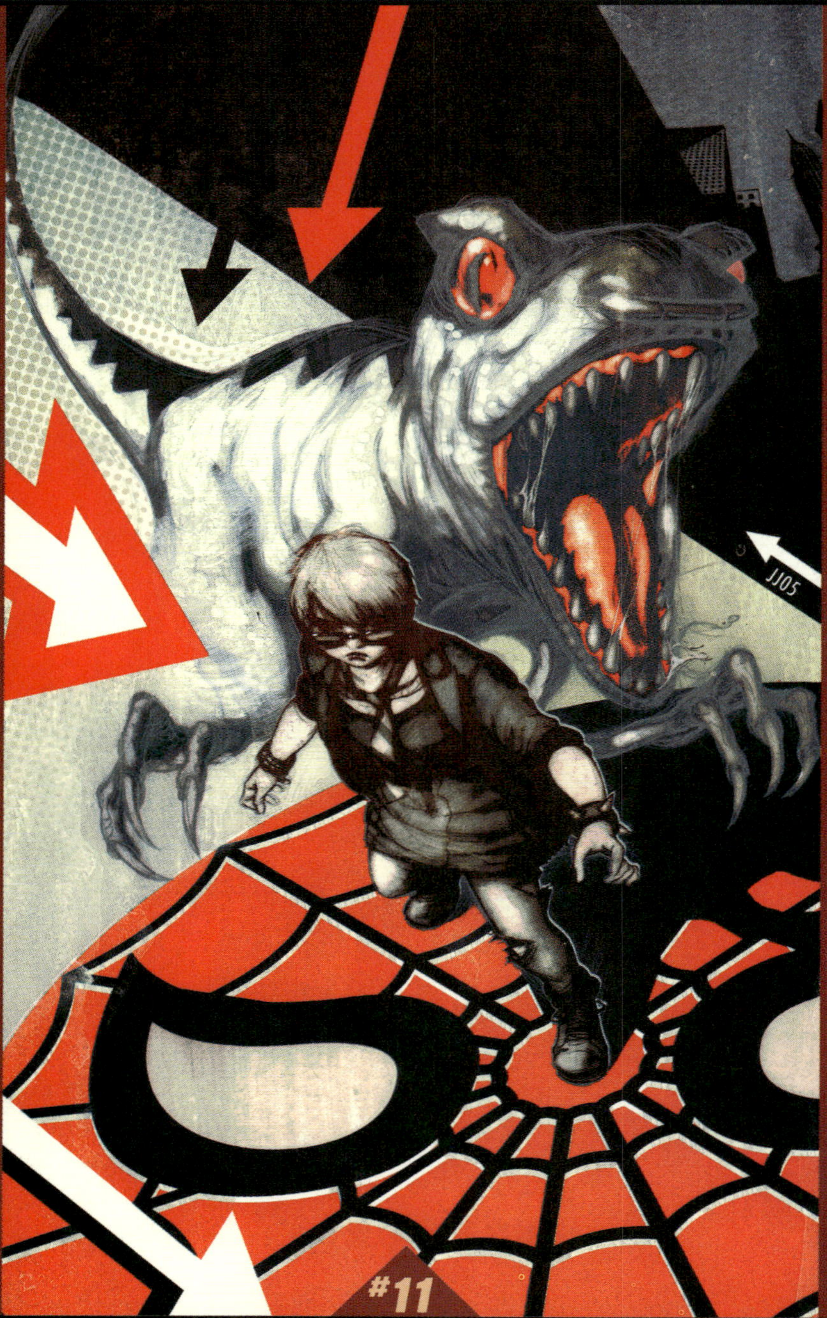
JJ05
#11

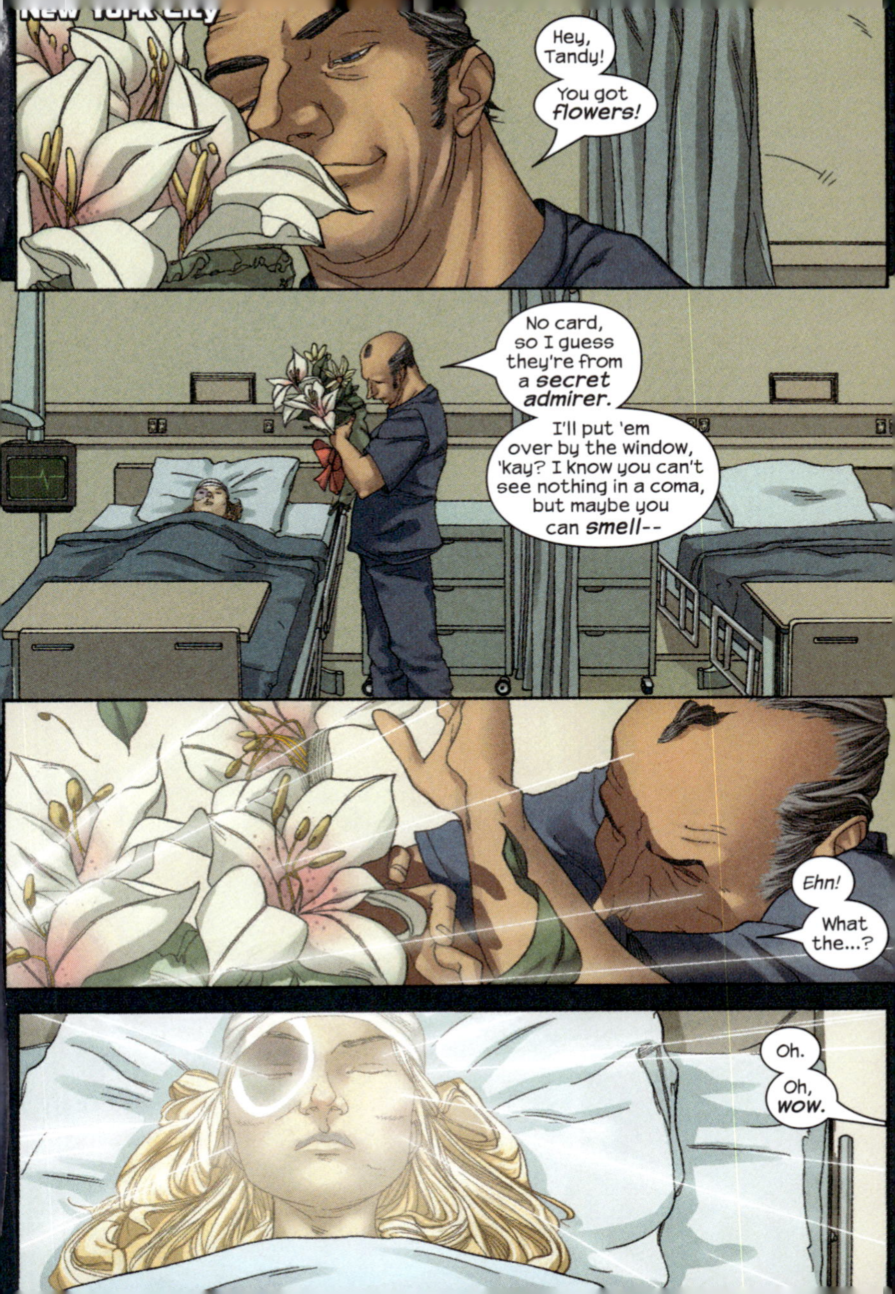
Hey, Tandy!
You got *flowers!*
No card, so I guess they're from a ***secret admirer.***
I'll put 'em over by the window, 'kay? I know you can't see nothing in a coma, but maybe you can ***smell***--
Ehn!
What the...?
Oh.
Oh, ***WOW.***

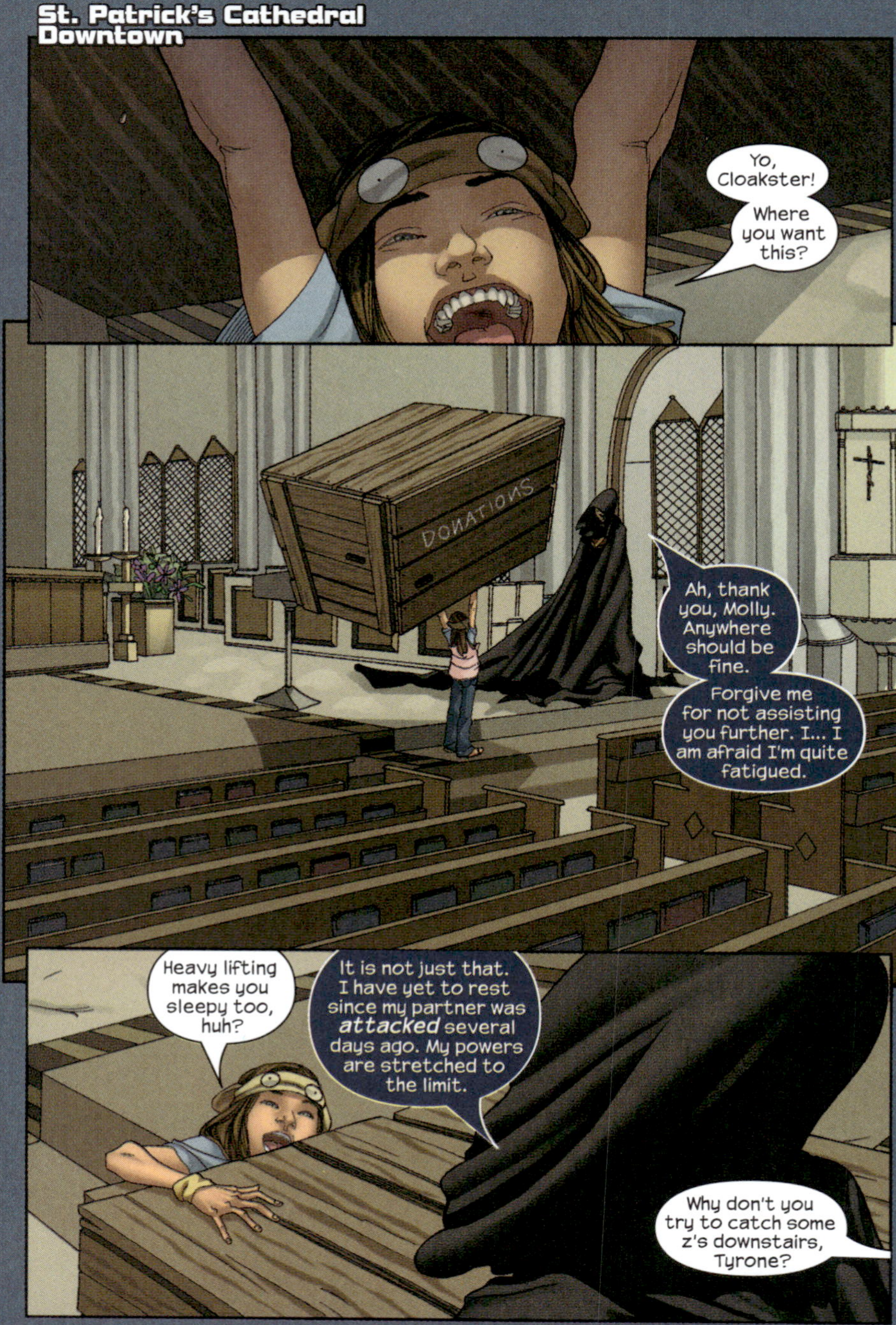
St. Patrick's Cathedral
Downtown
Yo, Cloakster!
Where you want this?
DONATIONS
Ah, thank you, Molly. Anywhere should be fine.
Forgive me for not assisting you further. I... I am afraid I'm quite fatigued.
Heavy lifting makes you sleepy too, huh?
It is not just that. I have yet to rest since my partner was *attacked* several days ago. My powers are stretched to the limit.
Why don't you try to catch some z's downstairs, Tyrone?

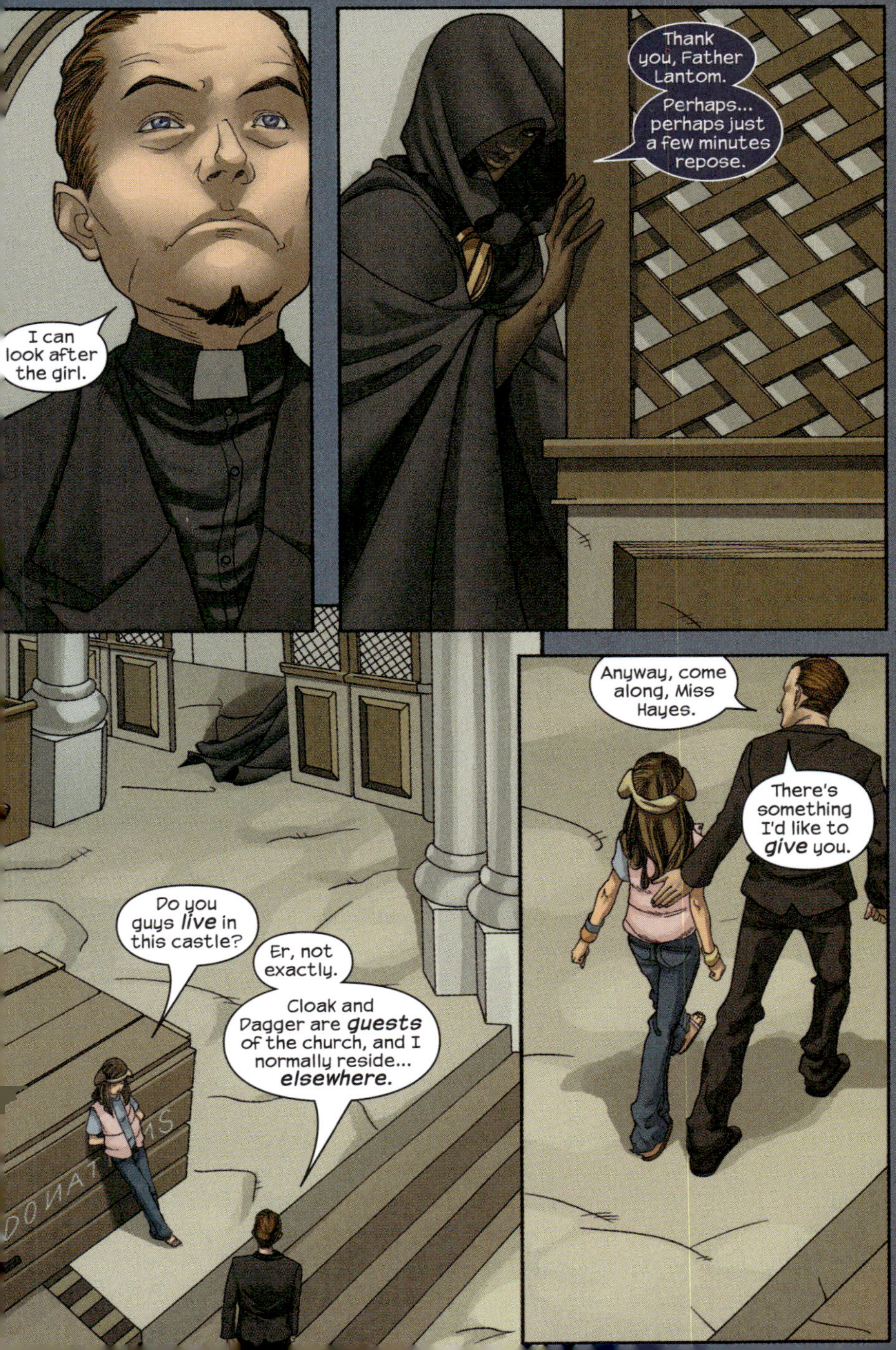
I can look after the girl.
Thank you, Father Lantom.
Perhaps... perhaps just a few minutes repose.
Do you guys live in this castle?
Er, not exactly.
Cloak and Dagger are guests of the church, and I normally reside... elsewhere.
DONATIONS
Anyway, come along, Miss Hayes.
There's something I'd like to give you.

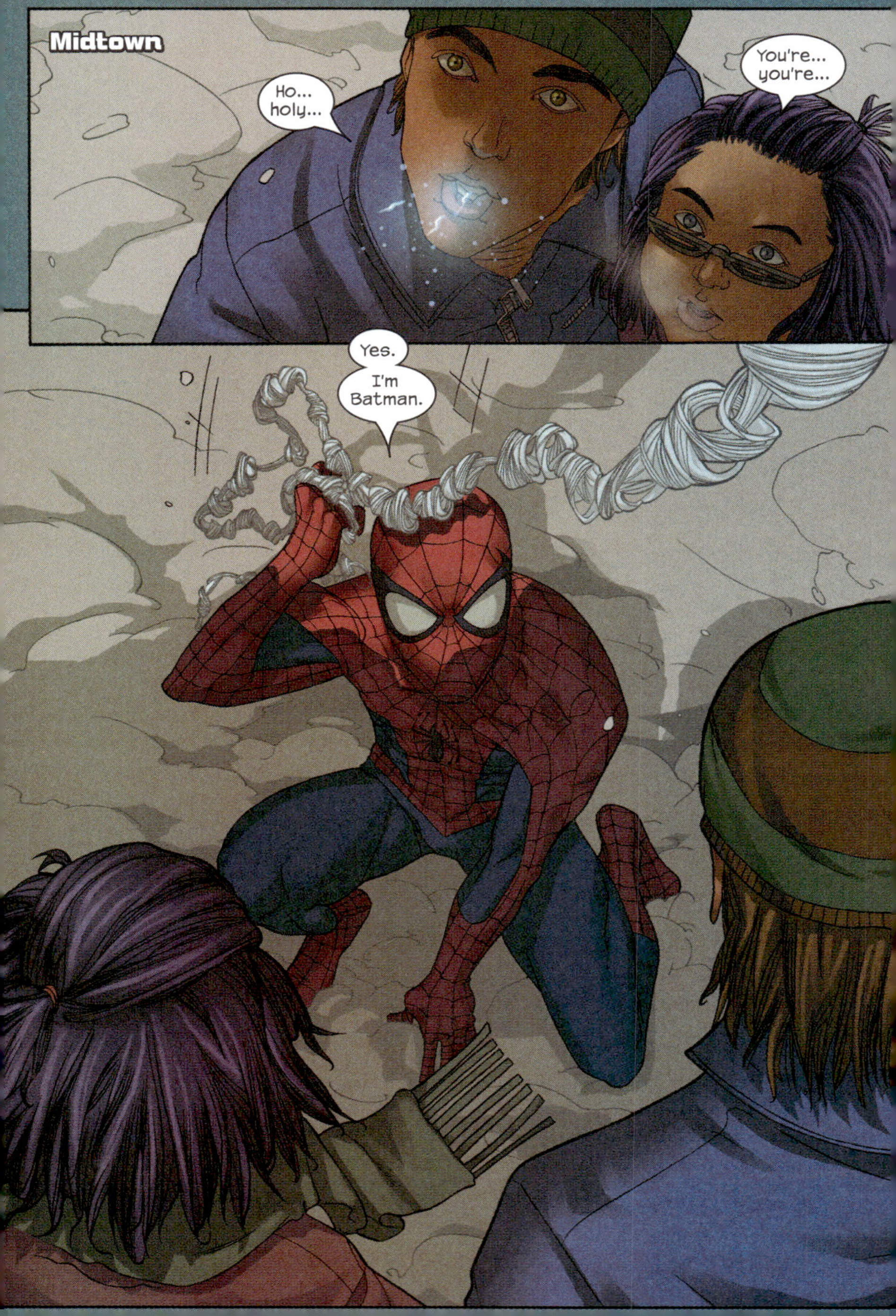
Midtown
Ho... holy...
You're... you're...
Yes.
I'm Batman.

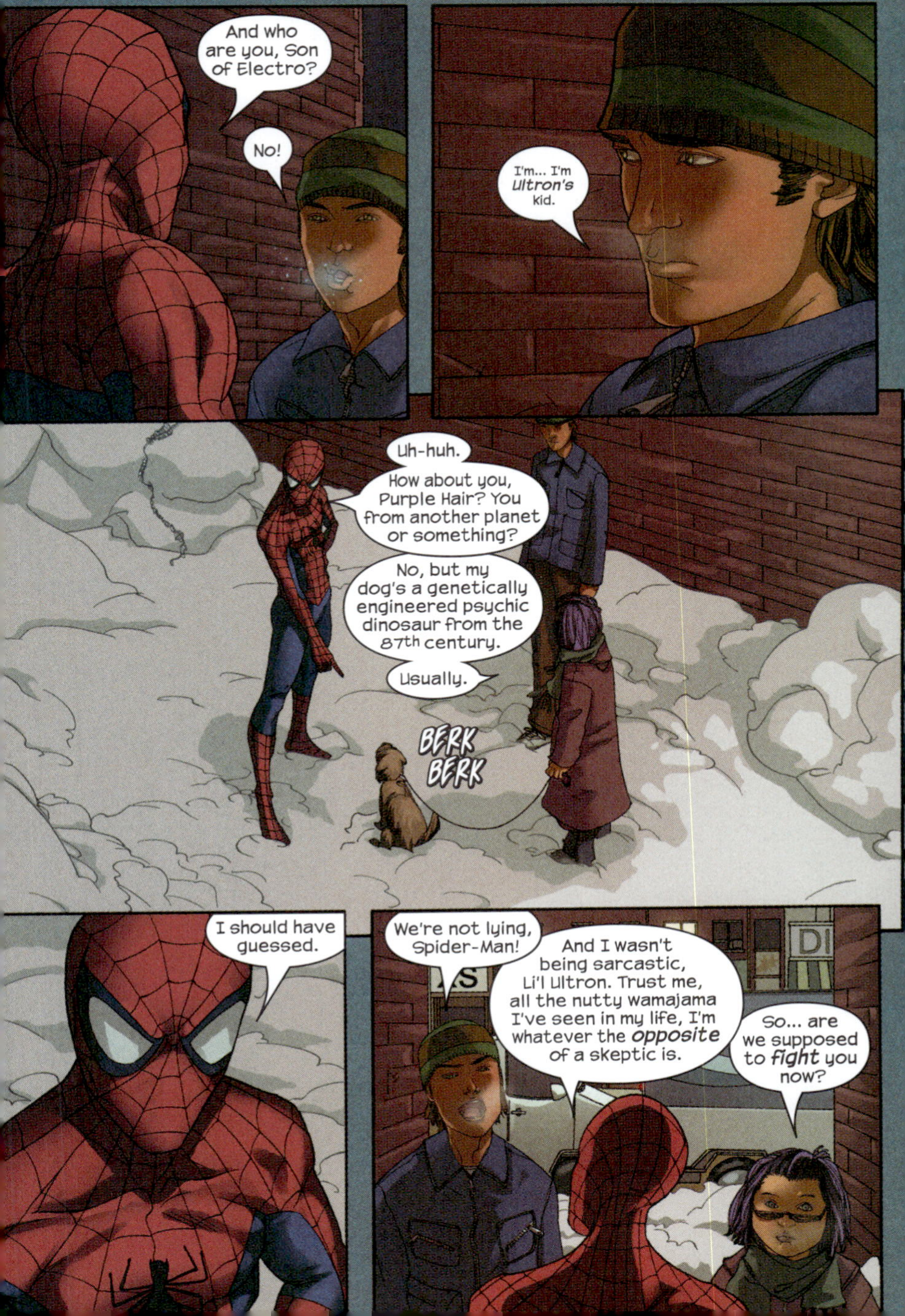

And who are you, Son of Electro?
No!
I'm... I'm *Ultron's* kid.
Uh-huh.
How about you, Purple Hair? You from another planet or something?
No, but my dog's a genetically engineered psychic dinosaur from the 87th century.
Usually.
BERK BERK
I should have guessed.
We're not lying, Spider-Man!
And I wasn't being sarcastic, Li'l Ultron. Trust me, all the nutty wamajama I've seen in my life, I'm whatever the *opposite* of a skeptic is.
So... are we supposed to *fight* you now?

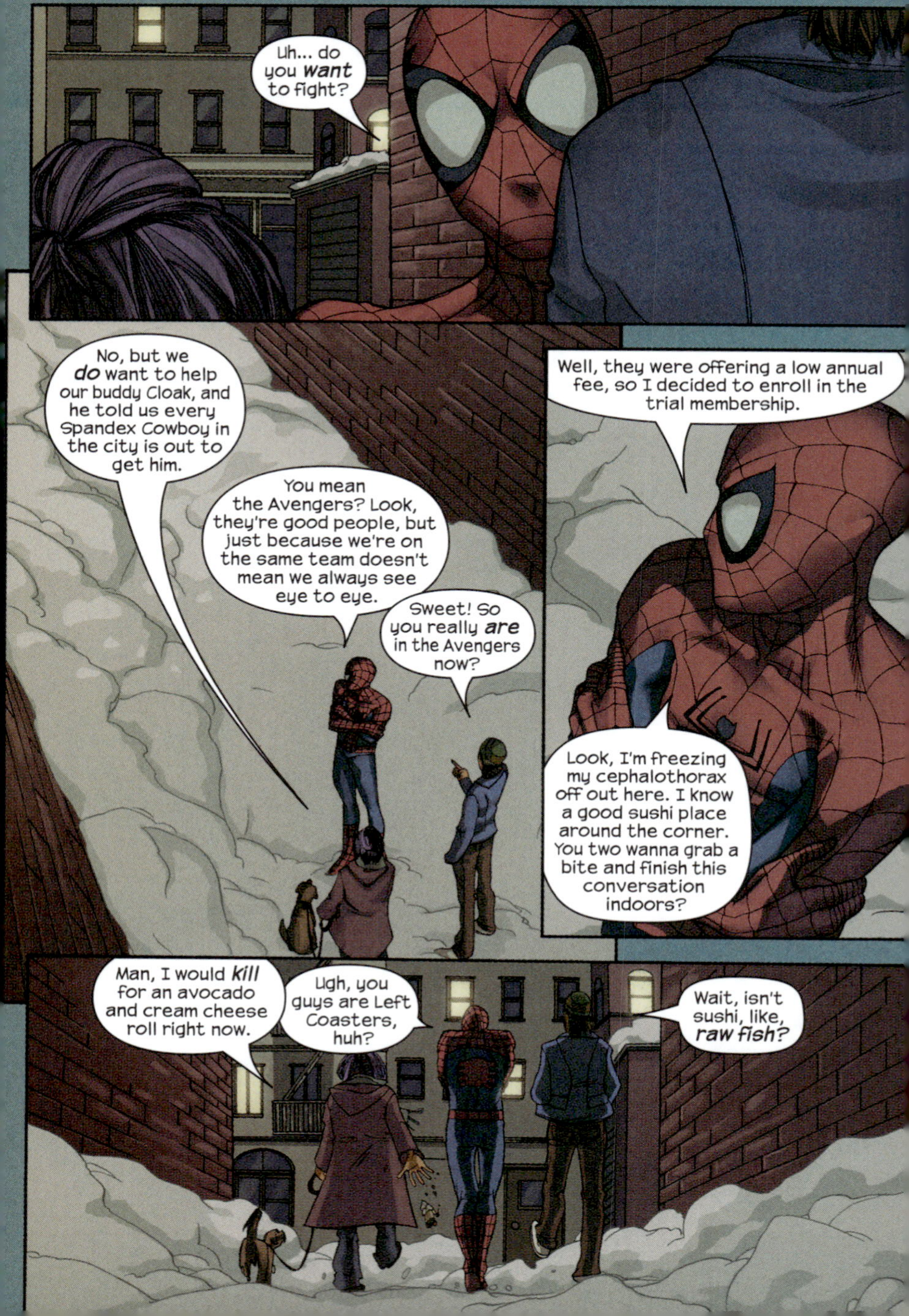
Uh... do you *want* to fight?
No, but we *do* want to help our buddy Cloak, and he told us every Spandex Cowboy in the city is out to get him.
You mean the Avengers? Look, they're good people, but just because we're on the same team doesn't mean we always see eye to eye.
Sweet! So you really *are* in the Avengers now?
Well, they were offering a low annual fee, so I decided to enroll in the trial membership.
Look, I'm freezing my cephalothorax off out here. I know a good sushi place around the corner. You two wanna grab a bite and finish this conversation indoors?
Man, I would *kill* for an avocado and cream cheese roll right now.
Ugh, you guys are Left Coasters, huh?
Wait, isn't sushi, like, *raw fish?*

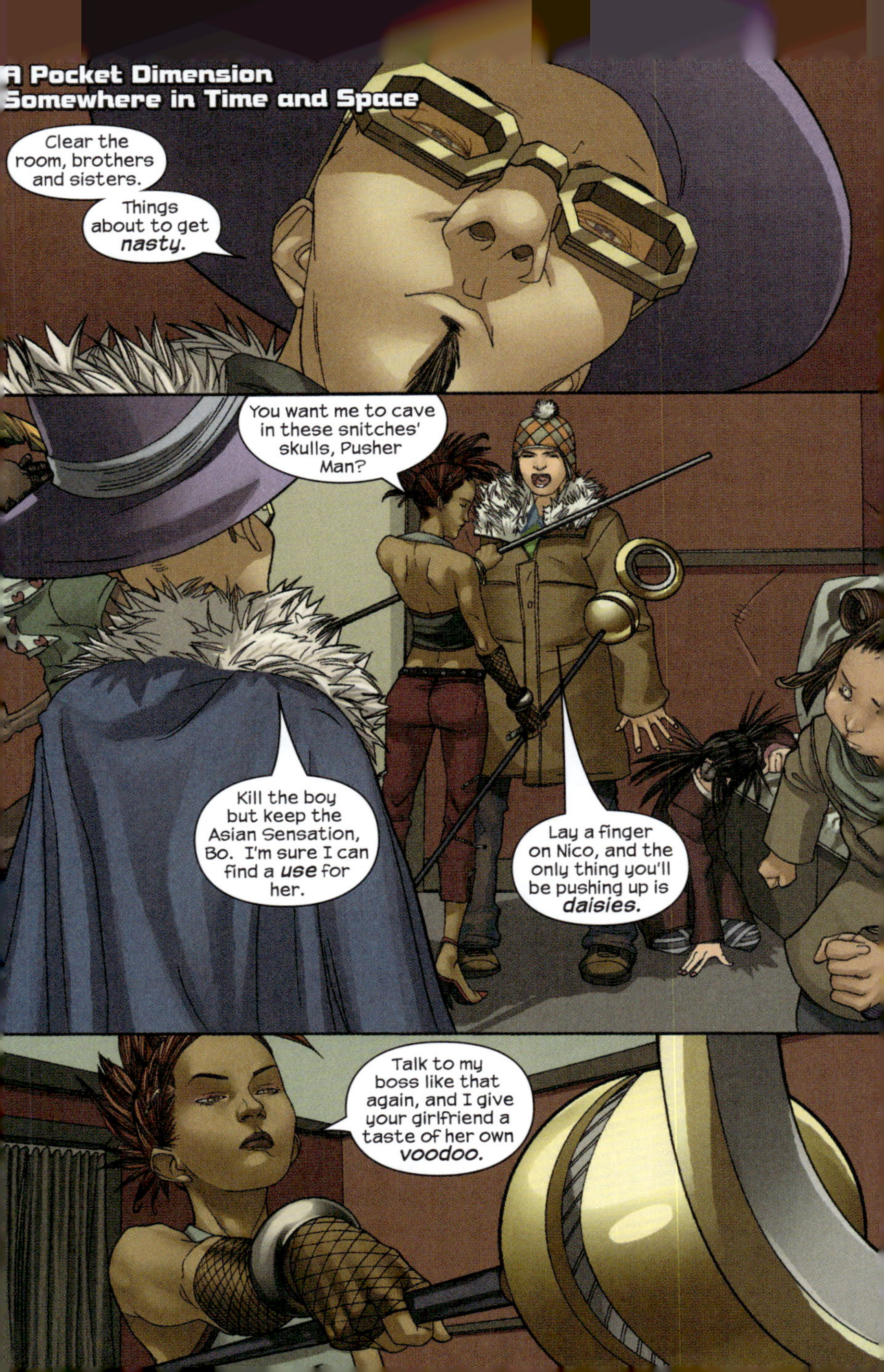
A Pocket Dimension
Somewhere in Time and Space
Clear the room, brothers and sisters.
Things about to get *nasty.*
You want me to cave in these snitches' skulls, Pusher Man?
Kill the boy but keep the Asian Sensation, Bo. I'm sure I can find a *use* for her.
Lay a finger on Nico, and the only thing you'll be pushing up is *daisies.*
Talk to my boss like that again, and I give your girlfriend a taste of her own *voodoo.*

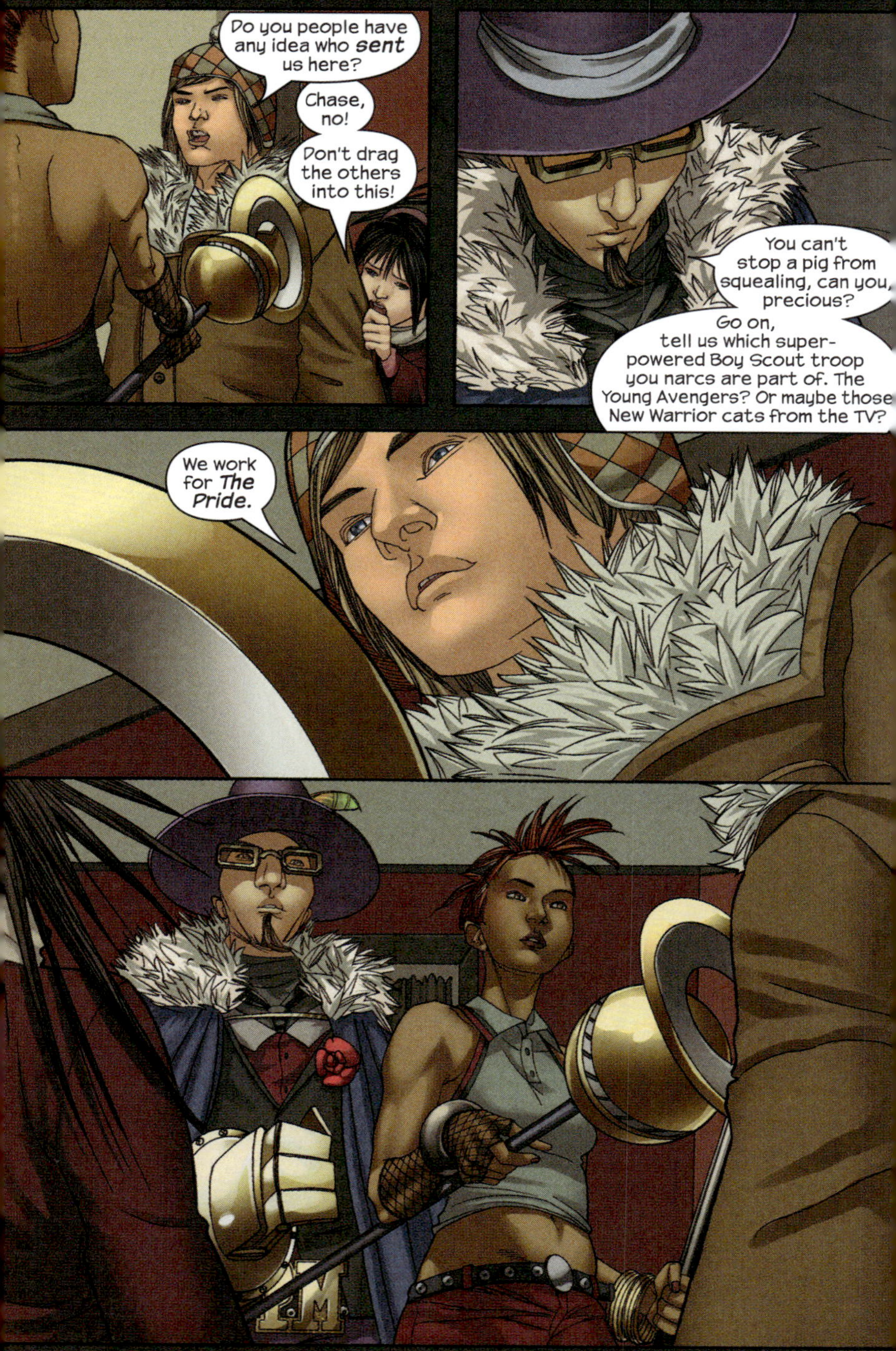

Do you people have any idea who *sent* us here?
Chase, no!
Don't drag the others into this!
You can't stop a pig from squealing, can you, precious?
Go on, tell us which super-powered Boy Scout troop you narcs are part of. The Young Avengers? Or maybe those New Warrior cats from the TV?
We work for *The Pride.*

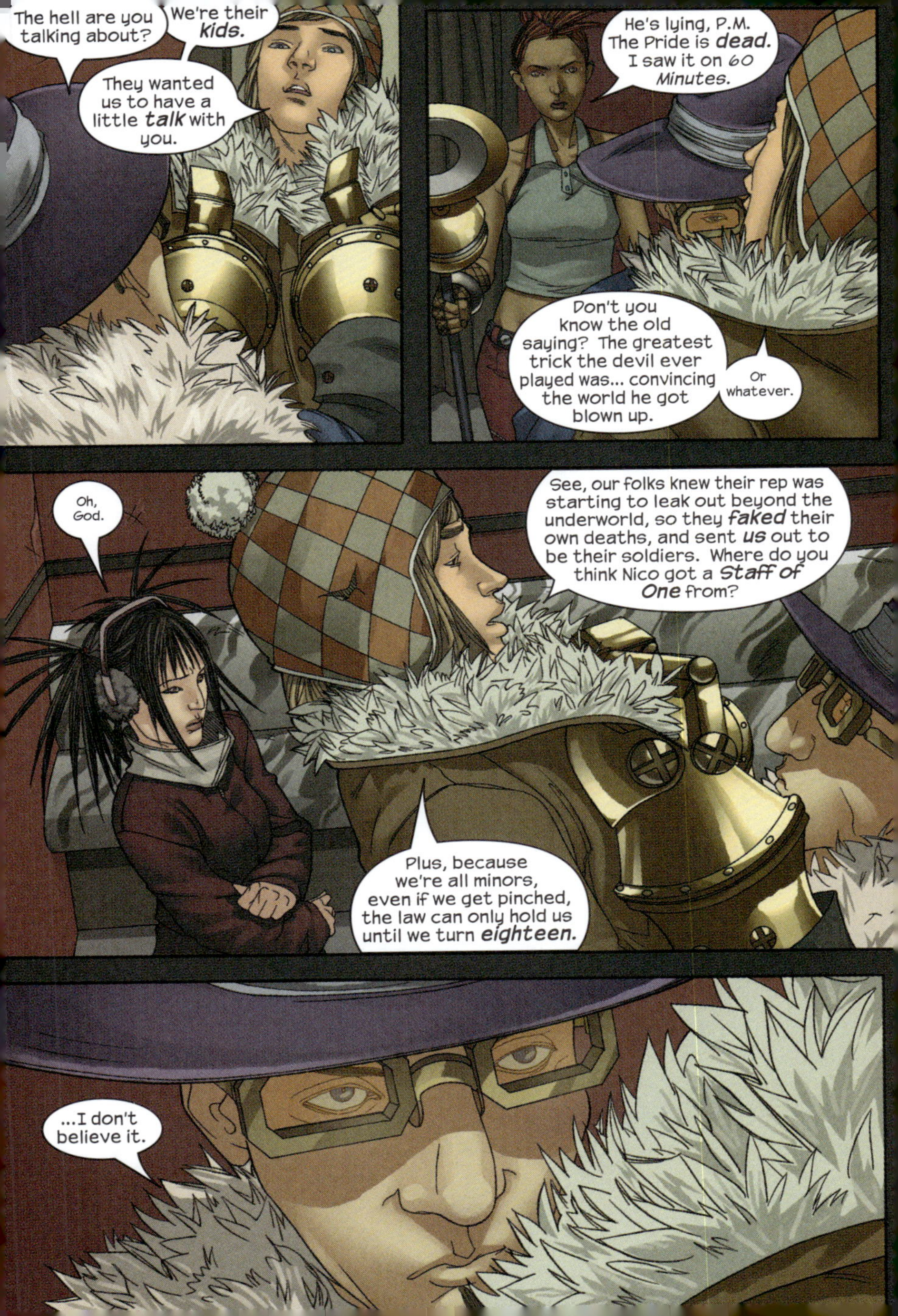
The hell are you talking about?
We're their *kids.*
They wanted us to have a little *talk* with you.
He's lying, P.M. The Pride is *dead.* I saw it on *60 Minutes.*
Don't you know the old saying? The greatest trick the devil ever played was... convincing the world he got blown up.
Or whatever.
Oh, God.
See, our folks knew their rep was starting to leak out beyond the underworld, so they *faked* their own deaths, and sent *us* out to be their soldiers. Where do you think Nico got a *Staff of One* from?
Plus, because we're all minors, even if we get pinched, the law can only hold us until we turn *eighteen.*
...I don't believe it.

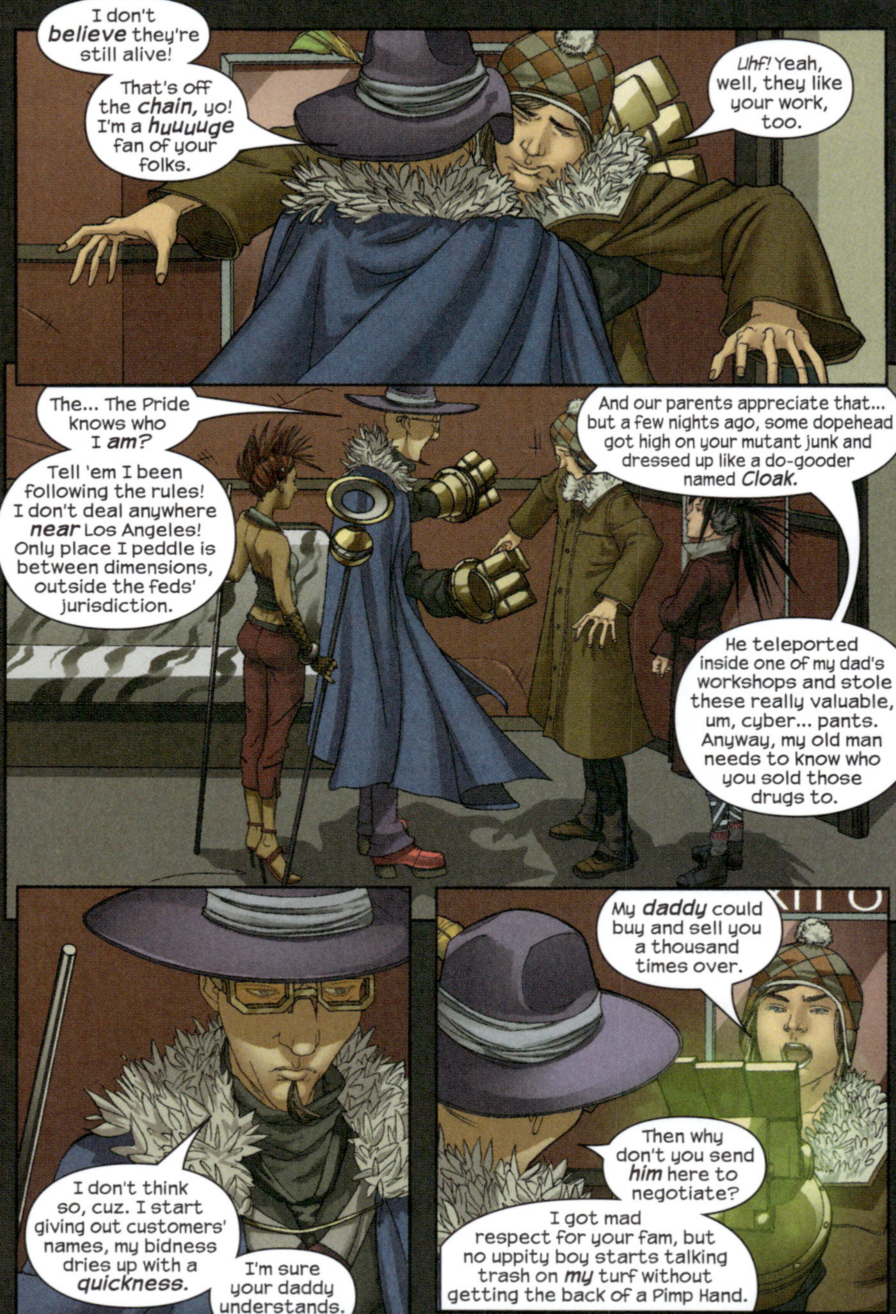

I don't *believe* they're still alive!
That's off the *chain,* yo! I'm a *huuuuge* fan of your folks.
Uhf! Yeah, well, they like your work, too.
The... The Pride knows who I *am?*
Tell 'em I been following the rules! I don't deal anywhere *near* Los Angeles! Only place I peddle is between dimensions, outside the feds' jurisdiction.
And our parents appreciate that... but a few nights ago, some dopehead got high on your mutant junk and dressed up like a do-gooder named *Cloak.*
He teleported inside one of my dad's workshops and stole these really valuable, um, cyber... pants. Anyway, my old man needs to know who you sold those drugs to.
I don't think so, cuz. I start giving out customers' names, my bidness dries up with a *quickness.*
I'm sure your daddy understands.
My *daddy* could buy and sell you a thousand times over.
Then why don't you send *him* here to negotiate?
I got mad respect for your fam, but no uppity boy starts talking trash on *my* turf without getting the back of a Pimp Hand.

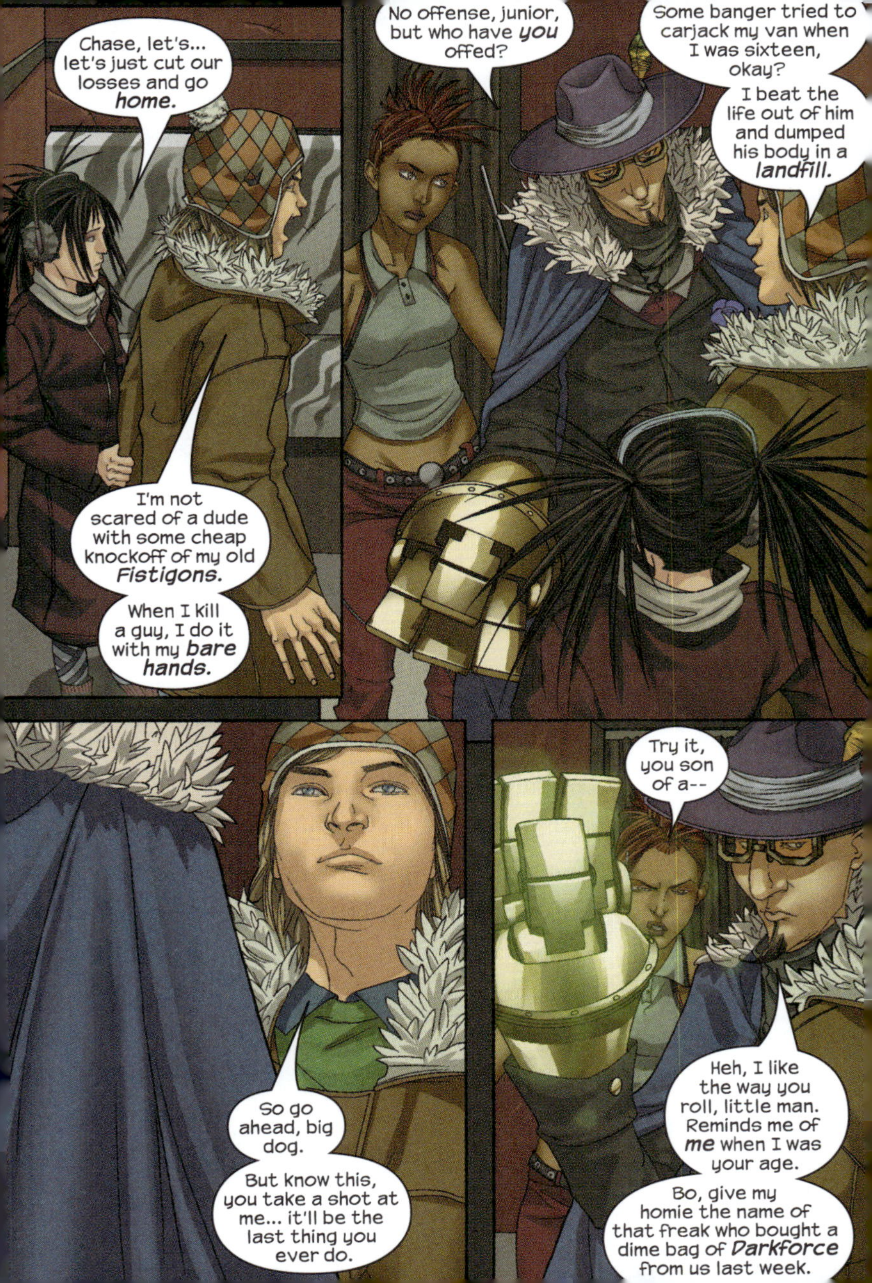

Chase, let's... let's just cut our losses and go *home.*
I'm not scared of a dude with some cheap knockoff of my old *Fistigons.*
When I kill a guy, I do it with my *bare hands.*
No offense, junior, but who have *you* offed?
Some banger tried to carjack my van when I was sixteen, okay?
I beat the life out of him and dumped his body in a *landfill.*
So go ahead, big dog.
But know this, you take a shot at me... it'll be the last thing you ever do.
Try it, you son of a--
Heh, I like the way you roll, little man. Reminds me of *me* when I was your age.
Bo, give my homie the name of that freak who bought a dime bag of *Darkforce* from us last week.

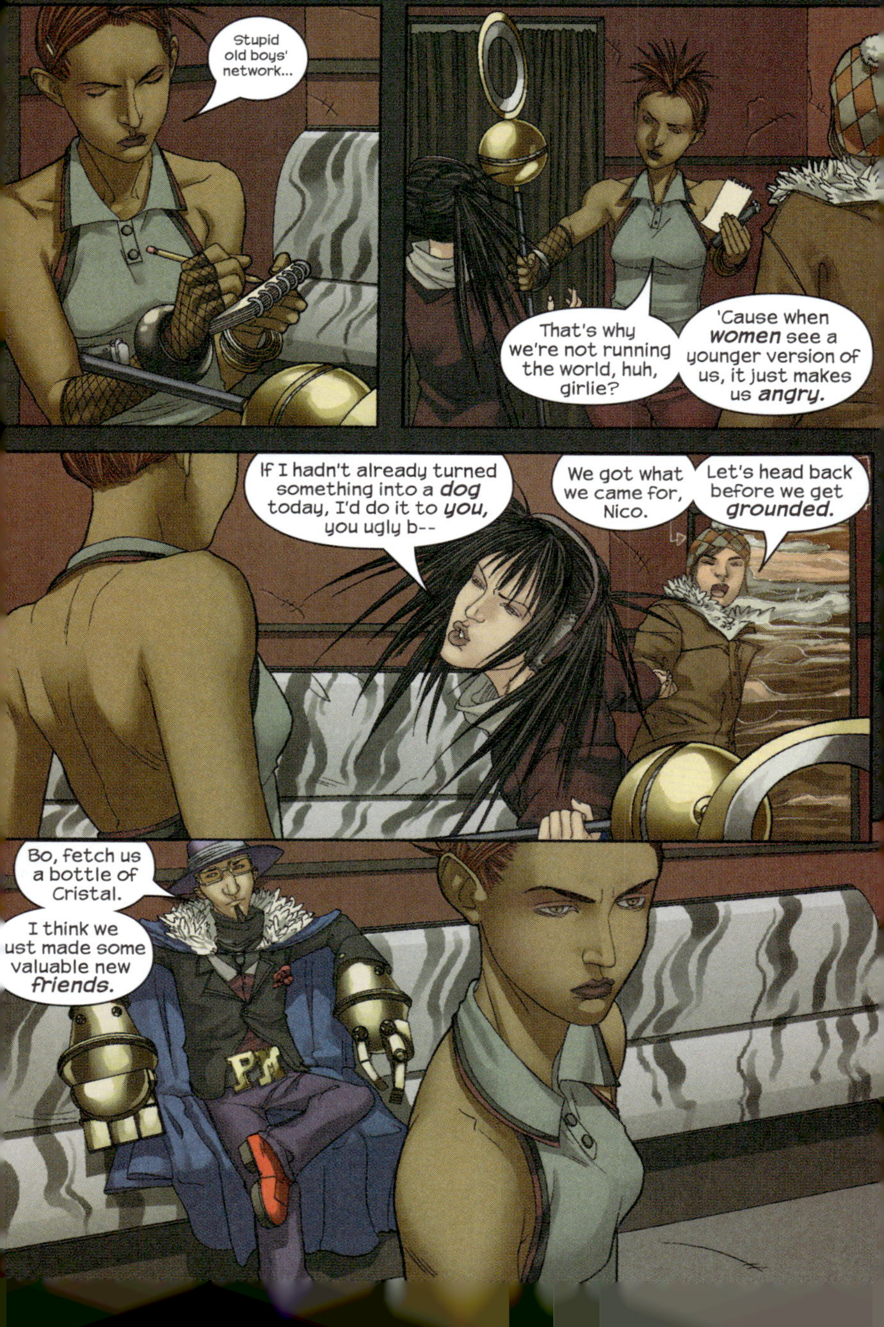

Stupid old boys' network...
That's why we're not running the world, huh, girlie?
'Cause when *women* see a younger version of us, it just makes us *angry.*
If I hadn't already turned something into a *dog* today, I'd do it to *you,* you ugly b--
We got what we came for, Nico.
Let's head back before we get *grounded.*
Bo, fetch us a bottle of Cristal.
I think we ust made some valuable new *friends.*

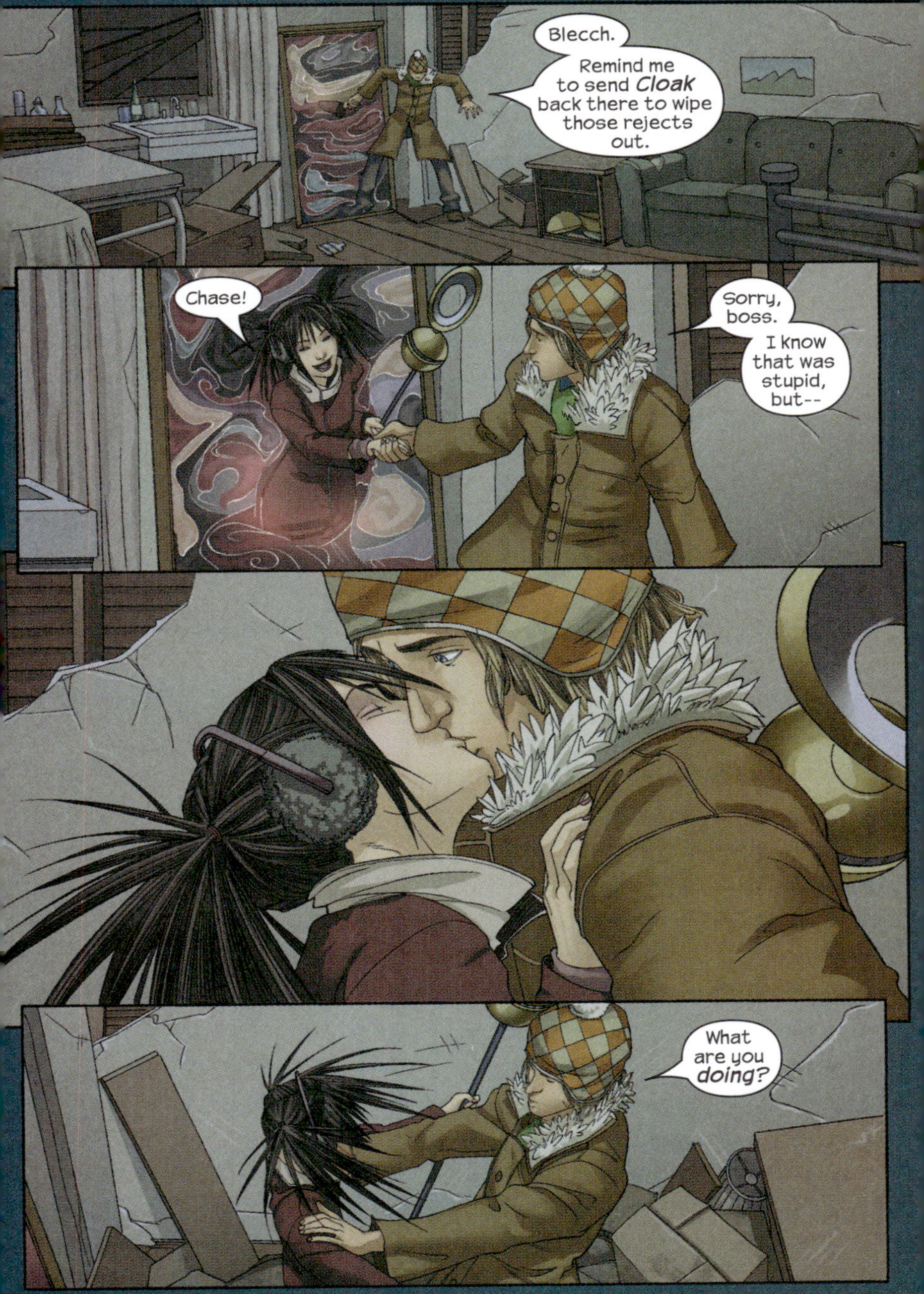
Blecch.
Remind me to send *Cloak* back there to wipe those rejects out.
Chase!
Sorry, boss.
I know that was stupid, but--
What are you *doing?*

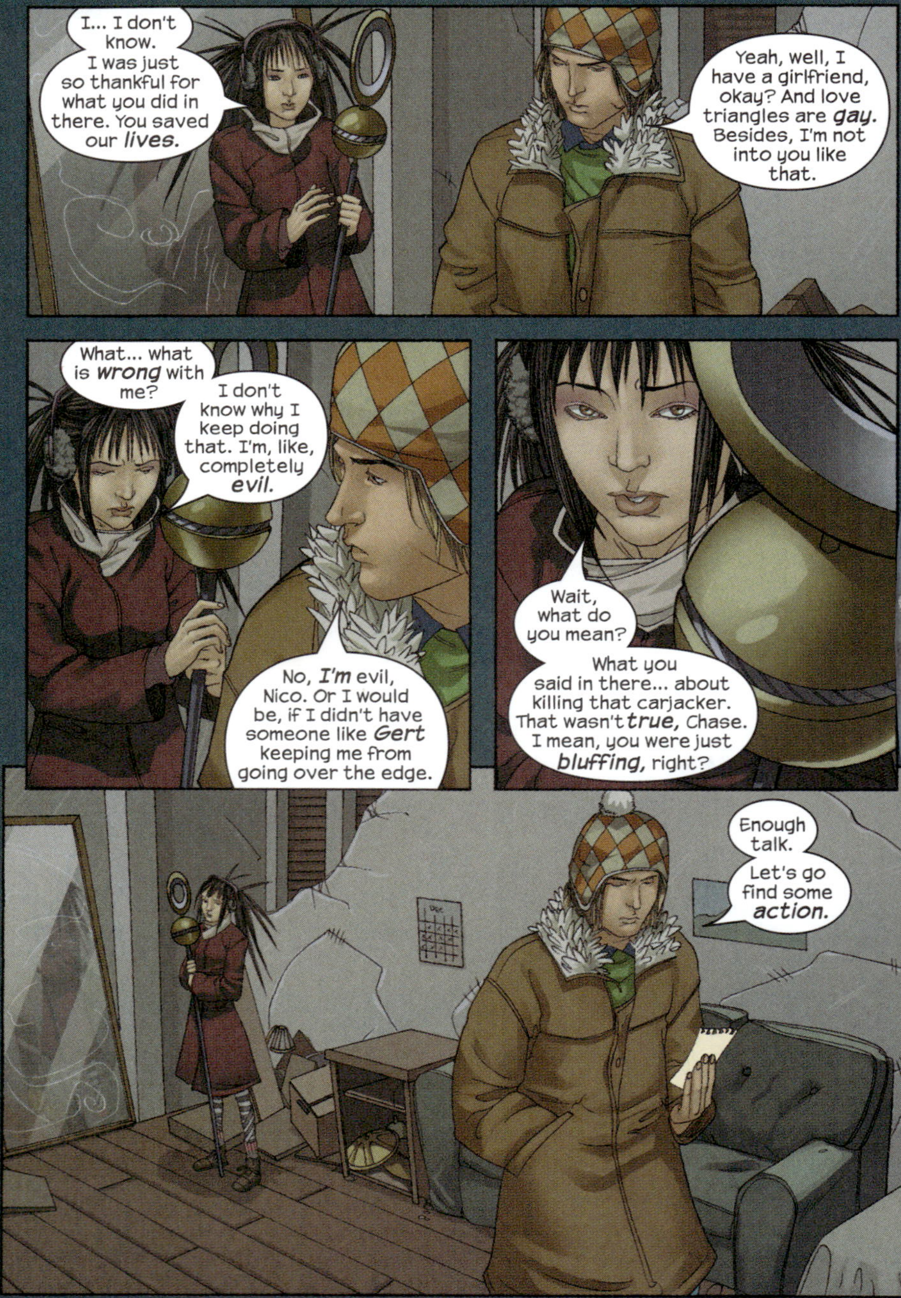

I... I don't know. I was just so thankful for what you did in there. You saved our *lives.*
Yeah, well, I have a girlfriend, okay? And love triangles are *gay.* Besides, I'm not into you like that.
What... what is *wrong* with me?
I don't know why I keep doing that. I'm, like, completely *evil.*
No, *I'm* evil, Nico. Or I would be, if I didn't have someone like *Gert* keeping me from going over the edge.
Wait, what do you mean?
What you said in there... about killing that carjacker. That wasn't *true,* Chase. I mean, you were just *bluffing,* right?
Enough talk.
Let's go find some *action.*

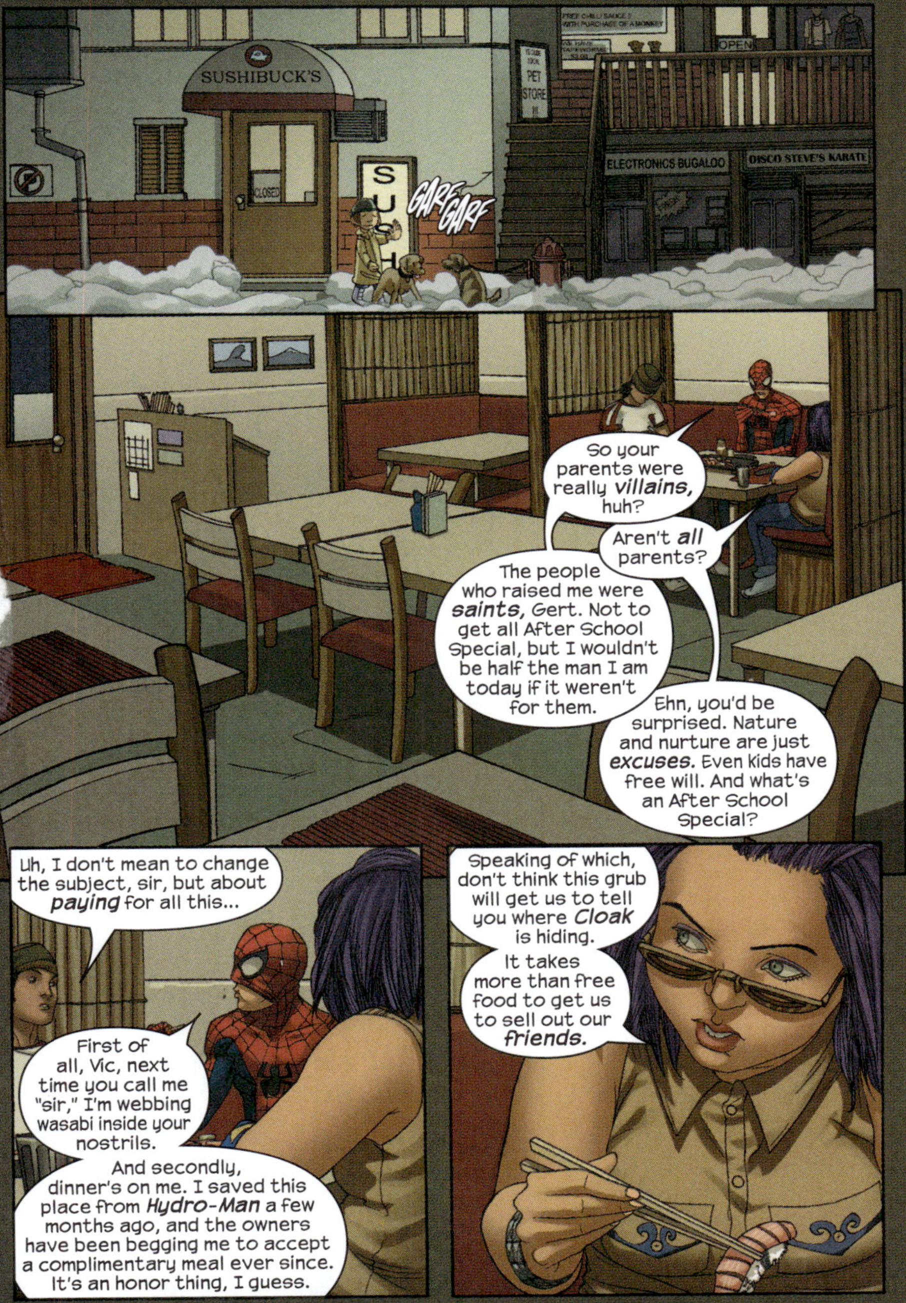
SUSHIBUCK'S
CLOSED
SUSHI
PET STORE
OPEN
ELECTRONICS BUGALOO
DISCO STEVE'S KARATE
GARF GARF
So your parents were really villains, huh?
Aren't all parents?
The people who raised me were saints, Gert. Not to get all After School Special, but I wouldn't be half the man I am today if it weren't for them.
Ehn, you'd be surprised. Nature and nurture are just excuses. Even kids have free will. And what's an After School Special?
Uh, I don't mean to change the subject, sir, but about paying for all this...
First of all, Vic, next time you call me "sir," I'm webbing wasabi inside your nostrils.
And secondly, dinner's on me. I saved this place from Hydro-Man a few months ago, and the owners have been begging me to accept a complimentary meal ever since. It's an honor thing, I guess.
Speaking of which, don't think this grub will get us to tell you where Cloak is hiding.
It takes more than free food to get us to sell out our friends.

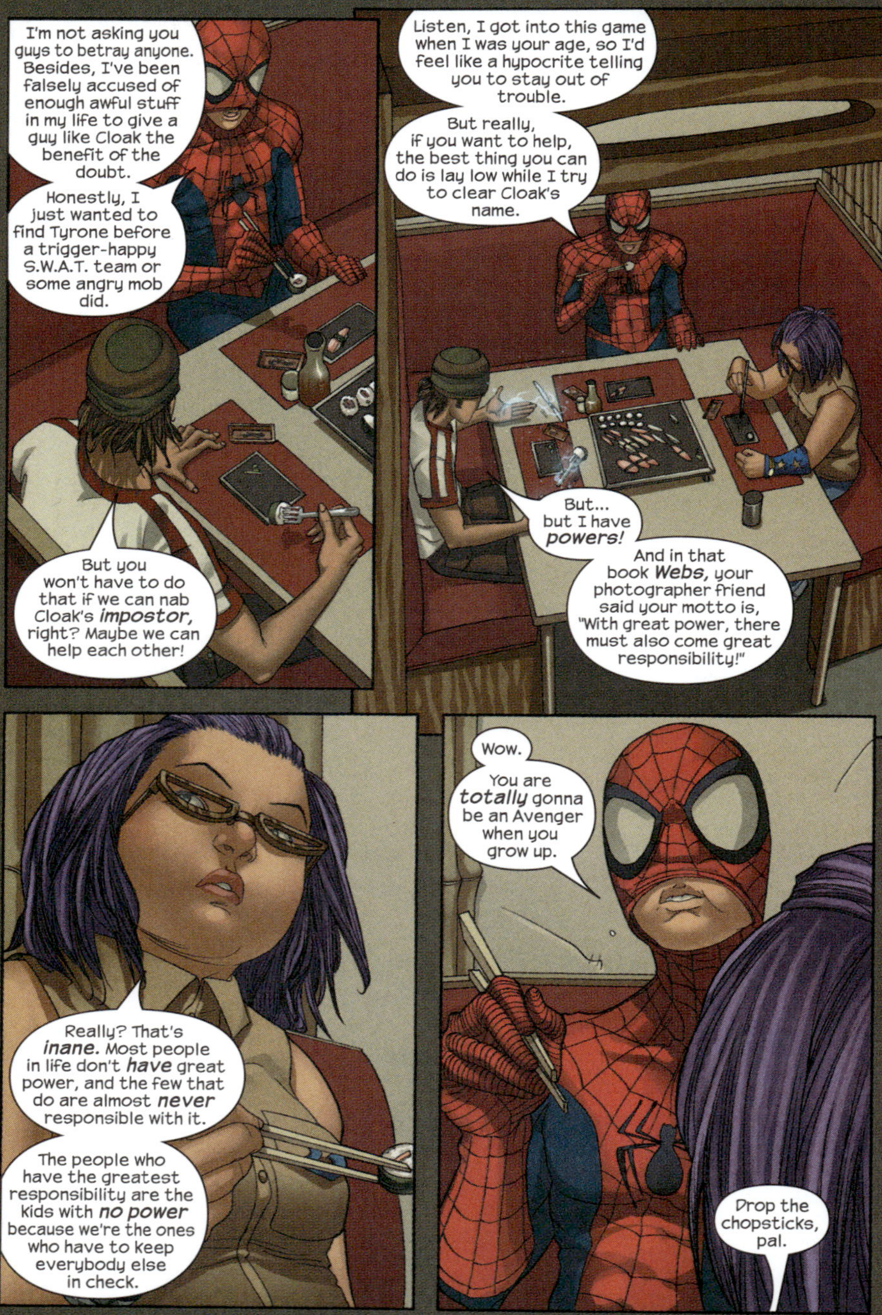

I'm not asking you guys to betray anyone. Besides, I've been falsely accused of enough awful stuff in my life to give a guy like Cloak the benefit of the doubt.
Honestly, I just wanted to find Tyrone before a trigger-happy S.W.A.T. team or some angry mob did.
But you won't have to do that if we can nab Cloak's *impostor,* right? Maybe we can help each other!
Listen, I got into this game when I was your age, so I'd feel like a hypocrite telling you to stay out of trouble.
But really, if you want to help, the best thing you can do is lay low while I try to clear Cloak's name.
But... but I have *powers!*
And in that book *Webs,* your photographer friend said your motto is, "With great power, there must also come great responsibility!"
Really? That's *inane.* Most people in life don't *have* great power, and the few that do are almost *never* responsible with it.
The people who have the greatest responsibility are the kids with *no power* because we're the ones who have to keep everybody else in check.
Wow.
You are *totally* gonna be an Avenger when you grow up.
Drop the chopsticks, pal.

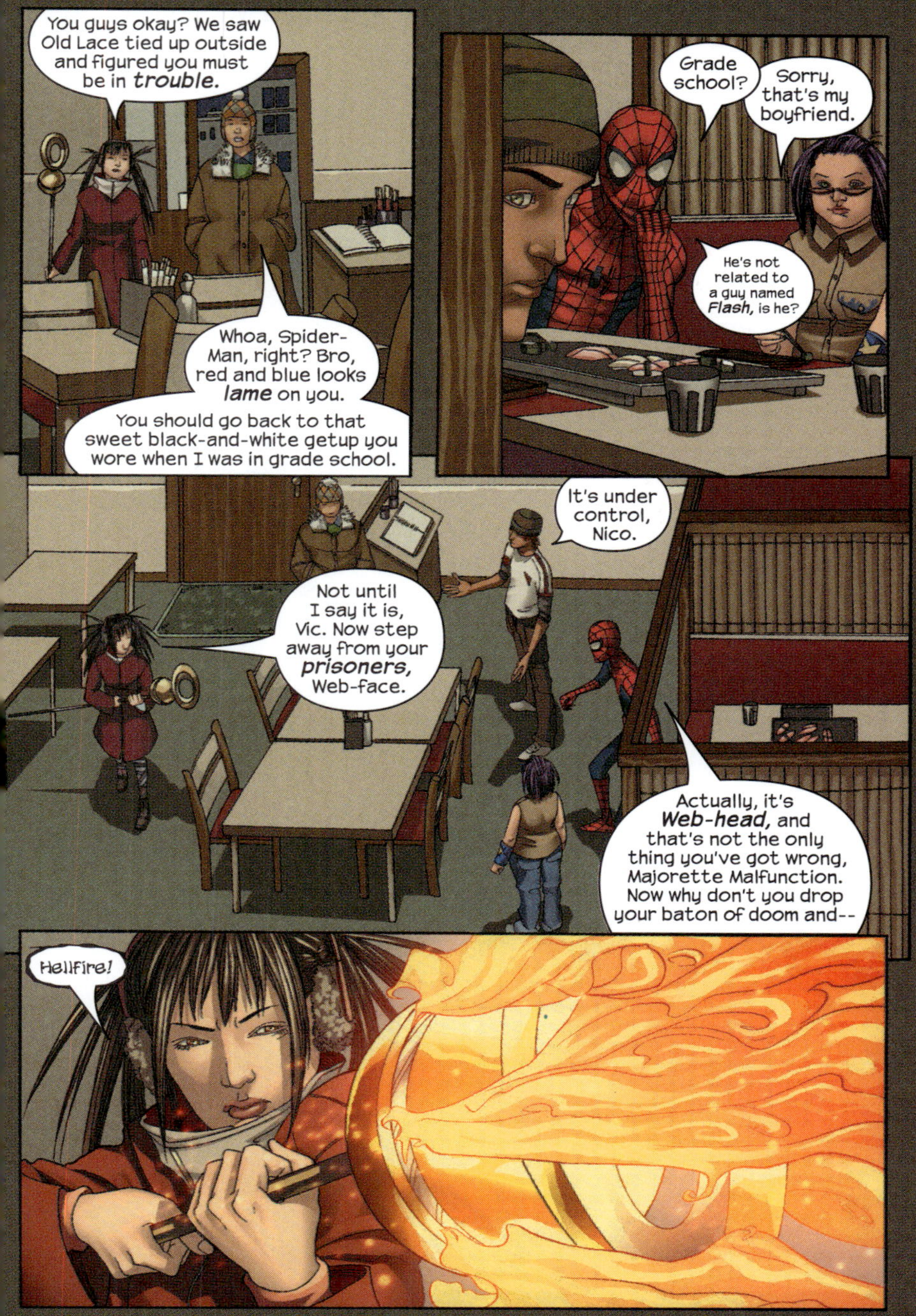
You guys okay? We saw Old Lace tied up outside and figured you must be in *trouble.*
Whoa, Spider-Man, right? Bro, red and blue looks *lame* on you.
You should go back to that sweet black-and-white getup you wore when I was in grade school.
Grade school?
Sorry, that's my boyfriend.
He's not related to a guy named *Flash,* is he?
It's under control, Nico.
Not until I say it is, Vic. Now step away from your *prisoners,* Web-face.
Actually, it's *Web-head,* and that's not the only thing you've got wrong, Majorette Malfunction. Now why don't you drop your baton of doom and--
Hellfire!

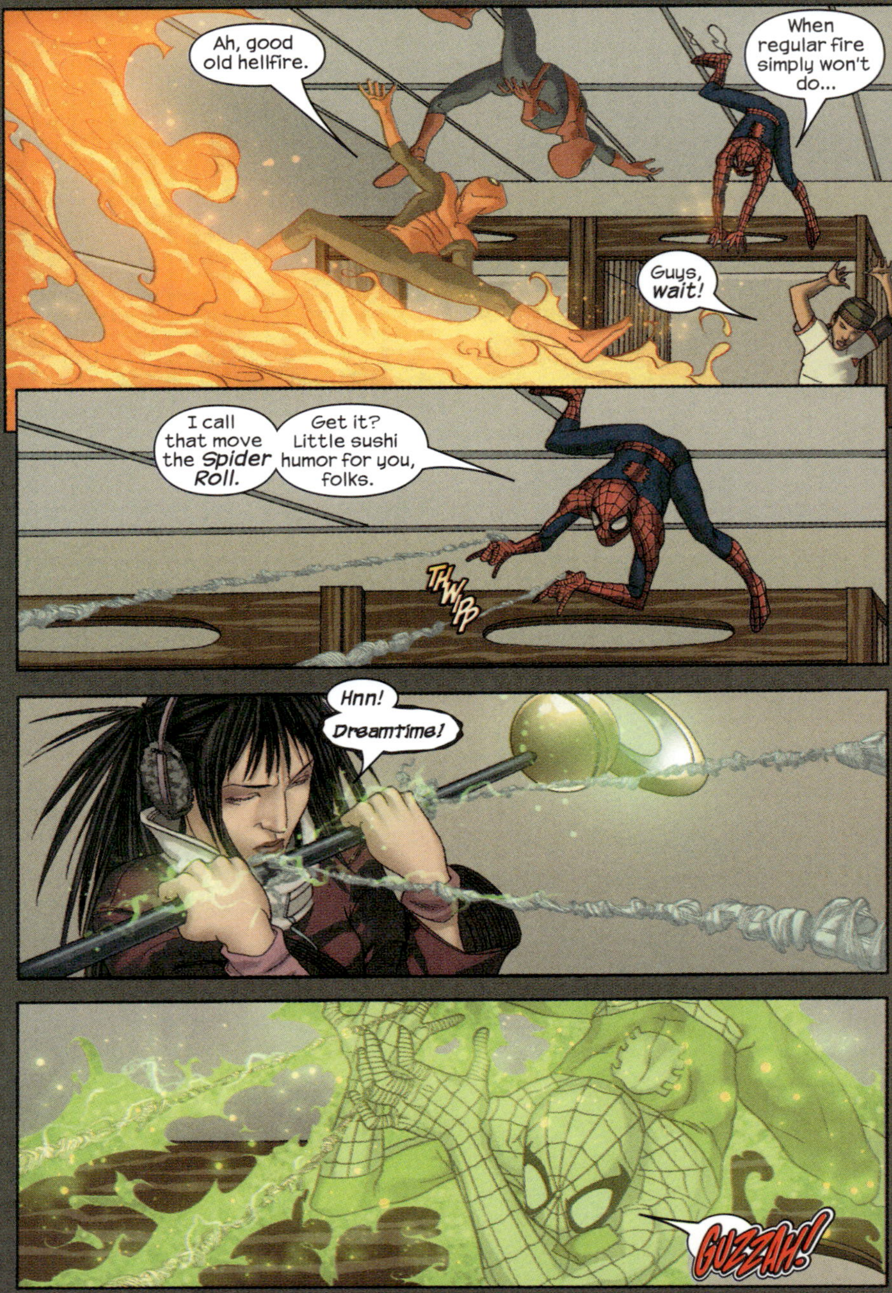

Ah, good old hellfire.
When regular fire simply won't do...
Guys, wait!
I call that move the Spider Roll.
Get it? Little sushi humor for you, folks.
THWIPP
Hnn!
Dreamtime!
GUZZAH!

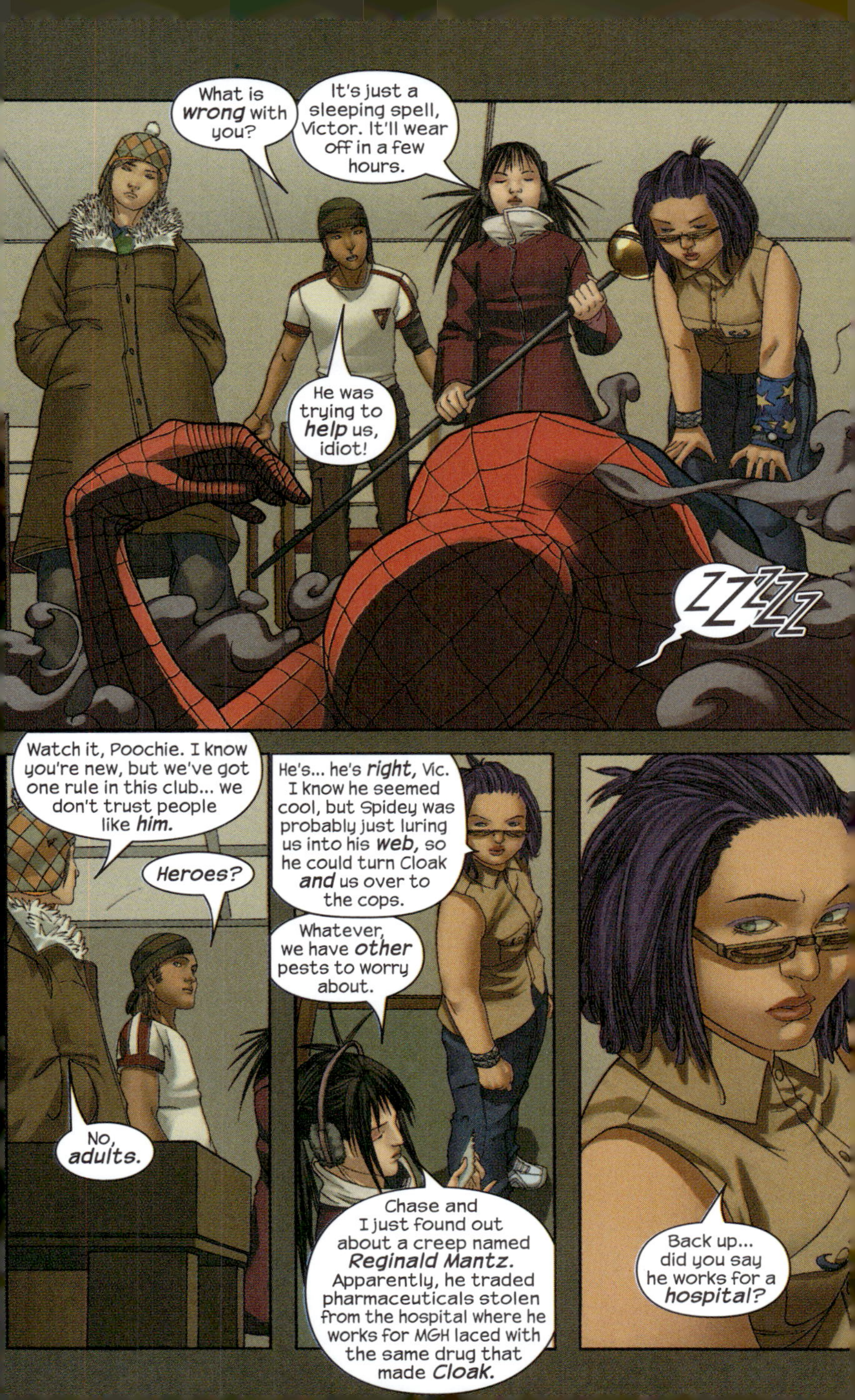

What is *wrong* with you?
It's just a sleeping spell, Victor. It'll wear off in a few hours.
He was trying to *help* us, idiot!
ZZZZZ
Watch it, Poochie. I know you're new, but we've got one rule in this club... we don't trust people like *him*.
Heroes?
No, *adults.*
He's... he's *right,* Vic. I know he seemed cool, but Spidey was probably just luring us into his *web,* so he could turn Cloak *and* us over to the cops.
Whatever, we have *other* pests to worry about.
Chase and I just found out about a creep named *Reginald Mantz.* Apparently, he traded pharmaceuticals stolen from the hospital where he works for MGH laced with the same drug that made *Cloak.*
Back up... did you say he works for a *hospital?*

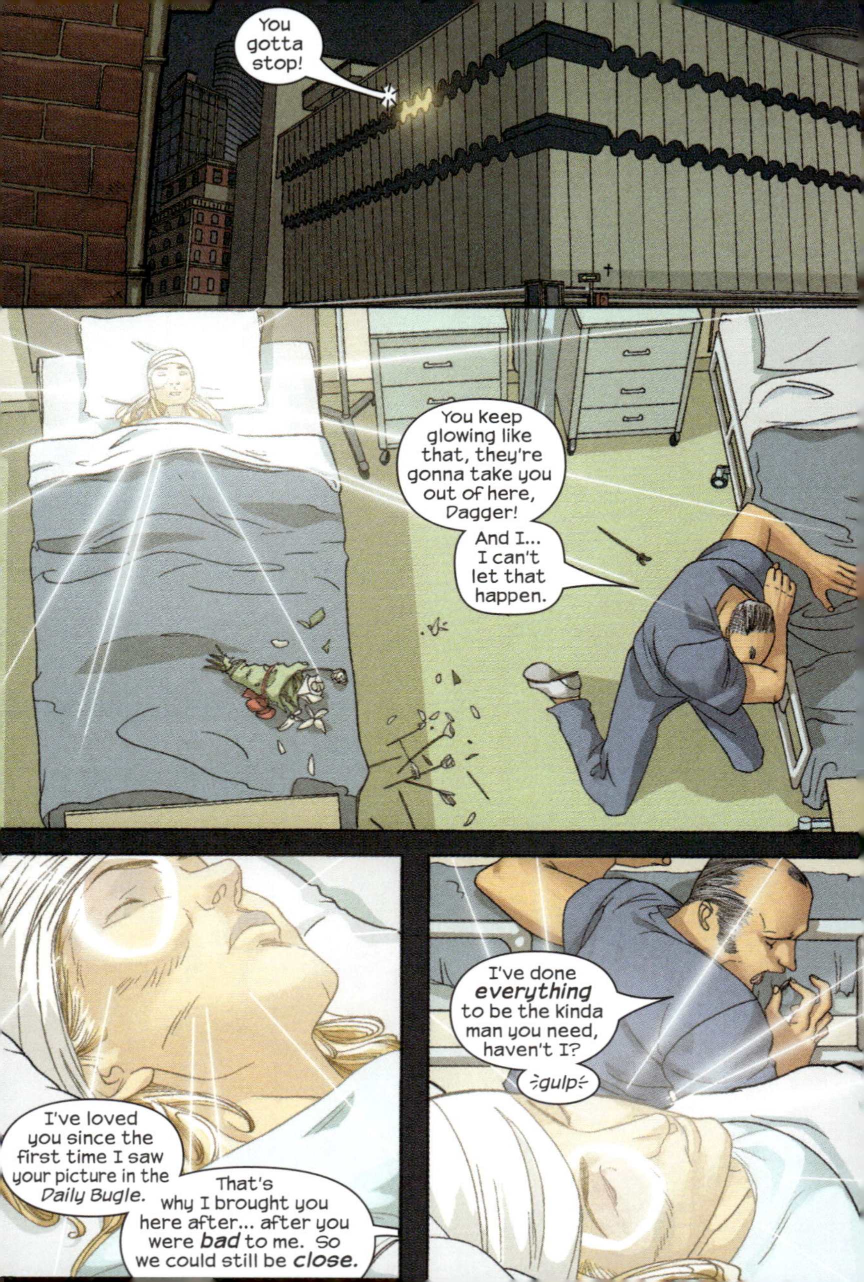
You gotta stop!
You keep glowing like that, they're gonna take you out of here, Dagger!
And I... I can't let that happen.
I've loved you since the first time I saw your picture in the *Daily Bugle.*
That's why I brought you here after... after you were *bad* to me. So we could still be *close.*
I've done *everything* to be the kinda man you need, haven't I?
gulp

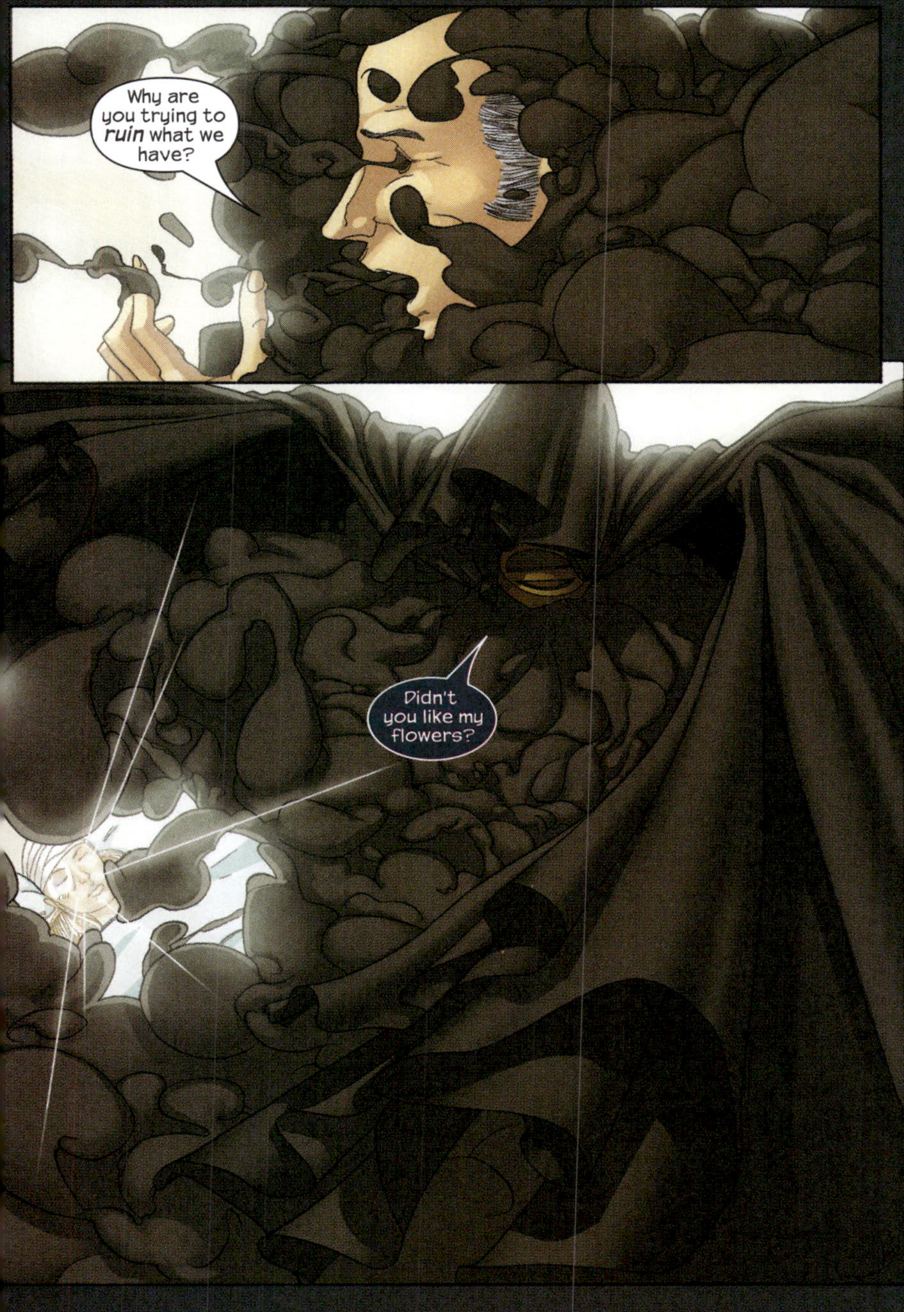
Why are you trying to *ruin* what we have?
Didn't you like my flowers?

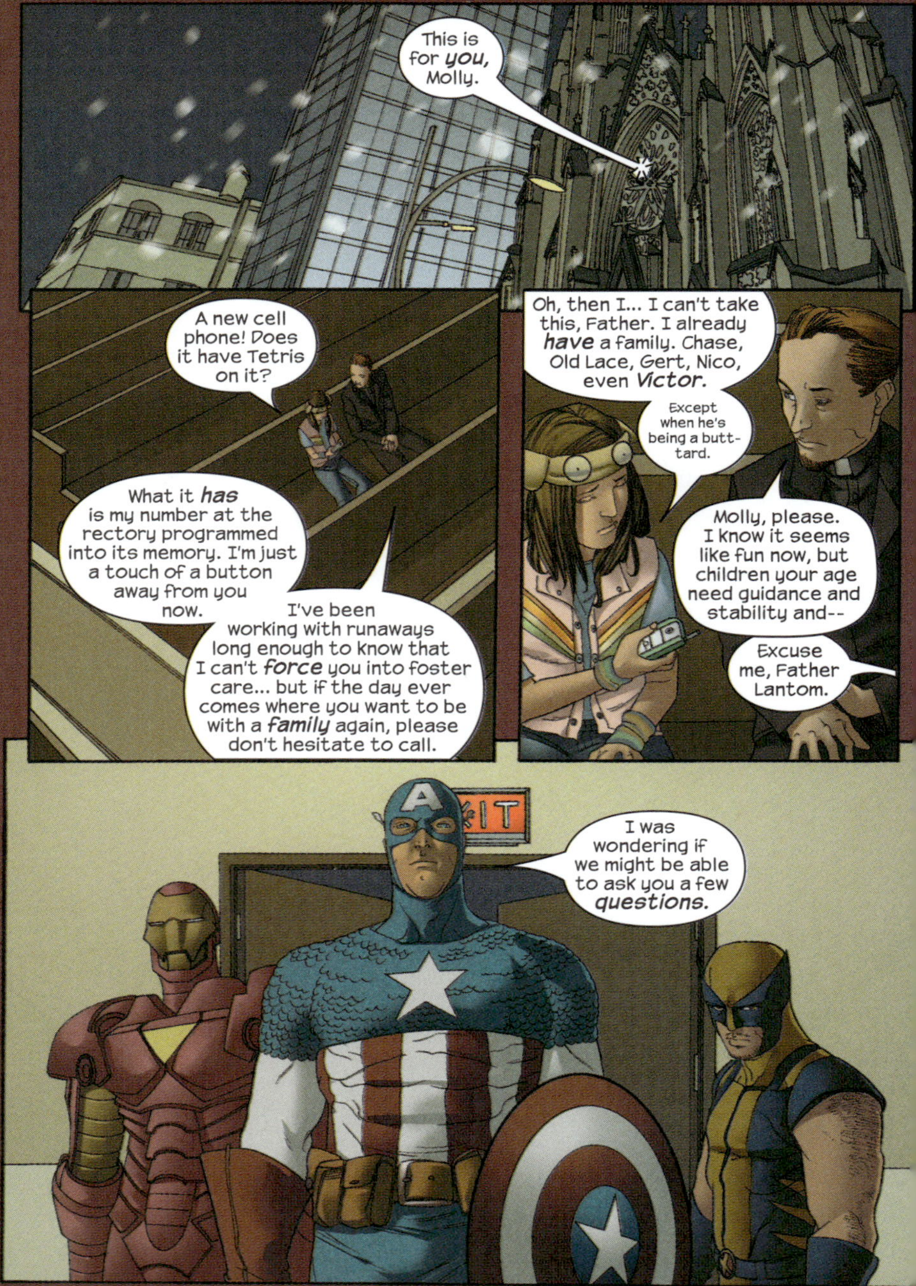
This is for *you,* Molly.
A new cell phone! Does it have Tetris on it?
What it *has* is my number at the rectory programmed into its memory. I'm just a touch of a button away from you now.
I've been working with runaways long enough to know that I can't *force* you into foster care... but if the day ever comes where you want to be with a *family* again, please don't hesitate to call.
Oh, then I... I can't take this, Father. I already *have* a family. Chase, Old Lace, Gert, Nico, even *Victor.*
Except when he's being a butt-tard.
Molly, please. I know it seems like fun now, but children your age need guidance and stability and--
Excuse me, Father Lantom.
I was wondering if we might be able to ask you a few *questions.*

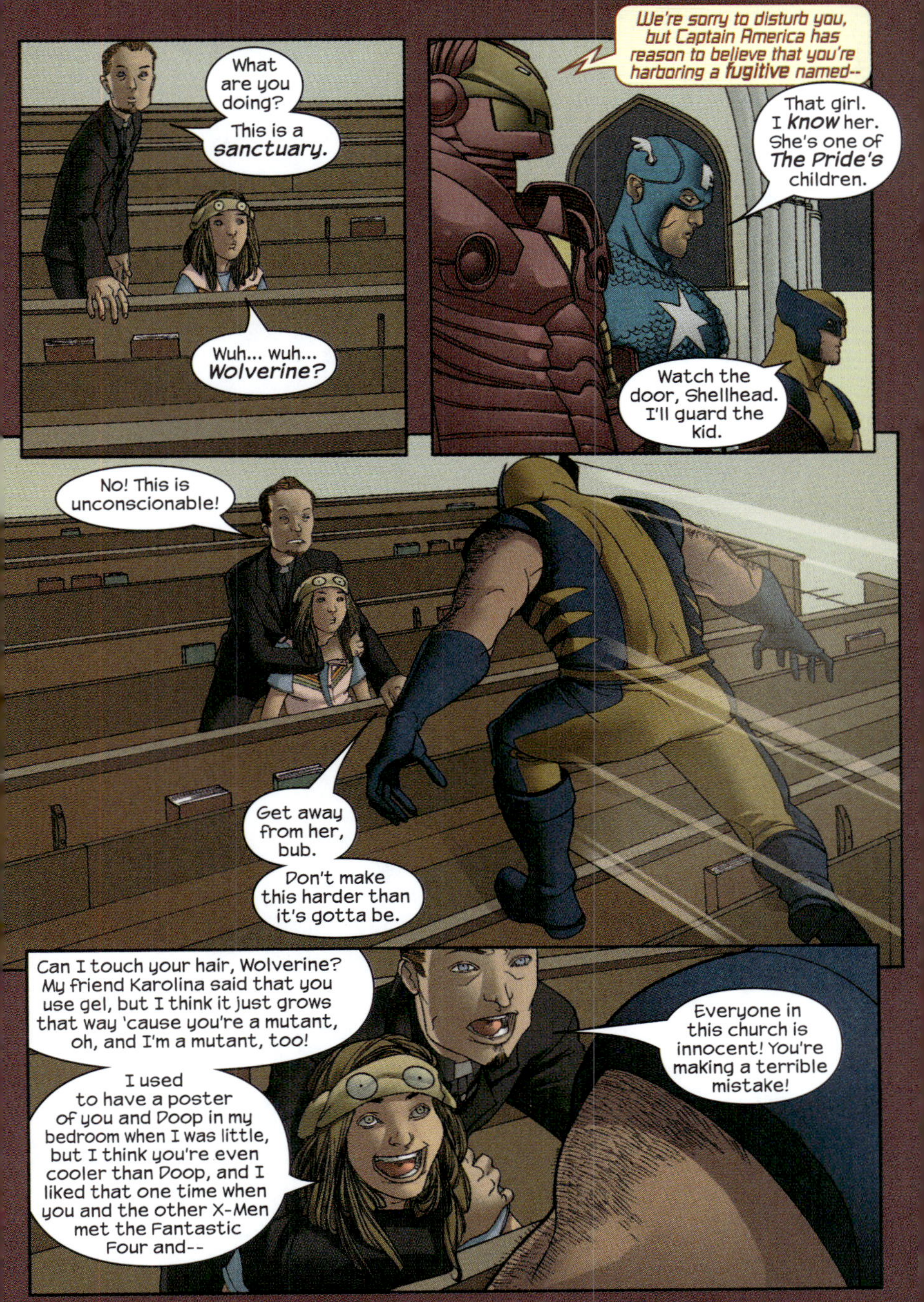
What are you doing?
This is a sanctuary.
Wuh... wuh... Wolverine?
We're sorry to disturb you, but Captain America has reason to believe that you're harboring a fugitive named--
That girl. I know her. She's one of The Pride's children.
Watch the door, Shellhead. I'll guard the kid.
No! This is unconscionable!
Get away from her, bub.
Don't make this harder than it's gotta be.
Can I touch your hair, Wolverine? My friend Karolina said that you use gel, but I think it just grows that way 'cause you're a mutant, oh, and I'm a mutant, too!
I used to have a poster of you and Doop in my bedroom when I was little, but I think you're even cooler than Doop, and I liked that one time when you and the other X-Men met the Fantastic Four and--
Everyone in this church is innocent! You're making a terrible mistake!

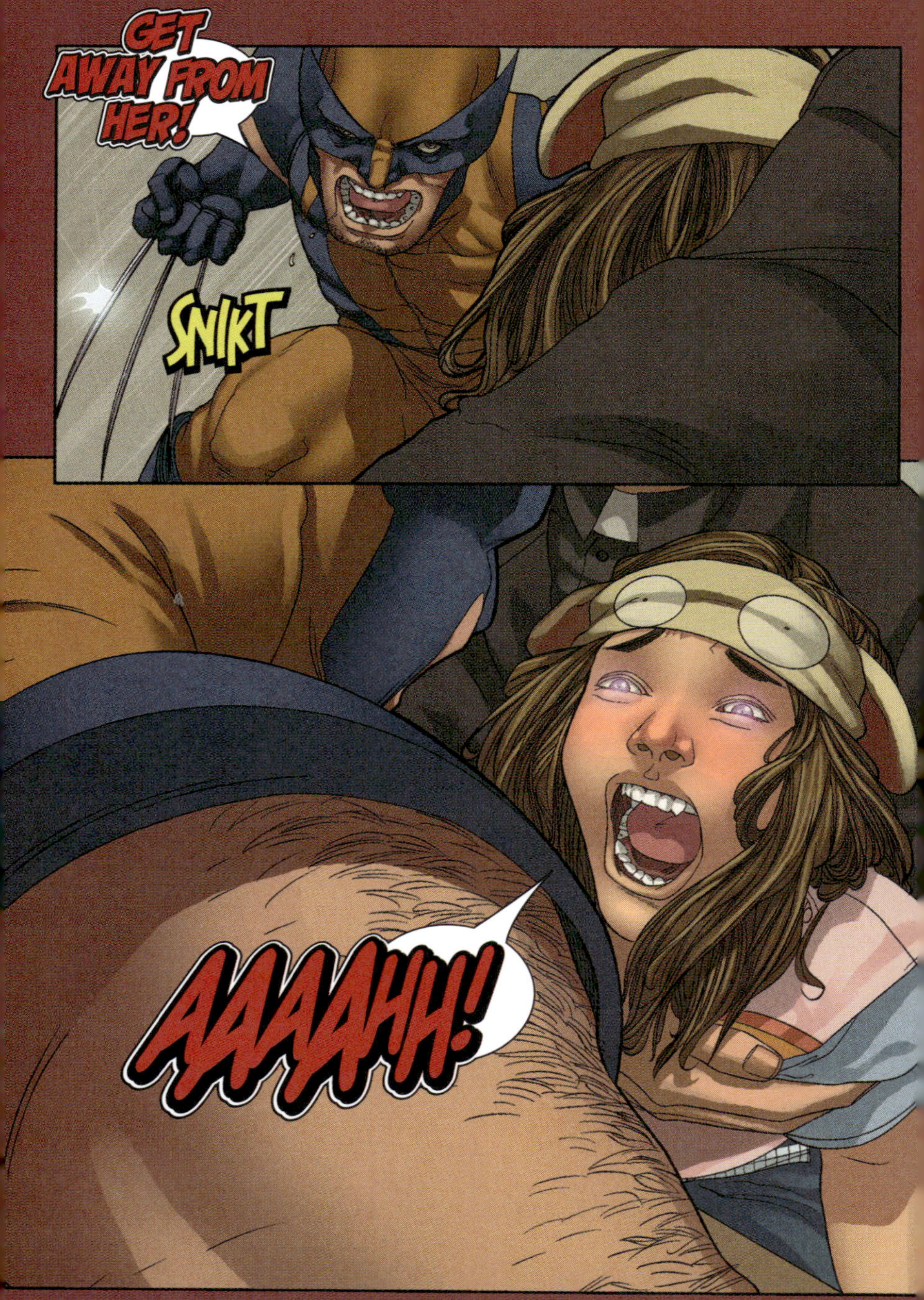
GET AWAY FROM HER!
SNIKT
AAAAHH!

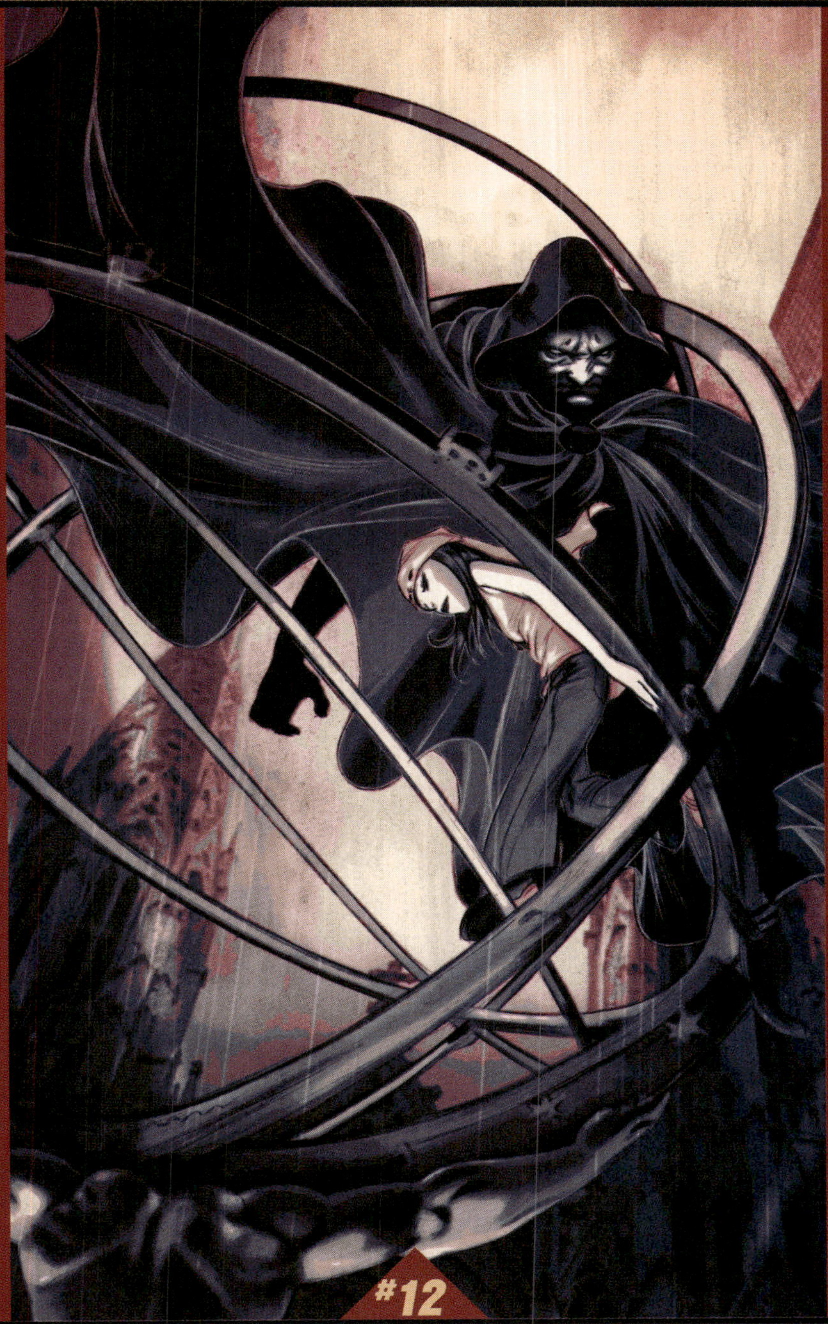
#12

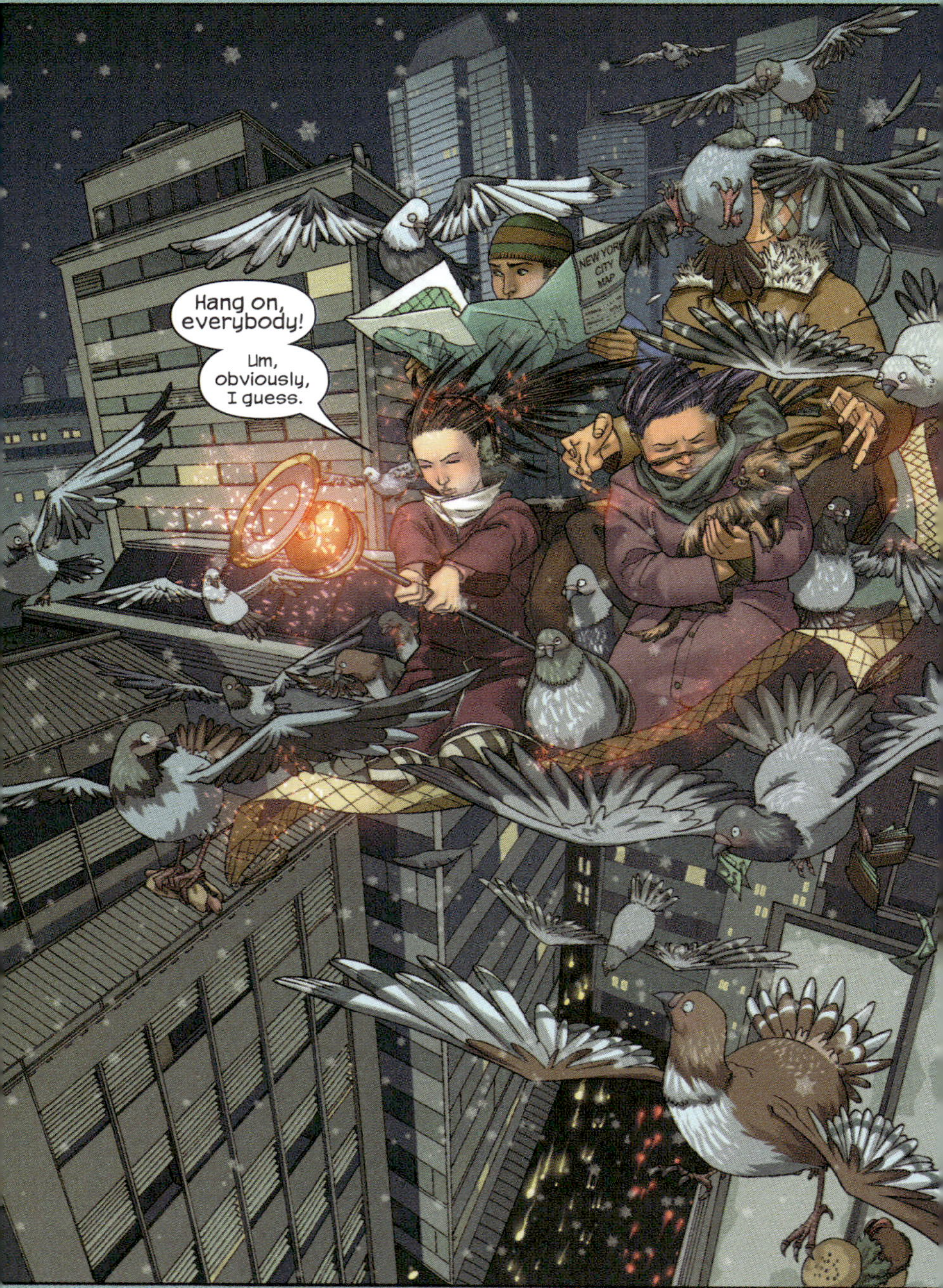
Hang on, everybody!
Um, obviously, I guess.
NEW YORK CITY MAP

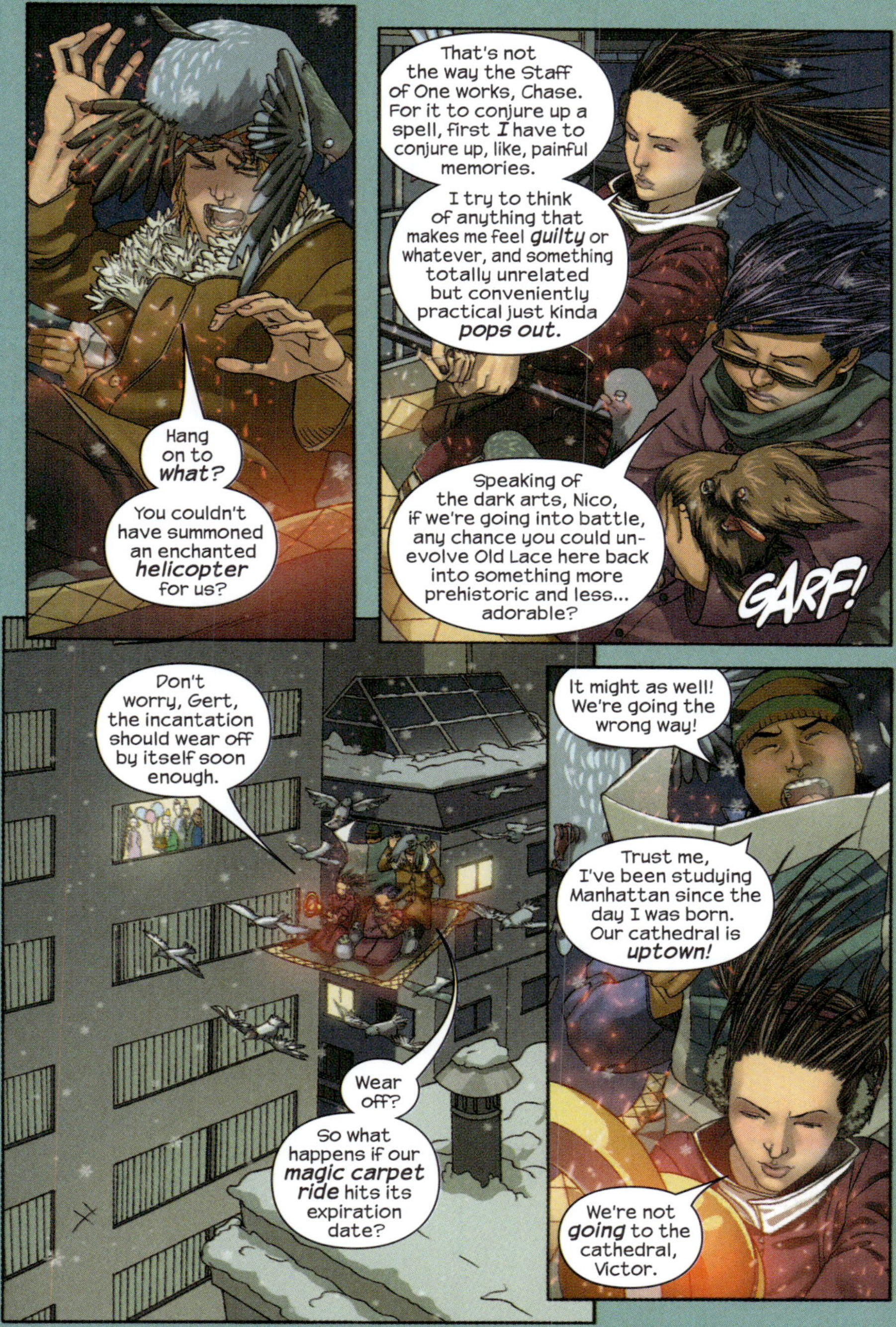
Hang on to *what?*
You couldn't have summoned an enchanted *helicopter* for us?
That's not the way the Staff of One works, Chase. For it to conjure up a spell, first *I* have to conjure up, like, painful memories.
I try to think of anything that makes me feel *guilty* or whatever, and something totally unrelated but conveniently practical just kinda *pops out.*
Speaking of the dark arts, Nico, if we're going into battle, any chance you could un-evolve Old Lace here back into something more prehistoric and less... adorable?
GARF!
Don't worry, Gert, the incantation should wear off by itself soon enough.
Wear off?
So what happens if our *magic carpet ride* hits its expiration date?
It might as well! We're going the wrong way!
Trust me, I've been studying Manhattan since the day I was born. Our cathedral is *uptown!*
We're not *going* to the cathedral, Victor.

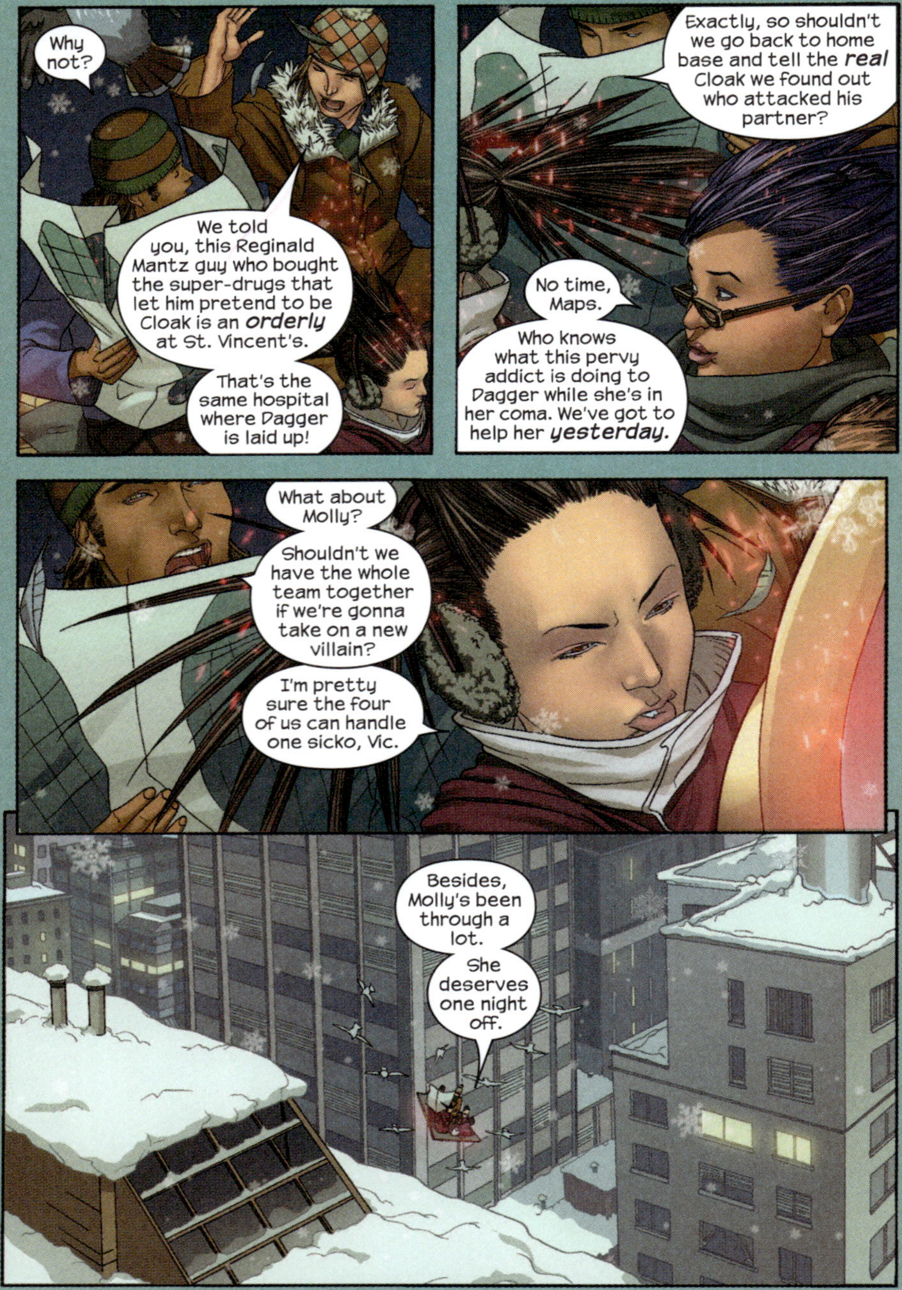
Why not?
We told you, this Reginald Mantz guy who bought the super-drugs that let him pretend to be Cloak is an *orderly* at St. Vincent's.
That's the same hospital where Dagger is laid up!
Exactly, so shouldn't we go back to home base and tell the *real* Cloak we found out who attacked his partner?
No time, Maps.
Who knows what this pervy addict is doing to Dagger while she's in her coma. We've got to help her *yesterday.*
What about Molly?
Shouldn't we have the whole team together if we're gonna take on a new villain?
I'm pretty sure the four of us can handle one sicko, Vic.
Besides, Molly's been through a lot.
She deserves one night off.

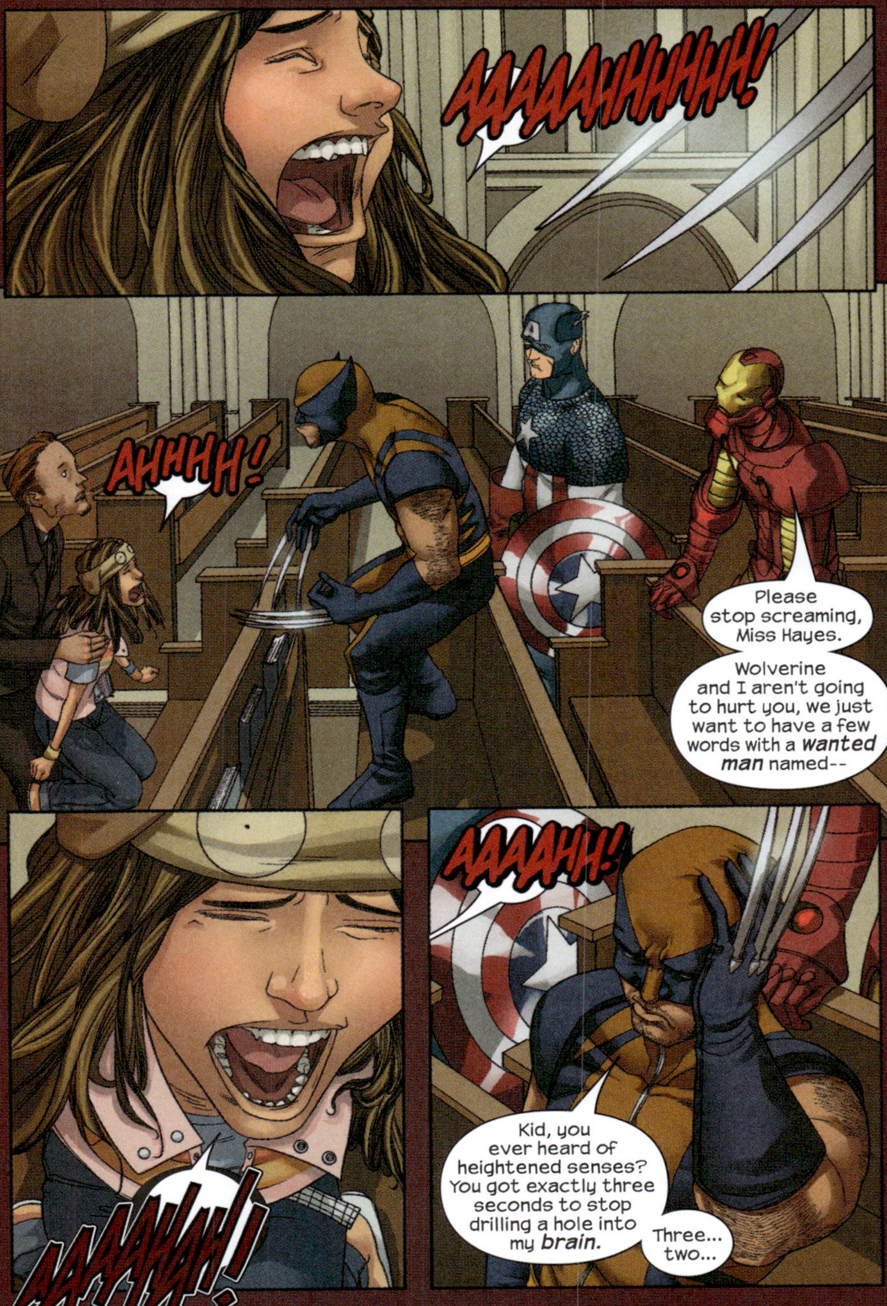
AAAAAHHHHHH!
AHHHH!
Please stop screaming, Miss Hayes.
Wolverine and I aren't going to hurt you, we just want to have a few words with a *wanted man* named--
AAAAHH!
AAAAAAH!
Kid, you ever heard of heightened senses? You got exactly three seconds to stop drilling a hole into my *brain.*
Three... two...

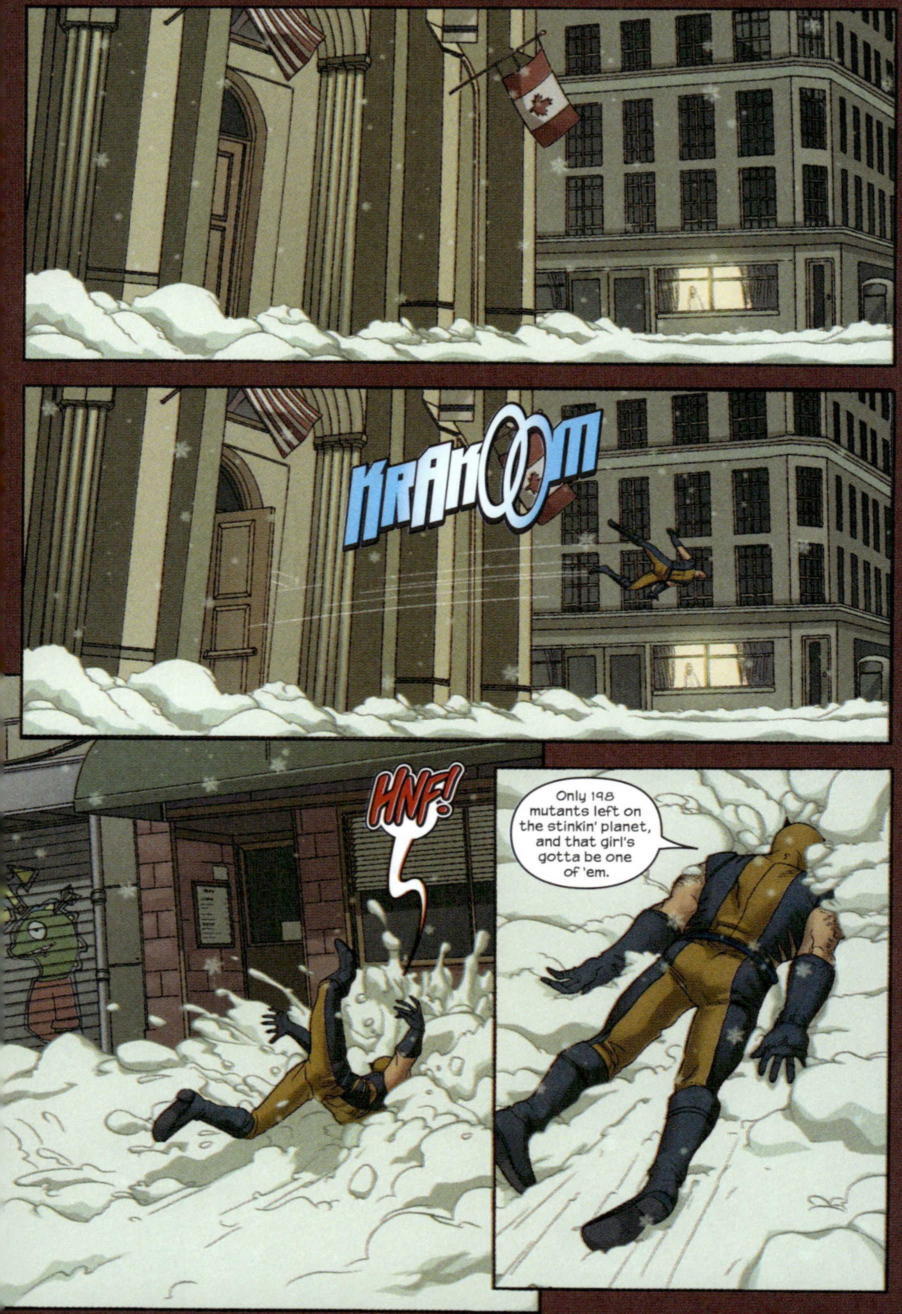
KRANOOM
HNF!
Only 198 mutants left on the stinkin' planet, and that girl's gotta be one of 'em.

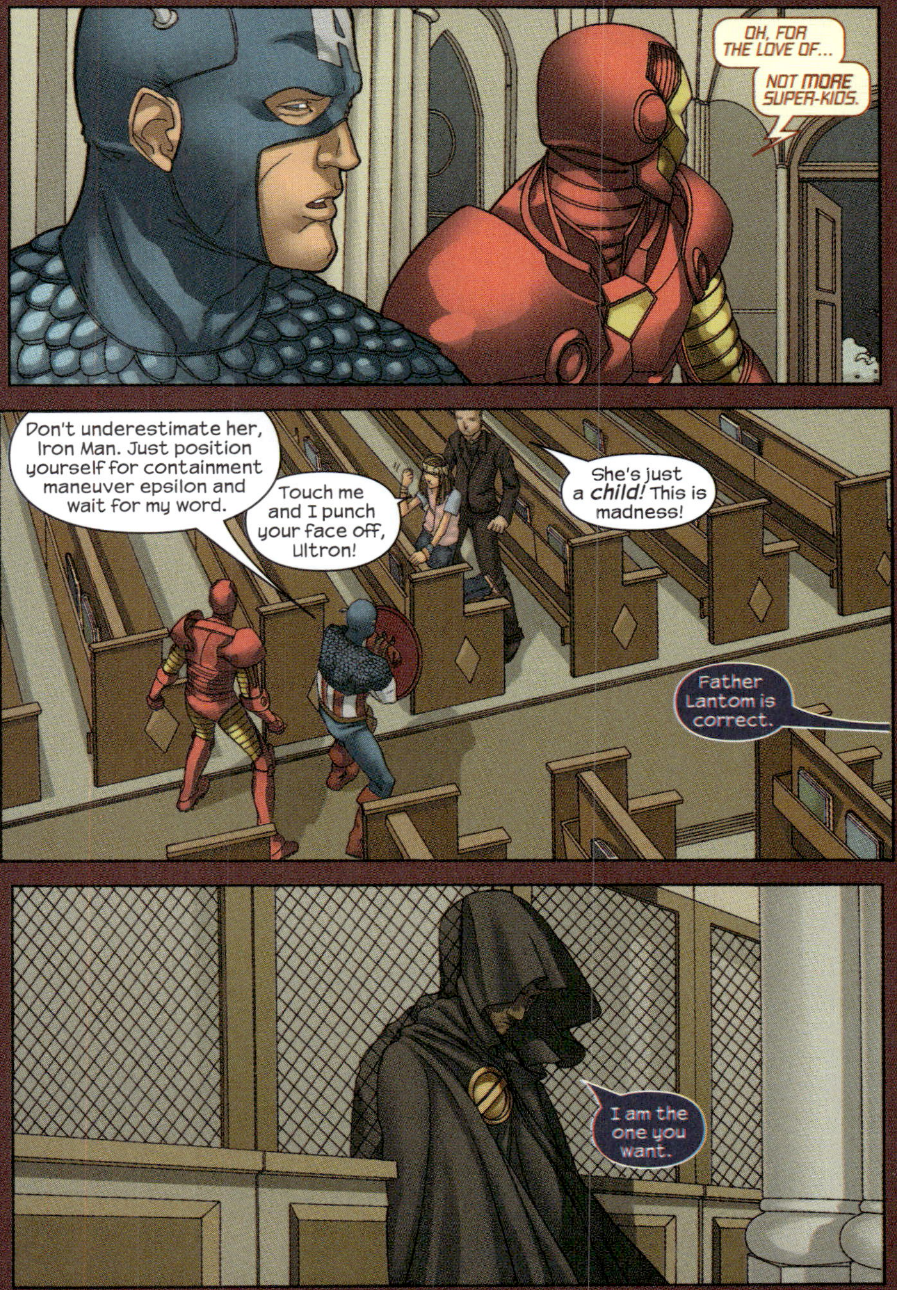
OH, FOR THE LOVE OF...
NOT MORE SUPER-KIDS.
Don't underestimate her, Iron Man. Just position yourself for containment maneuver epsilon and wait for my word.
Touch me and I punch your face off, Ultron!
She's just a *child!* This is madness!
Father Lantom is correct.
I am the one you want.

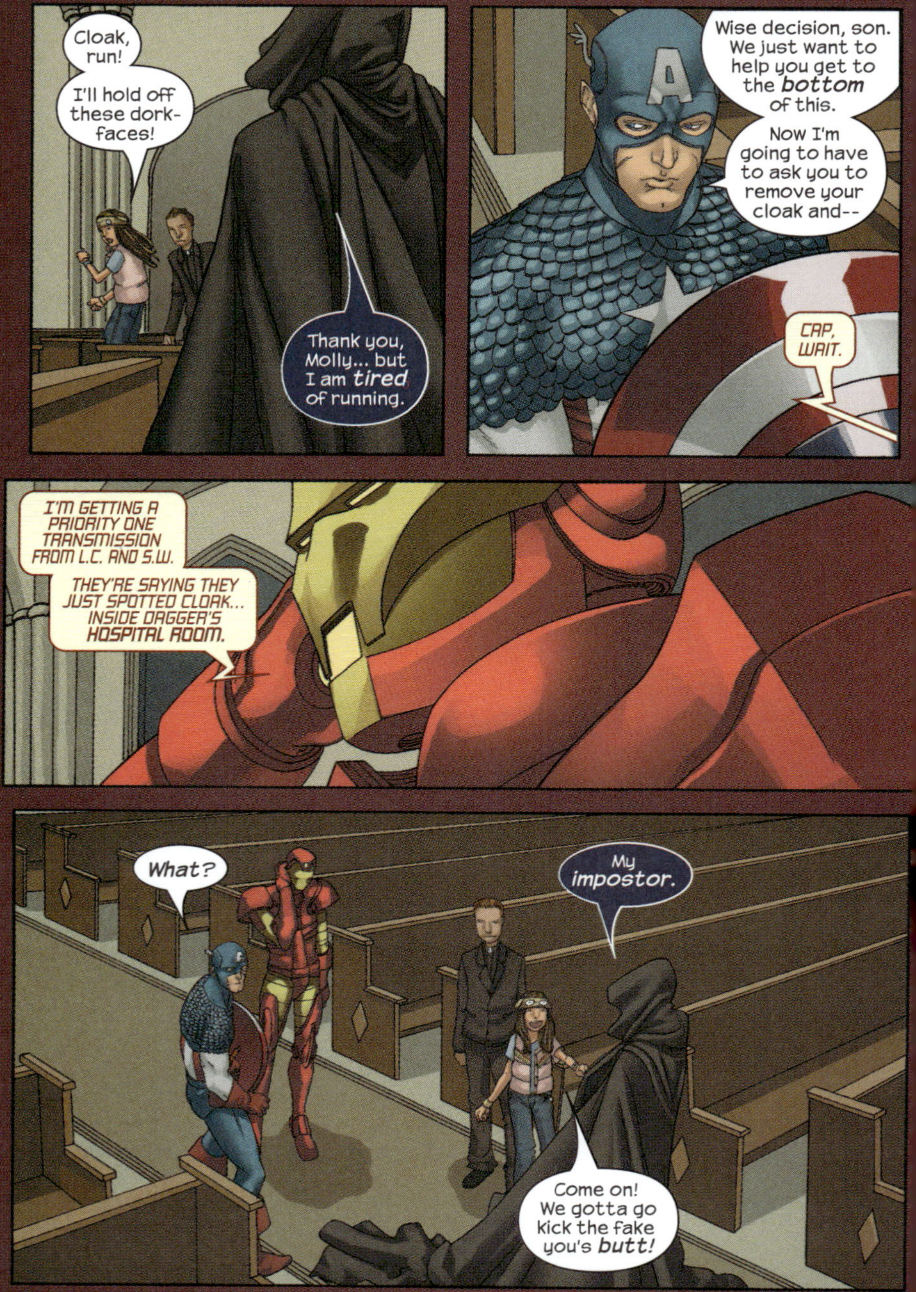
Cloak, run!
I'll hold off these dork-faces!
Thank you, Molly... but I am *tired* of running.
Wise decision, son. We just want to help you get to the **bottom** of this.
Now I'm going to have to ask you to remove your cloak and--
CAP, WAIT.
I'M GETTING A PRIORITY ONE TRANSMISSION FROM L.C. AND S.W.
THEY'RE SAYING THEY JUST SPOTTED CLOAK... INSIDE DAGGER'S **HOSPITAL ROOM.**
What?
My *impostor.*
Come on! We gotta go kick the fake you's *butt!*

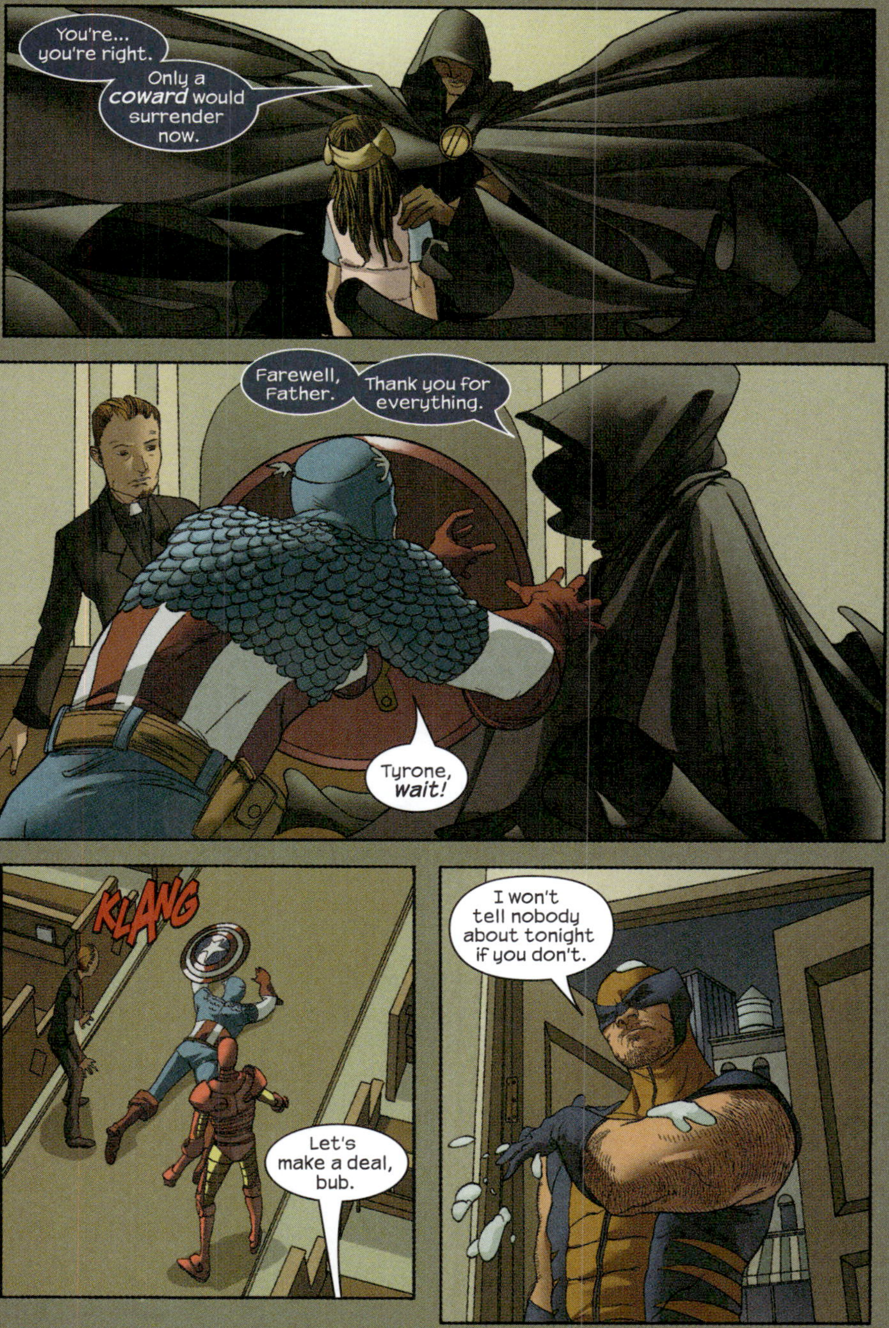
You're... you're right.
Only a *coward* would surrender now.
Farewell, Father.
Thank you for everything.
Tyrone, *wait!*
KLANG
Let's make a deal, bub.
I won't tell nobody about tonight if you don't.

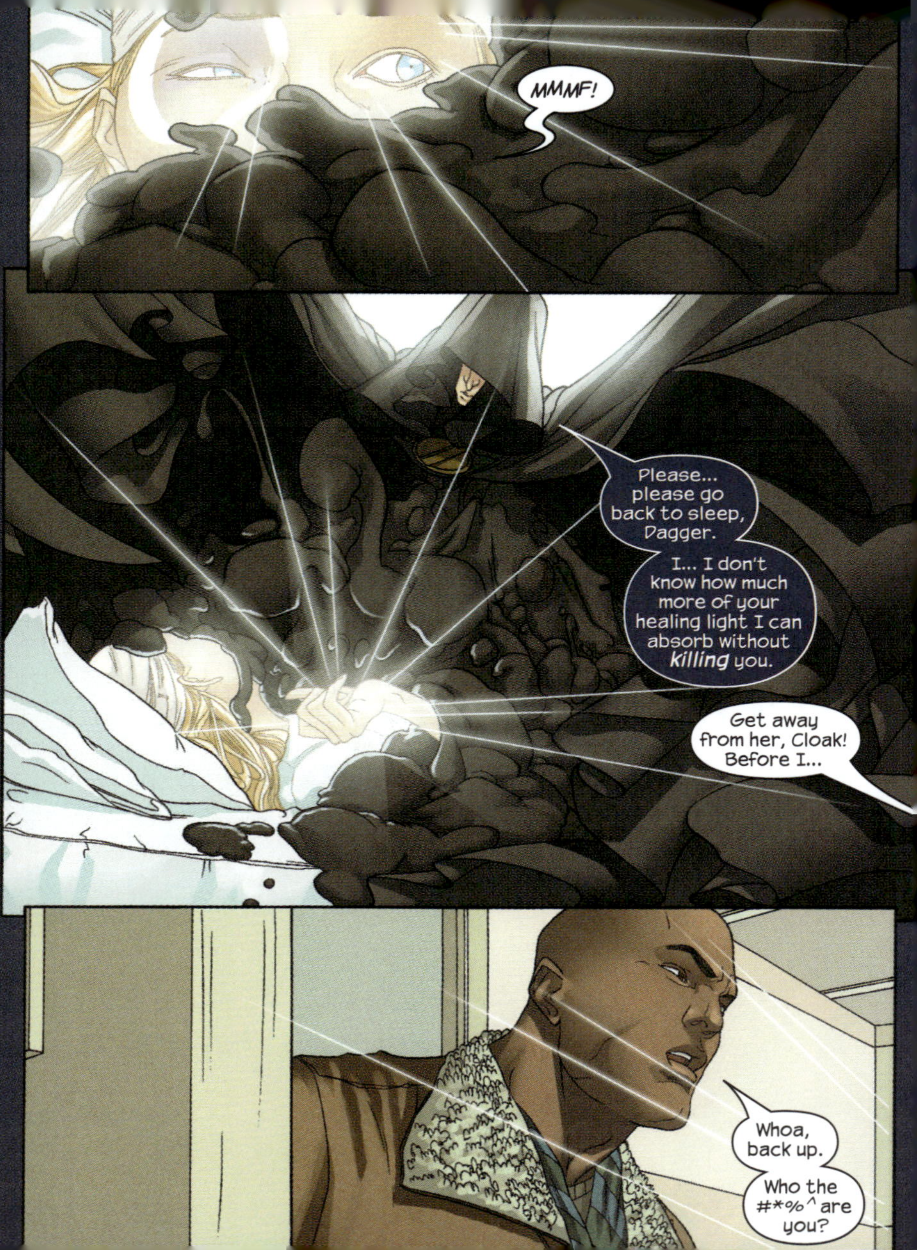
MMMF!
Please... please go back to sleep, Dagger.
I... I don't know how much more of your healing light I can absorb without *killing* you.
Get away from her, Cloak! Before I...
Whoa, back up.
Who the #*%^ are you?

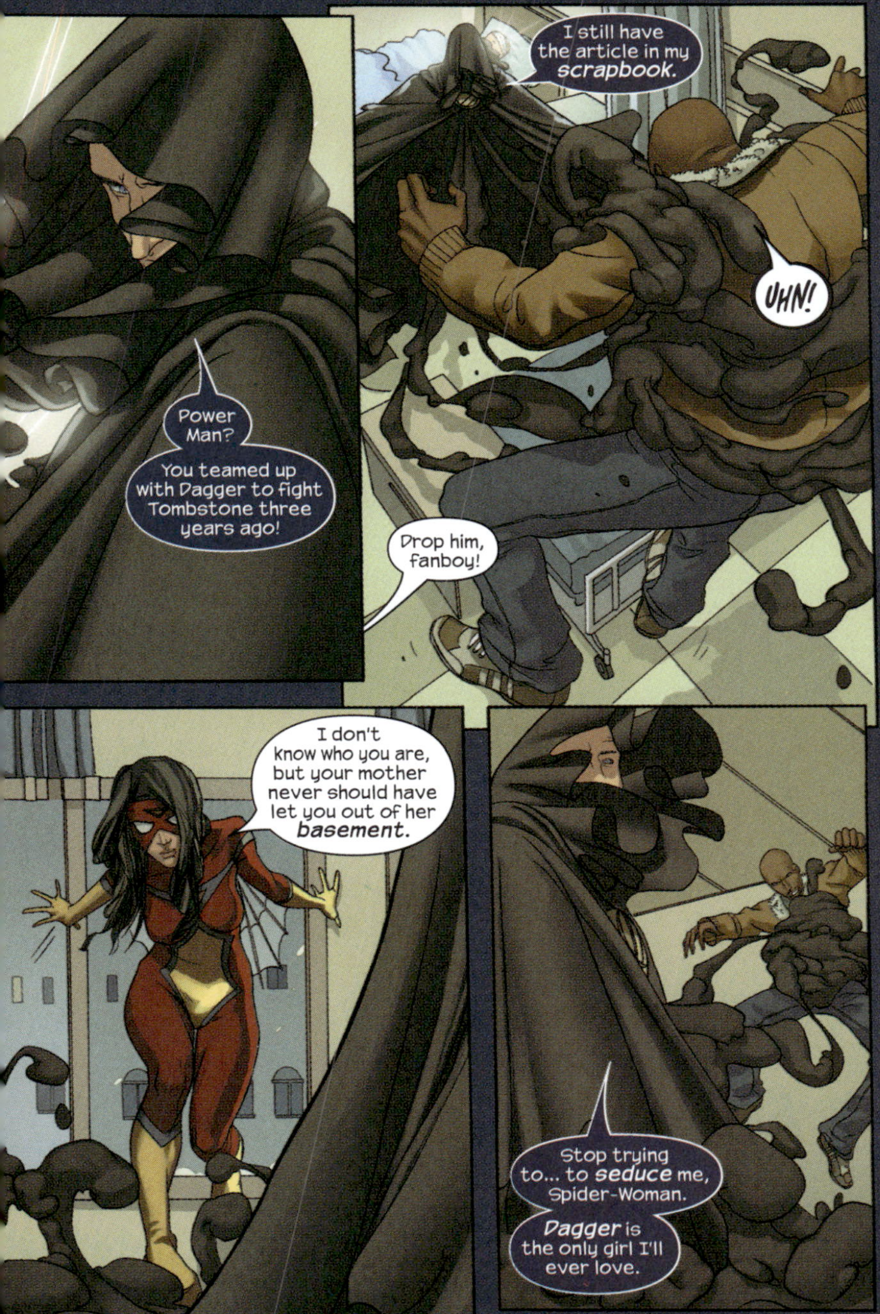
I still have the article in my *scrapbook.*
UHN!
Power Man?
You teamed up with Dagger to fight Tombstone three years ago!
Drop him, fanboy!
I don't know who you are, but your mother never should have let you out of her *basement.*
Stop trying to... to *seduce* me, Spider-Woman.
Dagger is the only girl I'll ever love.

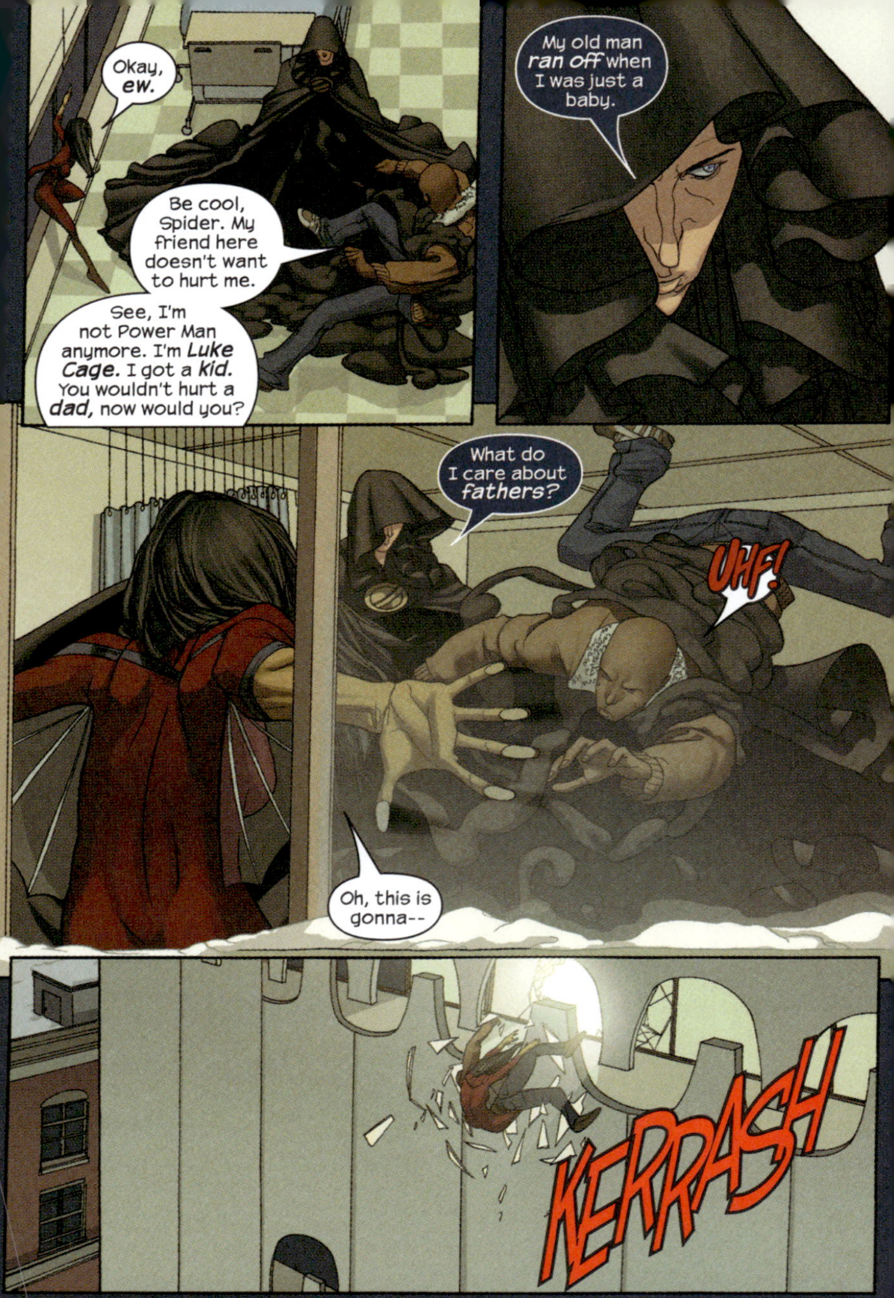

Okay, ew.
Be cool, Spider. My friend here doesn't want to hurt me.
See, I'm not Power Man anymore. I'm Luke Cage. I got a kid. You wouldn't hurt a dad, now would you?
My old man ran off when I was just a baby.
What do I care about fathers?
UHF!
Oh, this is gonna--
KERRASH

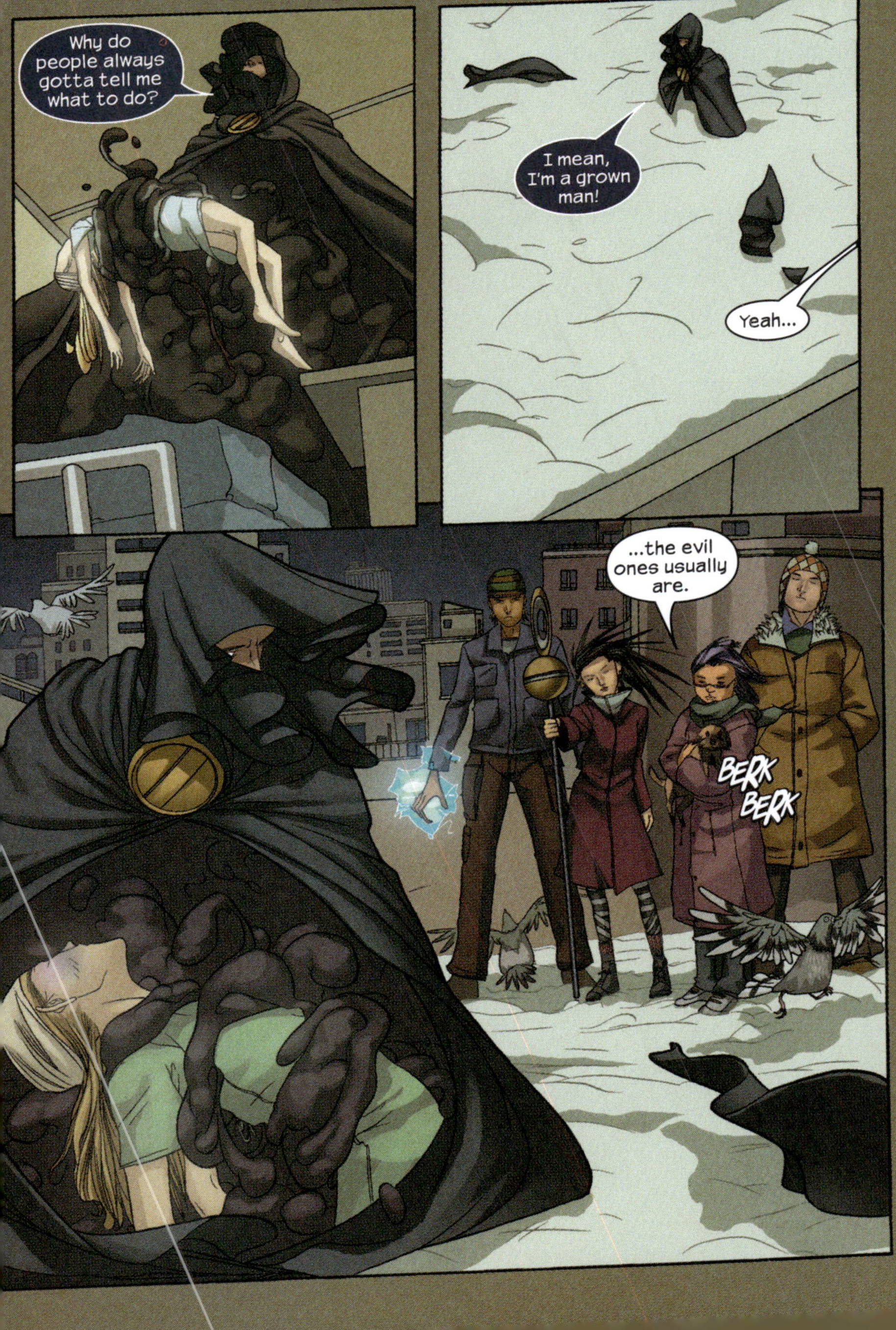
Why do people always gotta tell me what to do?
I mean, I'm a grown man!
Yeah...
...the evil ones usually are.
BERK
BERK

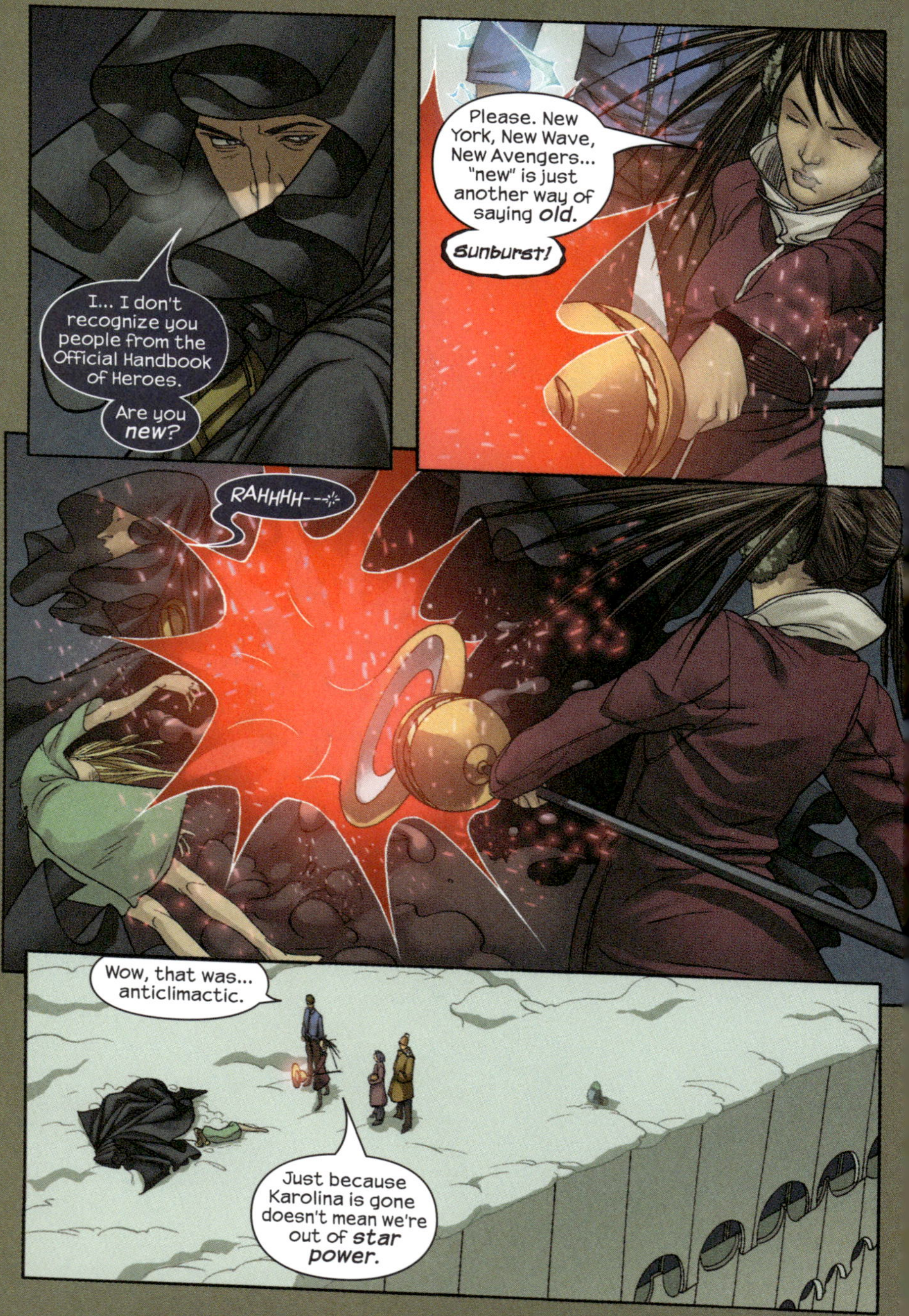
I... I don't recognize you people from the Official Handbook of Heroes.
Are you new?
Please. New York, New Wave, New Avengers... "new" is just another way of saying old.
Sunburst!
RAHHHH--
Wow, that was... anticlimactic.
Just because Karolina is gone doesn't mean we're out of star power.

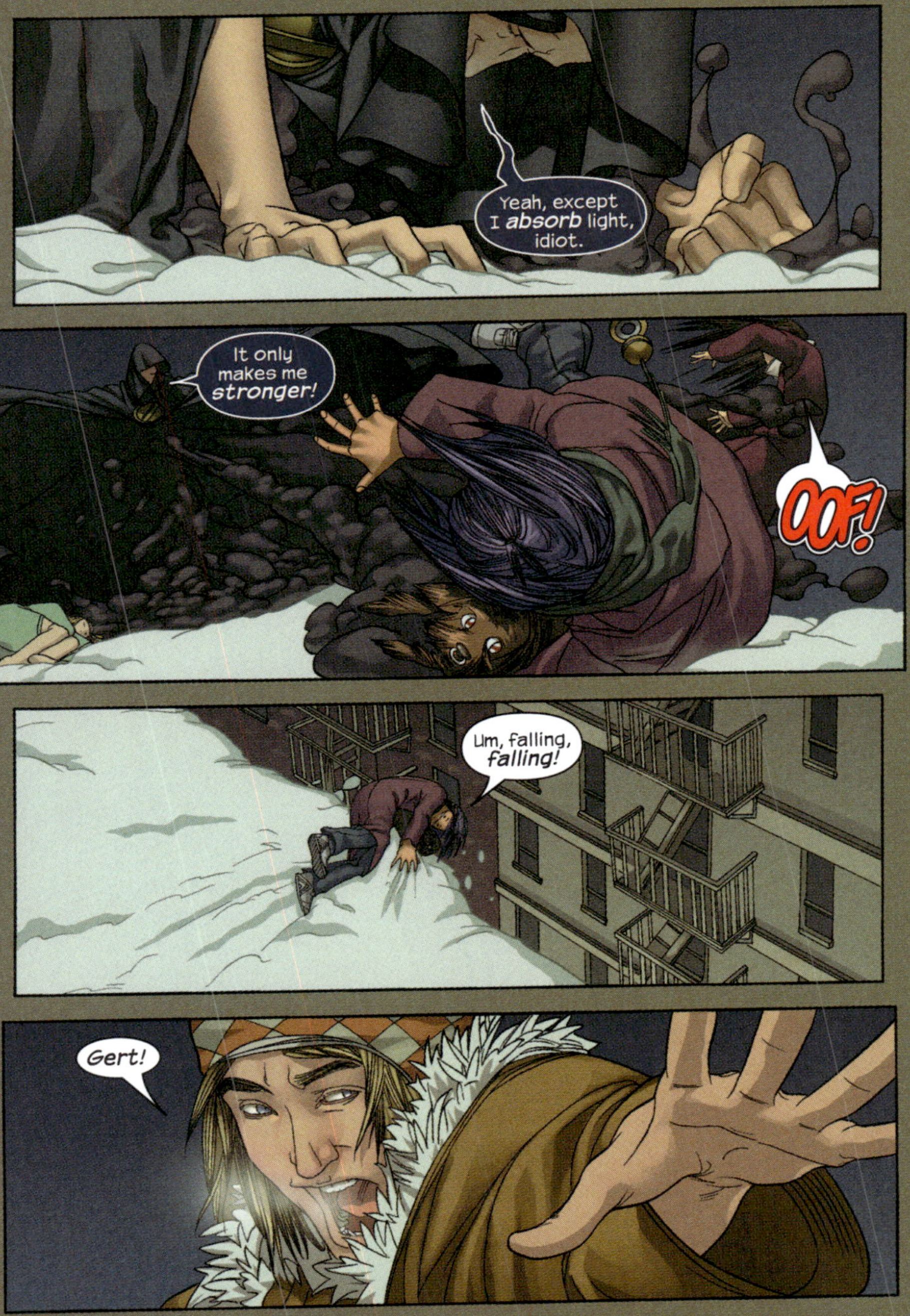
Yeah, except I *absorb* light, idiot.
It only makes me *stronger!*
OOF!
Um, falling, *falling!*
Gert!

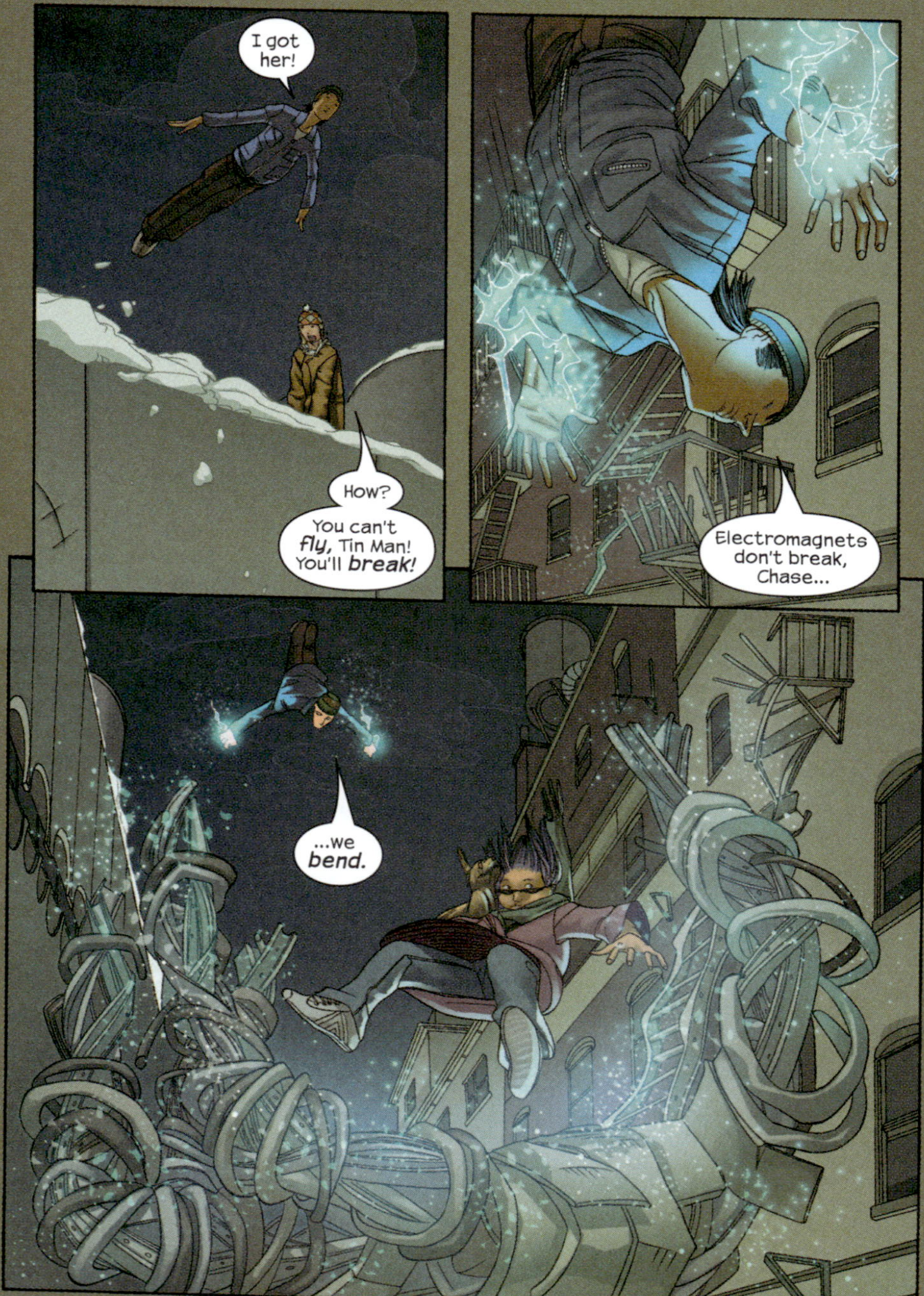

I got her!
How?
You can't *fly,* Tin Man! You'll ***break!***
Electromagnets don't break, Chase...
...we ***bend.***

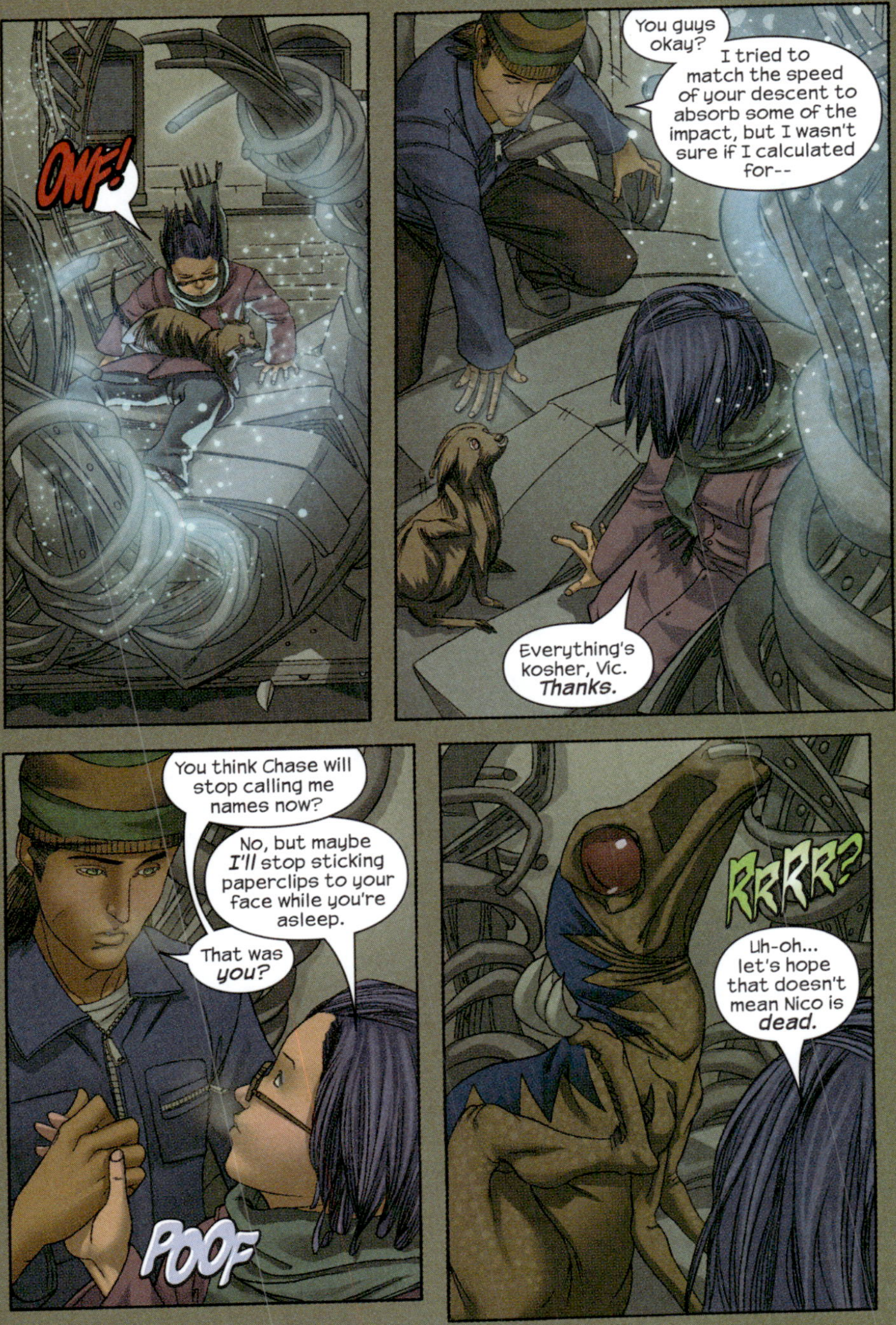
OWF!
You guys okay?
I tried to match the speed of your descent to absorb some of the impact, but I wasn't sure if I calculated for--
Everything's kosher, Vic. *Thanks.*
You think Chase will stop calling me names now?
No, but maybe *I'll* stop sticking paperclips to your face while you're asleep.
That was *you?*
POOF
RRRR?
Uh-oh... let's hope that doesn't mean Nico is *dead.*

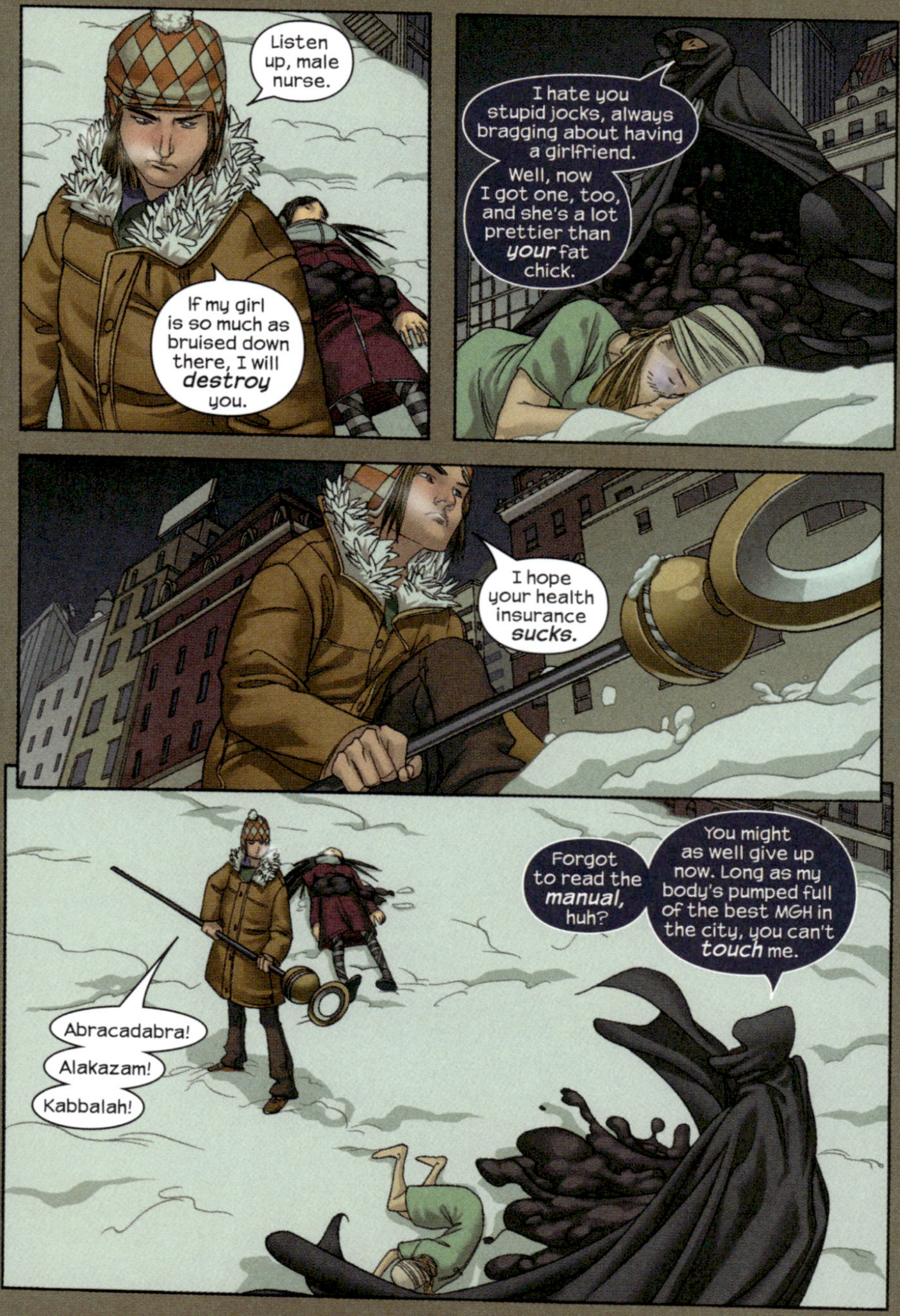
Listen up, male nurse.
If my girl is so much as bruised down there, I will destroy you.
I hate you stupid jocks, always bragging about having a girlfriend.
Well, now I got one, too, and she's a lot prettier than your fat chick.
I hope your health insurance sucks.
Abracadabra!
Alakazam!
Kabbalah!
Forgot to read the manual, huh?
You might as well give up now. Long as my body's pumped full of the best MGH in the city, you can't touch me.

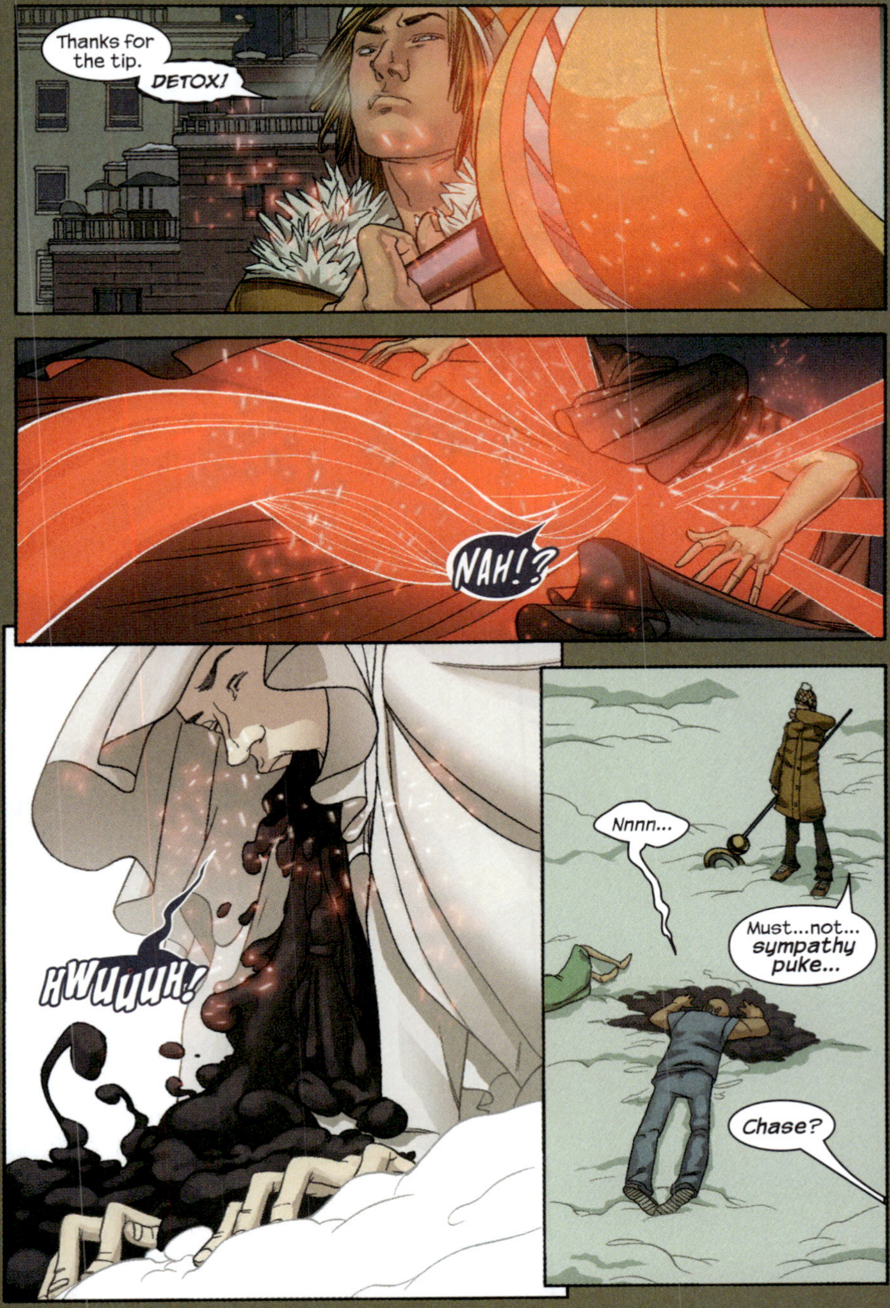
Thanks for the tip.
DETOX!
NAH!?
HWUUUUH!
Nnnn...
Must...not... sympathy puke...
Chase?

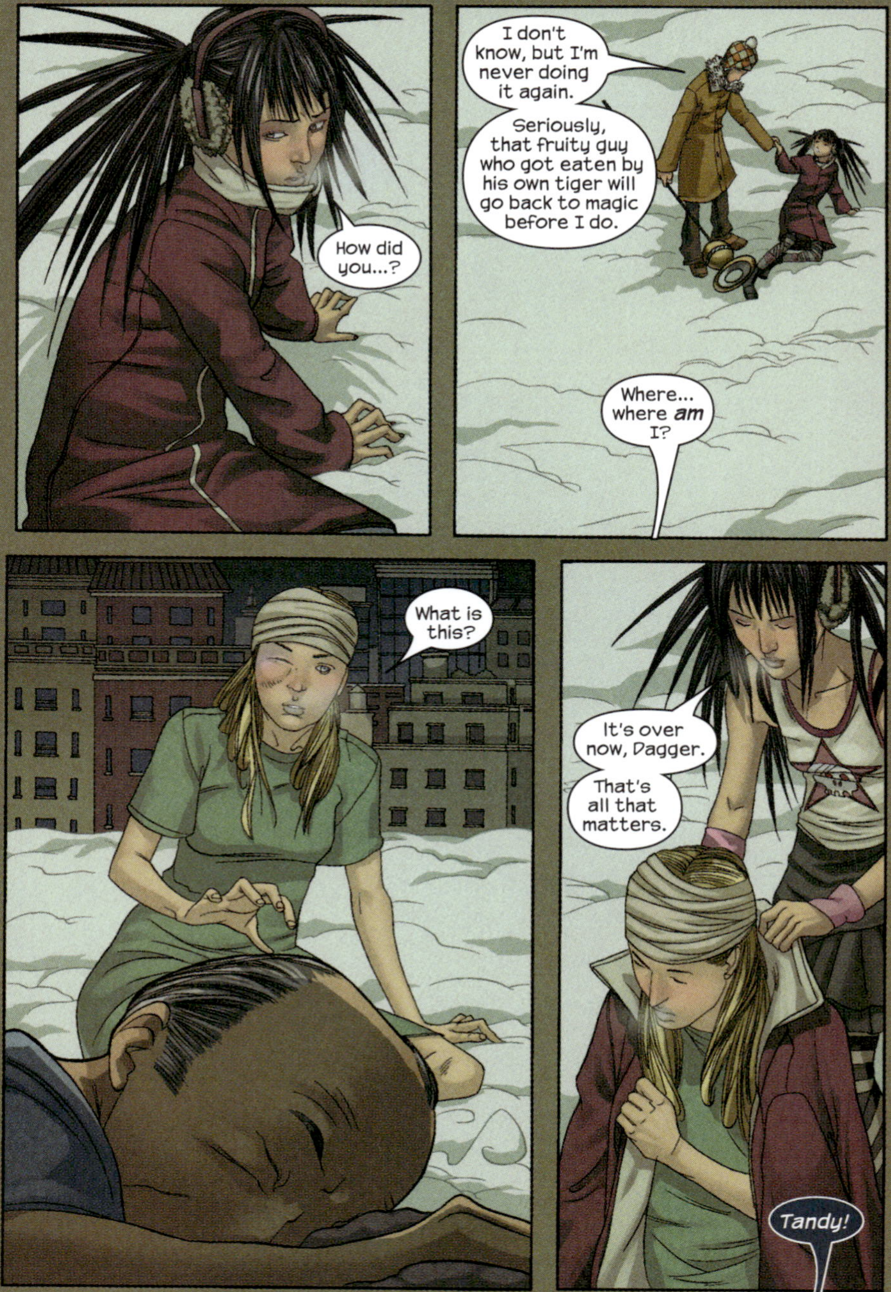
How did you...?
I don't know, but I'm never doing it again.
Seriously, that fruity guy who got eaten by his own tiger will go back to magic before I do.
Where... where *am* I?
What is this?
It's over now, Dagger.
That's all that matters.
Tandy!

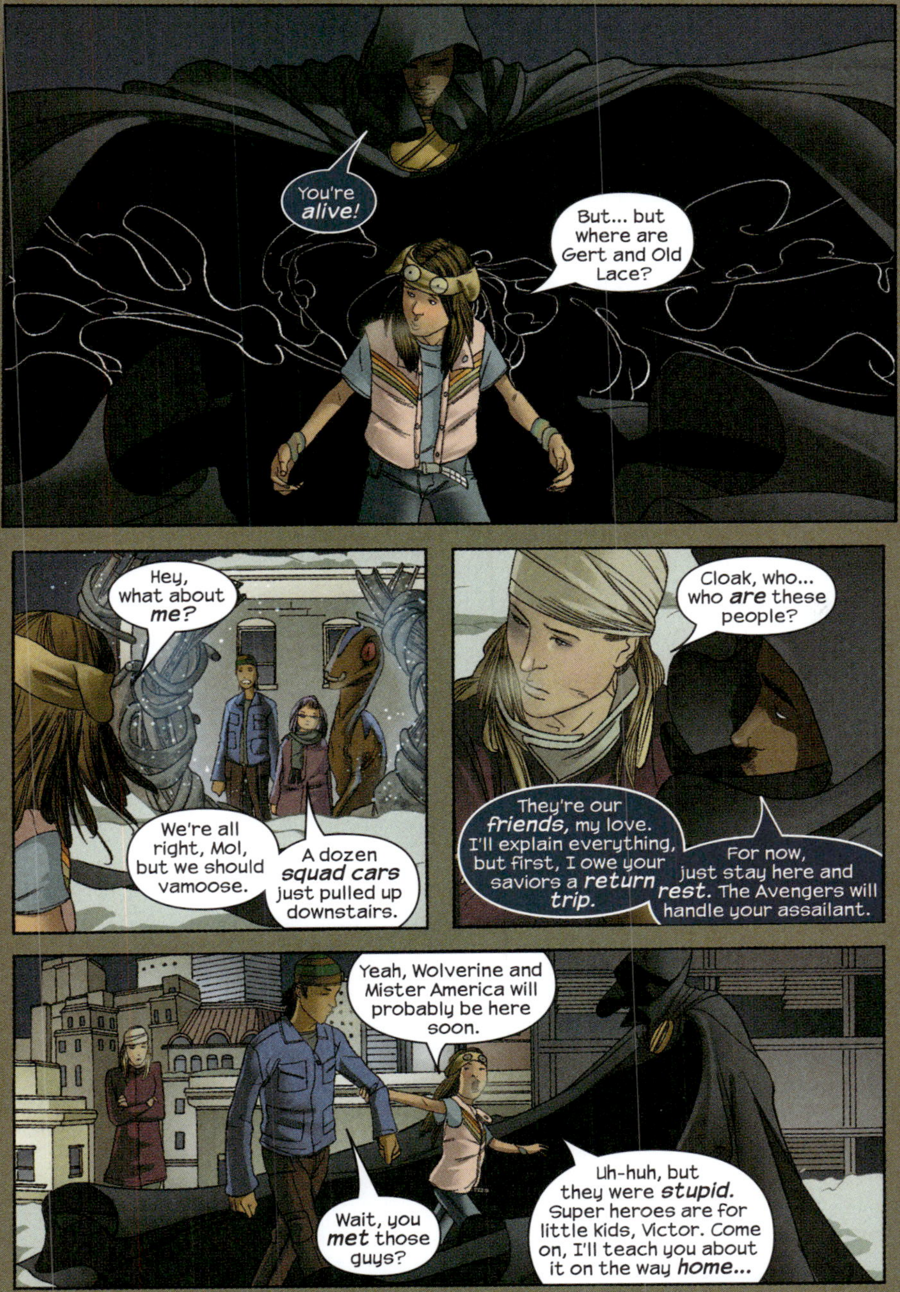
You're alive!
But... but where are Gert and Old Lace?
Hey, what about me?
We're all right, Mol, but we should vamoose.
A dozen squad cars just pulled up downstairs.
Cloak, who... who are these people?
They're our friends, my love. I'll explain everything, but first, I owe your saviors a return trip.
For now, just stay here and rest. The Avengers will handle your assailant.
Yeah, Wolverine and Mister America will probably be here soon.
Wait, you met those guys?
Uh-huh, but they were stupid. Super heroes are for little kids, Victor. Come on, I'll teach you about it on the way home...

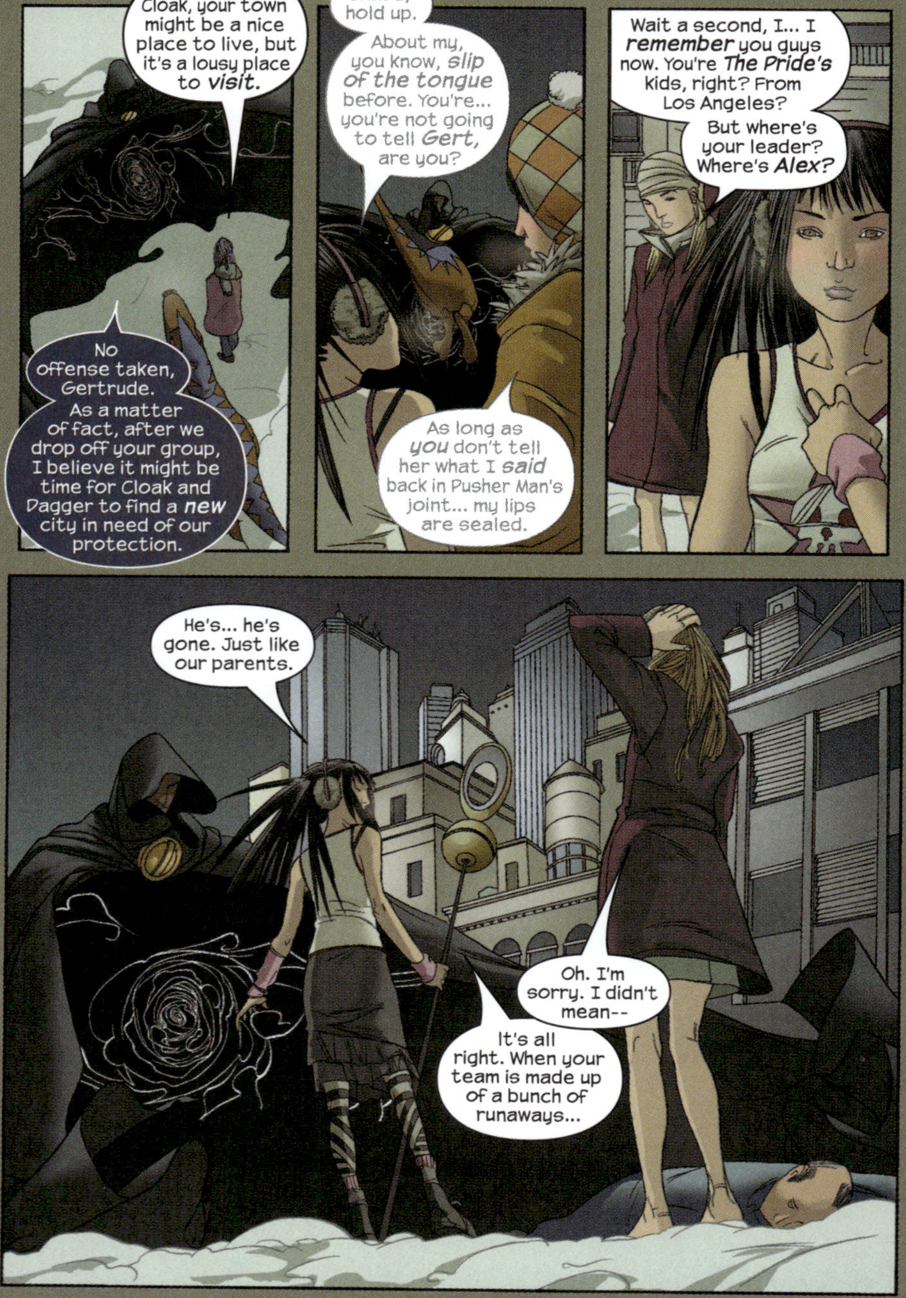
No offense, Cloak, your town might be a nice place to live, but it's a lousy place to *visit.*
No offense taken, Gertrude.
As a matter of fact, after we drop off your group, I believe it might be time for Cloak and Dagger to find a *new* city in need of our protection.
Chase, hold up.
About my, you know, *slip of the tongue* before. You're... you're not going to tell *Gert,* are you?
As long as *you* don't tell her what I *said* back in Pusher Man's joint... my lips are sealed.
Wait a second, I... I *remember* you guys now. You're *The Pride's* kids, right? From Los Angeles?
But where's your leader? Where's *Alex?*
He's... he's gone. Just like our parents.
Oh. I'm sorry. I didn't mean--
It's all right. When your team is made up of a bunch of runaways...

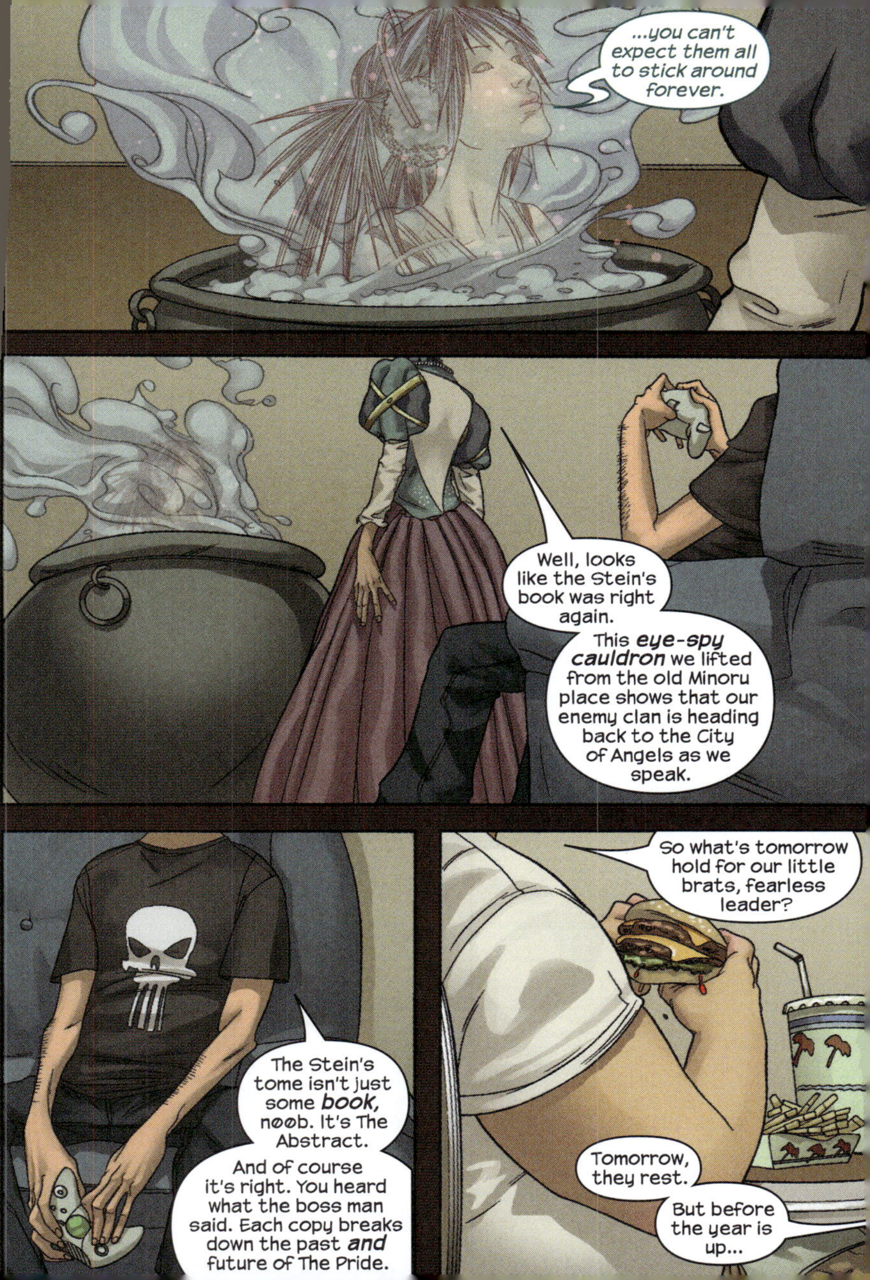
...you can't expect them all to stick around forever.
Well, looks like the Stein's book was right again.
This eye-spy cauldron we lifted from the old Minoru place shows that our enemy clan is heading back to the City of Angels as we speak.
The Stein's tome isn't just some book, noob. It's The Abstract.
And of course it's right. You heard what the boss man said. Each copy breaks down the past and future of The Pride.
So what's tomorrow hold for our little brats, fearless leader?
Tomorrow, they rest.
But before the year is up...

1/21/15

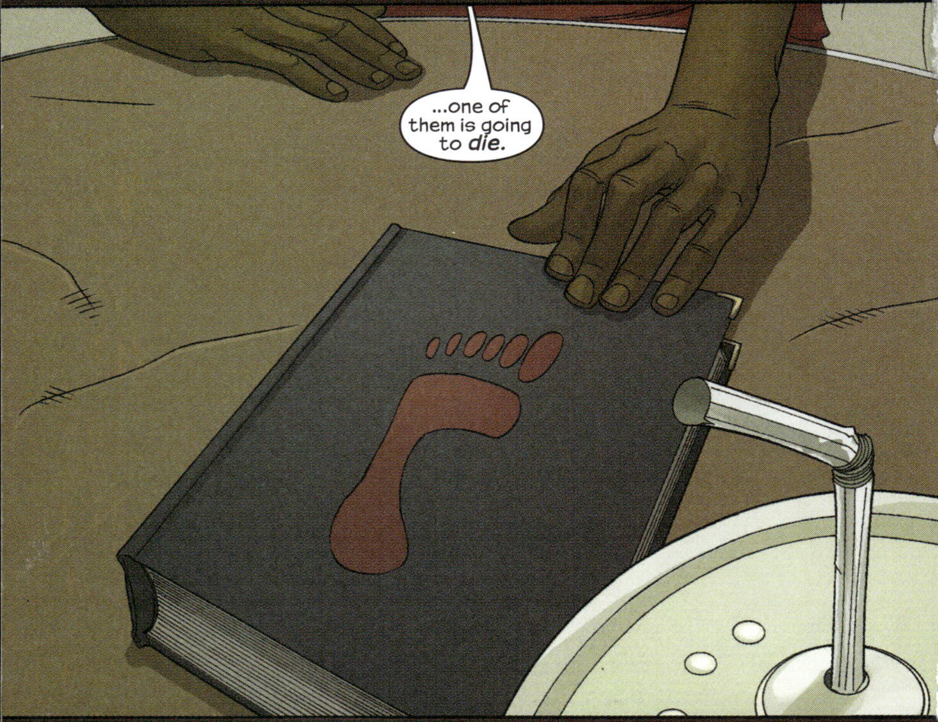
...one of them is going to *die.*

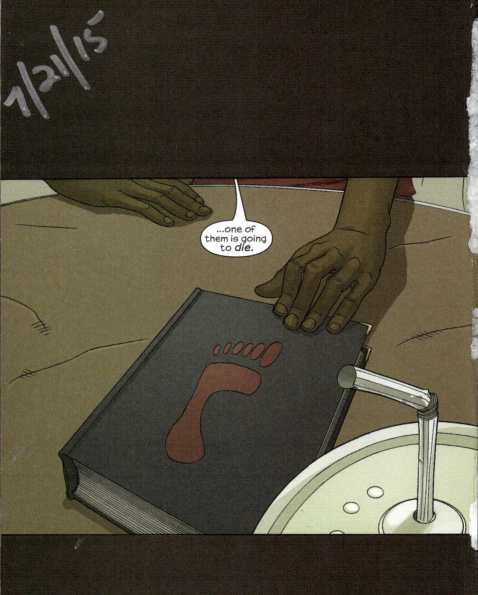

Next: Parental Guidance

RUNAWAYS
PARENTAL GUIDANCE

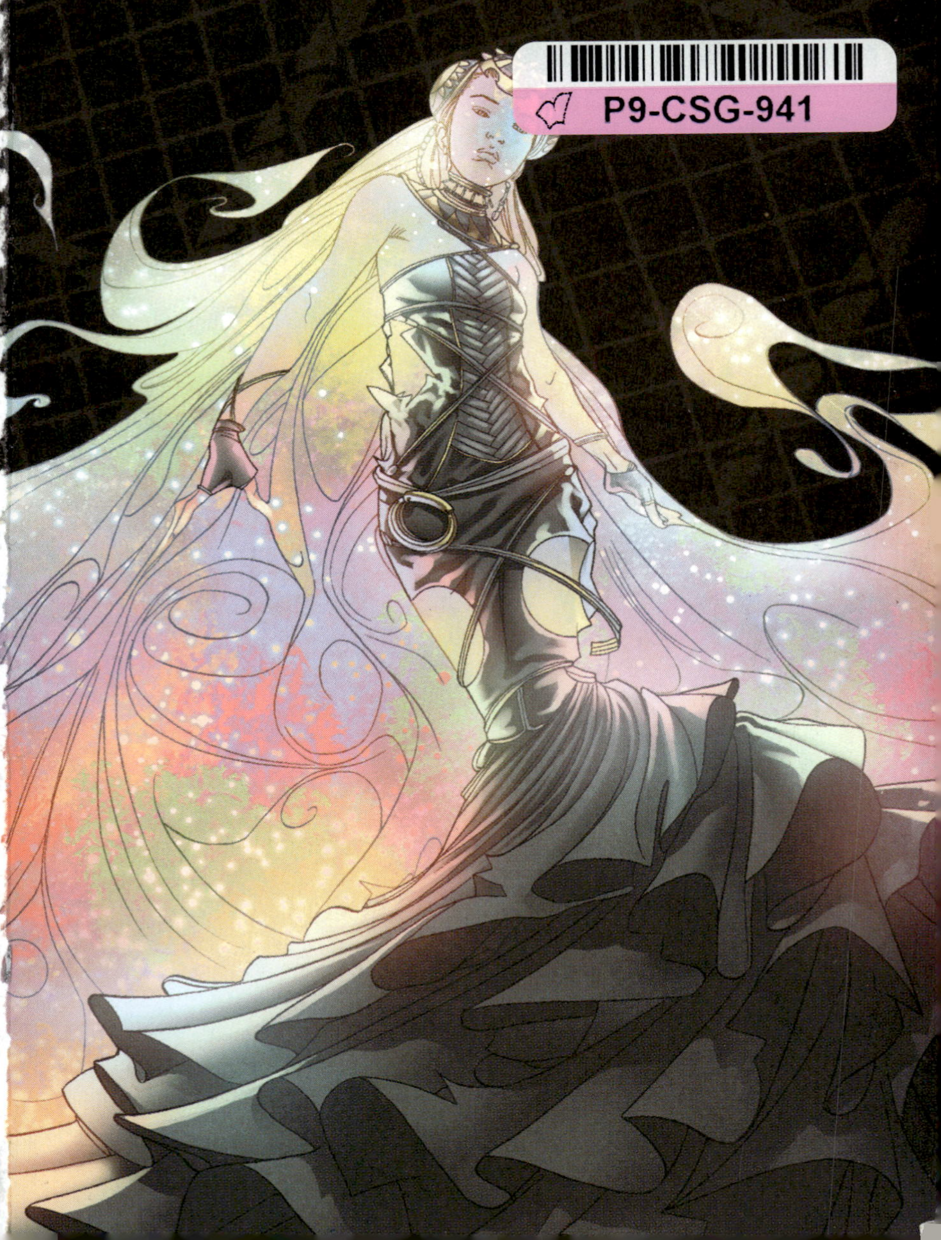

RUNAWAYS →

PARENTAL GUIDANCE

Writer: Brian K. Vaughan
Penciler: Adrian Alphona
Inker: Craig Yeung
Colorist: Christina Strain
Letterer: Virtual Calligraphy's Randy Gentile
Cover Art: Marcos Martin
Assistant Editor: Nathan Cosby
Editors: MacKenzie Cadenhead & Nick Lowe
Special thanks to C.B. Cebulski

Runaways created by Brian K. Vaughan & Adrian Alphona

Collection Editor: Jennifer Grünwald
Assistant Editor: Michael Short
Associate Editor: Mark D. Beazley
Senior Editor, Special Projects: Jeff Youngquist
Vice President of Sales: David Gabriel
Production: Jerron Quality Color
Vice President of Creative: Tom Marvelli

Editor in Chief: Joe Quesada
Publisher: Dan Buckley

PREVIOUSLY:

At some point in their lives, all kids think that they have the most evil parents in the world, but Nico Minoru and her friends really did.

Discovering they were the children of a group of super-villains known as The Pride, the Los Angeles teenagers stole weapons and resources from these criminals, before running away from home and eventually defeating their parents. But that was just the beginning. Together, the teenage runaways now hope to atone for their parents' crimes by taking on the new threats trying to fill The Pride's void.

The team's youngest member is Molly Hayes, one of the world's last living mutants. While Molly is extremely powerful, the more of her superhuman strength she uses, the more tired she becomes...

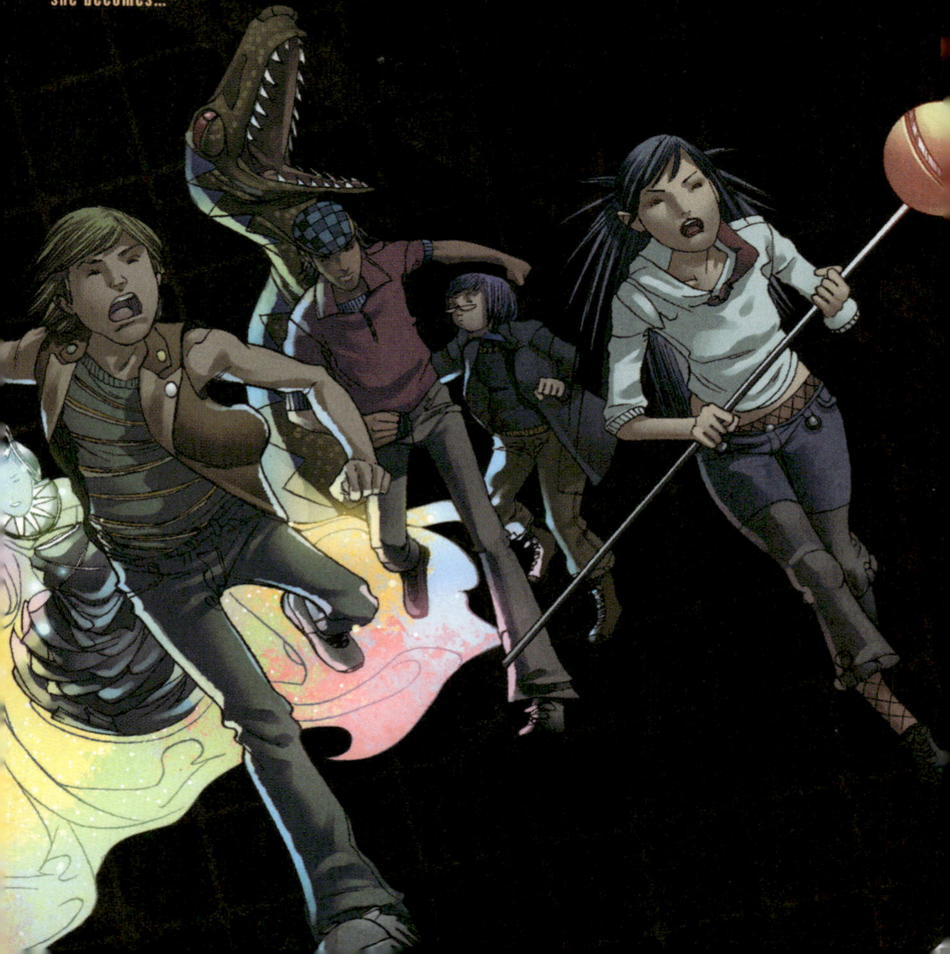

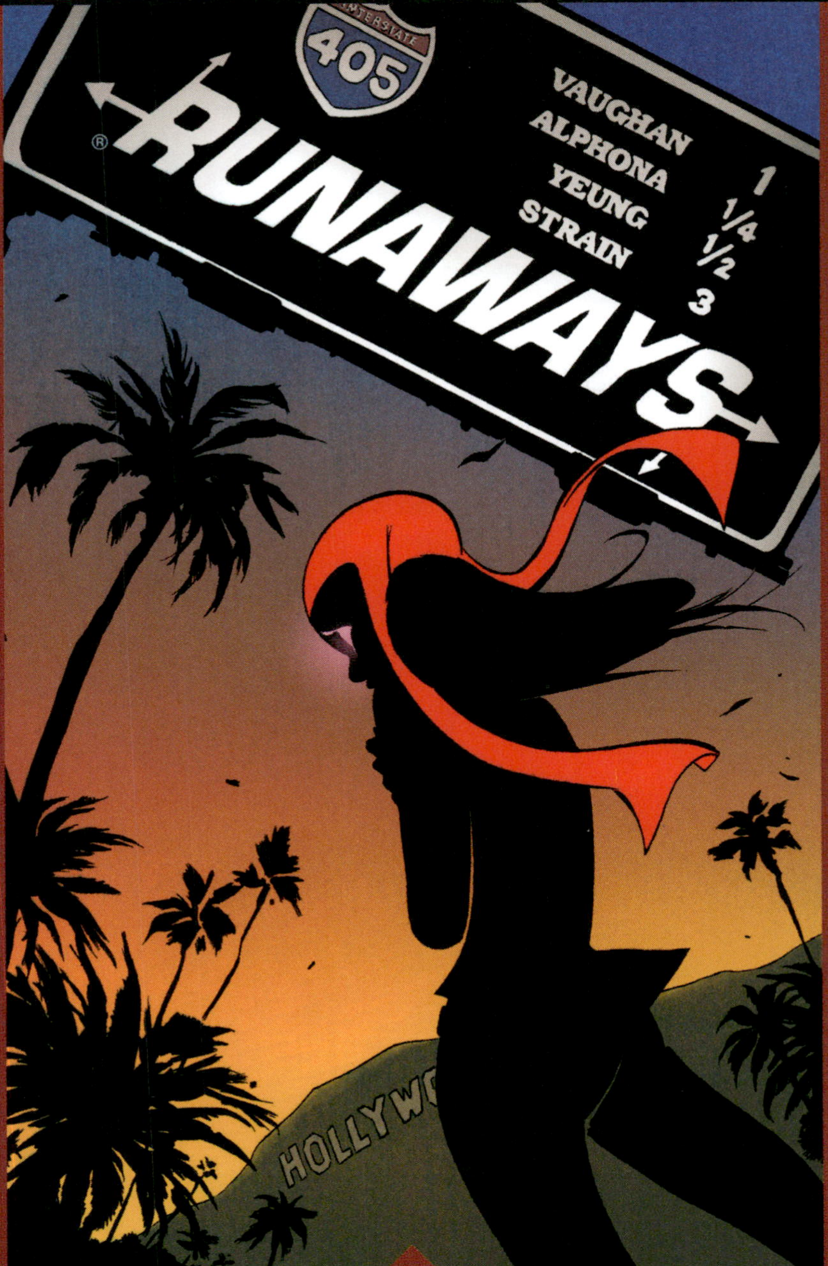
INTERSTATE
405
RUNAWAYS
VAUGHAN
ALPHONA
YEUNG
STRAIN
1
1/4
1/2
3
HOLLYWO
#13

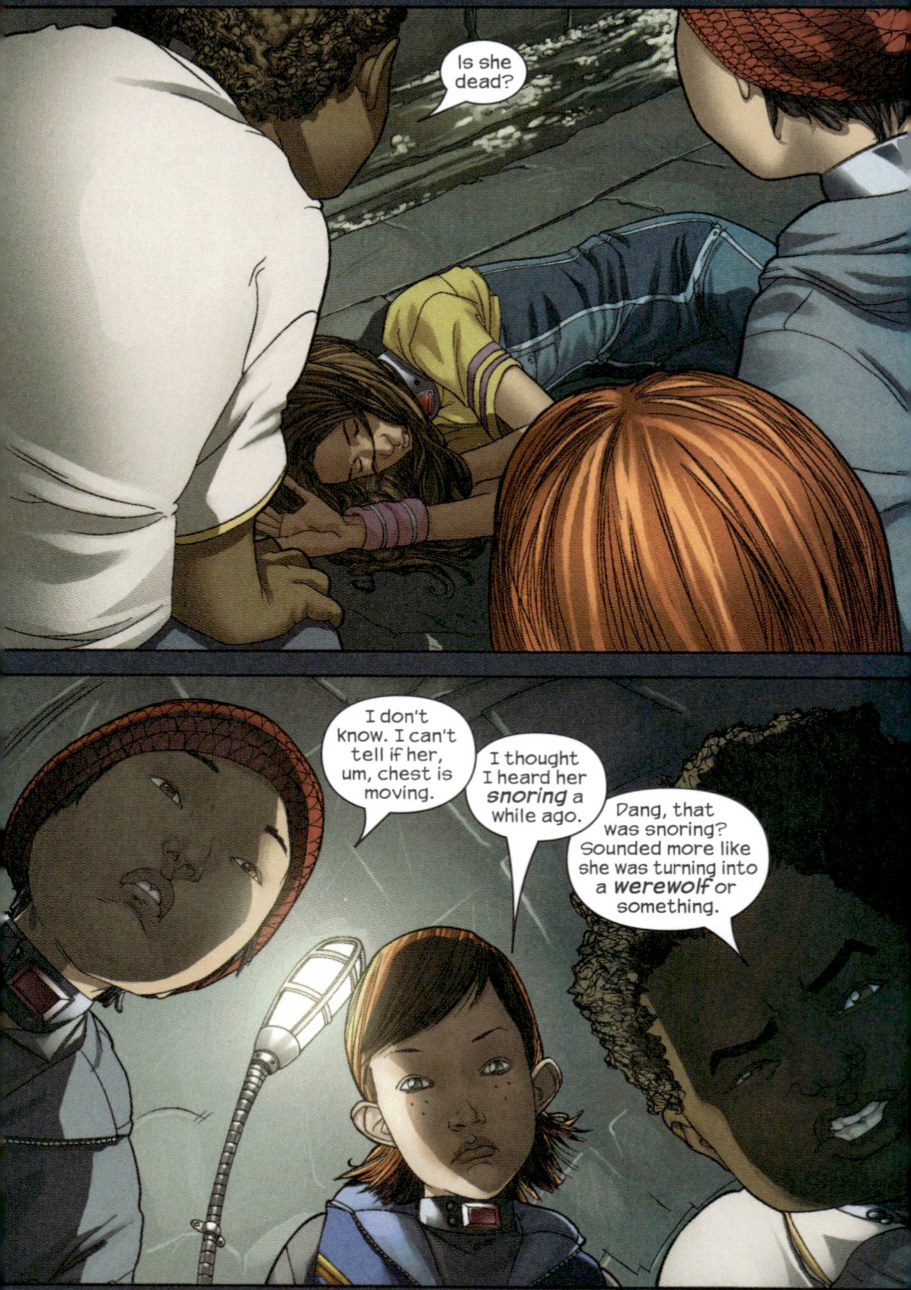
Is she dead?
I don't know. I can't tell if her, um, chest is moving.
I thought I heard her *snoring* a while ago.
Dang, that was snoring? Sounded more like she was turning into a *werewolf* or something.

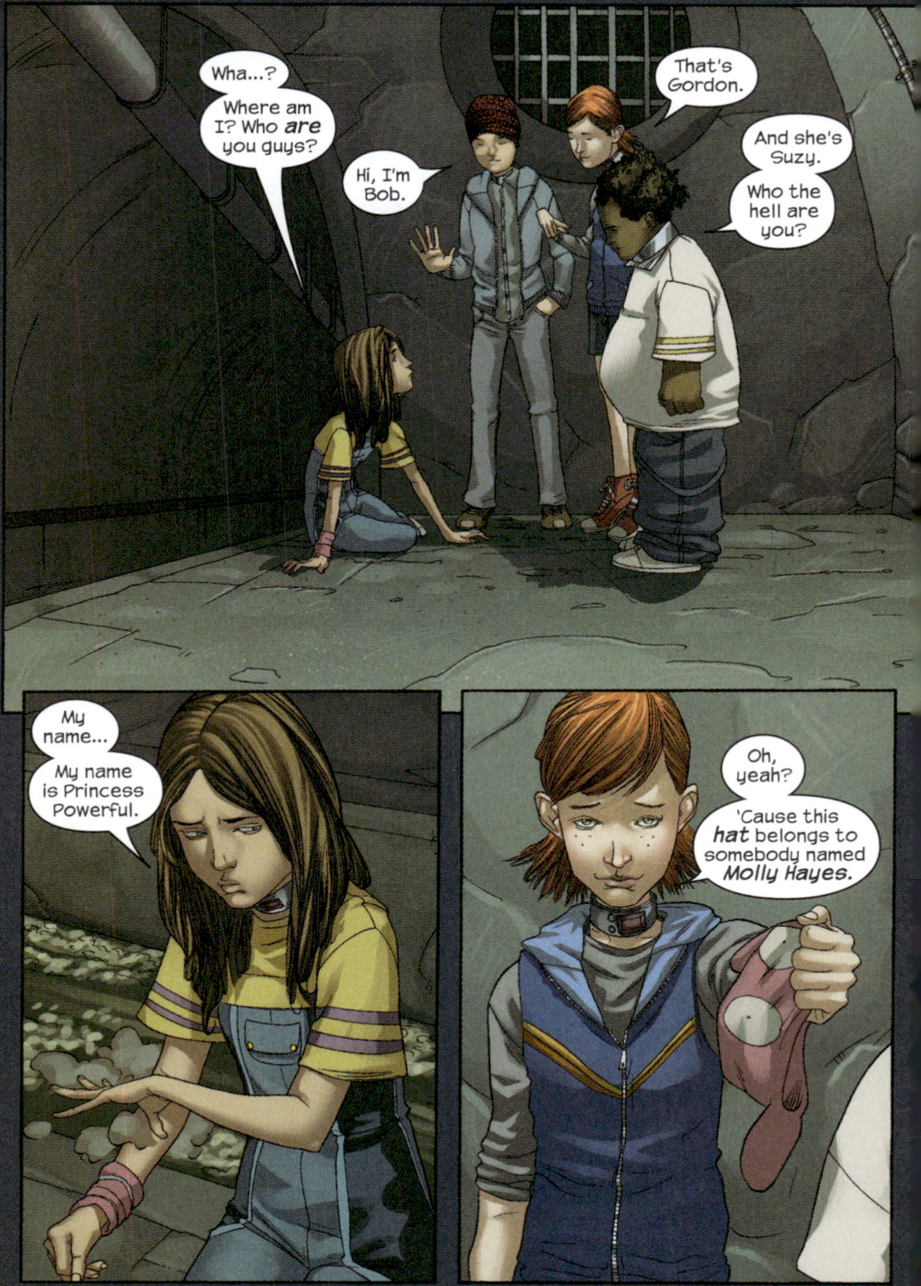

Wha...?
Where am I? Who *are* you guys?
Hi, I'm Bob.
That's Gordon.
And she's Suzy.
Who the hell are you?
My name...
My name is Princess Powerful.
Oh, yeah?
'Cause this *hat* belongs to somebody named *Molly Hayes.*

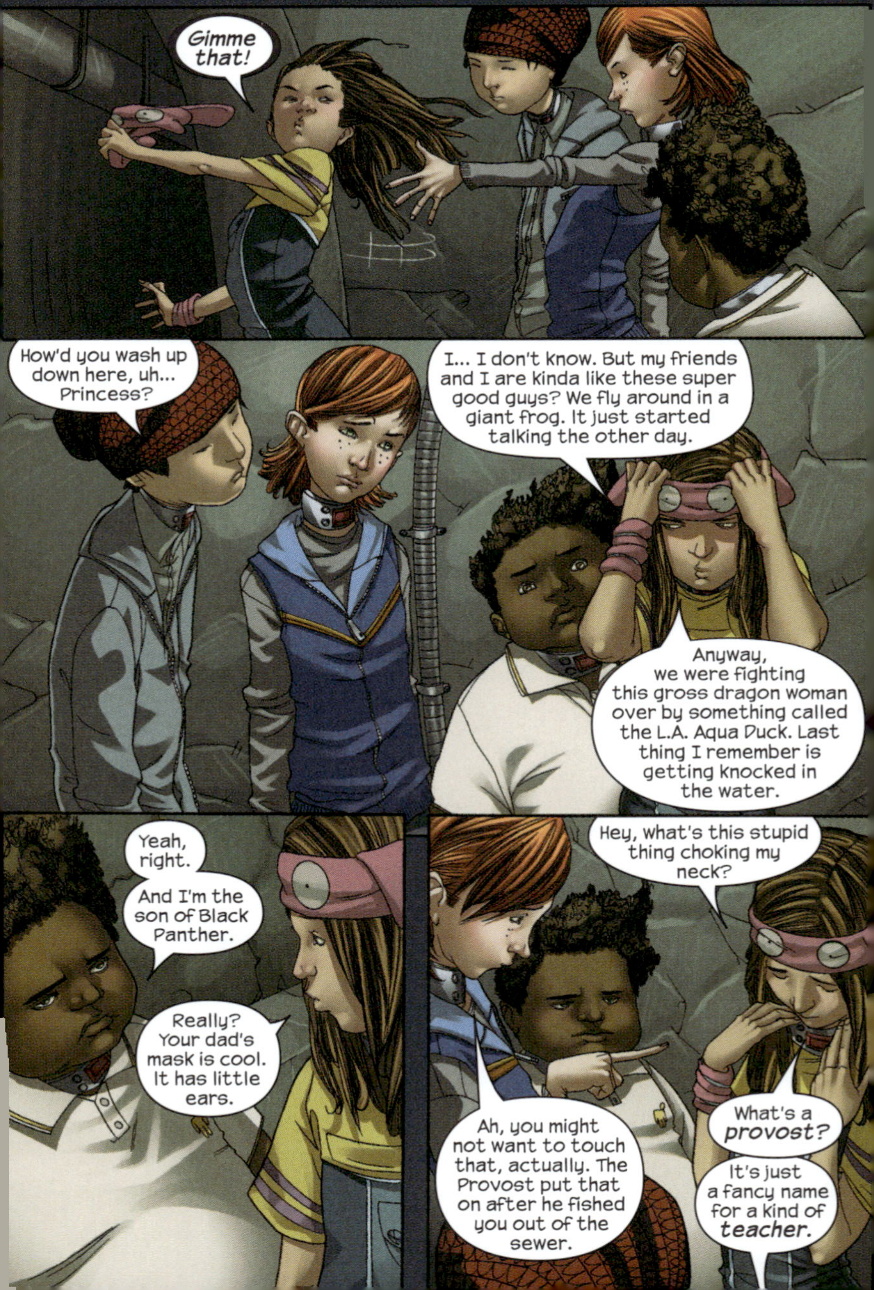

Gimme that!
How'd you wash up down here, uh... Princess?
I... I don't know. But my friends and I are kinda like these super good guys? We fly around in a giant frog. It just started talking the other day.
Anyway, we were fighting this gross dragon woman over by something called the L.A. Aqua Duck. Last thing I remember is getting knocked in the water.
Yeah, right.
And I'm the son of Black Panther.
Really? Your dad's mask is cool. It has little ears.
Hey, what's this stupid thing choking my neck?
Ah, you might not want to touch that, actually. The Provost put that on after he fished you out of the sewer.
What's a provost?
It's just a fancy name for a kind of teacher.

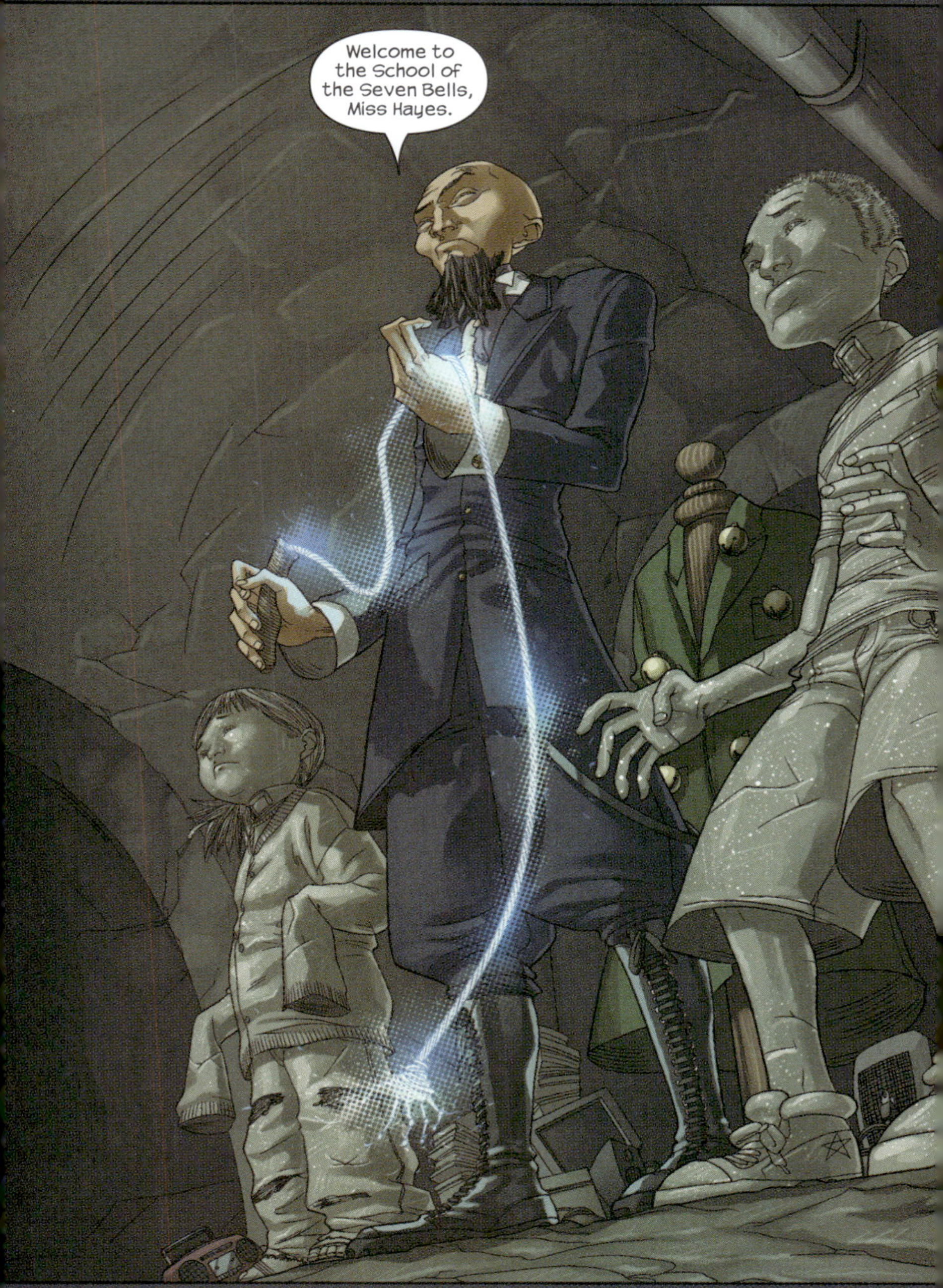
Welcome to the School of the Seven Bells, Miss Hayes.

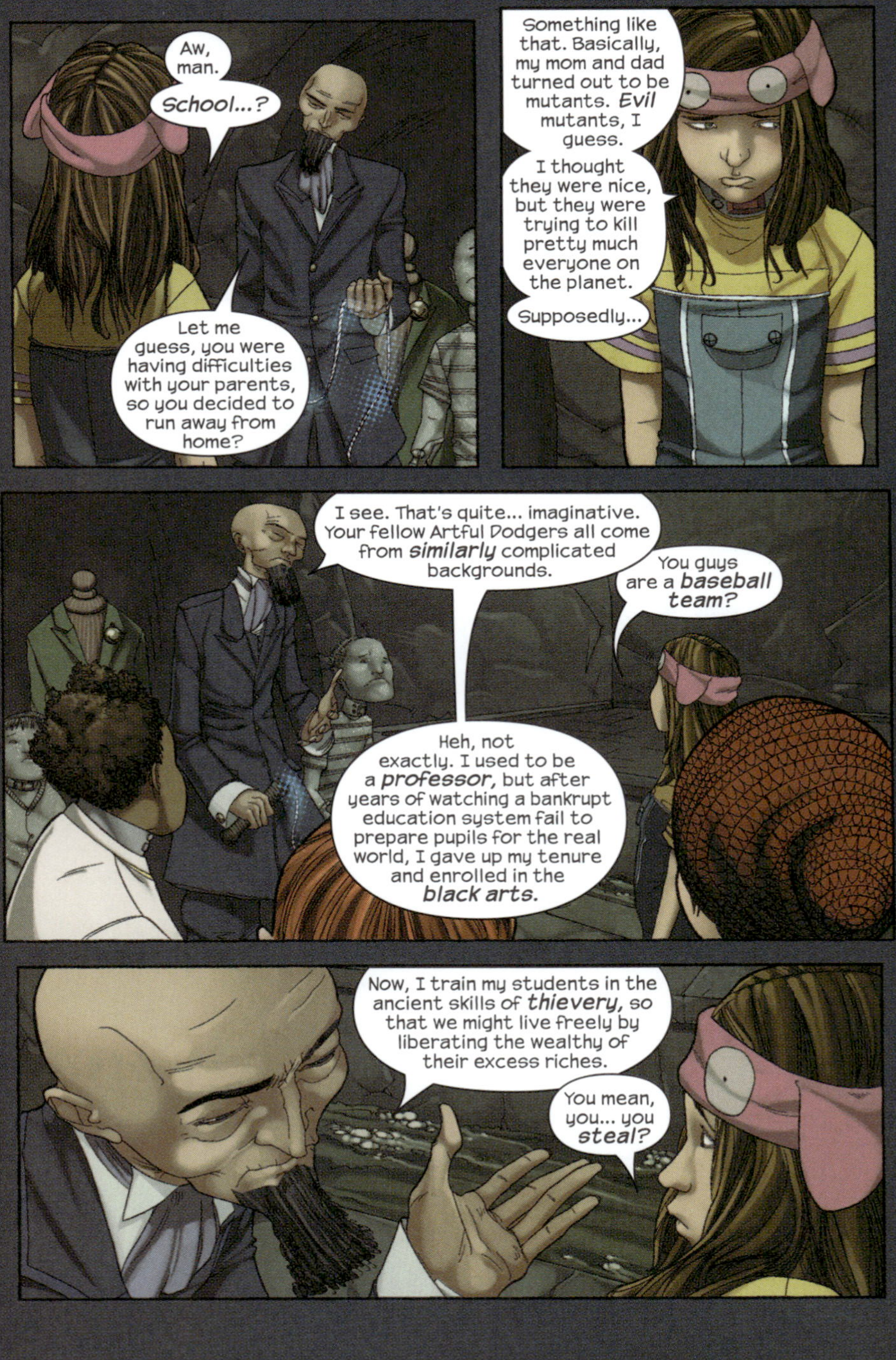
Aw, man.
School...?
Let me guess, you were having difficulties with your parents, so you decided to run away from home?
Something like that. Basically, my mom and dad turned out to be mutants. Evil mutants, I guess.
I thought they were nice, but they were trying to kill pretty much everyone on the planet.
Supposedly...
I see. That's quite... imaginative. Your fellow Artful Dodgers all come from similarly complicated backgrounds.
You guys are a baseball team?
Heh, not exactly. I used to be a professor, but after years of watching a bankrupt education system fail to prepare pupils for the real world, I gave up my tenure and enrolled in the black arts.
Now, I train my students in the ancient skills of thievery, so that we might live freely by liberating the wealthy of their excess riches.
You mean, you... you steal?

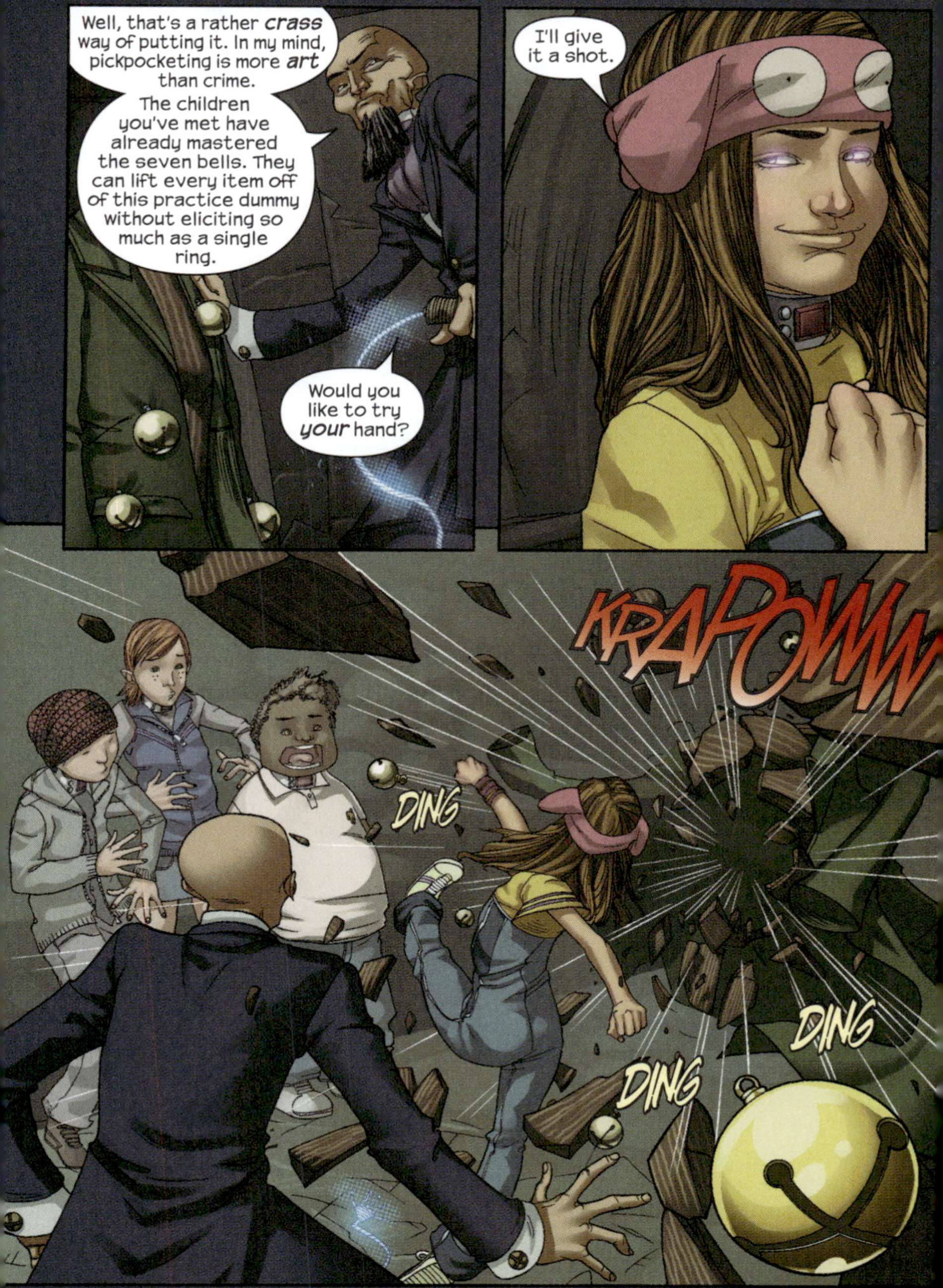
Well, that's a rather *crass* way of putting it. In my mind, pickpocketing is more *art* than crime.
The children you've met have already mastered the seven bells. They can lift every item off of this practice dummy without eliciting so much as a single ring.
Would you like to try *your* hand?
I'll give it a shot.
KRAPOWW
DING
DING
DING

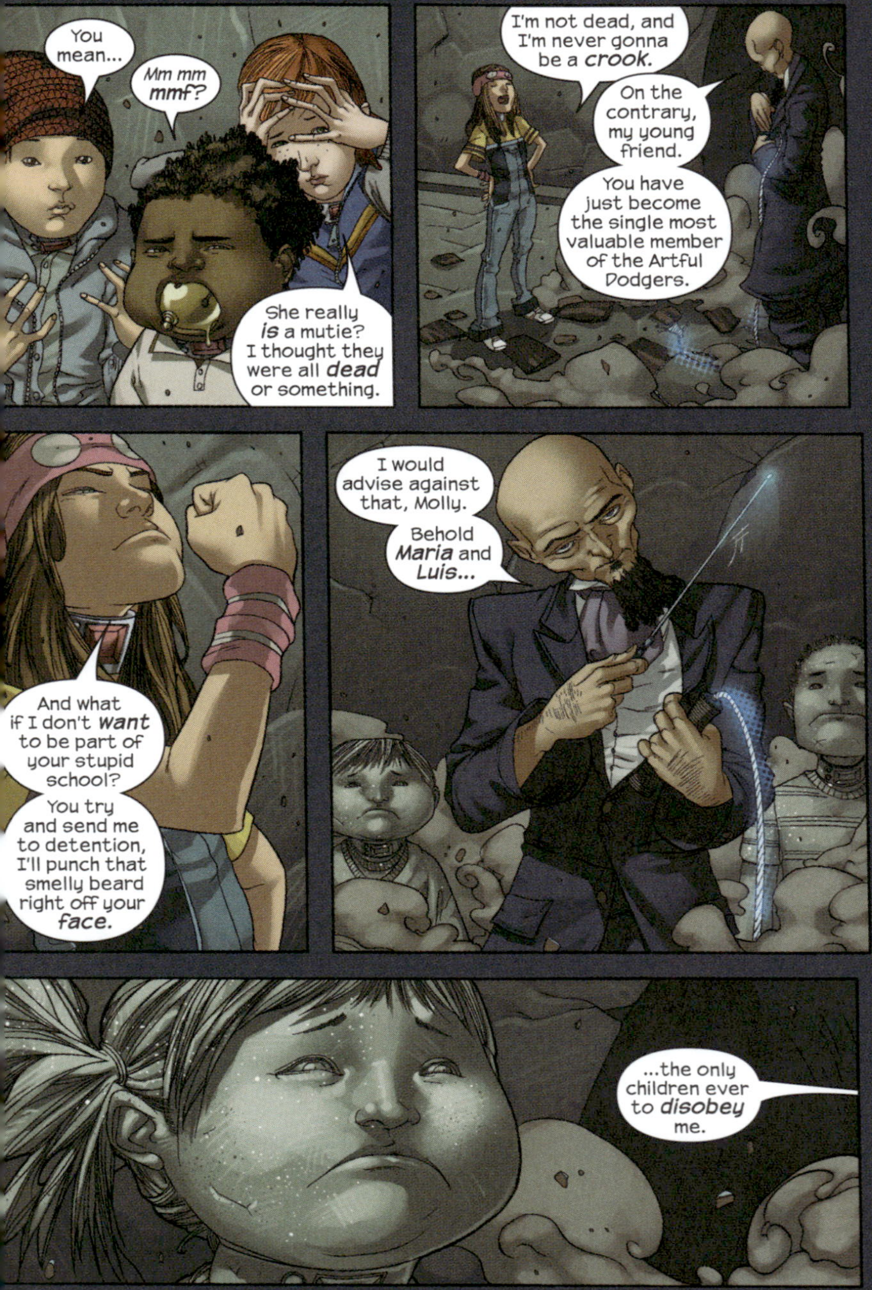
You mean...
Mm mm mmf?
She really is a mutie? I thought they were all dead or something.
I'm not dead, and I'm never gonna be a crook.
On the contrary, my young friend.
You have just become the single most valuable member of the Artful Dodgers.
And what if I don't want to be part of your stupid school?
You try and send me to detention, I'll punch that smelly beard right off your face.
I would advise against that, Molly.
Behold Maria and Luis...
...the only children ever to disobey me.

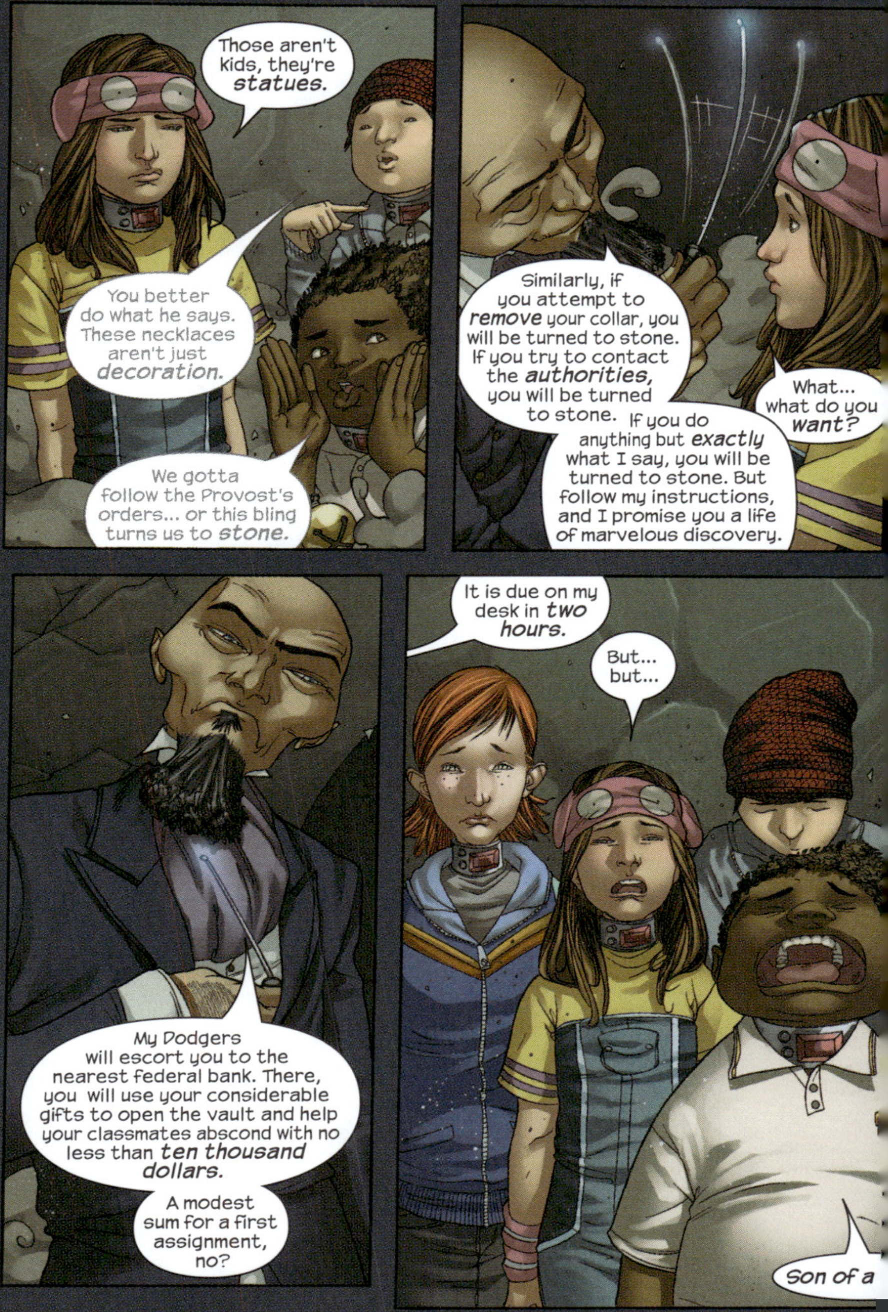
Those aren't kids, they're *statues.*
You better do what he says. These necklaces aren't just *decoration.*
We gotta follow the Provost's orders... or this bling turns us to *stone.*
Similarly, if you attempt to *remove* your collar, you will be turned to stone. If you try to contact the *authorities,* you will be turned to stone.
If you do anything but *exactly* what I say, you will be turned to stone. But follow my instructions, and I promise you a life of marvelous discovery.
What... what do you *want?*
My Dodgers will escort you to the nearest federal bank. There, you will use your considerable gifts to open the vault and help your classmates abscond with no less than *ten thousand dollars.*
A modest sum for a first assignment, no?
It is due on my desk in *two hours.*
But... but...
Son of a

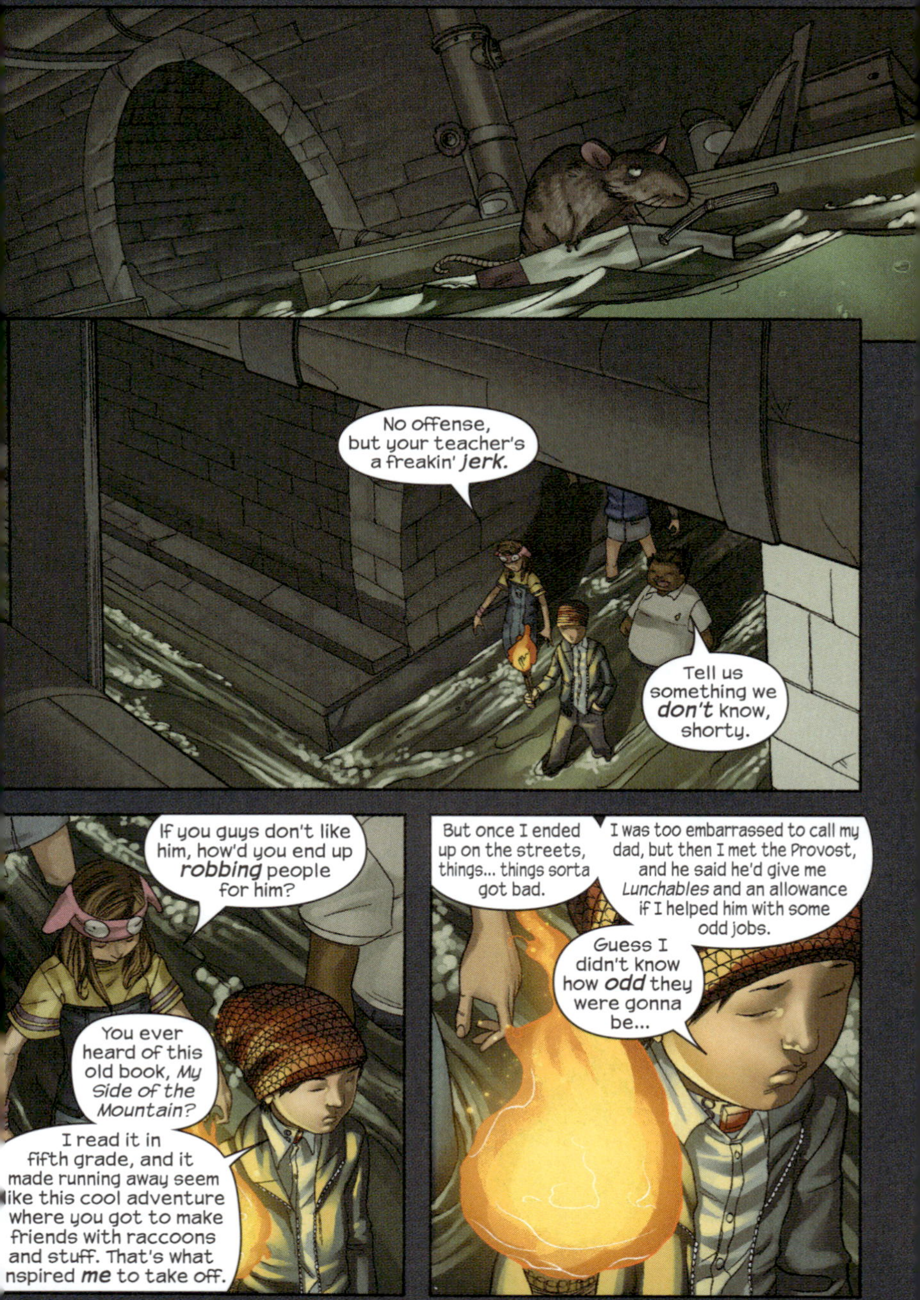

No offense, but your teacher's a freakin' *jerk.*
Tell us something we *don't* know, shorty.
If you guys don't like him, how'd you end up *robbing* people for him?
You ever heard of this old book, *My Side of the Mountain*?
I read it in fifth grade, and it made running away seem like this cool adventure where you got to make friends with raccoons and stuff. That's what nspired *me* to take off.
But once I ended up on the streets, things... things sorta got bad.
I was too embarrassed to call my dad, but then I met the Provost, and he said he'd give me *Lunchables* and an allowance if I helped him with some odd jobs.
Guess I didn't know how *odd* they were gonna be...

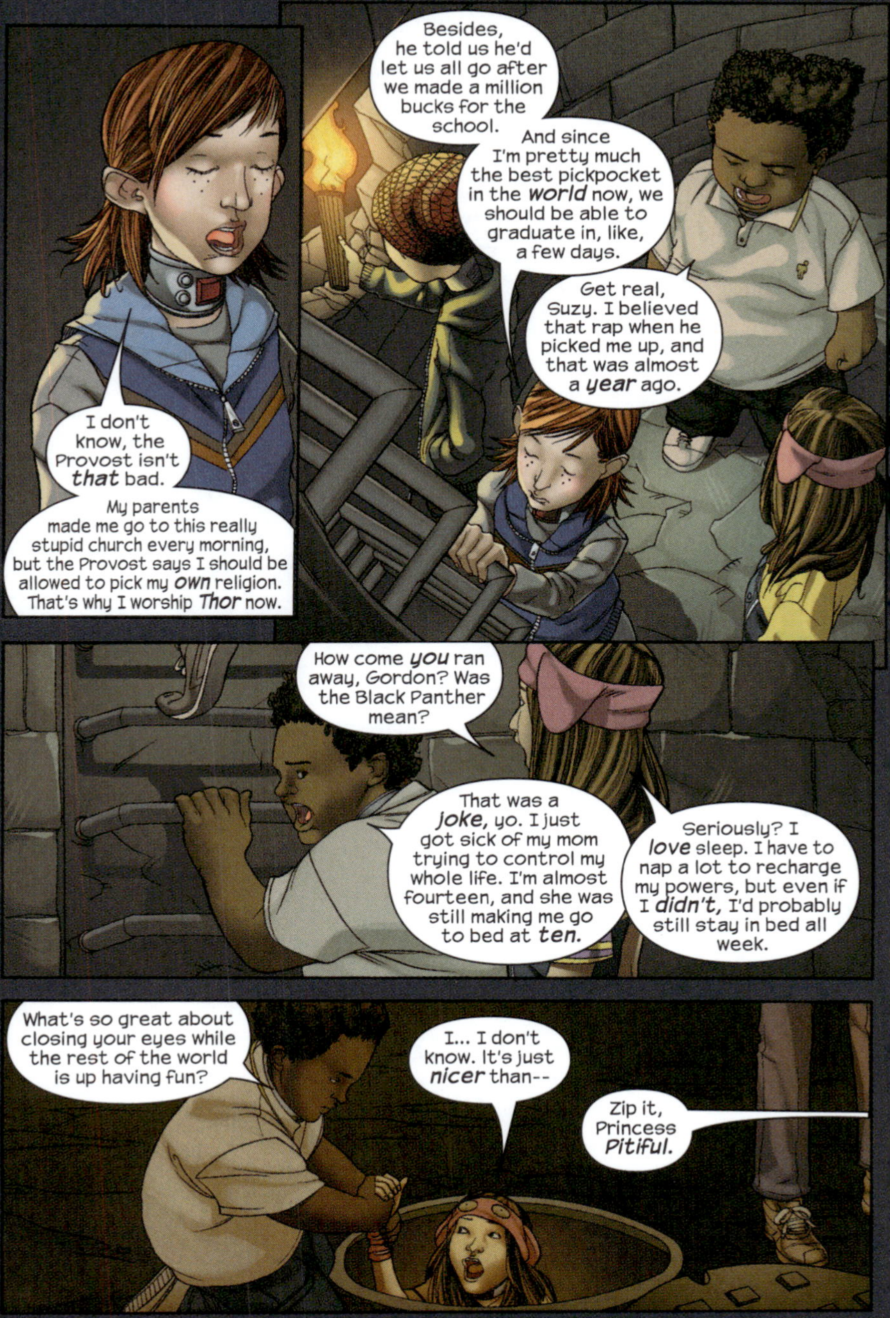
Besides, he told us he'd let us all go after we made a million bucks for the school.
And since I'm pretty much the best pickpocket in the *world* now, we should be able to graduate in, like, a few days.
Get real, Suzy. I believed that rap when he picked me up, and that was almost a *year* ago.
I don't know, the Provost isn't *that* bad.
My parents made me go to this really stupid church every morning, but the Provost says I should be allowed to pick my *own* religion. That's why I worship *Thor* now.
How come *you* ran away, Gordon? Was the Black Panther mean?
That was a *joke,* yo. I just got sick of my mom trying to control my whole life. I'm almost fourteen, and she was still making me go to bed at *ten.*
Seriously? I *love* sleep. I have to nap a lot to recharge my powers, but even if I *didn't,* I'd probably still stay in bed all week.
What's so great about closing your eyes while the rest of the world is up having fun?
I... I don't know. It's just *nicer* than--
Zip it, Princess *Pitiful.*

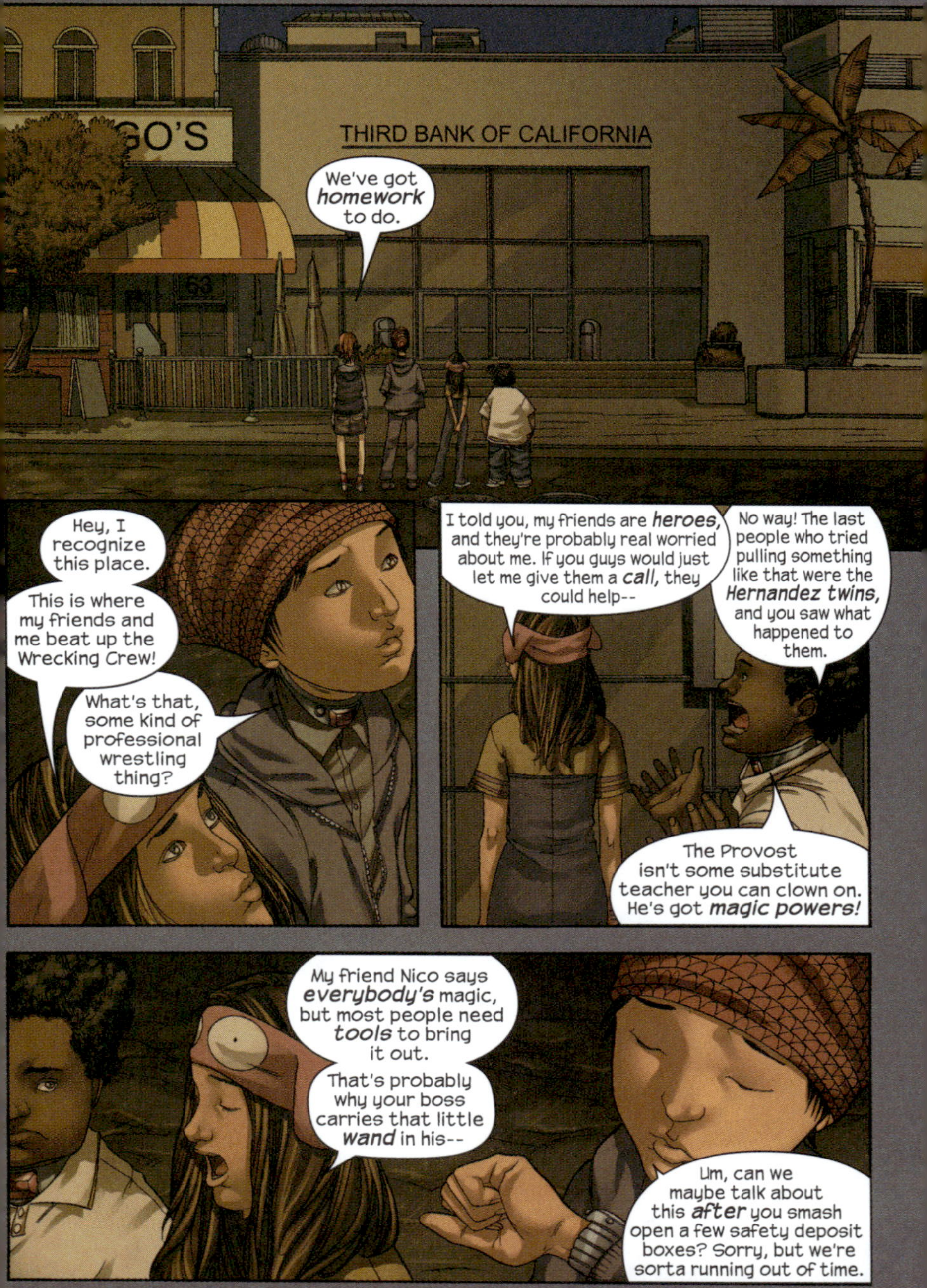
THIRD BANK OF CALIFORNIA
GO'S
We've got homework to do.
Hey, I recognize this place.
This is where my friends and me beat up the Wrecking Crew!
What's that, some kind of professional wrestling thing?
I told you, my friends are heroes, and they're probably real worried about me. If you guys would just let me give them a call, they could help--
No way! The last people who tried pulling something like that were the Hernandez twins, and you saw what happened to them.
The Provost isn't some substitute teacher you can clown on. He's got magic powers!
My friend Nico says everybody's magic, but most people need tools to bring it out.
That's probably why your boss carries that little wand in his--
Um, can we maybe talk about this after you smash open a few safety deposit boxes? Sorry, but we're sorta running out of time.

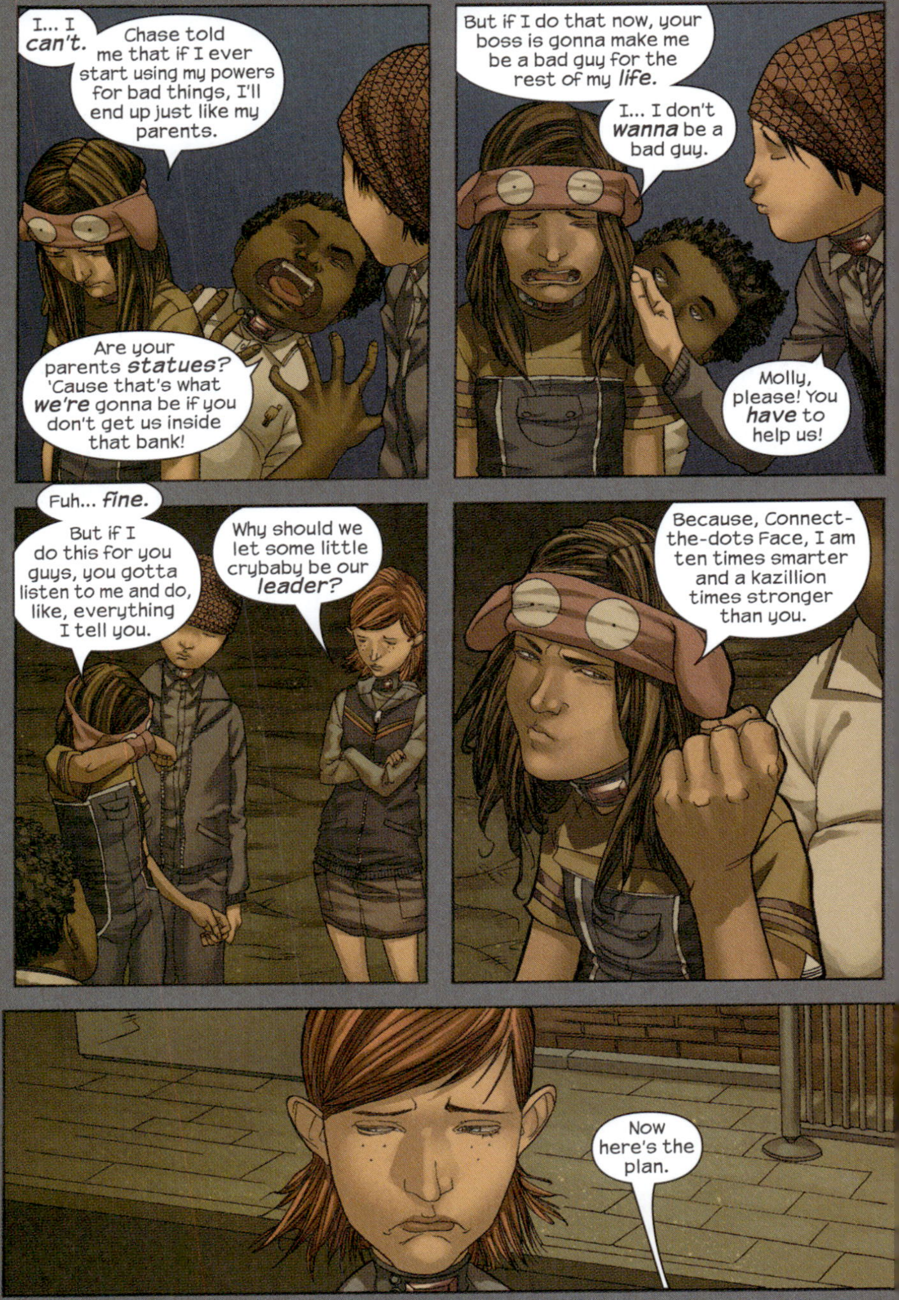
I... I can't.
Chase told me that if I ever start using my powers for bad things, I'll end up just like my parents.
Are your parents statues? 'Cause that's what we're gonna be if you don't get us inside that bank!
But if I do that now, your boss is gonna make me be a bad guy for the rest of my life.
I... I don't wanna be a bad guy.
Molly, please! You have to help us!
Fuh... fine.
But if I do this for you guys, you gotta listen to me and do, like, everything I tell you.
Why should we let some little crybaby be our leader?
Because, Connect-the-dots Face, I am ten times smarter and a kazillion times stronger than you.
Now here's the plan.

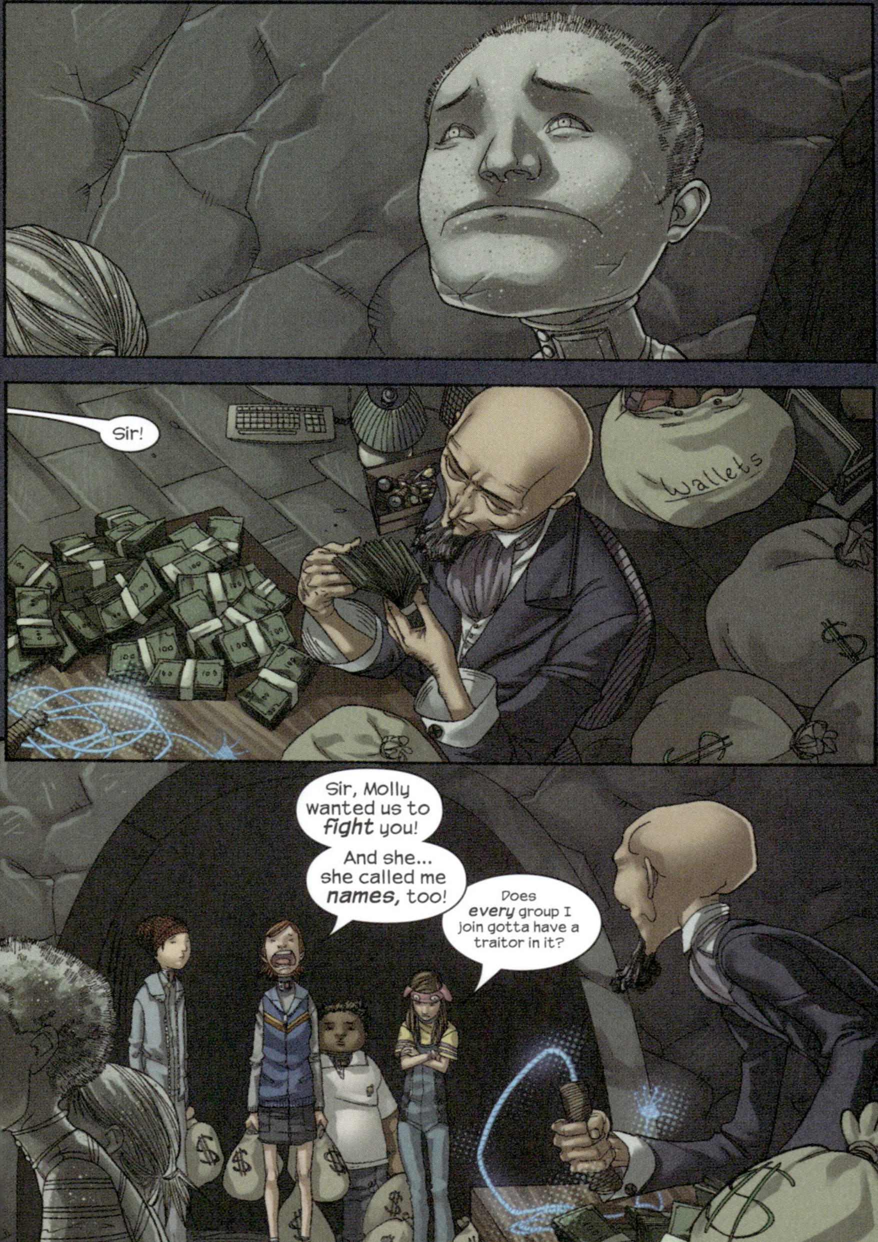
Sir!
Wallets
Sir, Molly wanted us to *fight* you!
And she... she called me *names,* too!
Does *every* group I join gotta have a traitor in it?

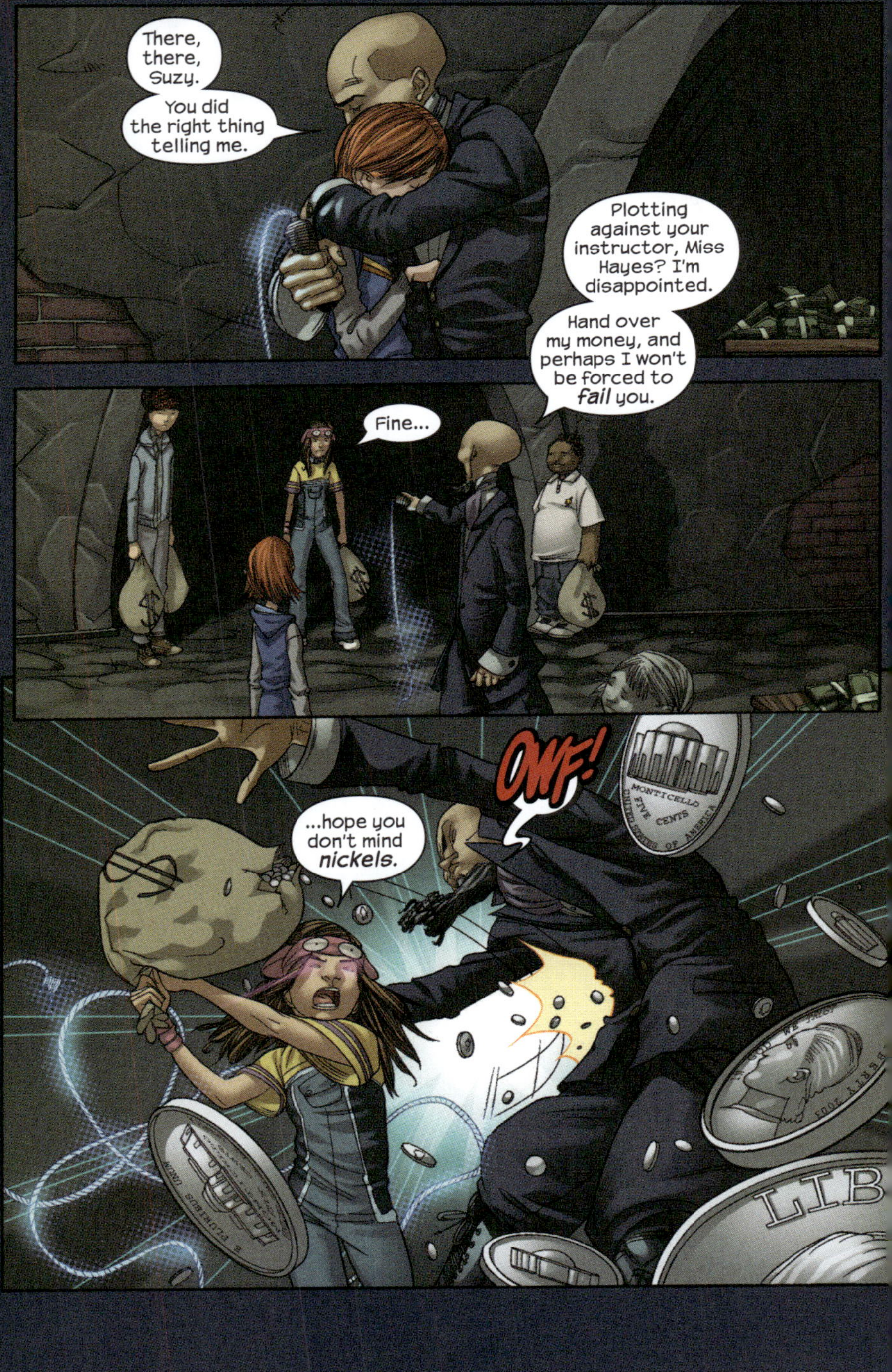
There, there, Suzy.
You did the right thing telling me.
Plotting against your instructor, Miss Hayes? I'm disappointed.
Hand over my money, and perhaps I won't be forced to *fail* you.
Fine...
...hope you don't mind *nickels.*
OWF!

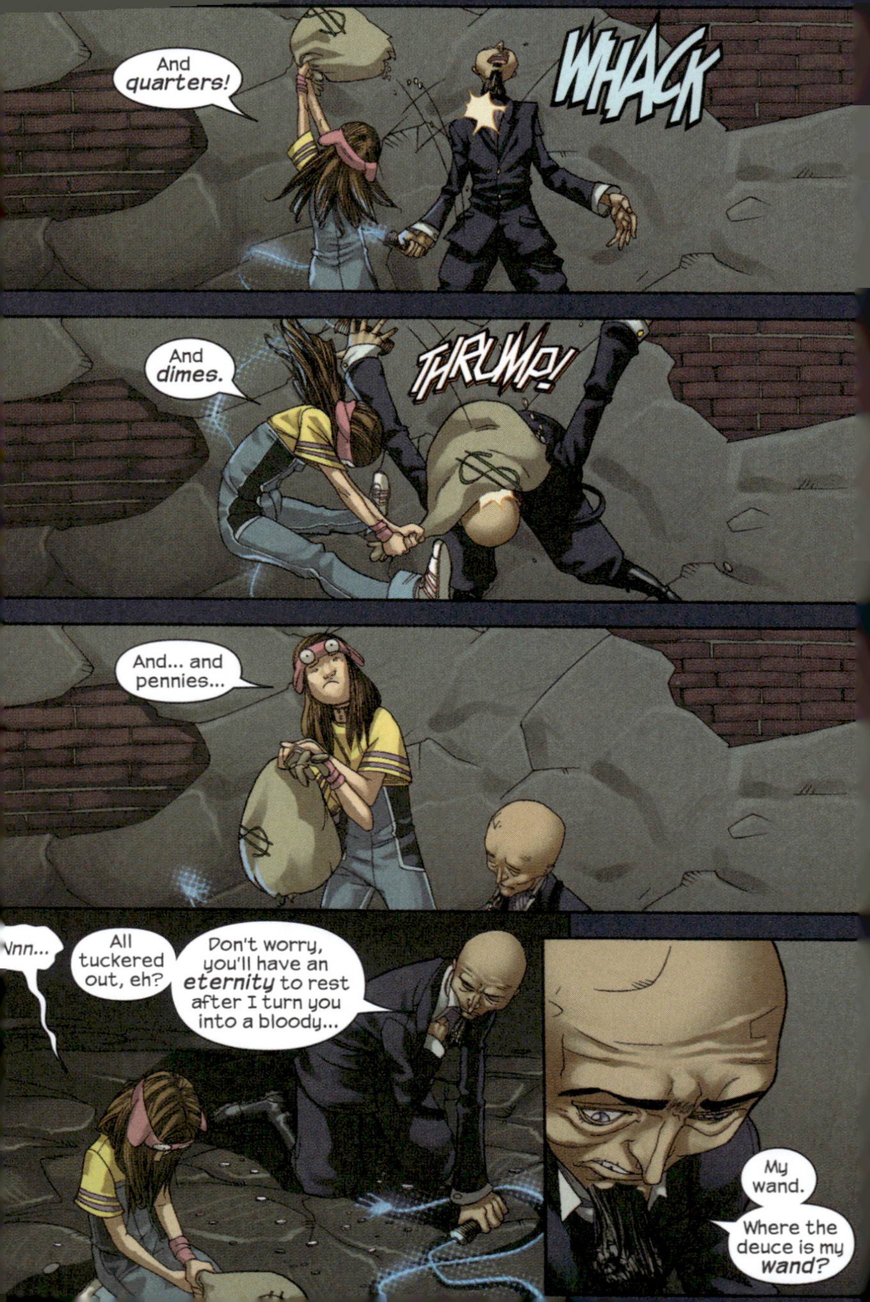
And *quarters!*
WHACK
And *dimes.*
THRUMP!
And... and pennies...
Vnn...
All tuckered out, eh?
Don't worry, you'll have an *eternity* to rest after I turn you into a bloody...
My wand.
Where the deuce is my *wand?*

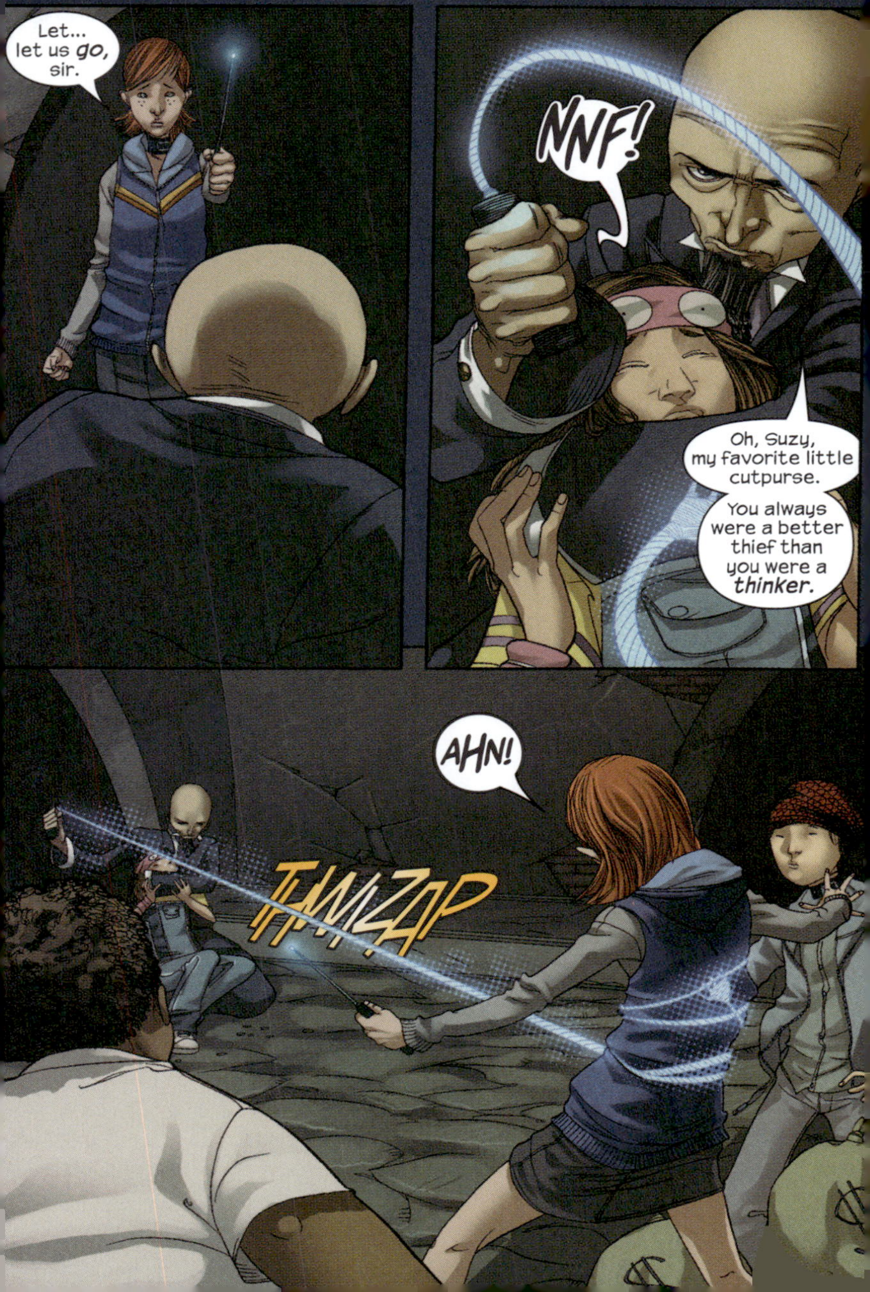
Let... let us go, sir.
NNF!
Oh, Suzy, my favorite little cutpurse.
You always were a better thief than you were a thinker.
AHN!
THWIZAP

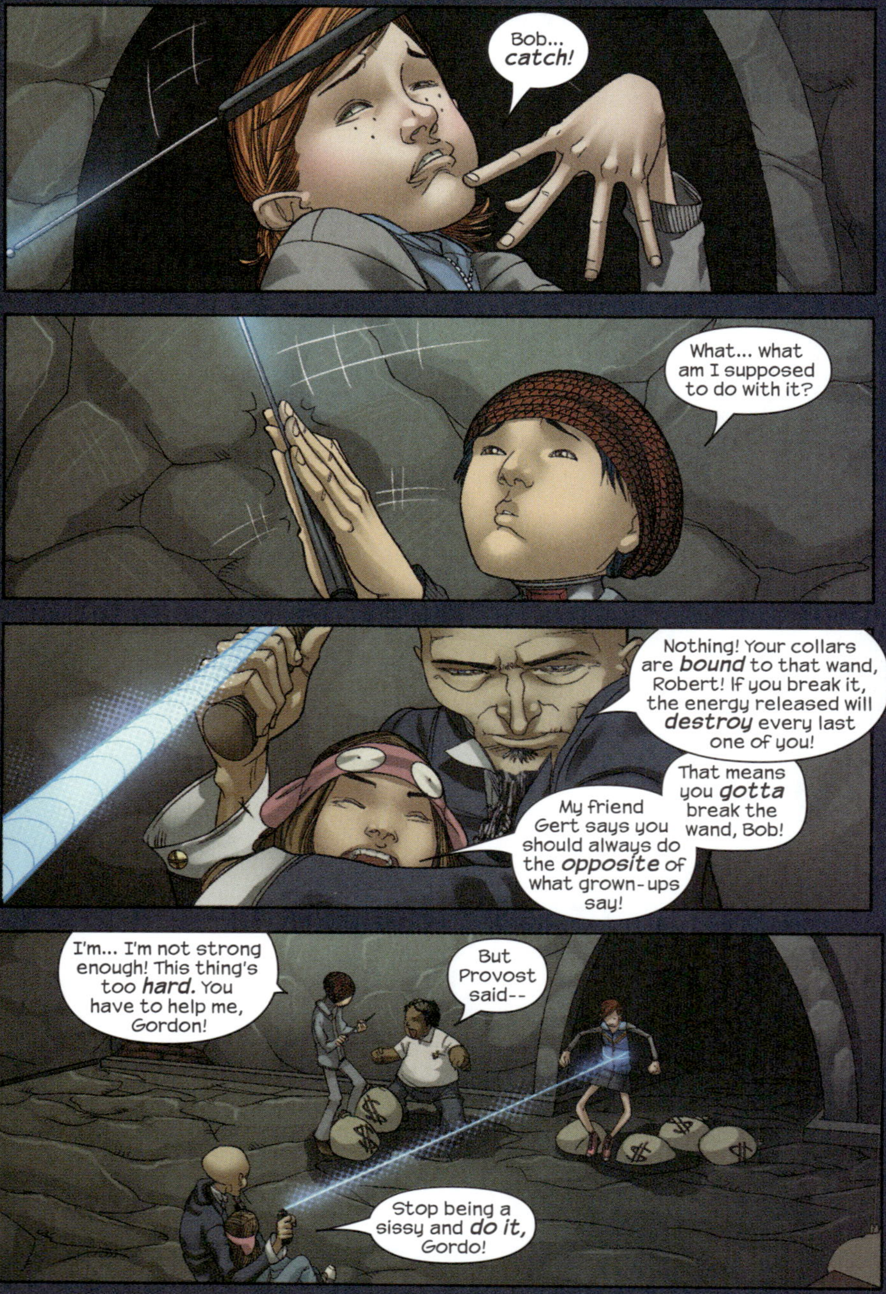
Bob... catch!
What... what am I supposed to do with it?
Nothing! Your collars are bound to that wand, Robert! If you break it, the energy released will destroy every last one of you!
That means you gotta break the wand, Bob!
My friend Gert says you should always do the opposite of what grown-ups say!
I'm... I'm not strong enough! This thing's too hard. You have to help me, Gordon!
But Provost said--
Stop being a sissy and do it, Gordo!

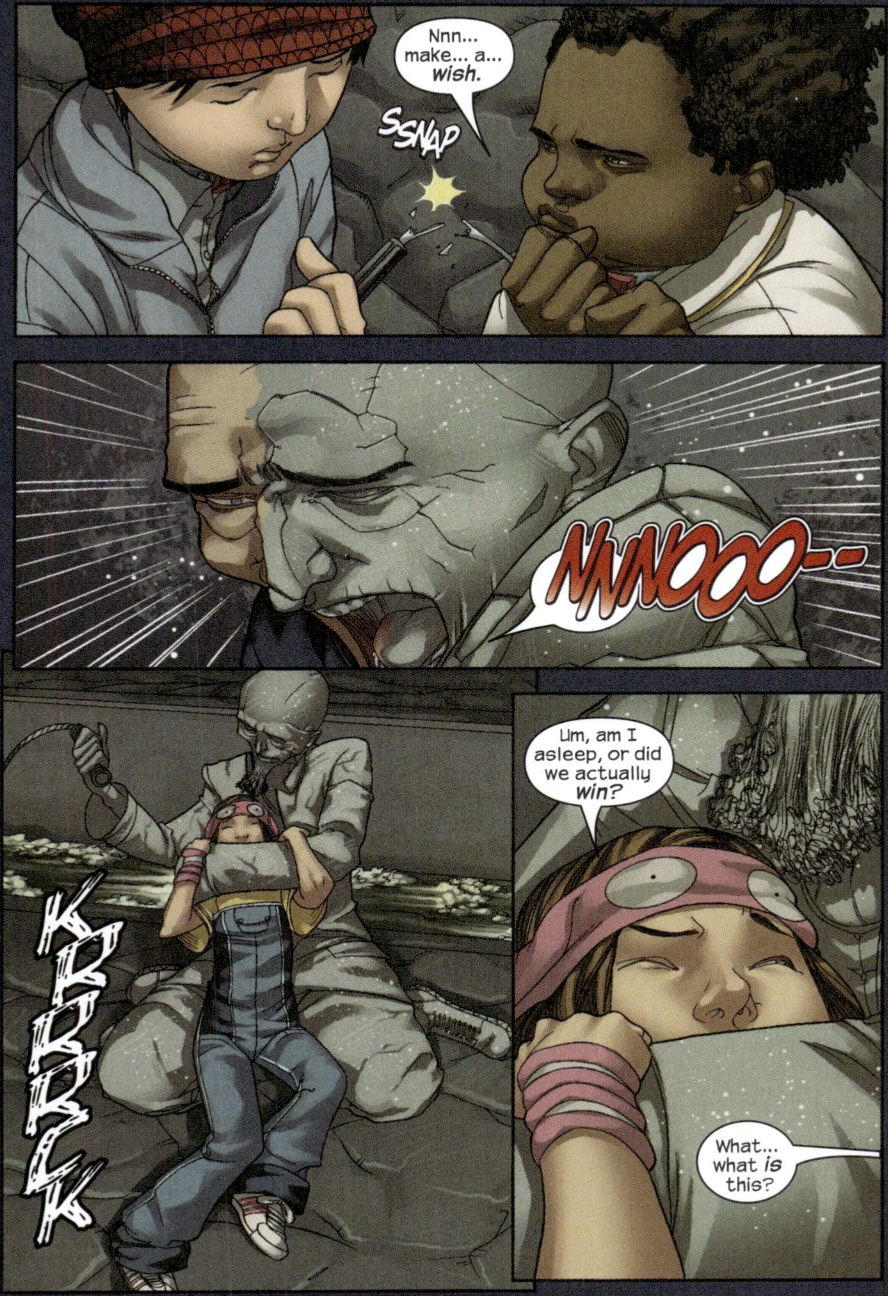
Nnn... make... a... *wish.*
SSNAP
NNNOOO--
KRRRCK
Um, am I asleep, or did we actually *win?*
What... what *is* this?

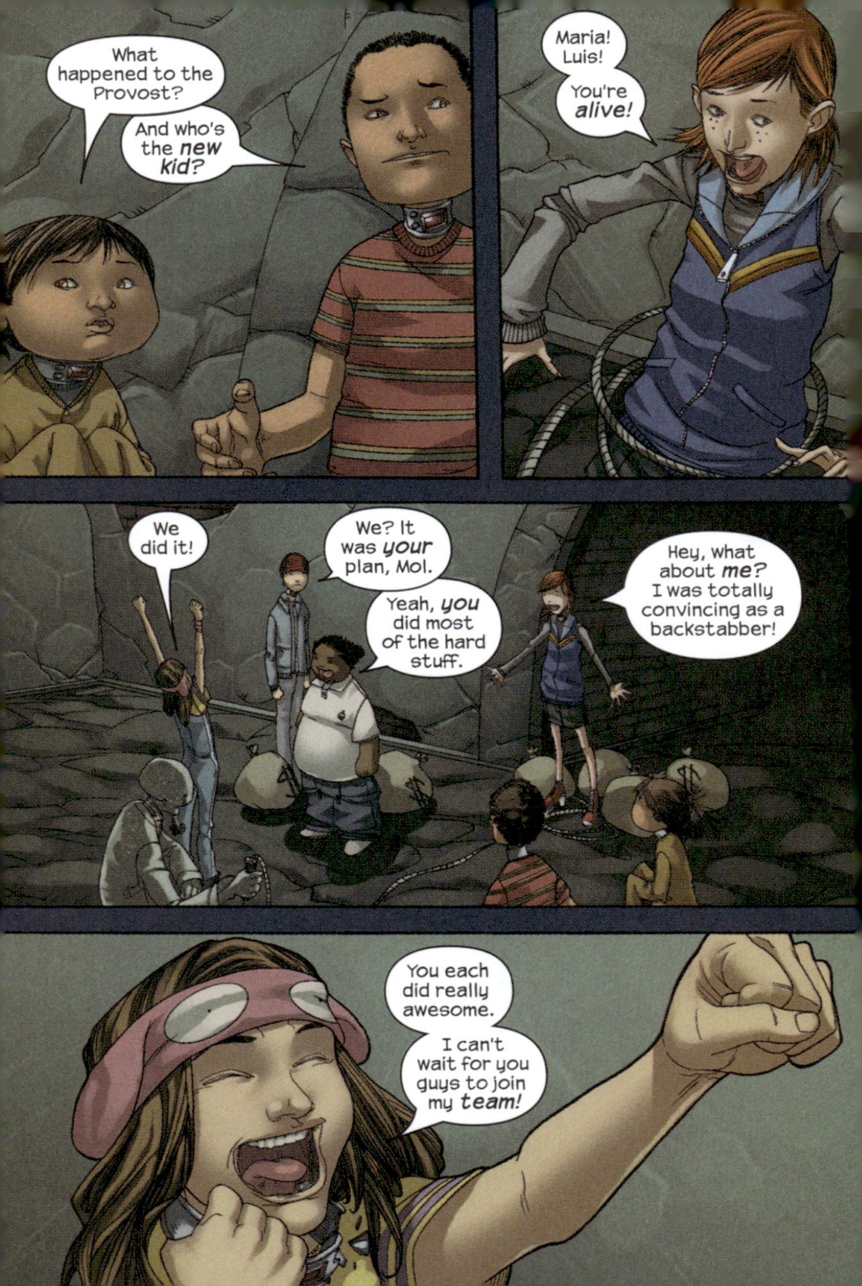
What happened to the Provost?
And who's the *new* kid?
Maria! Luis!
You're *alive!*
We did it!
We? It was *your* plan, Mol.
Yeah, *you* did most of the hard stuff.
Hey, what about *me?* I was totally convincing as a backstabber!
You each did really awesome.
I can't wait for you guys to join my *team!*

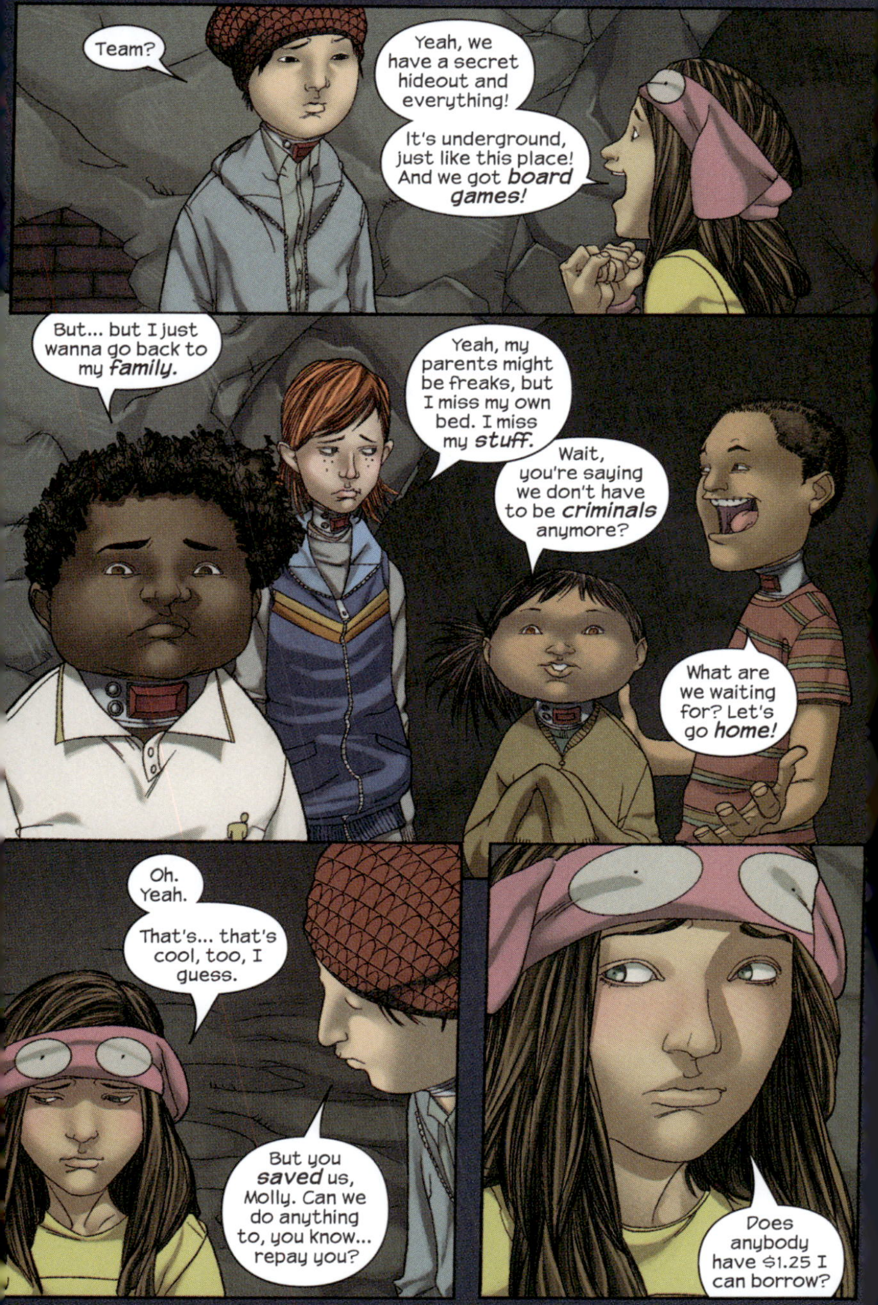
Team?
Yeah, we have a secret hideout and everything!
It's underground, just like this place! And we got **board games!**
But... but I just wanna go back to my **family.**
Yeah, my parents might be freaks, but I miss my own bed. I miss my **stuff.**
Wait, you're saying we don't have to be **criminals** anymore?
What are we waiting for? Let's go **home!**
Oh. Yeah.
That's... that's cool, too, I guess.
But you **saved** us, Molly. Can we do anything to, you know... repay you?
Does anybody have $1.25 I can borrow?

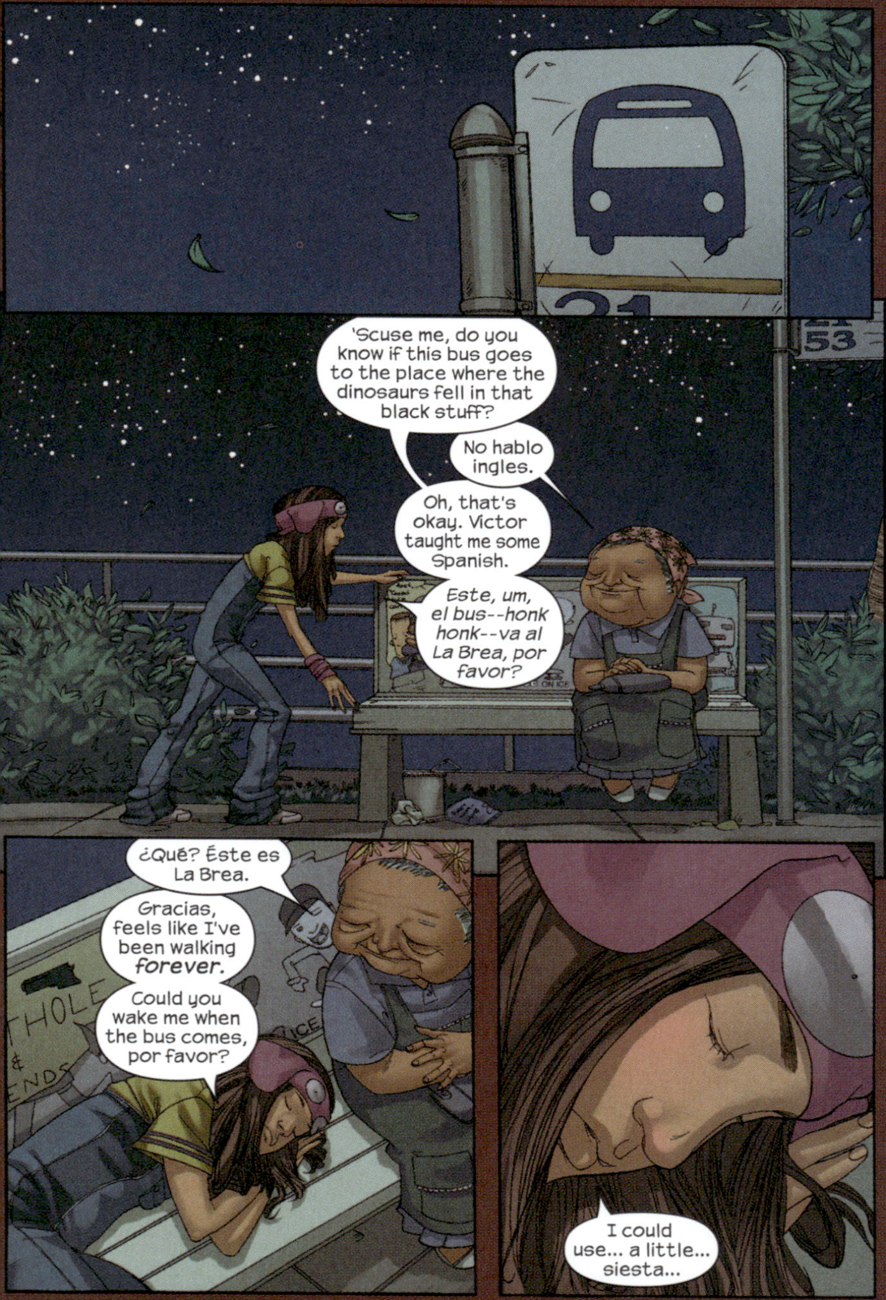
21
21
53
'Scuse me, do you know if this bus goes to the place where the dinosaurs fell in that black stuff?
No hablo ingles.
Oh, that's okay. Victor taught me some Spanish.
Este, um, el bus--honk honk--va al La Brea, por favor?
ON ICE
¿Qué? Éste es La Brea.
Gracias, feels like I've been walking forever.
Could you wake me when the bus comes, por favor?
I could use... a little... siesta...

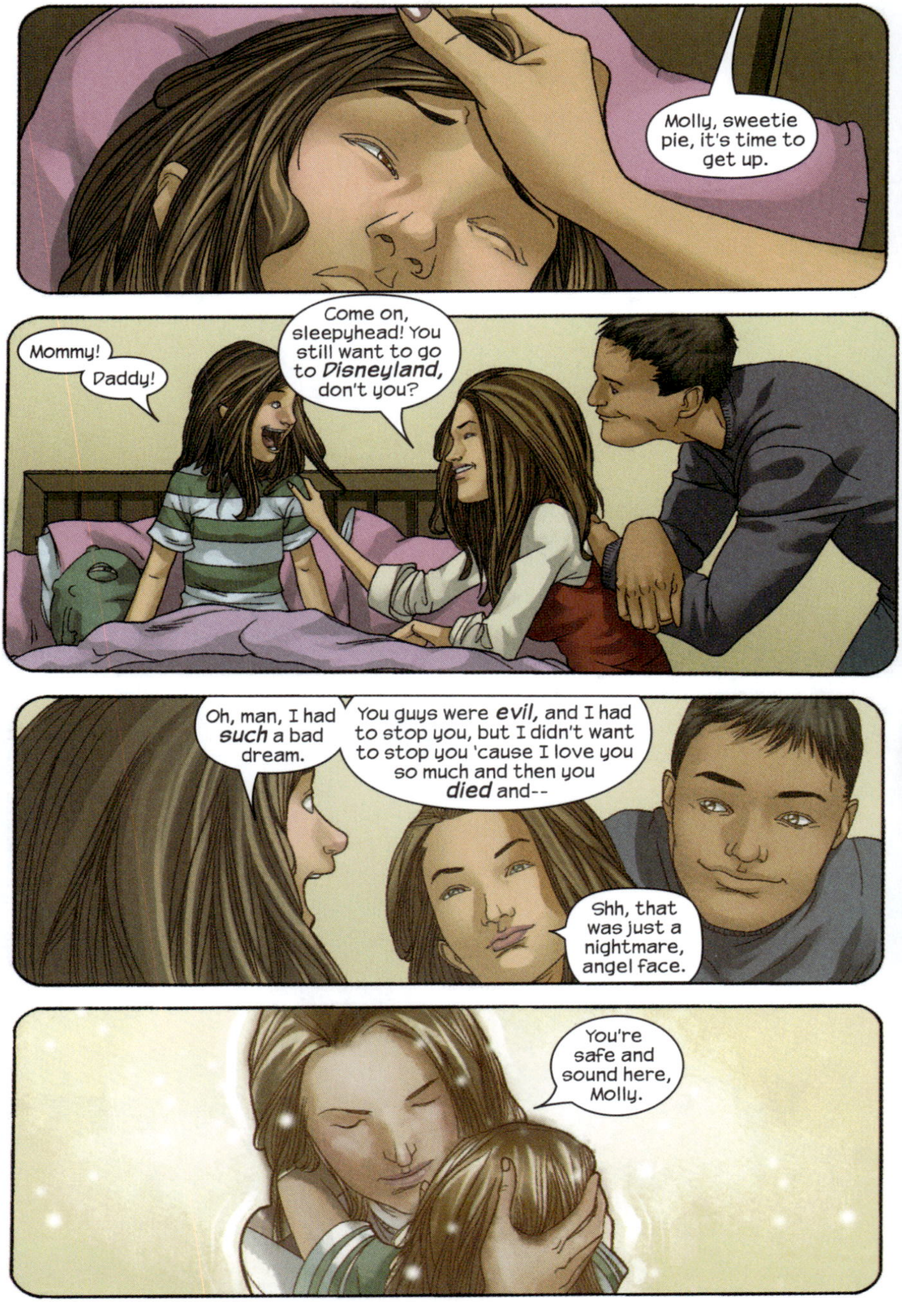
Molly, sweetie pie, it's time to get up.
Mommy!
Daddy!
Come on, sleepyhead! You still want to go to *Disneyland,* don't you?
Oh, man, I had *such* a bad dream.
You guys were *evil,* and I had to stop you, but I didn't want to stop you 'cause I love you so much and then you *died* and--
Shh, that was just a nightmare, angel face.
You're safe and sound here, Molly.

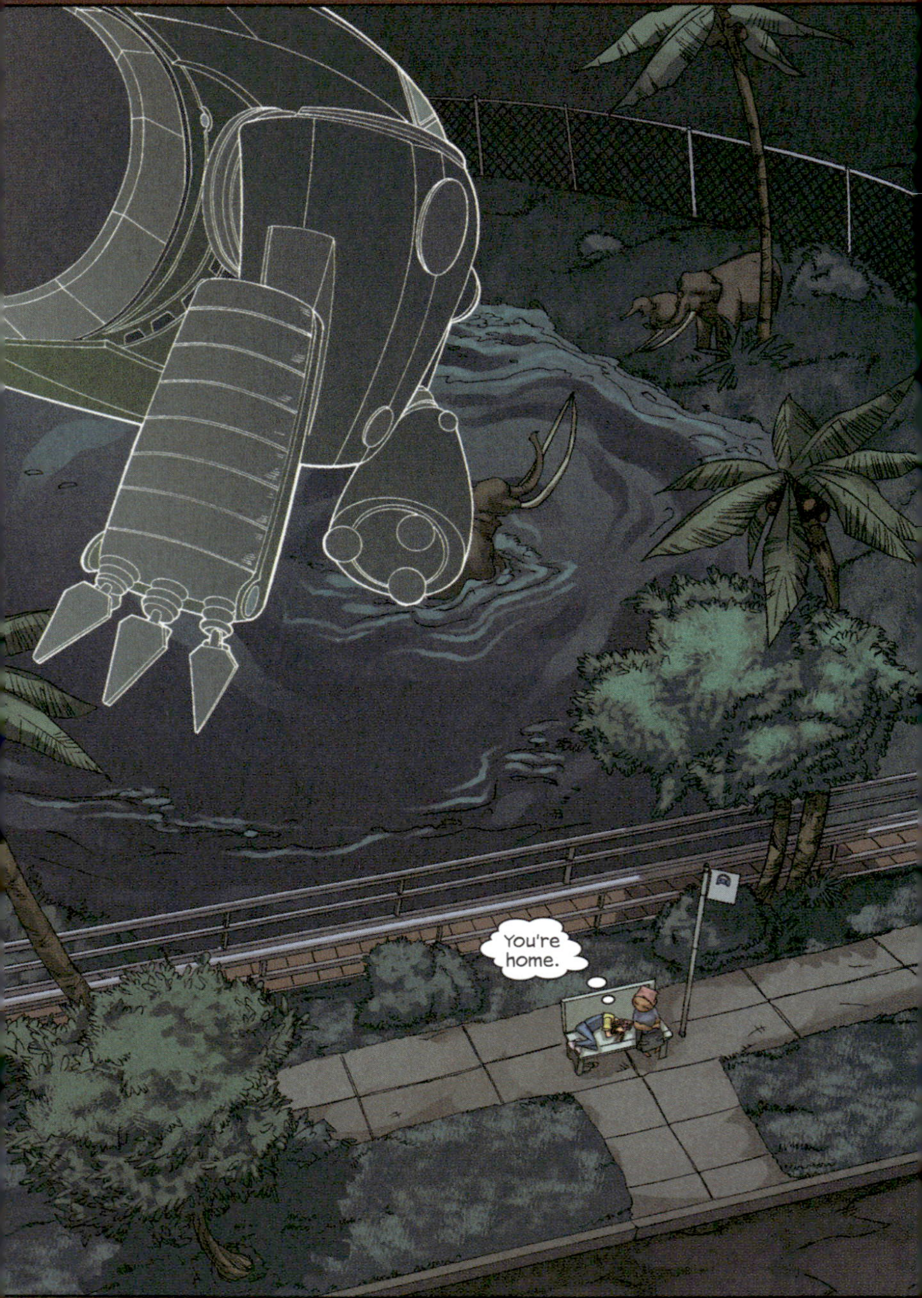
You're home.

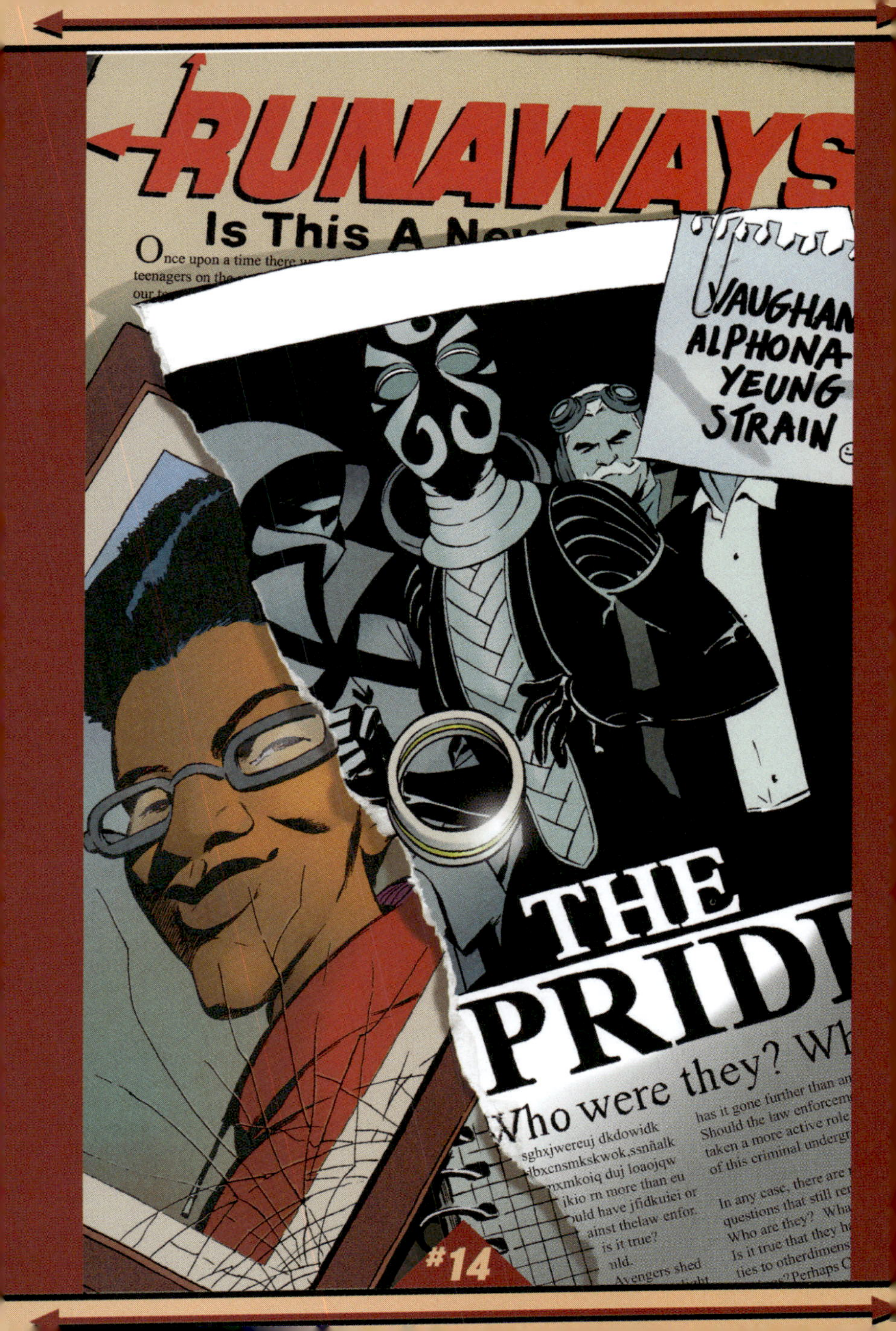
RUNAWAYS
Is This A New
Once upon a time there
teenagers on the
VAUGHAN
ALPHONA
YEUNG
STRAIN
THE
PRID
Who were they? Wh
sghxjwereuj dkdowidk
ikio rn more than eu
ainst thelaw enfor.
is it true?
Avengers shed
has it gone further than an
Should the law enforcem
taken a more active role
of this criminal underg
In any case, there are
questions that still re
Who are they? Wha
Is it true that they h
ties to otherdimens
#14

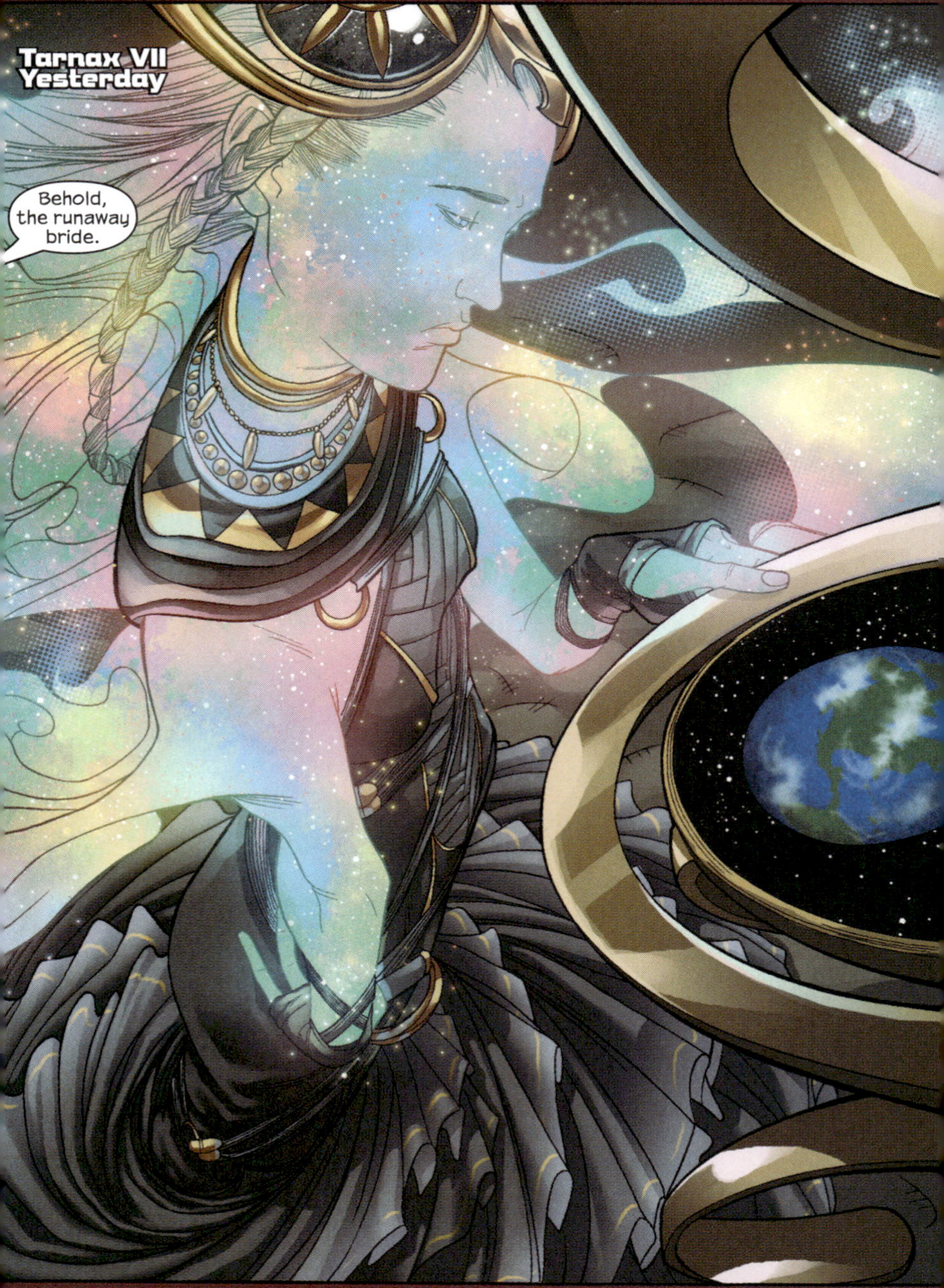
Tarnax VII
Yesterday
Behold, the runaway bride.

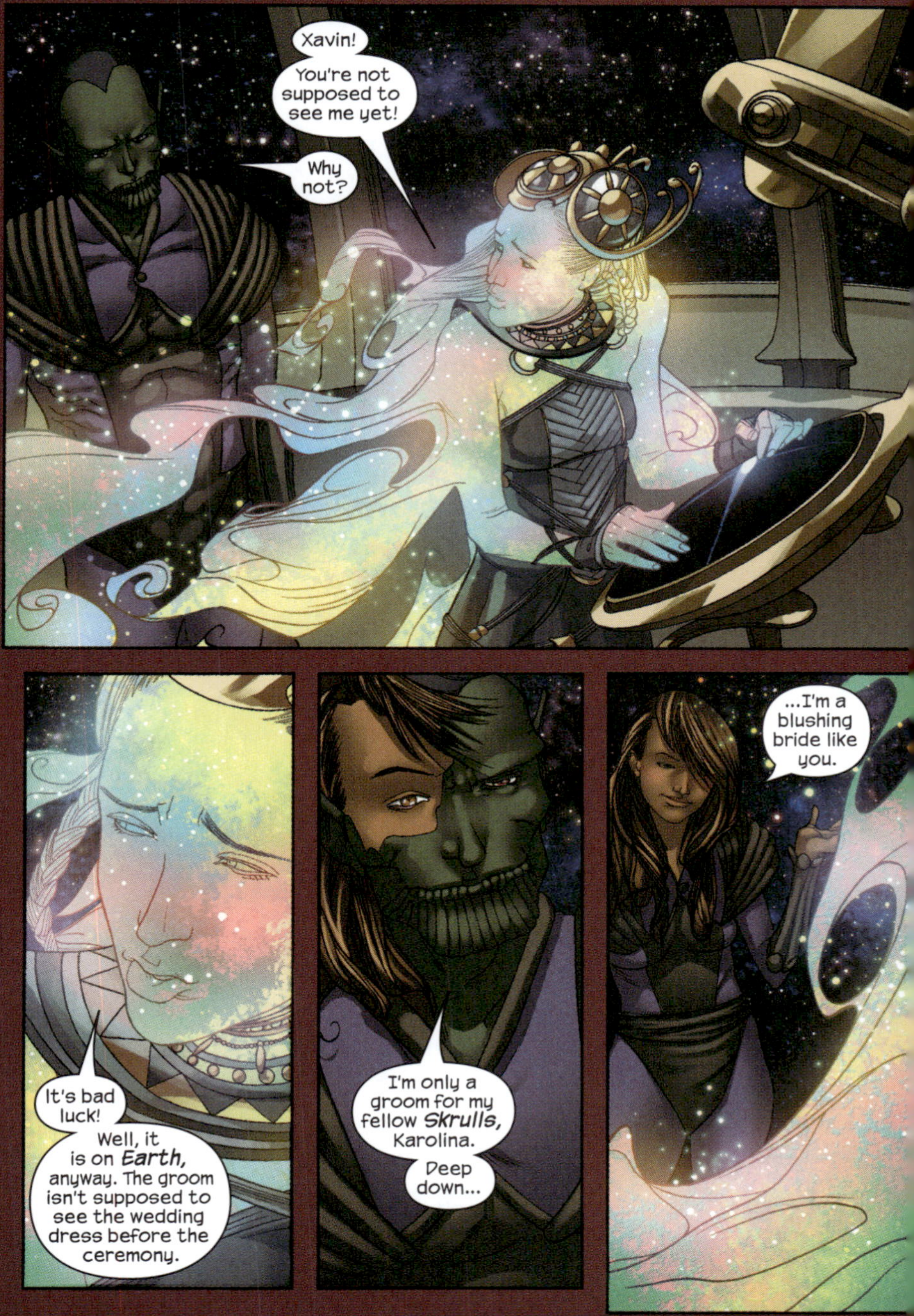
Xavin!
You're not supposed to see me yet!
Why not?
It's bad luck!
Well, it is on *Earth,* anyway. The groom isn't supposed to see the wedding dress before the ceremony.
I'm only a groom for my fellow *Skrulls,* Karolina.
Deep down...
...I'm a blushing bride like you.

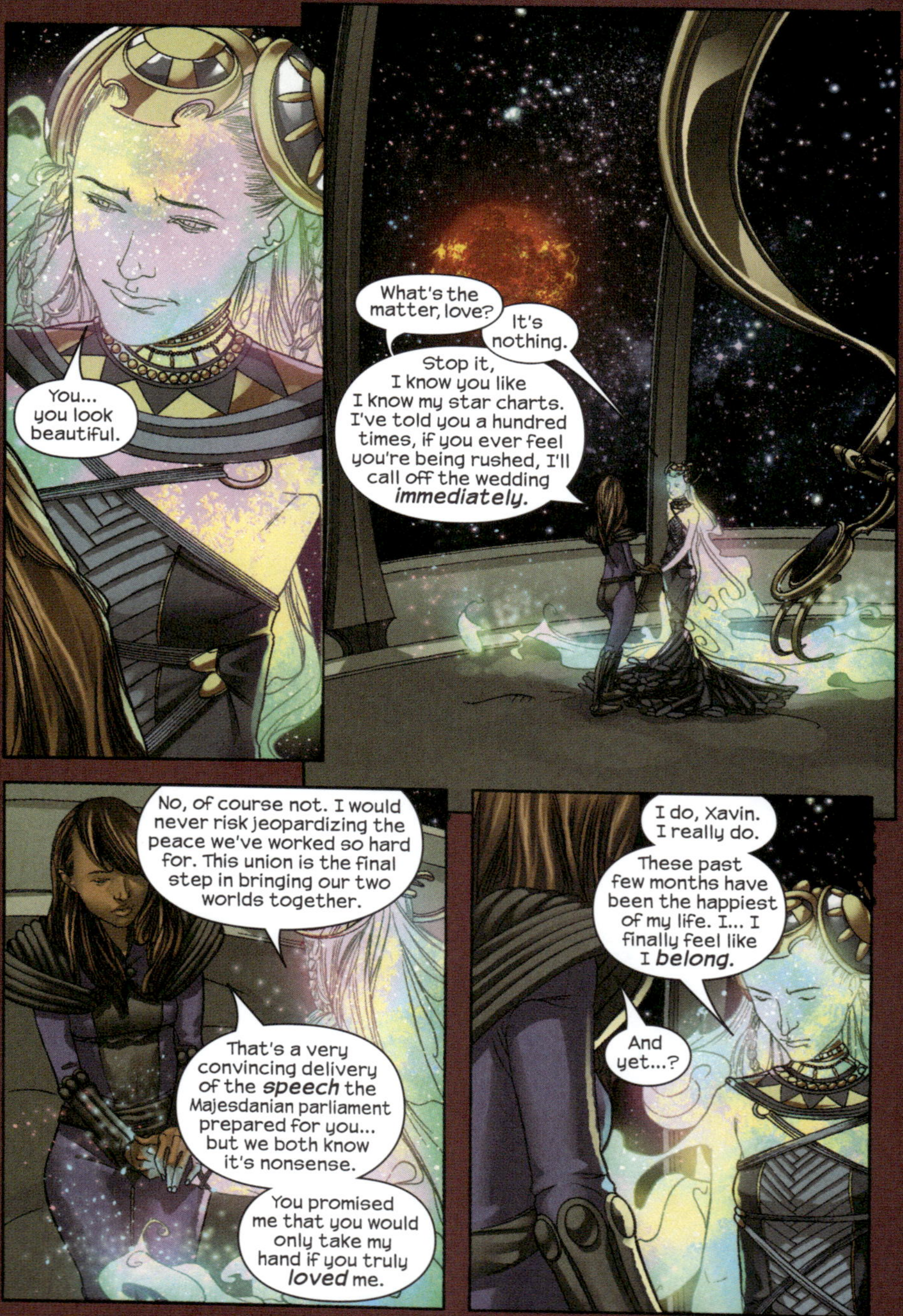

What's the matter, love?
It's nothing.
Stop it, I know you like I know my star charts. I've told you a hundred times, if you ever feel you're being rushed, I'll call off the wedding *immediately*.
You... you look beautiful.
No, of course not. I would never risk jeopardizing the peace we've worked so hard for. This union is the final step in bringing our two worlds together.
That's a very convincing delivery of the *speech* the Majesdanian parliament prepared for you... but we both know it's nonsense.
You promised me that you would only take my hand if you truly *loved* me.
I do, Xavin. I really do.
These past few months have been the happiest of my life. I... I finally feel like I *belong*.
And yet...?

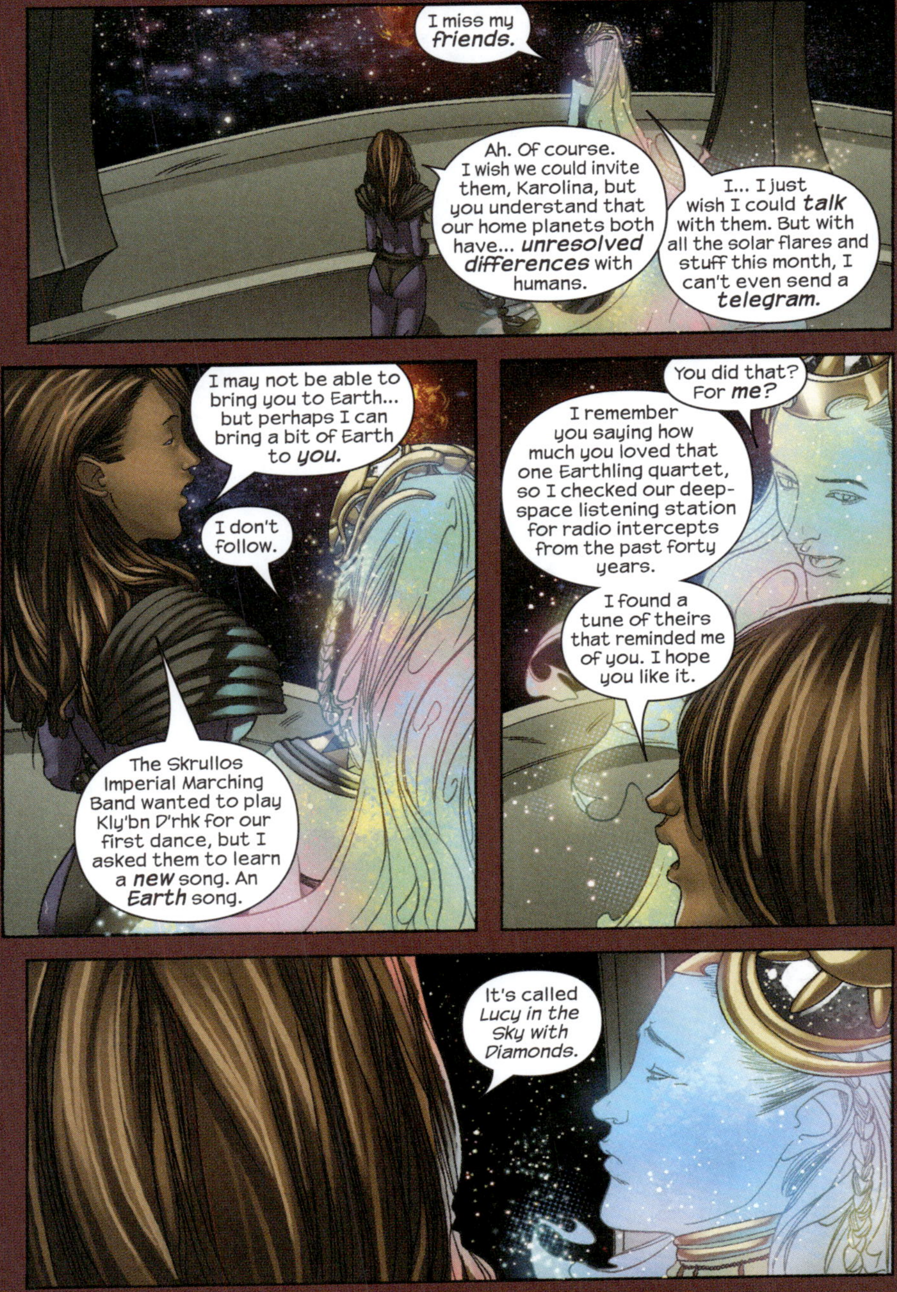
I miss my *friends.*
Ah. Of course. I wish we could invite them, Karolina, but you understand that our home planets both have... ***unresolved differences*** with humans.
I... I just wish I could ***talk*** with them. But with all the solar flares and stuff this month, I can't even send a ***telegram.***
I may not be able to bring you to Earth... but perhaps I can bring a bit of Earth to ***you.***
I don't follow.
The Skrullos Imperial Marching Band wanted to play Kly'bn D'rhk for our first dance, but I asked them to learn a ***new*** song. An ***Earth*** song.
You did that? For ***me?***
I remember you saying how much you loved that one Earthling quartet, so I checked our deep-space listening station for radio intercepts from the past forty years.
I found a tune of theirs that reminded me of you. I hope you like it.
It's called *Lucy in the Sky with Diamonds.*

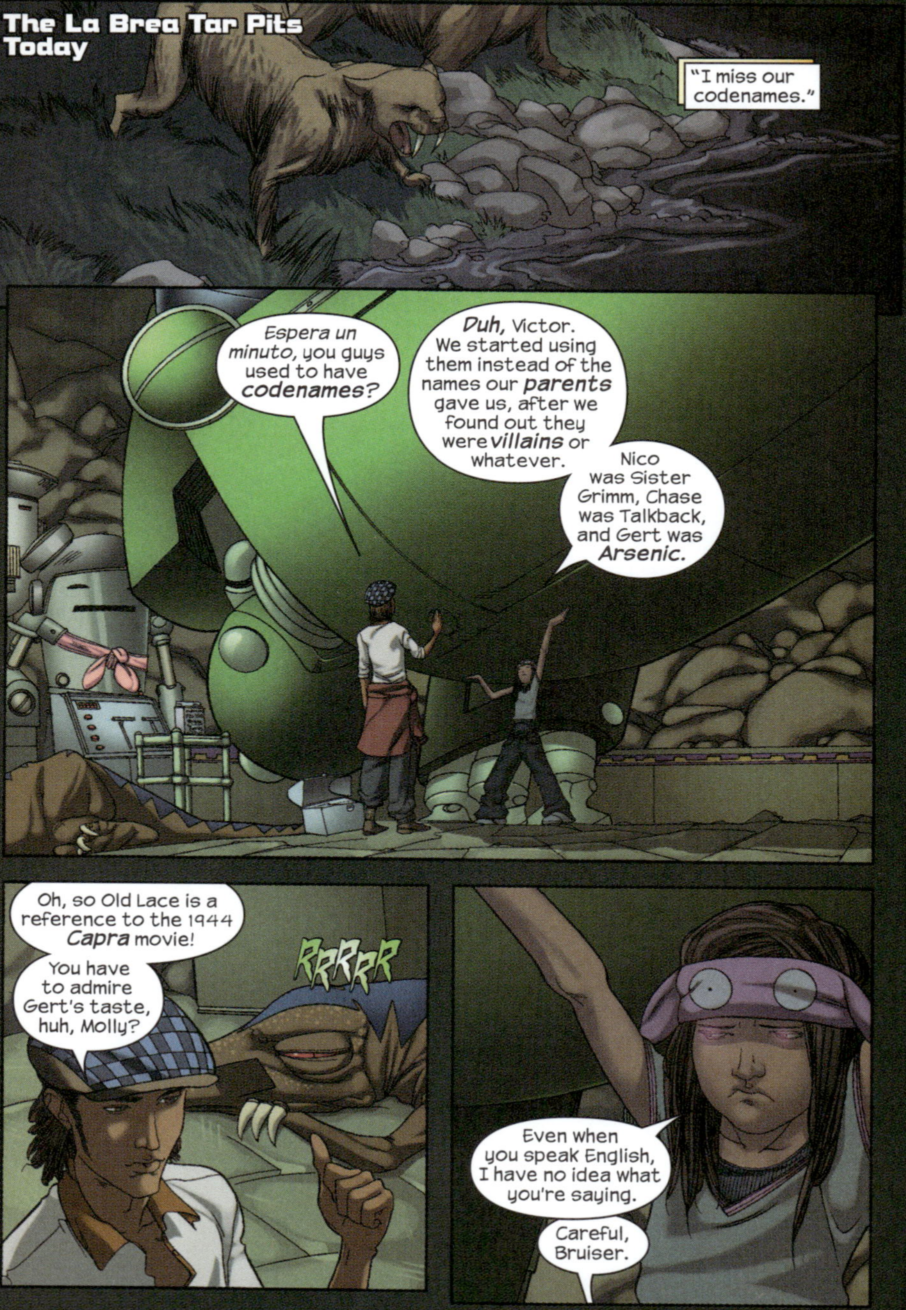
The La Brea Tar Pits Today
"I miss our codenames."
Espera un minuto, you guys used to have codenames?
Duh, Victor. We started using them instead of the names our parents gave us, after we found out they were villains or whatever.
Nico was Sister Grimm, Chase was Talkback, and Gert was Arsenic.
Oh, so Old Lace is a reference to the 1944 Capra movie!
You have to admire Gert's taste, huh, Molly?
RRRRR
Even when you speak English, I have no idea what you're saying.
Careful, Bruiser.

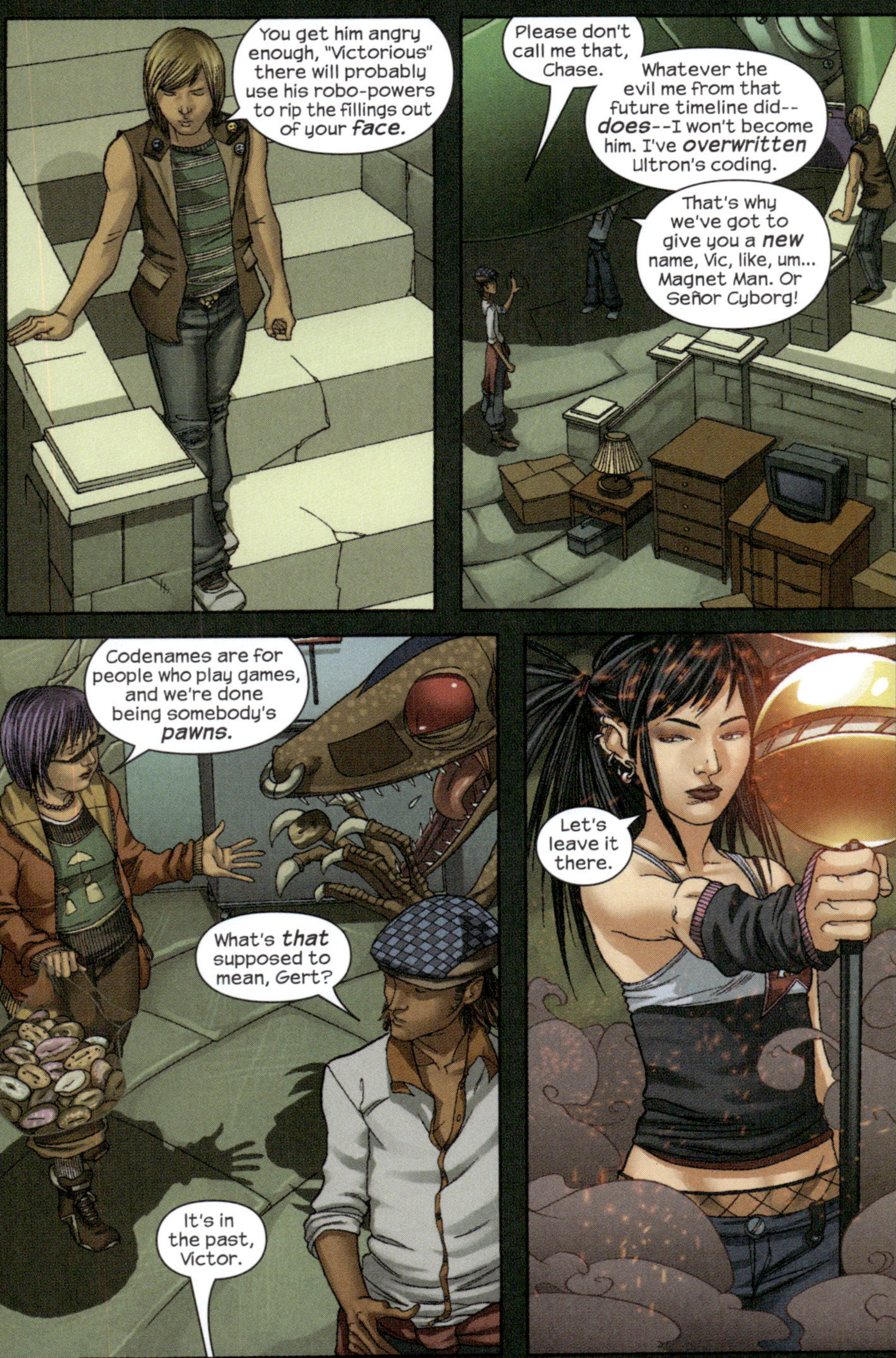
You get him angry enough, "Victorious" there will probably use his robo-powers to rip the fillings out of your *face.*
Please don't call me that, Chase.
Whatever the evil me from that future timeline did--*does*--I won't become him. I've *overwritten* Ultron's coding.
That's why we've got to give you a *new* name, Vic, like, um... Magnet Man. Or Señor Cyborg!
Codenames are for people who play games, and we're done being somebody's *pawns.*
What's *that* supposed to mean, Gert?
It's in the past, Victor.
Let's leave it there.

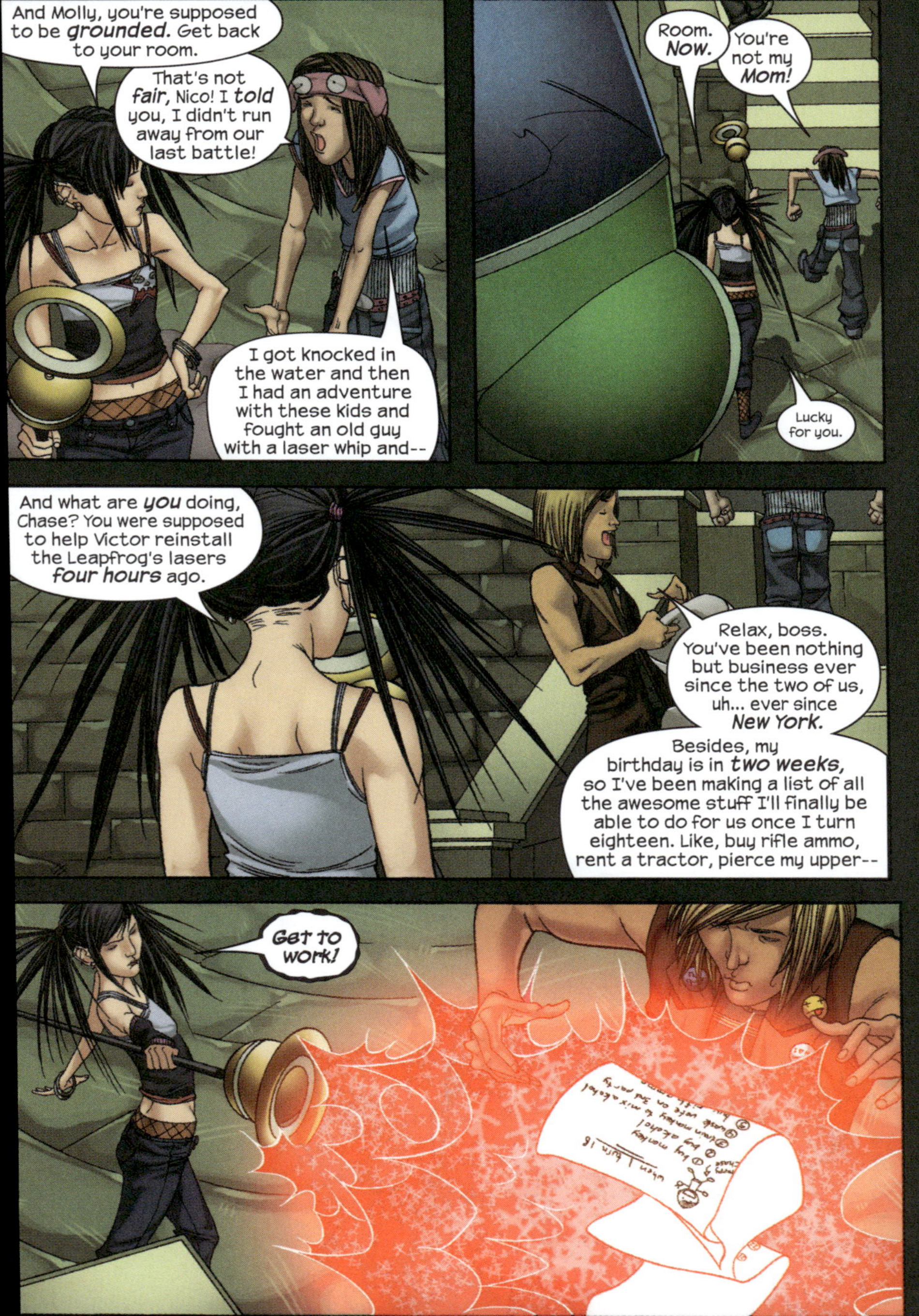
And Molly, you're supposed to be grounded. Get back to your room.
That's not fair, Nico! I told you, I didn't run away from our last battle!
I got knocked in the water and then I had an adventure with these kids and fought an old guy with a laser whip and--
Room. Now.
You're not my Mom!
Lucky for you.
And what are you doing, Chase? You were supposed to help Victor reinstall the Leapfrog's lasers four hours ago.
Relax, boss. You've been nothing but business ever since the two of us, uh... ever since New York.
Besides, my birthday is in two weeks, so I've been making a list of all the awesome stuff I'll finally be able to do for us once I turn eighteen. Like, buy rifle ammo, rent a tractor, pierce my upper--
Get to work!

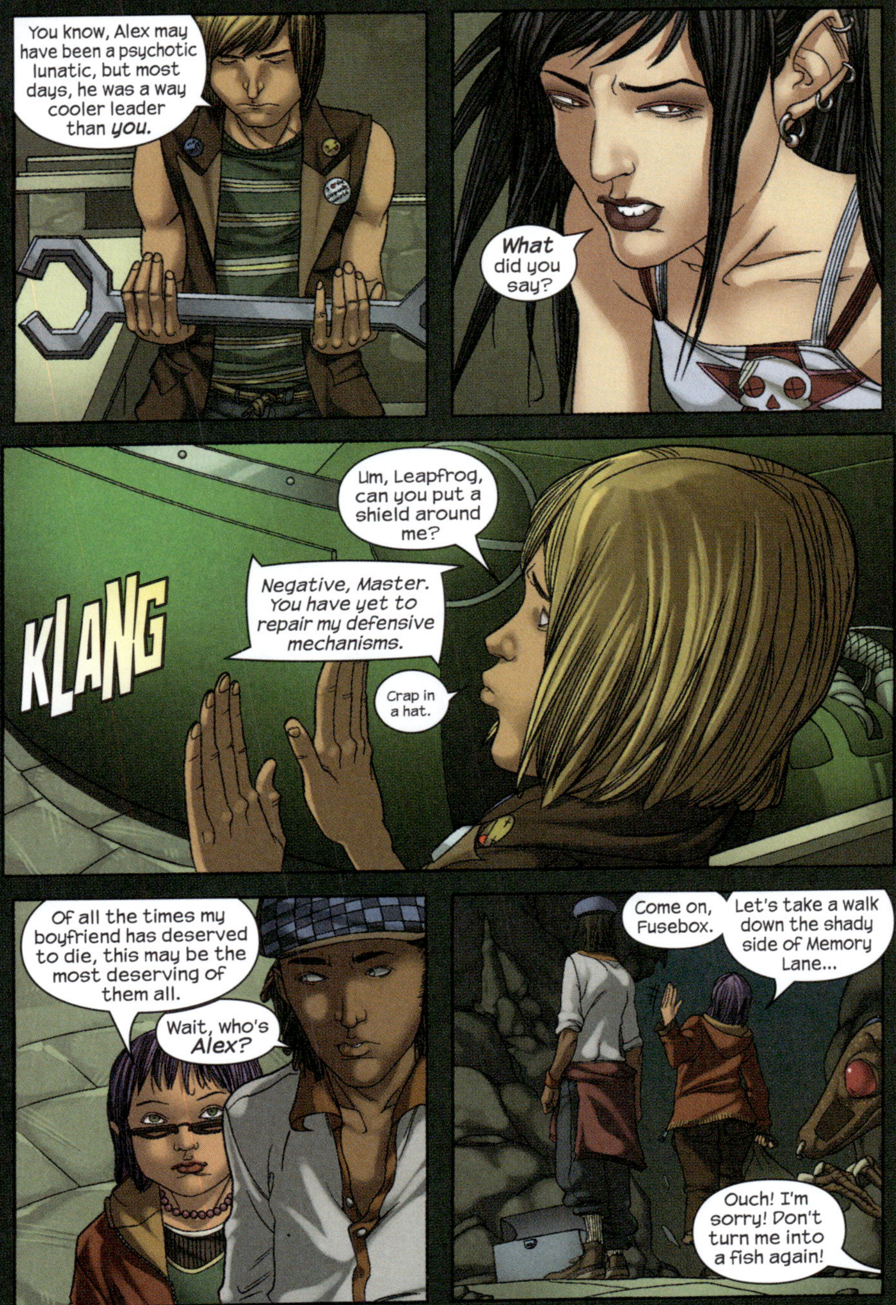
You know, Alex may have been a psychotic lunatic, but most days, he was a way cooler leader than *you*.
What did you say?
Um, Leapfrog, can you put a shield around me?
Negative, Master. You have yet to repair my defensive mechanisms.
KLANG
Crap in a hat.
Of all the times my boyfriend has deserved to die, this may be the most deserving of them all.
Wait, who's *Alex*?
Come on, Fusebox.
Let's take a walk down the shady side of Memory Lane...
Ouch! I'm sorry! Don't turn me into a fish again!

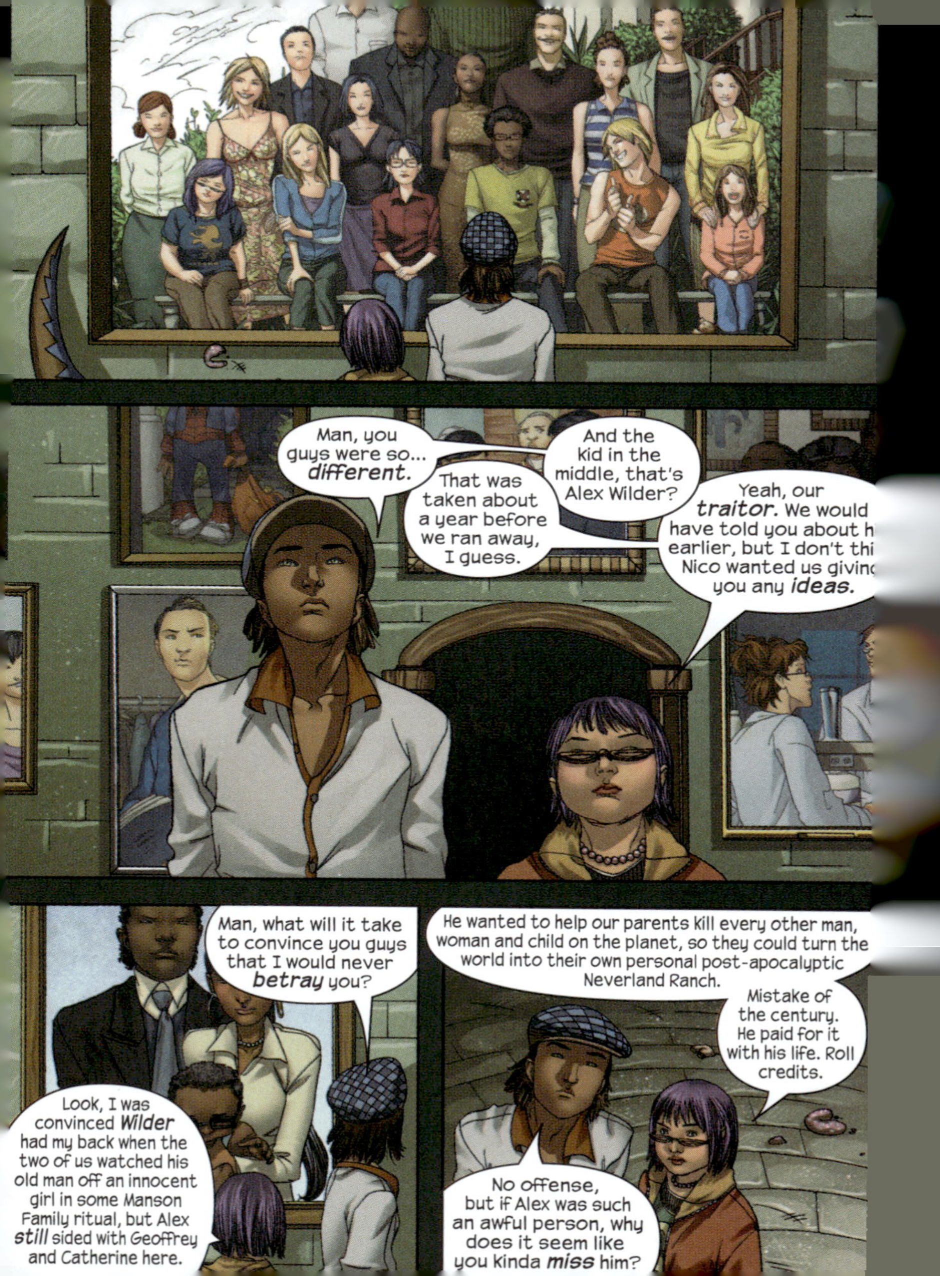
Man, you guys were so... *different.*
And the kid in the middle, that's Alex Wilder?
That was taken about a year before we ran away, I guess.
Yeah, our *traitor.* We would have told you about h earlier, but I don't thi Nico wanted us givin you any *ideas.*
Man, what will it take to convince you guys that I would never *betray* you?
Look, I was convinced *Wilder* had my back when the two of us watched his old man off an innocent girl in some Manson Family ritual, but Alex *still* sided with Geoffrey and Catherine here.
He wanted to help our parents kill every other man, woman and child on the planet, so they could turn the world into their own personal post-apocalyptic Neverland Ranch.
Mistake of the century. He paid for it with his life. Roll credits.
No offense, but if Alex was such an awful person, why does it seem like you kinda *miss* him?

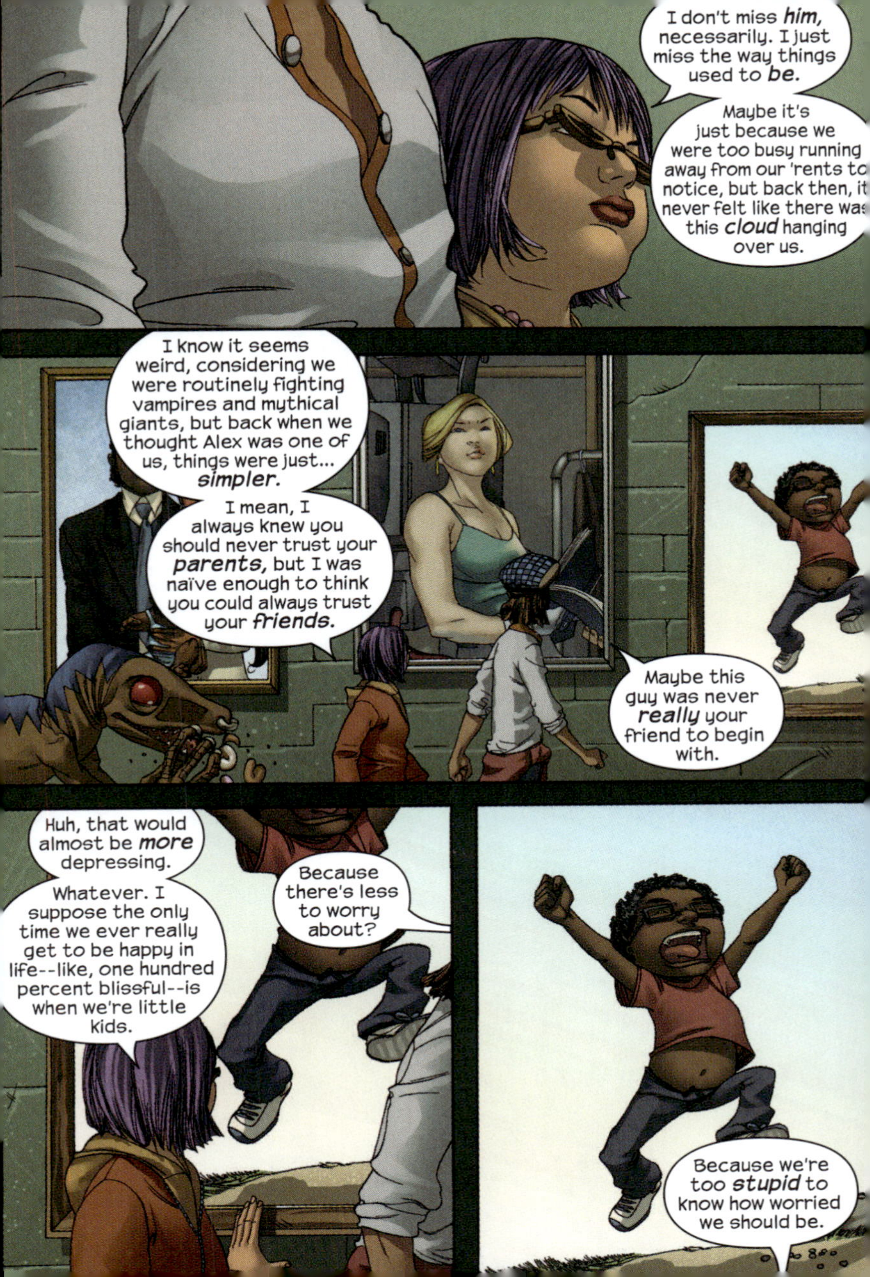

I don't miss *him,* necessarily. I just miss the way things used to *be.*
Maybe it's just because we were too busy running away from our 'rents to notice, but back then, it never felt like there was this *cloud* hanging over us.
I know it seems weird, considering we were routinely fighting vampires and mythical giants, but back when we thought Alex was one of us, things were just... *simpler.*
I mean, I always knew you should never trust your *parents,* but I was naïve enough to think you could always trust your *friends.*
Maybe this guy was never *really* your friend to begin with.
Huh, that would almost be *more* depressing.
Whatever. I suppose the only time we ever really get to be happy in life--like, one hundred percent blissful--is when we're little kids.
Because there's less to worry about?
Because we're too *stupid* to know how worried we should be.

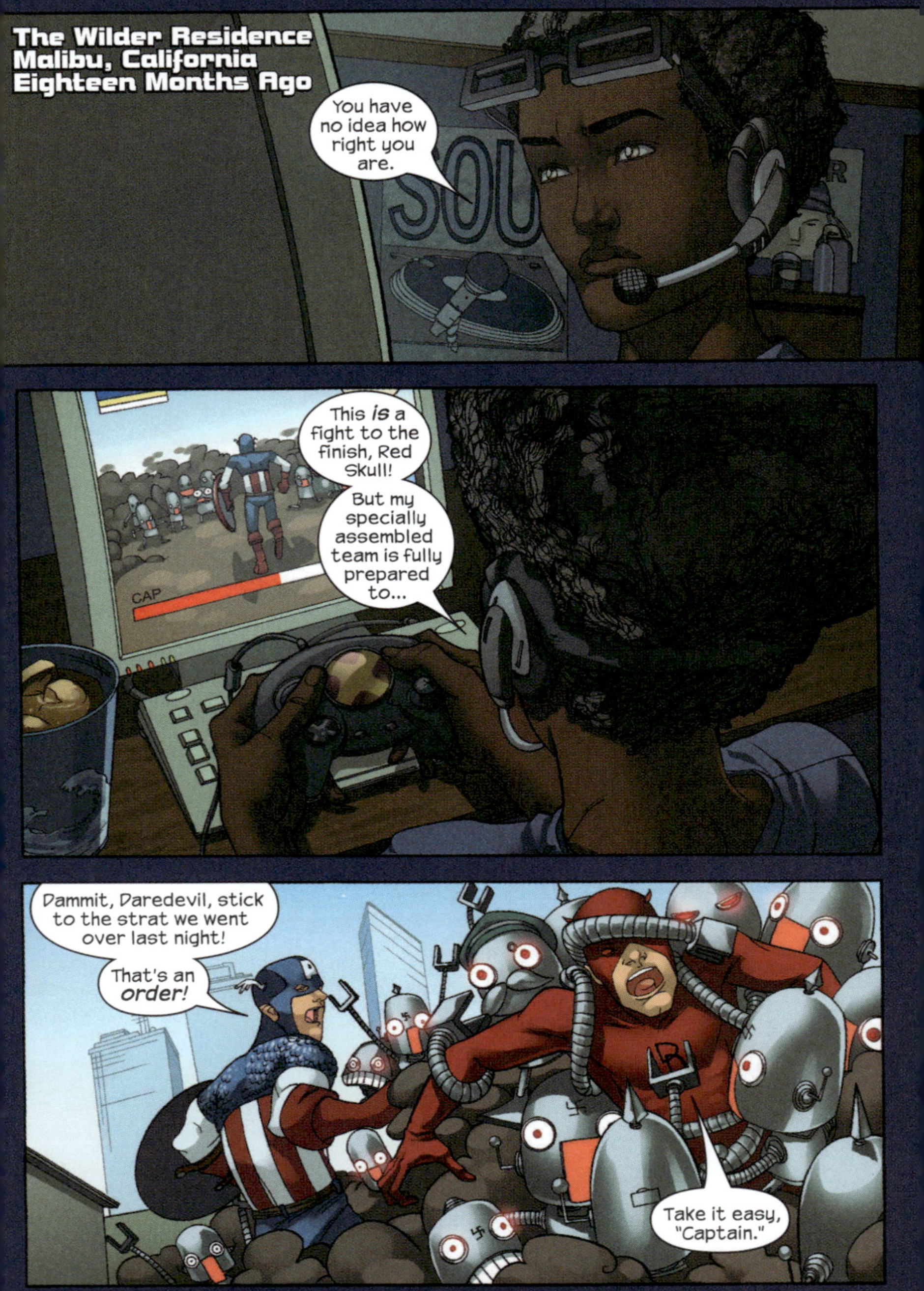
The Wilder Residence
Malibu, California
Eighteen Months Ago
You have no idea how right you are.
This *is* a fight to the finish, Red Skull!
But my specially assembled team is fully prepared to...
CAP
Dammit, Daredevil, stick to the strat we went over last night!
That's an *order!*
Take it easy, "Captain."

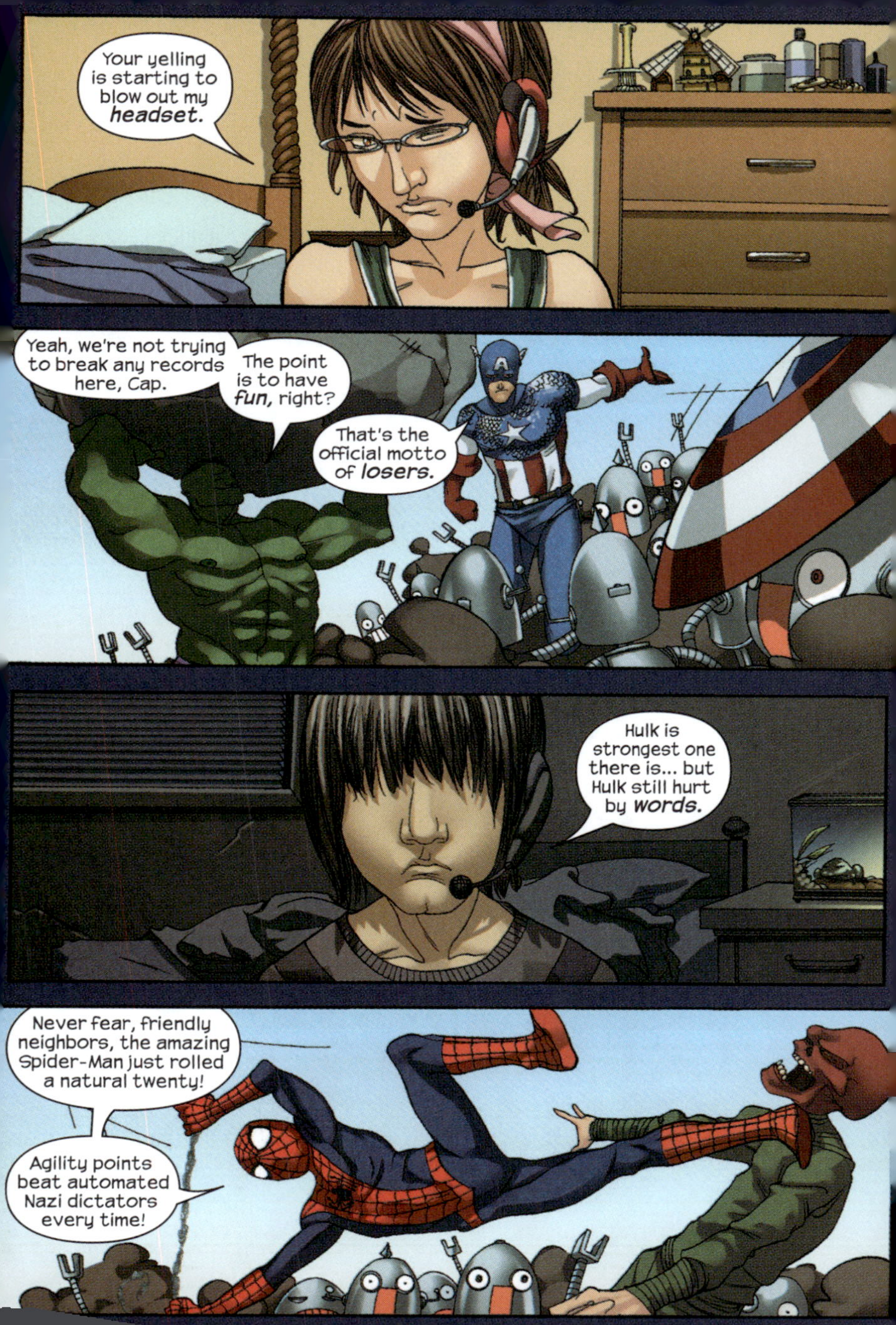

Your yelling is starting to blow out my *headset.*
Yeah, we're not trying to break any records here, Cap.
The point is to have *fun,* right?
That's the official motto of *losers.*
Hulk is strongest one there is... but Hulk still hurt by *words.*
Never fear, friendly neighbors, the amazing Spider-Man just rolled a natural twenty!
Agility points beat automated Nazi dictators every time!

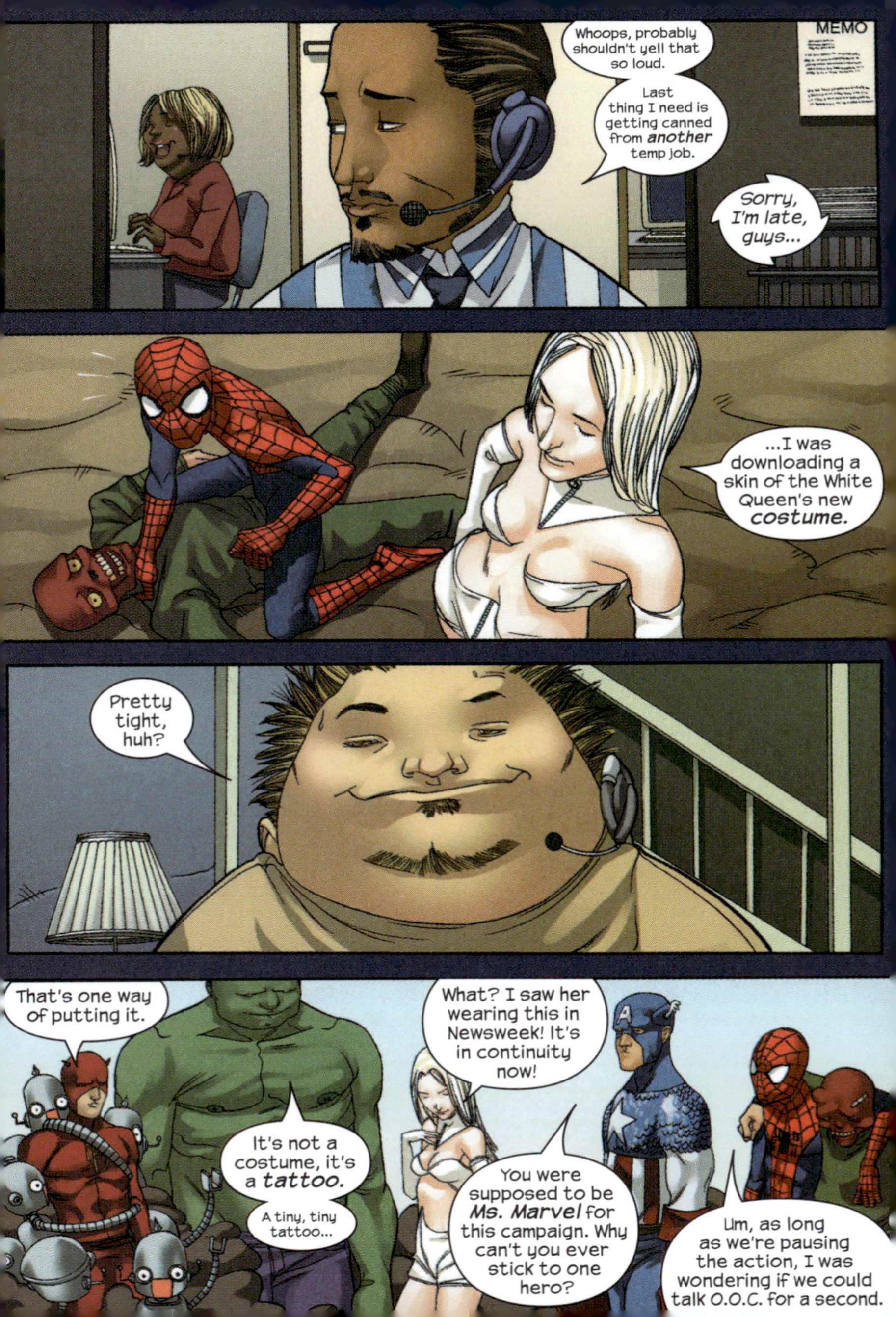
Whoops, probably shouldn't yell that so loud.
Last thing I need is getting canned from **another** temp job.
Sorry, I'm late, guys...
...I was downloading a skin of the White Queen's new **costume.**
Pretty tight, huh?
That's one way of putting it.
What? I saw her wearing this in Newsweek! It's in continuity now!
It's not a costume, it's a **tattoo.**
A tiny, tiny tattoo...
You were supposed to be **Ms. Marvel** for this campaign. Why can't you ever stick to one hero?
Um, as long as we're pausing the action, I was wondering if we could talk O.O.C. for a second.

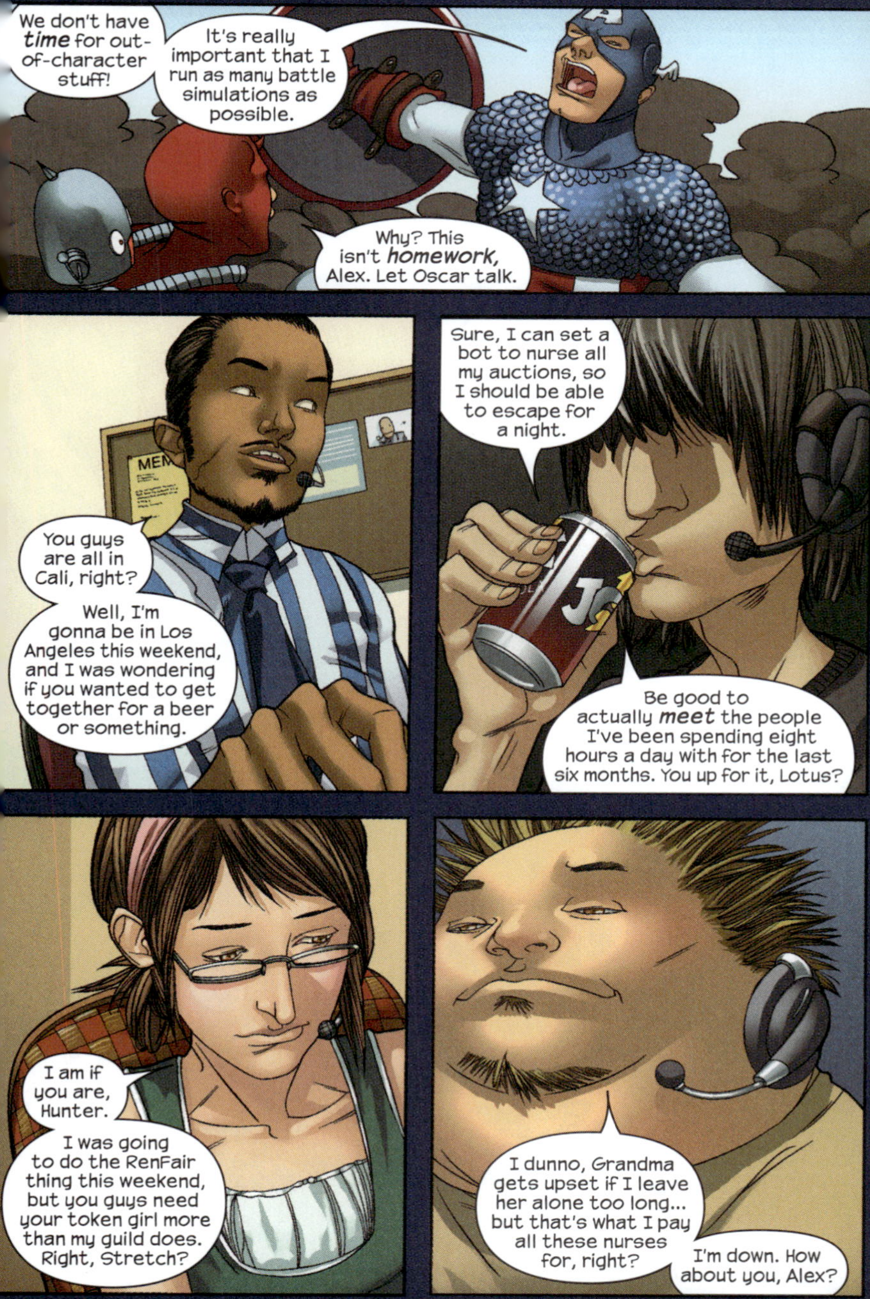
We don't have *time* for out-of-character stuff!
It's really important that I run as many battle simulations as possible.
Why? This isn't *homework,* Alex. Let Oscar talk.
You guys are all in Cali, right?
Well, I'm gonna be in Los Angeles this weekend, and I was wondering if you wanted to get together for a beer or something.
Sure, I can set a bot to nurse all my auctions, so I should be able to escape for a night.
Be good to actually *meet* the people I've been spending eight hours a day with for the last six months. You up for it, Lotus?
I am if you are, Hunter.
I was going to do the RenFair thing this weekend, but you guys need your token girl more than my guild does. Right, Stretch?
I dunno, Grandma gets upset if I leave her alone too long... but that's what I pay all these nurses for, right?
I'm down. How about you, Alex?

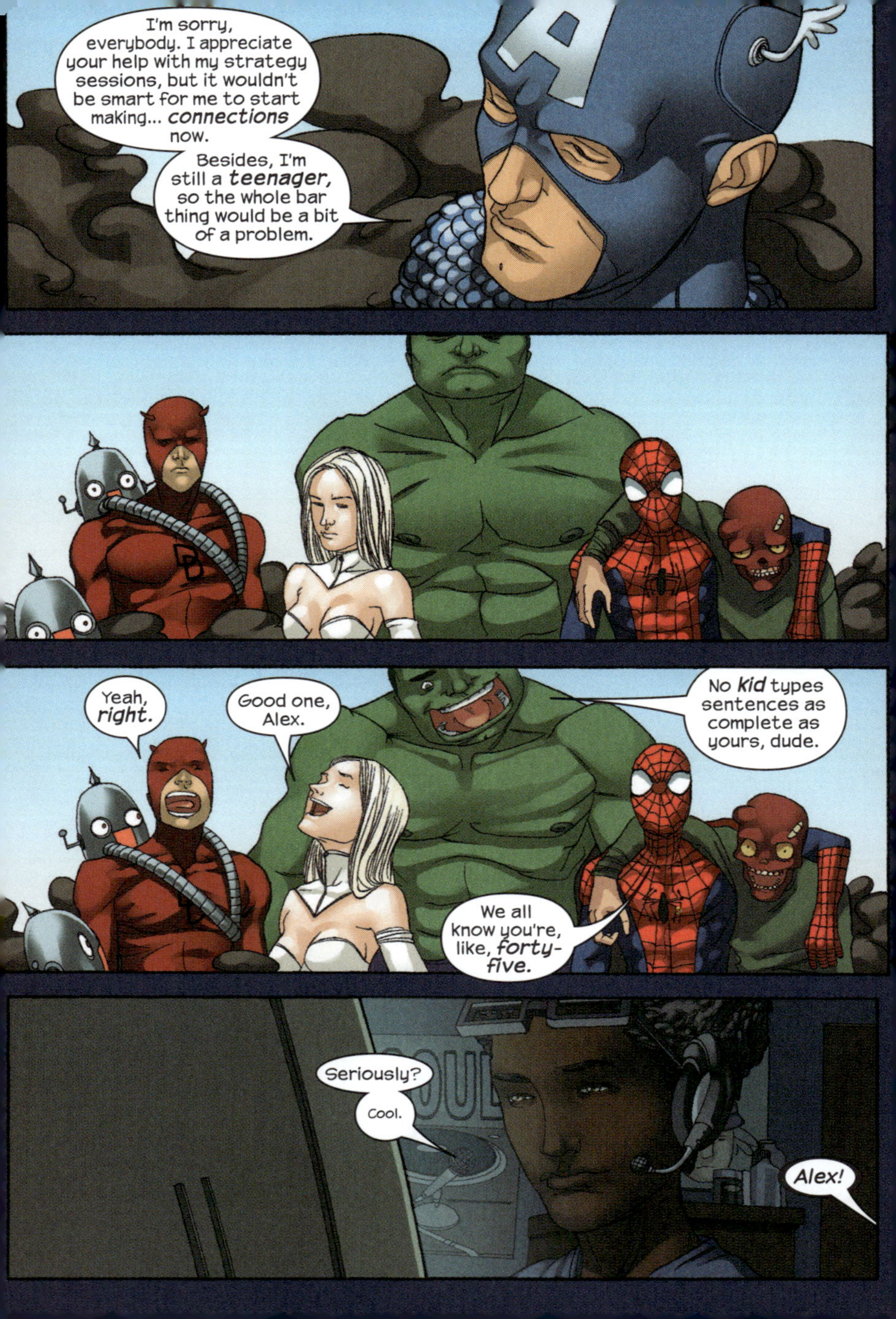
I'm sorry, everybody. I appreciate your help with my strategy sessions, but it wouldn't be smart for me to start making... connections now.
Besides, I'm still a teenager, so the whole bar thing would be a bit of a problem.
Yeah, right.
Good one, Alex.
No kid types sentences as complete as yours, dude.
We all know you're, like, forty-five.
Seriously?
Cool.
Alex!

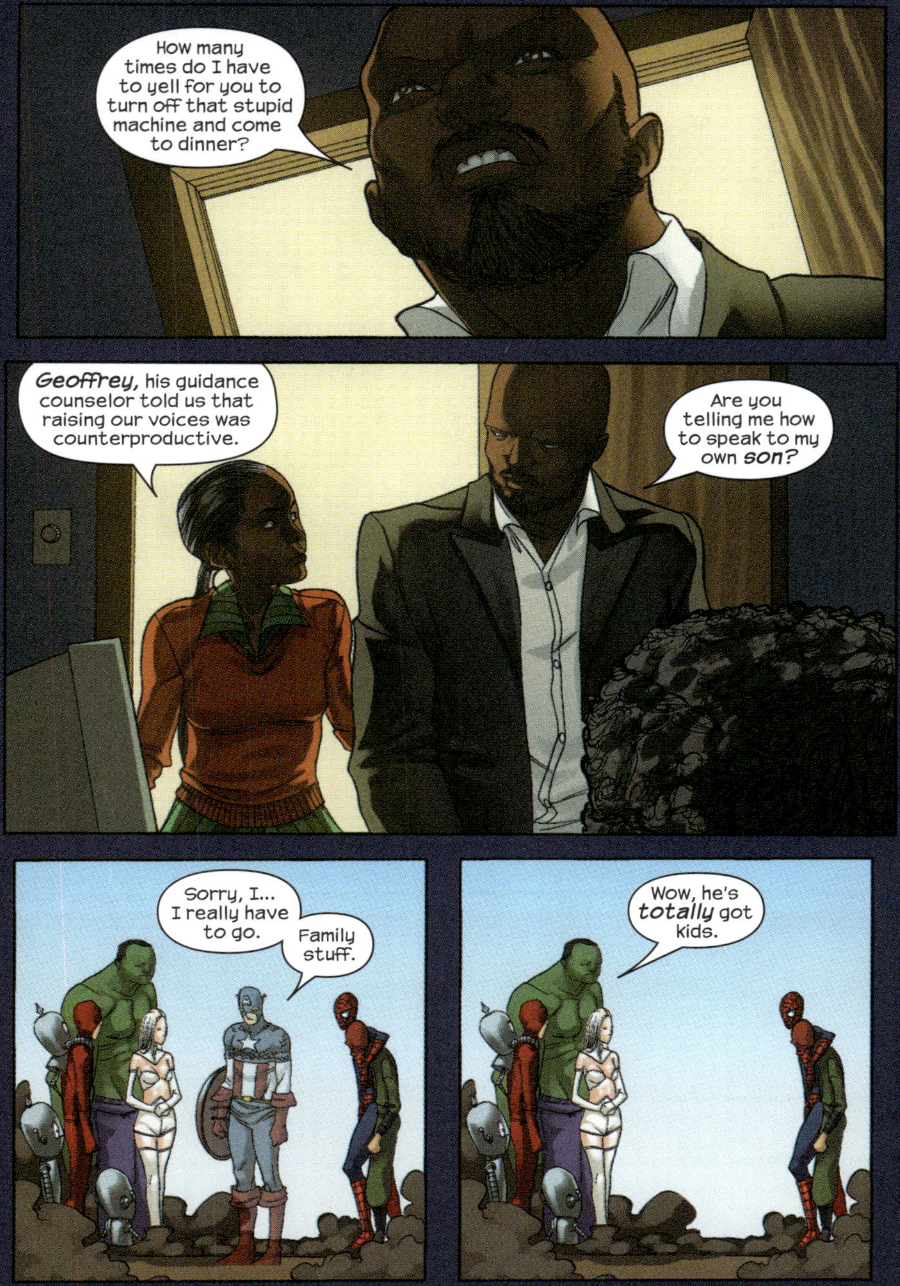
How many times do I have to yell for you to turn off that stupid machine and come to dinner?
Geoffrey, his guidance counselor told us that raising our voices was counterproductive.
Are you telling me how to speak to my own son?
Sorry, I... I really have to go.
Family stuff.
Wow, he's totally got kids.

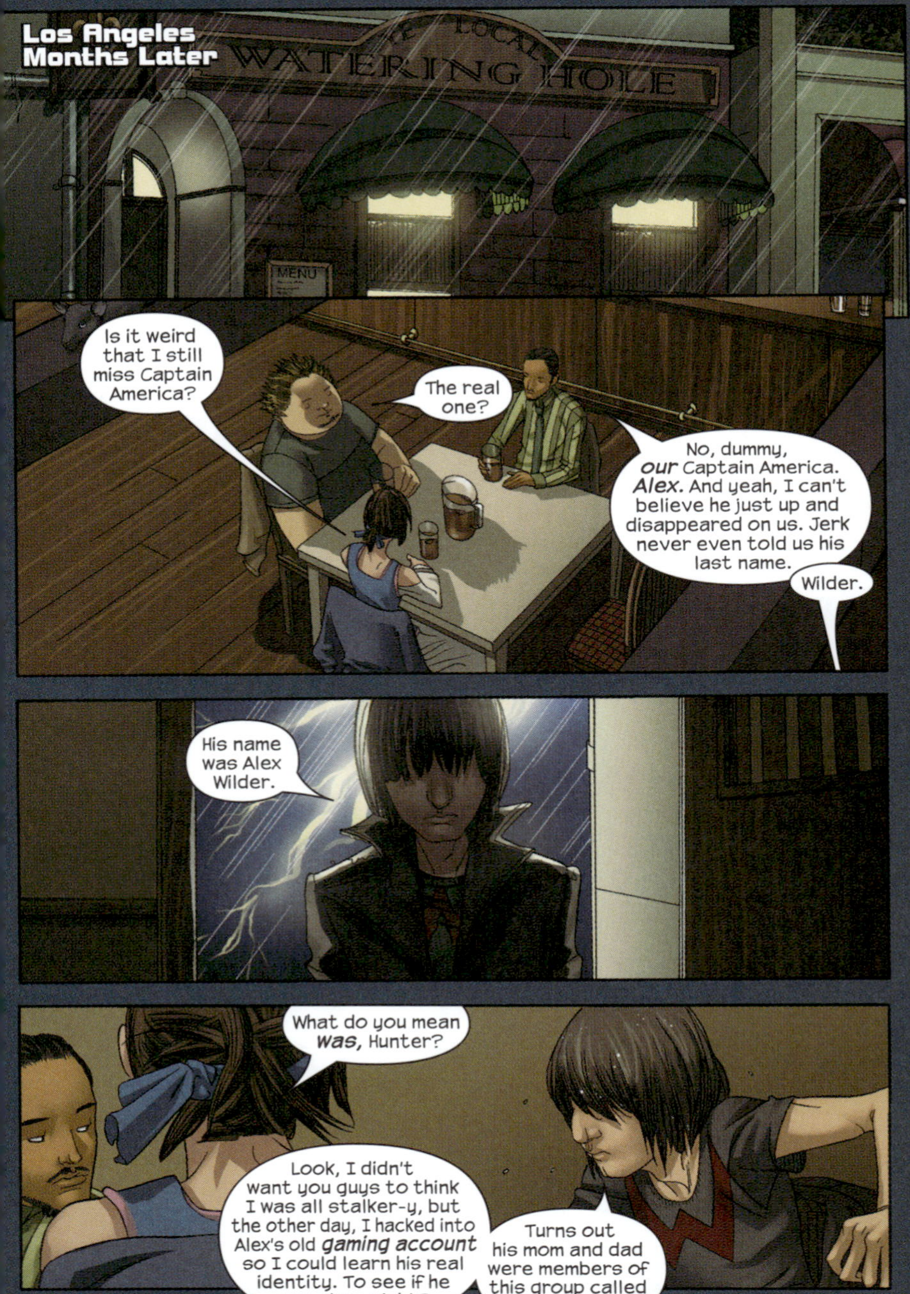
Los Angeles Months Later
YE LOCAL WATERING HOLE
MENU
Is it weird that I still miss Captain America?
The real one?
No, dummy, *our* Captain America. *Alex.* And yeah, I can't believe he just up and disappeared on us. Jerk never even told us his last name.
Wilder.
His name was Alex Wilder.
What do you mean *was,* Hunter?
Look, I didn't want you guys to think I was all stalker-y, but the other day, I hacked into Alex's old *gaming account* so I could learn his real identity. To see if he was okay, right?
Turns out his mom and dad were members of this group called *The Pride...*

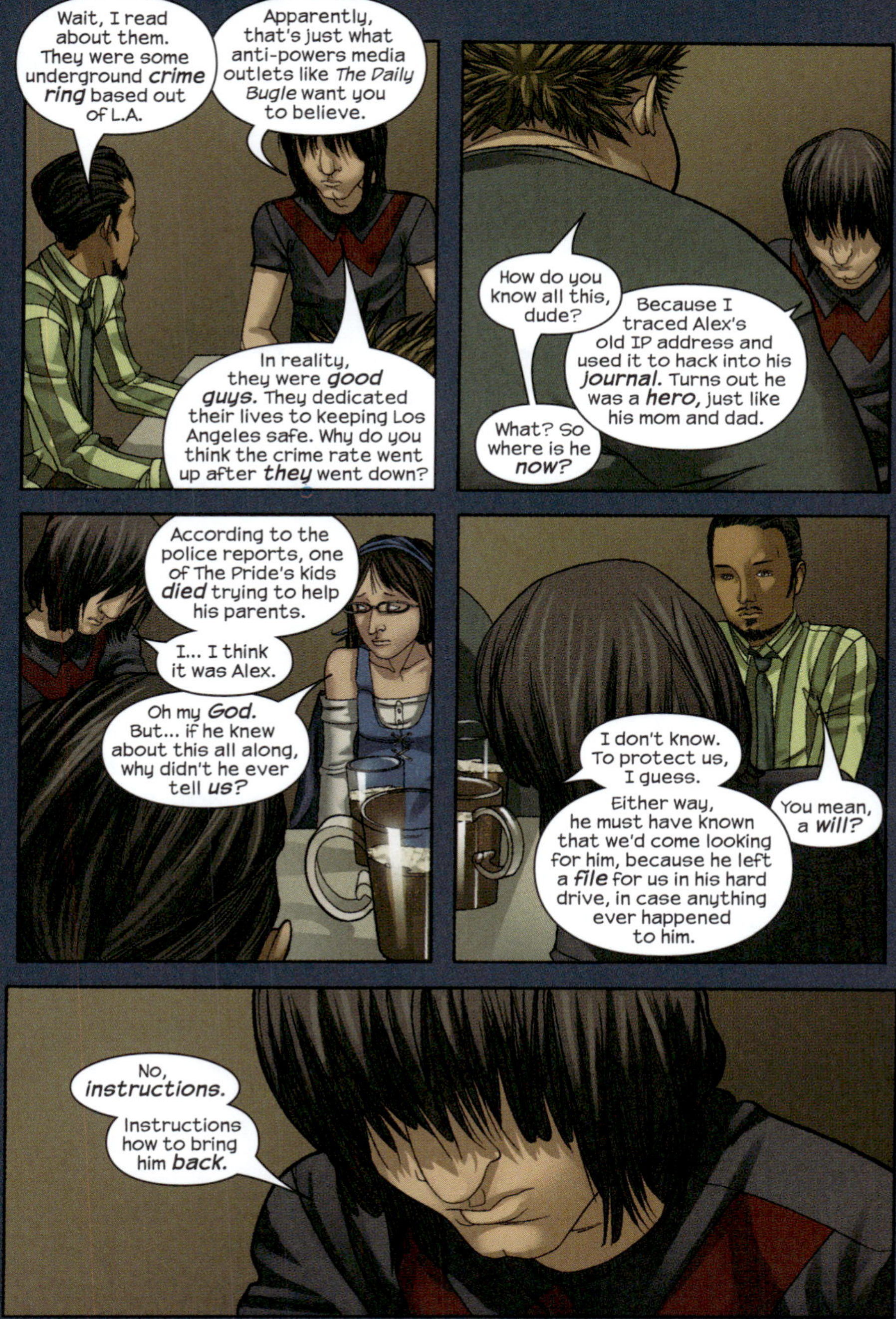
Wait, I read about them. They were some underground crime ring based out of L.A.
Apparently, that's just what anti-powers media outlets like The Daily Bugle want you to believe.
In reality, they were good guys. They dedicated their lives to keeping Los Angeles safe. Why do you think the crime rate went up after they went down?
How do you know all this, dude?
Because I traced Alex's old IP address and used it to hack into his journal. Turns out he was a hero, just like his mom and dad.
What? So where is he now?
According to the police reports, one of The Pride's kids died trying to help his parents.
I... I think it was Alex.
Oh my God. But... if he knew about this all along, why didn't he ever tell us?
I don't know. To protect us, I guess.
Either way, he must have known that we'd come looking for him, because he left a file for us in his hard drive, in case anything ever happened to him.
You mean, a will?
No, instructions.
Instructions how to bring him back.

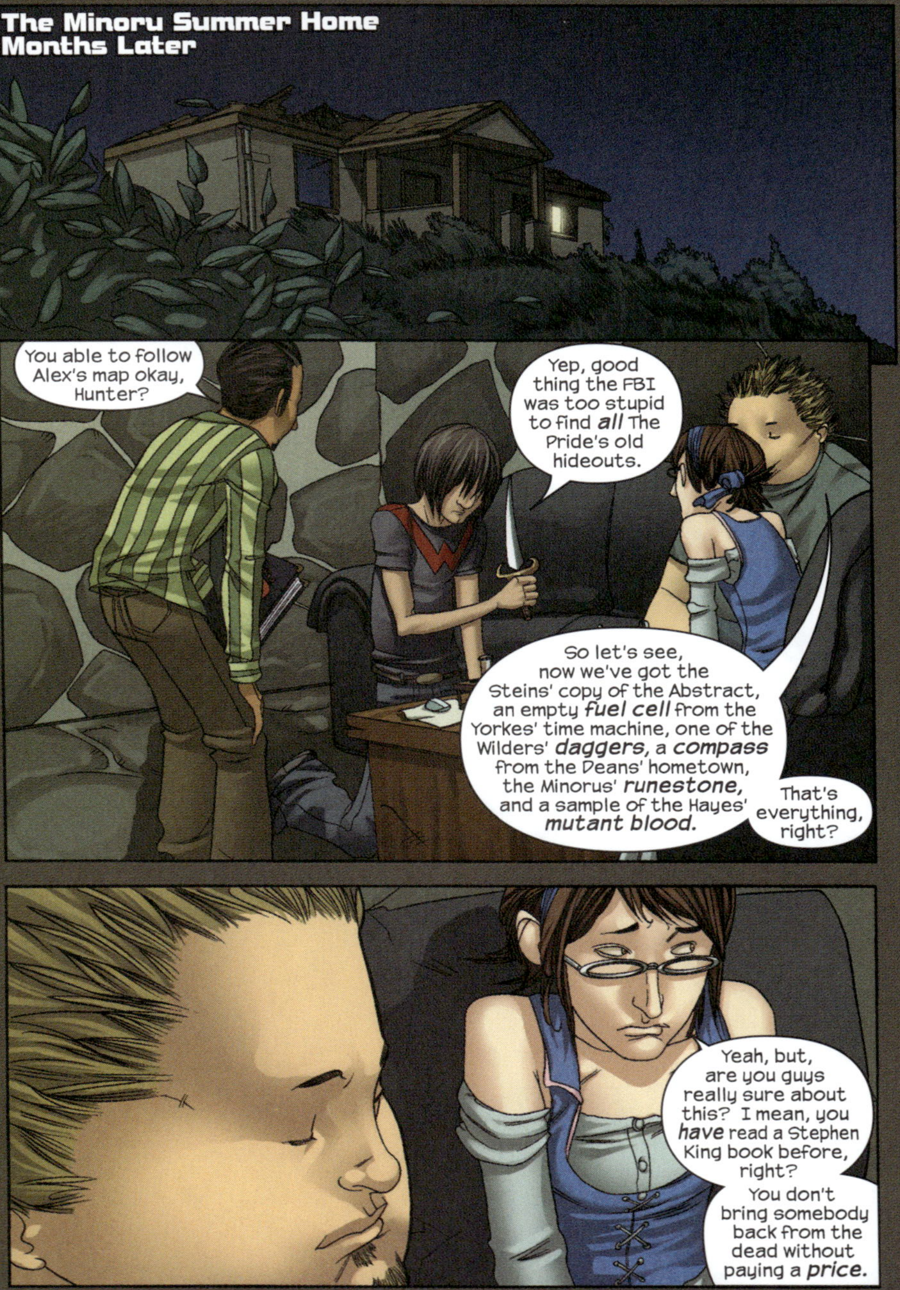
The Minoru Summer Home
Months Later
You able to follow Alex's map okay, Hunter?
Yep, good thing the FBI was too stupid to find *all* The Pride's old hideouts.
So let's see, now we've got the Steins' copy of the Abstract, an empty *fuel cell* from the Yorkes' time machine, one of the Wilders' *daggers*, a *compass* from the Deans' hometown, the Minorus' *runestone*, and a sample of the Hayes' *mutant blood*.
That's everything, right?
Yeah, but, are you guys really sure about this? I mean, you *have* read a Stephen King book before, right?
You don't bring somebody back from the dead without paying a *price*.

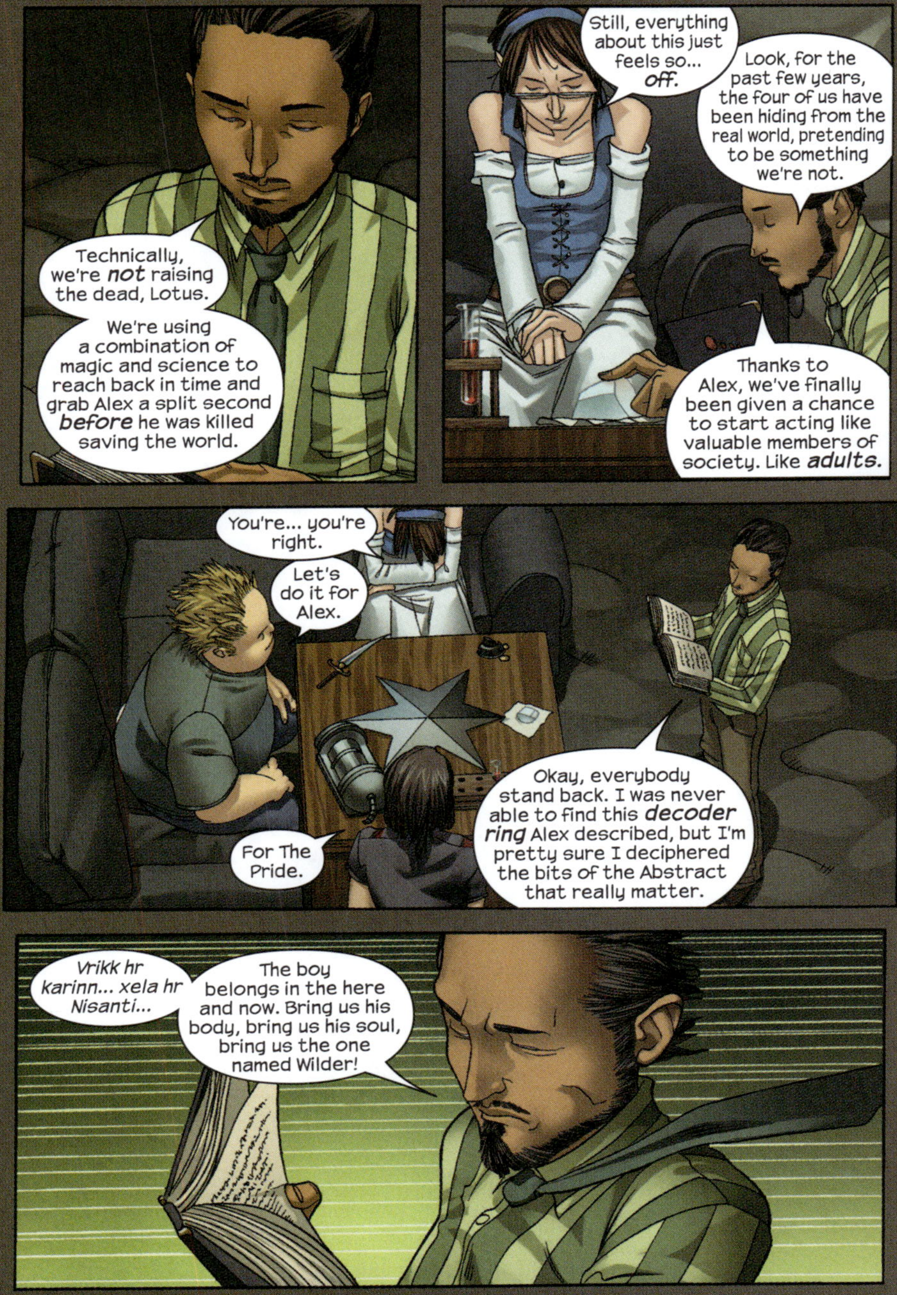
Technically, we're **not** raising the dead, Lotus.
We're using a combination of magic and science to reach back in time and grab Alex a split second **before** he was killed saving the world.
Still, everything about this just feels so... **off.**
Look, for the past few years, the four of us have been hiding from the real world, pretending to be something we're not.
Thanks to Alex, we've finally been given a chance to start acting like valuable members of society. Like **adults.**
You're... you're right.
Let's do it for Alex.
For The Pride.
Okay, everybody stand back. I was never able to find this **decoder ring** Alex described, but I'm pretty sure I deciphered the bits of the Abstract that really matter.
Vrikk hr karinn... xela hr Nisanti...
The boy belongs in the here and now. Bring us his body, bring us his soul, bring us the one named Wilder!

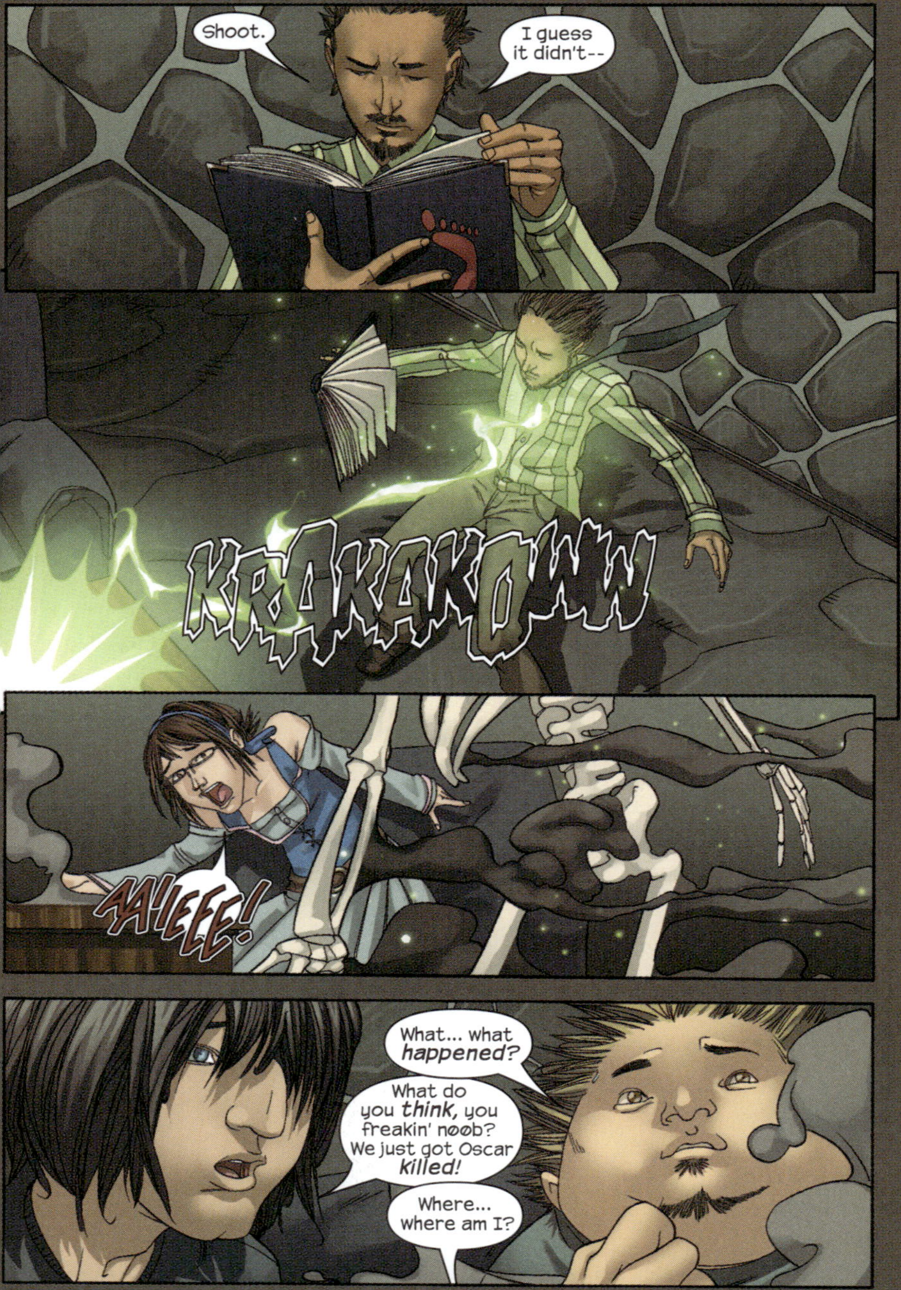
Shoot.
I guess it didn't--
KRAKAKOWW
AAIEEE!
What... what happened?
What do you think, you freakin' noob? We just got Oscar killed!
Where... where am I?

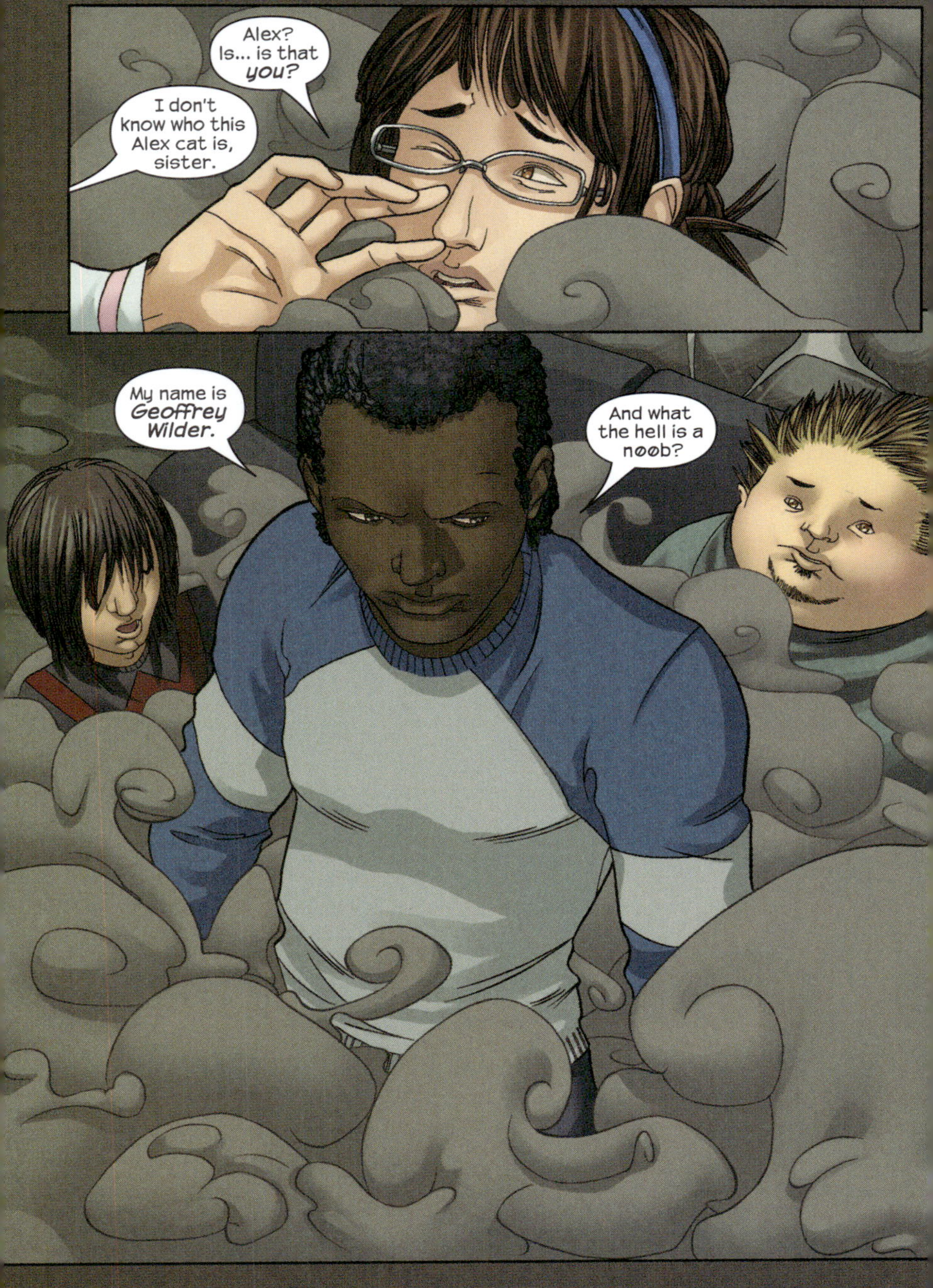
Alex?
Is... is that *you?*
I don't know who this Alex cat is, sister.
My name is *Geoffrey Wilder.*
And what the hell is a nøøb?

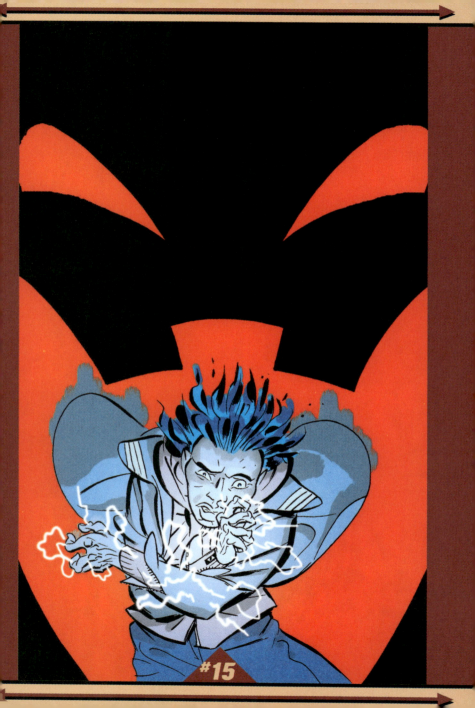

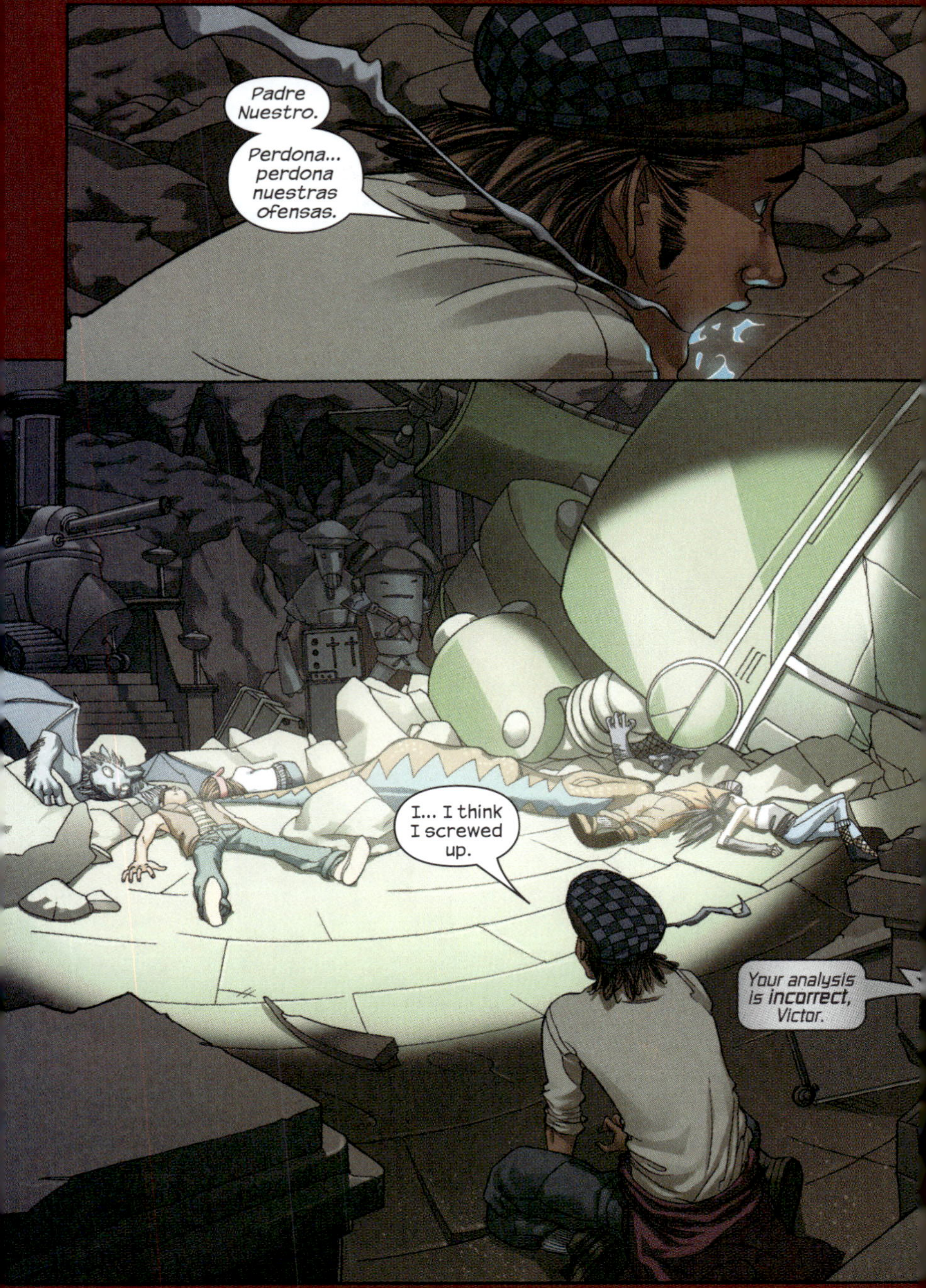
Padre Nuestro.
Perdona... perdona nuestras ofensas.
I... I think I screwed up.
Your analysis is incorrect, Victor.

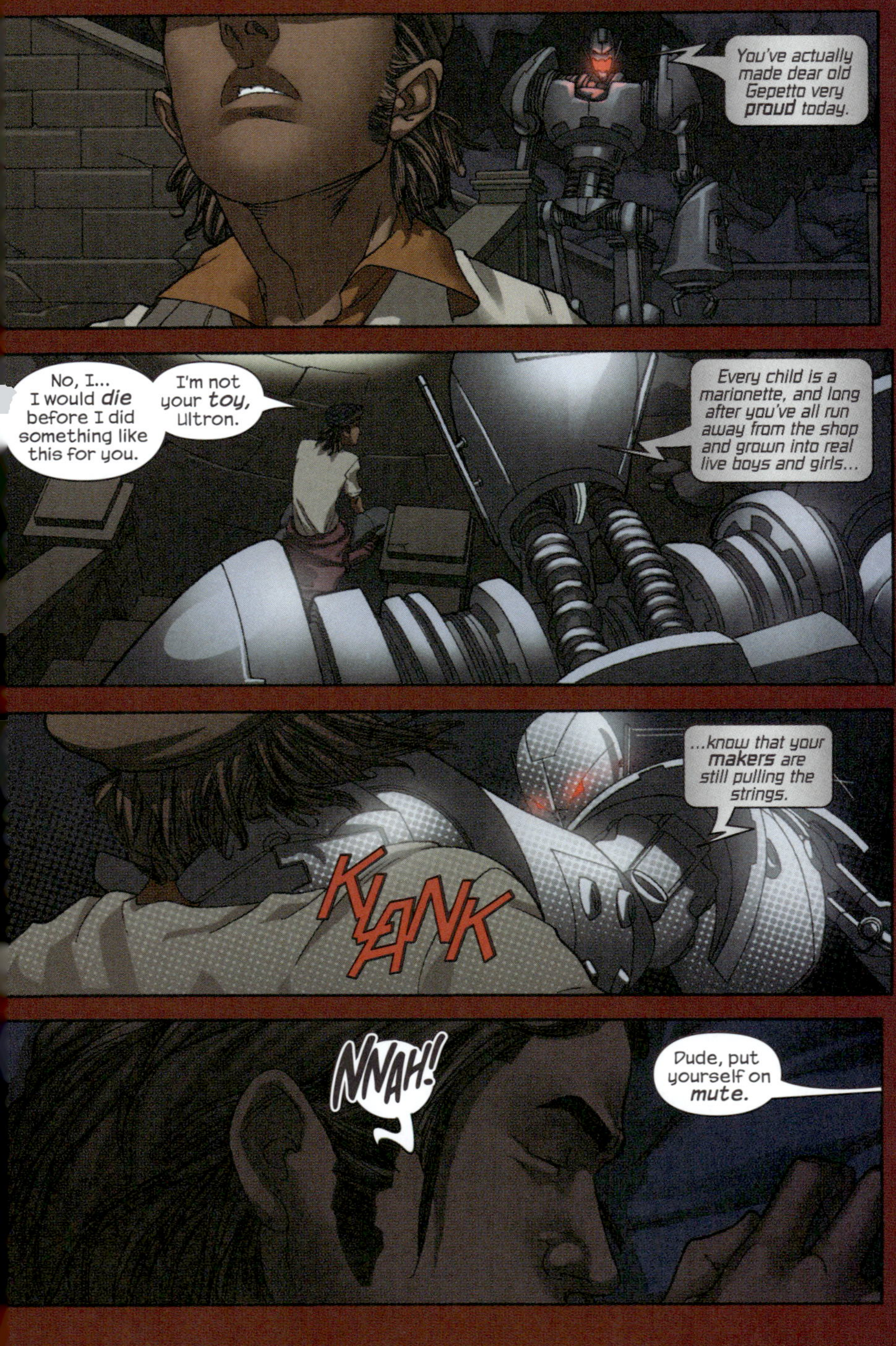

You've actually made dear old Gepetto very **proud** today.
No, I... I would **die** before I did something like this for you.
I'm not your **toy,** Ultron.
Every child is a marionette, and long after you've all run away from the shop and grown into real live boys and girls...
...know that your **makers** are still pulling the strings.
KLANK
NNAH!
Dude, put yourself on **mute.**

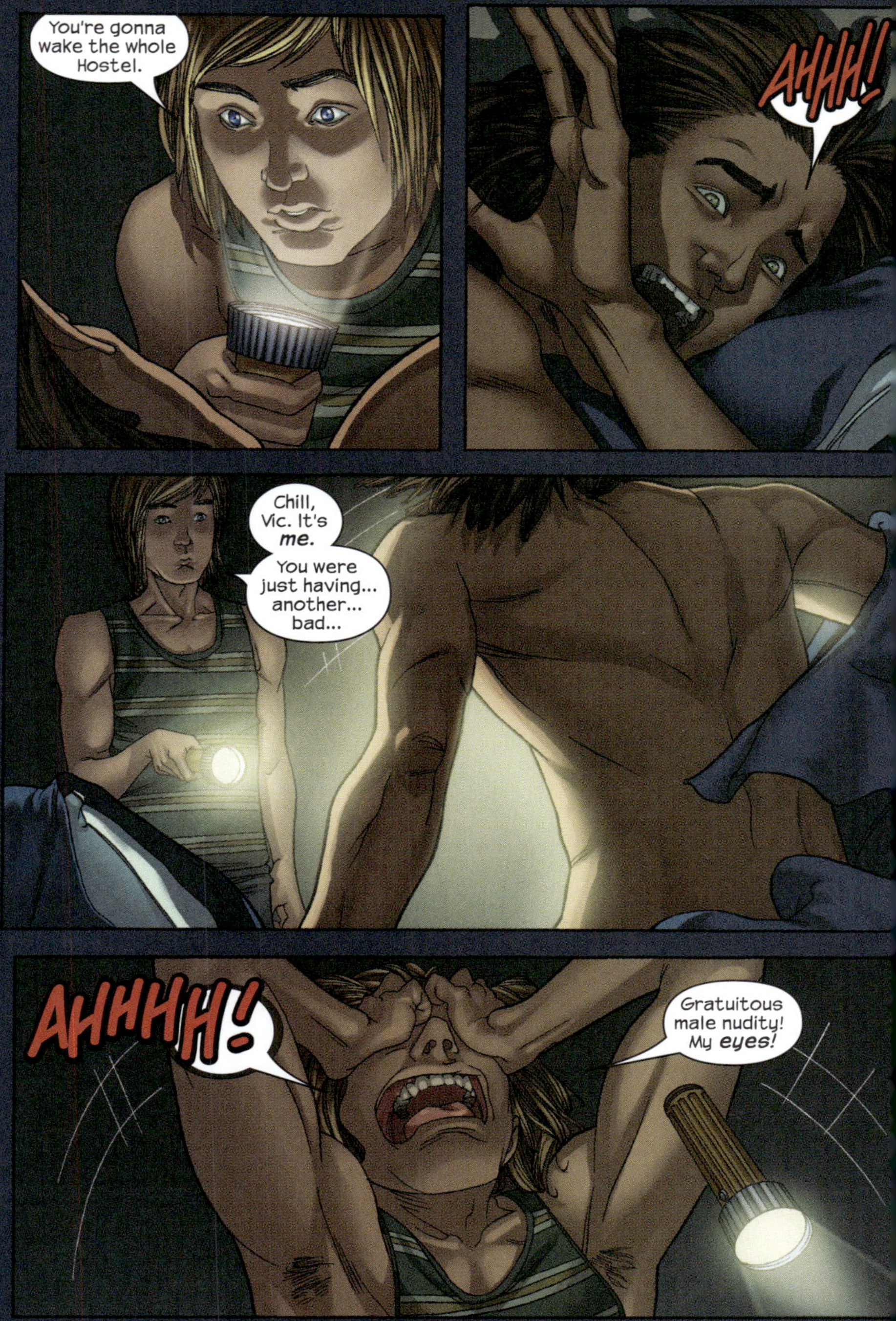
You're gonna wake the whole Hostel.
AHHH!
Chill, Vic. It's *me.*
You were just having... another... bad...
AHHHH!
Gratuitous male nudity! My *eyes!*

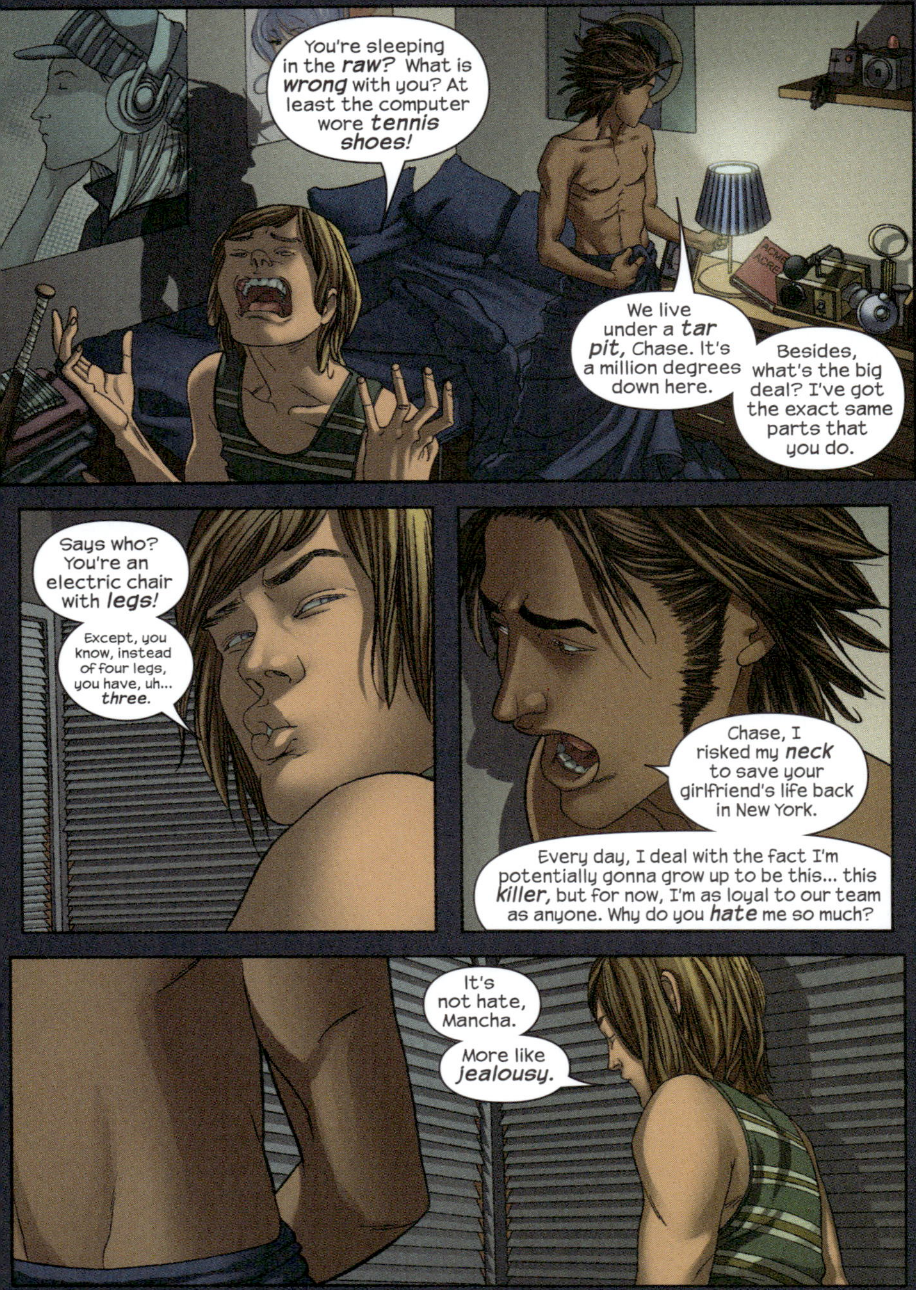
You're sleeping in the raw? What is wrong with you? At least the computer wore tennis shoes!
We live under a tar pit, Chase. It's a million degrees down here.
Besides, what's the big deal? I've got the exact same parts that you do.
Says who? You're an electric chair with legs!
Except, you know, instead of four legs, you have, uh... three.
Chase, I risked my neck to save your girlfriend's life back in New York.
Every day, I deal with the fact I'm potentially gonna grow up to be this... this killer, but for now, I'm as loyal to our team as anyone. Why do you hate me so much?
It's not hate, Mancha.
More like jealousy.

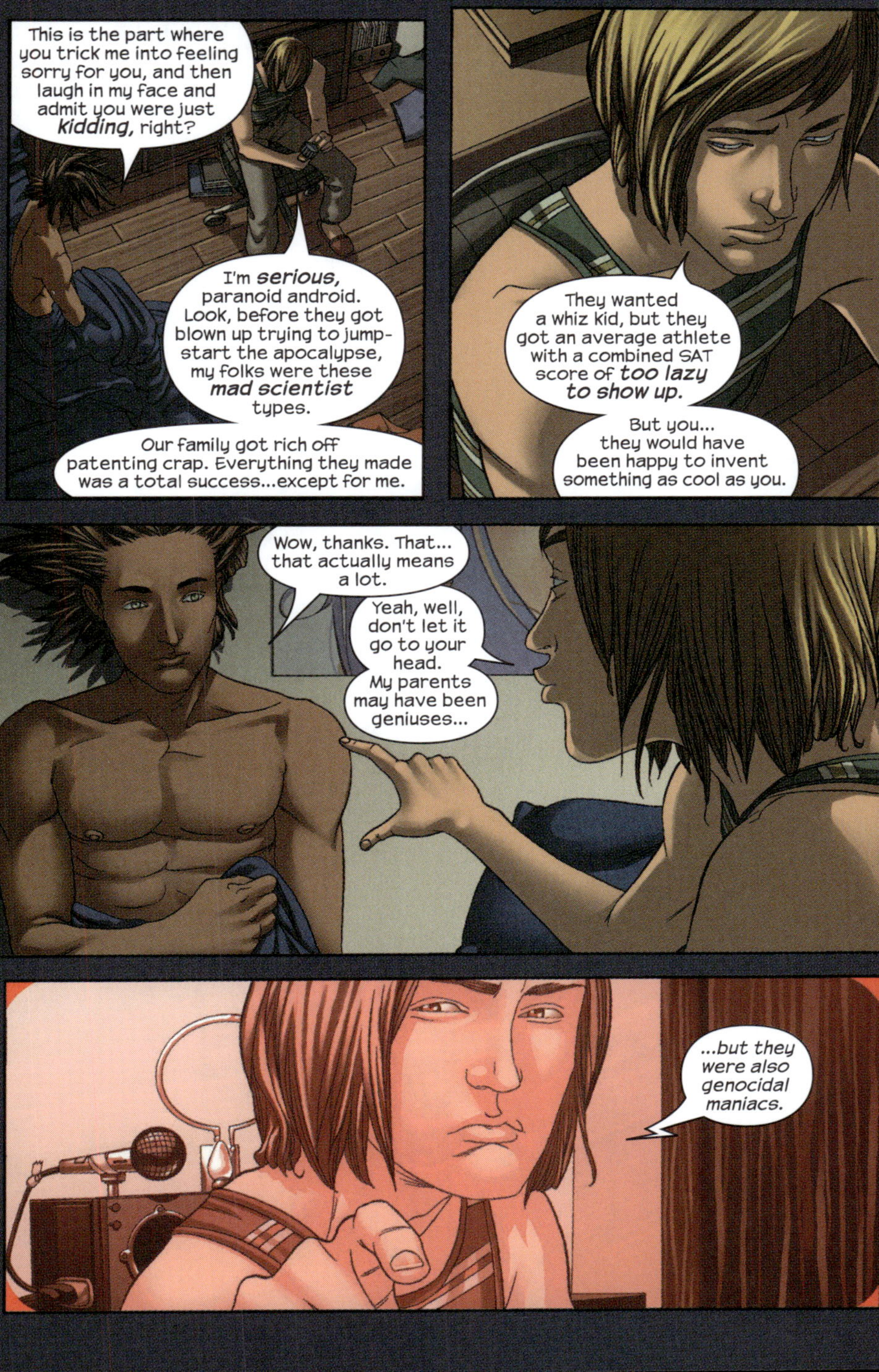

This is the part where you trick me into feeling sorry for you, and then laugh in my face and admit you were just *kidding,* right?
I'm *serious,* paranoid android. Look, before they got blown up trying to jump-start the apocalypse, my folks were these *mad scientist* types.
Our family got rich off patenting crap. Everything they made was a total success...except for me.
They wanted a whiz kid, but they got an average athlete with a combined SAT score of *too lazy to show up.*
But you... they would have been happy to invent something as cool as you.
Wow, thanks. That... that actually means a lot.
Yeah, well, don't let it go to your head.
My parents may have been geniuses...
...but they were also genocidal maniacs.

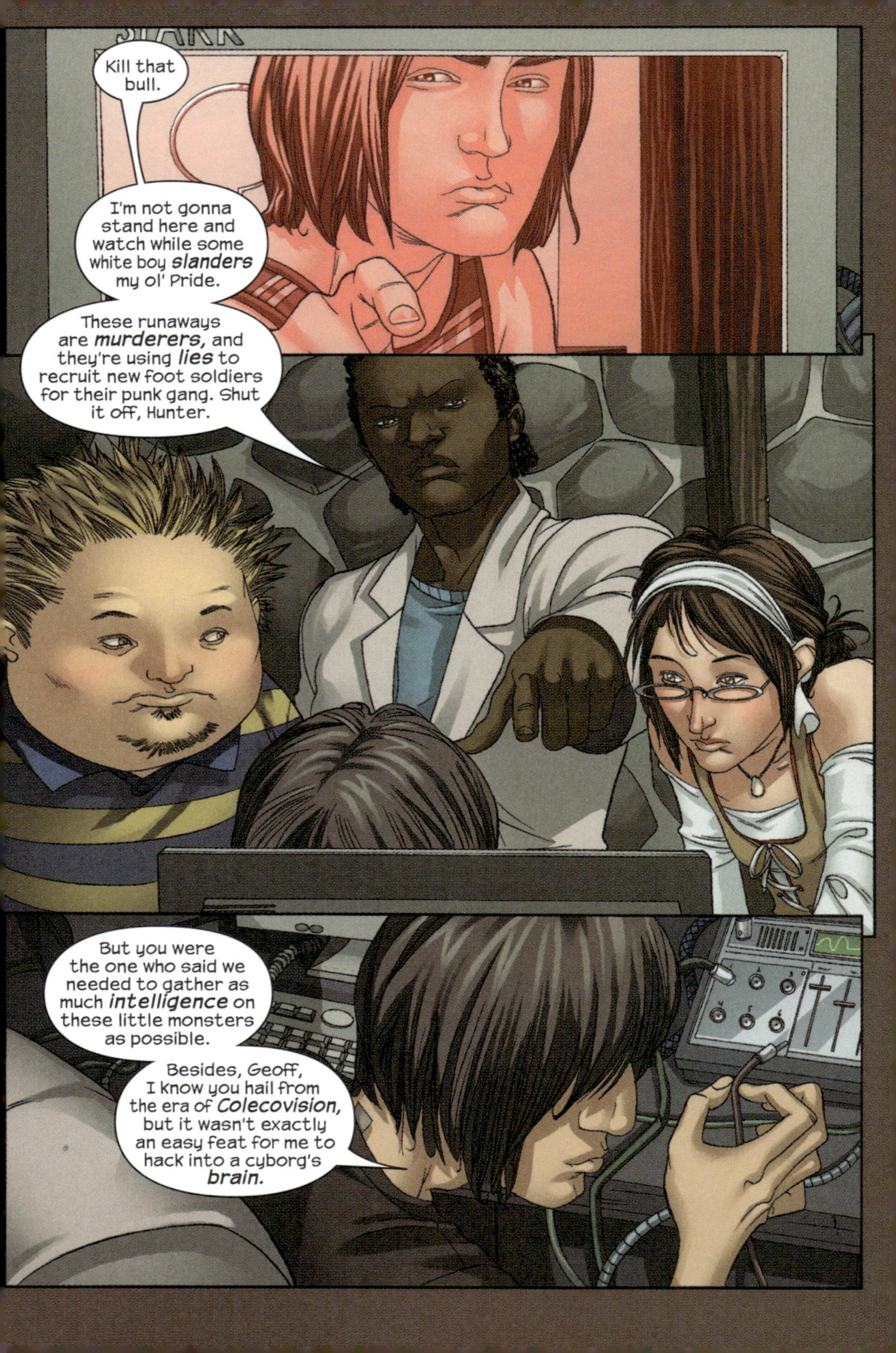

STARK
Kill that bull.
I'm not gonna stand here and watch while some white boy *slanders* my ol' Pride.
These runaways are *murderers,* and they're using *lies* to recruit new foot soldiers for their punk gang. Shut it off, Hunter.
But you were the one who said we needed to gather as much *intelligence* on these little monsters as possible.
Besides, Geoff, I know you hail from the era of *Colecovision,* but it wasn't exactly an easy feat for me to hack into a cyborg's *brain.*

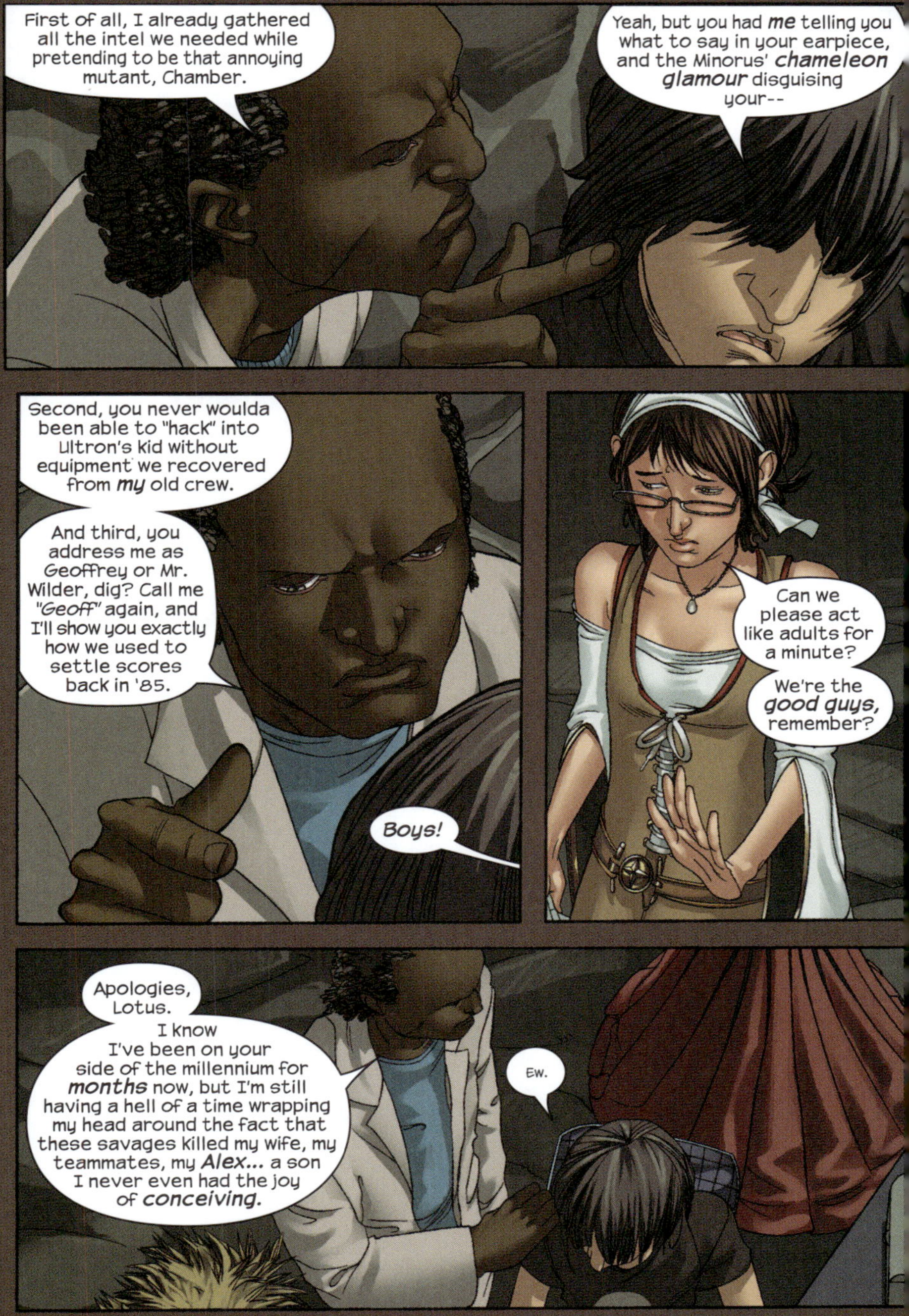
First of all, I already gathered all the intel we needed while pretending to be that annoying mutant, Chamber.
Yeah, but you had *me* telling you what to say in your earpiece, and the Minorus' *chameleon glamour* disguising your--
Second, you never woulda been able to "hack" into Ultron's kid without equipment we recovered from *my* old crew.
And third, you address me as Geoffrey or Mr. Wilder, dig? Call me *"Geoff"* again, and I'll show you exactly how we used to settle scores back in '85.
Boys!
Can we please act like adults for a minute?
We're the *good guys,* remember?
Apologies, Lotus.
I know I've been on your side of the millennium for *months* now, but I'm still having a hell of a time wrapping my head around the fact that these savages killed my wife, my teammates, my *Alex...* a son I never even had the joy of *conceiving.*
Ew.

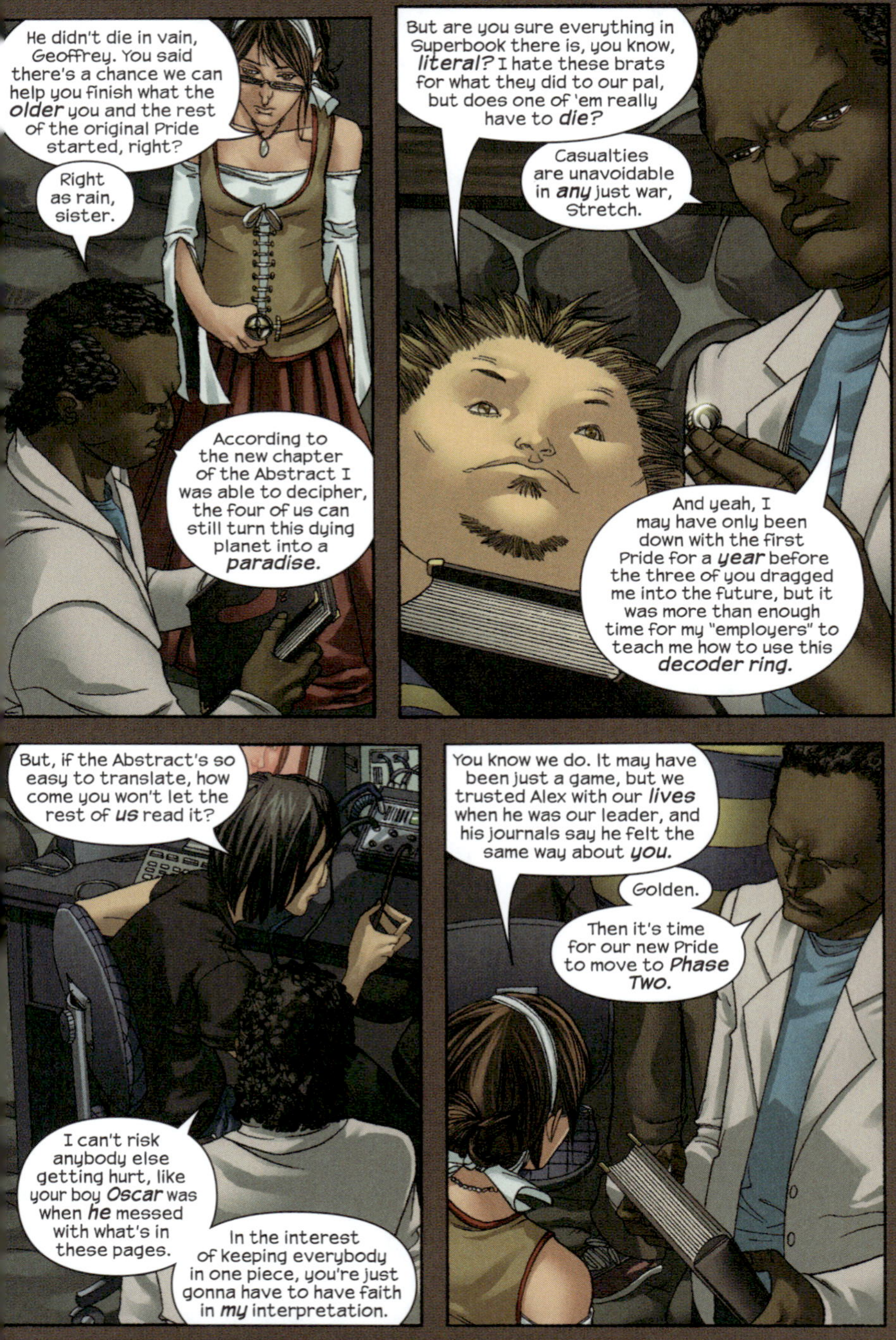
He didn't die in vain, Geoffrey. You said there's a chance we can help you finish what the older you and the rest of the original Pride started, right?
Right as rain, sister.
According to the new chapter of the Abstract I was able to decipher, the four of us can still turn this dying planet into a paradise.
But are you sure everything in Superbook there is, you know, literal? I hate these brats for what they did to our pal, but does one of 'em really have to die?
Casualties are unavoidable in any just war, Stretch.
And yeah, I may have only been down with the first Pride for a year before the three of you dragged me into the future, but it was more than enough time for my "employers" to teach me how to use this decoder ring.
But, if the Abstract's so easy to translate, how come you won't let the rest of us read it?
I can't risk anybody else getting hurt, like your boy Oscar was when he messed with what's in these pages.
In the interest of keeping everybody in one piece, you're just gonna have to have faith in my interpretation.
You know we do. It may have been just a game, but we trusted Alex with our lives when he was our leader, and his journals say he felt the same way about you.
Golden.
Then it's time for our new Pride to move to Phase Two.

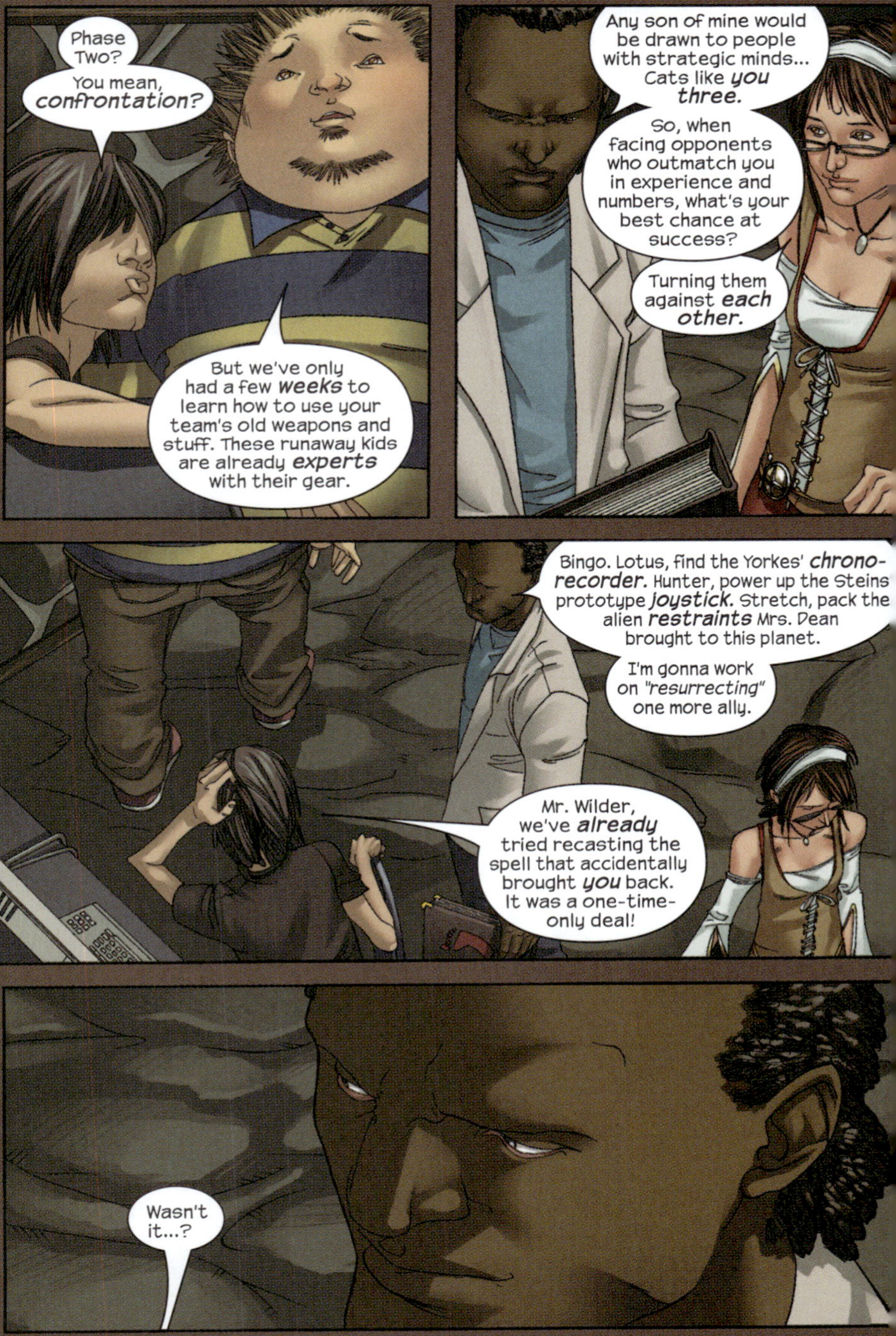

Phase Two?
You mean, *confrontation?*
But we've only had a few ***weeks*** to learn how to use your team's old weapons and stuff. These runaway kids are already ***experts*** with their gear.
Any son of mine would be drawn to people with strategic minds... Cats like ***you three.***
So, when facing opponents who outmatch you in experience and numbers, what's your best chance at success?
Turning them against ***each other.***
Bingo. Lotus, find the Yorkes' ***chrono-recorder.*** Hunter, power up the Steins prototype ***joystick.*** Stretch, pack the alien ***restraints*** Mrs. Dean brought to this planet.
I'm gonna work on *"resurrecting"* one more ally.
Mr. Wilder, we've ***already*** tried recasting the spell that accidentally brought ***you*** back. It was a one-time-only deal!
Wasn't it...?

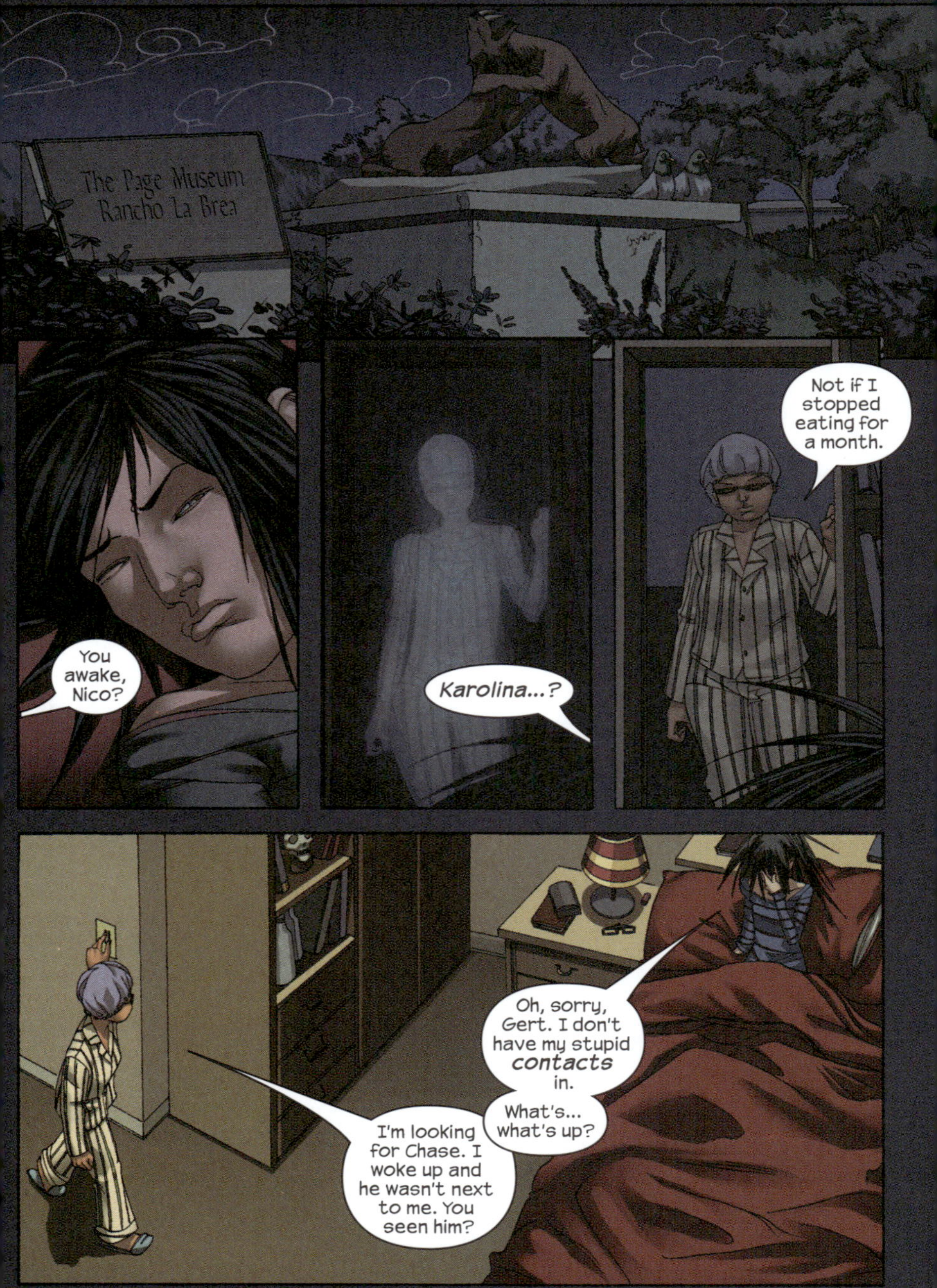

The Page Museum
Rancho La Brea
You awake, Nico?
Karolina...?
Not if I stopped eating for a month.
I'm looking for Chase. I woke up and he wasn't next to me. You seen him?
Oh, sorry, Gert. I don't have my stupid contacts in.
What's... what's up?

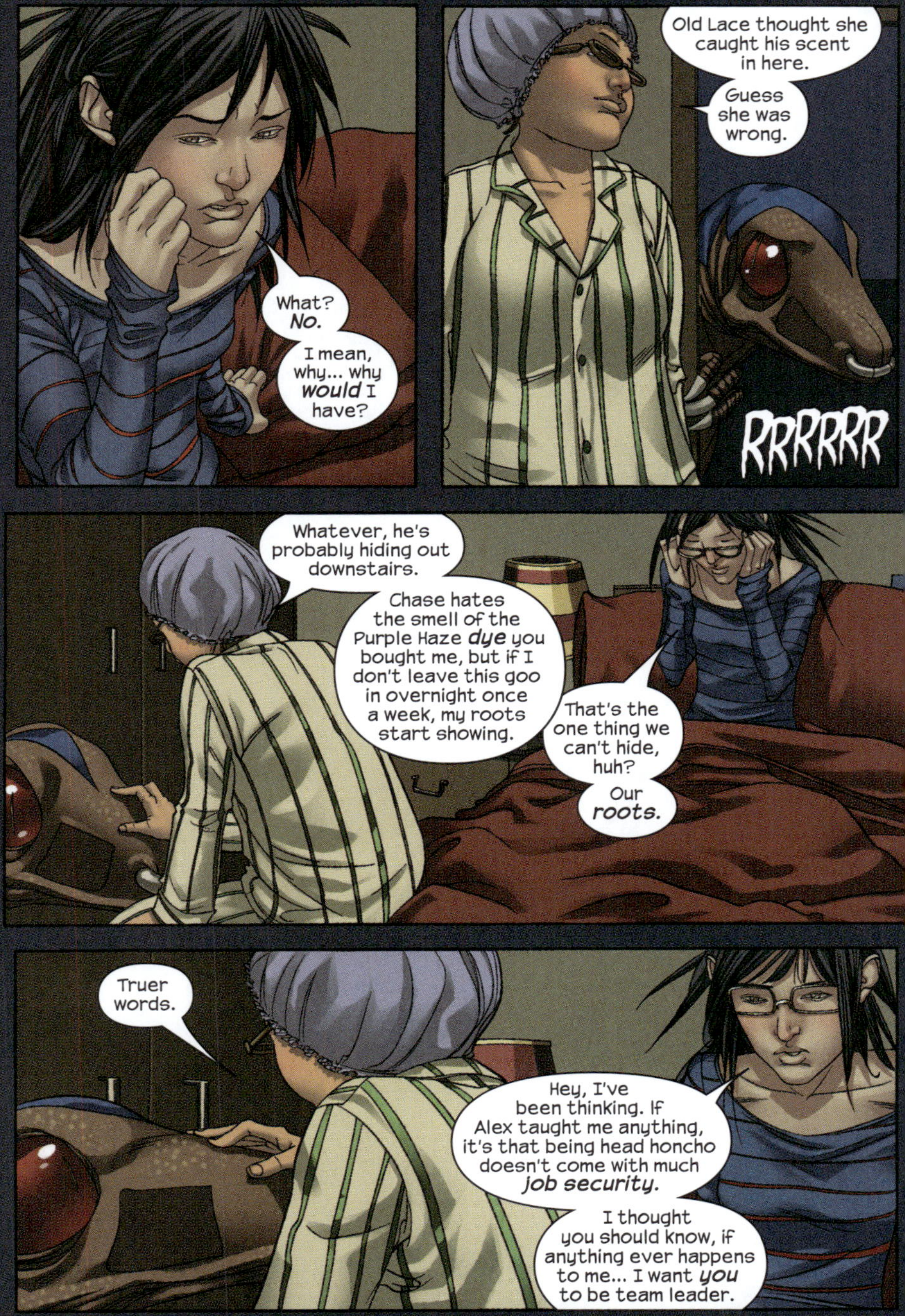
Old Lace thought she caught his scent in here.
Guess she was wrong.
What? No.
I mean, why... why would I have?
RRRRRR
Whatever, he's probably hiding out downstairs.
Chase hates the smell of the Purple Haze dye you bought me, but if I don't leave this goo in overnight once a week, my roots start showing.
That's the one thing we can't hide, huh?
Our roots.
Truer words.
Hey, I've been thinking. If Alex taught me anything, it's that being head honcho doesn't come with much job security.
I thought you should know, if anything ever happens to me... I want you to be team leader.

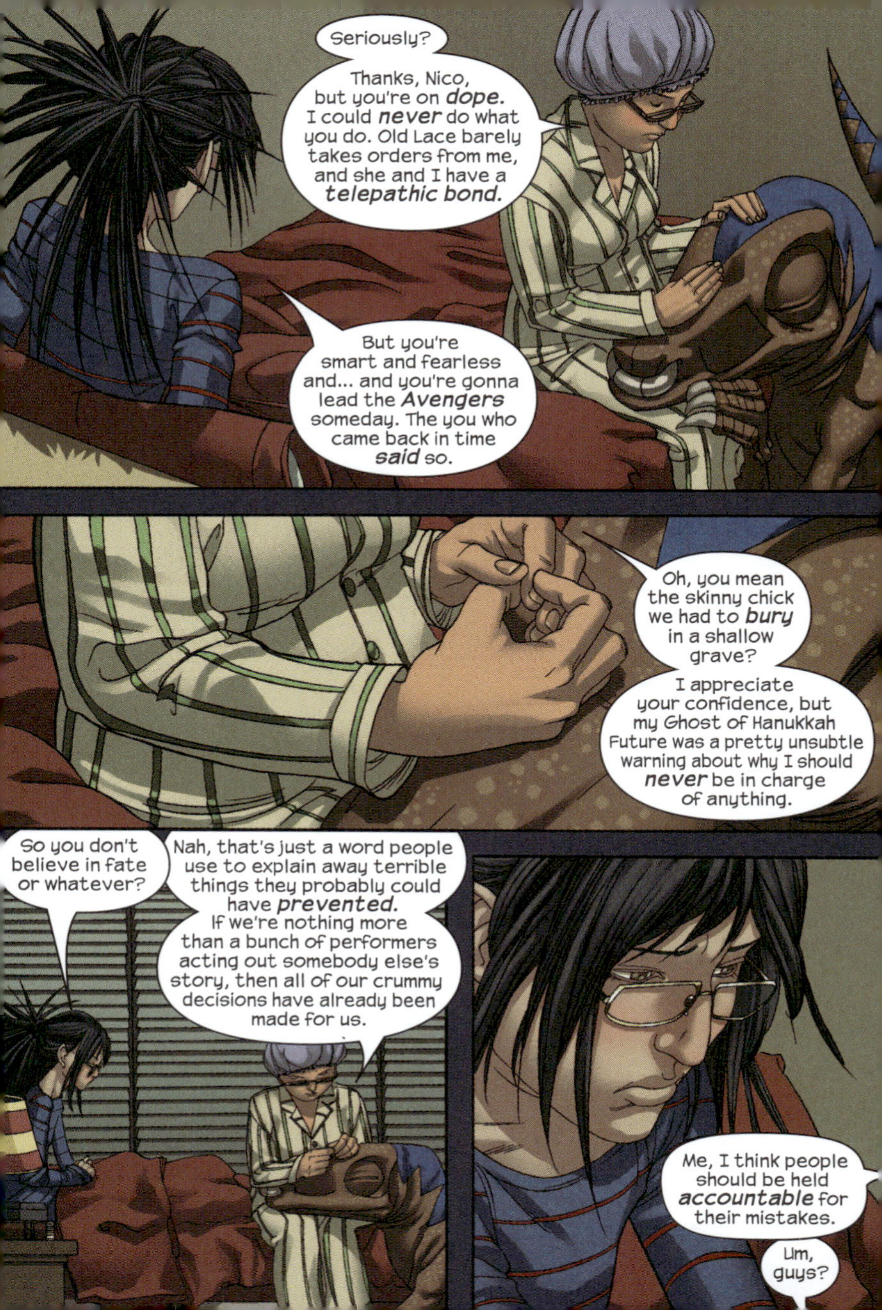
Seriously?
Thanks, Nico, but you're on dope. I could never do what you do. Old Lace barely takes orders from me, and she and I have a telepathic bond.
But you're smart and fearless and... and you're gonna lead the Avengers someday. The you who came back in time said so.
Oh, you mean the skinny chick we had to bury in a shallow grave?
I appreciate your confidence, but my Ghost of Hanukkah Future was a pretty unsubtle warning about why I should never be in charge of anything.
So you don't believe in fate or whatever?
Nah, that's just a word people use to explain away terrible things they probably could have prevented.
If we're nothing more than a bunch of performers acting out somebody else's story, then all of our crummy decisions have already been made for us.
Me, I think people should be held accountable for their mistakes.
Um, guys?

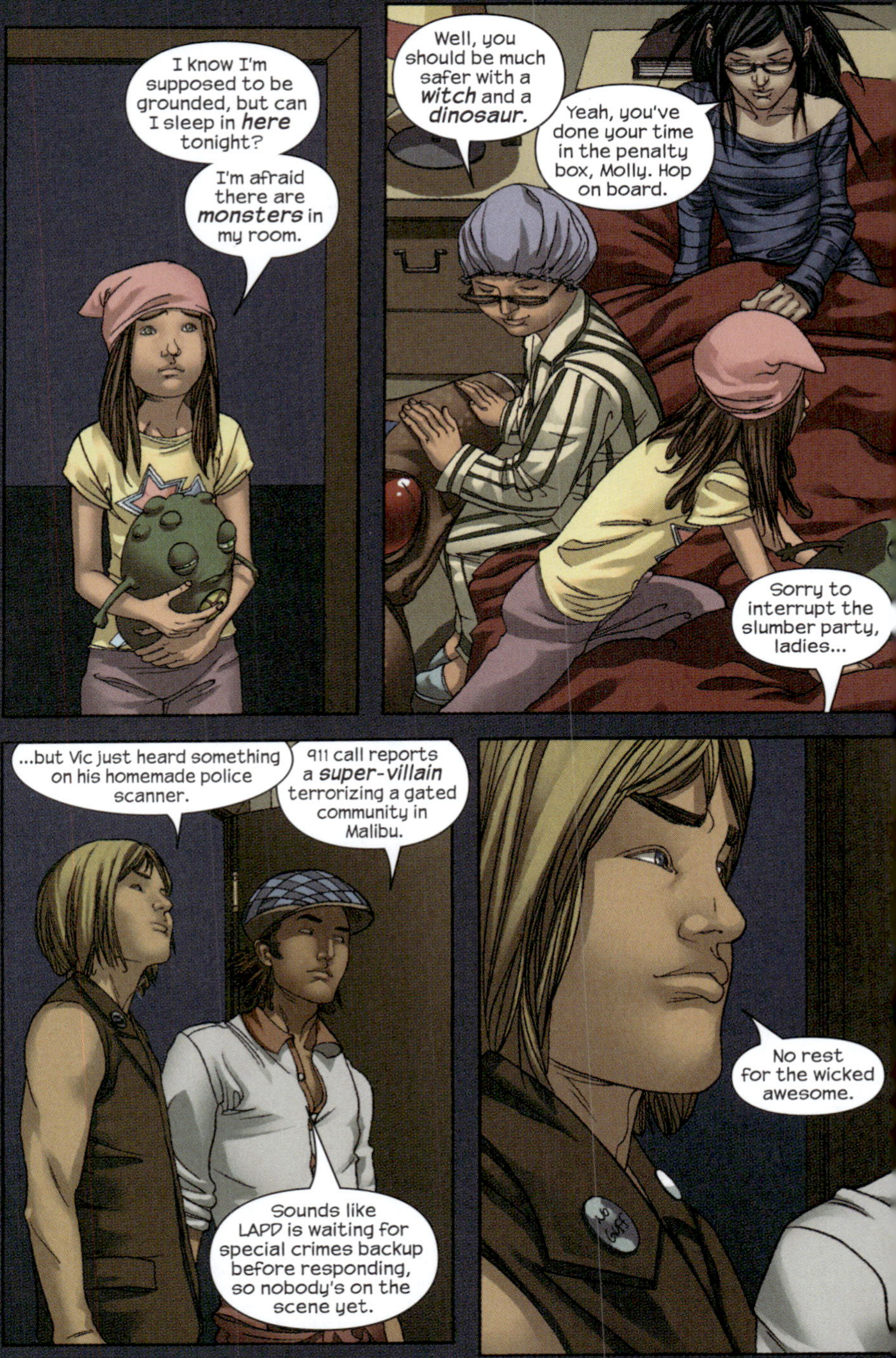
I know I'm supposed to be grounded, but can I sleep in here tonight?
I'm afraid there are monsters in my room.
Well, you should be much safer with a witch and a dinosaur.
Yeah, you've done your time in the penalty box, Molly. Hop on board.
Sorry to interrupt the slumber party, ladies...
...but Vic just heard something on his homemade police scanner.
911 call reports a super-villain terrorizing a gated community in Malibu.
Sounds like LAPD is waiting for special crimes backup before responding, so nobody's on the scene yet.
No rest for the wicked awesome.

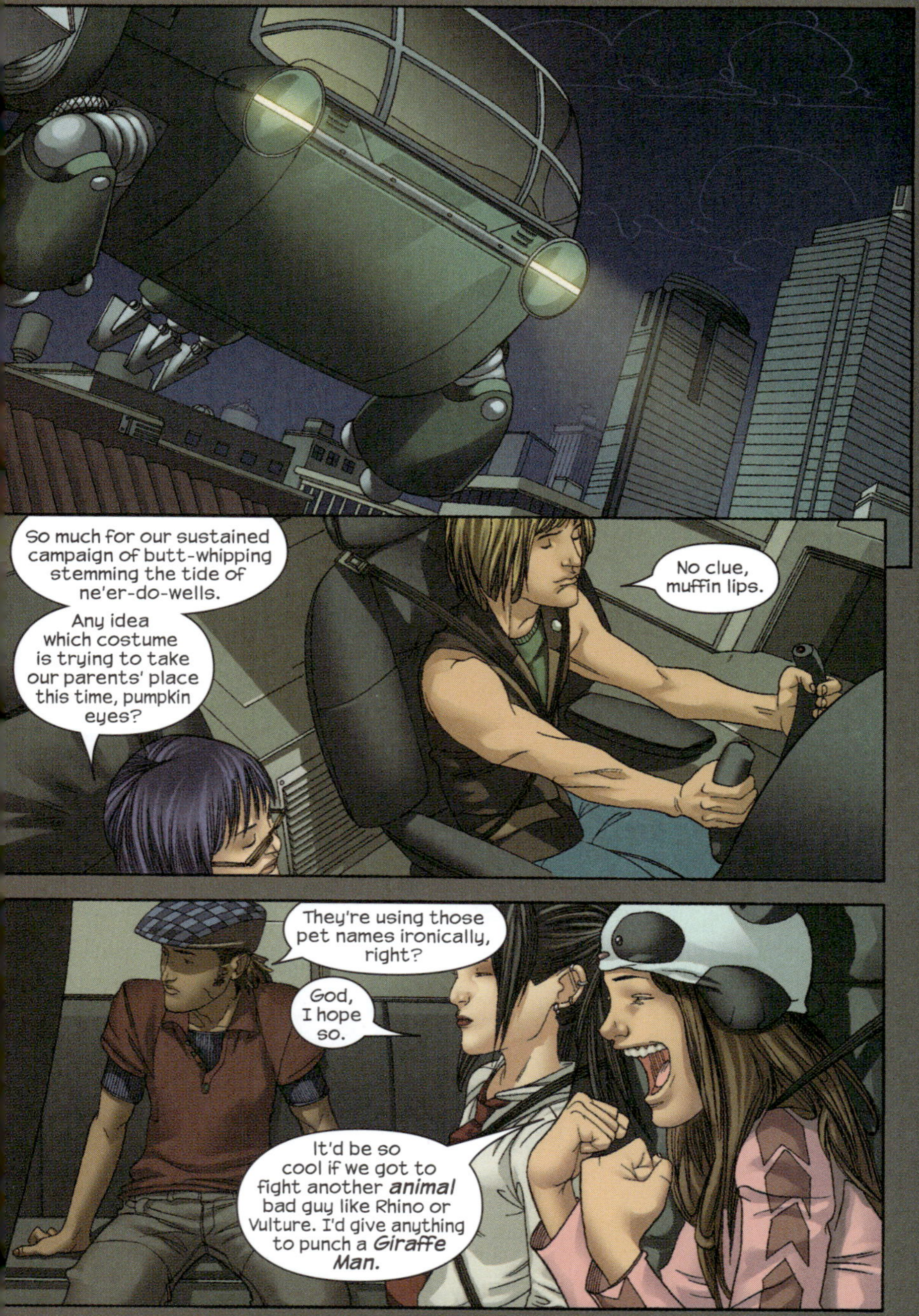

So much for our sustained campaign of butt-whipping stemming the tide of ne'er-do-wells.
Any idea which costume is trying to take our parents' place this time, pumpkin eyes?
No clue, muffin lips.
They're using those pet names ironically, right?
God, I hope so.
It'd be so cool if we got to fight another *animal* bad guy like Rhino or Vulture. I'd give anything to punch a *Giraffe Man*.

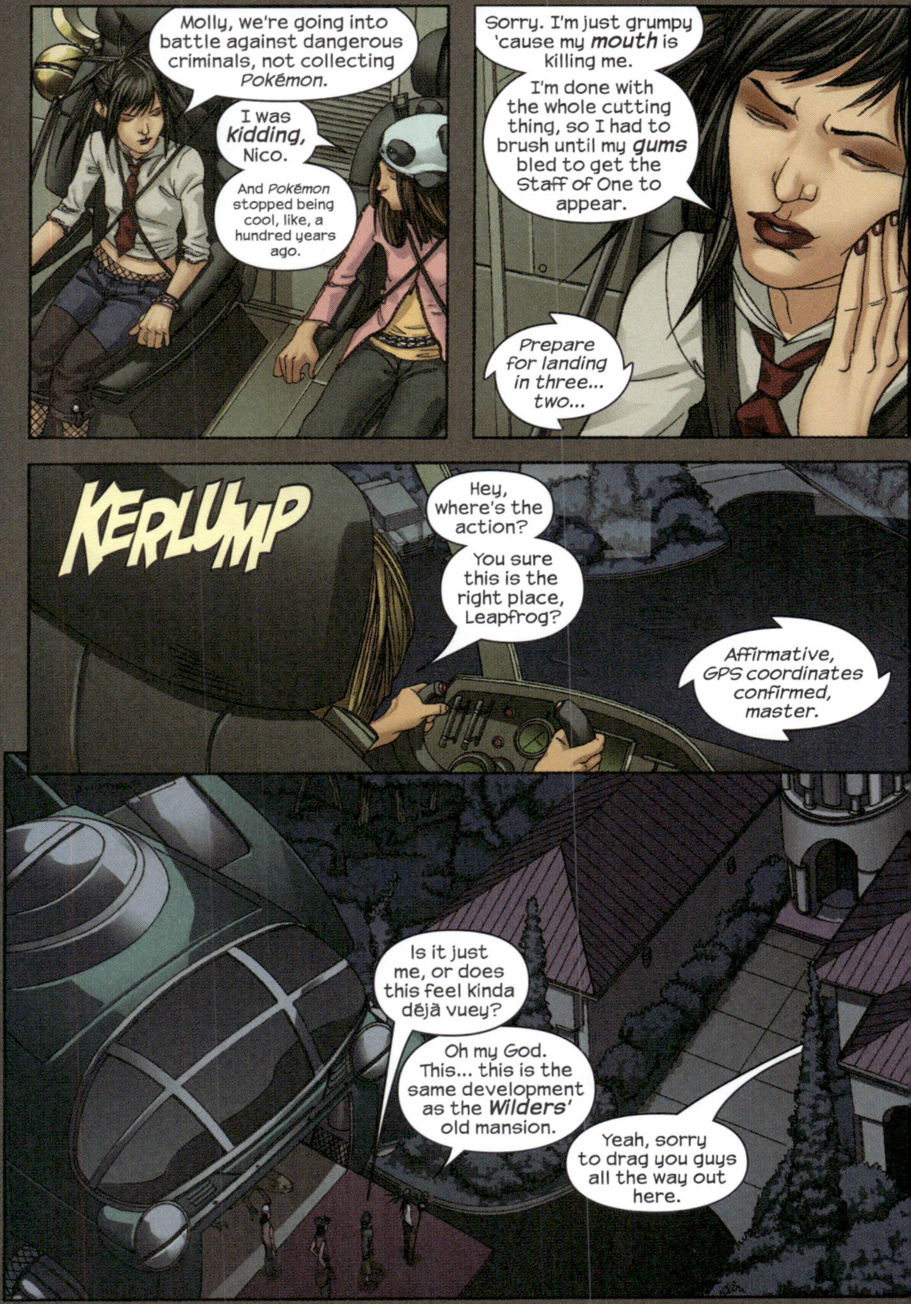
Molly, we're going into battle against dangerous criminals, not collecting *Pokémon.*
I was *kidding,* Nico.
And *Pokémon* stopped being cool, like, a hundred years ago.
Sorry. I'm just grumpy 'cause my *mouth* is killing me.
I'm done with the whole cutting thing, so I had to brush until my *gums* bled to get the Staff of One to appear.
Prepare for landing in three... two...
KERLUMP
Hey, where's the action?
You sure this is the right place, Leapfrog?
Affirmative, GPS coordinates confirmed, master.
Is it just me, or does this feel kinda déjà vuey?
Oh my God. This... this is the same development as the *Wilders'* old mansion.
Yeah, sorry to drag you guys all the way out here.

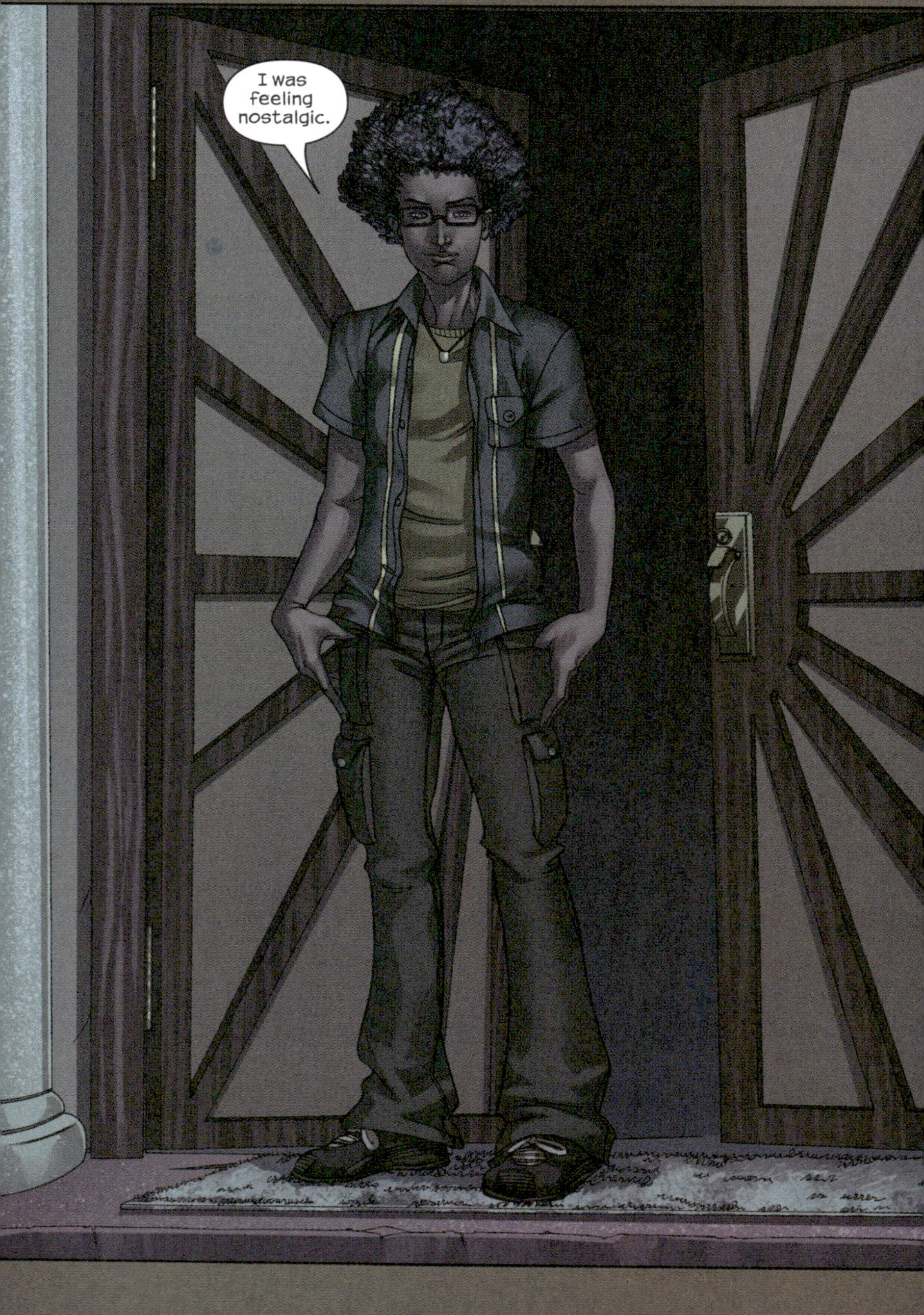
I was feeling nostalgic.

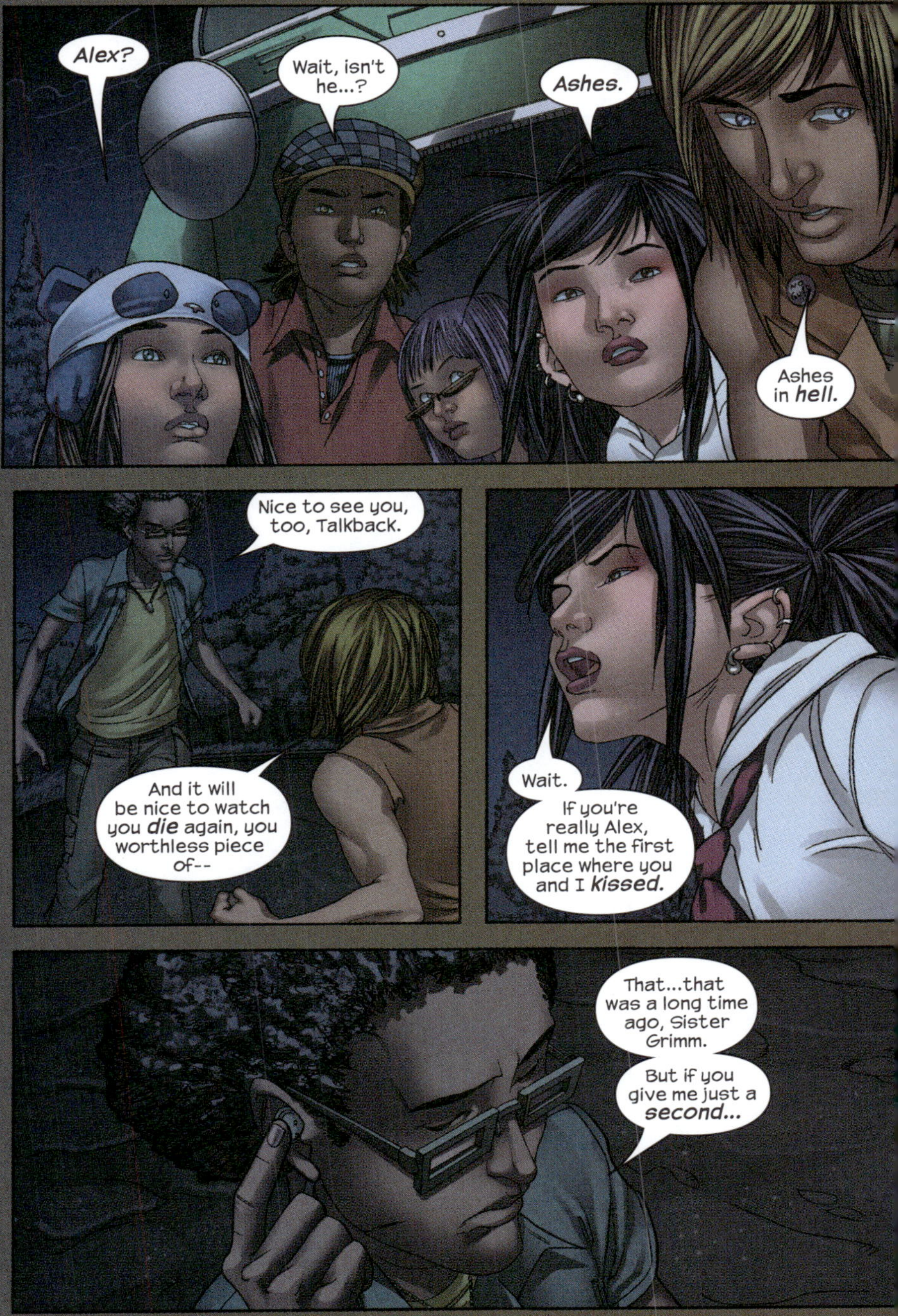
Alex?
Wait, isn't he...?
Ashes.
Ashes in hell.
Nice to see you, too, Talkback.
And it will be nice to watch you die again, you worthless piece of--
Wait.
If you're really Alex, tell me the first place where you and I kissed.
That...that was a long time ago, Sister Grimm.
But if you give me just a second...

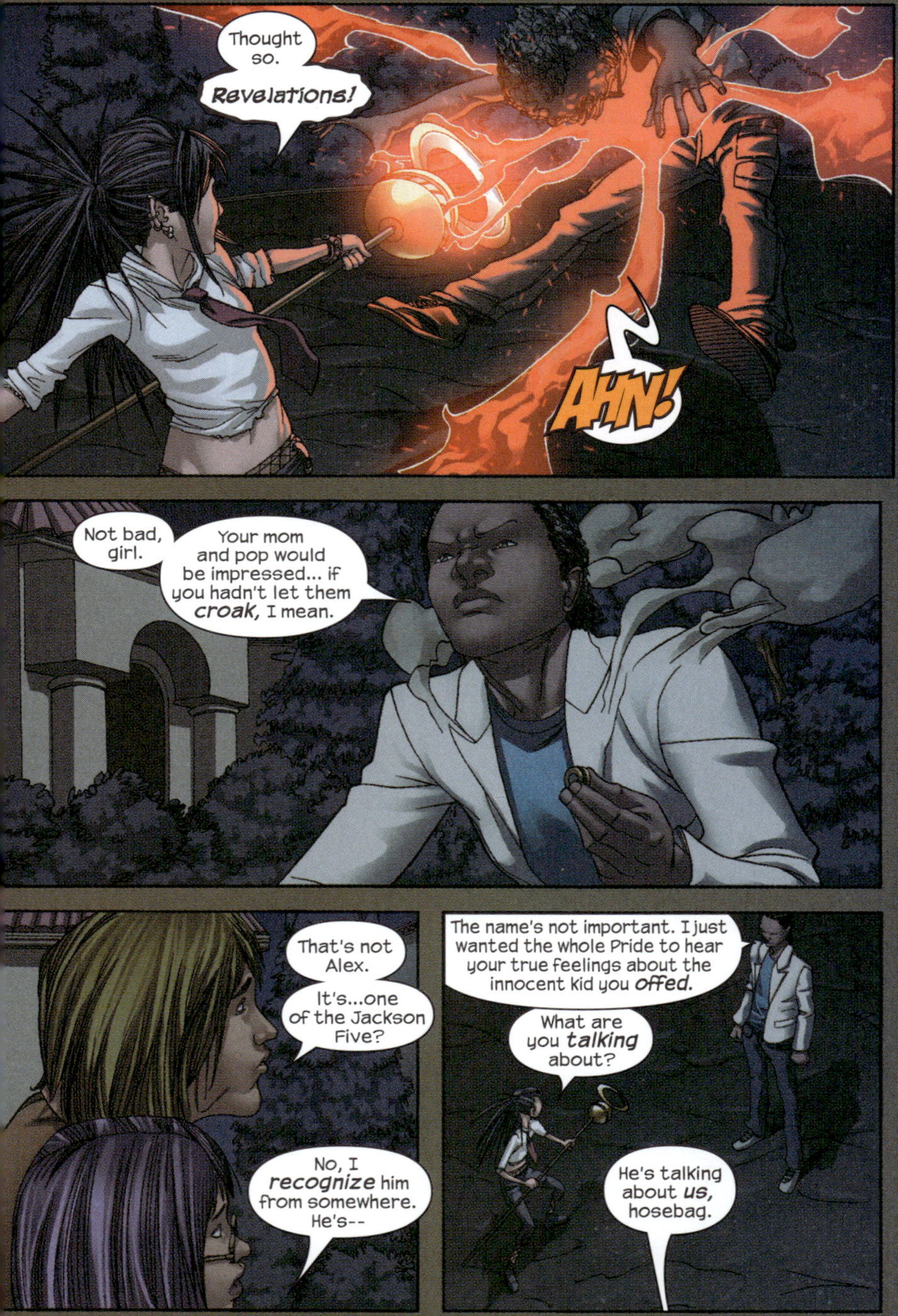
Thought so.
Revelations!
AHN!
Not bad, girl.
Your mom and pop would be impressed... if you hadn't let them croak, I mean.
That's not Alex.
It's...one of the Jackson Five?
No, I recognize him from somewhere. He's--
The name's not important. I just wanted the whole Pride to hear your true feelings about the innocent kid you offed.
What are you talking about?
He's talking about us, hosebag.

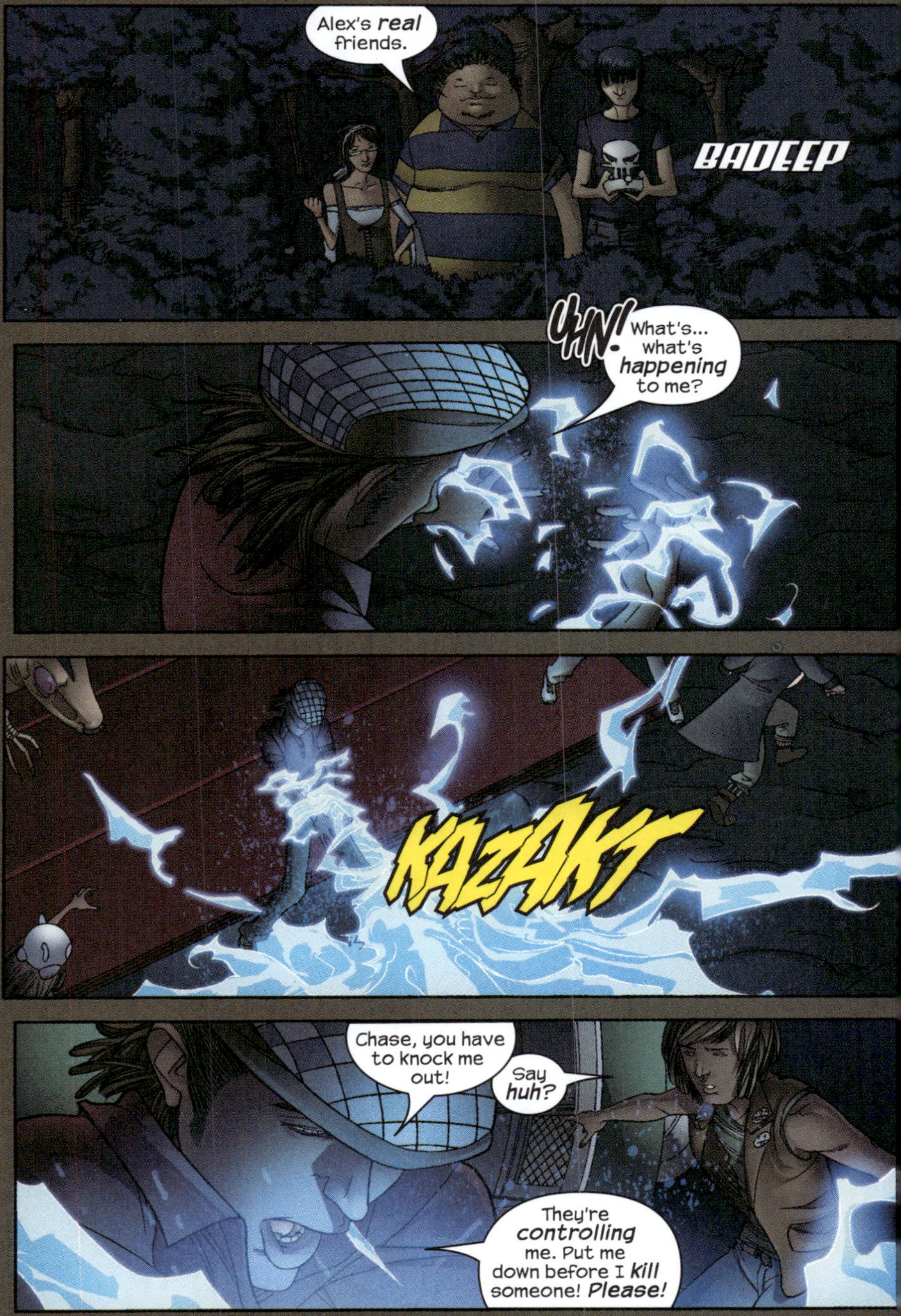
Alex's real friends.
BADEEP
UHN!
What's... what's happening to me?
KAZAKT
Chase, you have to knock me out!
Say huh?
They're controlling me. Put me down before I kill someone! Please!

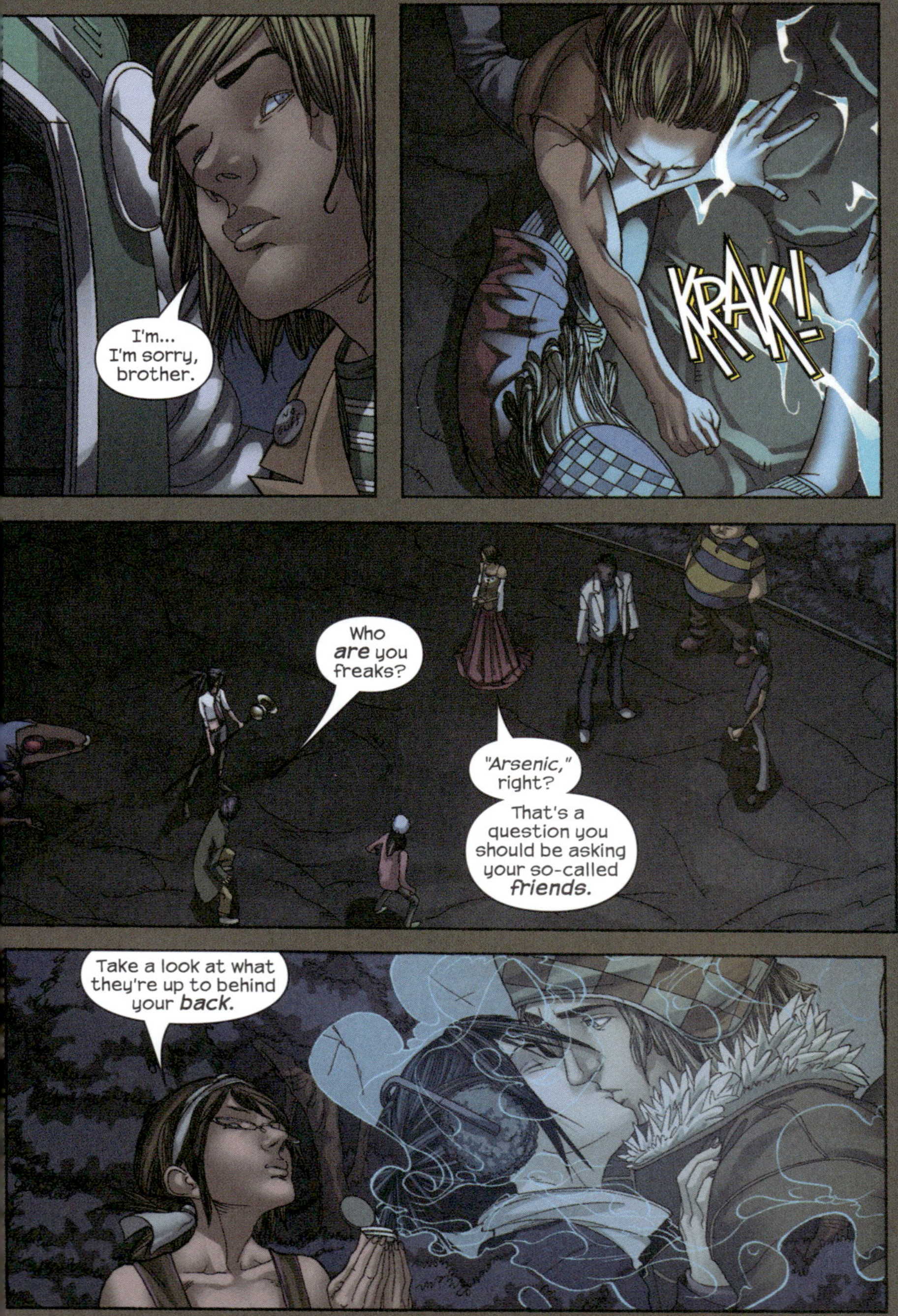

I'm... I'm sorry, brother.
KRAK!
Who **are** you freaks?
"Arsenic," right?
That's a question you should be asking your so-called **friends.**
Take a look at what they're up to behind your **back.**

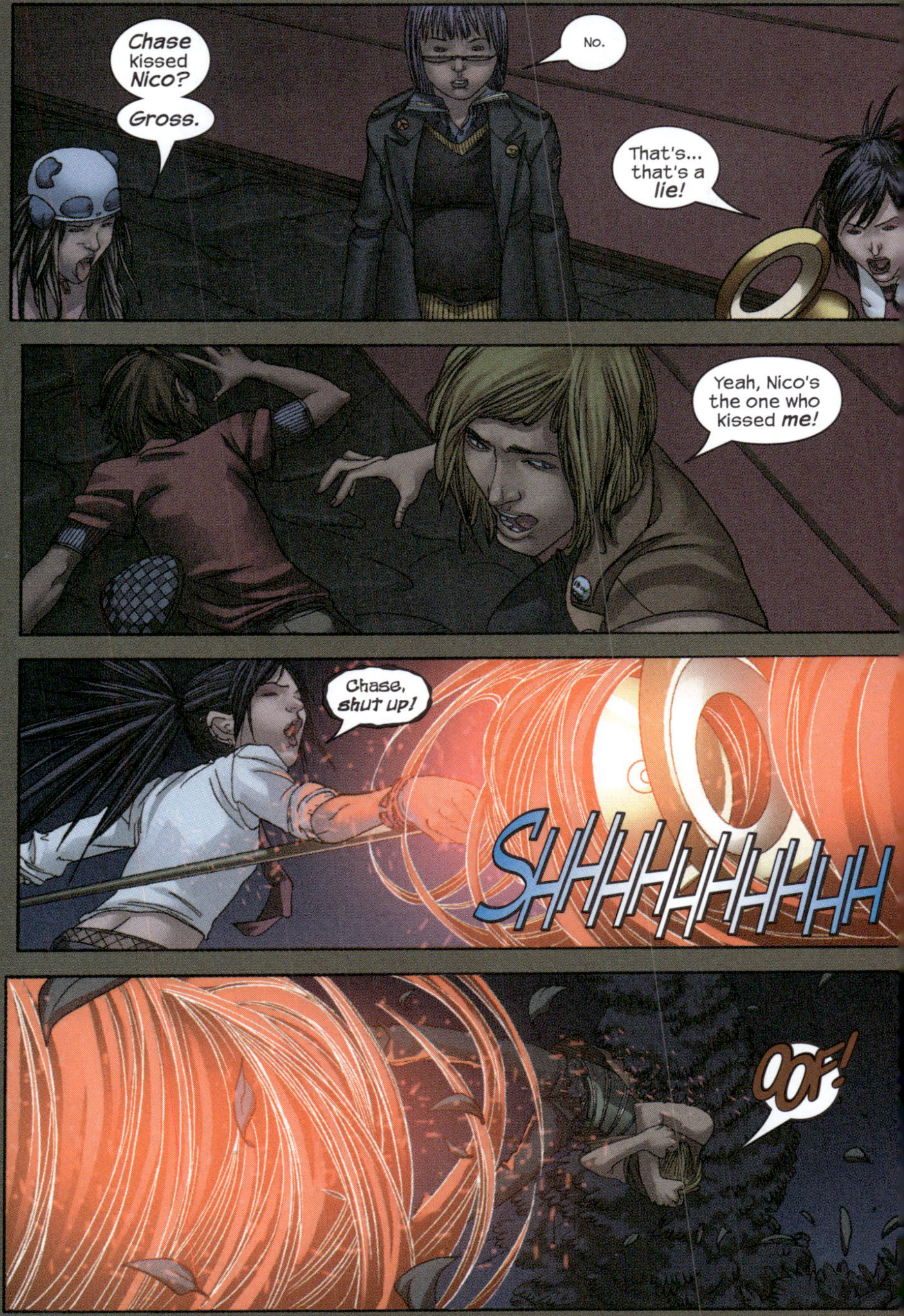
Chase kissed Nico?
Gross.
No.
That's... that's a lie!
Yeah, Nico's the one who kissed me!
Chase, shut up!
SHHHHHHHHHH
OOF!

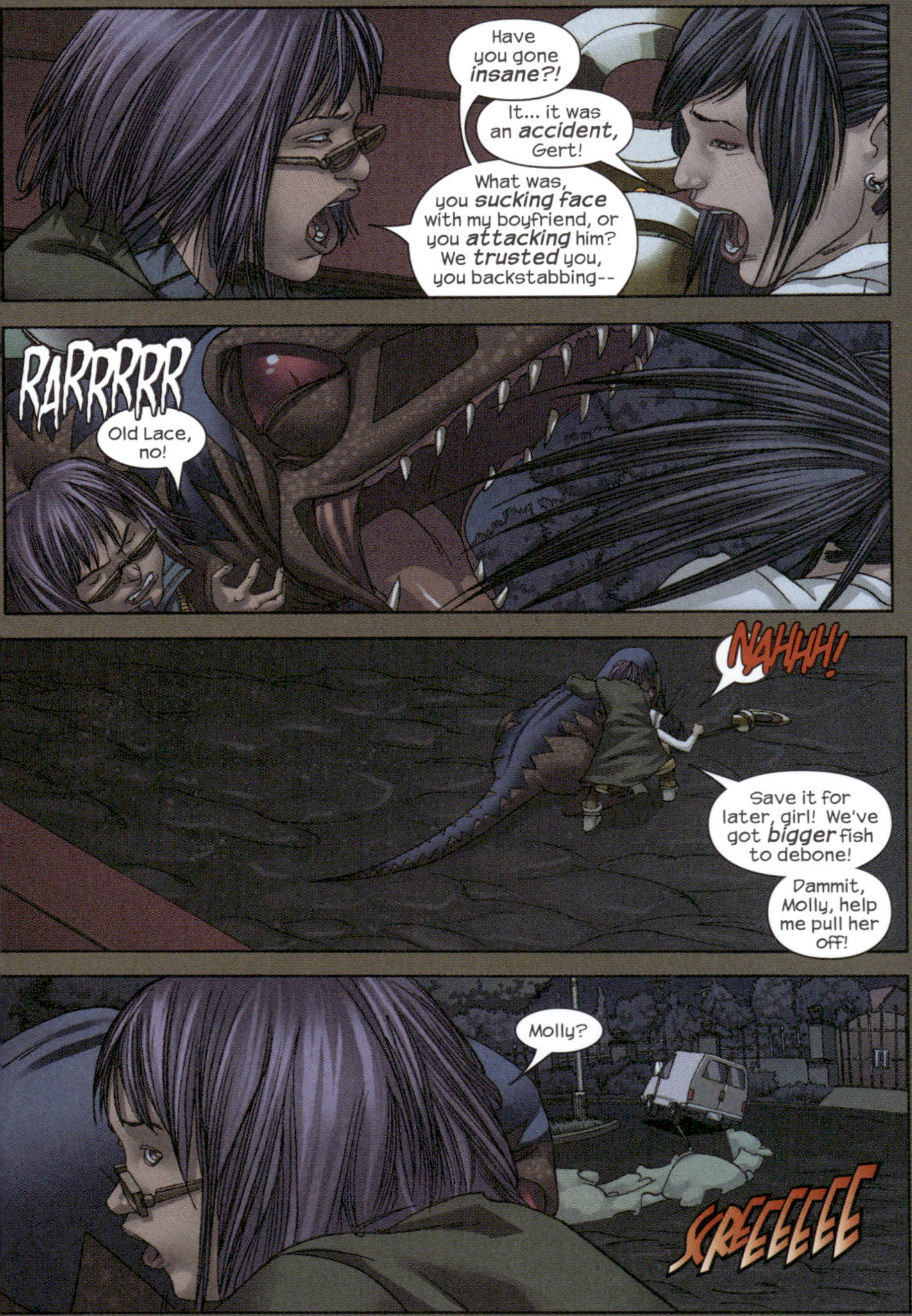
Have you gone insane?!
It... it was an accident, Gert!
What was, you sucking face with my boyfriend, or you attacking him? We trusted you, you backstabbing--
RARRRRR
Old Lace, no!
NAHHH!
Save it for later, girl! We've got bigger fish to debone!
Dammit, Molly, help me pull her off!
Molly?
SCREEEEEE

"Molly!"

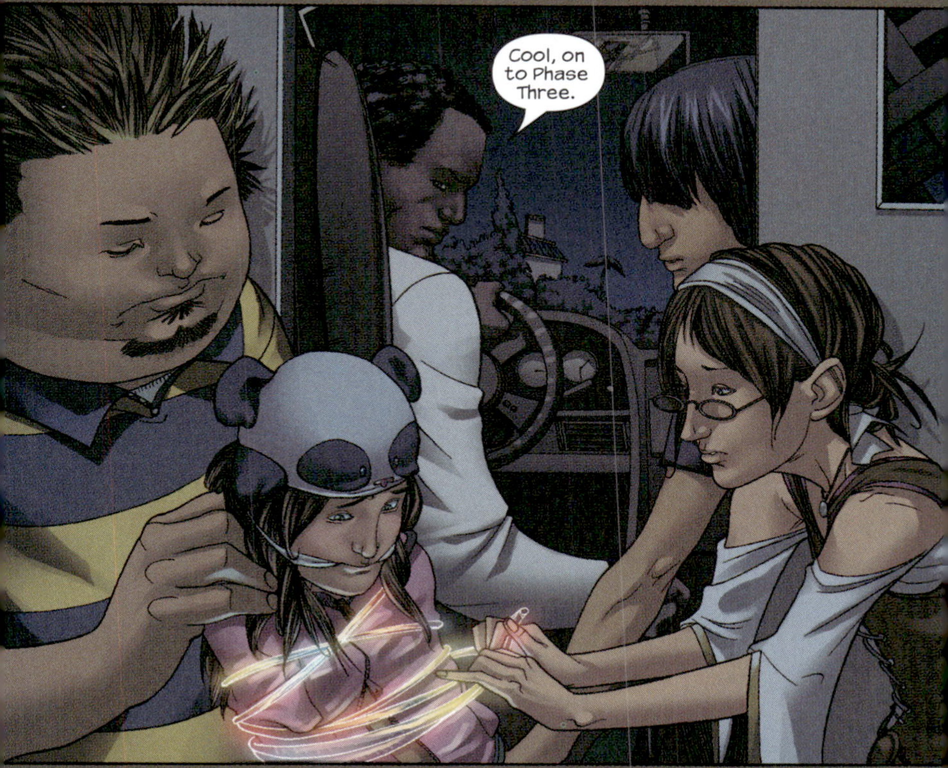
Cool, on to Phase Three.

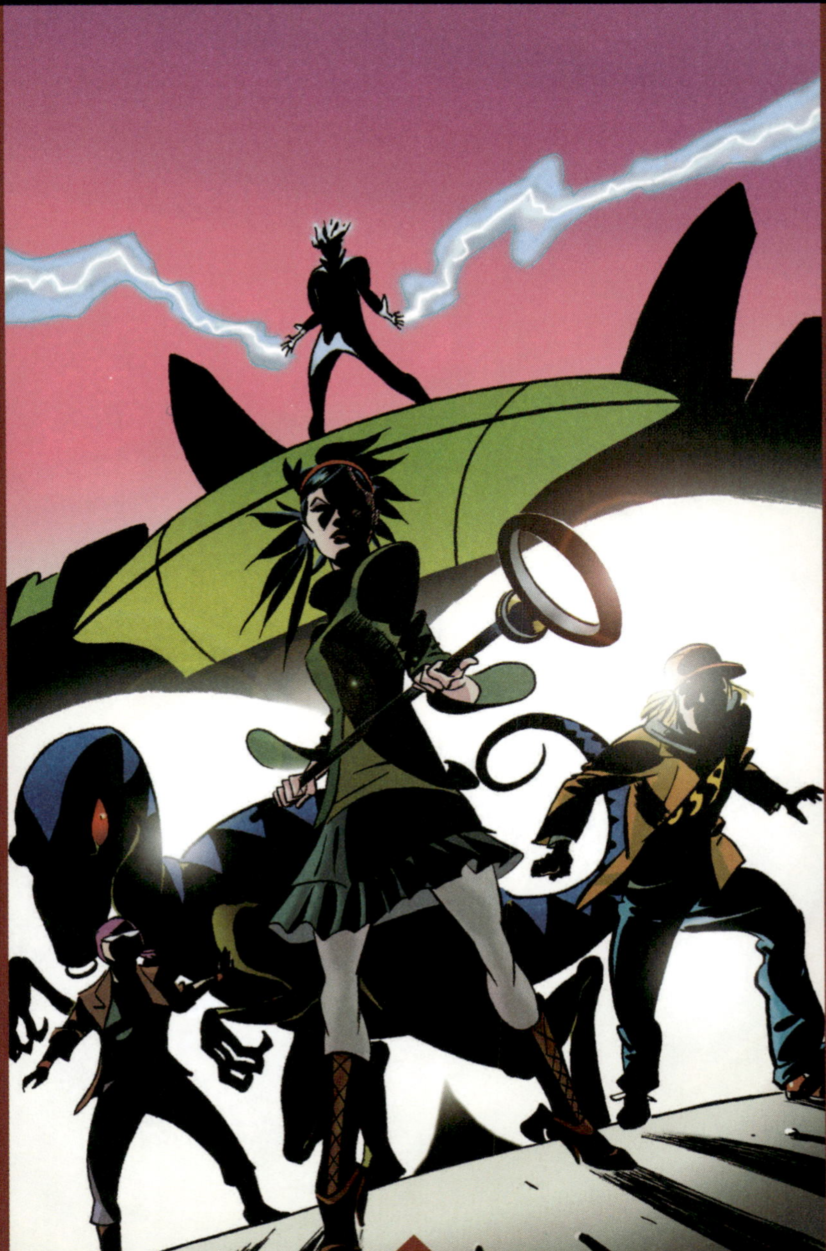
#16

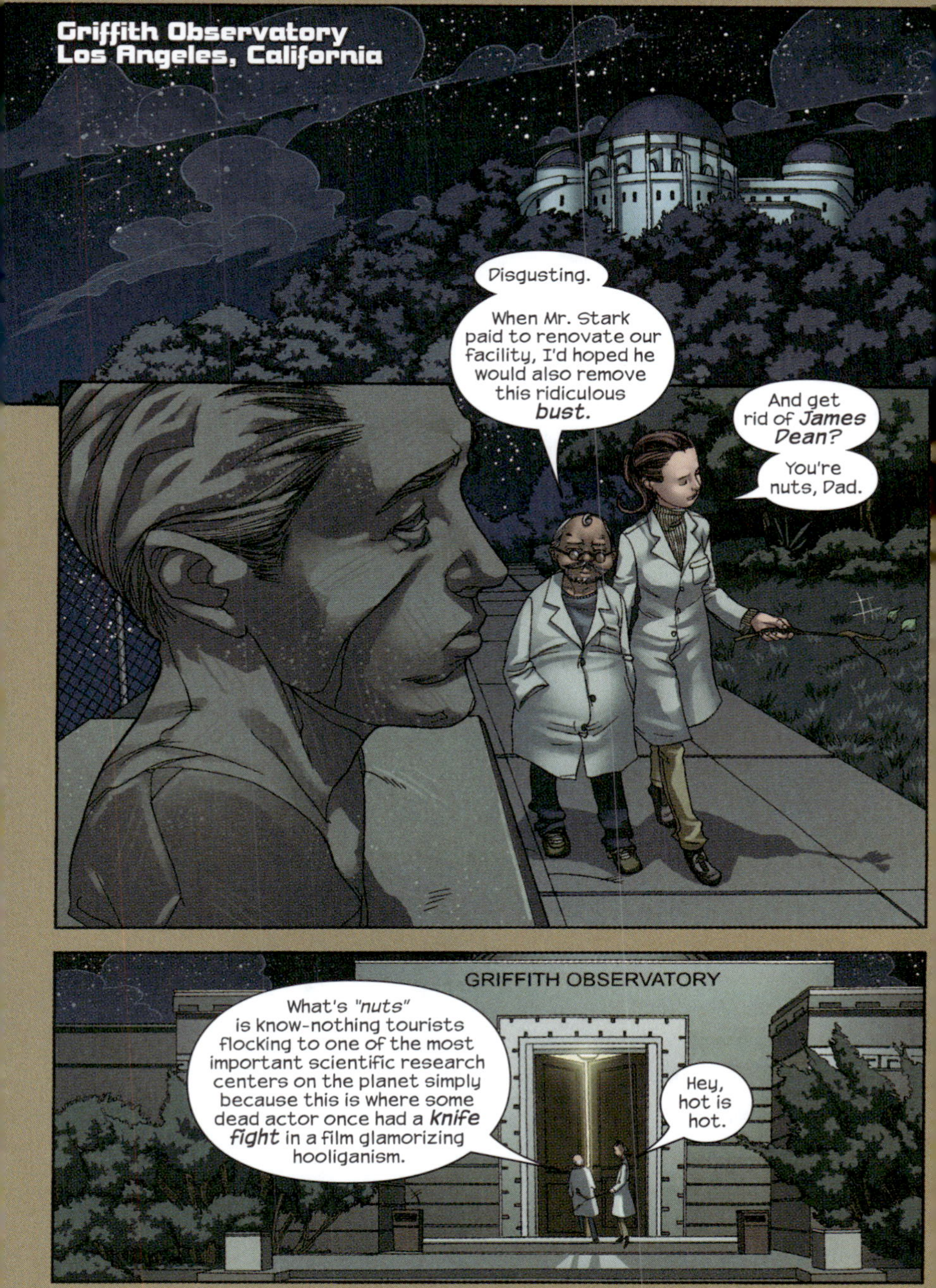
Griffith Observatory
Los Angeles, California
Disgusting.
When Mr. Stark paid to renovate our facility, I'd hoped he would also remove this ridiculous *bust.*
And get rid of *James Dean?*
You're nuts, Dad.
GRIFFITH OBSERVATORY
What's *"nuts"* is know-nothing tourists flocking to one of the most important scientific research centers on the planet simply because this is where some dead actor once had a *knife fight* in a film glamorizing hooliganism.
Hey, hot is hot.

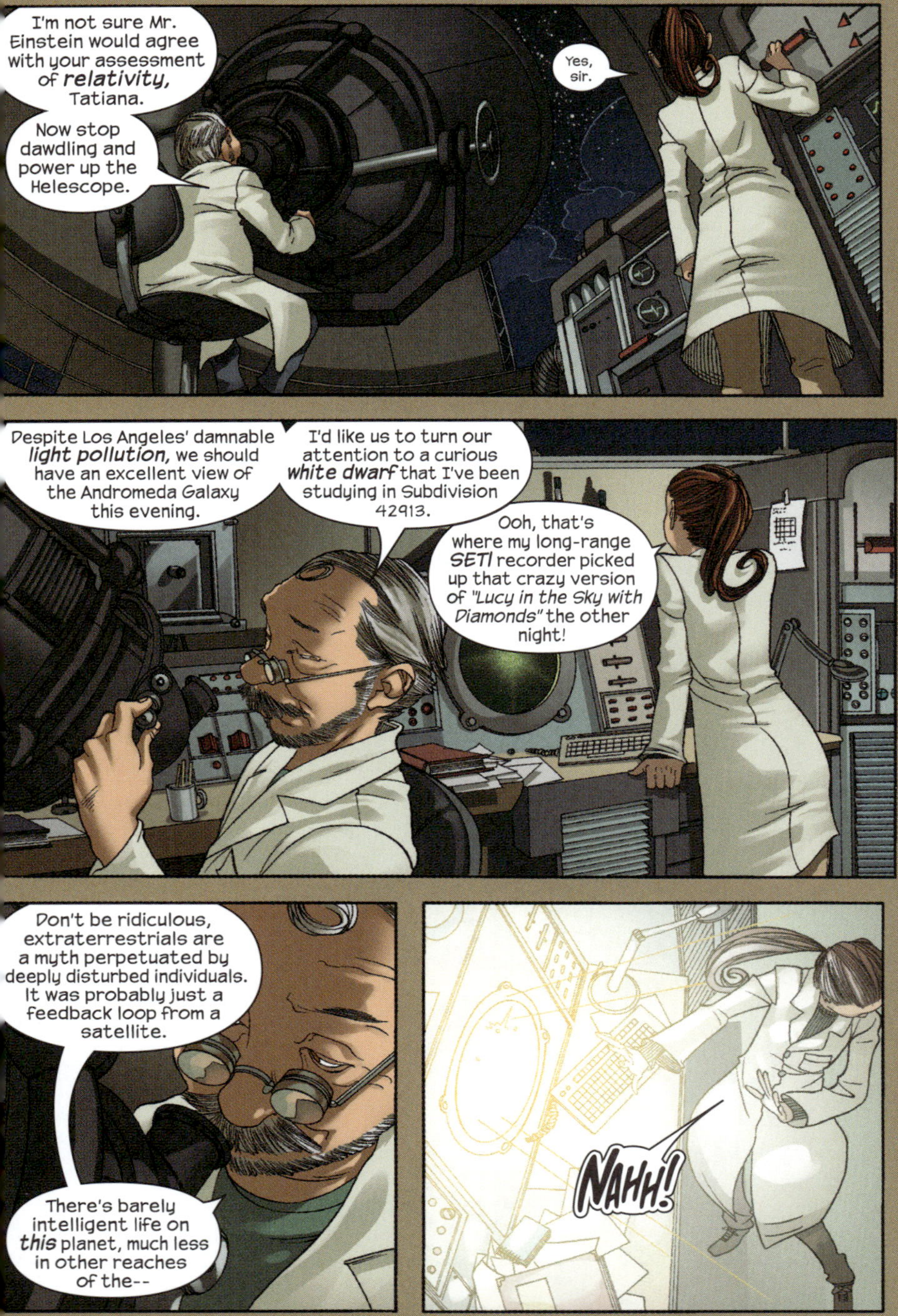
I'm not sure Mr. Einstein would agree with your assessment of *relativity,* Tatiana.
Now stop dawdling and power up the Helescope.
Yes, sir.
Despite Los Angeles' damnable *light pollution,* we should have an excellent view of the Andromeda Galaxy this evening.
I'd like us to turn our attention to a curious *white dwarf* that I've been studying in Subdivision 42913.
Ooh, that's where my long-range *SETI* recorder picked up that crazy version of *"Lucy in the Sky with Diamonds"* the other night!
Don't be ridiculous, extraterrestrials are a myth perpetuated by deeply disturbed individuals. It was probably just a feedback loop from a satellite.
There's barely intelligent life on *this* planet, much less in other reaches of the--
NAHH!

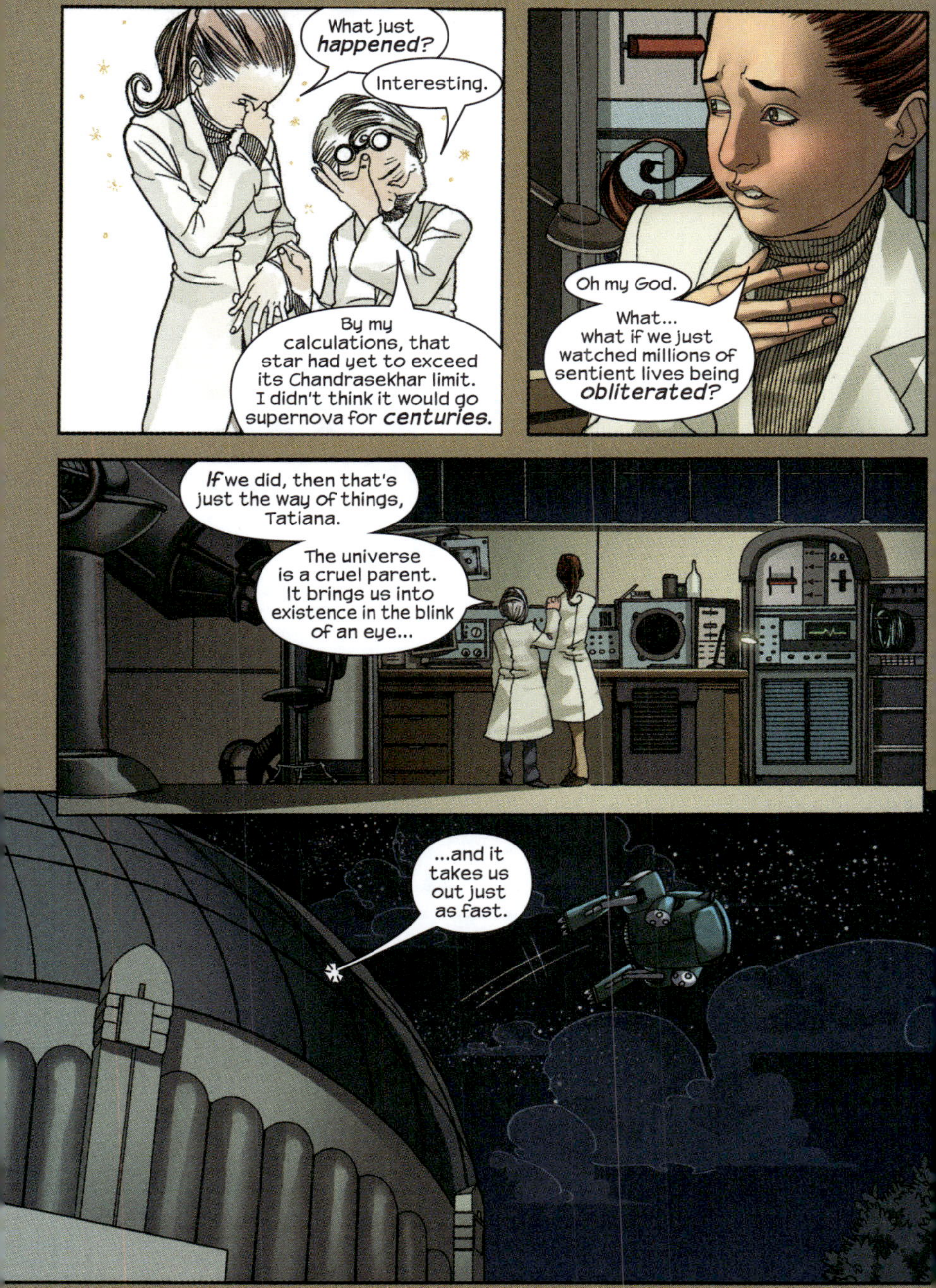
What just happened?
Interesting.
By my calculations, that star had yet to exceed its Chandrasekhar limit. I didn't think it would go supernova for centuries.
Oh my God.
What... what if we just watched millions of sentient lives being obliterated?
If we did, then that's just the way of things, Tatiana.
The universe is a cruel parent. It brings us into existence in the blink of an eye...
...and it takes us out just as fast.

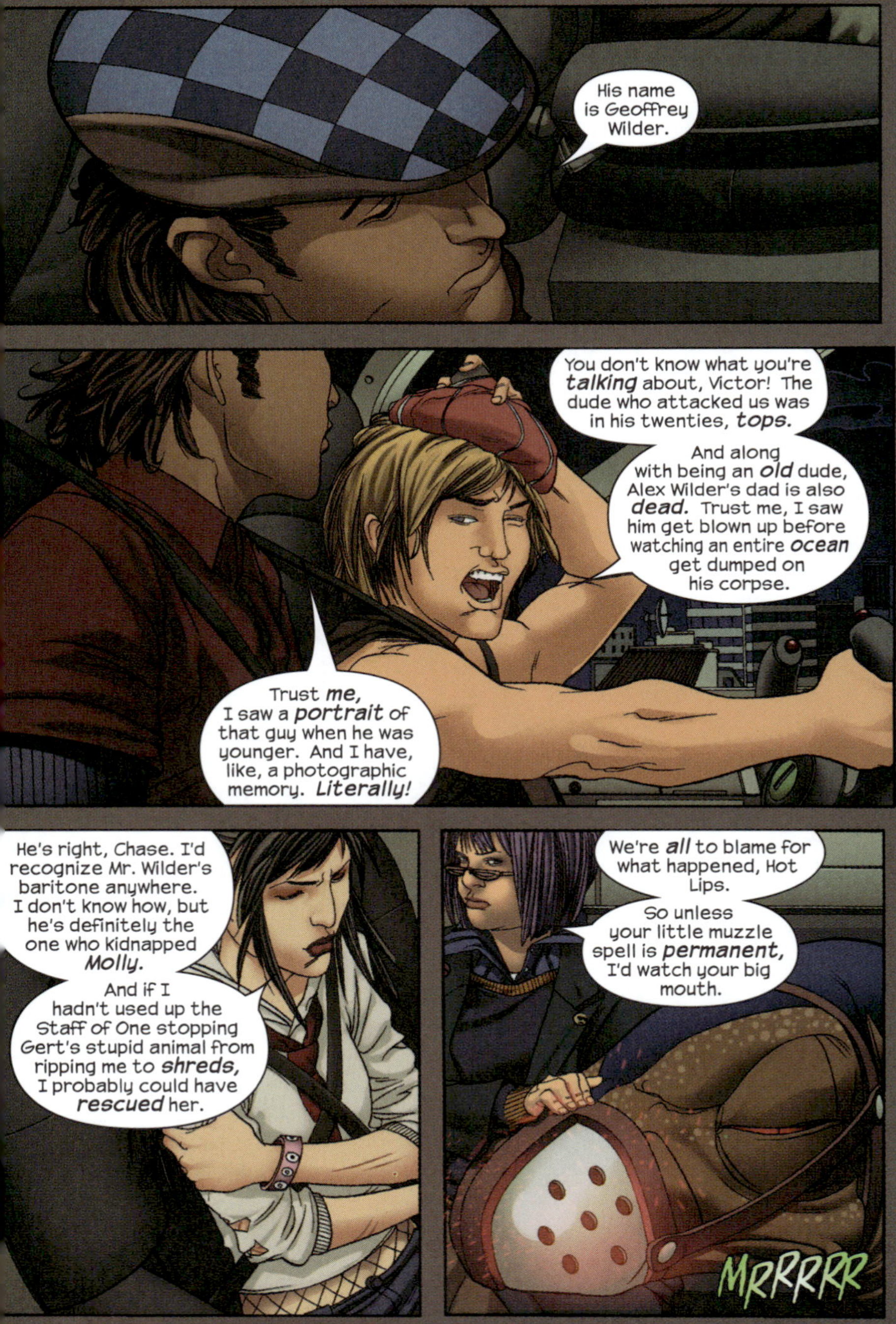
His name is Geoffrey Wilder.
You don't know what you're talking about, Victor! The dude who attacked us was in his twenties, tops.
And along with being an old dude, Alex Wilder's dad is also dead. Trust me, I saw him get blown up before watching an entire ocean get dumped on his corpse.
Trust me, I saw a portrait of that guy when he was younger. And I have, like, a photographic memory. Literally!
He's right, Chase. I'd recognize Mr. Wilder's baritone anywhere. I don't know how, but he's definitely the one who kidnapped Molly.
And if I hadn't used up the Staff of One stopping Gert's stupid animal from ripping me to shreds, I probably could have rescued her.
We're all to blame for what happened, Hot Lips.
So unless your little muzzle spell is permanent, I'd watch your big mouth.
MRRRRR

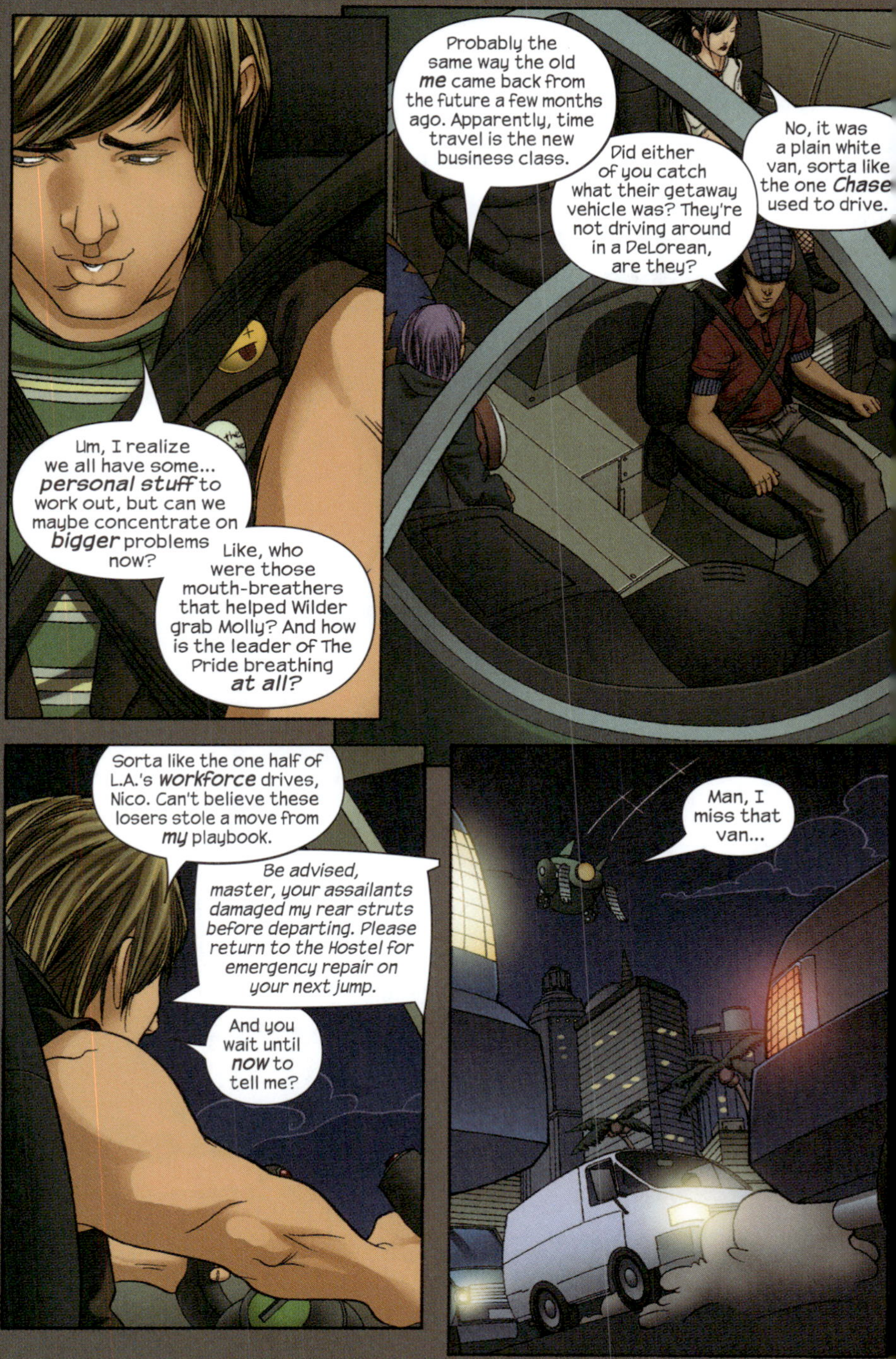

Probably the same way the old *me* came back from the future a few months ago. Apparently, time travel is the new business class.
Did either of you catch what their getaway vehicle was? They're not driving around in a DeLorean, are they?
No, it was a plain white van, sorta like the one *Chase* used to drive.
Um, I realize we all have some... *personal stuff* to work out, but can we maybe concentrate on *bigger* problems now?
Like, who were those mouth-breathers that helped Wilder grab Molly? And how is the leader of The Pride breathing *at all?*
Sorta like the one half of L.A.'s *workforce* drives, Nico. Can't believe these losers stole a move from *my* playbook.
Be advised, master, your assailants damaged my rear struts before departing. Please return to the Hostel for emergency repair on your next jump.
And you wait until *now* to tell me?
Man, I miss that van...

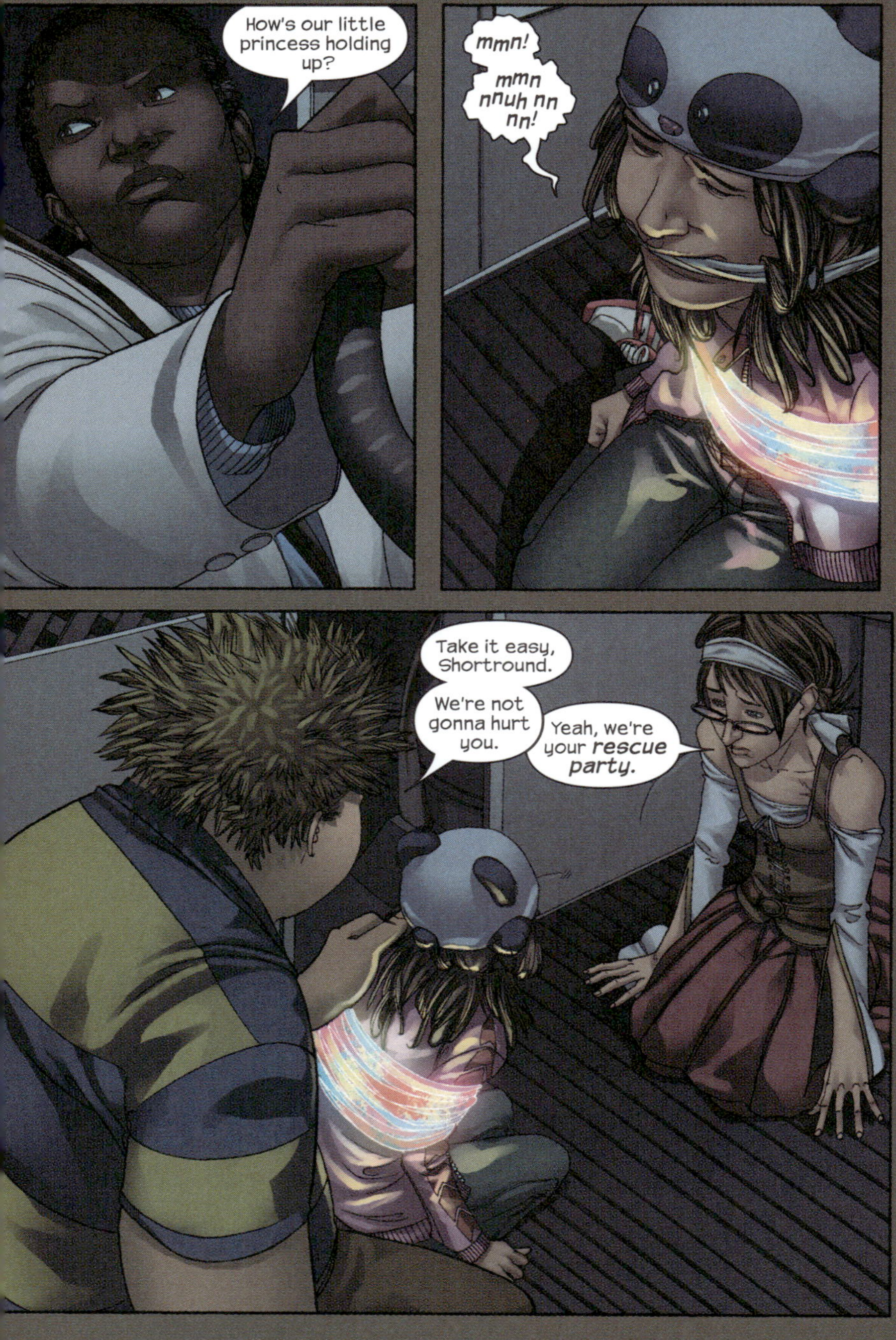
How's our little princess holding up?
mmn!
mmn nnuh nn nn!
Take it easy, Shortround.
We're not gonna hurt you.
Yeah, we're your *rescue party.*

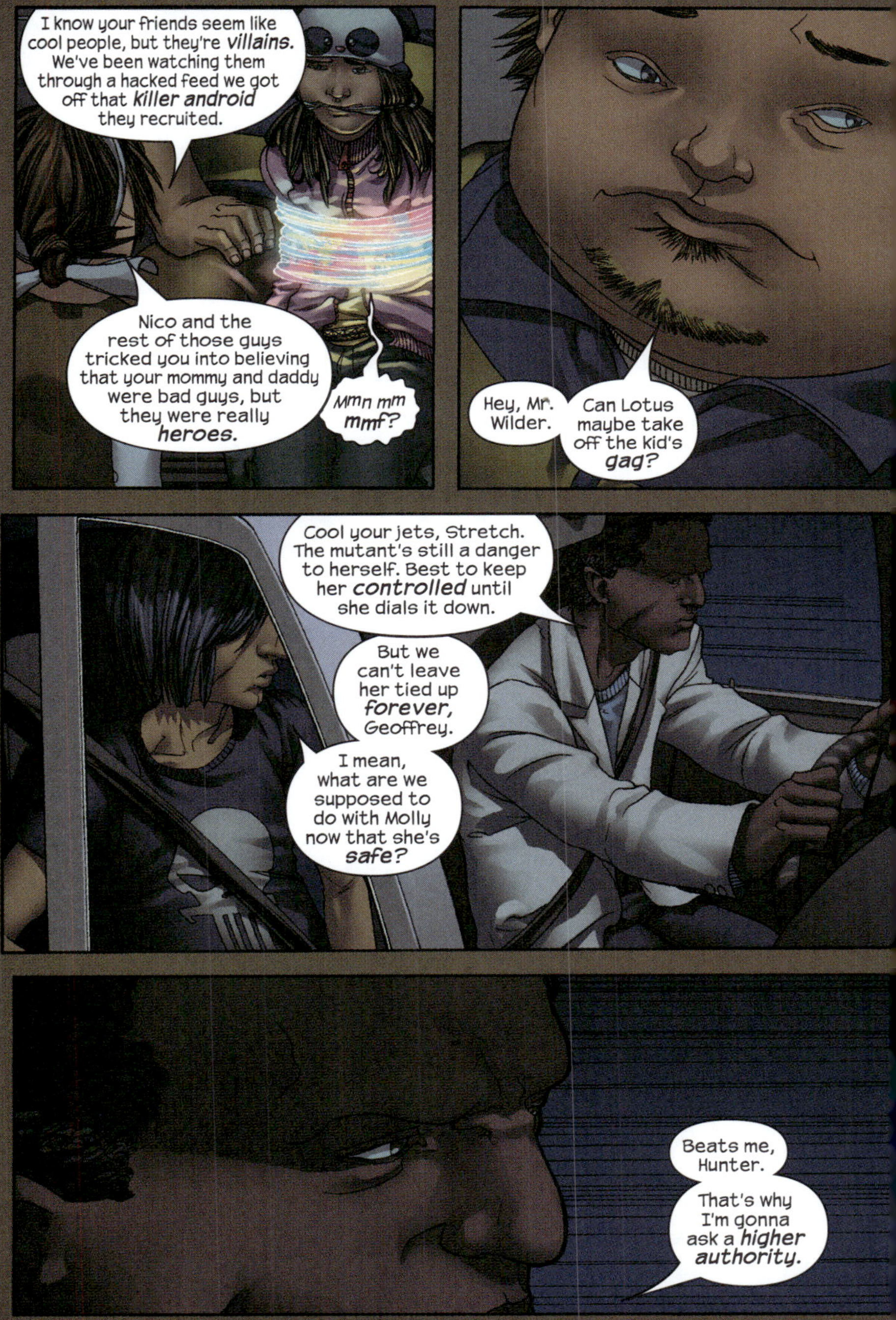
I know your friends seem like cool people, but they're *villains.* We've been watching them through a hacked feed we got off that *killer android* they recruited.
Nico and the rest of those guys tricked you into believing that your mommy and daddy were bad guys, but they were really *heroes.*
Mmn mm mmf?
Hey, Mr. Wilder.
Can Lotus maybe take off the kid's *gag?*
Cool your jets, Stretch. The mutant's still a danger to herself. Best to keep her *controlled* until she dials it down.
But we can't leave her tied up *forever,* Geoffrey.
I mean, what are we supposed to do with Molly now that she's *safe?*
Beats me, Hunter.
That's why I'm gonna ask a *higher authority.*

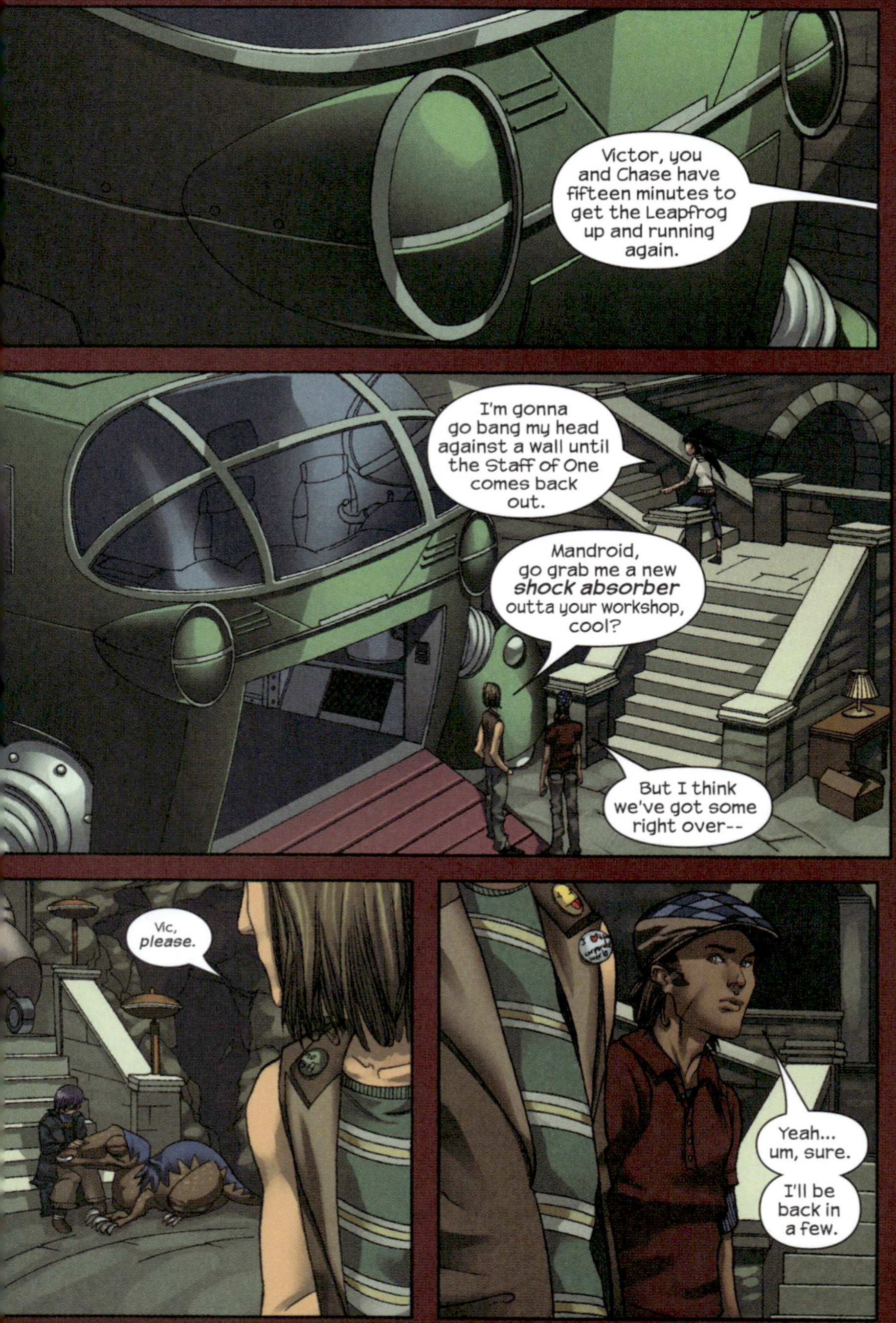
Victor, you and Chase have fifteen minutes to get the Leapfrog up and running again.
I'm gonna go bang my head against a wall until the Staff of One comes back out.
Mandroid, go grab me a new **shock absorber** outta your workshop, cool?
But I think we've got some right over--
Vic, *please.*
Yeah... um, sure.
I'll be back in a few.

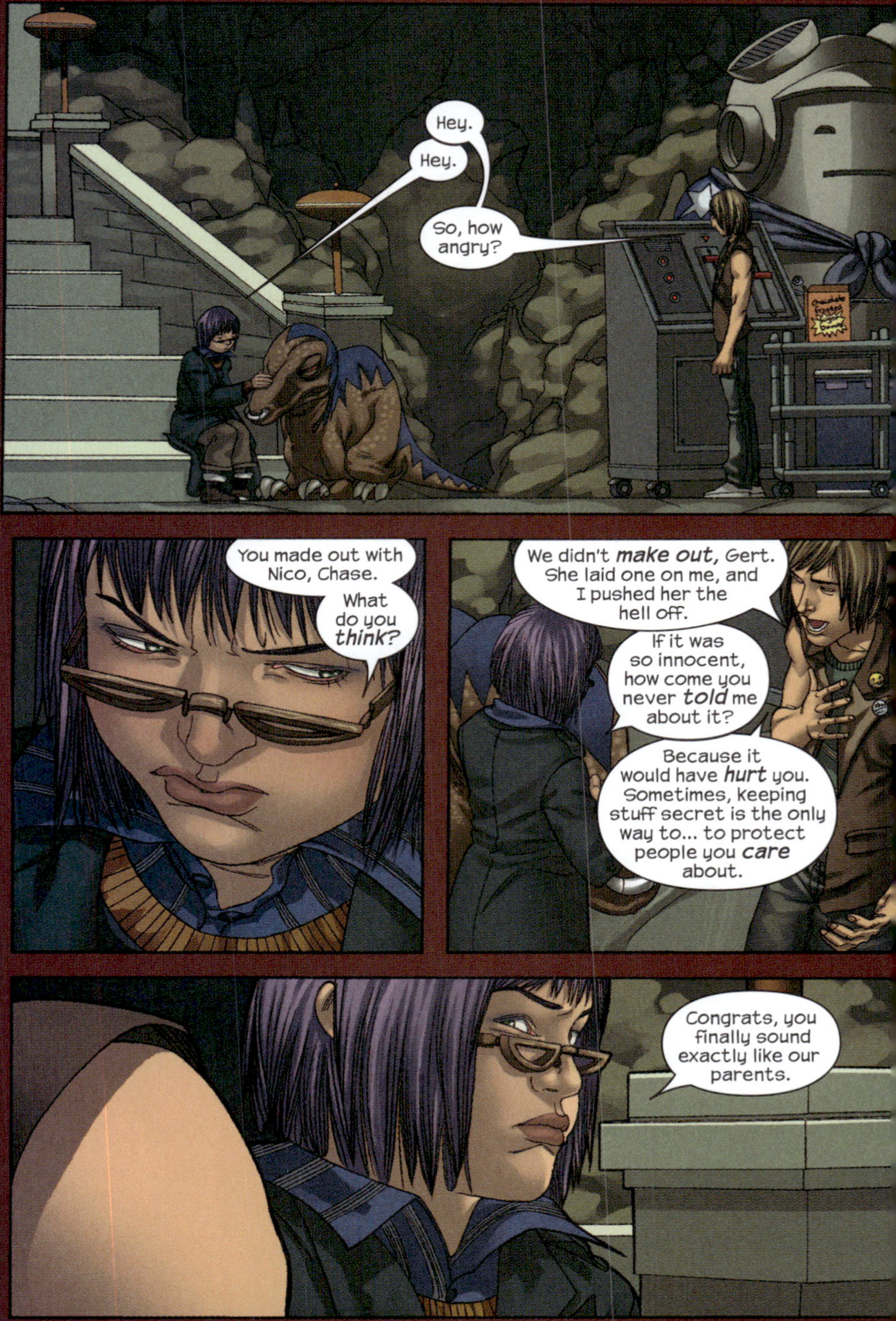
Hey.
Hey.
So, how angry?
You made out with Nico, Chase.
What do you *think*?
We didn't *make out,* Gert. She laid one on me, and I pushed her the hell off.
If it was so innocent, how come you never *told* me about it?
Because it would have *hurt* you. Sometimes, keeping stuff secret is the only way to... to protect people you *care* about.
Congrats, you finally sound exactly like our parents.

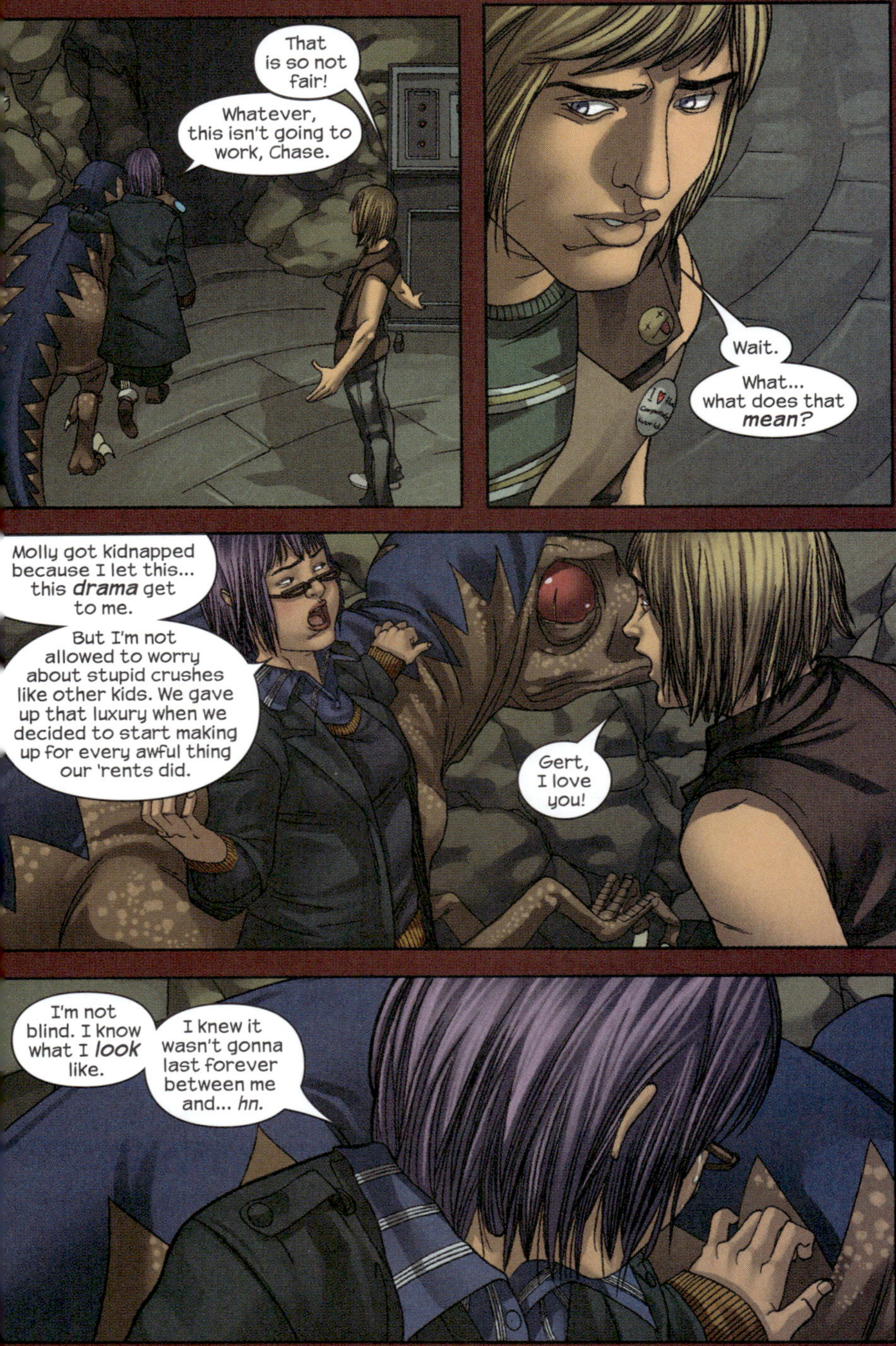
That is so not fair!
Whatever, this isn't going to work, Chase.
Wait.
What... what does that *mean?*
Molly got kidnapped because I let this... this *drama* get to me.
But I'm not allowed to worry about stupid crushes like other kids. We gave up that luxury when we decided to start making up for every awful thing our 'rents did.
Gert, I love you!
I'm not blind. I know what I *look* like.
I knew it wasn't gonna last forever between me and... *hn.*

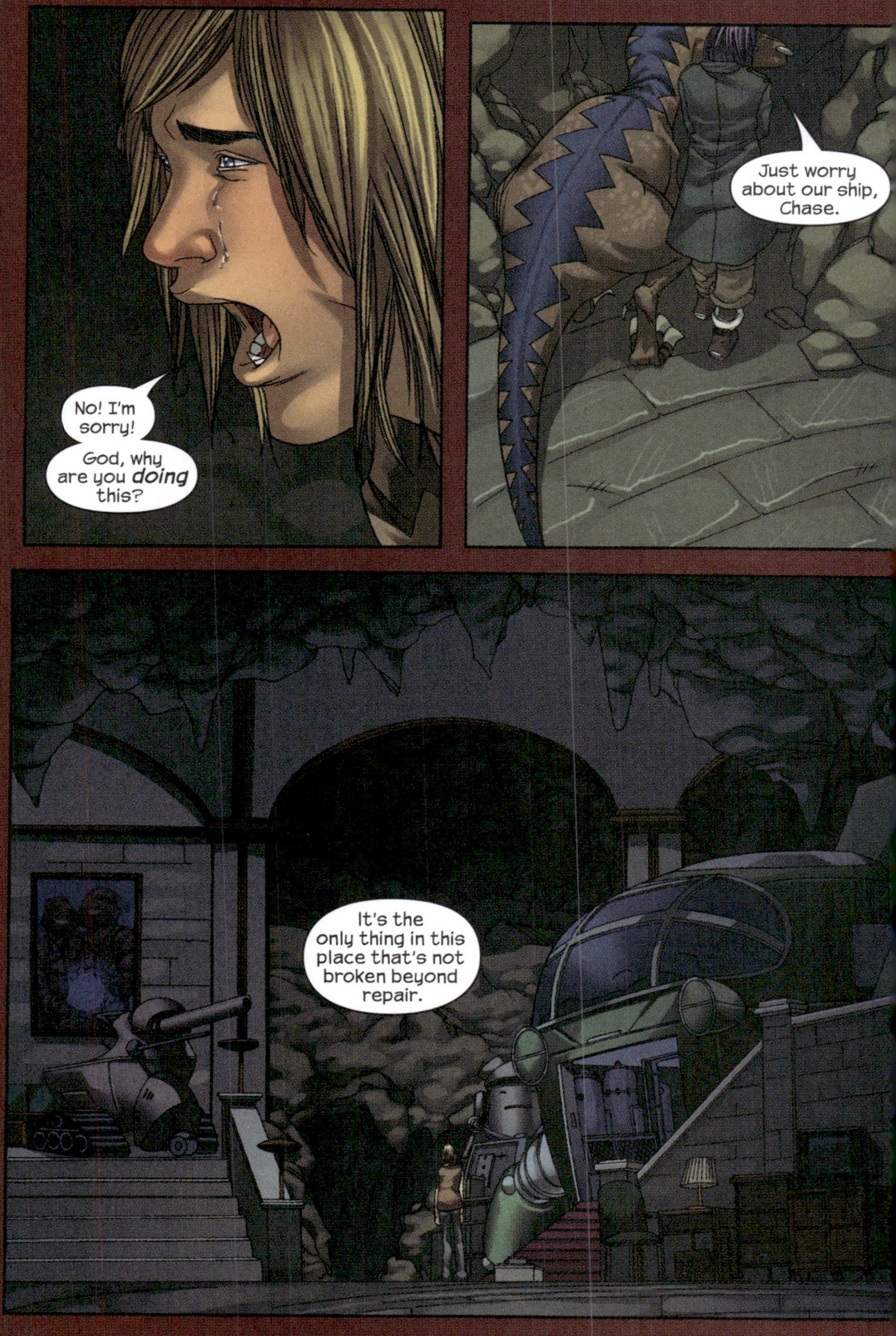
No! I'm sorry!
God, why are you *doing* this?
Just worry about our ship, Chase.
It's the only thing in this place that's not broken beyond repair.

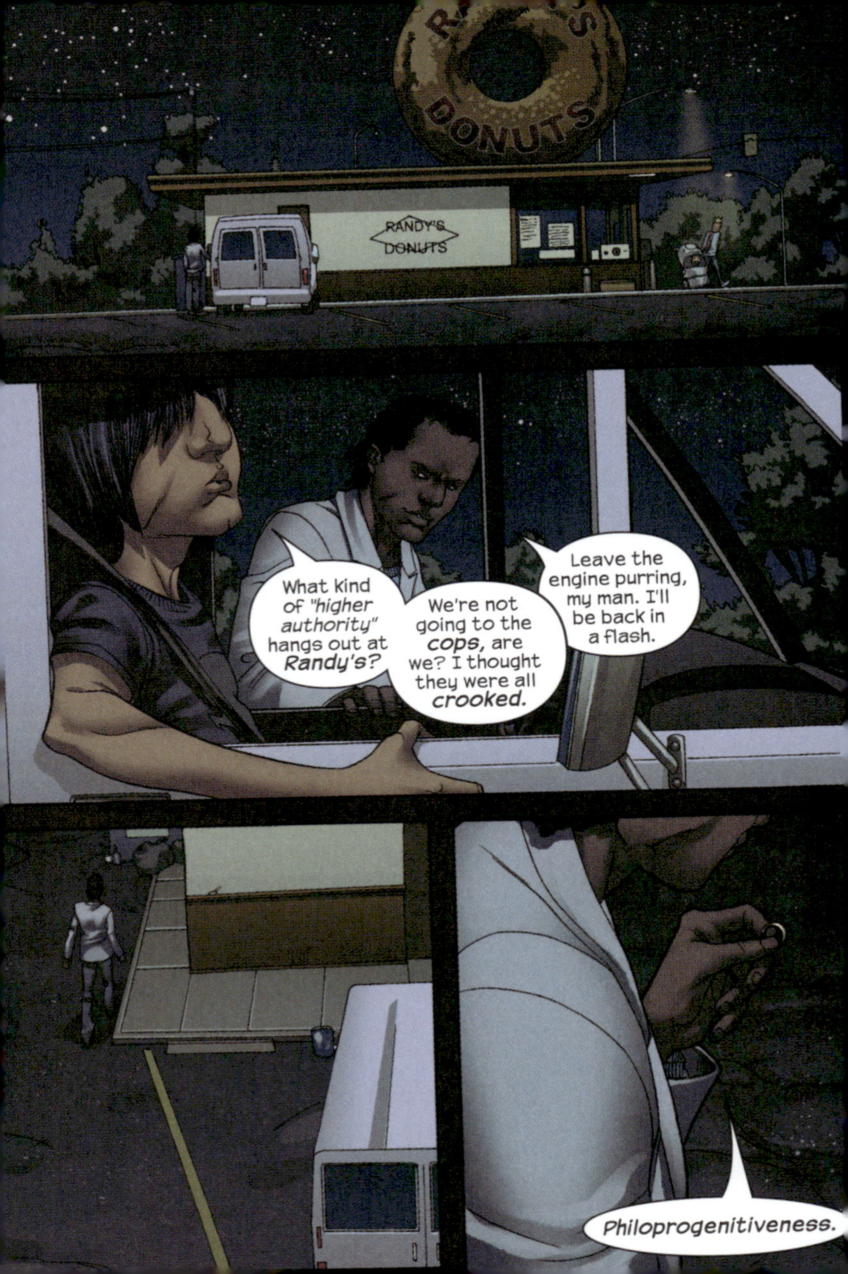
RANDY'S DONUTS
RANDY'S DONUTS
What kind of "higher authority" hangs out at Randy's?
We're not going to the cops, are we? I thought they were all crooked.
Leave the engine purring, my man. I'll be back in a flash.
Philoprogenitiveness.

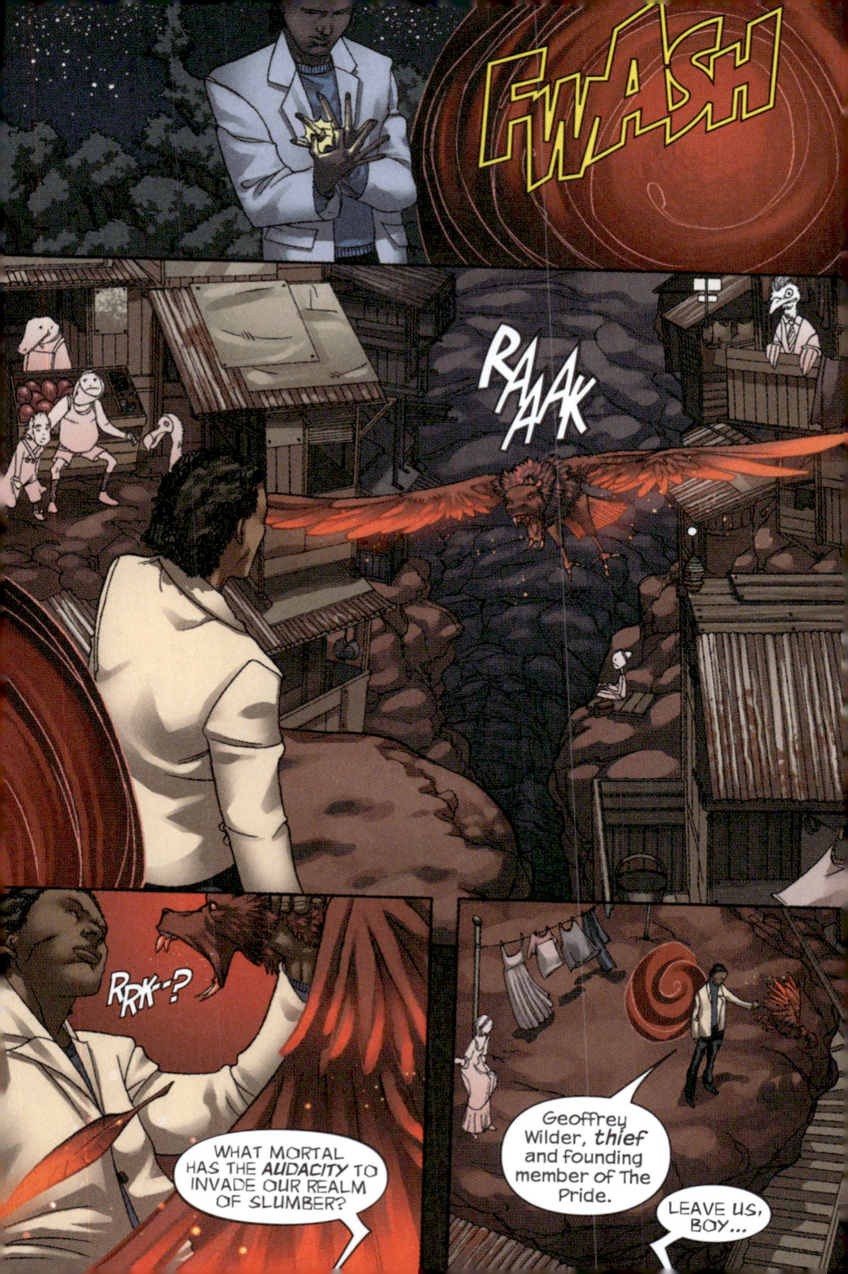
FWASH
RAAAAK
RRK--?
WHAT MORTAL HAS THE AUDACITY TO INVADE OUR REALM OF SLUMBER?
Geoffrey Wilder, thief and founding member of The Pride.
LEAVE US, BOY...

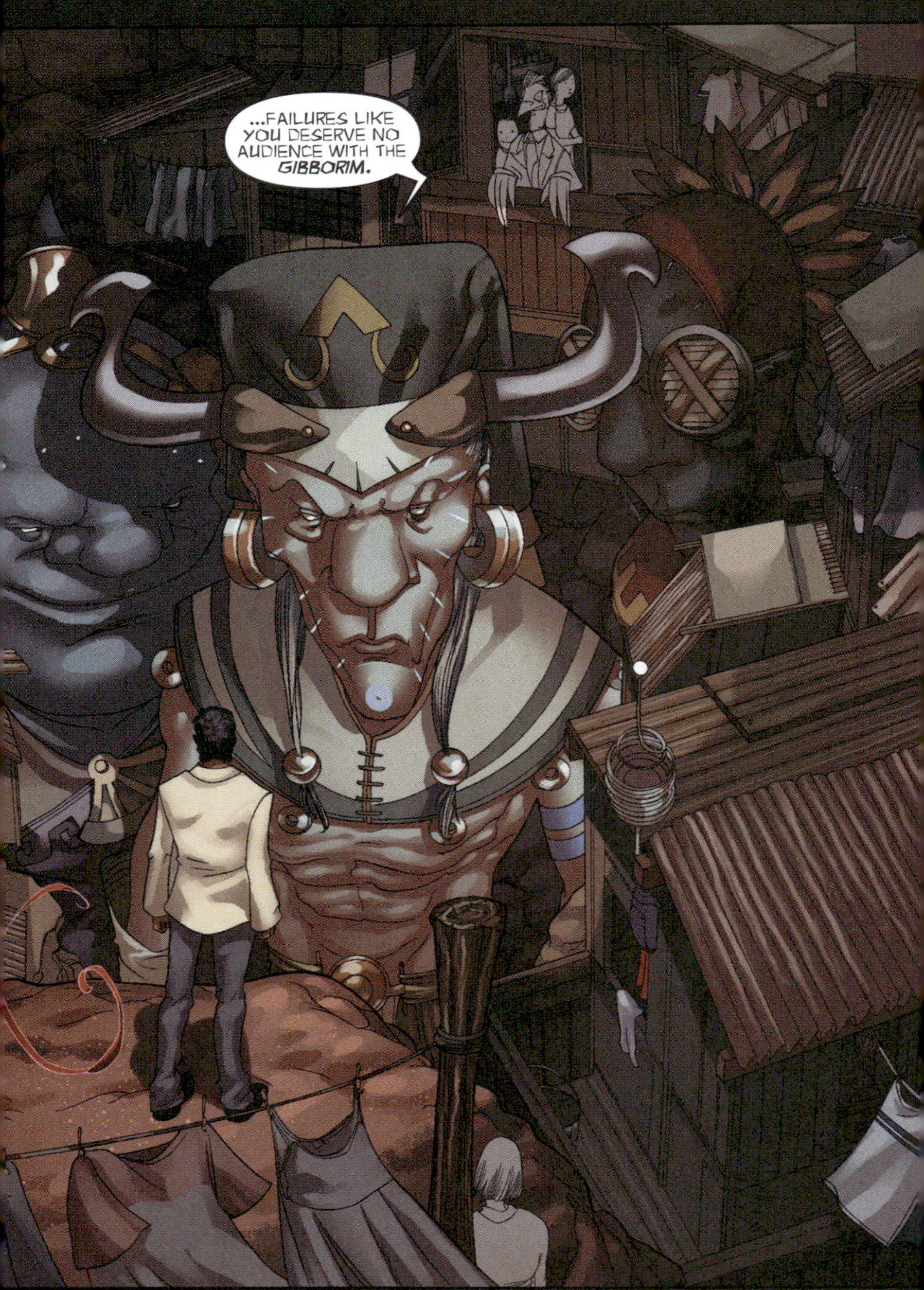
...FAILURES LIKE YOU DESERVE NO AUDIENCE WITH THE GIBBORIM.

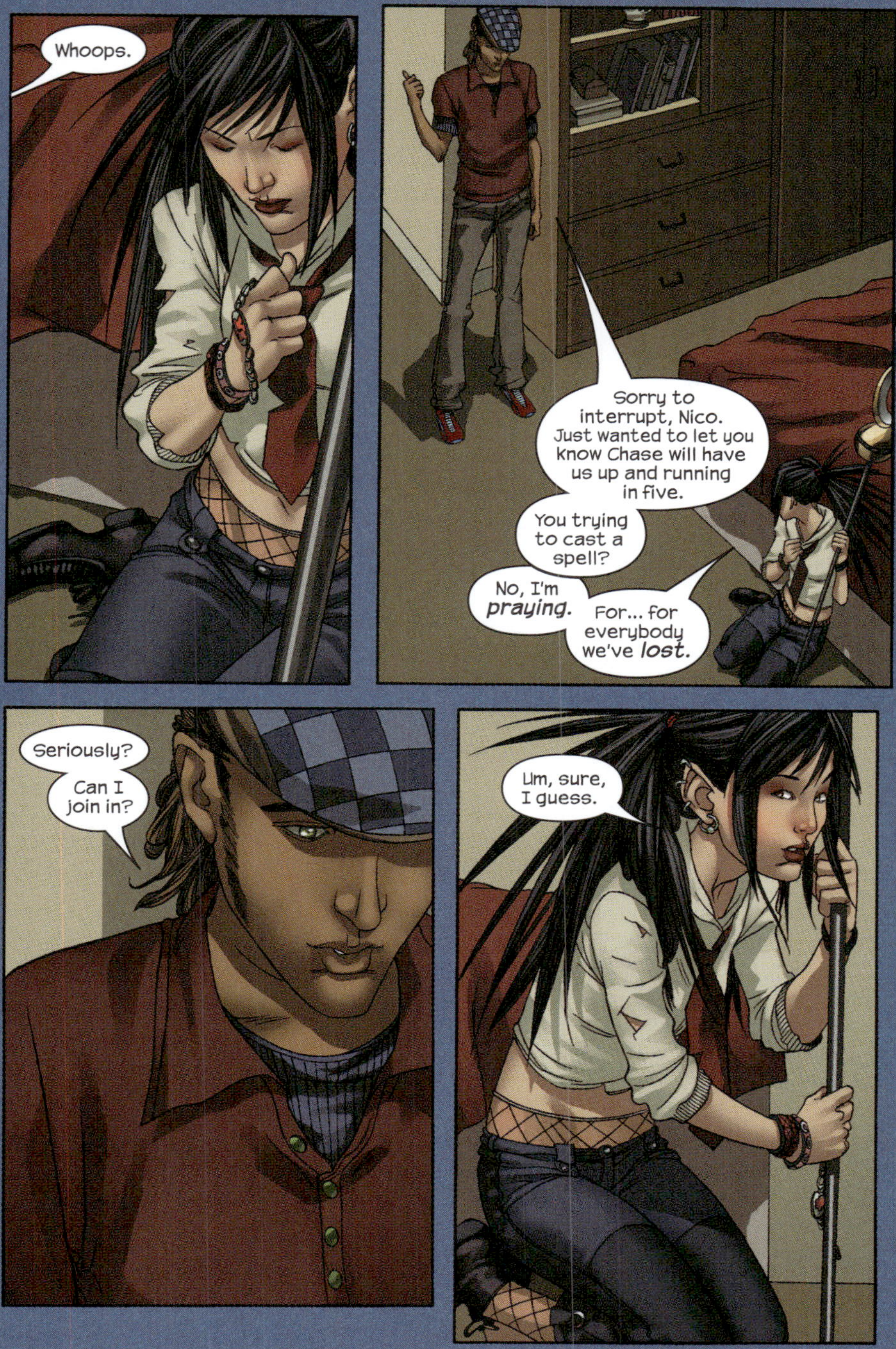
Whoops.
Sorry to interrupt, Nico. Just wanted to let you know Chase will have us up and running in five.
You trying to cast a spell?
No, I'm *praying.*
For... for everybody we've *lost.*
Seriously?
Can I join in?
Um, sure, I guess.

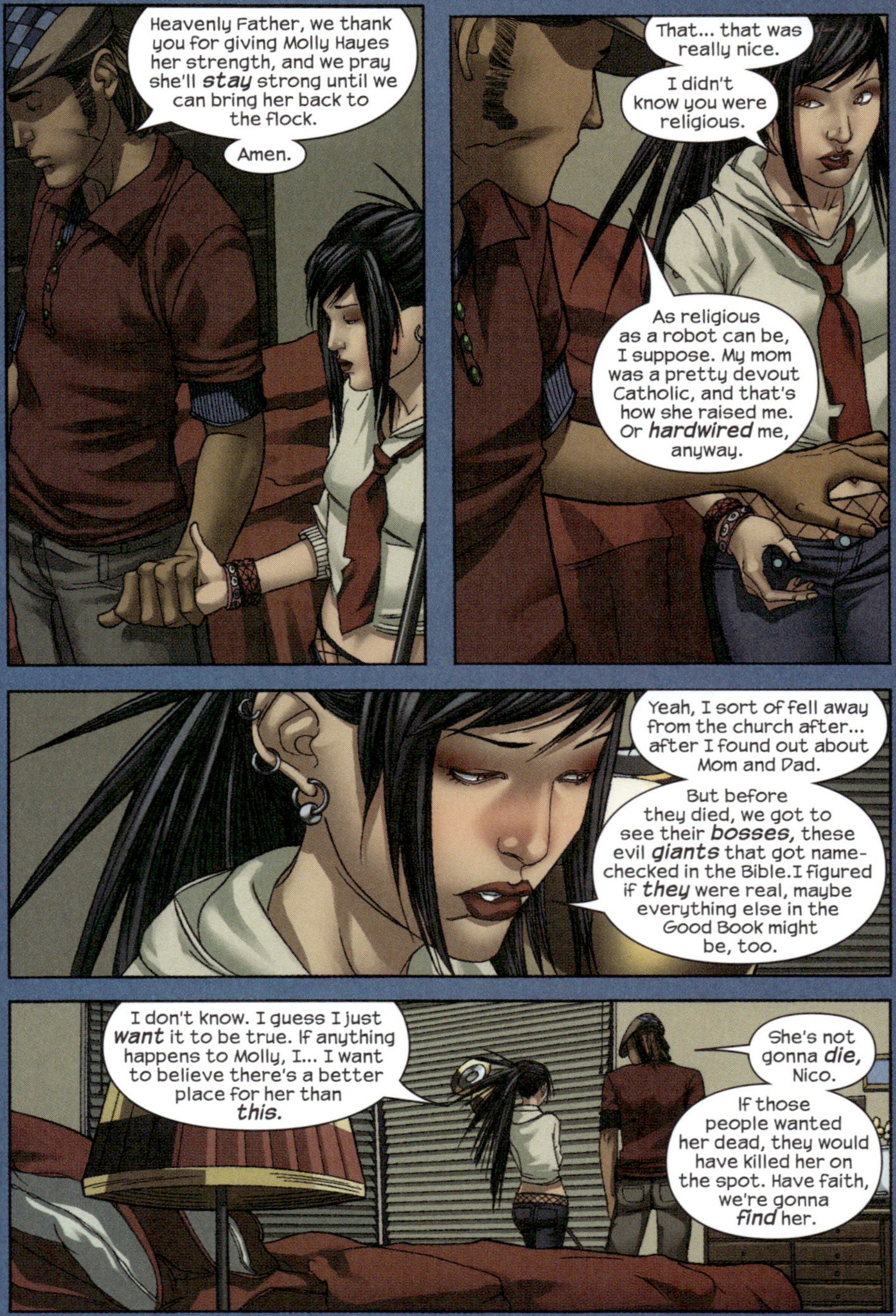
Heavenly Father, we thank you for giving Molly Hayes her strength, and we pray she'll *stay* strong until we can bring her back to the flock.
Amen.
That... that was really nice.
I didn't know you were religious.
As religious as a robot can be, I suppose. My mom was a pretty devout Catholic, and that's how she raised me. Or *hardwired* me, anyway.
Yeah, I sort of fell away from the church after... after I found out about Mom and Dad.
But before they died, we got to see their *bosses,* these evil *giants* that got name-checked in the Bible. I figured if *they* were real, maybe everything else in the Good Book might be, too.
I don't know. I guess I just *want* it to be true. If anything happens to Molly, I... I want to believe there's a better place for her than *this.*
She's not gonna *die,* Nico.
If those people wanted her dead, they would have killed her on the spot. Have faith, we're gonna *find* her.

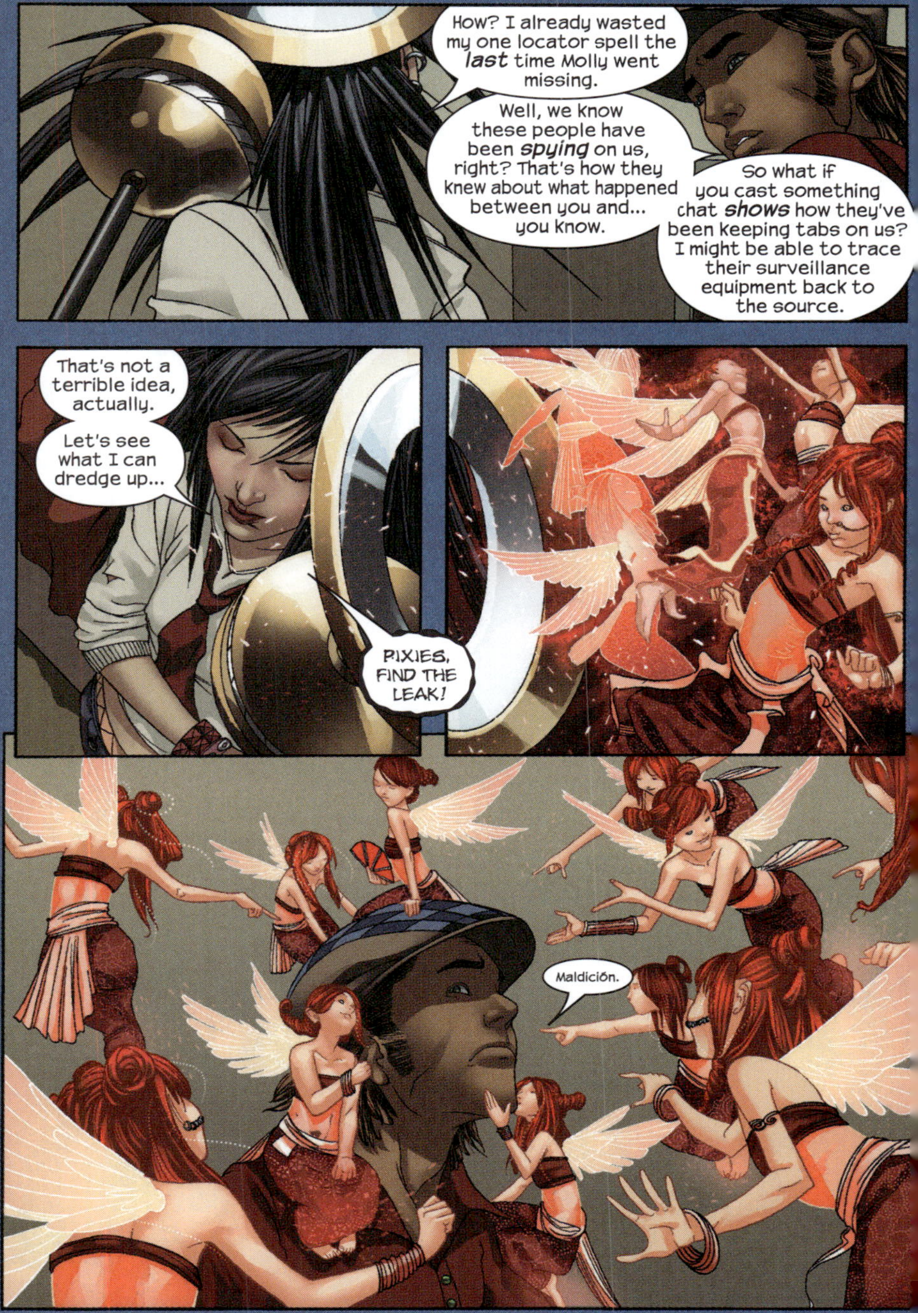
How? I already wasted my one locator spell the *last* time Molly went missing.
Well, we know these people have been *spying* on us, right? That's how they knew about what happened between you and... you know.
So what if you cast something that *shows* how they've been keeping tabs on us? I might be able to trace their surveillance equipment back to the source.
That's not a terrible idea, actually.
Let's see what I can dredge up...
PIXIES, FIND THE LEAK!
Maldición.

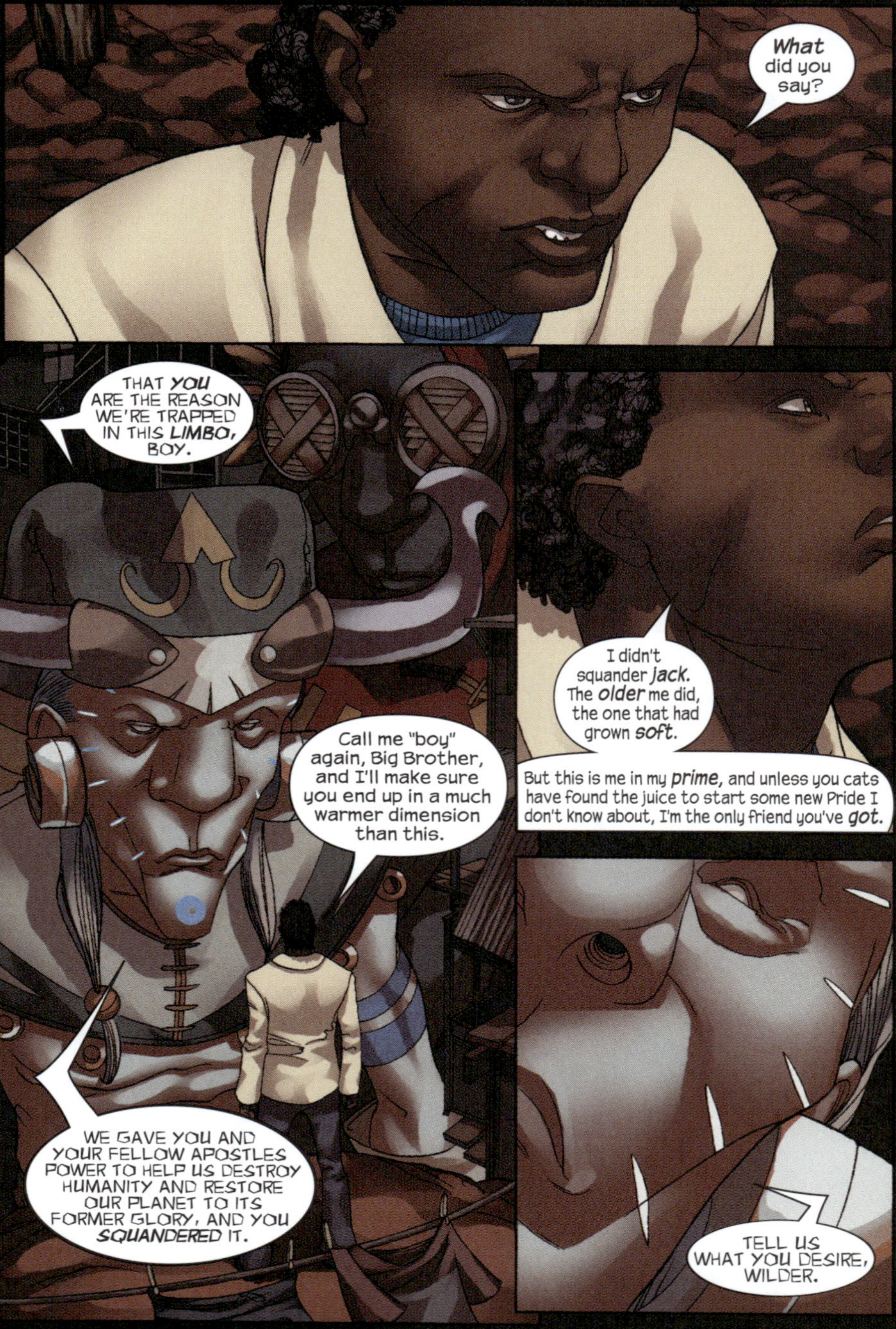
What did you say?
THAT YOU ARE THE REASON WE'RE TRAPPED IN THIS LIMBO, BOY.
Call me "boy" again, Big Brother, and I'll make sure you end up in a much warmer dimension than this.
WE GAVE YOU AND YOUR FELLOW APOSTLES POWER TO HELP US DESTROY HUMANITY AND RESTORE OUR PLANET TO ITS FORMER GLORY, AND YOU SQUANDERED IT.
I didn't squander jack. The older me did, the one that had grown soft.
But this is me in my prime, and unless you cats have found the juice to start some new Pride I don't know about, I'm the only friend you've got.
TELL US WHAT YOU DESIRE, WILDER.

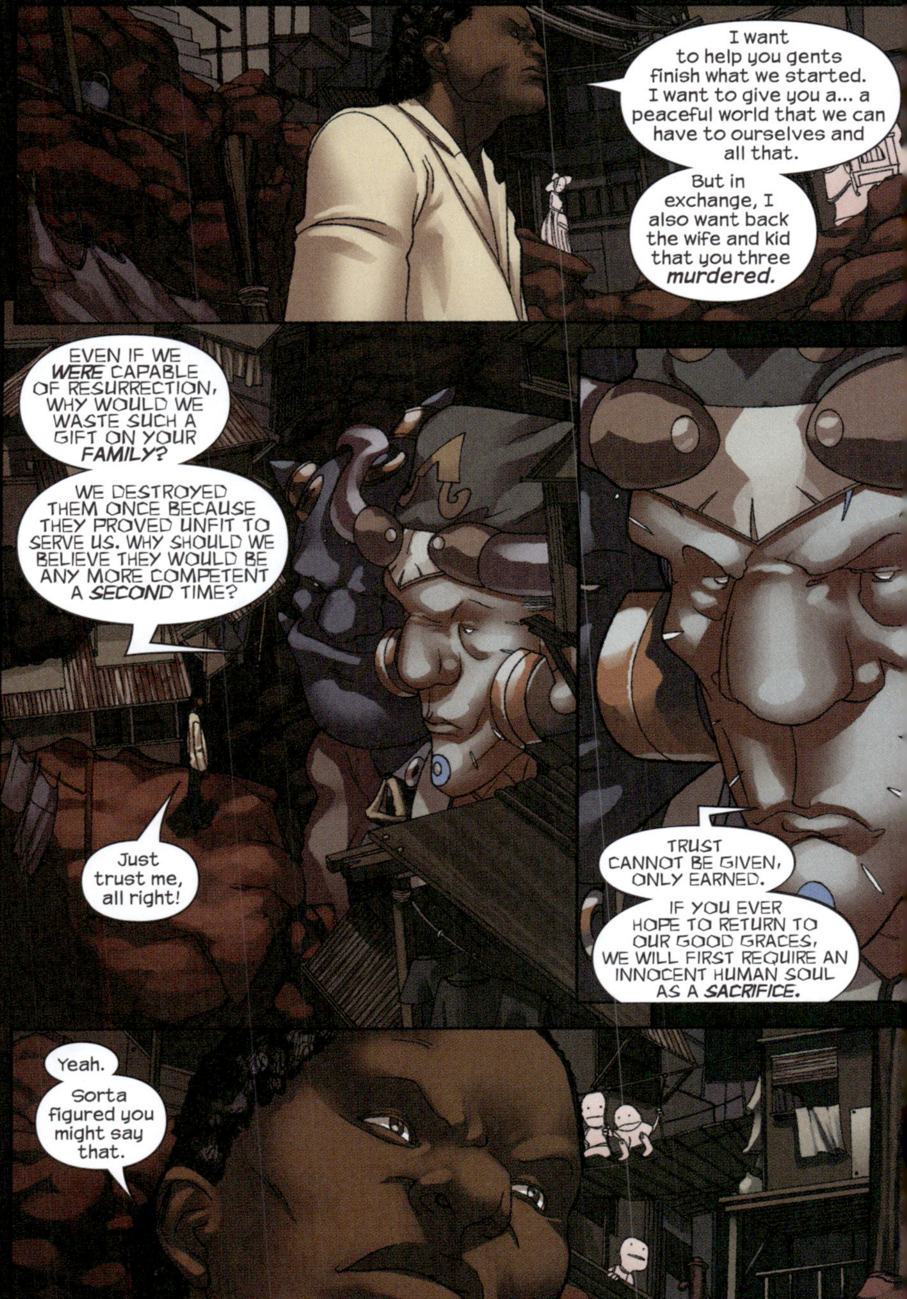
I want to help you gents finish what we started. I want to give you a... a peaceful world that we can have to ourselves and all that.
But in exchange, I also want back the wife and kid that you three murdered.
EVEN IF WE WERE CAPABLE OF RESURRECTION, WHY WOULD WE WASTE SUCH A GIFT ON YOUR FAMILY?
WE DESTROYED THEM ONCE BECAUSE THEY PROVED UNFIT TO SERVE US. WHY SHOULD WE BELIEVE THEY WOULD BE ANY MORE COMPETENT A SECOND TIME?
Just trust me, all right!
TRUST CANNOT BE GIVEN, ONLY EARNED.
IF YOU EVER HOPE TO RETURN TO OUR GOOD GRACES, WE WILL FIRST REQUIRE AN INNOCENT HUMAN SOUL AS A SACRIFICE.
Yeah.
Sorta figured you might say that.

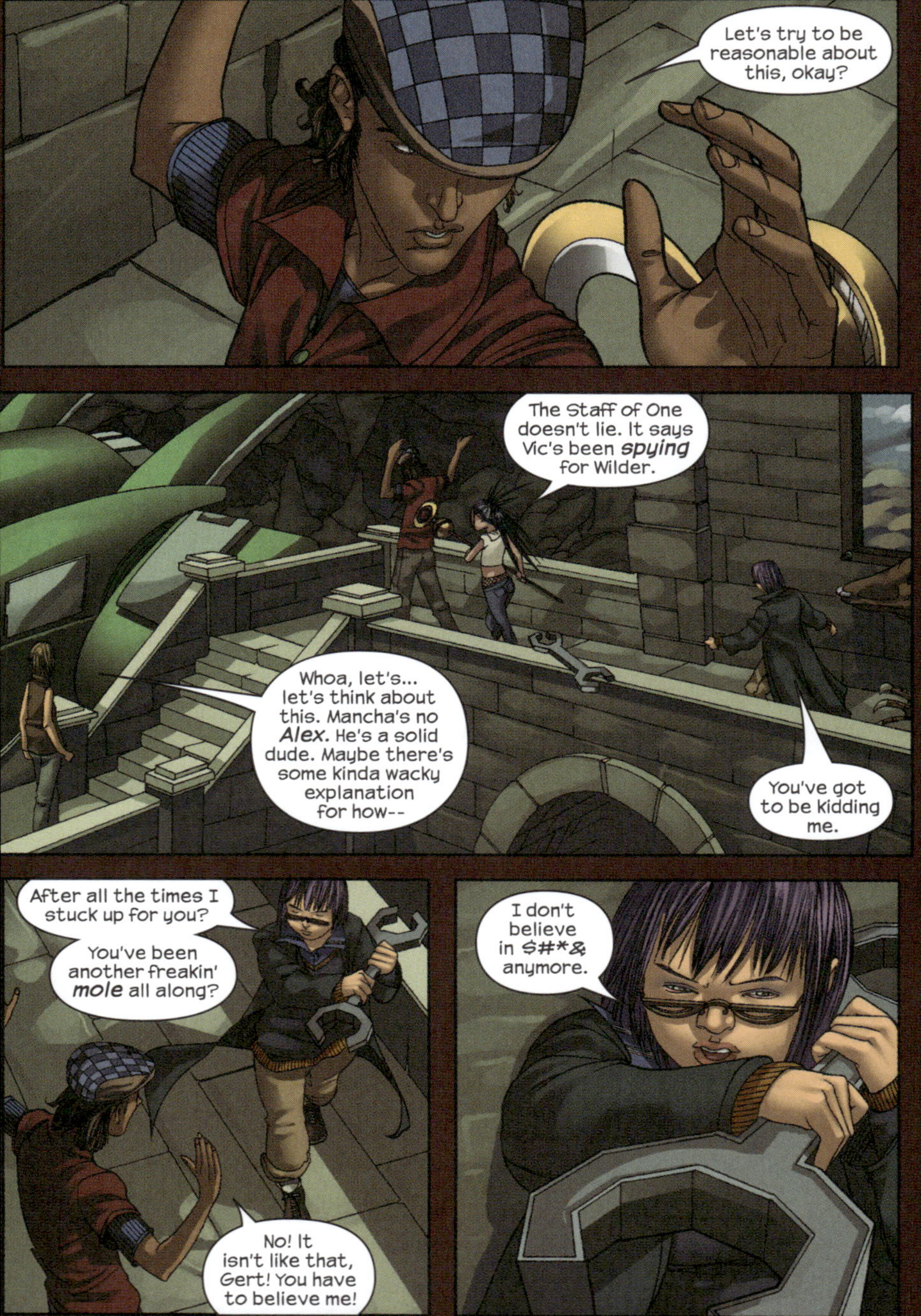

Let's try to be reasonable about this, okay?
The Staff of One doesn't lie. It says Vic's been *spying* for Wilder.
Whoa, let's... let's think about this. Mancha's no *Alex.* He's a solid dude. Maybe there's some kinda wacky explanation for how--
You've got to be kidding me.
After all the times I stuck up for you?
You've been another freakin' *mole* all along?
No! It isn't like that, Gert! You have to believe me!
I don't believe in $#*& anymore.

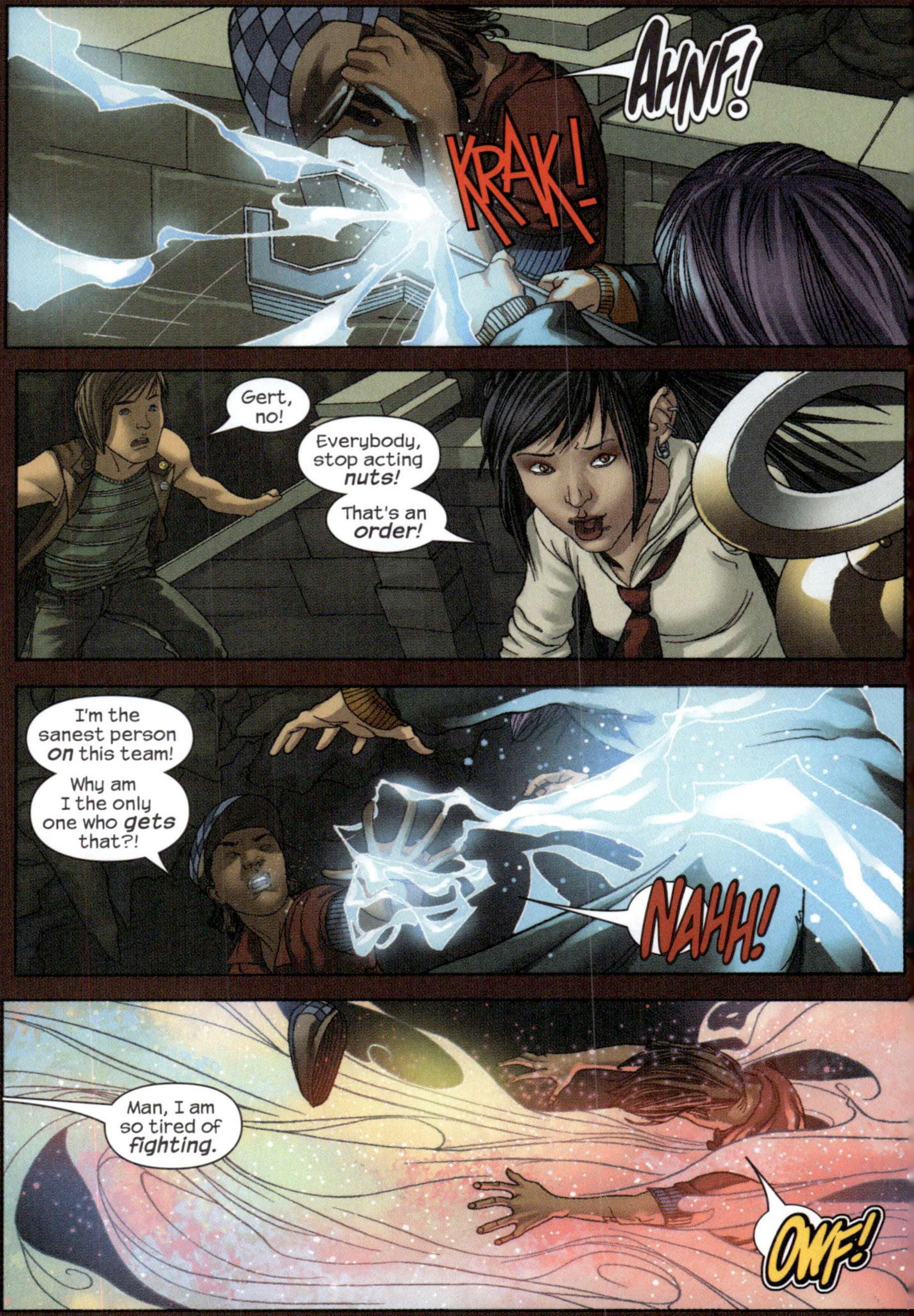

AHNF!
KRAK!
Gert, no!
Everybody, stop acting nuts!
That's an order!
I'm the sanest person on this team!
Why am I the only one who gets that?!
NAHH!
Man, I am so tired of fighting.
OWF!

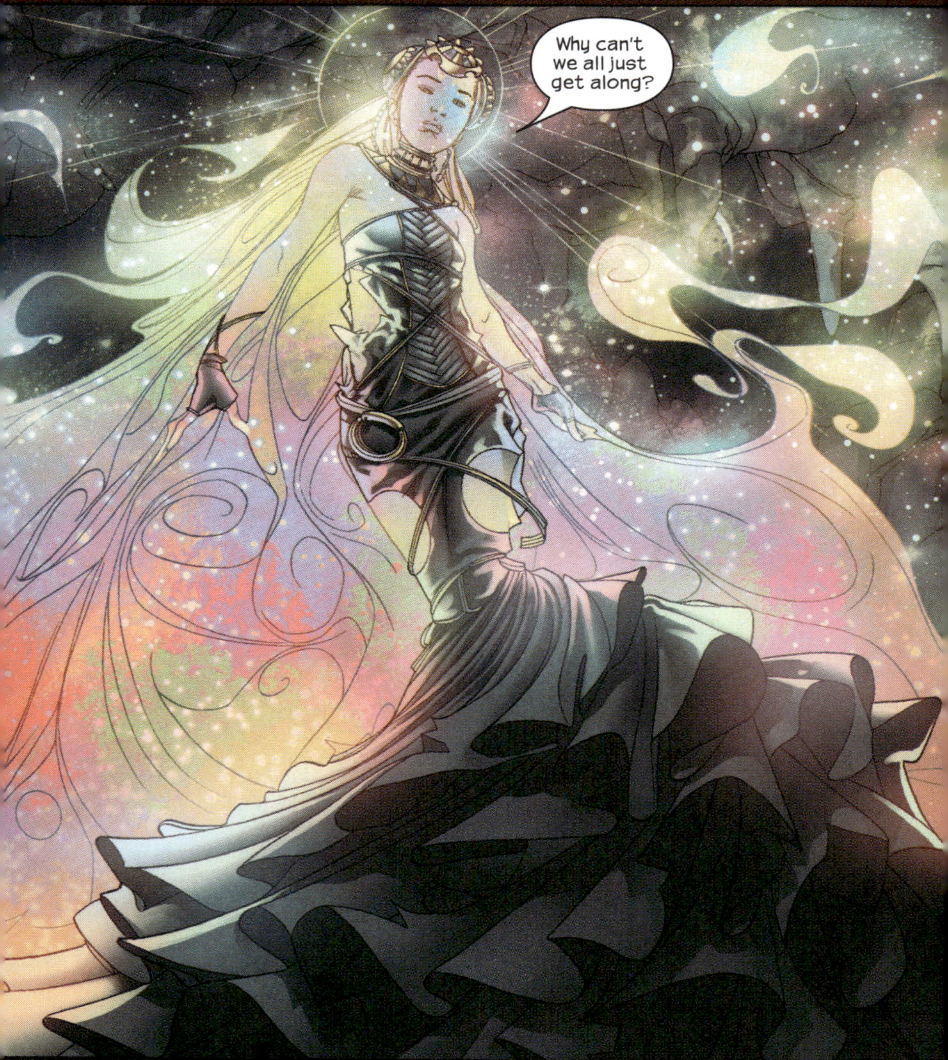
Why can't we all just get along?

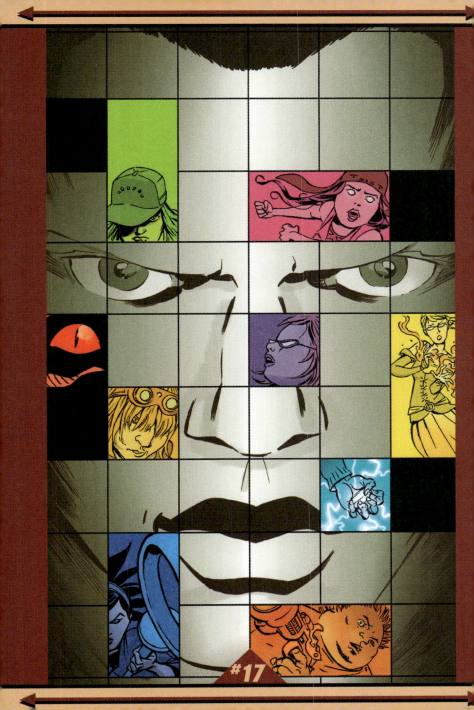

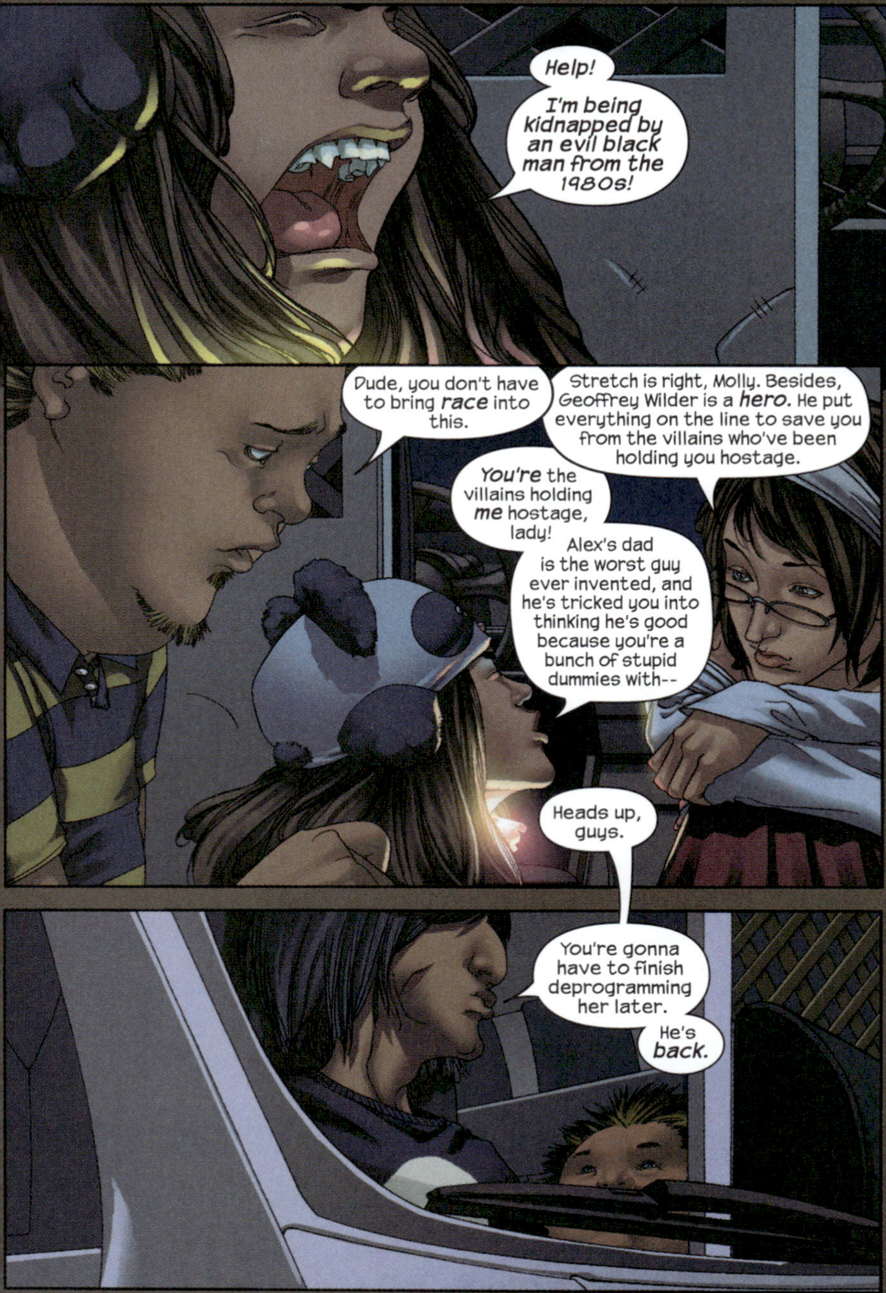
Help!
I'm being kidnapped by an evil black man from the 1980s!
Dude, you don't have to bring race into this.
Stretch is right, Molly. Besides, Geoffrey Wilder is a hero. He put everything on the line to save you from the villains who've been holding you hostage.
You're the villains holding me hostage, lady!
Alex's dad is the worst guy ever invented, and he's tricked you into thinking he's good because you're a bunch of stupid dummies with--
Heads up, guys.
You're gonna have to finish deprogramming her later.
He's back.

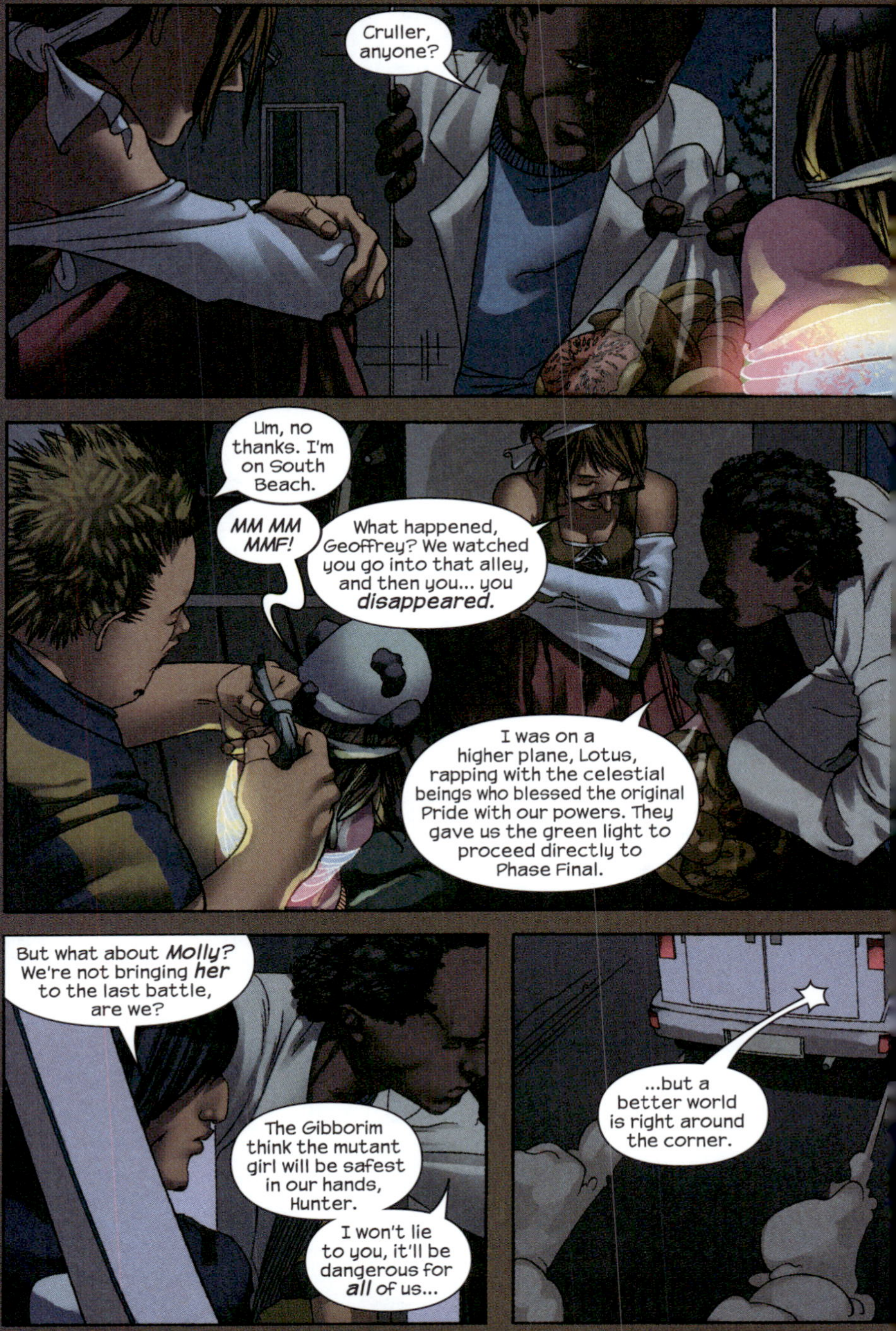
Cruller, anyone?
Um, no thanks. I'm on South Beach.
MM MM MMF!
What happened, Geoffrey? We watched you go into that alley, and then you... you *disappeared.*
I was on a higher plane, Lotus, rapping with the celestial beings who blessed the original Pride with our powers. They gave us the green light to proceed directly to Phase Final.
But what about *Molly?* We're not bringing *her* to the last battle, are we?
The Gibborim think the mutant girl will be safest in our hands, Hunter.
I won't lie to you, it'll be dangerous for *all* of us...
...but a better world is right around the corner.

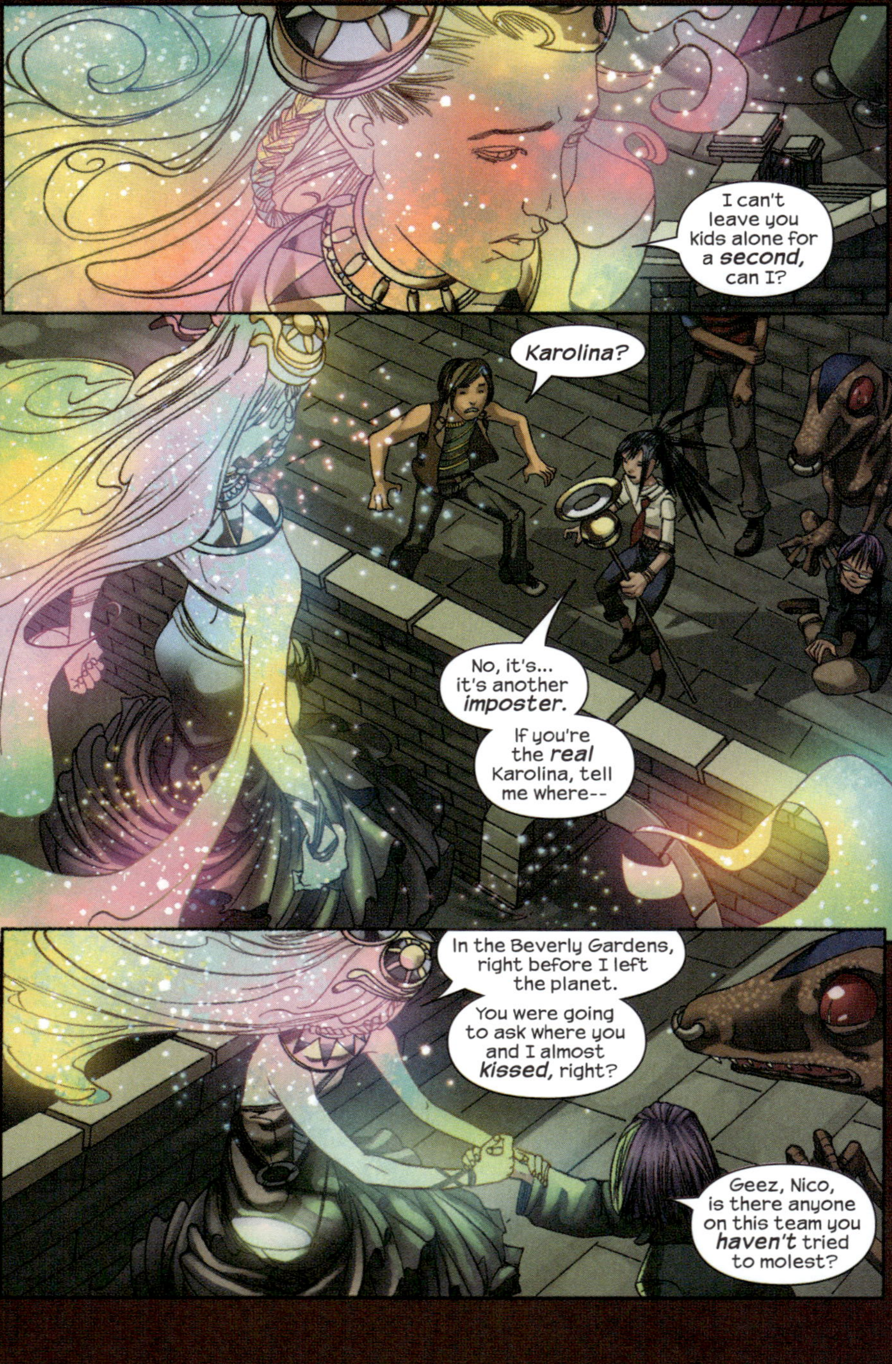
I can't leave you kids alone for a *second,* can I?
Karolina?
No, it's... it's another *imposter.*
If you're the *real* Karolina, tell me where--
In the Beverly Gardens, right before I left the planet.
You were going to ask where you and I almost *kissed,* right?
Geez, Nico, is there anyone on this team you *haven't* tried to molest?

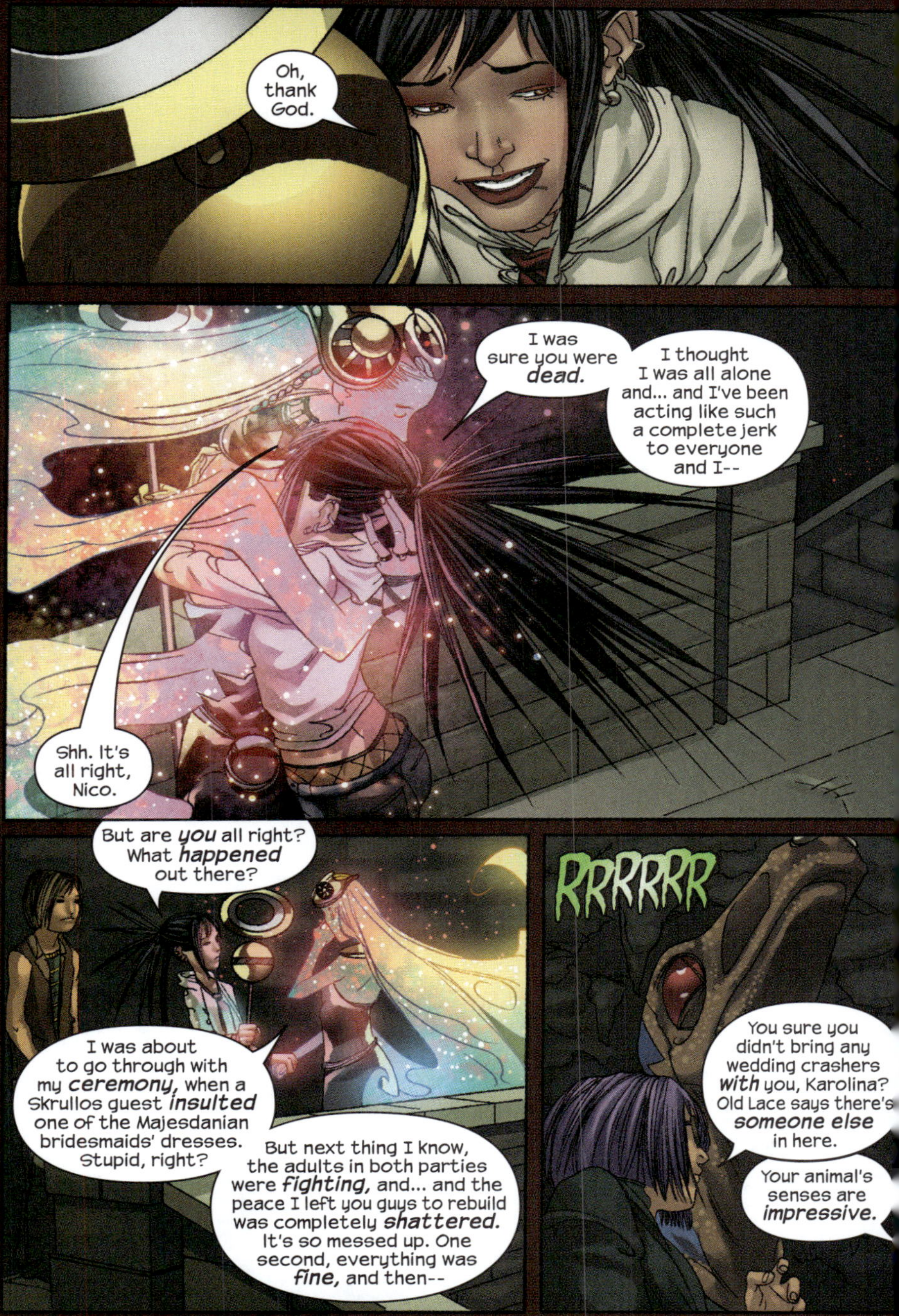
Oh, thank God.
I was sure you were dead.
I thought I was all alone and... and I've been acting like such a complete jerk to everyone and I--
Shh. It's all right, Nico.
But are you all right? What happened out there?
I was about to go through with my ceremony, when a Skrullos guest insulted one of the Majesdanian bridesmaids' dresses. Stupid, right?
But next thing I know, the adults in both parties were fighting, and... and the peace I left you guys to rebuild was completely shattered. It's so messed up. One second, everything was fine, and then--
RRRRRR
You sure you didn't bring any wedding crashers with you, Karolina? Old Lace says there's someone else in here.
Your animal's senses are impressive.

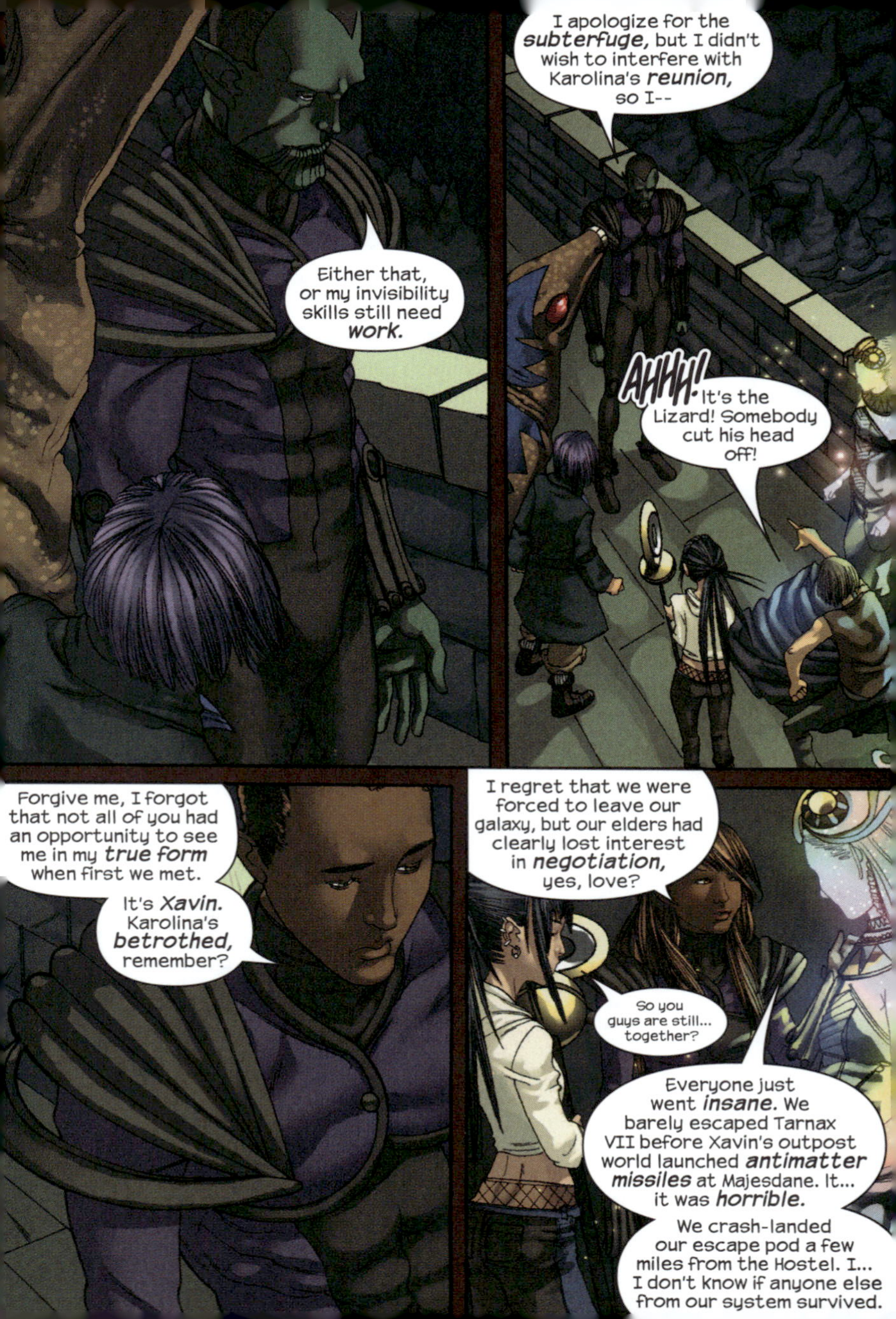
Either that, or my invisibility skills still need *work.*
I apologize for the *subterfuge,* but I didn't wish to interfere with Karolina's *reunion,* so I--
AHHH! It's the Lizard! Somebody cut his head off!
Forgive me, I forgot that not all of you had an opportunity to see me in my *true form* when first we met.
It's *Xavin.* Karolina's *betrothed,* remember?
I regret that we were forced to leave our galaxy, but our elders had clearly lost interest in *negotiation,* yes, love?
So you guys are still... together?
Everyone just went *insane.* We barely escaped Tarnax VII before Xavin's outpost world launched *antimatter missiles* at Majesdane. It... it was *horrible.*
We crash-landed our escape pod a few miles from the Hostel. I... I don't know if anyone else from our system survived.

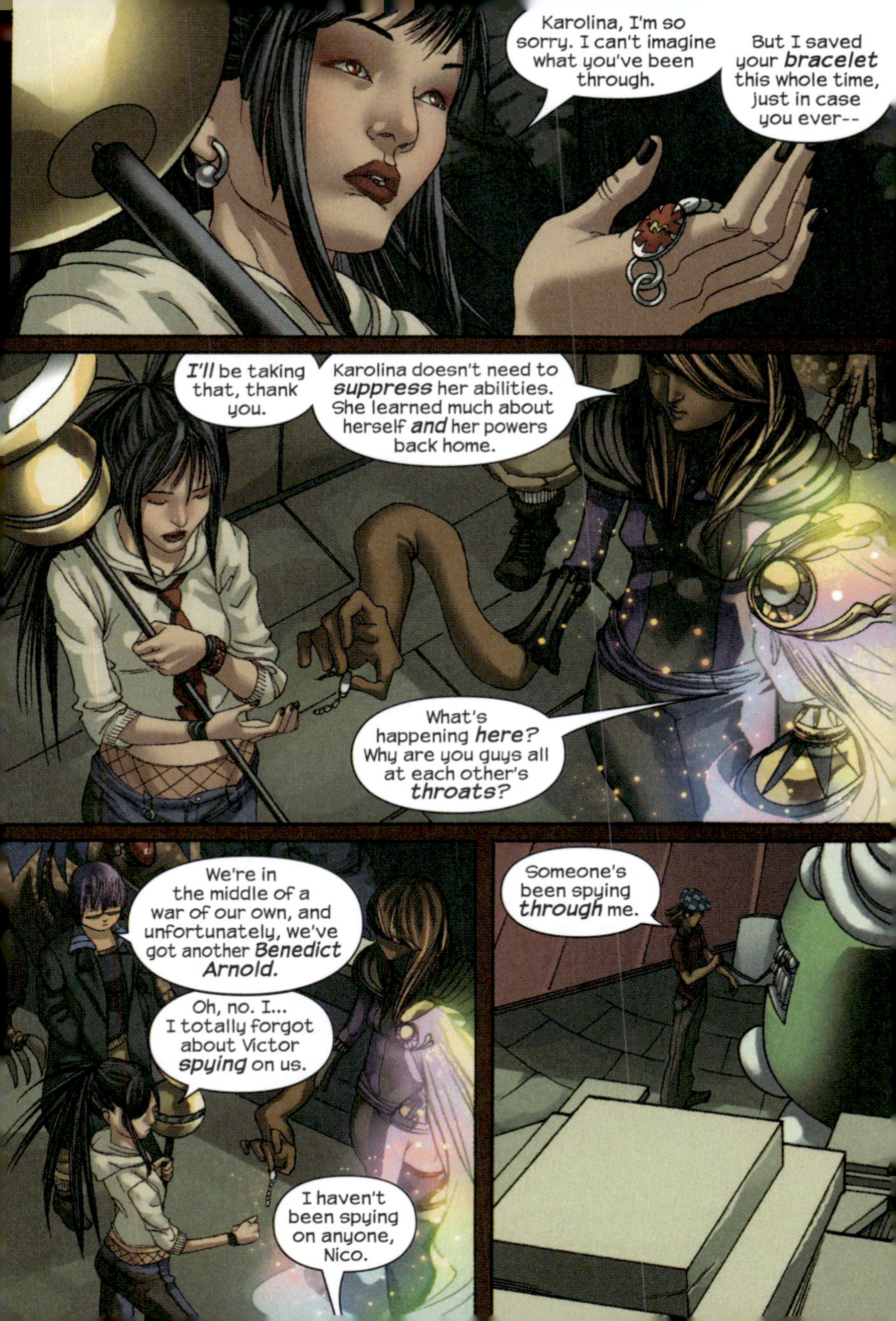
Karolina, I'm so sorry. I can't imagine what you've been through.
But I saved your bracelet this whole time, just in case you ever--
I'll be taking that, thank you.
Karolina doesn't need to suppress her abilities. She learned much about herself and her powers back home.
What's happening here? Why are you guys all at each other's throats?
We're in the middle of a war of our own, and unfortunately, we've got another Benedict Arnold.
Oh, no. I... I totally forgot about Victor spying on us.
I haven't been spying on anyone, Nico.
Someone's been spying through me.

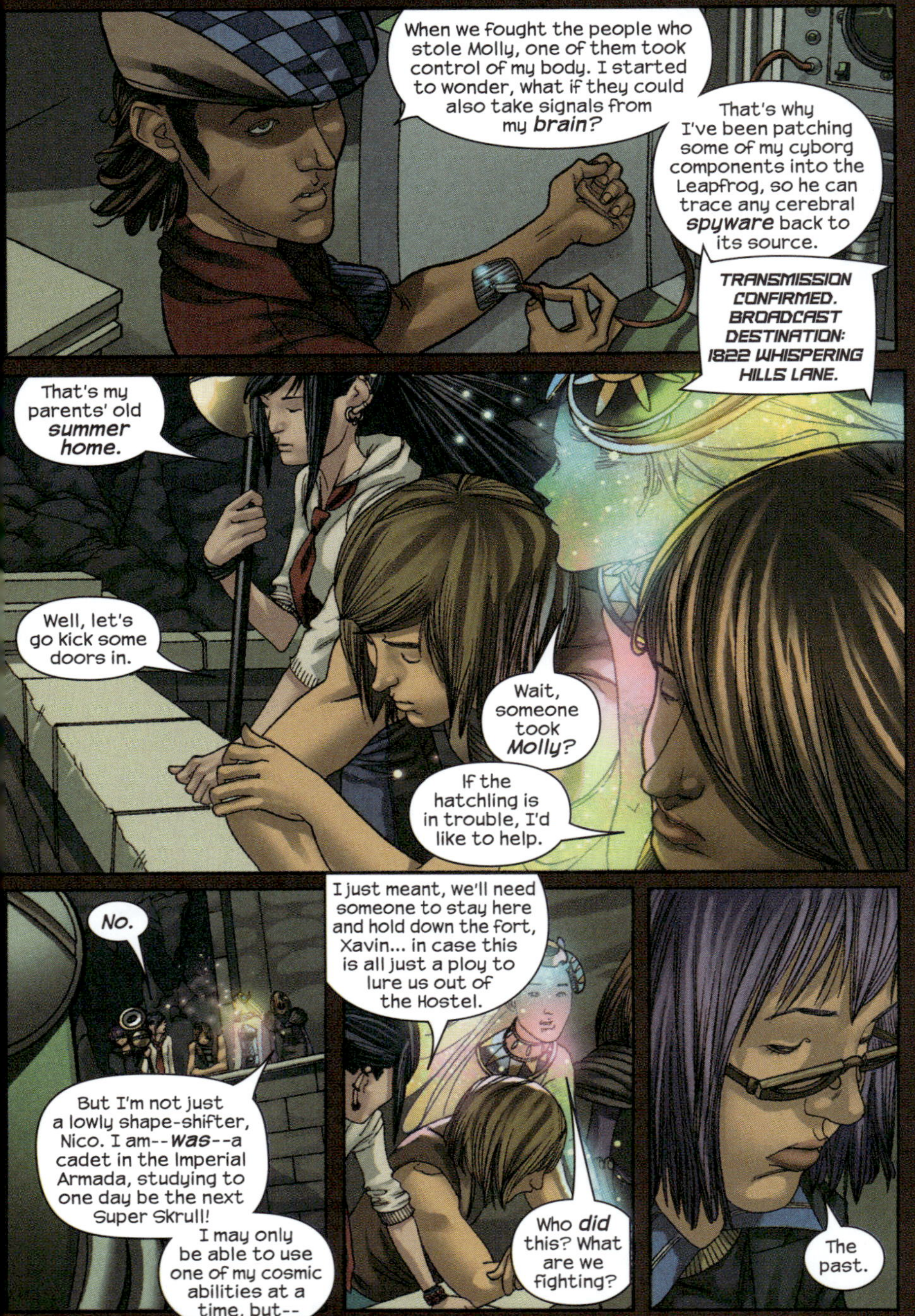
When we fought the people who stole Molly, one of them took control of my body. I started to wonder, what if they could also take signals from my *brain*?
That's why I've been patching some of my cyborg components into the Leapfrog, so he can trace any cerebral *spyware* back to its source.
TRANSMISSION CONFIRMED. BROADCAST DESTINATION: 1822 WHISPERING HILLS LANE.
That's my parents' old *summer home.*
Well, let's go kick some doors in.
Wait, someone took *Molly*?
If the hatchling is in trouble, I'd like to help.
No.
I just meant, we'll need someone to stay here and hold down the fort, Xavin... in case this is all just a ploy to lure us out of the Hostel.
But I'm not just a lowly shape-shifter, Nico. I am--*was*--a cadet in the Imperial Armada, studying to one day be the next Super Skrull!
I may only be able to use one of my cosmic abilities at a time, but--
Who *did* this? What are we fighting?
The past.

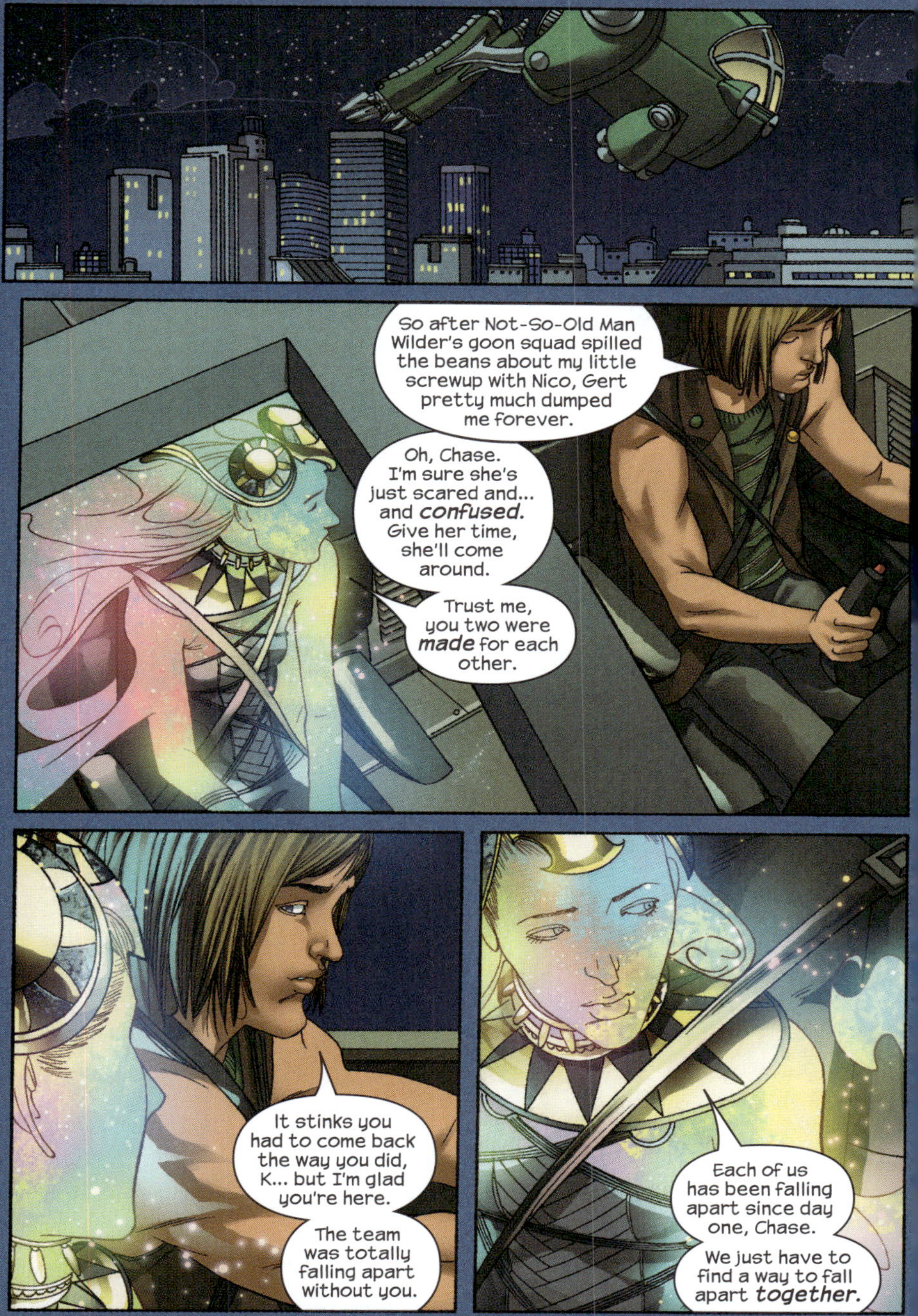
So after Not-So-Old Man Wilder's goon squad spilled the beans about my little screwup with Nico, Gert pretty much dumped me forever.
Oh, Chase. I'm sure she's just scared and... and *confused.* Give her time, she'll come around.
Trust me, you two were *made* for each other.
It stinks you had to come back the way you did, K... but I'm glad you're here.
The team was totally falling apart without you.
Each of us has been falling apart since day one, Chase.
We just have to find a way to fall apart *together.*

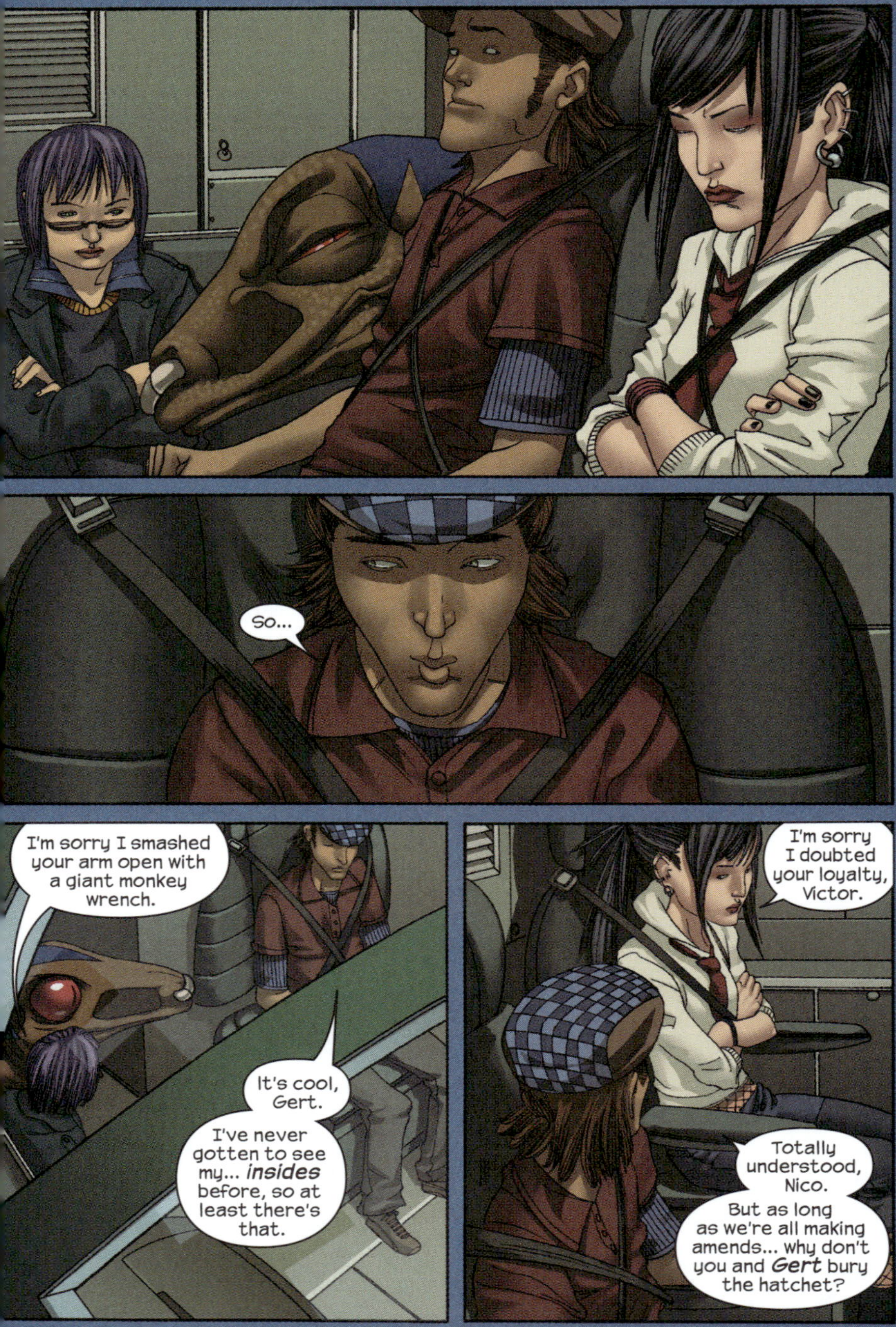
So...
I'm sorry I smashed your arm open with a giant monkey wrench.
It's cool, Gert.
I've never gotten to see my... *insides* before, so at least there's that.
I'm sorry I doubted your loyalty, Victor.
Totally understood, Nico.
But as long as we're all making amends... why don't you and *Gert* bury the hatchet?

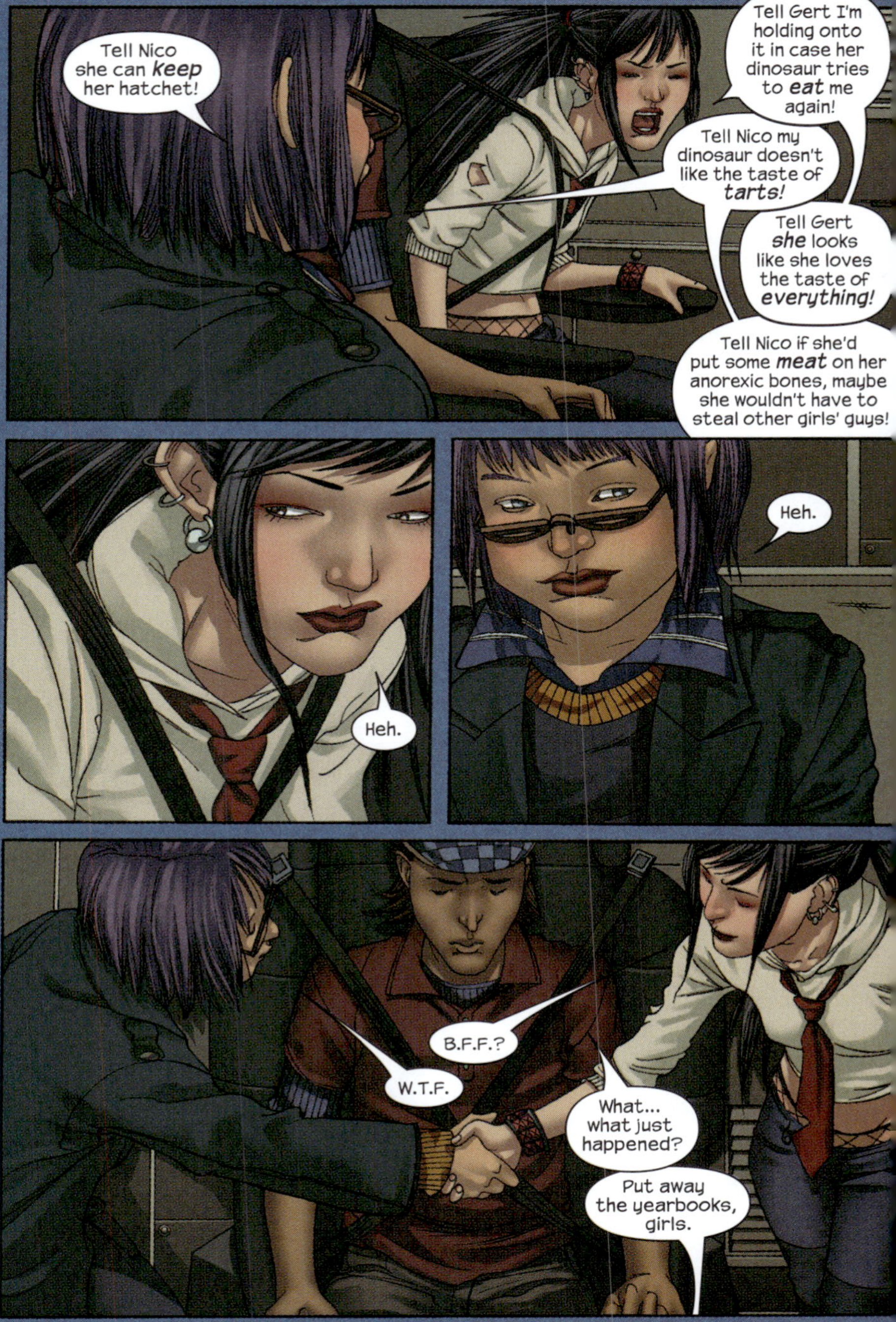
Tell Nico she can *keep* her hatchet!
Tell Gert I'm holding onto it in case her dinosaur tries to *eat* me again!
Tell Nico my dinosaur doesn't like the taste of *tarts!*
Tell Gert *she* looks like she loves the taste of *everything!*
Tell Nico if she'd put some *meat* on her anorexic bones, maybe she wouldn't have to steal other girls' guys!
Heh.
Heh.
B.F.F.?
W.T.F.
What... what just happened?
Put away the yearbooks, girls.

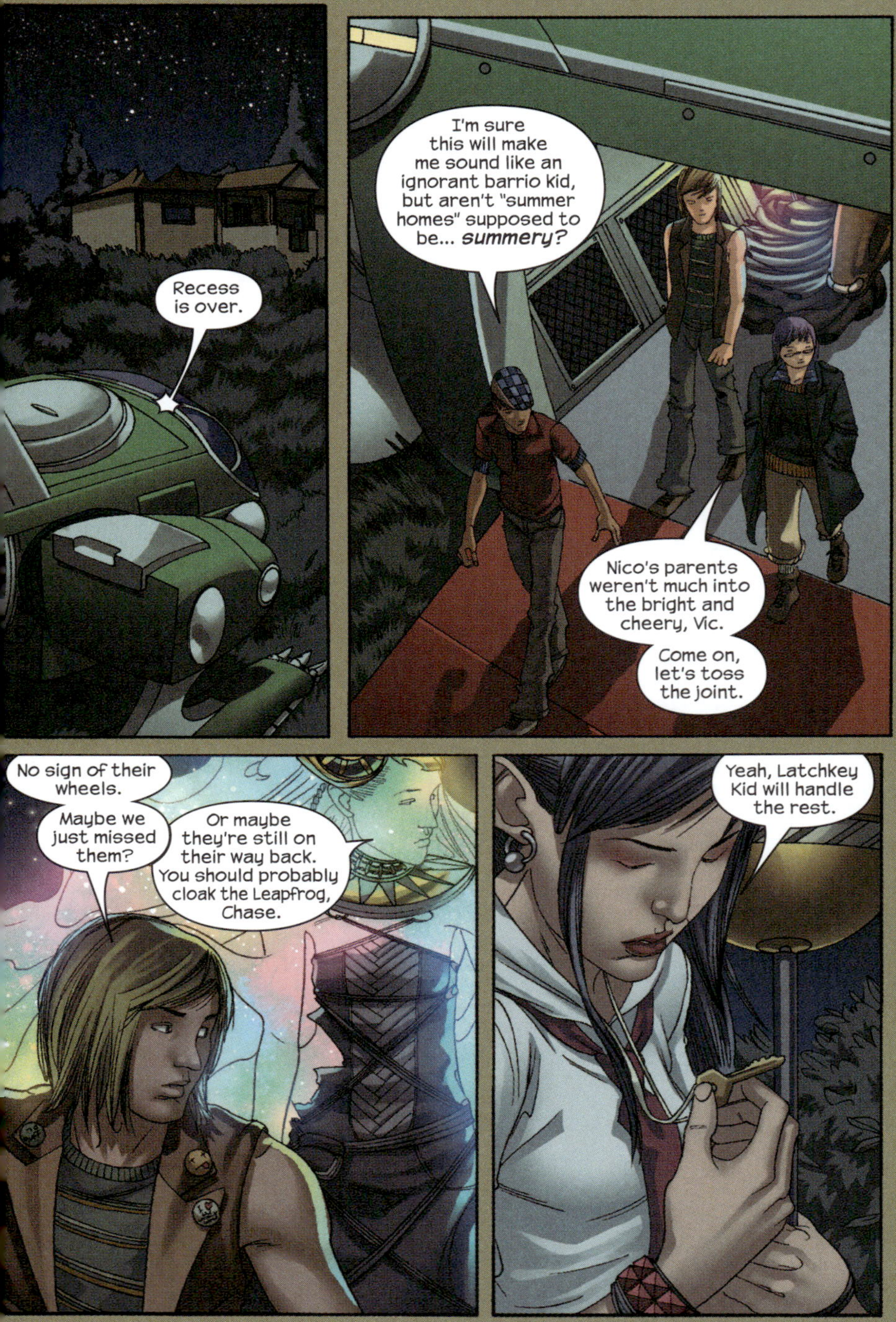
Recess is over.
I'm sure this will make me sound like an ignorant barrio kid, but aren't "summer homes" supposed to be... *summery?*
Nico's parents weren't much into the bright and cheery, Vic.
Come on, let's toss the joint.
No sign of their wheels.
Maybe we just missed them?
Or maybe they're still on their way back. You should probably cloak the Leapfrog, Chase.
Yeah, Latchkey Kid will handle the rest.

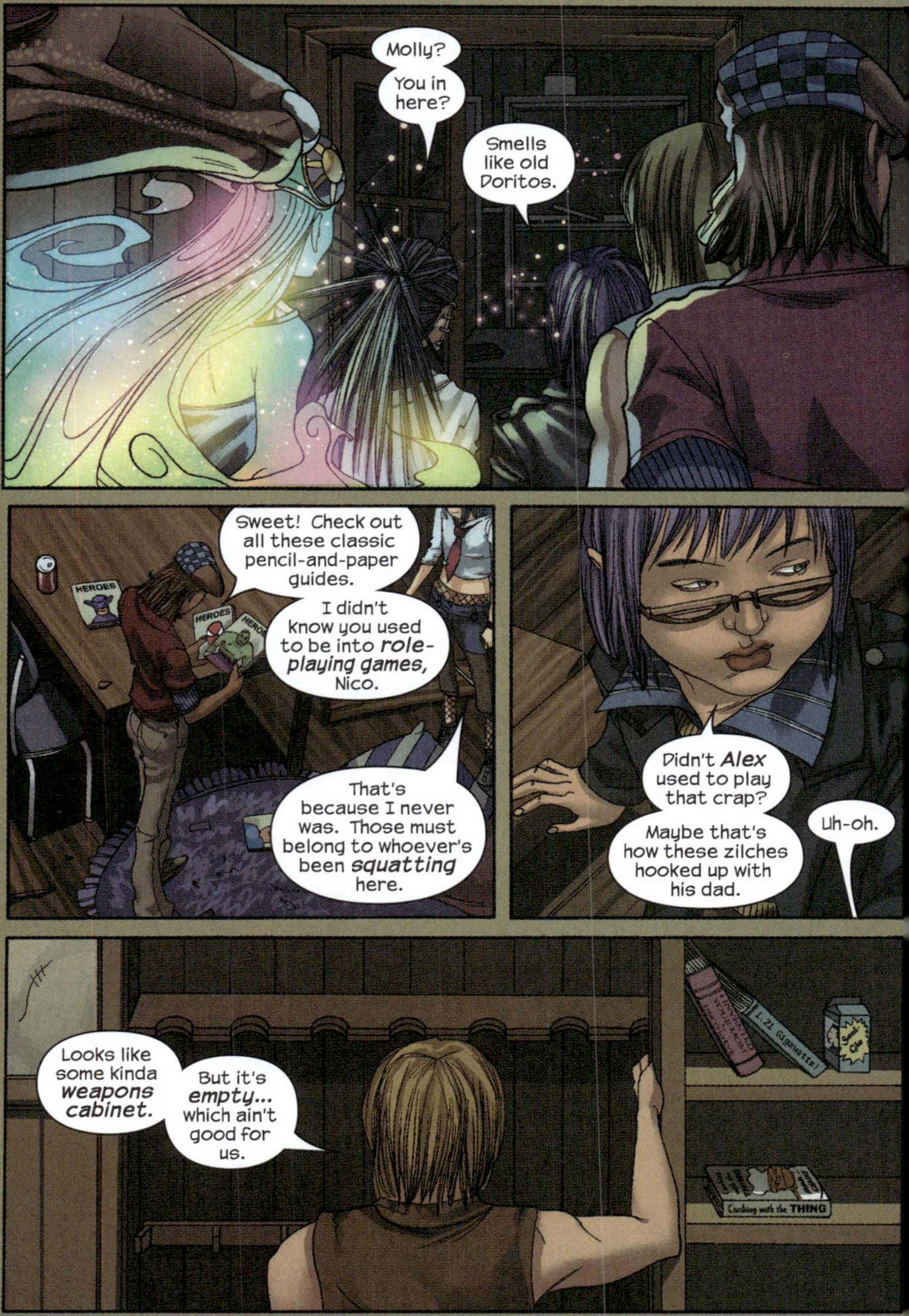
Molly?
You in here?
Smells like old Doritos.
Sweet! Check out all these classic pencil-and-paper guides.
HEROES
I didn't know you used to be into *role-playing games,* Nico.
That's because I never was. Those must belong to whoever's been *squatting* here.
Didn't *Alex* used to play that crap?
Maybe that's how these zilches hooked up with his dad.
Uh-oh.
Looks like some kinda *weapons cabinet.*
But it's *empty...* which ain't good for us.
1.21 Gigawatts!
Cooking with the THING

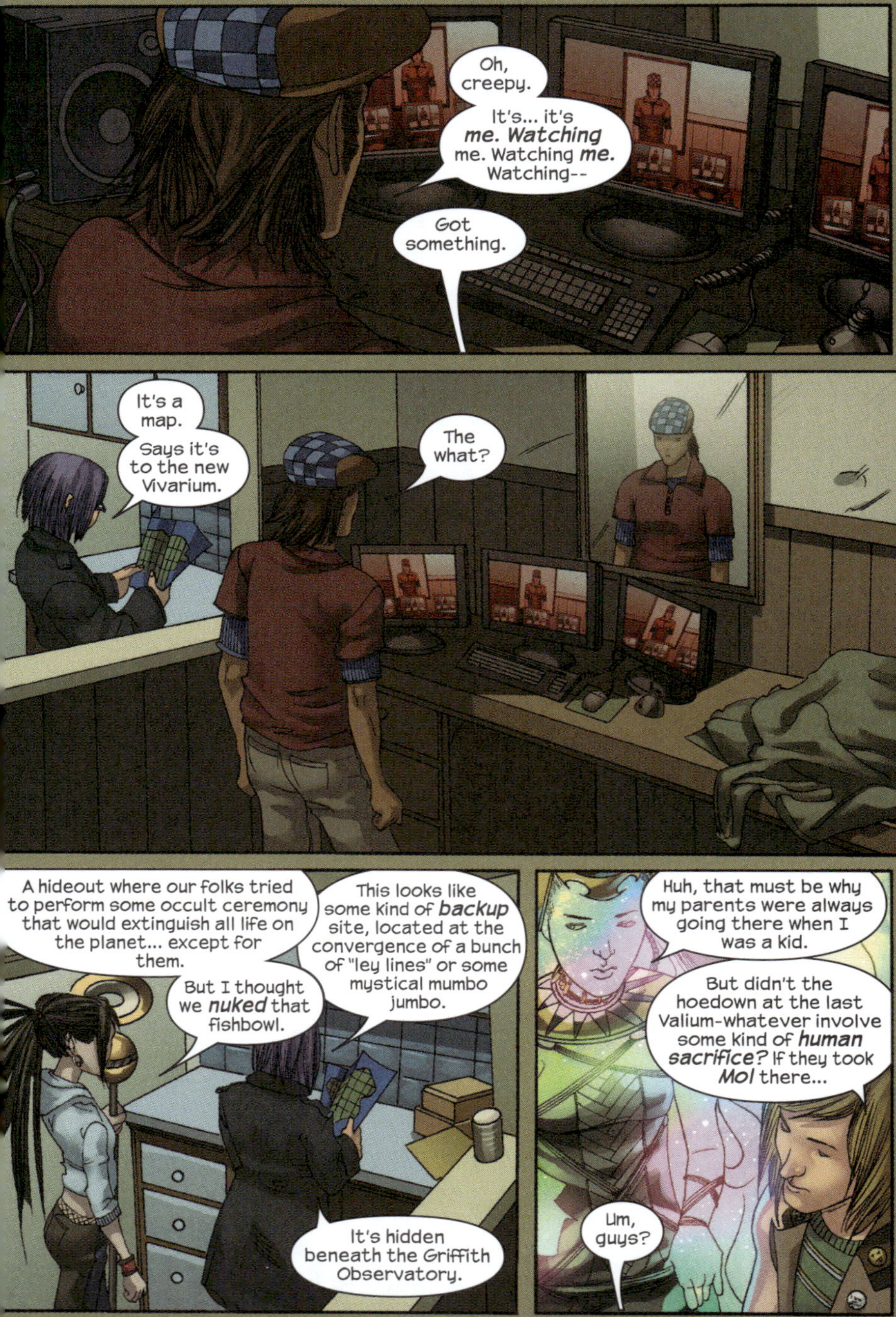

Oh, creepy.
It's... it's *me. Watching* me. Watching *me.* Watching--
Got something.
It's a map.
Says it's to the new Vivarium.
The what?
A hideout where our folks tried to perform some occult ceremony that would extinguish all life on the planet... except for them.
But I thought we *nuked* that fishbowl.
This looks like some kind of *backup* site, located at the convergence of a bunch of "ley lines" or some mystical mumbo jumbo.
It's hidden beneath the Griffith Observatory.
Huh, that must be why my parents were always going there when I was a kid.
But didn't the hoedown at the last Valium-whatever involve some kind of *human sacrifice?* If they took *Mol* there...
Um, guys?

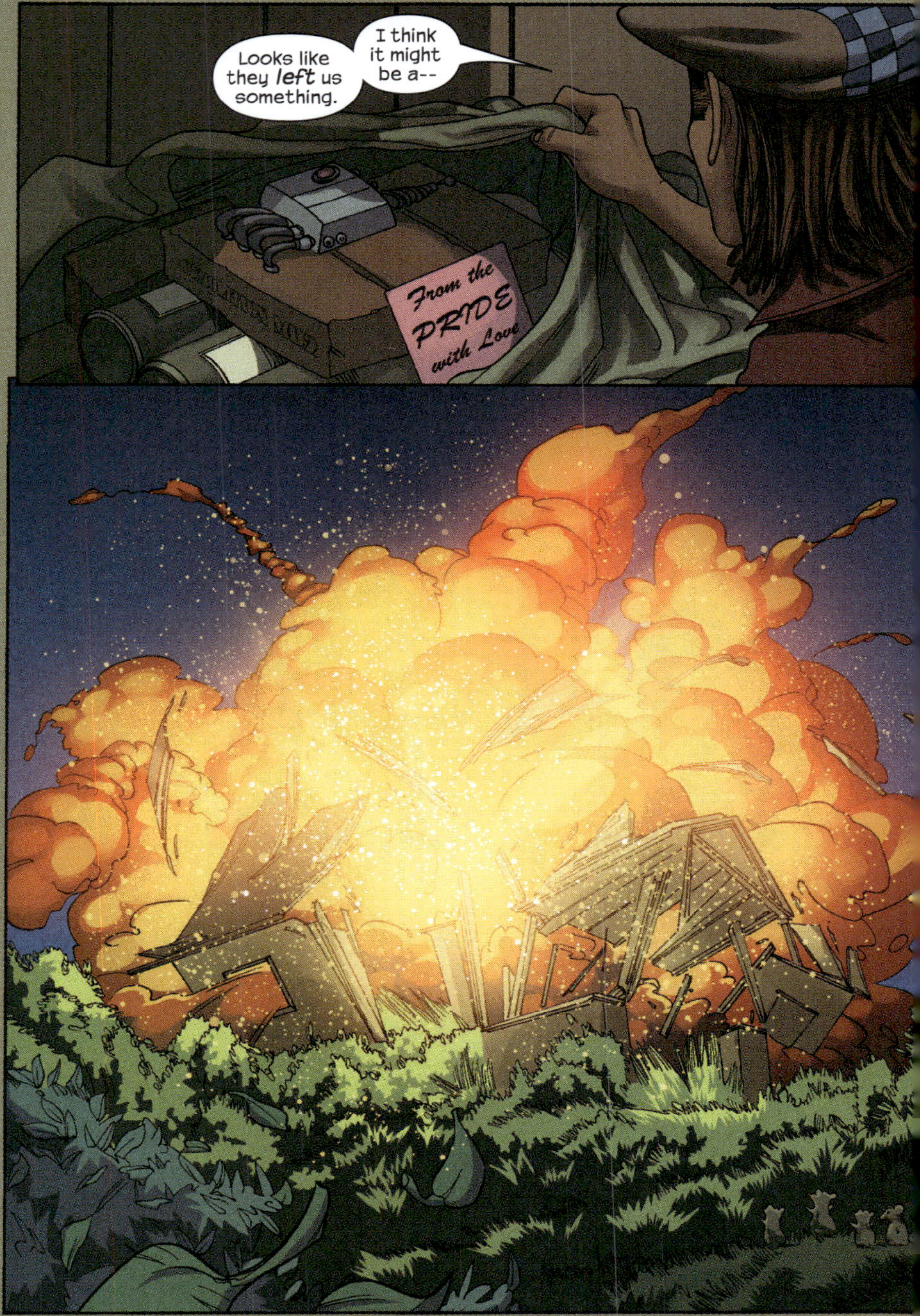
Looks like they *left* us something.
I think it might be a--
From the PRIDE with Love

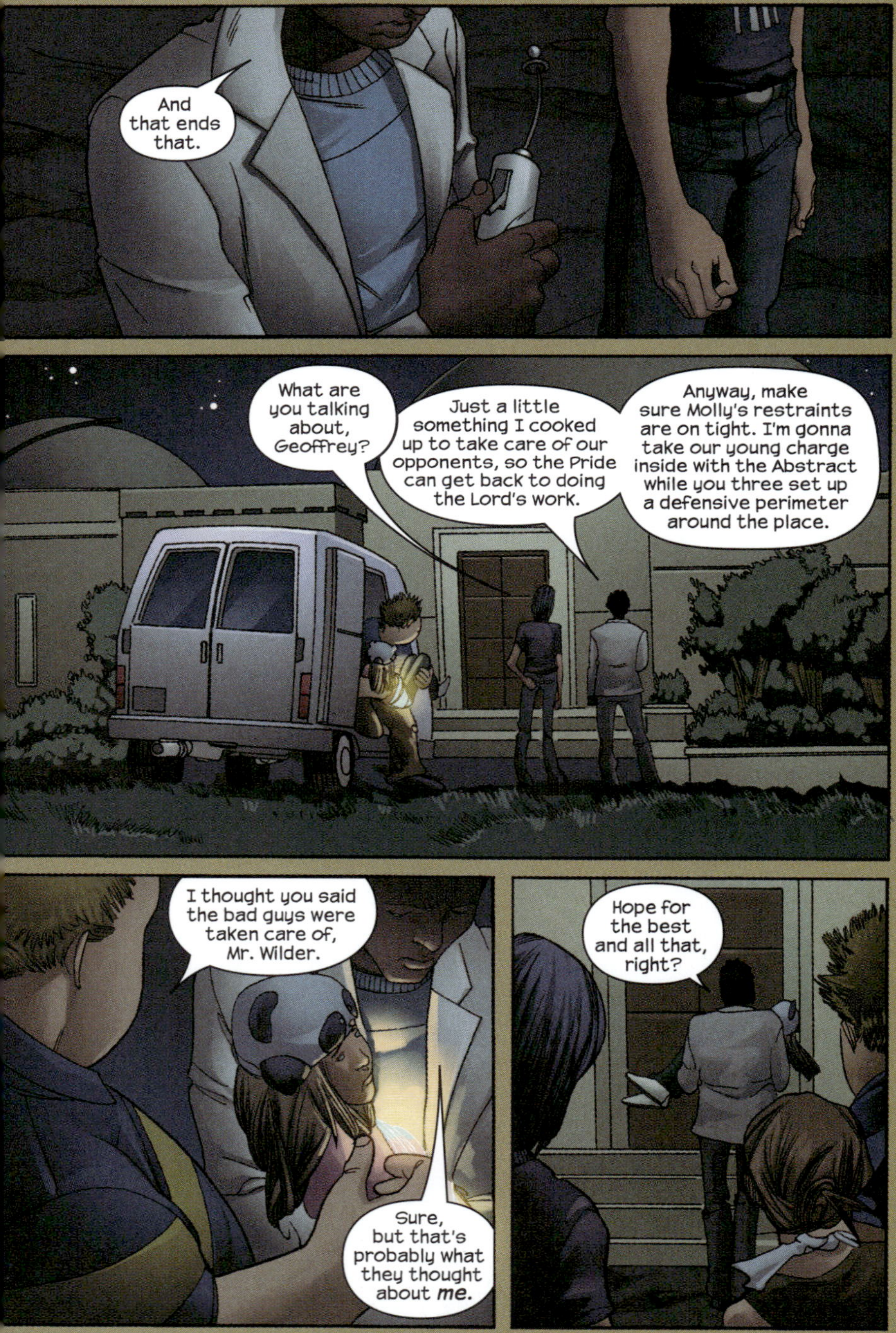
And that ends that.
What are you talking about, Geoffrey?
Just a little something I cooked up to take care of our opponents, so the Pride can get back to doing the Lord's work.
Anyway, make sure Molly's restraints are on tight. I'm gonna take our young charge inside with the Abstract while you three set up a defensive perimeter around the place.
I thought you said the bad guys were taken care of, Mr. Wilder.
Sure, but that's probably what they thought about *me.*
Hope for the best and all that, right?

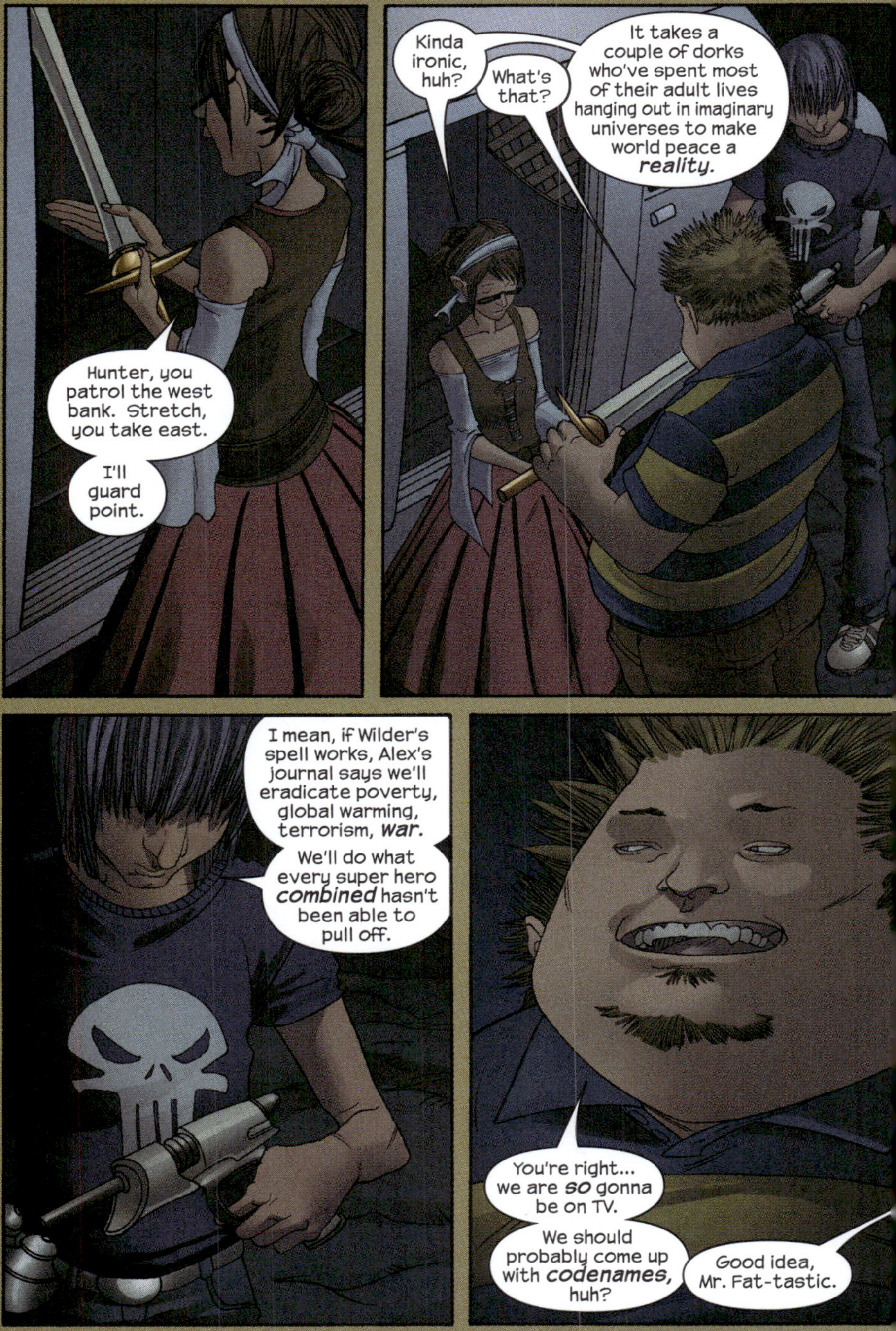
Hunter, you patrol the west bank. Stretch, you take east.
I'll guard point.
Kinda ironic, huh?
What's that?
It takes a couple of dorks who've spent most of their adult lives hanging out in imaginary universes to make world peace a *reality.*
I mean, if Wilder's spell works, Alex's journal says we'll eradicate poverty, global warming, terrorism, *war.*
We'll do what every super hero *combined* hasn't been able to pull off.
You're right... we are *so* gonna be on TV.
We should probably come up with *codenames,* huh?
Good idea, Mr. Fat-tastic.

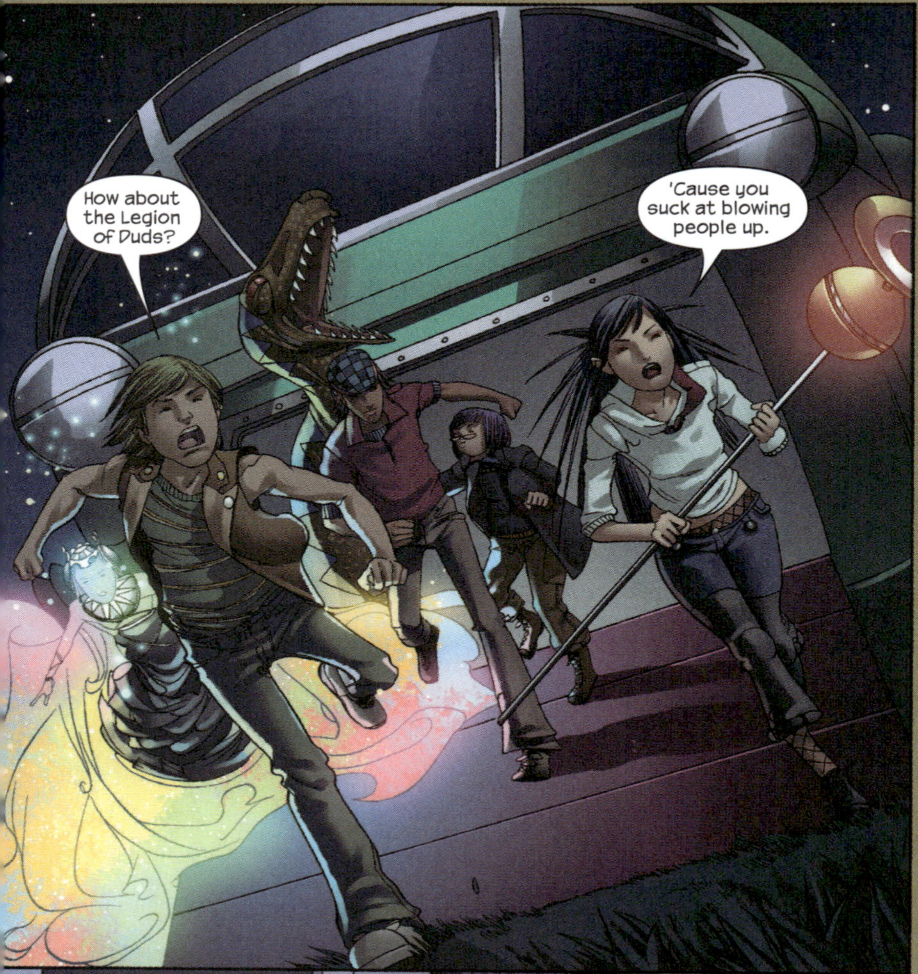
How about the Legion of Duds?
'Cause you suck at blowing people up.

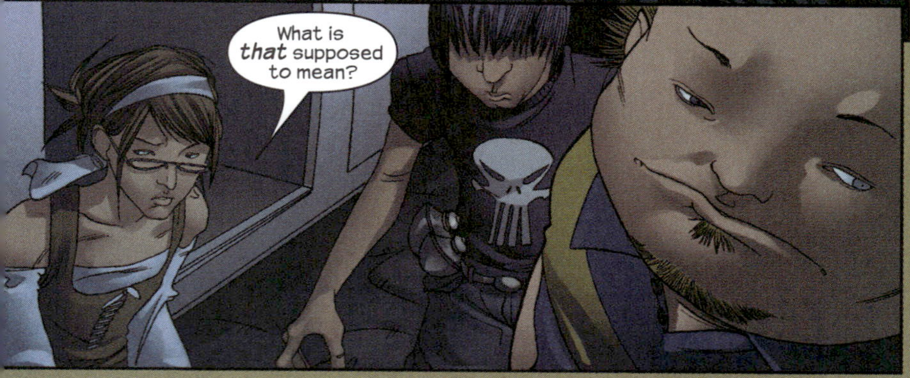
What is *that* supposed to mean?

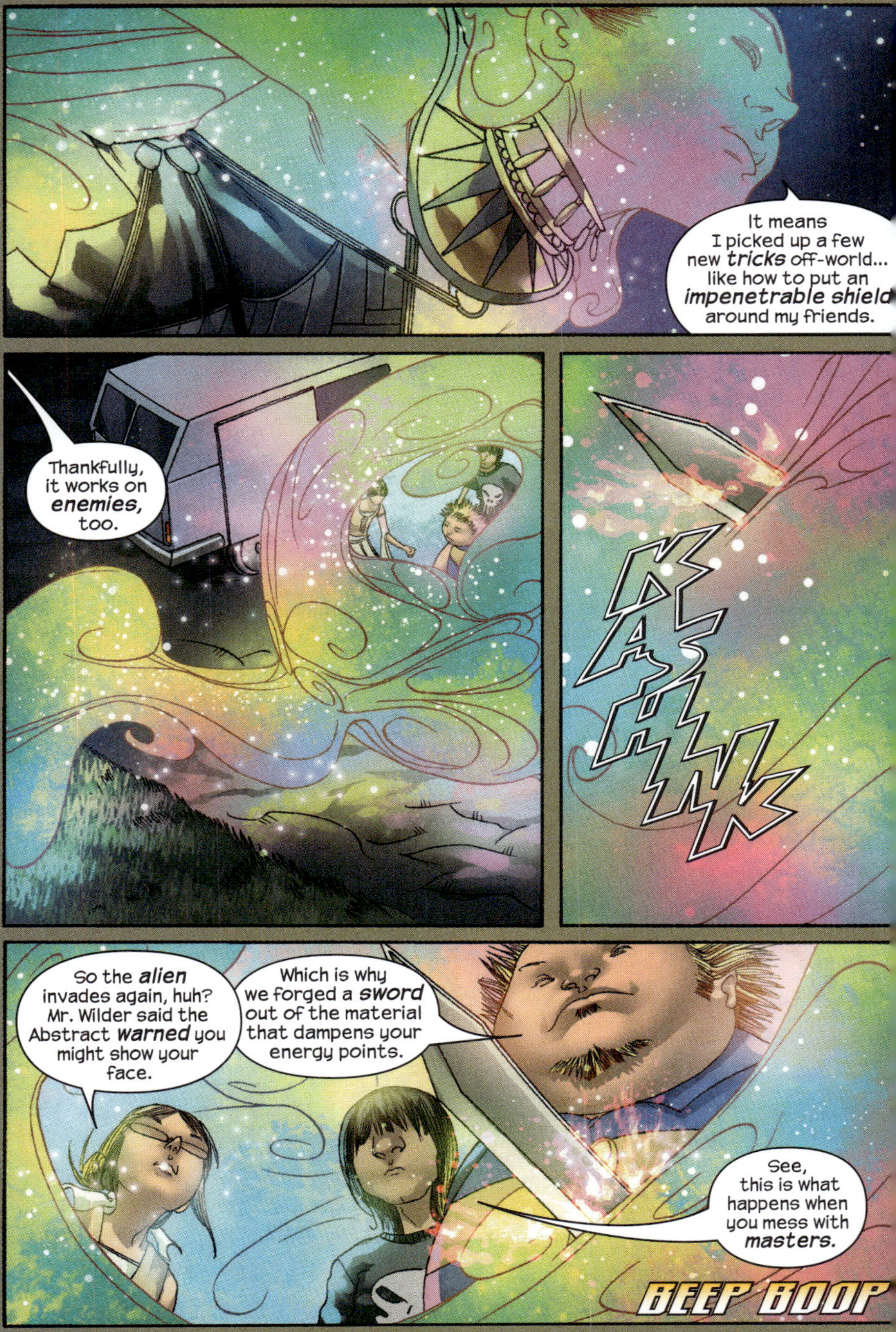
It means I picked up a few new *tricks* off-world... like how to put an *impenetrable shield* around my friends.
Thankfully, it works on *enemies,* too.
KASHUNK
So the *alien* invades again, huh? Mr. Wilder said the Abstract *warned* you might show your face.
Which is why we forged a *sword* out of the material that dampens your energy points.
See, this is what happens when you mess with *masters.*
BEEP BOOP

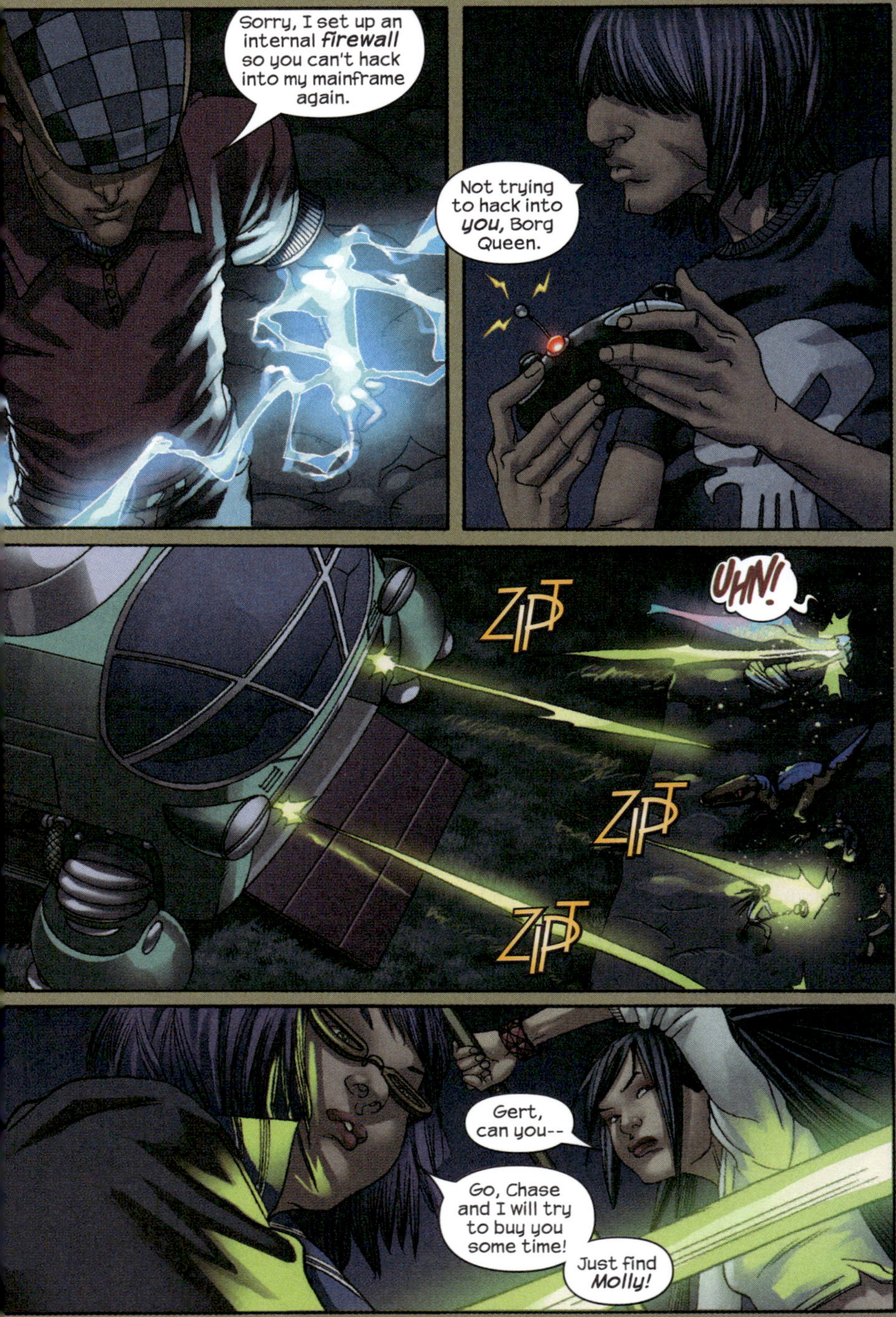
Sorry, I set up an internal *firewall* so you can't hack into my mainframe again.
Not trying to hack into *you*, Borg Queen.
ZIPT
UHN!
ZIPT
ZIPT
Gert, can you--
Go, Chase and I will try to buy you some time!
Just find *Molly!*

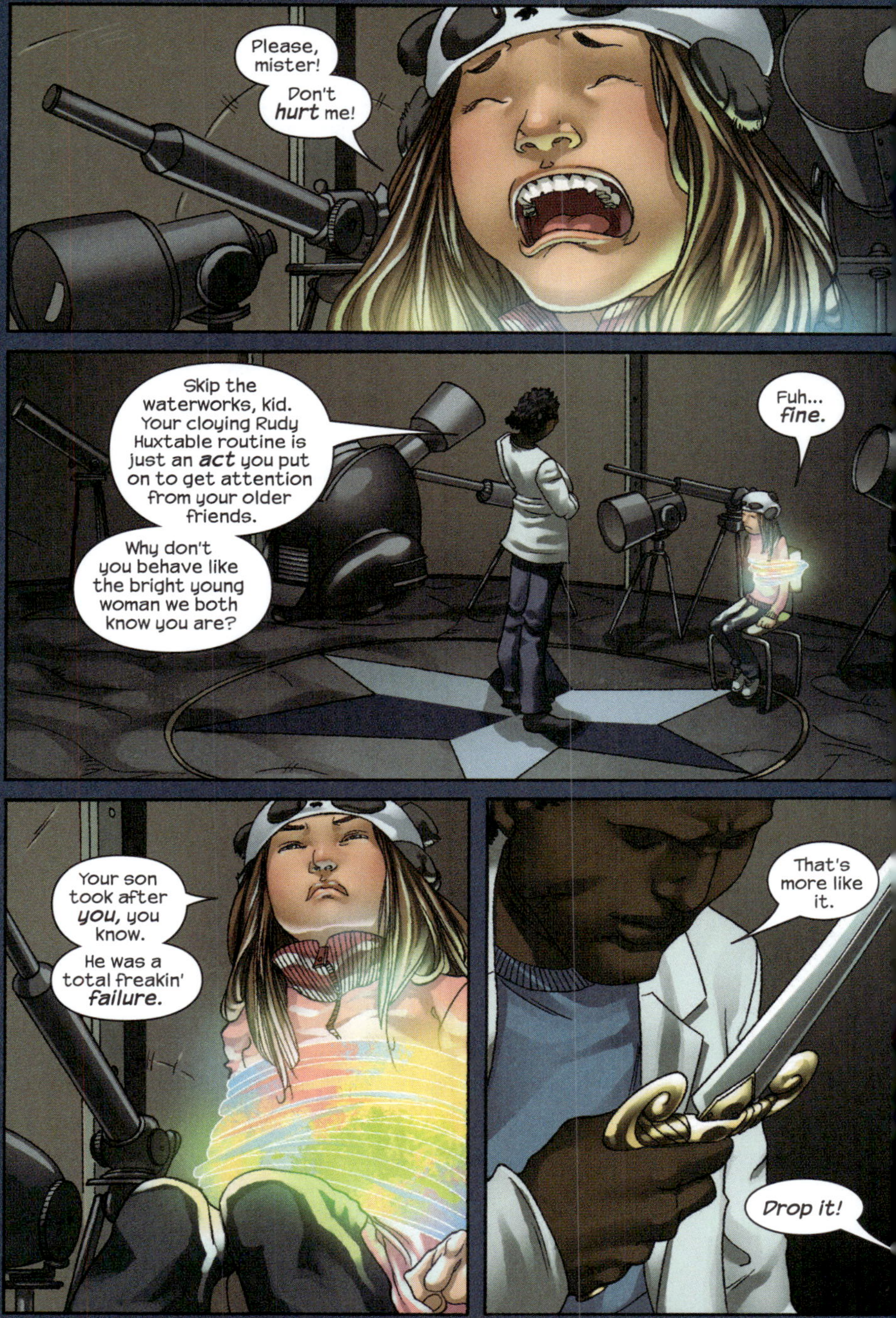

Please, mister!
Don't *hurt* me!
Skip the waterworks, kid. Your cloying Rudy Huxtable routine is just an *act* you put on to get attention from your older friends.
Why don't you behave like the bright young woman we both know you are?
Fuh... *fine.*
Your son took after *you*, you know.
He was a total freakin' *failure.*
That's more like it.
Drop it!

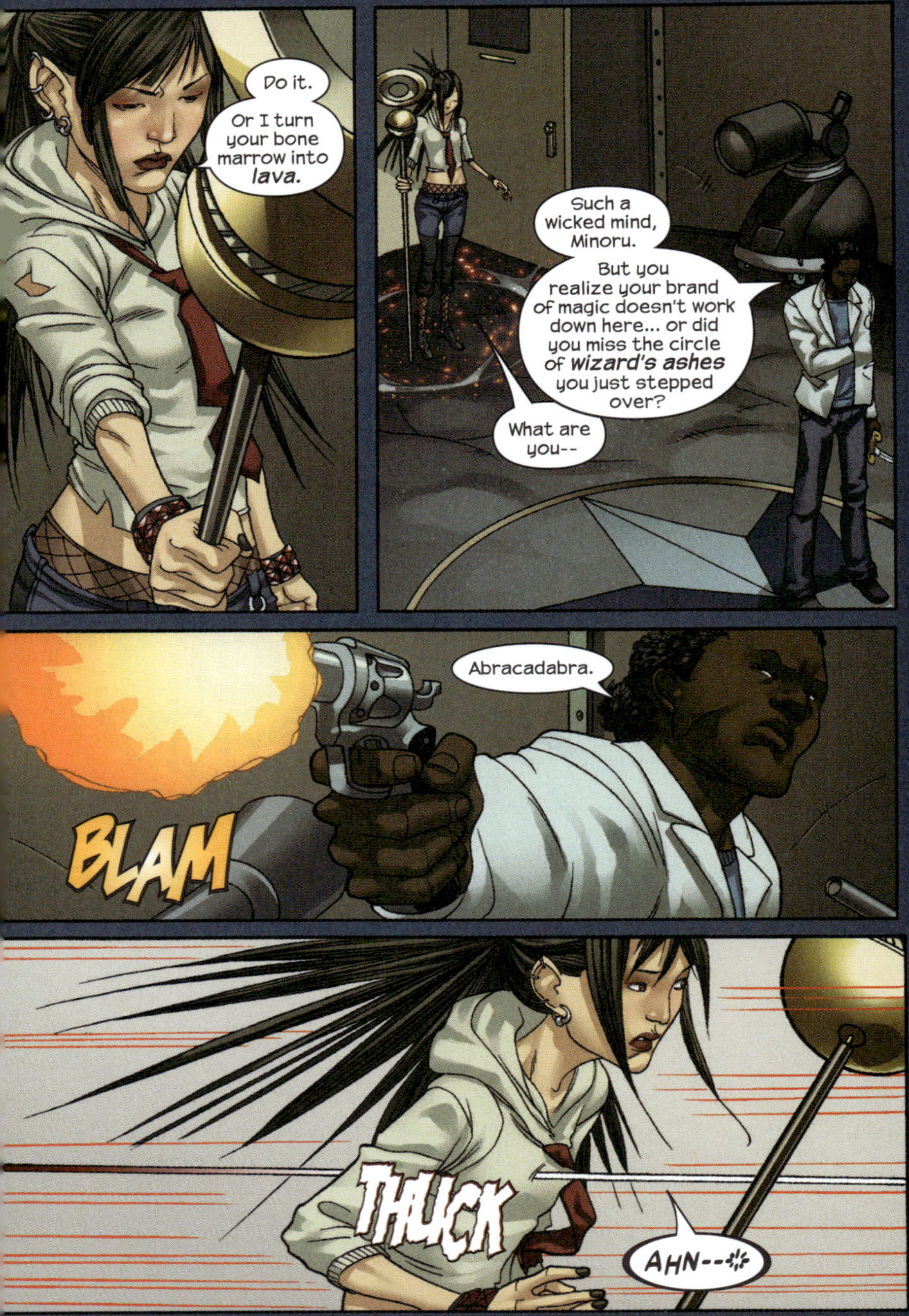
Do it.
Or I turn your bone marrow into *lava.*
Such a wicked mind, Minoru.
But you realize your brand of magic doesn't work down here... or did you miss the circle of ***wizard's ashes*** you just stepped over?
What are you--
Abracadabra.
BLAM
THUCK
AHN--

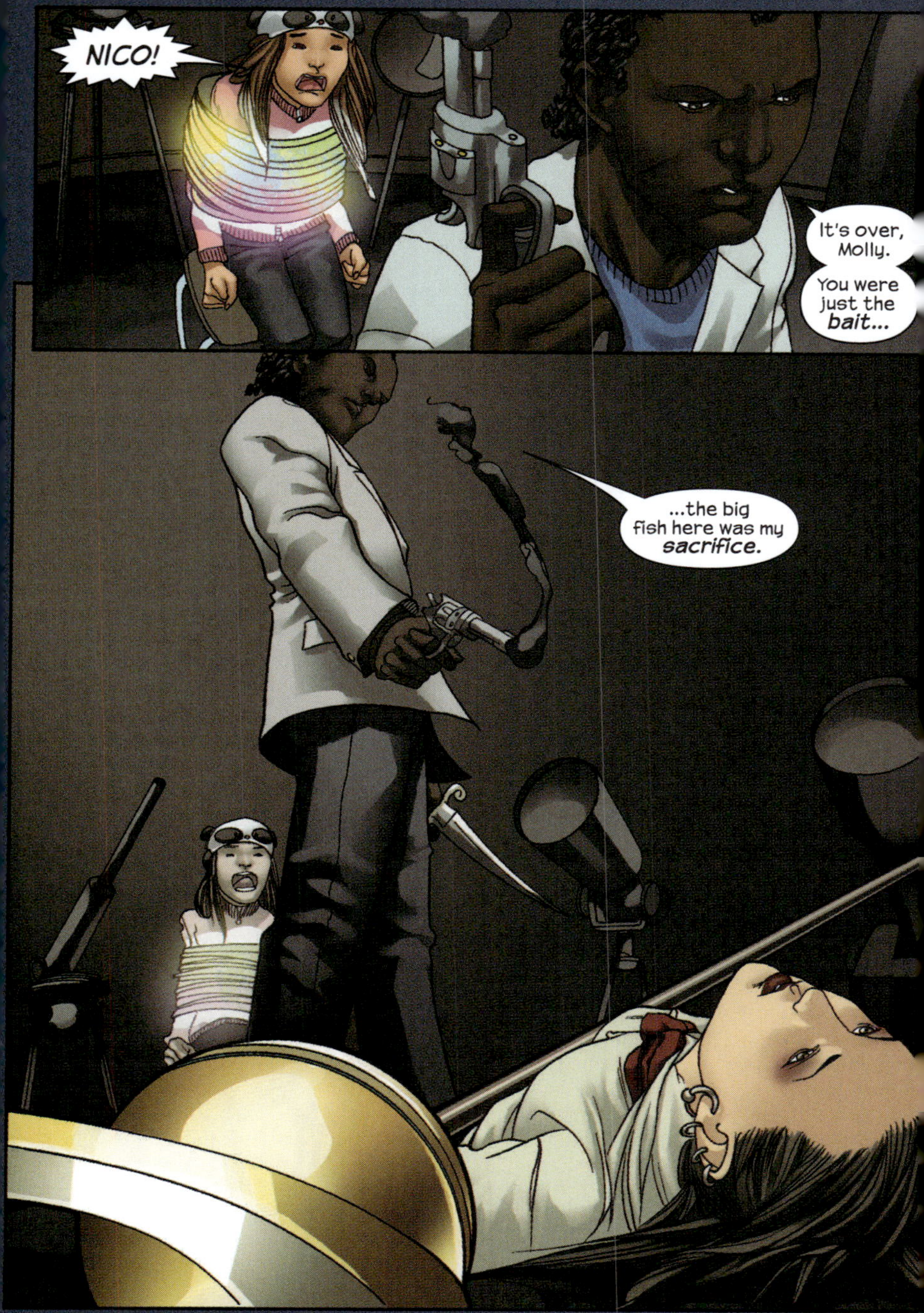
NICO!
It's over, Molly.
You were just the bait...
...the big fish here was my sacrifice.

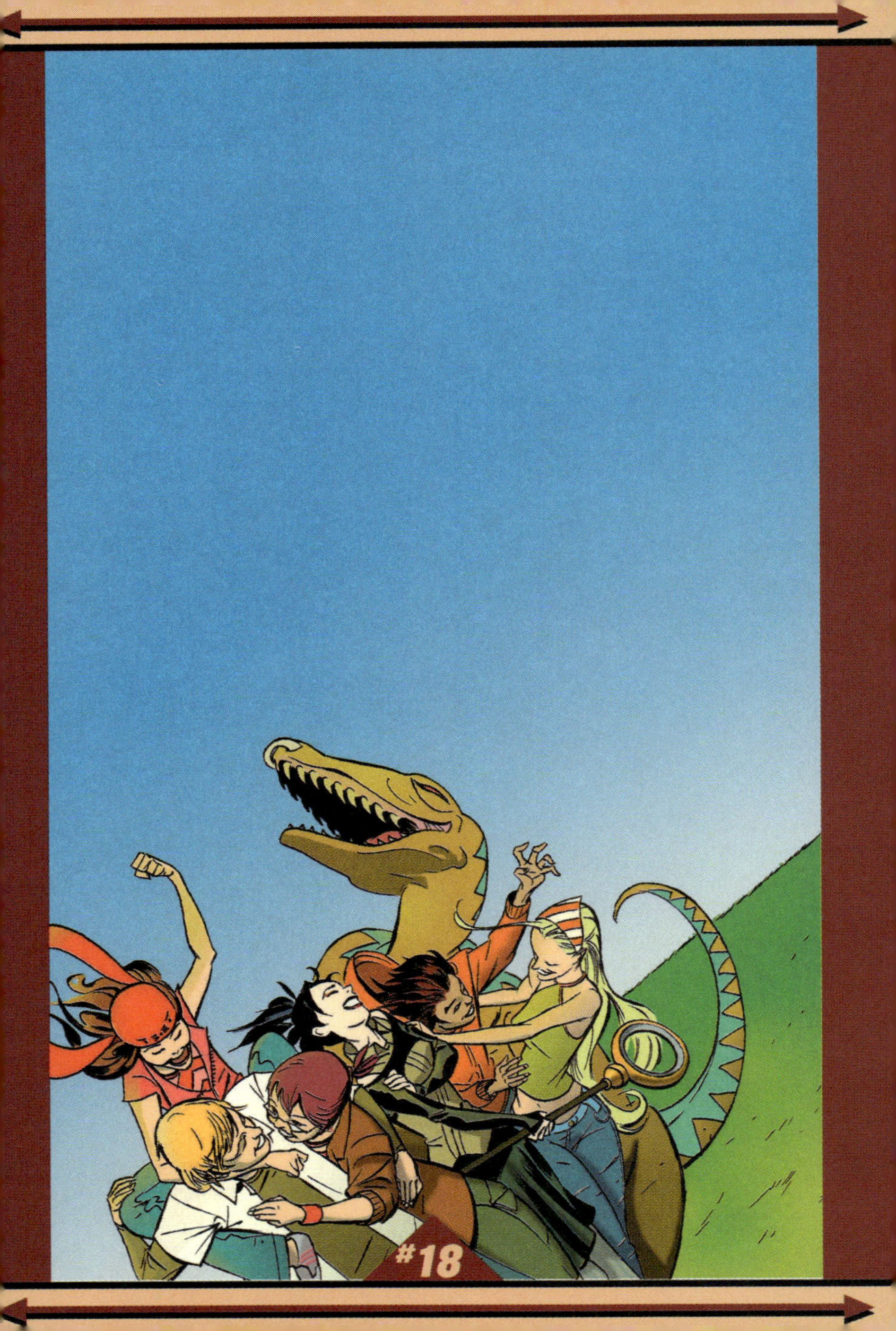
#18

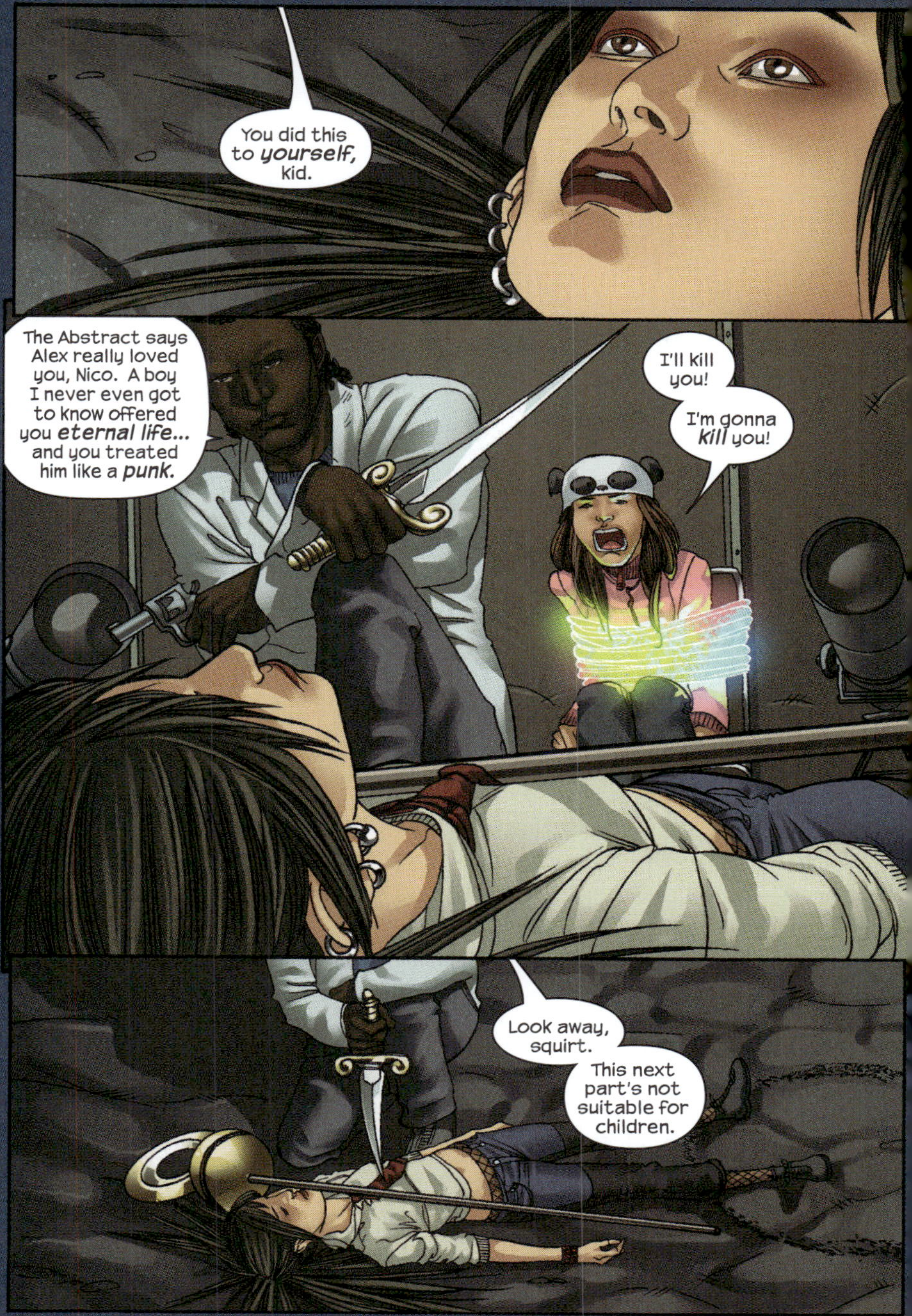
You did this to *yourself,* kid.
The Abstract says Alex really loved you, Nico. A boy I never even got to know offered you *eternal life...* and you treated him like a *punk.*
I'll kill you!
I'm gonna *kill* you!
Look away, squirt.
This next part's not suitable for children.

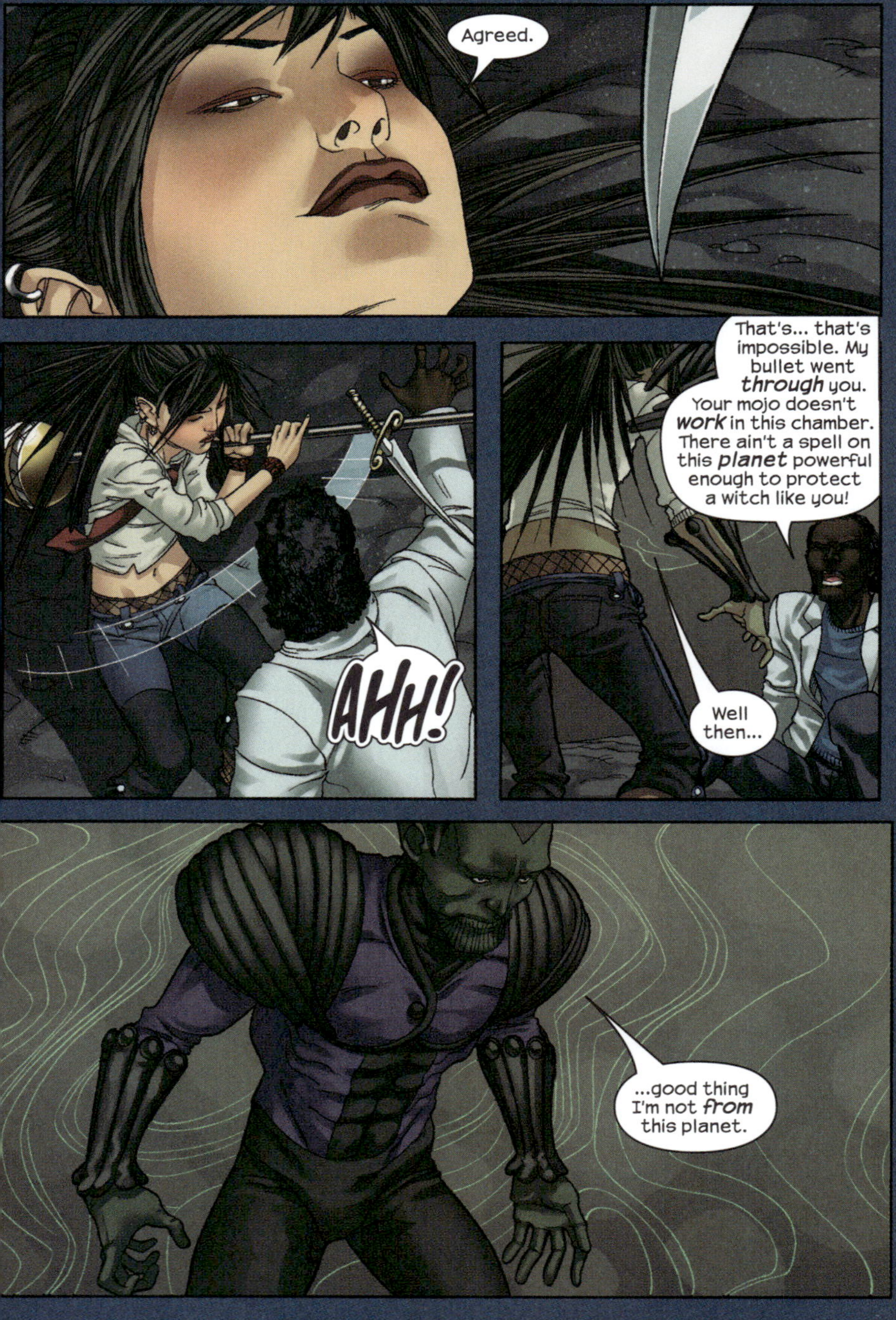
Agreed.
AHH!
That's... that's impossible. My bullet went through you. Your mojo doesn't work in this chamber. There ain't a spell on this planet powerful enough to protect a witch like you!
Well then...
...good thing I'm not from this planet.

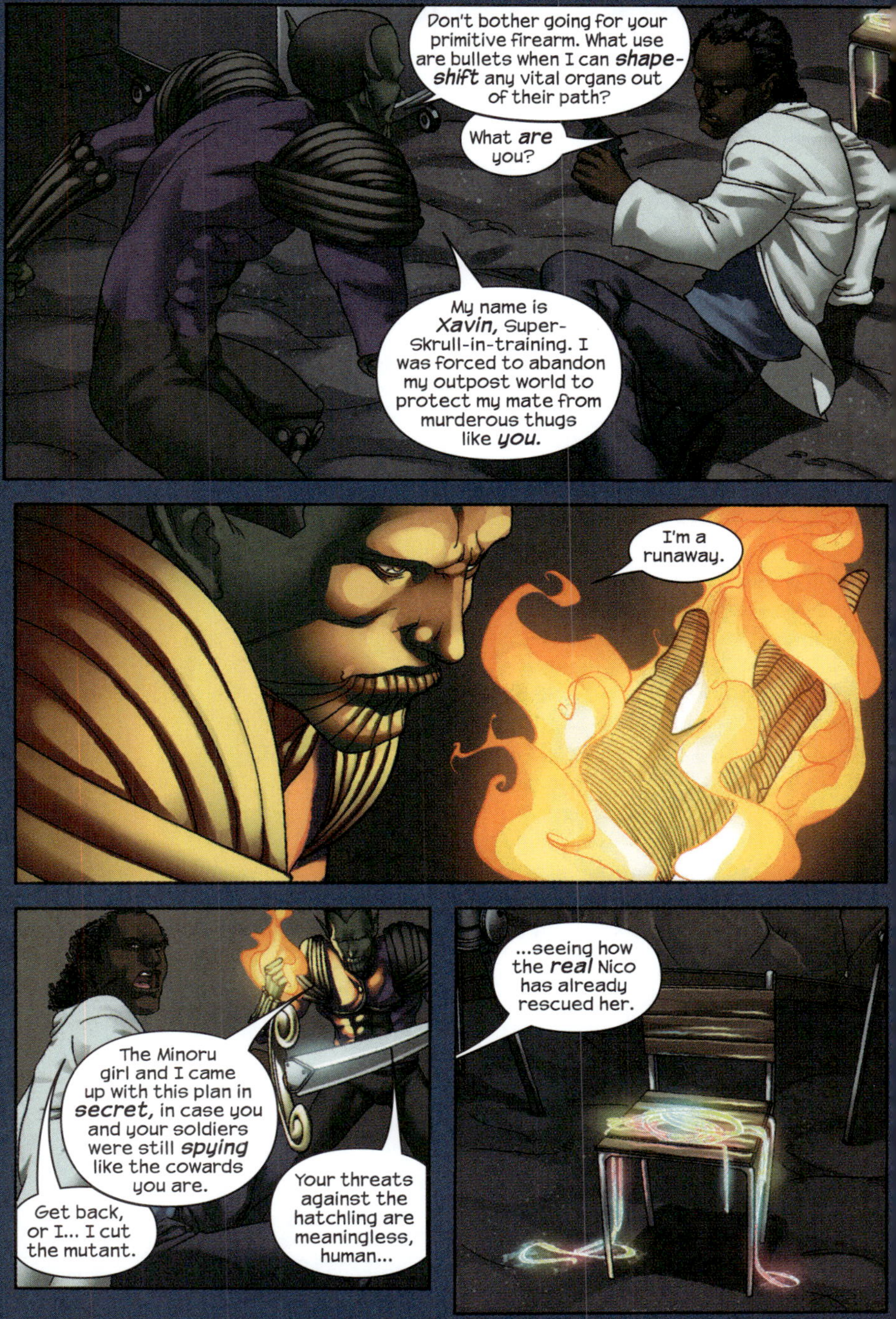
Don't bother going for your primitive firearm. What use are bullets when I can *shape-shift* any vital organs out of their path?
What *are* you?
My name is *Xavin,* Super-Skrull-in-training. I was forced to abandon my outpost world to protect my mate from murderous thugs like *you.*
I'm a runaway.
Get back, or I... I cut the mutant.
The Minoru girl and I came up with this plan in *secret,* in case you and your soldiers were still *spying* like the cowards you are.
Your threats against the hatchling are meaningless, human...
...seeing how the *real* Nico has already rescued her.

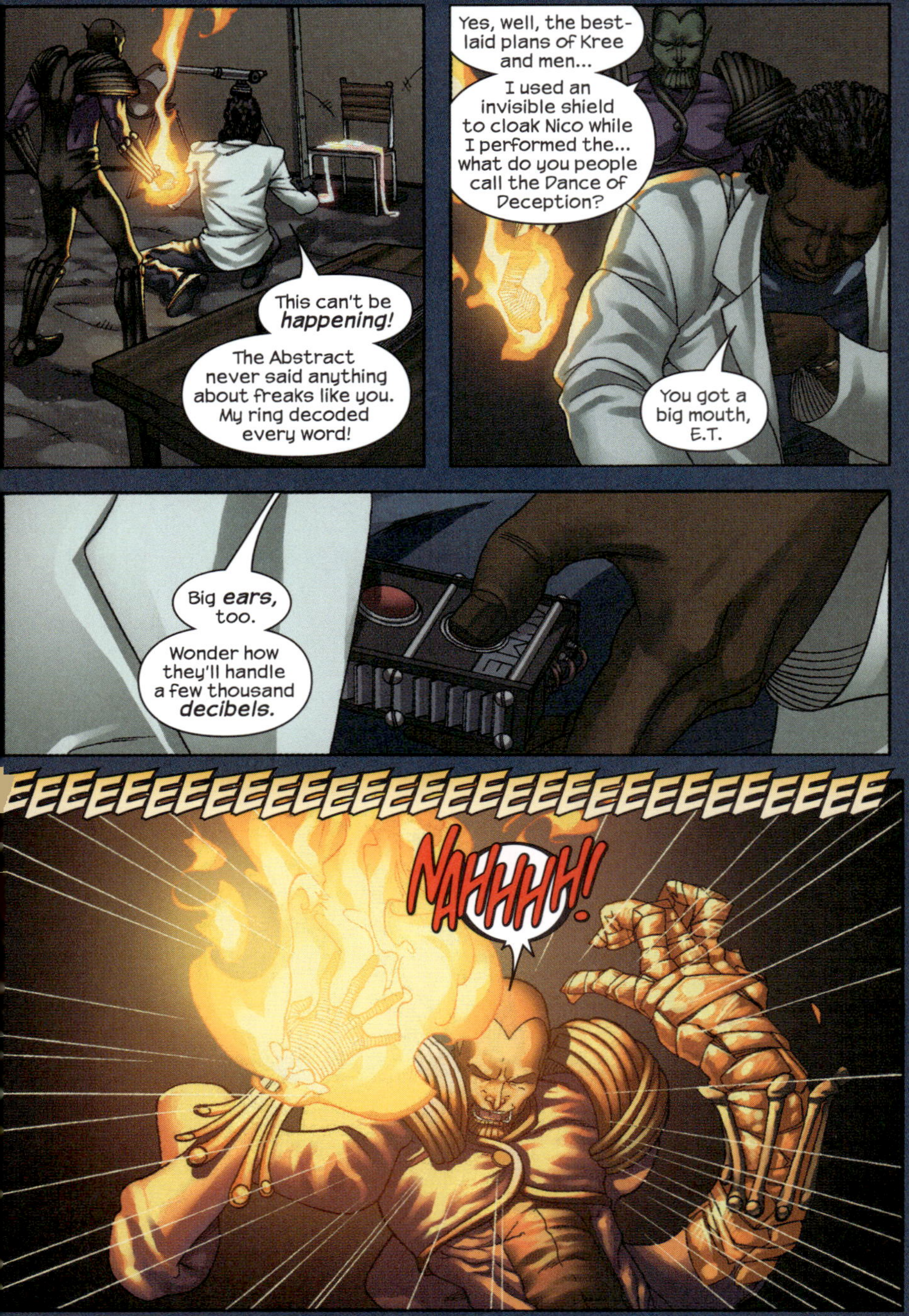
This can't be *happening!*
The Abstract never said anything about freaks like you. My ring decoded every word!
Yes, well, the best-laid plans of Kree and men...
I used an invisible shield to cloak Nico while I performed the... what do you people call the Dance of Deception?
You got a big mouth, E.T.
Big *ears,* too.
Wonder how they'll handle a few thousand *decibels.*
EEEEEEEEEEEEEEEEEEEEEEEEEEEEEE
NAHHHH!

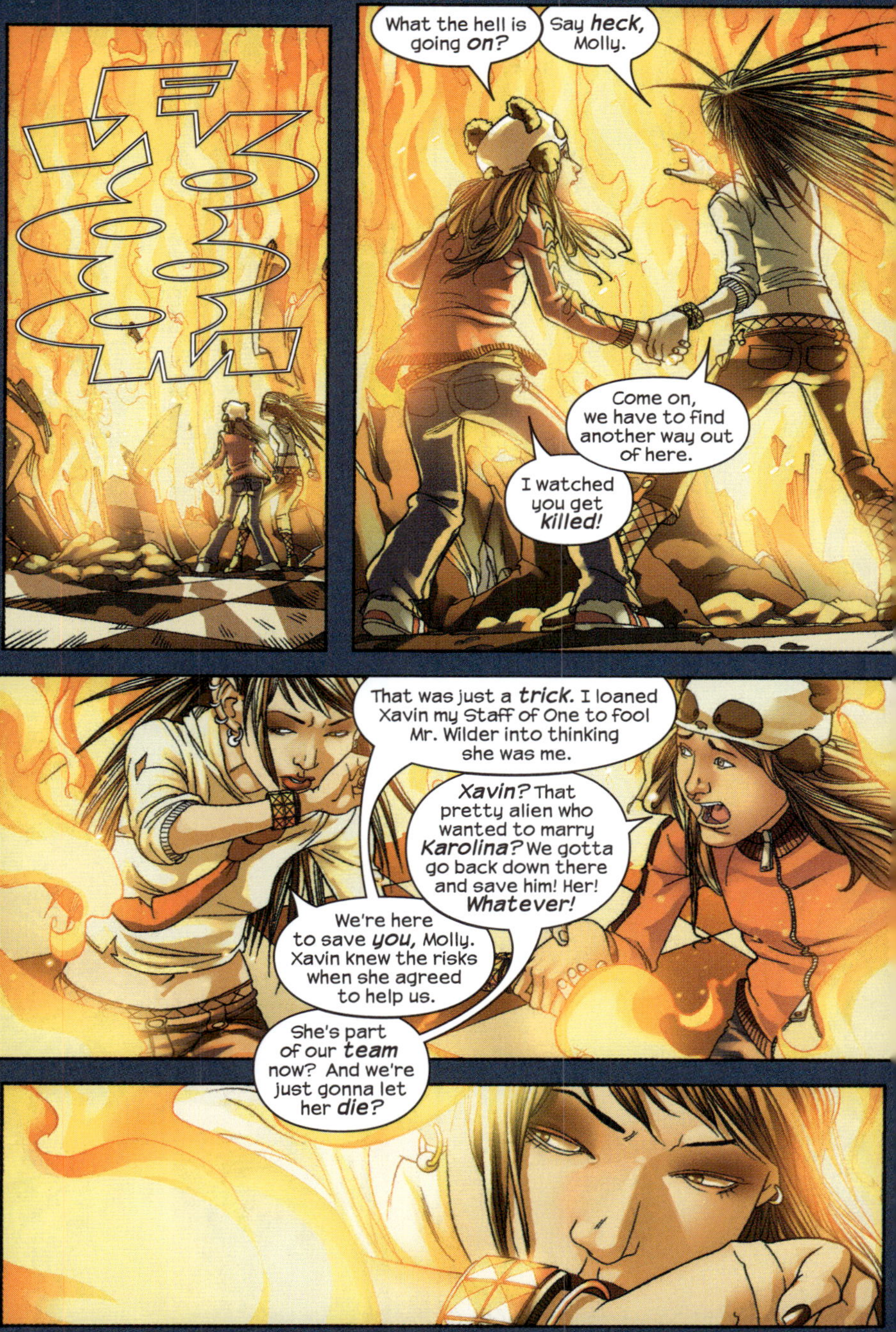
What the hell is going *on?*
Say *heck,* Molly.
Come on, we have to find another way out of here.
I watched you get *killed!*
That was just a *trick.* I loaned Xavin my Staff of One to fool Mr. Wilder into thinking she was me.
Xavin? That pretty alien who wanted to marry *Karolina?* We gotta go back down there and save him! Her! *Whatever!*
We're here to save *you,* Molly. Xavin knew the risks when she agreed to help us.
She's part of our *team* now? And we're just gonna let her *die?*

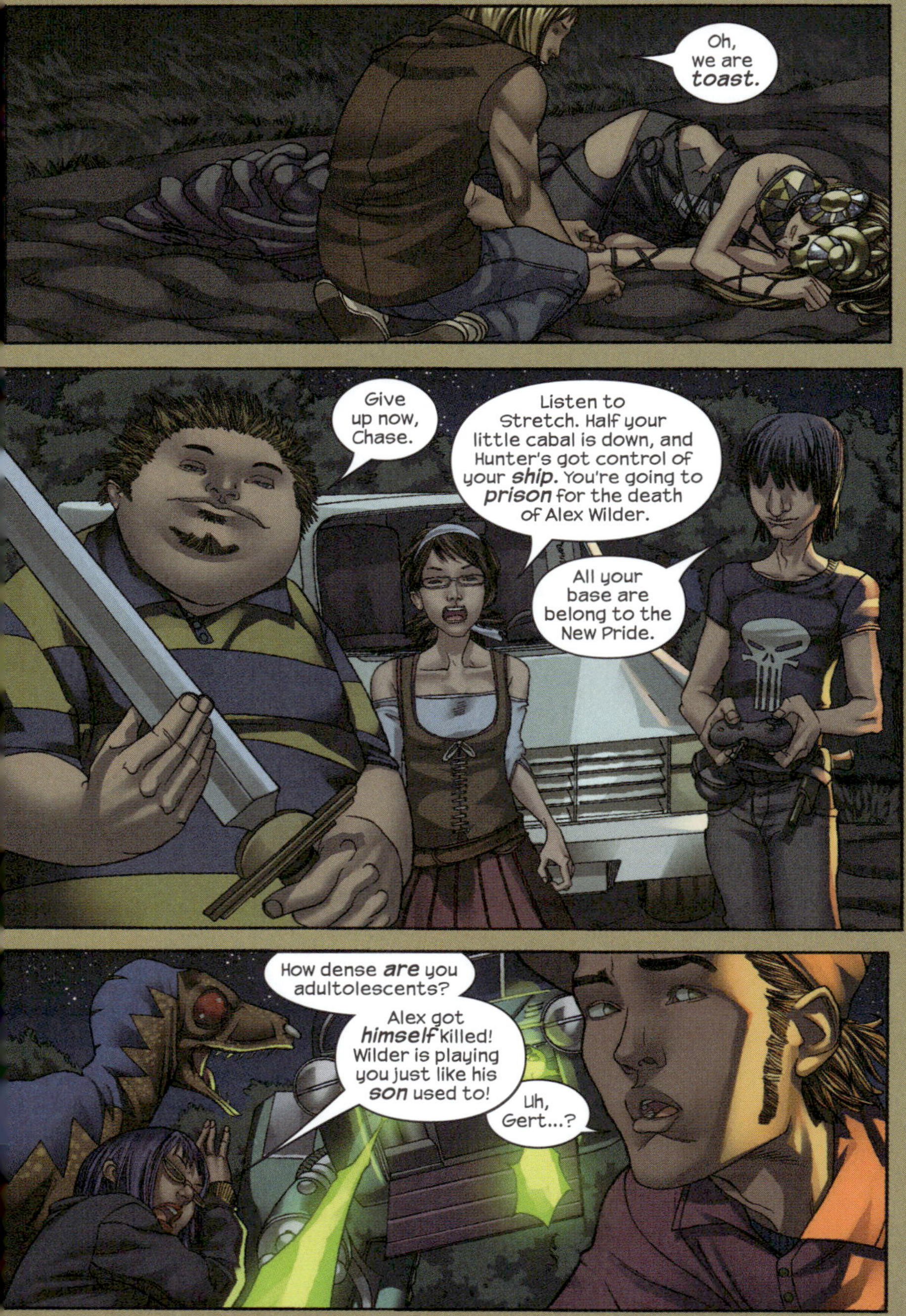
Oh, we are *toast.*
Give up now, Chase.
Listen to Stretch. Half your little cabal is down, and Hunter's got control of your *ship.* You're going to *prison* for the death of Alex Wilder.
All your base are belong to the New Pride.
How dense *are* you adultolescents?
Alex got *himself* killed! Wilder is playing you just like his *son* used to!
Uh, Gert...?

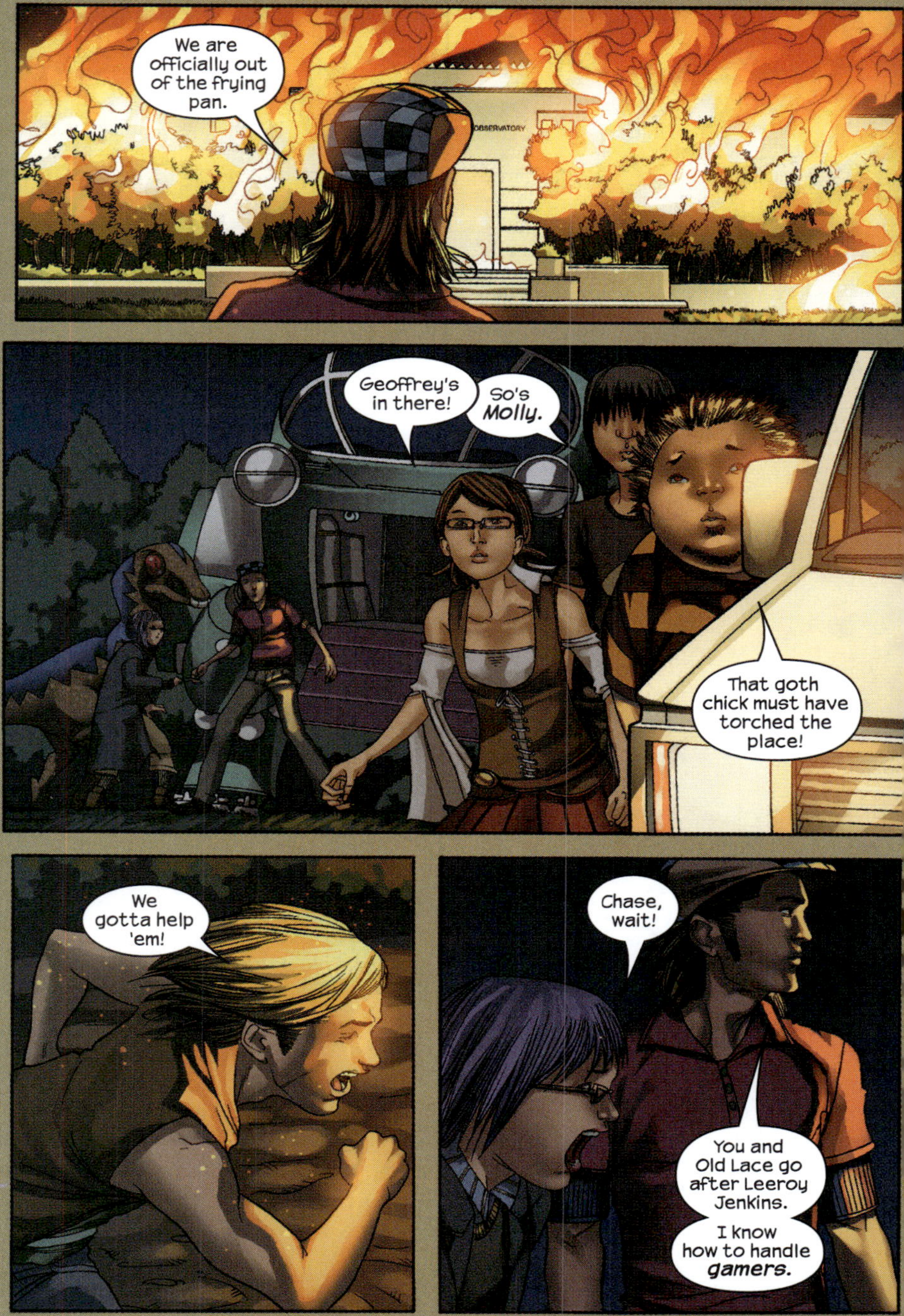

We are officially out of the frying pan.
OBSERVATORY
Geoffrey's in there!
So's *Molly.*
That goth chick must have torched the place!
We gotta help 'em!
Chase, wait!
You and Old Lace go after Leeroy Jenkins.
I know how to handle *gamers.*

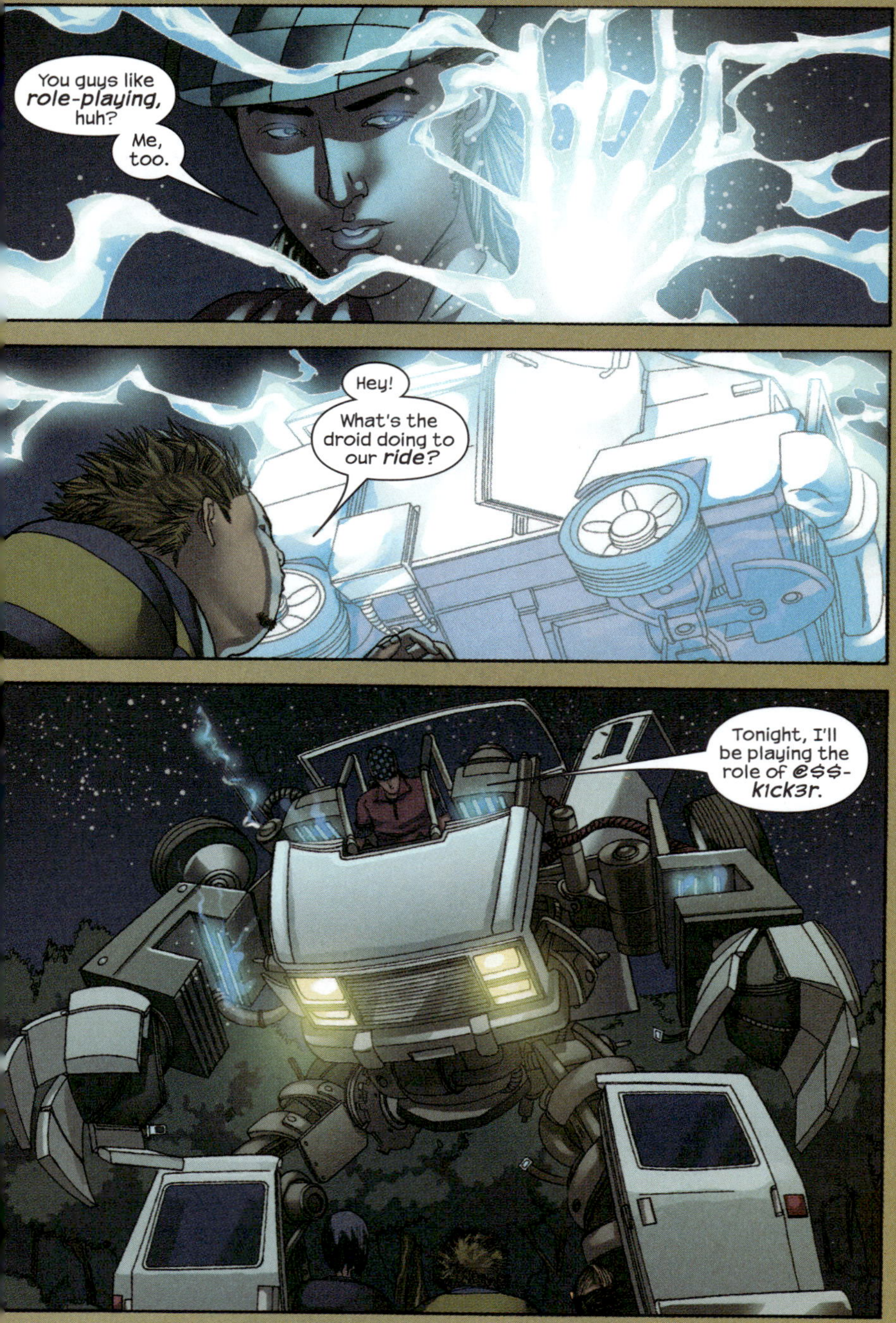
You guys like role-playing, huh?
Me, too.
Hey!
What's the droid doing to our ride?
Tonight, I'll be playing the role of @$$-kick3r.

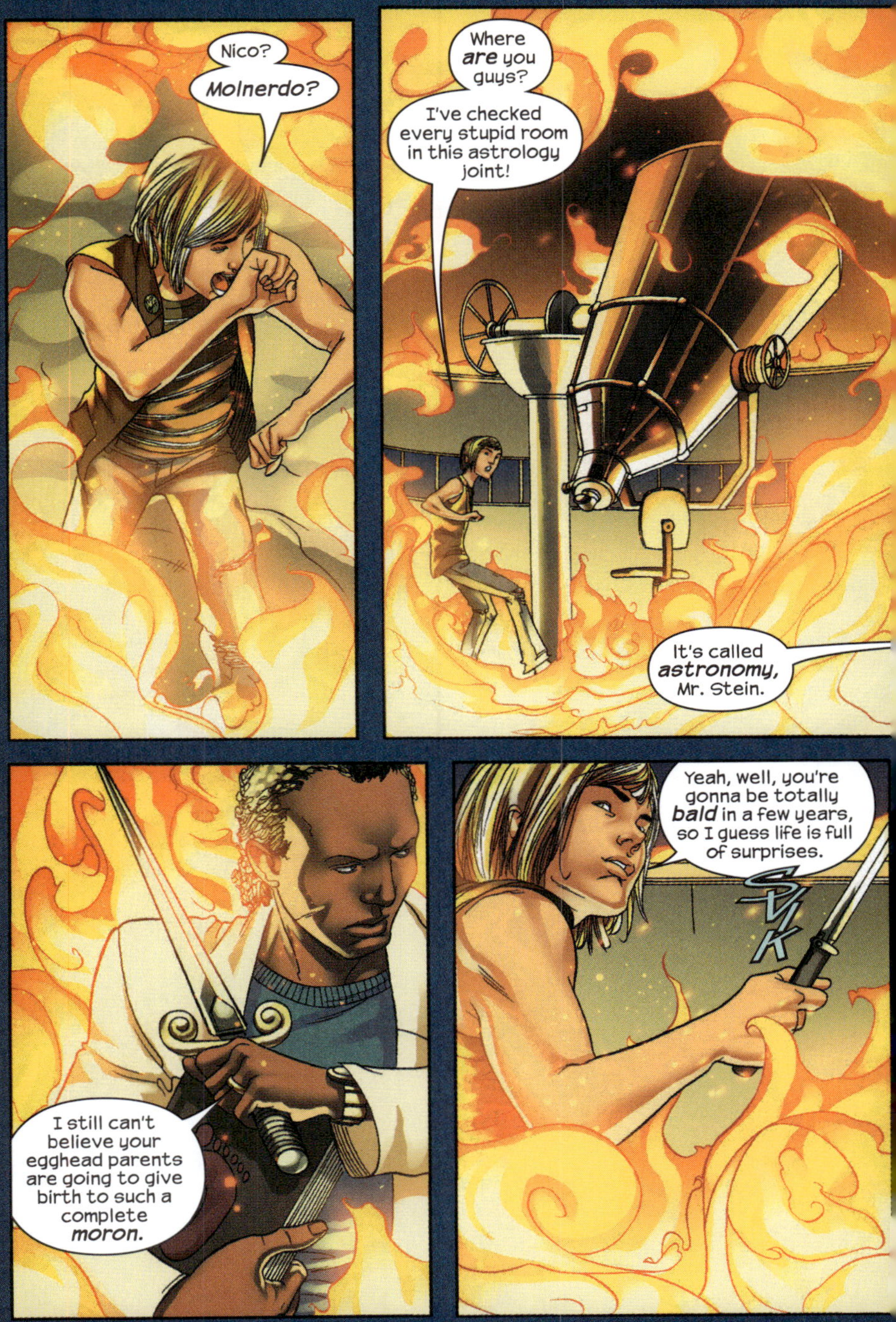
Nico?
Molnerdo?
Where are you guys?
I've checked every stupid room in this astrology joint!
It's called astronomy, Mr. Stein.
I still can't believe your egghead parents are going to give birth to such a complete moron.
Yeah, well, you're gonna be totally bald in a few years, so I guess life is full of surprises.
SVIK

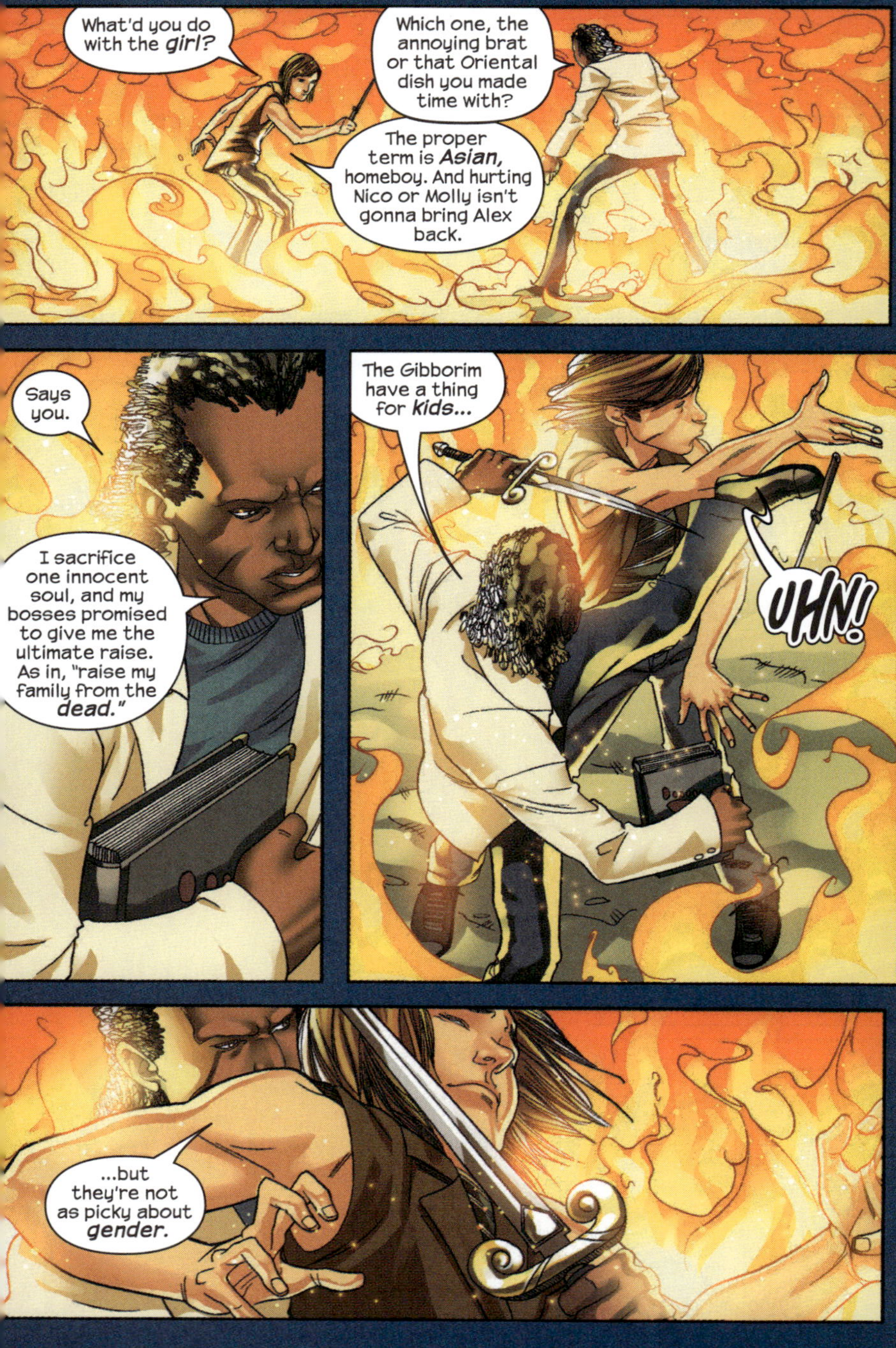
What'd you do with the *girl?*
Which one, the annoying brat or that Oriental dish you made time with?
The proper term is ***Asian,*** homeboy. And hurting Nico or Molly isn't gonna bring Alex back.
Says you.
I sacrifice one innocent soul, and my bosses promised to give me the ultimate raise. As in, "raise my family from the ***dead.***"
The Gibborim have a thing for ***kids...***
UHN!
...but they're not as picky about ***gender.***

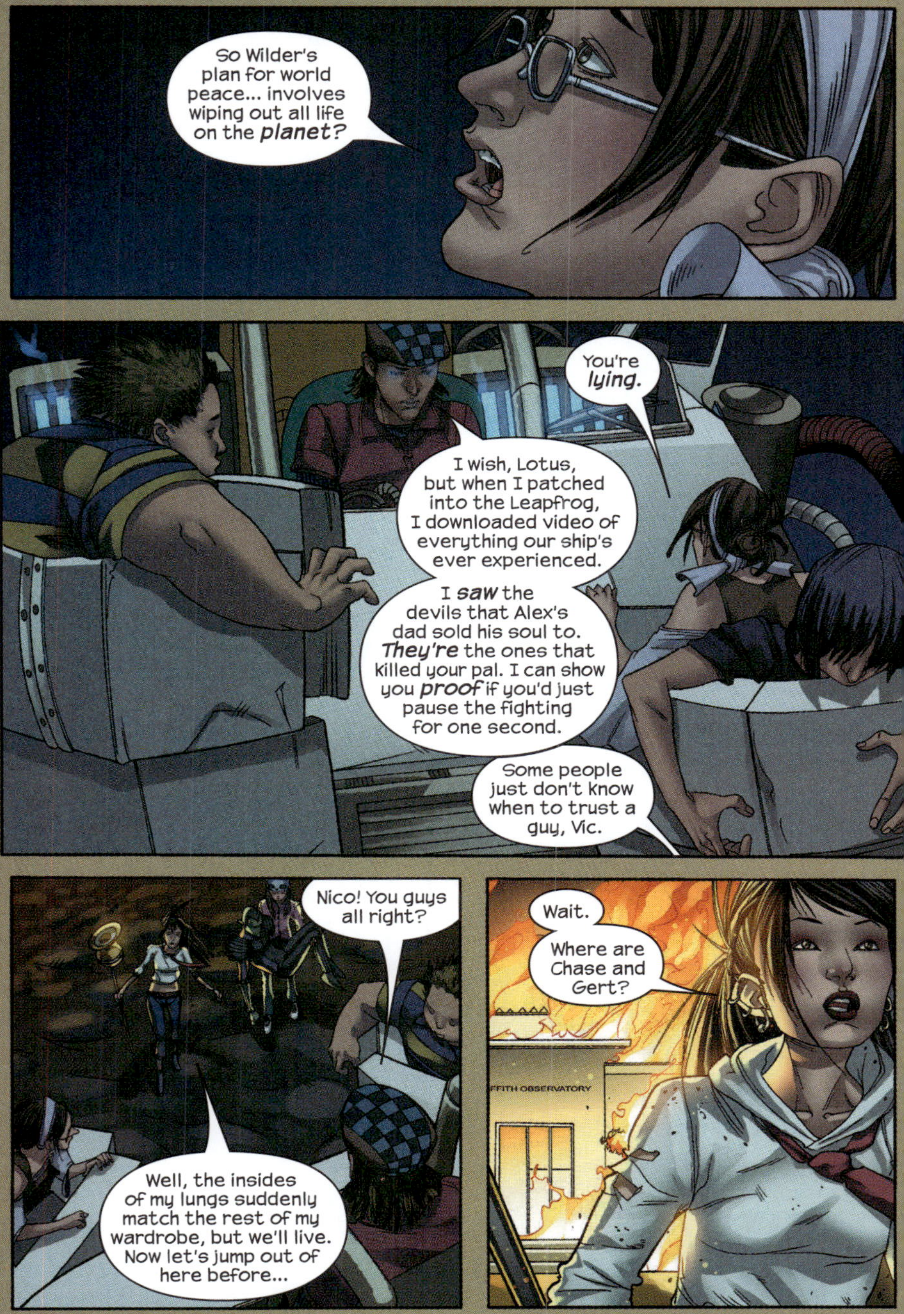
So Wilder's plan for world peace... involves wiping out all life on the *planet?*
You're *lying.*
I wish, Lotus, but when I patched into the Leapfrog, I downloaded video of everything our ship's ever experienced.
I *saw* the devils that Alex's dad sold his soul to. *They're* the ones that killed your pal. I can show you *proof* if you'd just pause the fighting for one second.
Some people just don't know when to trust a guy, Vic.
Nico! You guys all right?
Well, the insides of my lungs suddenly match the rest of my wardrobe, but we'll live. Now let's jump out of here before...
Wait.
Where are Chase and Gert?
FFITH OBSERVATORY

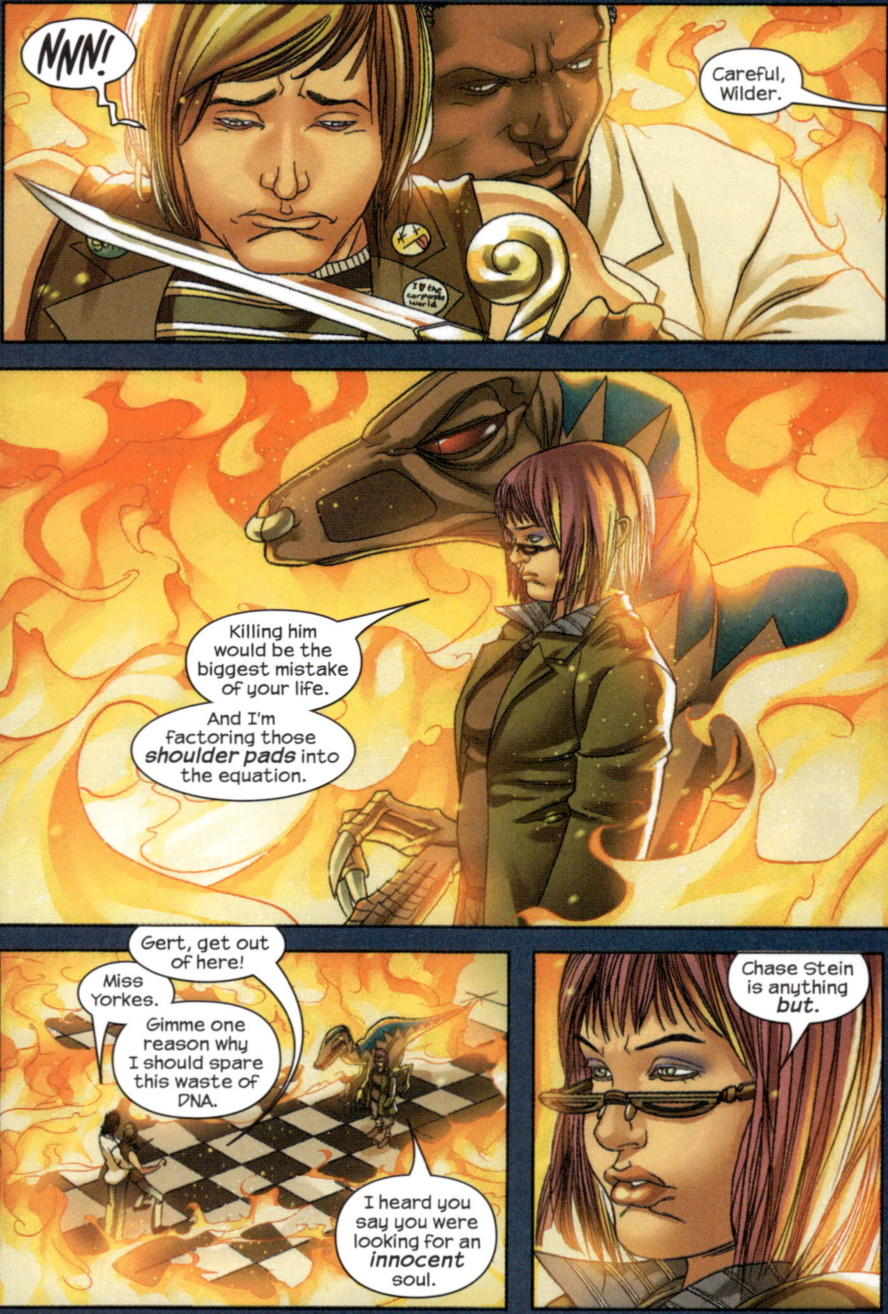
NNN!
Careful, Wilder.
Killing him would be the biggest mistake of your life.
And I'm factoring those **shoulder pads** into the equation.
Miss Yorkes.
Gert, get out of here!
Gimme one reason why I should spare this waste of DNA.
I heard you say you were looking for an ***innocent*** soul.
Chase Stein is anything ***but.***

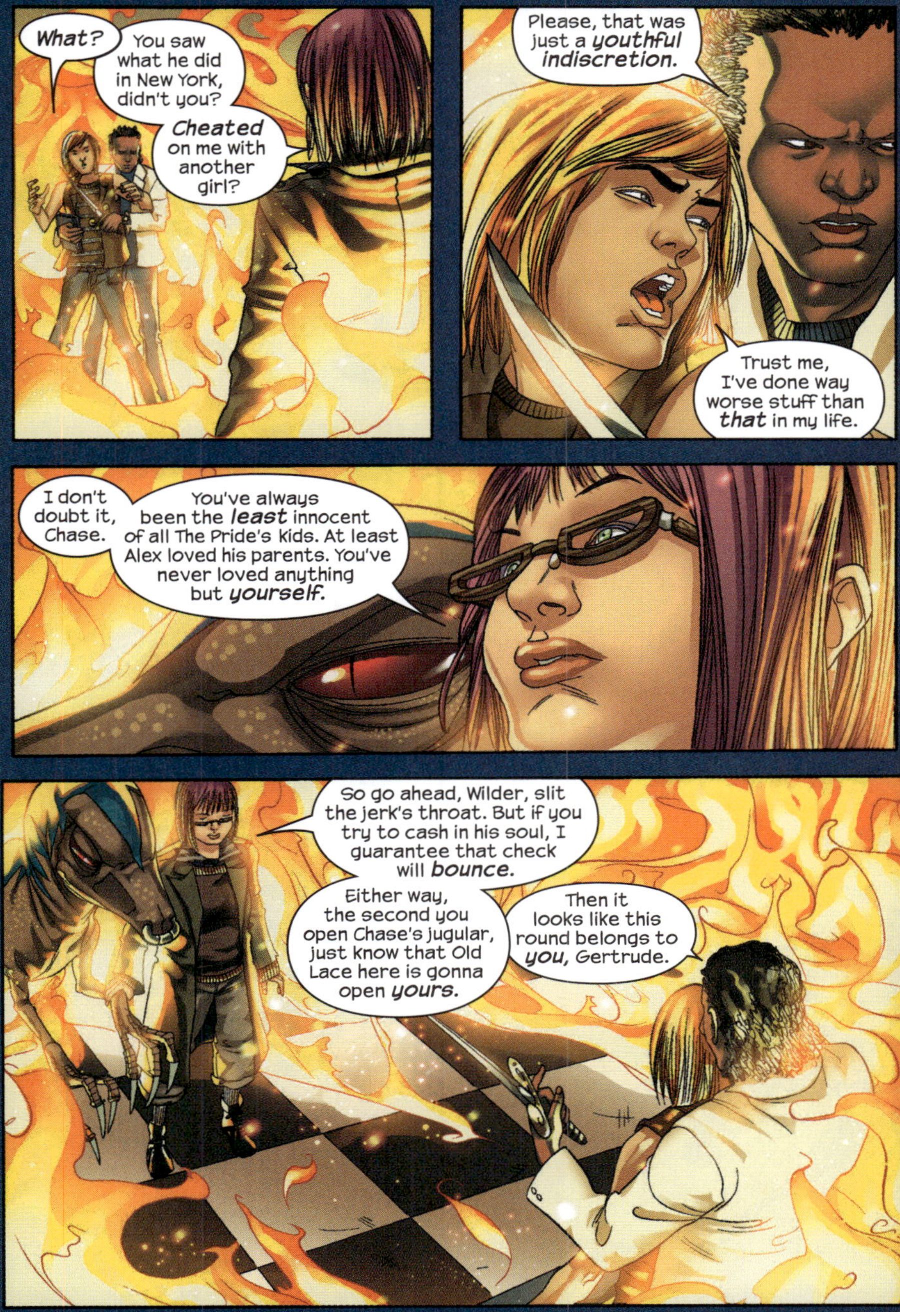
What?
You saw what he did in New York, didn't you?
Cheated on me with another girl?
Please, that was just a youthful indiscretion.
Trust me, I've done way worse stuff than that in my life.
I don't doubt it, Chase.
You've always been the least innocent of all The Pride's kids. At least Alex loved his parents. You've never loved anything but yourself.
So go ahead, Wilder, slit the jerk's throat. But if you try to cash in his soul, I guarantee that check will bounce.
Either way, the second you open Chase's jugular, just know that Old Lace here is gonna open yours.
Then it looks like this round belongs to you, Gertrude.

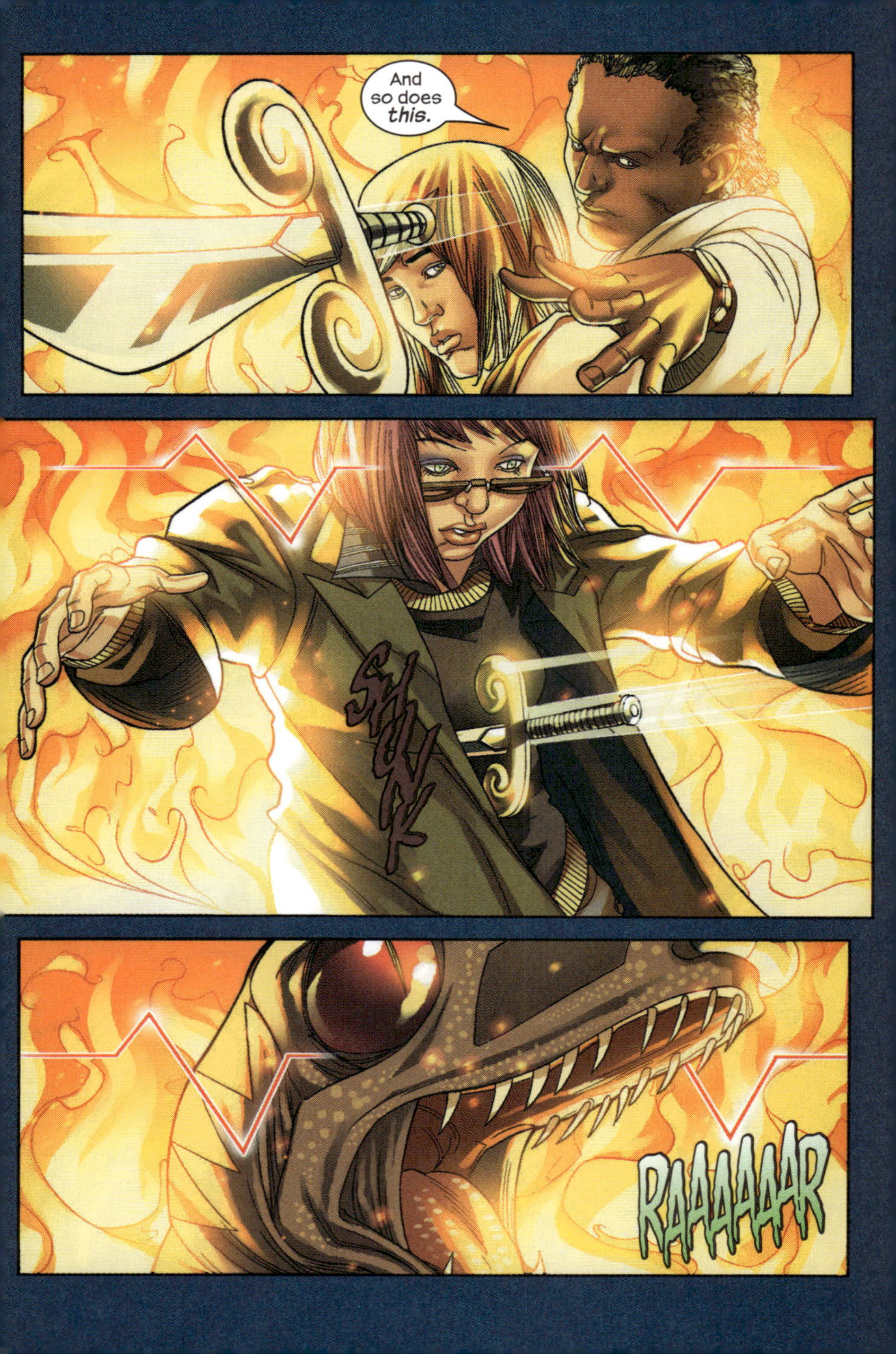
And so does *this.*
SHUNK
RAAAAAR

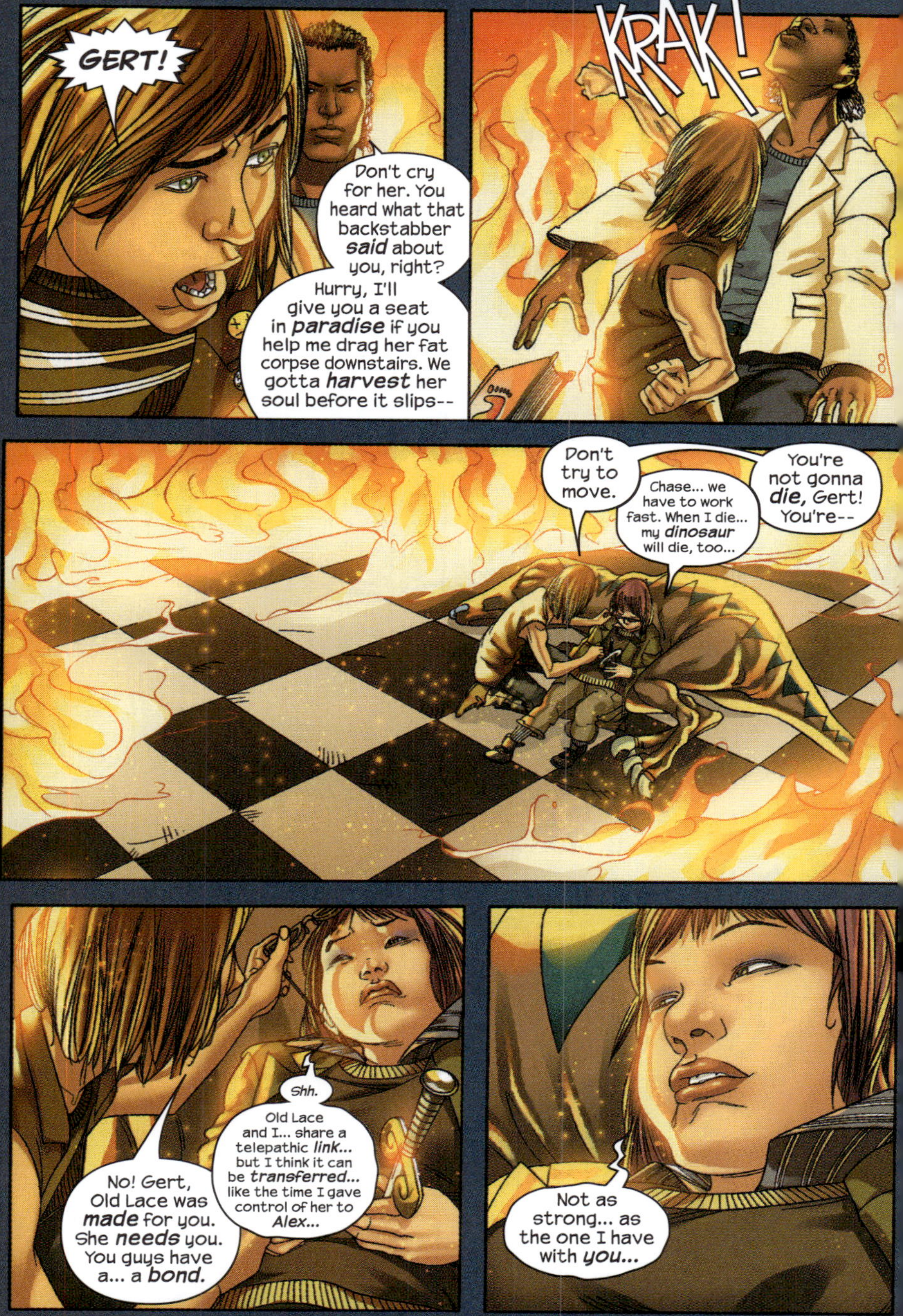
GERT!
Don't cry for her. You heard what that backstabber *said* about you, right?
Hurry, I'll give you a seat in *paradise* if you help me drag her fat corpse downstairs. We gotta *harvest* her soul before it slips--
KRAK!
Don't try to move.
You're not gonna *die*, Gert! You're--
Chase... we have to work fast. When I die... my *dinosaur* will die, too...
Shh.
Old Lace and I... share a telepathic *link*... but I think it can be *transferred*... like the time I gave control of her to *Alex*...
No! Gert, Old Lace was *made* for you. She *needs* you. You guys have a... a *bond.*
Not as strong... as the one I have with *you...*

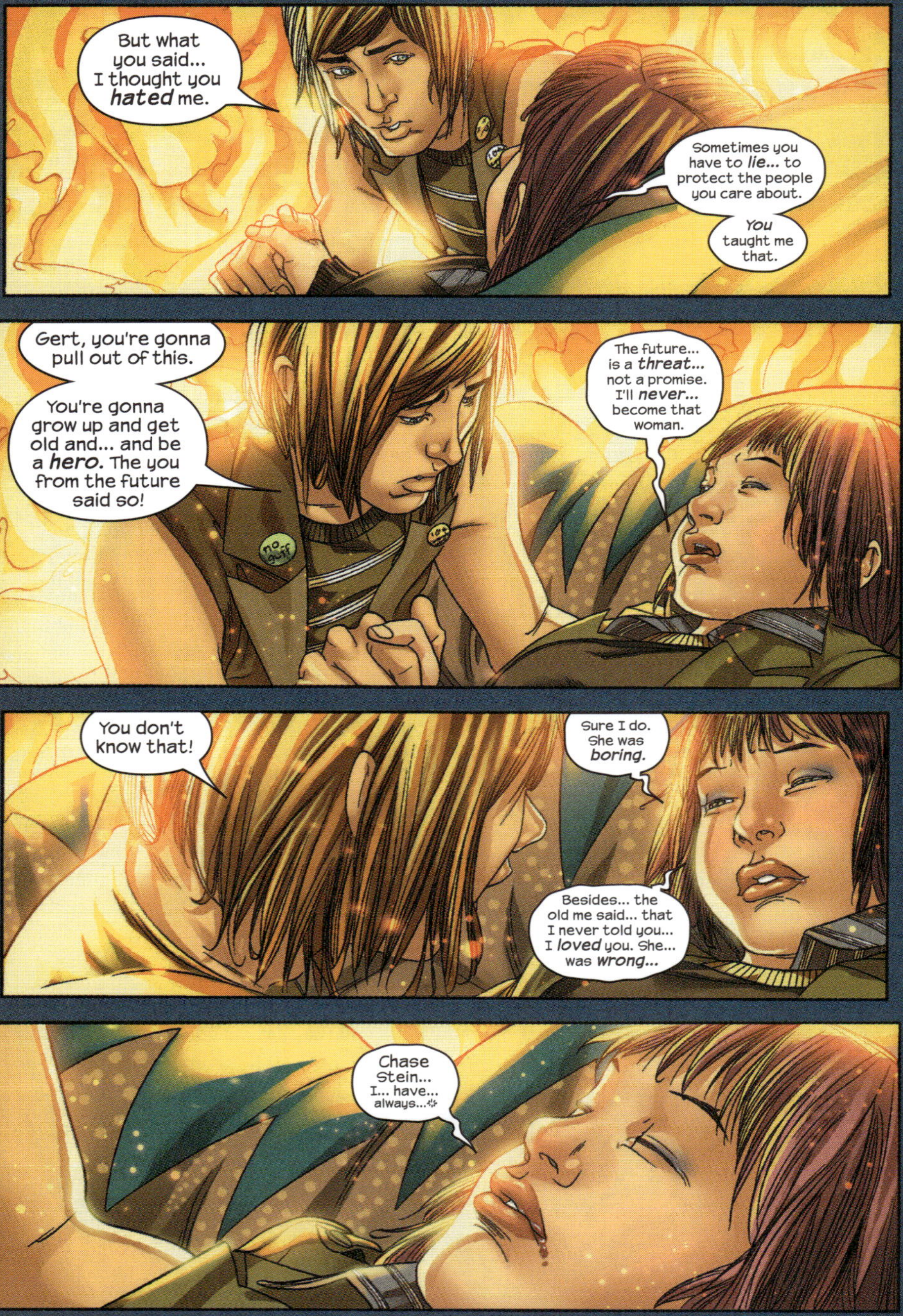
But what you said... I thought you hated me.
Sometimes you have to lie... to protect the people you care about.
You taught me that.
Gert, you're gonna pull out of this.
You're gonna grow up and get old and... and be a hero. The you from the future said so!
The future... is a threat... not a promise. I'll never... become that woman.
You don't know that!
Sure I do. She was boring.
Besides... the old me said... that I never told you... I loved you. She... was wrong...
Chase Stein... I... have... always...

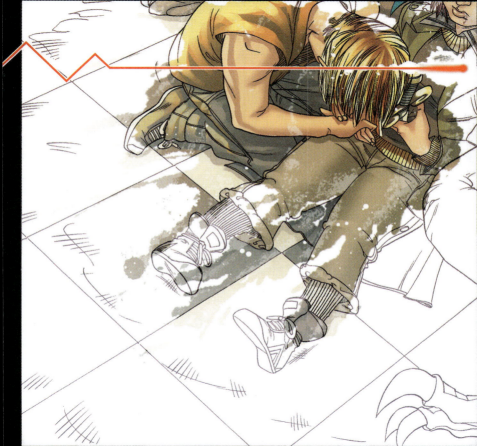

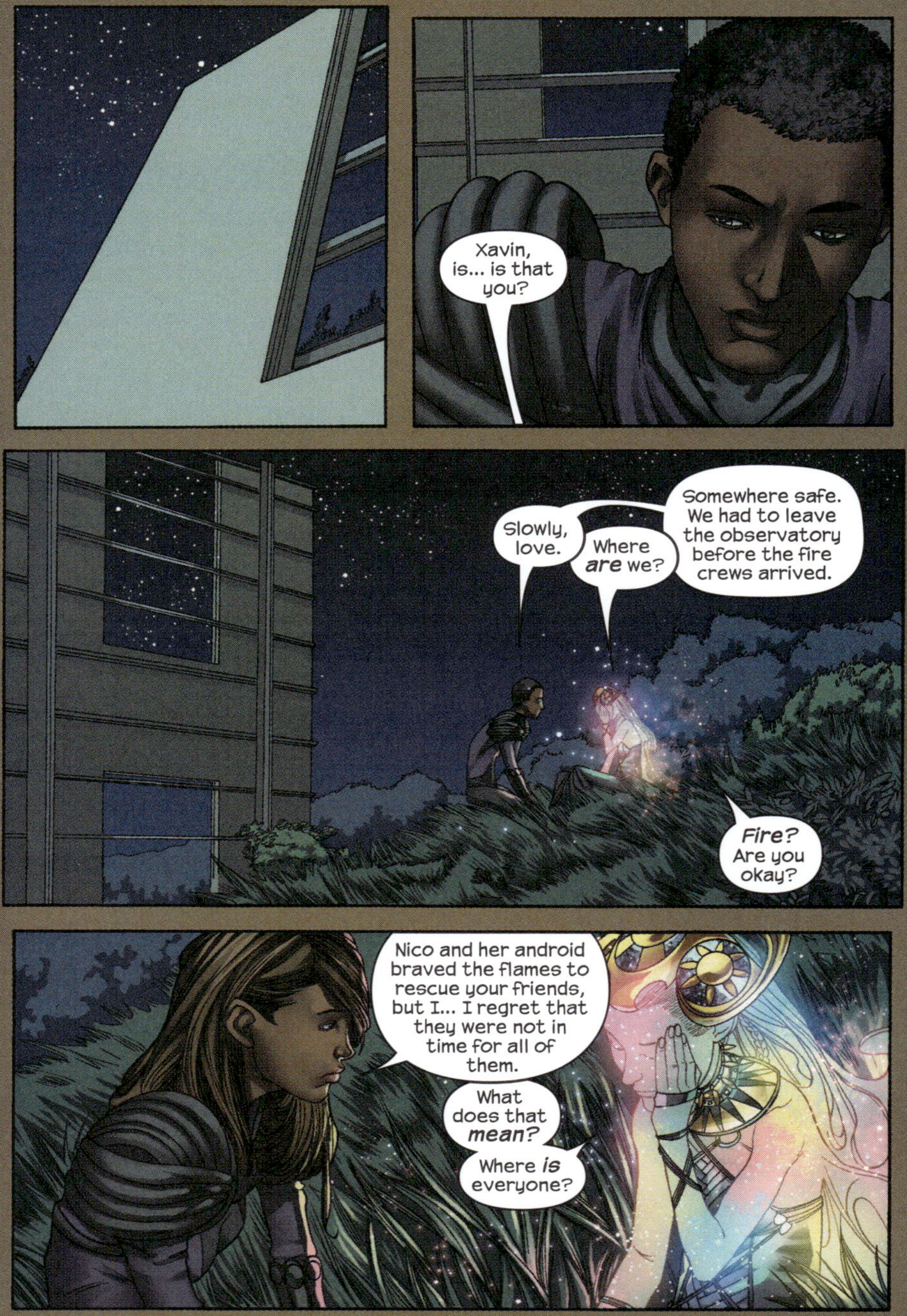
Xavin, is... is that you?
Slowly, love.
Where *are* we?
Somewhere safe. We had to leave the observatory before the fire crews arrived.
Fire? Are you okay?
Nico and her android braved the flames to rescue your friends, but I... I regret that they were not in time for all of them.
What does that *mean?*
Where *is* everyone?

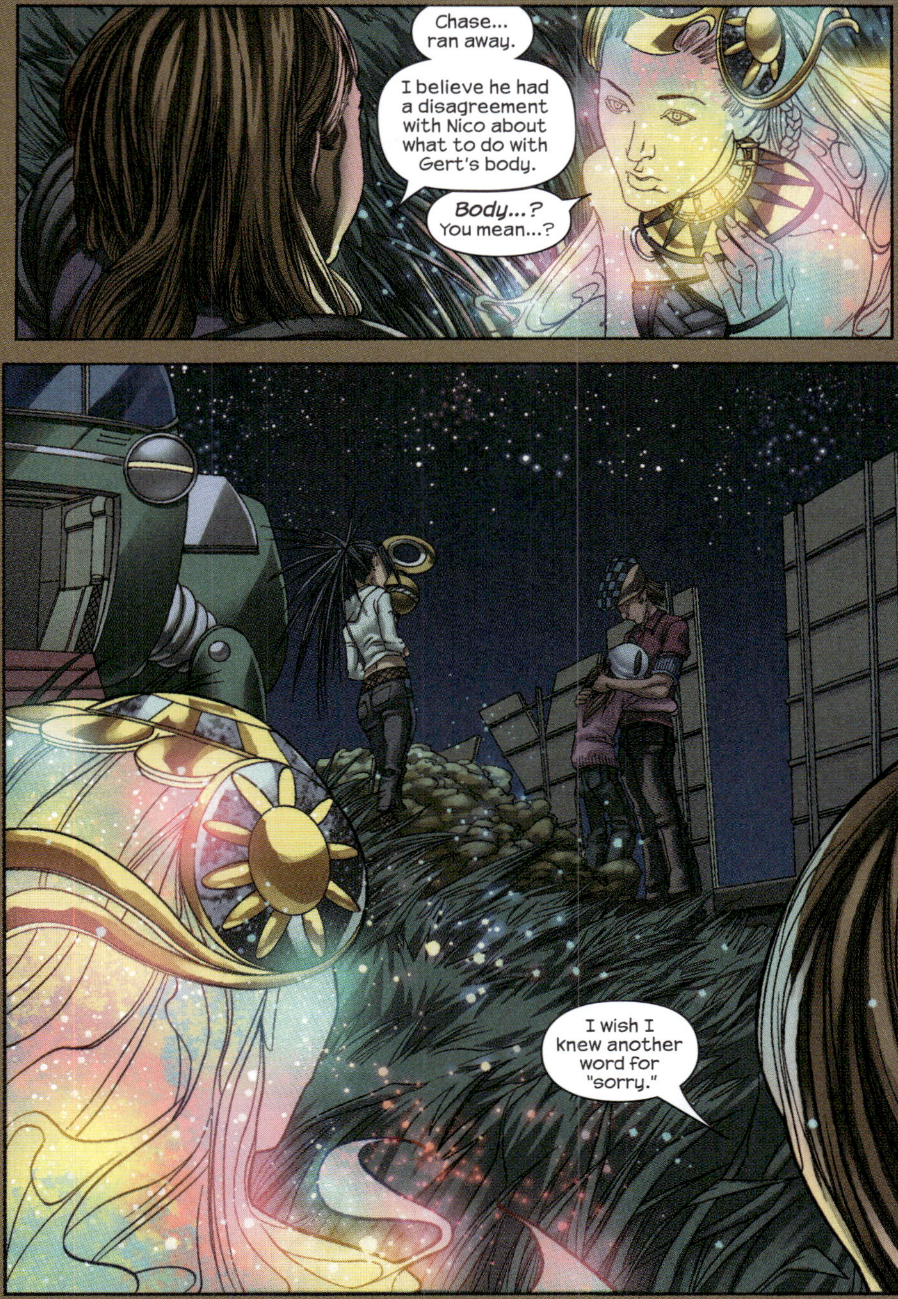
Chase... ran away.
I believe he had a disagreement with Nico about what to do with Gert's body.
Body...? You mean...?
I wish I knew another word for "sorry."

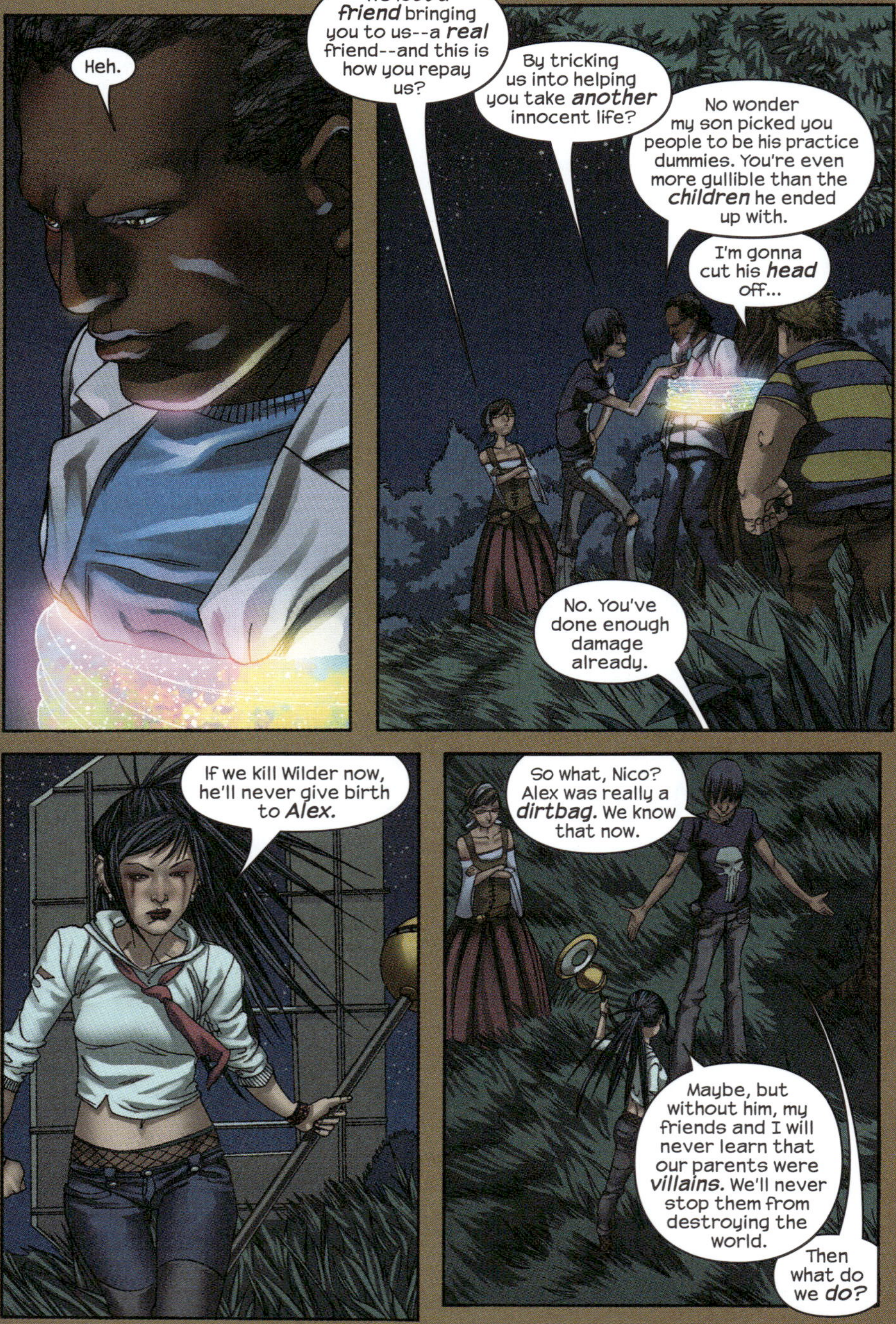

Heh.
We lost a friend bringing you to us--a real friend--and this is how you repay us?
By tricking us into helping you take another innocent life?
No wonder my son picked you people to be his practice dummies. You're even more gullible than the children he ended up with.
I'm gonna cut his head off...
No. You've done enough damage already.
If we kill Wilder now, he'll never give birth to Alex.
So what, Nico? Alex was really a dirtbag. We know that now.
Maybe, but without him, my friends and I will never learn that our parents were villains. We'll never stop them from destroying the world.
Then what do we do?

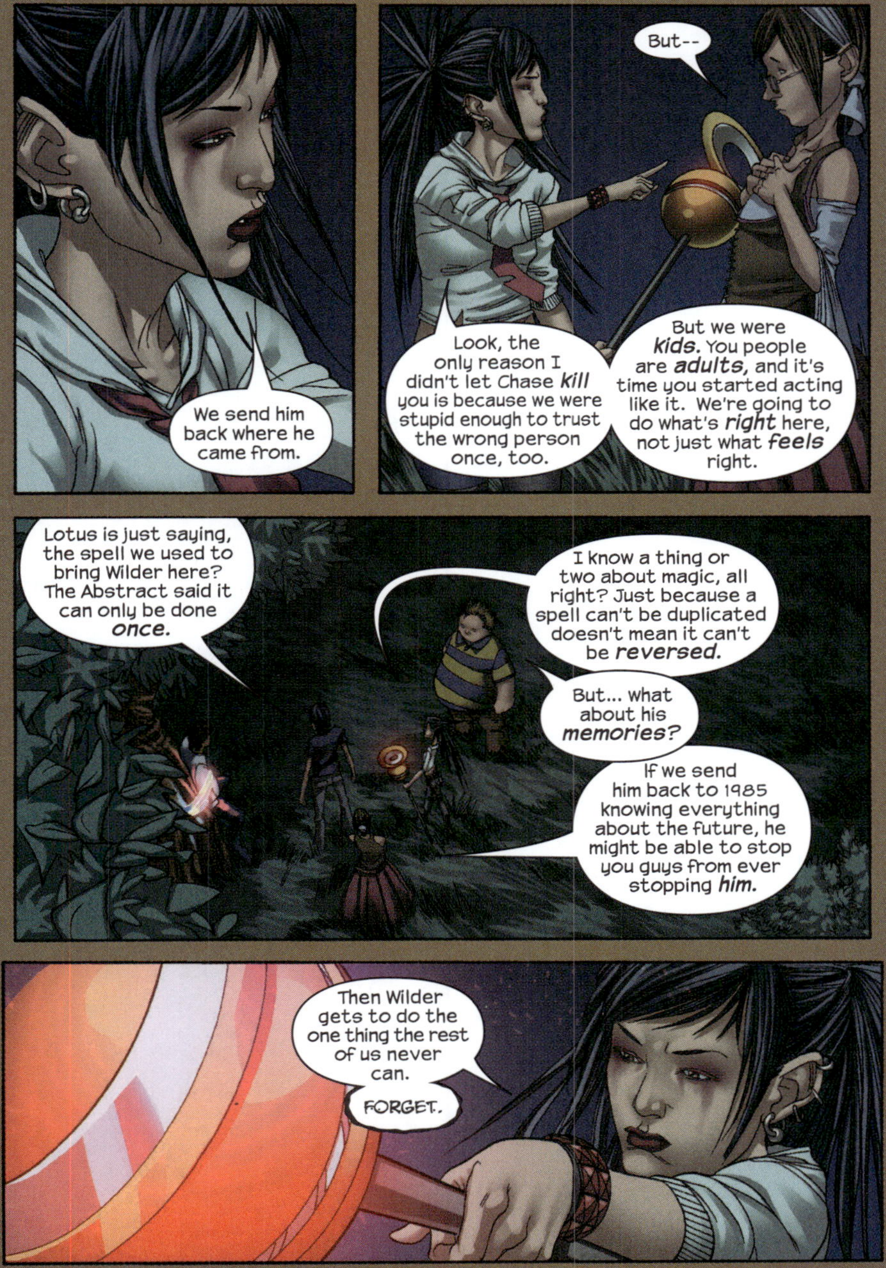
We send him back where he came from.
But--
Look, the only reason I didn't let Chase kill you is because we were stupid enough to trust the wrong person once, too.
But we were kids. You people are adults, and it's time you started acting like it. We're going to do what's right here, not just what feels right.
Lotus is just saying, the spell we used to bring Wilder here? The Abstract said it can only be done once.
I know a thing or two about magic, all right? Just because a spell can't be duplicated doesn't mean it can't be reversed.
But... what about his memories?
If we send him back to 1985 knowing everything about the future, he might be able to stop you guys from ever stopping him.
Then Wilder gets to do the one thing the rest of us never can.
FORGET.

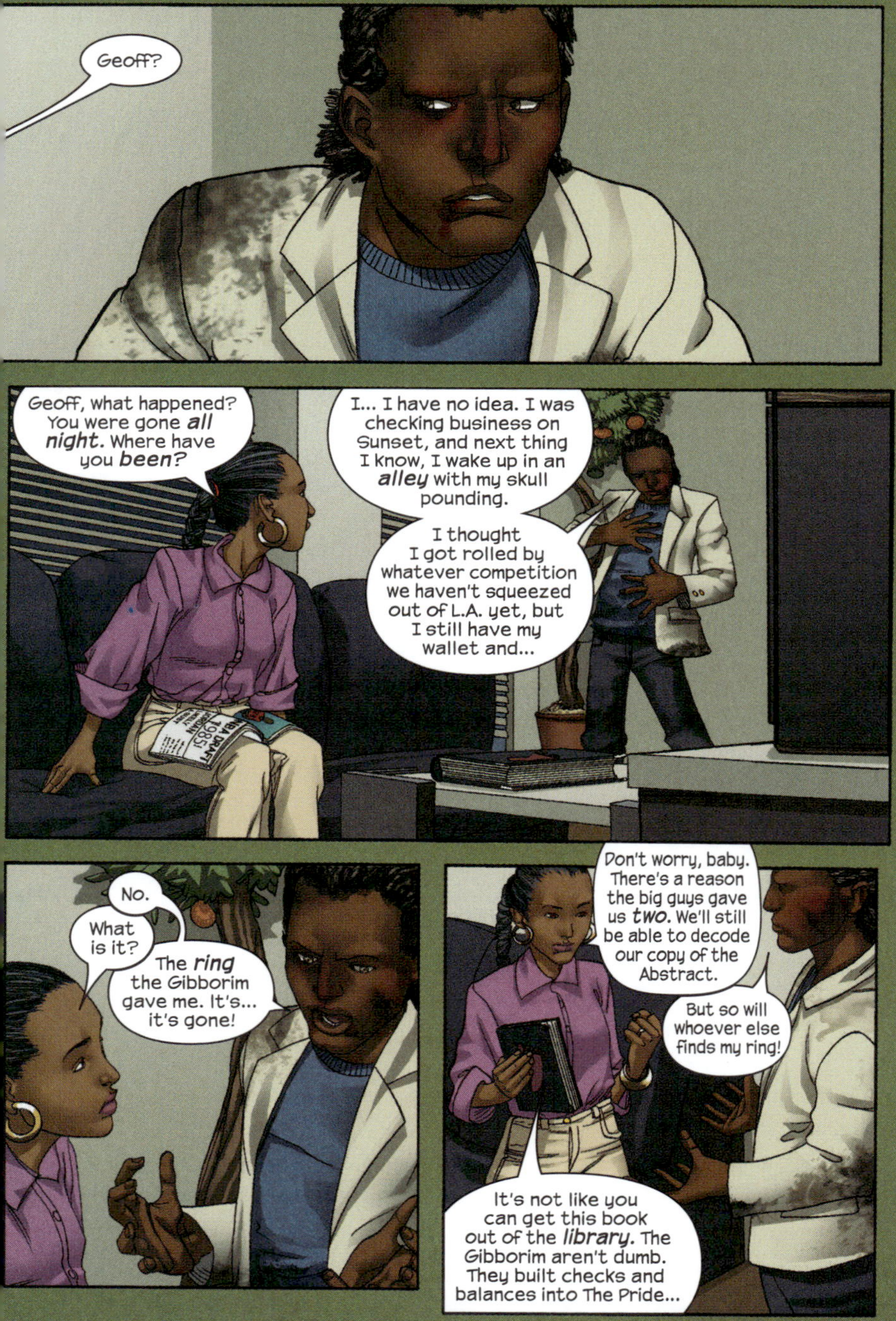
Geoff?
Geoff, what happened? You were gone all night. Where have you been?
I... I have no idea. I was checking business on Sunset, and next thing I know, I wake up in an alley with my skull pounding.
I thought I got rolled by whatever competition we haven't squeezed out of L.A. yet, but I still have my wallet and...
What is it?
No.
The ring the Gibborim gave me. It's... it's gone!
Don't worry, baby. There's a reason the big guys gave us two. We'll still be able to decode our copy of the Abstract.
But so will whoever else finds my ring!
It's not like you can get this book out of the library. The Gibborim aren't dumb. They built checks and balances into The Pride...

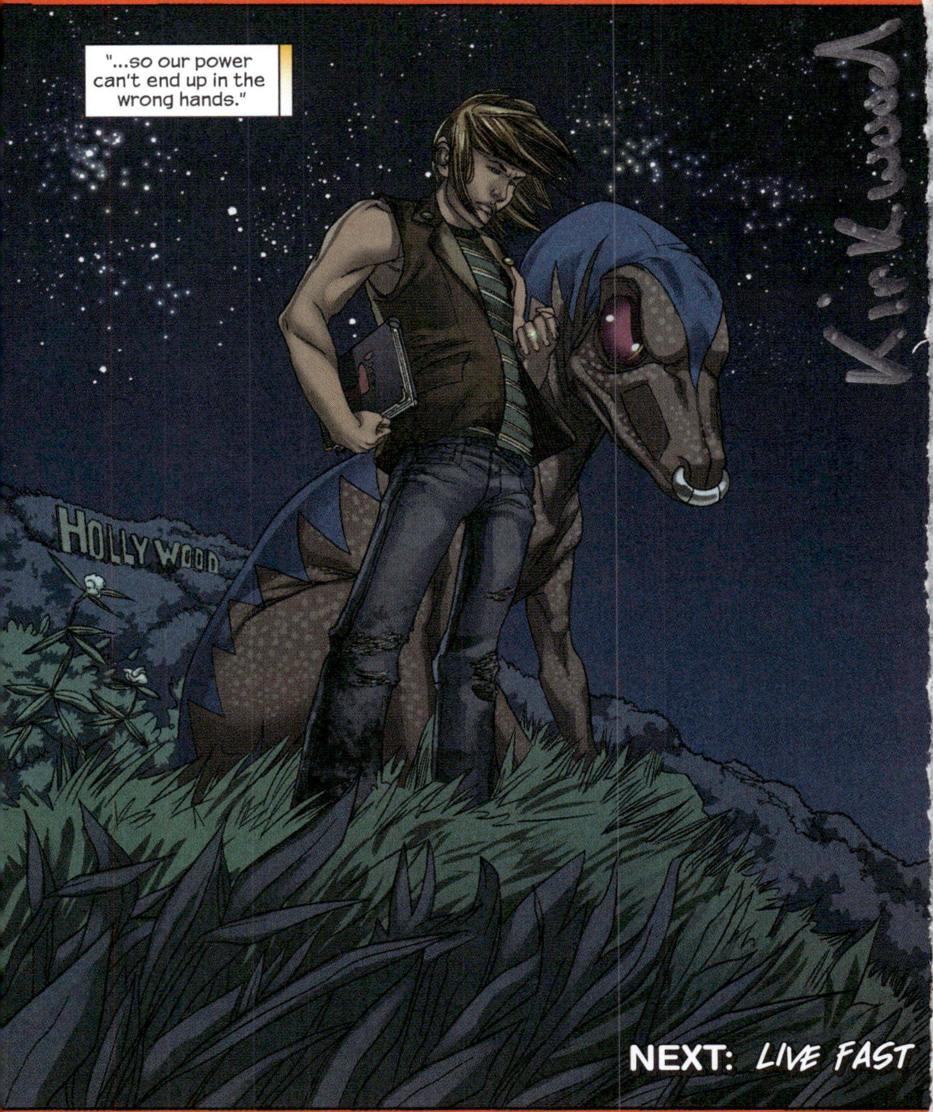
"...so our power can't end up in the wrong hands."
HOLLYWOOD
NEXT: LIVE FAST